Sovereign Ladies

ALSO BY MAUREEN WALLER

1700: Scenes from London Life

Ungrateful Daughters: The Stuart Princesses
Who Stole Their Father's Crown

London 1945: Life in the Debris of War

Sovereign Ladies

Sex, Sacrifice, and Power — The Six Reigning Queens of England

MAUREEN WALLER

ST. MARTIN'S GRIFFIN

NEW YORK

www.stmartins.com

Library of Congress Cataloging-in-Publication Data

Waller, Maureen.
    Sovereign ladies : sex, sacrifice, and power—the six reigning queens of England / Maureen Waller. — 1st St. Martin's Griffin ed.
       p. cm.
    First published in Great Britain in 2006 by John Murray; first published in the U.S. by St. Martin's Press in 2007.
    Includes bibliographical references and index.
    ISBN-13: 978-0-312-38608-5
    ISBN-10: 0-312-38608-7
    1. Queens—Great Britain—Biography. 2. Great Britain—Kings and rulers—Biography. I. Title.
DA28.2.W35 2008
942.009'9—dc22
[B]

                                                  2008036883

First published in Great Britain in 2006 by
John Murray (Publishers), a division of Hodder Headline

First published in the United States in 2007 as *Sovereign Ladies:
The Six Reigning Queens of England* by St. Martin's Press

First St. Martin's Griffin Edition: December 2008

10 9 8 7 6 5 4 3 2 1

For Brian, who made it possible . . .
and Charles Spicer, who loves English history.

Contents

PART TWO: *House of Stuart*

MARY II
b. 1662, r. 1689–1694

ANNE
b. 1665, r. 1702–1714

PART THREE: *House of Hanover*

VICTORIA
b. 1819, r. 1837–1901

PART FOUR: *House of Windsor*

ELIZABETH II
b. 1926, r. 1952–

List of Illustrations

Acknowledgements

I should like to thank my agent, Jonathan Lloyd, and my publishers, Roland Philipps and Charles Spicer, for their input and enthusiasm for this project. I am grateful to Morag Lyall for copy-editing the script, and to Rowan Yapp and the rest of the team at John Murray. I also wish to thank those who were kind enough to give me confidential interviews to discuss our present Queen.

Enormous thanks, as ever, go to my husband, Brian MacArthur, for his boundless support. He has lived with the six queens for far too long.

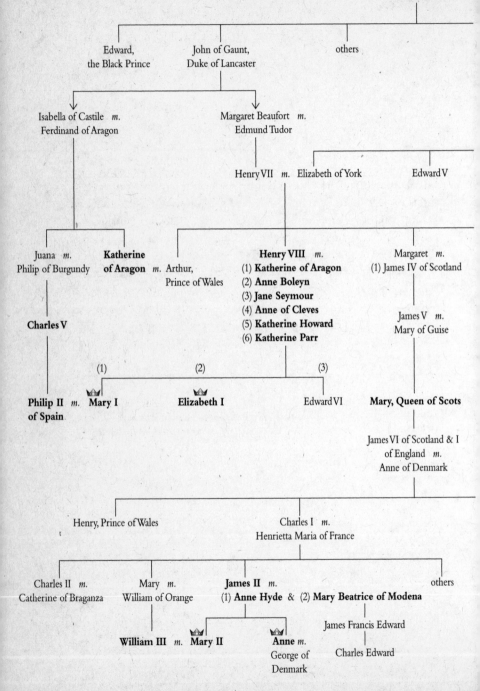

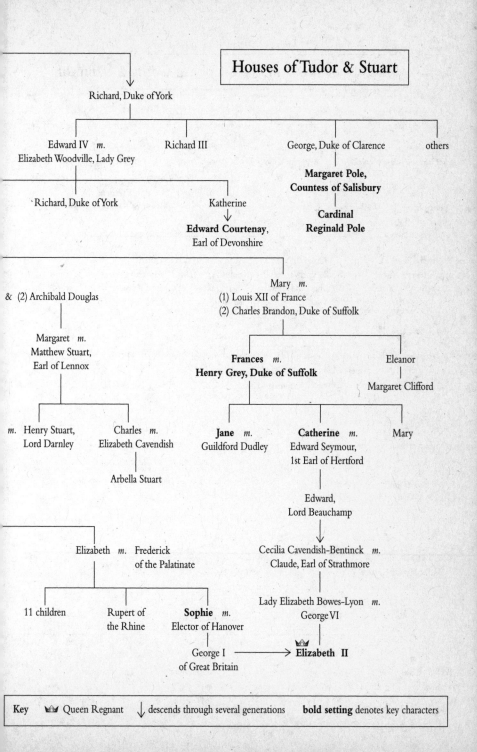

Houses of Tudor & Stuart

Richard, Duke of York

Edward IV *m.*
Elizabeth Woodville, Lady Grey

Richard III

George, Duke of Clarence

others

**Margaret Pole,
Countess of Salisbury**

Richard, Duke of York

Katherine

Edward Courtenay,
Earl of Devonshire

**Cardinal
Reginald Pole**

& (2) Archibald Douglas

Mary *m.*
(1) Louis XII of France
(2) Charles Brandon, Duke of Suffolk

Margaret *m.*
Matthew Stuart,
Earl of Lennox

Frances *m.*
Henry Grey, Duke of Suffolk

Eleanor

Margaret Clifford

m. Henry Stuart,
Lord Darnley

Charles *m.*
Elizabeth Cavendish

Jane *m.*
Guildford Dudley

Catherine *m.*
Edward Seymour,
1st Earl of Hertford

Mary

Arbella Stuart

Edward,
Lord Beauchamp

Elizabeth *m.* Frederick
of the Palatinate

Cecilia Cavendish-Bentinck *m.*
Claude, Earl of Strathmore

11 children

Rupert of
the Rhine

Sophie *m.*
Elector of Hanover

Lady Elizabeth Bowes-Lyon *m.*
George VI

George I
of Great Britain

Elizabeth II

Key   Queen Regnant   ↓ descends through several generations   **bold setting** denotes key characters

Houses of Hanover, Saxe-Coburg-Gotha & Windsor

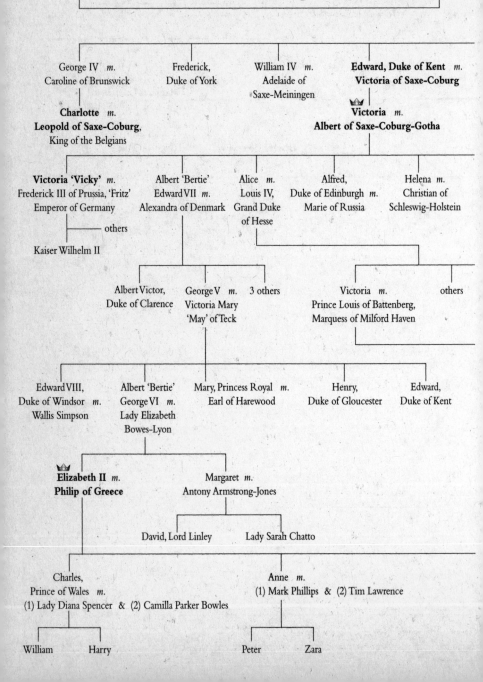

George IV *m.*
Caroline of Brunswick

Charlotte *m.*
Leopold of Saxe-Coburg,
King of the Belgians

Frederick,
Duke of York

William IV *m.*
Adelaide of
Saxe-Meiningen

Edward, Duke of Kent *m.*
Victoria of Saxe-Coburg

Victoria *m.*
Albert of Saxe-Coburg-Gotha

Victoria 'Vicky' *m.*
Frederick III of Prussia, 'Fritz'
Emperor of Germany

———— others

Kaiser Wilhelm II

Albert 'Bertie'
Edward VII *m.*
Alexandra of Denmark

Alice *m.*
Louis IV,
Grand Duke
of Hesse

Alfred,
Duke of Edinburgh *m.*
Marie of Russia

Helena *m.*
Christian of
Schleswig-Holstein

Albert Victor,
Duke of Clarence

George V *m.*
Victoria Mary
'May' of Teck

3 others

Victoria *m.*
Prince Louis of Battenberg,
Marquess of Milford Haven

others

Edward VIII,
Duke of Windsor *m.*
Wallis Simpson

Albert 'Bertie'
George VI *m.*
Lady Elizabeth
Bowes-Lyon

Mary, Princess Royal *m.*
Earl of Harewood

Henry,
Duke of Gloucester

Edward,
Duke of Kent

Elizabeth II *m.*
Philip of Greece

Margaret *m.*
Antony Armstrong-Jones

David, Lord Linley

Lady Sarah Chatto

Charles,
Prince of Wales *m.*
(1) Lady Diana Spencer & (2) Camilla Parker Bowles

Anne *m.*
(1) Mark Phillips & (2) Tim Lawrence

William

Harry

Peter

Zara

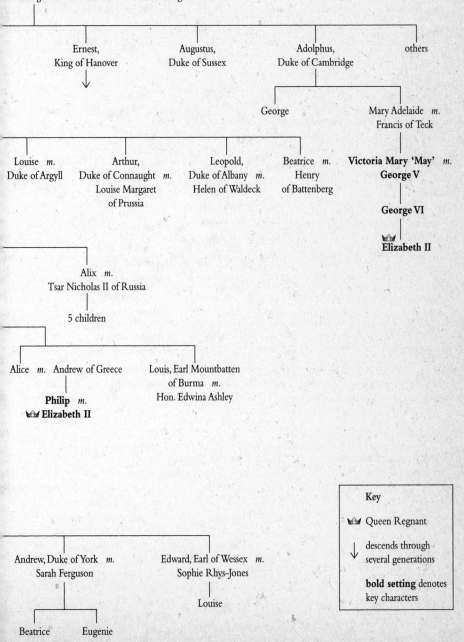

Sophie of Hanover

George I of Great Britain

George III   *m.*   Charlotte of Mecklenburg-Strelitz

Ernest,
King of Hanover

Augustus,
Duke of Sussex

Adolphus,
Duke of Cambridge

others

George

Mary Adelaide   *m.*
Francis of Teck

Louise   *m.*
Duke of Argyll

Arthur,
Duke of Connaught   *m.*
Louise Margaret
of Prussia

Leopold,
Duke of Albany   *m.*
Helen of Waldeck

Beatrice   *m.*
Henry
of Battenberg

Victoria Mary 'May'   *m.*
George V

George VI

Elizabeth II

Alix   *m.*
Tsar Nicholas II of Russia

5 children

Alice   *m.*   Andrew of Greece

Louis, Earl Mountbatten
of Burma   *m.*
Hon. Edwina Ashley

Philip   *m.*
Elizabeth II

Andrew, Duke of York   *m.*
Sarah Ferguson

Edward, Earl of Wessex   *m.*
Sophie Rhys-Jones

Louise

Beatrice   Eugenie

Key

Queen Regnant

↓   descends through
several generations

bold setting denotes
key characters

Table of Sovereigns since the Norman Conquest

HOUSE	NAME	ACCESSION	YEARS ON THRONE	CONSORT
Norman	William I	1066	21	Matilda of Flanders
	William II	1087	13	
	Henry I	1100	35	(1) Matilda of Scotland
				(2) Adele of Louvain
	Matilda, daughter of Henry I			Geoffrey Plantagenet
	Lady of the English (not crowned or anointed)			
	Stephen,	1135	19	
	son of Adela, daughter of William I			Matilda of Boulogne
Plantagenet	Henry II	1154	35	Eleanor of Aquitaine
	Richard I	1189	10	Berengaria of Navarre
	John	1199	17	(1) Hadwisa of Gloucester
				(2) Isabella of Angoulême
	Henry III	1216	56	Eleanor of Provence
	Edward I	1272	35	(1) Eleanor of Castile
				(2) Margaret of France
	Edward II	1307	20	Isabella of France
	Edward III	1327	50	Philippa of Hainault
	Richard II	1377	22	(1) Anne of Bohemia
				(2) Isabella of France
Lancaster	Henry IV	1399	14	(1) Mary de Bohun
				(2) Joan of Navarre
	Henry V	1413	9	Catherine of France
	Henry VI	1422	39	Margaret of Anjou
York	Edward IV	1461	22	Elizabeth Woodville
	Edward V	1483	2 years 2 months	
	Richard III	1483	2	Anne Neville
Tudor	Henry VII	1485	24	Elizabeth of York
	Henry VIII	1509	38	(1) Katherine of Aragon
				(2) Anne Boleyn
				(3) Jane Seymour
				(4) Anne of Cleves
				(5) Katherine Howard
				(6) Katherine Parr

	Edward VI	1547	6	
	Mary I	1553	5	Philip II of Spain
	Elizabeth I	1558	45	
Stuart	James I	1603	22	Anne of Denmark
	Charles I	1625	24	Henrietta Maria of France
	Commonwealth and Protectorate			
	Charles II	1660	25	Catherine of Braganza
	James II	1685	4	(1) Anne Hyde (2) Mary of Modena
	William III & Mary II	1689	6	
	William III	1694	7	
	Anne	1702	12	George of Denmark
Hanover	George I	1714	13	Sofia Dorothea of Zell
	George II	1727	33	Caroline of Anspach
	George III	1760	60	Charlotte of Mecklenburg-Strelitz
	George IV	1820	10	Caroline of Brunswick
	William IV	1830	7	Adelaide of Saxe-Meiningen
	Victoria	1837	64	Albert of Saxe-Coburg- Gotha
Saxe-Coburg-Gotha				
	Edward VII	1901	9	Alexandra of Denmark
	George V	1910	26	Victoria Mary 'May' of Teck
Windsor (1917)				
	Edward VIII	1936	(abdicated same year)	
	George VI	1936	16	Elizabeth Bowes-Lyon
	Elizabeth II	1952		Philip Mountbatten (formerly Prince Philip of Greece), created Duke of Edinburgh

Introduction

'Famous have been the reigns of our Queens. Some of the
greatest periods in our history have unfolded under their sceptre'
Winston Spencer Churchill, 1952

'THE ENGLISH LIKE Queens,' the old Duchess of Coburg remarked
cheerfully when she received news of the birth of her granddaughter, the future Queen Victoria. Indeed, by the early nineteenth
century the English greeted the accession of a young female sovereign
with relief. Victoria's sex was very much to her advantage. Even in 1936,
the year of the abdication crisis, the nation contemplated the eventual
succession of the young Princess Elizabeth with happy anticipation,
assuming she would emulate the qualities of her great-great-grandmother Victoria, while, in the aftermath of the Second World War, it
was optimistically believed she would recreate a new Elizabethan age.

It had not always been so. England had no Salic law, barring a
woman from the throne, but in practice the idea of female sovereignty
was anathema. It was assumed that a female succession would plunge
the country into civil war, as, indeed, it had when in the early twelfth
century Henry I had died, leaving the crown to his daughter, Matilda.
Although Henry had had his barons swear to accept her, and Matilda,
who had been married to the Holy Roman Emperor, was no
ingénue, the hereditary principle was not yet established, and it was
easy for her cousin Stephen – one of the boys, as it were, and not even
the eldest son – to snatch the crown.

'Great by birth, greater by marriage, greatest in her offspring' ran
the epitaph for Matilda, who was never crowned or anointed queen.
Nor did she ever call herself Queen. Possibly she thought the term,

derived from the Saxon *cwen*, inappropriate, since hitherto it had applied only to queens consort, or possibly she hesitated to call herself Queen before a coronation had taken place. At any rate, the title she used was Lady of the English. There can be no clearer indication than her epitaph that as a woman she was seen merely as a vessel through whom the right to the crown would pass from one male to another, from her father Henry I to her son, Henry II. As she was a woman, it was assumed she would be unable to fulfil a king's primary function – that of active military leader – even though for nineteen years she courageously and determinedly fought her cause.

Four centuries later Henry VIII was confronted with the same problem, since his wife had failed – as he saw it – to provide him with a son. In theory, his daughter Mary could have fulfilled the same role as Matilda, a vessel to be used for the perpetuation of a masculine dynasty, had Henry married her off early enough. Indeed, Henry's own claim to the throne derived from two women: his grandmother, Margaret Beaufort, and his mother, Elizabeth, representing the rival claims of Lancaster and York, both of whom had ceded their rights to the men. Unfortunately, Henry's mind was far too conventional to accept the idea of a female succession and he failed to see the possibilities before him.

For someone as macho as Henry VIII, a daughter was a dent on his manhood, a deep injury to his self-esteem and hence to the glory of the monarchy, of which he was the personification. He would overturn Church and state to get a son, but, ironically, he was still succeeded – after the six-year minority of Edward VI – by two daughters. If the first failed to confound the prejudice against female rule, the second, Elizabeth I, was arguably the greatest sovereign in our history.

Contrast the childhoods of the first two Tudor queens regnant, Mary I and Elizabeth I, with the cocooned existence of the future Elizabeth II in the twentieth century, recalled in the saccharine account of Crawfie, her governess. Henry VIII threatened to chop off his daughter Mary's head if she did not submit to his will, declaring her mother's marriage 'by God's law and man's law incestuous and unlawful' and herself a bastard. By the time she was three, Elizabeth's status had changed from inheritrix of England to bastard; at thirteen, under suspicion of treason, she pitted her wits against the Council, and won; by the time she was twenty-one she was her sister's prisoner in the Tower, under threat of death. Their cousin, Lady Jane Grey, proclaimed Queen but never crowned and anointed, was only seventeen when she went to the scaffold, the innocent victim of ambitious and unscrupulous schemes to usurp the crown in her name.

Mary I and Elizabeth I came to the throne at a time of enormous religious upheaval. Everything that had brought comfort in previous centuries – the age-old traditions of the Church, which embraced kings, nobles and commoners in the whole body of Christendom from the cradle to the grave and beyond – had been stripped away, just as the reassuringly familiar figure of the King was replaced by a woman. How to assuage the anxiety that female rule generated, and how were these female sovereigns to overcome the drawbacks of their sex?

A tradition reaching back to Aristotle held that women were morally and physically inferior to men and therefore unfit to rule. The prejudice was strongly embedded in Christianity. The traditional Pauline doctrine of the Church – 'I gyve no licence to a woman to be a teacher nor to have authorite of the man, but to be in silence' – had applied to queens consort as well as commoners. Indeed, it was Matilda's authoritative personality that earned her the reputation of being 'proud' and alienated the Londoners, whose support was crucial if she was to be crowned. The preponderance of queens regnant and female regents in the mid sixteenth century, in England, Scotland, France and the Low Countries, coinciding with intense religious conflict, fuelled the debate.

John Knox's bitter diatribe, *The First Blast of the Trumpet against the Monstrous Regiment of Women*, was a vicious attack on female rule generally, although specifically targeted at three Catholic queens, among them Mary Tudor. 'It is a thinge most repugnant in nature, that women rule and governe over men,' he ranted, 'that a woman promoted to sit in the seate of God, that is, to teache, to judge or to reigne above man, is a monster in nature, contumelie to God, and a thing most repugnant to his will and ordinance.' In Knox's world, authority was equated with maleness; femaleness and rule were mutually contradictory.

The anomaly of female rule, for which there was no precedent, was partially addressed in England in the year of Mary I's accession with the passing of the Act Concerning Regal Power, which recognized the authority of a queen regnant by parliamentary statute. Parliament declared that the rule of Mary, and of future queens regnant, was as authoritative as that of a male monarch. The Act not only declared a queen regnant equal to a king, but also – radically – a woman, albeit a particular one, the equal of a man. It called the office 'kingly' and authorized a female sovereign to do anything a king could do 'as King'. This may be interpreted as meaning that a queen regnant was legally a king, that is, male, for the purpose of ruling. It appeared to dismiss all consideration of the alleged natural inferiority of women, perhaps because the crown is a corporation and not subject to the defects of mortality; that is, the monarch has a second, and wholly functional, body politic.

This medieval notion of the King's two bodies – the one immortal, part of the enduring body politic, the other mortal and open to human frailties – was useful in defining a female sovereign's dual role as ruler and wife. For the purpose of governing, Mary was a magistrate, superior to her earthly husband; as a woman and as a wife, in her mortal body, she was subordinate to her husband, whose gender lent him superiority. Elizabeth I would adopt the theory of the two bodies and exploit it for her own purposes. Her 'natural body' was that of a woman, subject to the weaknesses of her sex; her 'body politic' was that of a king, carrying the strength and masculine spirit of the best of her male predecessors: 'and though I am a woman, I have as good a courage answerable to my place as ever my father had.'

Patriarchal societies regard an anomalously powerful woman with suspicion, disquiet and revulsion – or with intense fascination, awe and devotion. In order to function successfully in a man's world, Elizabeth realized she would have to present herself as an extraordinary woman, not just an honorary male, but someone who could transcend nature itself by assuming a dual sexual identity as both king and queen. Yes, she had 'the body but of a weak and feeble woman', she admitted, but she also had 'the heart and stomach of a king'. In truth, Robert Cecil concluded at the end of her life, she was both 'more than a man and less than a woman'. Elizabeth's queenship was pure theatre, but the role she played, de-sexed and elevated above the norm, took an enormous amount of ingenuity. It was inevitable, perhaps, that as her powers began to wane in her last decade there should be a resurgence of misogyny, manifesting itself in an increase of witchcraft trials.

Elizabeth's success made queenship respectable, but there was little gratitude. 'If by chance she should die,' the French ambassador commented during the last decade of her reign – a time of war, poor harvests, inflation and impatience with an old woman's rule – 'it is certain that the English would never again submit to the rule of a woman.' History proved him wrong, of course. While the English nobility have rigidly adhered to the practice of primogeniture, whereby estates pass through the male line, so respectable has queenship become that the present royal family's Way Ahead Committee is discussing the possibility of altering the rules of inheritance to allow the monarch's eldest child, regardless of gender, to succeed.

Although Elizabeth made concessions to male discomfort at being commanded by a woman by making frequent references to her 'womanly weakness' – usually an implicit invitation to view her otherwise – succeeding queens regnant were both less brilliant and less alarming. During the seventeenth century patriarchal sentiments hardened. The publication of Robert Filmer's *Patriarcha* in 1680 ensured that Mary II would be forever entrapped in familial models and expected patterns of behaviour. She has always been judged as an appendage to the men in her life – as too bad a daughter and too good a wife – rather than on her own merits.

In a dual monarchy unique in English history, Mary accepted without question the subordinate role, even though she, not William, had the superior claim to the throne. When Parliament offered them joint sovereignty at a ceremony in the Banqueting House in February 1689, William answered for both of them, while Mary kept silent. Her role was to look good and curtsey. A natural diffidence, partly attributable to her limited education, and unquestioning acceptance of patriarchal ideas of female inferiority, meant that she underestimated her own abilities as a shrewd political operator and has in turn been underrated by posterity.

The demeanour of Anne, Victoria and Elizabeth II at their

accession evoked the chivalric protectiveness of their male counsellors. Elizabeth I had shown that an image of feminine vulnerability, properly exploited, could arouse the gallantry and loyalty of the gentlemen of England. Less artfully, but just as effectively, Anne addressed her first Parliament in her melodious voice, blushing as she spoke, which some considered very becoming in a woman. 'Never any woman spoke more audibly or with better grace,' one member noted approvingly.

When she ascended the throne after her grandfather and two uncles – a lunatic, a profligate and a buffoon – the eighteen-year-old Victoria's youthful femininity disarmed the monarchy's fiercest critics. She was a virgin with decorative appeal. The twenty-five-year-old Elizabeth II, with her beauty, serenity and amenability, inspired the same urge to place her on a pedestal. 'All the film people in the world, if they scoured the globe, could not have found anyone so suited to the part,' her elderly Prime Minister, Winston Churchill, marvelled. Neither Victoria nor Elizabeth II had any hesitation in using her femininity where it served her purposes to do so. Indeed, Victoria was highly skilled at exploiting the chivalrous instincts of her ministers to shield her whenever there was something she did not want to do.

Five of England's six queens regnant reigned before other women gained a political voice or the vote. The sixth, Elizabeth II, had been on the throne twenty-seven years before the election of the first woman Prime Minister, Margaret Thatcher. A queen regnant is an anomaly, an exception: all six believe they have God's divine sanction to rule, marking them apart, especially from other women. The presence of a female sovereign is not the signal for other women to start wielding power – far from it. By presenting herself as an extraordinary woman, Elizabeth I reinforced the inferior position of other women. In the late nineteenth century Victoria was vociferous in her hostility to the very notion of female advancement, telling Gladstone: 'The Queen is most anxious to enlist every one who can speak or write to join in checking this mad, wicked folly of "Women's Rights", with all its attendant horrors, on which her poor feeble sex is bent.'

In spite of wielding a power unique among women, queens regnant were prevented by their sex from active engagement in war. Traditionally, in the pre-coronation procession a king rode on horseback, symbolizing his readiness as a military leader. Mary I and, subsequently, Elizabeth I, appeared in the procession in a litter rather than on horseback; they wore white cloth of gold and went 'in their hair' – the symbols of purity and fertility adopted by queens consort. Her long hair worn loose reassured the onlookers that the queen regnant intended to marry and prove fruitful.

Like Elizabeth I, Anne was a Protestant queen engaged in a war with the most powerful Catholic king on earth. She had at her service the greatest military genius of the age in John Churchill, Duke of Marlborough, the hero of Blenheim. Less than forty years later, George II was the last British king who actually went into battle, at Dettingen. During the Crimean War Victoria, who was proud to be a soldier's daughter, confessed: 'I regret exceedingly not to be a man and to be able to fight in the war . . . I consider that there is no finer death for a man than on the battlefield.' She was more belligerent than her ministers. A year or so before her death at eighty-one, during the Boer War, she was proclaiming: 'We are not interested in the possibility of defeat. It does not exist.'

Elizabeth II is head of the armed forces, but as a constitutional monarch she is there, as Walter Bagehot described in the nineteenth century, 'to be consulted, to encourage and to warn': she is powerless to prevent war if her government decides on it. So discreet has she been about the content of her weekly audiences with her Prime Ministers that we can only speculate as to her views on the Suez debacle of 1956 or the Iraq War.

If queens regnant cannot be leaders in war, they are identified with the nation and its successes, and their patriotism is crucial. When she addressed her troops at Tilbury, Elizabeth I boasted that not only did she have 'the heart and stomach of a king', but 'of a king of England too' and took 'foul scorn that Parma or any prince of Europe should dare to invade the borders of my realm'. Mary II confessed to Sophie of Hanover that 'a woman is but a very useless and helpless creature . . . in times of war', but discovered in herself 'an old English inclination to the love and honour of the nation'. Like Elizabeth, Anne could boast she was 'mere English'. 'As I know my heart to be entirely English, I can very sincerely assure you there is not anything you can expect or desire from me which I shall not be ready to do for the happiness and prosperity of England.' Victoria was fiercely patriotic and a determined advocate of British interests. 'I really cannot say how proud I feel to be the Queen of such a nation,' she admitted.

Traditionally a queen's first duty has been to marry and produce an heir. Only Elizabeth I declined to do so. It took a very bold and courageous woman in the sixteenth century to elect not to marry at all. Elizabeth confessed with almost modern insight: 'There is a strong idea in the world that a woman cannot live unless she is married, or at all events that if she refrains from marriage she does so for some bad reason.'

A queen who would not be a wife and mother had to become something else. Elizabeth made great play of being married to England, of being both spouse and mother of her people. 'To conclude, I am already bound unto a husband, which is the kingdom of England,' she told a parliamentary delegation urging her to marry. Consciously or otherwise, she found she could rely on her sex to tap into the emotional power behind the image of wife-mother, particularly the most sacred mother of all, the Virgin Mary. The bejewelled statue of the Virgin, so abruptly cast out at the Reformation, was replaced by the gorgeously bejewelled and attired figure of the Queen at court. Like the Virgin before her she was carried in procession for her people to worship. Once she was no longer a fertile queen, her chastity became closely associated with England's impregnability; her virginity was the guarantee of the nation's welfare.

How does a queen reconcile her supremacy with a husband who must walk two steps behind her? The constitution does not recognize the consort of a queen. There is no defined role for him; he must forge his own. Victoria's Albert decided to subsume his identity in hers, as a strong husband manager who would not compete for attention with his wife. 'Whilst a female sovereign has a great many disadvantages in comparison with a king,' he conceded, 'yet, if she is married and her husband understands and does his duty, her position . . . has many compensating advantages, and, in the long run, will be found to be even stronger than that of a male sovereign.'

This did not mean that Albert was going to accept Victoria as he found her. First he had to break her will and mould her into an image of becoming womanhood. Not only was the carefully contrived image of wife and mother misleading, disguising the fact that Victoria exerted a masculine power in government, but it ensured that other women would remain in the domestic sphere. While Albert was alive, Victoria seemed to collude in her own diminishment: 'I am every day more convinced that we women, if we are to be good women, feminine and amiable and domestic, are not fitted to reign.' She had become dangerously dependent on Albert, so much so that her long seclusion after his death precipitated the most dangerous swing towards republicanism since she had come to the throne.

Motherhood raises the status of a queen, but queens are as much prisoners of biology as other women. The pressure to produce an heir was often overwhelming. In November 1554 Mary I sat under the cloth of estate in the Great Chamber at Whitehall 'richly apparelled, and her belly laid out, that all men might see that she was with child'. It was a tragic illusion. So desperate was she to have a child that she suffered one of the most public and humiliating cases of pseudocyesis – phantom pregnancy – in history. In losing control of her body, she exposed the person of the sovereign as all too fallible and lowered the prestige of the monarchy. Anne was equally unlucky. She had seventeen pregnancies and not one of her children survived her; most of them died in the womb in the later stages of pregnancy or in the first few days of life.

Victoria loathed the whole business of childbearing. 'I think these ladies who are always *enceinte* quite disgusting,' she wrote to her eldest daughter, 'it is more like a rabbit or a guinea pig than anything else and really it is not very nice.' She had nine children herself, the birth of the last two being eased by the administration of 'the blessed chloroform'. If, hitherto, Christian society had regarded women's suffering in childbirth as their just punishment for Eve's disobedience in the Garden of Eden – 'I will greatlie multiplie thy sorowe and thy conception, with sorowe shall thou beare thy children' – Queen Victoria's approval of the new panacea made it respectable for other women to follow suit. But like other 'respectable' women, Victoria had no knowledge of contraception. Could she not just have fun in bed, she asked her doctor after the birth of her last child, without the consequences? Only Elizabeth II emerged fit and well enough to ask for her boxes within a day or two of giving birth.

With or without children, queens are mothers of their people. When Mary I addressed the Londoners at Guildhall during Wyatt's rebellion she did so as their 'Queen and mother', 'not for having borne you as my children, but full of more than motherly love towards you since the day you chose me as your Queen and mistress'. Elizabeth I assured Parliament that 'though after my death you may have many stepdames, yet shall you never have any a more mother than I mean to be unto you all.' Anne, who had ruined her health in a forlorn attempt to give England an heir, would instead become the mother of her people. Her coronation sermon was preached on Isaiah 49: 23: 'And kings shall be thy nursing fathers, and their queens thy nursing mothers.' As long as she lived, she promised her First Lord of the Treasury, it 'shall be my endeavour to make my country and my friends easy'.

Victoria's apotheosis as Queen-Empress at the time of the Golden Jubilee owed a great deal to her carefully nurtured image as the imperial mother-figure to which millions of people of diverse races and religions could relate, as well as being in her own family the matriarch whom so many of Europe's crowned heads called simply 'Grandmama'.

Like mothers for their children, queens were suffused with love for their people, giving expression to that love in a way that kings did not. 'There is no jewel, be it never so rich a price, which I set before this jewel – I mean your loves,' Elizabeth I said in her Golden Speech, 'and though God has raised me high, yet this I count the glory of my crown: that I have reigned with your loves.'

For all Elizabeth's fine words, however, the legacy of childless queens was unease. Doubts about the efficacy of female rule rear their head whenever insecurity creeps in. It is no coincidence that towards the end of Mary I's reign there were rumours of 'sightings' of the boy-King Edward VI, arising from subconscious longing for the return of a king. Resentment at Elizabeth's refusal to name a successor gave rise to malicious slanders about her: that she and Leicester had children and that she went on progress every summer to give birth to those children. Similarly, Victoria's 'invisibility' during her widowhood fuelled the John Brown scandal. Rumour had it that the Highlander was the Queen's stallion, that they were secretly married and that they had a child together.

There is one moral standard for men, another for women. Kings are applauded for their mistresses, but no suggestion of scandal must touch a queen. Just as queens have to be exemplars of moral probity, so too, like women in the workplace generally, do they have to work twice as hard as men. All six queens have been hard-working, diligent, conscientious and dutiful. They believe they have been entrusted by God with a special responsibility. 'I know also that I must seek to discharge myself of that great burden that God hath laid upon me,' Elizabeth I declared, 'for of them to whom much is committed, much is required.'

Long before women had their own careers, Victoria was frustrated by the conflicting demands of her role as queen and as the mother of a large, fatherless family. 'And for a woman alone to be head of so large a family and at the same time reigning Sovereign is I can assure you almost more than human strength can bear,' she complained. By placing her duty to the country before her children, Elizabeth II perhaps fell short as a mother when her children were young. When she came to the throne, the National Federation of Women's Institutes passed a resolution urging that the nation 'should endeavour not to overwork our beloved young Queen, remembering that she has her duties also as a wife and mother', while the *Lancet* argued that she should be able to put her family life first, only attending the most important ceremonial occasions. She showed no inclination to take the advice.

The Queen is the embodiment of the nation, the universal representative of society, and it is in her we see our better selves reflected. The divorces of three of her four children and the Prince of Wales's admission of adultery on national television meant that the House of Windsor could no longer sell itself as the model family. Daylight had indeed been let in on the magic.

The most photographed woman in the world, Elizabeth II has been with most of us all our lives. She is ubiquitous. When she is referred to in the United States, it is simply as the Queen, in Germany *Die Königin*, in France *La Reine*; there is no need to specify the country. Like Victoria's, her head is on the coinage, the banknotes and the postage stamps. Unlike Victoria, she has lived her life under the relentless gaze of the camera lens. Her coronation in 1953 was the first time millions of people around the world saw the crown placed on the head of a queen; she was the first sovereign to be crowned, literally, 'in the sight of the people', through the new, intrusive medium of television. Elizabeth I had initiated the walkabout; this Elizabeth was in the living room as well. We probably see her face more often than we do that of our own mothers. She has even entered our dreams.

Longevity helps. Had Victoria died in 1870 her reign would have been considered in no way remarkable, perhaps even a bit of a failure; while in our own time Elizabeth II has weathered the worst – her annus horribilis in 1992 and the public backlash after the death of Diana, Princess of Wales, in 1997 – and seems to be entering a more serene ninth decade. As a queen who is politically impartial, she may well be judged one of the most politically accomplished women of her time.

England's queens regnant have presided over some of the greatest triumphs and events in our history. Three of them have given their name to an era. They have encouraged the growth of overseas empire, inspired cultural achievement, made possible a glorious and bloodless revolution, and almost always been equated with good government. A queen who became a queen-empress reigned over the greatest global empire the world has ever seen. Even after an era of imperial disintegration, the present Queen of Great Britain and Northern Ireland is Queen of sixteen other countries and Head of a Commonwealth comprising fifty-three countries – a family of nations she has helped shape and nurtured with almost maternal love. If there is a threat to her sovereignty from the encroaching European Union or incipient republicanism, she sails on unfalteringly, her majesty unimpaired, her sense of duty undiminished, so much so that any discussions about ending the monarchy are put on hold while she lives.

Today, more than four centuries after England gained its first female sovereign, queenship remains one of our greatest assets.

PART ONE: *House of Tudor*

MARY I
b. 1516, r. 1553–1558

I

Princess

WHEN THEY ARE born, princesses are expected to live happily ever after. They seldom do. Mary Tudor was a cherished only child, the darling of her family. Heiress presumptive to her mighty father, King Henry VIII, she was betrothed first to one great prince, then an emperor. But she was not the son her father wanted. Bewitched by the seductive charms of another woman, Henry banished his wife, good Queen Katherine, sending her to the unhealthiest place of confinement in all England. Cruelly separated from her beloved mother, Mary found herself alienated from her father, who withdrew his affection. She was degraded from princess to bastard. Her 'wicked' stepmother ordered her to wait on the sibling who had supplanted her as the heir of England, and threatened to force her into a base marriage or poison her. Her father, who had overturned Church and state to replace her with a son, was determined to have her submission and would not scruple to chop off her head.

All that seemed far away on a glorious May morning in 1515, when King Henry VIII and Queen Katherine, accompanied by their gorgeously attired courtiers, rode out from Greenwich Palace, up Shooters Hill and disappeared into the forest. Henry, a golden giant of a man, had always taken a childlike pleasure in May Day, rising at dawn to gather may and green boughs to mark the beginning of summer. Once, disguised as Robin Hood and his merry men, Henry and his cronies had burst into the Queen's chamber, sending her ladies scurrying with fright. Katherine, far more mature than her husband, smiled indulgently at the prank, pretending surprise. Now, deep in the forest, the royal party was greeted by 200 of the palace guard in green costumes masquerading as Robin Hood and his outlaws. Proud of their skill as bowmen, which had won the English the battles of Crécy and Agincourt, they fired a volley of arrows before the admiring company. Robin Hood then led the royal couple into an arbour decorated with flowers and aromatic herbs, where a great feast of venison and wine had been laid. On the way back to Greenwich, the party was met by the Queen of the May, who sang to them.

It was, of course, a fertility festival. Just over nine months later, on 18 February 1516, the Queen gave birth to a daughter at the riverside palace of Greenwich, where she and Henry had been privately married shortly after his accession seven years before. Katherine had already lost several babies, not least her first-born son. Pilgrimages to the shrine of Our Lady of Walsingham to pray for an heir had not proved fruitful, until now. Any disappointment at the child's sex was outweighed by the fact that she was healthy and likely to live.

The christening was held three days later with great pomp and solemnity at the nearby Church of the Observant Friars. Four knights held the canopy of estate over the baby Princess, who was wrapped so tightly against the cold that not even her face was visible. Under all the layers, she wore an exquisite christening robe, which her mother had brought from Spain. She was carried in the arms of the Countess of Surrey, flanked by the premier dukes, Thomas Howard, Duke of Norfolk, representing the old nobility, and Charles Brandon, Duke of Suffolk, the King's boon companion and parvenu husband of his favourite sister.

The procession stopped at the church door, where the priest blessed and named the child, and then proceeded into the church, richly hung with jewelled cloth of arras gleaming in the light of hundreds of candles. A brazier provided warmth, as the infant had to be dipped naked into the silver font, brought specially from Canterbury for the occasion. After the baptism, Margaret Pole, Countess of Salisbury, daughter of that Plantagenet Duke of Clarence who was drowned in a butt of malmsey, stood godmother at the confirmation. From the front of the church, the herald proclaimed the style and title of the Princess: 'God give good life and long unto the right high, right noble, and right excellent princess Mary, princess of England and daughter of our sovereign lord and king.'

After taking refreshment, the torch-lit procession returned in the same order to the palace to be met by Henry in the presence chamber.

It was not customary for the King of England to attend his child's baptism, while the Queen was still confined to her lying-in chamber, where she would remain until her 'churching', the purification ceremony that took place a month after the birth. To honour the King's children was to honour the King and Mary received many rich christening gifts: a gold cup from her godfather Thomas Wolsey, Cardinal Archbishop of York, a commoner of low birth but her father's indefatigable servant; a gold pomander from her aunt and namesake, Mary, Dowager Queen of France and Duchess of Suffolk; a gold spoon from her godmother and great-aunt, the Lady Katherine Courtenay, daughter of Edward IV and sister of the King's late mother, Elizabeth of York; and from her other godmother, the Duchess of Norfolk, a richly illuminated primer. After receiving her mother's blessing, the infant was taken away to the nursery in the Queen's apartments, where she would remain until she was weaned.

The Venetian ambassador, Sebastian Guistinian, took his time in coming to court to congratulate the King on the birth of his daughter. 'Had it been a son,' he told the Doge, 'it would not have been fit to delay.' He had the temerity to tell Henry that, of course, the Republic would much rather the child had been a boy. The remark must have irritated Henry, but his reply was determinedly optimistic. If 'it were a daughter this time, by the grace of God the sons will follow'.

All queens were under pressure to bear a male heir – indeed, it was their prime function – but for Katherine there was the added burden of knowing that her marriage was contentious. She was the widow of Henry's brother, Arthur, and although she maintained that her marriage to Arthur had not been consummated and a papal dispensation had been issued for Henry and Katherine to marry, there were lingering doubts about the propriety of the marriage. By the standards of the time, Katherine, at thirty-one, six years older than her husband, was already old for childbearing. She had a string of failed pregnancies behind her and time was running out.

For someone as macho as Henry VIII, a daughter was a deep injury to his self-esteem and hence to the glory of the monarchy, of which he was the personification. One of the most magnificent princes in Europe, Henry had used his charisma, his ebullient personality and his father's carefully hoarded millions to restore the monarchy to unprecedented heights and splendour, but what guarantee of its future if he did not have a son to succeed him? Was the King not the nation's leader in war; had he not personally led a military campaign in France to regain the conquests of his predecessors? How on earth could a woman do that?

Katherine knew different, sharing none of her husband's doubts about female sovereignty. When she herself was acting regent during Henry's absence in France, the English army won a resounding victory over the Scots at Flodden. Triumphant, she had sent the bloodstained coat of the slain James IV to Henry as a trophy. She had the example of her own mother, Isabella, before her. Isabella had not just been Queen of Castile and León in her own right, but also a warrior-queen. Katherine, the youngest of Isabella's children, had spent much of her childhood with her mother in military camps and she had been with both her parents at the conquest of Granada in 1492. Exhibiting a zeal for religious purity which would be mirrored in her granddaughter, Mary of England, Isabella had not rested until she had made Spain wholly Christian, eradicating Islam, forcing the Moors and the Jews either to convert or to leave. In that same year, she had also funded a Genoese seaman, Christopher Columbus, on a voyage that would end in the discovery of the New World in the Americas. It is reasonable to assume that Katherine regaled her daughter with stories of the great queen who was her grandmother, as she began quietly steering her towards her destiny as Queen of England.

Royal children were traditionally given their own establishments, but as a precious only child Mary was rarely too far away from the court, so that Katherine could visit her frequently. In this way, she forged a close bond with her daughter, getting to know her, as Henry did not, as a person. It was Katherine who probably taught Mary her letters and prayers, setting an example in religious devotion, and who later brought her influence to bear on her education.

Following the movements of the court, Mary's household made its circular progress from one royal manor to another in the Home Counties. It seems that Henry, fastidious and fearful of infection, was an early believer that cleanliness was a key to good health. Instructions for Mary's living arrangements paid particular attention to hygiene, 'so that everything about her be pure, sweet, clean and wholesome, as to so great a princess doth appertain; all corruption, evil airs, and things noisome and unpleasant, to be eschewed.'

As each residence was vacated to be 'sweetened', the Princess travelled on to the next by litter or barge, her gold cloth of estate denoting her royal status, her miniature throne of gold and silver, the little gold cushions for her feet, her tapestries, feather beds, coffers and plate following in a procession of carts. Only on great festivals such as Christmas – the most important in the Church and the court calendars – was Mary brought to join her parents at court. The twelve days of Christmas were a time of feasting and play-acting. There was a Lord of Misrule – a mock king with his own jester – and mummers with brightly coloured costumes and bells to delight a small princess.

On New Year's Day the King and Queen would exchange presents and make gifts of cash or plate to the chief personages of the realm and the officers of their households. Presents to Mary listed in the accounts were those valuables deemed worthy of her status or designed to impress; only one, a tree covered in gold spangles from a poor woman of Greenwich, was likely to have captured the imagination of a child. Christmas ended on 6 January, the Feast of the Epiphany, which began with a dramatic religious service recalling the recognition of Christ by the Three Kings, followed by feasting. Appropriately, the King and Queen wore their crowns on this day. The festivities that night were the most sumptuous of the whole year, including a pageant prepared by the Master of the Revels.

Mary would also be brought to court on particular diplomatic occasions. It was then that her boisterous father would proudly display the lovely little delicate blonde creature and make a fuss of her. The vainglorious Henry, so used to applause, desired the world to rejoice at the accomplishments of his daughter, which reflected well on him. She had inherited his passion for music. The King's Musik was the finest royal orchestra in Europe and his court resounded to the sound of trumpets, flutes, shawms, rebecs, tabourets, sackbuts, lutes and viols. As a small child held in her father's arms, Mary spotted among the crowd Friar Dionysio Memo, the organist of St Mark's, Venice, who had been invited to England to 'wait upon the King in his chamber'. Crying, 'Priest, priest!' she imperiously indicated that Memo should play for her. Something of a musical prodigy, she would be summoned to perform for foreign dignitaries, looking her over as a possible bride for one of their princes.

For all Mary's prettiness, charm and intelligence, however, she was not the boy Henry wanted and he was reluctant to recognize her as his successor. There was no precedent for female sovereignty in England. The Wars of the Roses, between the rival houses of York and Lancaster, were sufficiently recent for Henry to fear that everything he and his father had accomplished in establishing the Tudor dynasty and unifying the country under a strong monarchy would be thrown into jeopardy. Henry's mind was far too conventional to take seriously the idea of a female successor.

If Henry was at best ambivalent about female sovereignty, he had no compunction about treating his daughter as a valuable marriageable asset. Perhaps if he married her young, he might be succeeded by a grandson, rather as Henry I through his daughter Matilda had been succeeded by Henry II. There was an inherent danger in the marriage strategy, however. If he married her to a foreigner, England might lose its independence; if he married her to an Englishman – say, to Reginald Pole, the son of Mary's governess the Countess of Salisbury and a scion of the House of York – it could cause jealousy and faction at home.

While Mary was young, Henry could cynically use her as a pawn on the chessboard of international diplomacy. It is surely significant that he called her his 'pearl of the world' – an ornament, a treasure to be expended for the good of his kingdom. It was the fate of royal women. The idea that as a mere female she needed a husband must have been imprinted on Mary's consciousness from her earliest childhood.

At the age of two and a half she was betrothed to the Dauphin, a babe in arms, in a spectacular ceremony at Greenwich. Dressed in cloth of gold with a black velvet cap on her silver curls, the bejewelled child held out her small finger as the red-robed bulk of Cardinal Wolsey slipped a diamond ring on to it. When the Frenchman representing the Dauphin slipped the ring down to the end of her finger in a final act of solemnity, Mary, thinking he was her bridegroom, tried to kiss him.

She was six when that engagement was broken off in favour of an even grander alliance. The newly elected Holy Roman Emperor, Charles V, had inherited the Habsburg lands of his grandfather Maximilian in central and eastern Europe, the Low Countries from his father Philip the Fair of Burgundy, Aragon from his grandfather Ferdinand, and Castile and the Spanish Empire in the New World from his still living, but insane, mother Juana. He was, quite simply, the most powerful man in the world – and Katherine's nephew.

When Charles came to Greenwich in June 1522 Mary was waiting with her mother and the other ladies at the hall door to greet him. He knelt for his aunt's blessing, according to the Spanish custom. Flaxen-haired with brilliant dark eyes and the ungainly, under-slung Habsburg jaw, Charles was a serious young man, given to melancholy. Sixteen years older than his intended bride, he was evidently kind to Mary, because she remembered him all her life, until they died within weeks of each other. Henry resisted the Emperor's request that Mary be sent to Spain to be prepared for her future position as his consort, telling him that 'the young princess is not meet as yet to bear the pains of the sea, nor strong enough to be transported into the air of another country.' Besides, there was no one more suitable than her mother, a daughter of the royal house of Spain, to prepare her.

It was time for her education in England to begin in earnest. A memo later prepared for her governess, Margaret Pole, Countess of Salisbury, outlined her routine. Mary's first duty must be to serve God. She was 'to use moderate exercise, taking open air in gardens, sweet and wholesome places, and walks (which may conduce unto her health, solace and comfort)'. She was to practise her music – on the lute, harpsichord and virginals – and study French and Latin, but not so intensely as to make her tired. 'At other seasons to dance, and among the rest to have good respect to her diet, which is meet to be pure, well prepared, dressed and served with comfortable, joyous, and merry communication, in all honourable and virtuous manner.'

It does not sound too arduous, yet she was receiving the best education available for a woman in England at that time. Her parents' friend, Sir Thomas More, had been chiefly responsible for popularizing the concept of a classical education for women and it became fashionable in court circles to extol the capabilities of the 'weaker sex'. Katherine herself was one of the best-educated women in Europe, being well read in history, theology, philosophy, the classics and canon law and being able to converse easily in Latin. She was more than Henry's match intellectually. On a visit to Oxford in 1523 she met her compatriot, Juan Luis Vives of Valencia, who had become Reader in Latin, Greek and Rhetoric at Cardinal College. He presented the Queen with his *A Plan of Study for Children* and was duly rewarded with an invitation to spend Christmas at Windsor and a request to draw up a programme of studies for Mary.

It is not clear if Vives actually taught Mary, but he compiled his seminal book, *De Institutione Christianae Feminae*, as the central platform in her education. Its philosophy probably played a significant part in moulding her adult mind. Vives was offering a radical departure in education for women, but for a future woman ruler it had its limitations. He did not have huge confidence in the female sex and he made no concessions to Mary's future position: 'a woman is a fraile thinge and of weake discretion and that may lightly be disceyved.'

Vives sought to provide a way of changing women's experience within the restricted roles allowed by the patriarchal society of the time: he had no ambition to change their status. Crucially, he followed the traditional, Pauline teaching of the Church: 'I gyve no licence to a woman to be a teacher nor to have authorite of the man,' Vives wrote, 'but to be in silence.' Women were worth teaching and capable of learning, he maintained, but only so that they could be more virtuous. Hence the use of moral sayings in his second work dedicated to Mary, the *Satellitium*, as a way of encouraging moral action. Chastity was everything for a woman: not just abstinence from sex, but a purity of mind without even a consciousness of carnal desire.

Vives' brief for Mary seems to have been to prepare her for the inevitable dynastic marriage, when her superior education would enable her to give learned and wise counsel to a husband ruling in her name, rather as her mother had done when first married to the young and inexperienced Henry. Mary's education reinforced what she had already imbibed from all her father's marriage plans for her: her sense of inferiority and helplessness as a woman, the idea that she could not trust her own judgement, but must be dependent, the unfitness of her sex for sovereignty. No one, not even her mother, envisaged a queen ruling without the support and guidance of a husband.

In 1525 Charles V jilted Mary in favour of their cousin, Isabella of Portugal; Mary might be heir to a kingdom, but Isabella could provide the cash-strapped Emperor with capital and an immediate heir. Henry vented his fury at this international humiliation on Katherine, who turned forty this year. Prematurely aged, her looks and figure gone, she had long ceased to please him, and it was clear that he could no longer hope for a male heir from her. He toyed with the idea of legitimizing his son by Bessie Blount. Not sure which way to turn, he sent Mary to Ludlow to preside in vice-regal splendour over the Welsh Marches, rather as his brother Arthur had done when first married to Katherine. Mary was not actually created Princess of Wales, although some who wished to flatter – Vives, for instance, who dedicated the *Satellitium* to 'Mary, Princeps Cambriae' – referred to her as such.

Mary's departure for Ludlow might have been Henry's way of punishing Katherine or removing the girl from her mother's influence. Katherine missed her sorely. She kept up a deliberately cheerful front, writing to beg for a glimpse of her Latin homework. 'For it shall be a great comfort to me to see you keep your Latin and fair writing and all.'

Mary was once more a disposable asset, although the fact that she was still his sole heir and not far off the lawful age of cohabitation – twelve for a girl – made her future use in the marriage game increasingly hazardous. The husband he had in mind for her now was Francis I of France, a syphilitic lecher who was only two years younger than Henry. Not relishing the prospect of marrying a twelve-year-old, Francis made a counter-proposal, offering his younger son, Henri of Orléans. In April 1527 Mary was summoned back to court for inspection. At the culmination of the festivities she danced with the principal French ambassador, while her father took as his partner one of the Queen's maids of honour, Mistress Anne Boleyn, daughter of the diplomat Sir Thomas Boleyn of Blickling in Norfolk and Hever Castle in Kent.

If Mary noticed Mistress Boleyn at all, she might have wondered why she of all the ladies had been chosen, other than that she could converse with the visitors in her excellent French. She would not have been aware of the impact this fascinating creature had made from the moment she arrived at the English court. In spite of her expressive, coal-black eyes, shining mass of auburn-tinted dark hair and elegance, Anne was not conventionally beautiful. Her face was long and narrow and her skin has been described as sallow. Brought up in the courts of Burgundy and France, however, she knew how to make the best of herself, with an exquisite sense of style. She had a confidence and sophistication that English women lacked. She was clever and well read, a witty and engaging conversationalist, and possessed an indefinable sexual allure. The sheltered Mary would have been amazed to learn that her father was truly smitten, that he had been bombarding Mistress Boleyn with love letters for over a year and that the two had plighted their troth that very January.

Oblivious of the fact that she had just met the woman who would poison her life, Mary was the belle of the ball and still, apparently, her father's joy. When she finished dancing, he took great pleasure in pulling off 'her cap and the net being displaced, a profusion of silver tresses as beautiful as ever seen on human head fell over her shoulders'.

While dutifully admiring her charms, the French calculated that Mary was so thin and underdeveloped that she would not be ready for marriage for at least two years. Worse, the Bishop of Tarbes, acting on rumours that Henry was thinking of repudiating Katherine, raised the shattering question whether Henry, in putting Mary forward as his heir, was not ignoring the possibility that his marriage was invalid and his daughter therefore born out of wedlock. He merely crystallized doubts Henry had been harbouring for some time.

Twelve days after the court ball, Cardinal Wolsey opened the secret trial of the King's marriage, summoning Henry to answer charges of living in sin with his brother's wife. It was so secret that Henry did not even have the courtesy to inform his wife of nearly twenty years that it was happening. The timing could not have been worse, however, because on 6 May 1527 Imperial troops sacked Rome and Pope Clement VII became, to all intents and purposes, a prisoner of Katherine's nephew, Emperor Charles.

Her status and prospects suddenly uncertain, the curtain came down on Mary's happy childhood.

2

Bastard

Princess mary was on the brink of adolescence when the question of her parents' divorce arose. After being adulated as a princess and a precious only child, she spent her youth – the best part of a decade – in a state of uncertainty, fear, anger, misery and humiliation. It was to embitter her life.

Mary allied herself firmly with her mother over the divorce and took her cue in blaming the whore Anne Boleyn for the transformation of her father's character and the alienation of his affections. Denied the quick divorce he had taken for granted, frustrated at every turn by papal prevarication and the stubborn refusal of Katherine to co-operate, Mary's once fun-loving and generous father became cruel and tyrannical, a monster she no longer recognized.

In considering his childlessness, Henry had convinced himself that he was under God's displeasure. Did it not say in Leviticus 20: 21: 'If a man shall take his brother's wife, it is an unclean thing: he hath uncovered his brother's nakedness; they shall be childless'? In vain, Katherine argued that they were not childless, they had Mary. Henry brushed this aside; she was a girl, she did not count. 'Although we have had the lady Mary, singular both in beauty and shape, by the most noble lady Katherine,' he pontificated, 'yet that marriage cannot be legitimate which gives us such pain and torment of conscience.'

Henry's mistake had been to question the validity of his marriage, rather than laying before Katherine the very real threat – as he saw it – to the peace and unity of the realm if he were to be succeeded by a daughter and gently persuading her to step aside, leaving him free to remarry. Katherine might have been more amenable if it had not been so blatantly obvious that Henry was moved not so much by his conscience as by lust for Anne Boleyn. Stubborn, courageous, implacably convinced of the rightness of her cause, Katherine could never accept that her marriage was invalid, for that would be to imply that she had been nothing but Henry's whore and her daughter a bastard. She had powerful international allies and the weight of public opinion on her side – particularly the women, for if the King could repudiate his wife, what security did they have? She looked to Rome for justice and, failing that, to God.

Officially, Katherine still presided as queen at court, but Anne had as good as usurped her position and, on her visits to her parents, Mary would have noticed how marginalized her mother had become. The tension was palpable. It was not altogether surprising, therefore, that in the spring of 1531, shortly after parting from her mother, Mary fell ill. The Milanese ambassador reported that she had 'what the physicians call hysteria'. 'Hysteria', in contemporary parlance, indicates a menstrual disorder, but whether it signalled the onset of puberty, or a particular malfunction brought on by stress is not clear. Ever after, Mary would suffer from amenorrhoea, the irregularity or cessation of menstrual periods, which sixteenth-century physicians described as 'strangulation of the womb' or 'suffocation of the mother'. The disorder included depression – 'heaviness, fear and sorrowfulness' – headaches, vomiting, palpitations, difficulty in breathing and abdominal swelling. There is also a suggestion that the emotional disturbance of her parents' divorce caused an eating disorder. In due course, Mary would suffer – like her grandmother Isabella and her cousin Charles – from a profound melancholy.

Concerned for Mary, Katherine pleaded with Henry to bring her to Greenwich. He replied that she might go to her daughter – and stay there. She would not leave him for her daughter or anyone else in the world, she assured him. But Henry had other ideas. On the morning of 14 July 1531, when they were at Windsor, Henry and Anne and their party rode out, ostensibly on a hunting trip, leaving Katherine behind in the suddenly silent castle. They did not return. After twenty-two years of marriage, Henry had not even bothered – or been too shamefaced and embarrassed – to bid her farewell in person. Mary was allowed to go to her mother at Windsor and the two enjoyed one last extended holiday together. Then Katherine was ordered to go to the More, a run-down manor in Hertfordshire, while Mary was to leave for Richmond before Henry and Anne returned to Windsor. During the five years that remained of Katherine's life, mother and daughter were never to see each other again.

Mary's circumstances did not immediately alter. Small, but well proportioned, with a pretty face and a beautiful complexion, and a surprisingly gruff and mannish voice for such a delicate girl, the fifteen-year-old held court at Richmond. The Master of the Great Wardrobe was still providing her with clothes fit for a princess: gowns of cloth of silver tissue, purple and black velvet and crimson satin, kirtles of gold and silver, velvet shoes and Spanish gloves, Holland cloth for smocks and ribbon for trim. Henry sent her gifts of pocket money and even contrived to meet her on one or two occasions – furtively, it seems, as Anne's spies were never far behind. Ironically, just as Mary became ready for marriage, the question of her legitimacy scotched a dynastic match.

In January 1533 Anne, who had withheld her sexual favours until she was sure that marriage would be forthcoming, triumphantly told Henry that she was pregnant. It was imperative that the child – and Henry was sure it would be a son – was born in wedlock, so that they went through a secret marriage ceremony. In May Thomas Cranmer, the former Boleyn chaplain who had been appointed Archbishop of Canterbury, held a court at Dunstable, where on his own authority he declared the King's first marriage null and void. Convocation meekly fell in with royal demands. Katherine had never envisaged that Henry would bypass Rome in his quest for a divorce, but by 1533, under the influence of Anne and the Boleyn faction with their Lutheran sympathies and with legislation masterminded by his new man, the ruthless Thomas Cromwell, he was effectively cutting himself off from the papacy. As the imprisoned Pope ruefully realized, Henry had stumbled on his own solution and England was hastening towards heresy and schism.

Jealous and tempestuous, Anne was relentless in her enmity towards Katherine. Not content with all the jewels Henry had showered on her, she must have Katherine's too. She knew just where to wound, demanding the beautiful christening robe that Katherine had brought from Spain. Even though Mary was now technically a bastard, Anne saw her as a threat to her unborn child. She boasted that she would make her a maid of honour, or perhaps 'give her too much dinner' – poison her – or 'marry her to some varlet'. Once the child was born, Mary would be expendable.

The Imperial ambassador, Eustace Chapuys, Katherine and Mary's friend, could hardly contain his glee when on 7 September 1533 Anne gave birth to a girl. Henry was furious. In the sixteenth century it was not understood that the man determined the sex of a child. To Henry, it was another dent on his manhood. 'Am I not a man like others – am I not? Am I not?' he shouted at Chapuys, when he had the temerity to suggest that there was no guarantee of children, even with a new wife.

If the child had been a boy, he would have taken precedence without question and Mary would have been relatively safe, but with the birth of another girl, who by rights should take second place to an elder sister, the persecution of Mary began in earnest. Elizabeth was given Mary's former title: she was to be Princess of England, inheritrix of the realm. A few months later the Act of Succession stated that the children of Henry and his 'most dearly and entirely beloved wife Queen Anne' were to be considered the King's lawful heirs. In lieu of sons, the crown was to devolve upon Elizabeth and her lawfully begotten children. Although Mary was not named specifically in the Act, the implications were obvious. In future she was to be known merely as the Lady Mary, the King's daughter.

It was hardly a recipe for harmony between the sisters. Two months after Elizabeth's birth, Anne followed up her threat that the King's dispossessed daughter should wait upon her child. A deputation led by Anne's uncle, the Duke of Norfolk, arrived at New Hall, where Mary was staying, and broke up her establishment. She was to be taken to Hatfield, as a member of her sister's household.

Here, Norfolk asked if she would go and pay her respects to her sister, the Princess. Mary replied that she knew of no other princess in England except herself. 'Have you no message for the King?' he asked.

'None,' she replied, 'except that the Princess of Wales, his daughter, asked for his blessing.'

'That is a message I dare not take,' Norfolk told her.

'Then go away, my lord, and leave me alone.'

And so, concluded Chapuys in his report to the Emperor, 'she retired to weep in her chamber, as she does continuously.' Mary had been given the worst room in the house, unworthy even of a maid of honour.

She now concentrated all her energies on defying her father. She could never approve the revolutionary doctrine, contained in the Act in Restraint of Appeals, that 'this realm of England is an Empire . . . governed by one supreme head and king', to whom the body politic, both spiritual and temporal, 'be bounden and owe to bear next to God a natural and humble obedience'. Nor with the Act of Supremacy, which acknowledged Henry, his heirs and successors, to be the Supreme Head of the Church of England, with authority 'to reform and redress all errors, heresies and abuses of the same'. Still Catholic, her father had severed England's thousand-year allegiance to the papacy. His power and strength as King of England could only be enhanced by the aggregation of all allegiance, spiritual and temporal, to himself. This meant he held sway not just over his people's mortal lives, but also their souls. Not only did Mary not agree, but she embraced the Catholic faith and allegiance to Rome with renewed fervour as part of her loyalty to her mother.

Under the tyranny of her father and stepmother, her efforts were expended on the negative. In this way, she was as much an affliction to herself as to those around her. She refused to give up her title of Princess, even when Henry sent Cromwell and other heavies to force her to do so. When Anne heard she was taking her meals in her room, she forced her to dine in public, where she had to sit in an inferior place to Elizabeth. When the household was moving from one residence to another, Elizabeth was given the best litter, while Mary had to follow in a shabbier one. But Mary was never prepared to yield precedence to her sister without a struggle. To do so would be interpreted as a tacit admission of the other's rights and abandonment of her own.

Whenever Henry came to visit Elizabeth, Mary was confined to her room, but on one such occasion she went up on to the leads of the roof to catch a glimpse of him as he left. Seeing her there on her knees, with her hands joined either in prayer or supplication, Henry bowed to her and touched his hat. His fawning courtiers duly followed his example, saluting her respectfully.

Lady Shelton, Anne's aunt, had charge of Mary. When Norfolk and Lord Rochford, Anne's brother, reprimanded her for 'behaving to the Princess with too much respect and kindness, saying that she ought only to be treated as a bastard', Lady Shelton replied that 'even if Mary were only the bastard of a poor gentleman, she deserved honour and good treatment for her goodness and virtues.' Anne urged her to slap Mary's face every time she claimed to be the true princess, reminding her of 'the cursed bastard that she was'.

Once or twice, Anne tried to change tack, inviting Mary to honour her as queen, saying that it would be a means of reconciliation with her father. Mary haughtily replied that she knew of no queen in England except her mother. She had a tendency – which grew more marked with age – to see everything in terms of black and white. She rebuffed Anne's overtures without considering that Anne had troubles of her own: Henry's constant philandering which had begun when she was pregnant with Elizabeth, the pressure on her to bear a son – so intense that in 1534 she may have been suffering from a false pregnancy – her knowledge of her unpopularity, and her fear for her daughter's security in a hostile world.

Fearful that her father would put her to death, as he had many others for refusing to acknowledge the Act of Succession, Mary was pleading with Chapuys to find a way for her to flee the country. Flight was the natural reflex of a young woman goaded beyond endurance and in terror of her life. So desperate was Mary that she told Chapuys that she would cross the Channel in a sieve if necessary. Knowing what a valuable asset Mary would be in the hands of a foreign power, Henry had her and the ports watched, so that there was no realistic possibility of escape.

Two days before her nineteenth birthday, Mary fell dangerously ill. As she lay in pain surrounded by enemies, she heard them say that they hoped she would die. Anne had declared on many occasions that she meant to kill Mary, saying, 'She is my death, and I am hers; so I will take care that she shall not laugh at me after my death.' Rumour had it that Mary had been poisoned, but Henry's physician, Dr Butts, more accurately attributed her condition to her 'ill treatment'. He advised Henry to send her to her mother, so that he would be freed from all suspicion if she died.

By now, Katherine was in her final place of confinement, Kimbolton in Huntingdonshire – isolated, damp, pestilential and gloomy. She was pleading with Cromwell to send Mary to her, so that she could nurse her in the same bed. A little comfort and cheer would 'be half the cure', she promised. 'I have found this by experience, being ill of the same sickness.'

Henry was not prepared to risk the consequences. His only hope of forcing Mary to renounce her title and claim to the throne was by isolating her, cutting her off from those who loved her. He suspected the worst of Katherine: 'She is of such high courage,' he said, 'that, with her daughter at her side, she might raise an army and take the field against me with as much spirit as her mother Isabella.' On the contrary, Katherine was tormented by the fact that her principled stand on her marriage had driven Henry and England away from the true Church. She had no intention of harming her adopted country further by inciting civil war.

By late 1535 Anne was expecting another child. A son would mean her final triumph over Katherine, perhaps even the death of Katherine, for did not an old prophecy say that a Queen of England would be burned at this time? She wrote boasting to Lady Shelton that it no longer mattered whether Mary bowed to her father's wishes or not, 'for if I have a son, as I hope shortly, I know what will happen to her'. The letter was left lying around for Mary to read.

In January 1536 Katherine died. She had been reduced to living in one room with a handful of attendants; fearing poison, her food was cooked on the fire in front of her. She wrote a last loving letter to Henry, beseeching him to be a good father to Mary. Informed bluntly of her mother's death by Lady Shelton, Mary retired to her room to mourn alone. Naturally she did not attend the funeral. Katherine was buried at Peterborough as Princess Dowager, with the officiating bishop mendaciously claiming that she had admitted on her deathbed that she had never been legally married to the King.

It was on the day of Katherine's funeral that Anne lost the child who would have been her saviour. The foetus was about three and a half months old and was judged to be male. When Henry visited her, he told her ominously that 'he saw clearly that God did not wish to give him male children'. There would be no more chances. In Henry's mind, God was frowning on a marriage that, given that Anne's sister had once been his mistress, was every bit as incestuous as the union between Henry and Katherine. While Katherine was alive, Henry could not afford to dispose of Anne without being obliged to take his first wife back. His passion assuaged, he had quickly begun to tire of Anne, muttering that he had been 'seduced by witchcraft'. At the beginning of May she was suddenly arrested and tried on trumped-up charges of adultery and incest with her brother. The sentence for a queen condemned for high treason was to be burned alive, just as the old prophecy predicted, but in a rare show of mercy Henry had it commuted to beheading.

If Mary felt her stepmother's death would clear the way for reconciliation with her father, she was sadly mistaken. When Queen Jane Seymour, whom Henry married with indecent haste within days of Anne's execution, pleaded with him to make peace with Mary, he told her she was a fool and that she should be thinking of the advancement of her own children. Jane replied that she *was* thinking of them, in that the country could only be at peace if he did right by Mary. The people had always loved her and regarded her as the rightful heir. Only Cromwell really understood that there could be no turning back the clock; that Henry was utterly committed to the royal supremacy. He had no intention of validating his first marriage, or of returning to Rome; indeed, the wealth of the Church in England lay temptingly before him, his for the taking.

Mary had a following in England and powerful relatives abroad; she was a potential figurehead of opposition in an increasingly restless realm. The people were uneasy at the King's drift away from the religious sureties they had always known and were about to become more so: in 1536 the Pilgrimage of Grace, the most dangerous rebellion of Henry's reign, was to break out in the North. The destruction of the monasteries had begun: the inmates were being cast out, the beautiful buildings stripped of their valuables and despoiled, their treasures dispersed, leaving barren scars on the landscape. Monastic property, amounting to one-quarter of the land of England, was appropriated by the crown, triggering off the biggest land grab since the Conquest. Now, the aristocracy, the gentry and aspiring lawyers and merchants could literally buy into the Reformation, for which of them would want to return to the Roman allegiance if it meant returning their newly acquired property?

The destruction of the monasteries would be followed by the abolition of pilgrimages, shrines, holy relics and the use of candles or tapers before images. In Canterbury, one of the most famous places of pilgrimage in Europe, the tomb of Thomas à Becket – 'a rebel and a traitor to his prince' – would be ransacked, the fabulous jewels that had been the gifts of kings and other pilgrims sent in twenty-six carts to London to be presented to the King, the saint's bones consigned to a bonfire. In Walsingham, to whose shrine Henry himself had walked barefoot as a young man to offer a great ruby, the ancient wooden statue of the Virgin would be removed and sent to London, where it would be ceremoniously burned along with other notable images.

It was one thing to destroy, another to erase the much loved images and traditions of centuries from the people's hearts and minds.

Conscious of her symbolic importance, Henry was determined to make an example of Mary. He wanted nothing less than her acknowledgement of the royal supremacy and the invalidity of her mother's marriage and her own illegitimacy, as reiterated in the new Act of Succession of 1536. It was a matter of state, but also personal. In a patriarchal society, a girl owed her father unquestioning obedience, as she would later do a husband. It irked Henry that Mary had taken her mother's side in the divorce. If he could not have her love, he would certainly have her abject submission. If it meant breaking her will and threatening her death, so be it.

When Mary did not immediately hear from her father, she wrote to Cromwell, asking him to intercede for her. 'Nobody dared to speak for me as long as that woman lived,' she told him, but now she hoped that he would be the means of reconciliation with her father, assuring him of her desire to obey the King as far as her conscience allowed. Oblivious to the fact that she was taking quite the wrong approach in placing her conscience before the King, Mary followed this up a few days later with a letter to Henry himself. She begged his blessing and forgiveness for her past offences, 'in as humble and lowly a manner as a child can'. It was by no means humble enough. Mary assured him that she would obey him in all things 'next to God', 'humbly beseech-ing your Highness to consider that I am but a woman and your child, who hath committed her soul only to God, and her body to be ordered in this world as it shall stand with your pleasure'.

To Henry, it sounded like Katherine all over again.

Cromwell drafted a letter of submission which Mary merely had to copy and sign. She returned a letter in which she declared herself 'most humbly prostrate before the feet of your most excellent Majesty', his most obedient, repentant and humble child who was 'ready, next to Almighty God, to put herself totally at his gracious mercy'. In a covering letter, Mary thanked Cromwell and told him she had followed his advice, in so far as God allowed. She had done 'the utmost my conscience will suffer me' and could do no more.

Needless to say, Cromwell's original draft had said nothing about Almighty God – an insertion that rendered the submission useless. Furious, Cromwell warned her that unless she complied he would wash his hands of her for good. Beginning at last to understand how perilous her situation was, Mary faithfully copied the draft again 'without adding or minishing' and returned it to Cromwell. She was leaving the letter unsealed, she told him, as she could not bear to write a second copy for Cromwell. 'For the pain in my head and teeth hath troubled me so sore these two or three days, and doth yet so continue, that I have very small rest, day or night.'

Henry was still not satisfied. He sent a commission, headed by the Duke of Norfolk, to Hunsdon, with a set of articles for Mary's signa-ture and full authority to use any tactic to bully her into submission. The document stated that 'the said lady Mary hath sundry times and of long continuance showed herself so obstinate towards the King's Majesty, her sovereign lord and father, and so disobedient unto the laws . . . that she seemed a monster in nature.' She was to renounce the authority of the Bishop of Rome, as the Pope was now called in England, and to recognize and accept the King to be Supreme Head 'in earth under Christ of this Church of England'. She was to submit to all his laws 'like a true subject . . . and maintain them to her power'. Finally, she was to acknowledge the marriage between the King and her mother, 'the late Princess Dowager', to have been 'by God's law and man's law incestuous and unlawful'.

For Mary to give in to the last demand would be to dishonour her mother. Nor could she agree to repudiate the Pope. Through all her misery, Mary had clung to the religion her mother upheld to the end, and would continue to do so with increasing ardour. She refused to sign. Norfolk and the other commissioners now turned nasty. She was such an unnatural daughter, said one, that he doubted if she was even the King's bastard. Another added that if she were *his* daughter, he would beat her to death. He would knock her head against a wall until it was as soft as a boiled apple. They told her she was a traitor to the King and his laws and would be punished accordingly. Then they left, telling her that she had four days to think it over.

Trapped and in fear of her life, she seemed to have no alternative than to give way to her father's demands. Chapuys advised her to submit. God looked more at the intentions than the deeds of men, he told her, and perhaps if she swallowed her principles now she would save herself in order to serve Him better in the future. Late on the fourth night, Mary signed, without looking at the paper. She had been beaten into submission, mentally if not physically. To make matters worse, the papal absolution she secretly sought was not forthcoming. Nothing could alter the fact that she had betrayed the mother she loved and revered. The betrayal would haunt her for the rest of her life, while her father's terror tactics left her psychologically scarred.

Mary's return to favour was heralded by a meeting with the King and Queen. Henry had not seen his daughter to speak to for five years, since she was fifteen. 'There was nothing but conversing with the Princess in private,' Chapuys reported, 'and with such love and affection and such brilliant promises for the future that no father could have behaved better.' Jane, who had served Queen Katherine as a maid of honour, was predisposed to treat Mary with genuine kindness, showing her so much deference that she would take her by the hand, so that they could both pass through a door together, rather than take precedence herself. Meanwhile, Henry pressed a draft for 1,000 crowns into his daughter's hand, for 'her little pleasures', with the assurance that there would be plenty more.

Now she was the predominant sister again – for the Act of Succession of 1536 had rendered Elizabeth a bastard as well – Mary did not forget her little half-sister, a motherless child just turned three. Although she could never quite forgive Elizabeth for innocently usurping her place as Princess of England or forget the humiliations she had endured at the hands of Anne Boleyn, she was kind enough to remind Henry of her existence, commending her as 'such a child toward as I doubt not but your Highness shall have cause to rejoice of in time coming'.

Mary must have been profoundly relieved when in October 1537 Queen Jane, after a labour of fifty hours, gave the King a male heir. The focus of attention moved away from her on to the longed-for son. He was named after St Edward the Confessor and proclaimed Duke of Cornwall and Earl of Chester in a magnificent christening ceremony, at which Mary had the honour of being godmother. It was after midnight when the torch-lit procession reached the Queen's apartments, where she lay in bed feverish. Mary presented her godson with a gold cup and gave a generous sum to the midwife, the nurse and the rockers.

Days after her great triumph, the twenty-nine-year-old Jane died of puerperal fever. Hating sickness and death and any reminders of it, Henry fled to Hampton Court, leaving Mary to supervise the funeral arrangements and to act as chief mourner, sitting in vigils by the coffin, saying Masses for the departed soul, and following the hearse as it was taken in torch-lit, night-time procession in stages to its final resting place in the Garter Chapel at Windsor.

For the rest of her father's reign, Mary fulfilled the role of first lady at his court whenever he was between wives. He seems to have been grateful for her company and lavished jewellery on her. Whether or not she ever forgave him for his treatment of her and her mother, she was careful to show him all outward signs of deference and obedience. She helped his last wife, Katherine Parr, nurse him, his temper rendered ever more irascible by the pain of his ulcerous leg. At Christmas 1545 he was touched by her thoughtfulness when she gave him a bespoke wooden chair, beautifully upholstered, to accommodate his giant bulk.

Living mainly at court, Mary's Privy Purse expenses reveal the serene existence of a high-born lady. She received innumerable gifts for her table: a swan from Lady Butler and a hogshead of wine from

Lady Lisle, pears from Chapman the gardener at Hampton Court and a quince pie from Master Parry. The country people left gifts of strawberries, cherries and cucumbers, while the keepers of the Great Park at Windsor presented her with a buck and a stag. Knowing her love of gardening, the King's gardener at Greenwich offered her herbs and flowers. Someone else gave her roses. There was a gift of rose water, perhaps used to sweeten the closet where her robes were kept. A London woman brought a bird in a cage to please her, while some Venetian visitors left her a looking glass – a great novelty.

Mary's was a musical household, with money paid to someone 'comyng from London for mending of my lady graces virgynnalle'. Every month there was the expense of 'shaving of Jane fooles hedde'. This female jester, Jane the Fool, had to be kitted out with new shoes and hose, presumably part of her clown costume. The servant of John 'Poticary' – John the Apothecary – was paid for 'bringing stuff to my lady grace soundry tymes', while a surgeon would come from London 'to lett my lady grace bloode'. Christopher, the keeper of Mary's greyhounds, had to be given money for their meat and, since only ladies' lapdogs were allowed inside the court, for their kennels. There are many little gifts to Elizabeth – a box embroidered with silver and 'a pomander of golde with a diall in yt' – presumably some sort of timepiece. One day Elizabeth received ten shillings 'to play w'all'. Mary amply fulfilled the obligation of a great lady to dispense alms. There was money to be distributed 'amonge the prisons in London', 'to a scoler of Cambridge' and 'to a pore priest' – perhaps a former monk ejected from his monastery.

Mary loved children and stood godmother to a great many, often those of her servants and quite humble people. She must have profoundly regretted that she was not a mother herself. An unmarried woman was an anomaly, but, as ever, she was powerless to change her fate. Remembering Vives' instruction that 'it is not comely for a mayde to desire marriage and moche lesse to shew herselfe to longe therefor' she must wait for her father to choose a husband for her.

The English candidate for her hand, the one her mother had favoured, Reginald Pole, son of Mary's old governess the Countess of Salisbury, was in exile. He had publicly criticized Henry and allowed himself to be caught up in a papal scheme for an invasion of England, involving Henry's overthrow and Pole's marriage to Mary. Henry, whose cruelty remained undiminished, decided to eliminate the last tiresome remnants of the House of York, whose royal blood, mad-cap schemes and reactionary politics posed a threat to his young heir, Edward. Pole's elder brother, together with a Courtenay and a Neville, were executed, while his sixty-nine-year-old mother, who had been a second mother to Mary, was hacked to death in a botched execution.

As far as Catholic Europe was concerned, Mary was Henry's rightful, legitimate heir. Edward, born of a marriage that had taken place while England was in schism, was not considered the legal heir by Catholic purists, but Mary did not agree with this. She loved her little brother and saw no reason why he should not succeed their father. Henry had indeed restored her to her place in the succession, after Edward and before Elizabeth, but, never one to admit a wrong, he did not go so far as to reverse the bastard status of either of his daughters.

He was still using the adult Mary in the diplomatic marriage game, just as he had when she was a small child, first pretending to consider the Emperor's proposal of Dom Luiz, younger brother of the King of Portugal, then veering off towards a French alliance. Only one man, Duke Philip of Bavaria, a Lutheran, came to woo Mary in person, asking Henry for her hand in marriage and offering to do military service for him. The courtship came to nothing.

As Mary ruefully admitted to one of her chamber women, the marriage negotiations for this husband or that would continue, but 'nothing would be got from them but fine words, for she would be, while her father lived, only Lady Mary, the unhappiest lady in Christendom'.

Realizing that the world would be a difficult place for his daughters when he was dead, Henry made generous provision for them in his will. When he died in January 1547, Mary discovered that she was a great landed magnate in her own right. Probably considering herself too old at thirty-one for marriage, she no doubt looked forward to a future spent in peace and relative obscurity. In this modest hope she was to be both disappointed and confounded.

3

Rebel

IN THE SUMMER OF 1553 Mary's brother, the boy-King Edward VI, lay dying. He was showing symptoms of advanced tuberculosis: lethargy, racking cough, spitting of blood and the ejection of foul greenish-yellow and black phlegm. Once more the question of the succession loomed. A fervent Protestant far to the left of his father, Edward was tormented by the prospect of his Catholic sister Mary succeeding him and overturning all the godly work of recent years. Indeed, there were far too many prominent courtiers who had done well out of the Reformation and had too big a stake in the regime to contemplate a return to the old religion, of which Mary was the undoubted representative. It was an easy matter for the ruthless and ambitious regent, John Dudley, Duke of Northumberland, to play on those fears and persuade Edward to set aside his late father's will and devise his own plan for the succession.

Through most of Edward's six-year reign, Mary had fought a war of attrition. A great landed magnate in East Anglia, she avoided the court, playing no part in politics, which were driven by the ambition and greed of the key protagonists: first, Edward's maternal uncle, Edward Seymour, Duke of Somerset, then, after his overthrow, by John Dudley, Earl of Warwick, who seized power late in 1549, sending his erstwhile rival to the scaffold two years later. A magnetic personality with several sons of his own, Warwick — soon created Duke of Northumberland — quickly gained ascendancy over Edward, who looked up to him with genuine admiration. Unlike Somerset, who kept the boy short of pocket money, Northumberland knew how to win Edward's gratitude and loyalty, flattering him by listening to his opinions and giving him an illusion of a greater say in affairs, pandering to his rigid Protestant beliefs.

Somerset had been determined to carry the Reformation in England to its logical conclusion. In a few months he had virtually eradicated the seasonal rituals of the Church, abolishing the feast days and ceremonies and expunging prayers to individual saints. The existence of purgatory was denied, prayers for the dead were forbidden. The chantries and guilds, where Masses had been offered up for the dead, were destroyed, their wealth forfeit to the crown.

Over the next few years, the parish churches were systematically stripped of their Catholic furnishings: their high altars and side altars, their statues, rood screens and holy water stoups. The perpetrators embarked on an orgy of destruction. Exquisite gold and silver objects were smashed for easier transport; lovely carvings were hacked to pieces; richly coloured medieval wall paintings and the 'Doom' – the Last Judgement – above the altar whitewashed. Even as Edward lay dying, processions of carts were trundling towards London, replete with the last treasures of the old religion, lovingly lavished on the Church for centuries by a devout people and the pride of every parish.

There would be no need for such excess and distraction in the new, simplified Church of England. Now the pulpit took prominent place and the parishioners were expected to concentrate on the word; the emphasis was on the ear, on hearing the word of God, not on the vision or the senses. In March 1549 it was announced that the Latin Mass was to be replaced by a new communion service in English contained in Archbishop Cranmer's first Book of Common Prayer, to come into effect at Whitsun; in 1552 a second, more radical, Prayer Book would replace it. The Mass was outlawed.

Mary refused to have anything to do with the new-fangled Prayer Book, continuing to have the old Latin Mass – her chief consolation in life – said in her household at least twice a day and welcoming any who wished to attend. Only the protection of her cousin, Emperor Charles, enabled her to flout the law so blatantly. Realizing, however, that Northumberland would be a much more ruthless opponent than Somerset, Mary raised the question of her escape with the Imperial ambassador, Van der Delft. Would the Emperor help her and give her refuge? Mary had always laboured under the illusion that Charles cared about her happiness and security, when in fact his support for her cause was only ever self-interested. She could be a useful tool in

England to serve Habsburg interests; if she left England, she had no chance whatsoever of becoming Queen.

In the event, the escape plan went badly wrong. Mary was supposed to steal away in the night on a small trading vessel, which would come up the Blackwater to Maldon in Essex, near where she was staying, on the pretext of selling corn. The vessel was to take her out to the Imperial fleet lingering off Harwich, ostensibly on the hunt for pirates, for the crossing to Flanders. In response to local unrest and rumours that the Emperor was planning to invade England on Mary's behalf, the country was in a heightened state of alert with roads, harbours and creeks carefully watched. Nevertheless, Mary could have made her escape if she had not dithered when it came to the crucial moment. She was still in the middle of her packing, she told the Imperial agent, Dubois, she needed more time. The controller of her household, Sir Robert Rochester, fuelled her fears, exaggerating the dangers. Dubois could wait no longer, slipping out of England as silently as he had entered. 'What shall we do? What is to become of me?' Mary kept repeating, once she realized that prevarication had lost her the chance of rescue.

She had no alternative than to make the best of the situation in England. She placed all her hopes on Edward's coming of age and proving more reasonable than his Council, but in this she was to be sadly disabused. He was a cold, imperious little prig, promising to be every bit as autocratic as his father. She was shocked and saddened to receive a blistering letter from him accusing her of denying his sovereignty. Her crime was the more heinous because she was his sister, he told her, giving an unacceptable example to his subjects. 'I will see my laws strictly obeyed,' he concluded, 'and those who break them shall be watched and denounced.' It did not bode well for her future.

In March 1551 she reluctantly obeyed a summons to court, arriving at her London lodging, the Hospital of St John at Clerkenwell, attended by a vast train of gentlemen and ladies, all ostentatiously sporting a black rosary. It was a reminder, if any were needed, of her loyalty to the old religion. Her following was already referred to as the 'Marian faction'. Londoners flocked to welcome her, showing the Council that she was as popular as ever.

She received a less fulsome welcome at court, where she was forced to defend herself during more than two hours of heated argument with Edward and the Council. She could not have broken his laws, she insisted, since as a minor he had not made those laws. 'There are two things, body and soul,' she told him. 'Although my soul belongs to God, I offer my body to the King's service; might it please him to take away my life rather than the old religion.' Edward had no wish to make a martyr of his sister and any further moves against her were forestalled by the Emperor's threat to declare war on England if Mary were forbidden to practise her religion. It was a bluff, but not one the English could afford to call.

It was all the more suspicious, therefore, when in February 1553 Northumberland suddenly switched tack and started courting Mary's favour. When she visited the ailing Edward at court, the new Imperial ambassador told Charles, 'the Duke of Northumberland and the members of the Council went to receive her even to the outer gate of the palace, and did duty and obeisance to her as if she had been Queen of England.'

Northumberland must already have guessed that Edward's disease was fatal. His plan was to lull Mary into a false sense of security that, in the event of her brother's death, she would be Queen with his assistance. It is unlikely that she was fooled even for a minute, as Northumberland systematically began making plans to hijack the crown. He was confident that he could manipulate the King to do his bidding when the time came. He was less sanguine about the Council, some of whose members actively disliked him, were wary of his ambition and suspicious of his intentions. The Imperial ambassador was keeping a close eye on Edward's decline, while at the same time reporting to Charles the ominous news that Northumberland 'has found means to ally and bind his son, my Lord Guildford, to the Duke of Suffolk's eldest daughter, whose mother is the third heiress to the crown by the testamentary dispositions of the late King, and has no heirs male'. It did not take a genius to work out what this presaged.

Lady Jane Grey, eldest of three daughters of Lady Frances Brandon and Henry Grey, Marquis of Dorset and Duke of Suffolk in right of his wife, was a pert and precocious girl of fourteen. Her mother was Henry VIII's niece, elder daughter of Mary, the Dowager Queen of France and Duchess of Suffolk; her father was a descendant of Edward

IV's commoner Queen, Elizabeth Woodville, whose first husband and the father of her two eldest sons had been a Grey. Jane was one of the best-educated women of the Tudor period: her education, a generation on from Mary's, had been far more exacting, at the hands of reformist tutors from Cambridge University. Like Edward, she was a fervent Protestant. Indeed, she had never known or practised the old religion. She was already corresponding with notable Protestant scholars in Switzerland and learning Hebrew so that she could read the Old Testament in the original.

The only kindness and affection Jane seems to have received during her strict upbringing had been during a spell in the household of the Queen Dowager, Katherine Parr, who took the serious, studious girl under her wing. Katherine's fourth husband, the dangerously volatile Lord Admiral Thomas Seymour, younger brother of Protector Somerset, had bought Jane's wardship, promising her ambitious parents that he would marry her to the King. Of course, the scheme came to nothing, as he had neither the power nor the ability to bring it off. Fond as he was of Lady Jane, Edward had always maintained that when he married it would be to a foreign princess 'well stuffed'. Somerset had had his troublesome brother executed for high treason after his failed attempt to capture the person of the King, and Jane was returned to her parents' strict disciplinarian regime.

The Suffolks were not unusual in treating their daughter with severity, in an age that believed that to spare the rod was to spoil the child. Vives had recommended that daughters, in particular, needed a firm hand. Children were also expected to show their parents unquestioning obedience and deference. Jane was highly intelligent, articulate and opinionated and a little too forceful in voicing those opinions, often to the outrage of the adults around her.

When Mary thoughtfully sent her a gift of gorgeous fabric for a new gown for the visit of the Dowager Queen of Scotland, Mary of Guise, to the English court – a visit, incidentally, which Mary boycotted, to the irritation of Emperor Charles, who felt she showed poor political sense in not making an appearance – Jane, who affected the plain garb and lack of adornment of a Protestant maiden, turned her nose up, saying, 'What shall I do with it?' 'Marry, wear it!' one of her ladies reproved her. On another occasion in Mary's private chapel,

Jane asked her companion why she genuflected before the altar. When she explained that she was showing reverence before the sacrament – the Real Presence, according to Catholic theology – Jane mockingly asked how that could be, when the baker had made the communion bread that morning?

When the Lady Elizabeth's Cambridge tutor, Roger Ascham, paid a visit to Jane at her home in Leicestershire, she assumed an air of superior disdain at the activities of her parents, who were hunting in the park, while she was curled up with a copy of Plato. She was a typical adolescent at odds with her parents, complaining to the sympathetic Ascham about her lot in life. She loved learning, she told him, because her tutor, John Aylmer, was such a pleasant contrast to her parents. Nothing she ever did pleased them.

> For when I am in the presence of either Father or Mother, whether I speak, keep silence, sit, stand or go, eat, drink, be merry or sad, be sewing, playing, dancing, or doing anything else, I must do it as it were in such weight, measure and number, even so perfectly as God made the world; or else I am so sharply taunted, so cruelly threatened, yea presently sometimes with pinches, nips and bobs and other ways . . . that I think myself in hell.

When Northumberland offered his fifth and only unmarried son, Guildford, to the Suffolks for Jane's hand, they had no hesitation in accepting, presumably because he was holding out the prospect of the crown for their daughter. Jane herself objected strongly to the proposed marriage, because she was already contracted to Lord Hertford, the eldest son of the late Duke of Somerset. When argument, blows and threats failed to sway her, her mother whipped her until Jane gave her sullen consent. Jane already disliked the Dudleys and, despite his tall, fair good looks, she was to find Guildford a spoilt, petulant Mummy's boy.

A sumptuous double wedding between Jane and Guildford and her sister Catherine and Lord Herbert, son of Lord Pembroke, whom Northumberland wanted to woo as an ally, took place at Durham House on the Strand on Whit Sunday, 25 May 1553. Neither Mary nor Elizabeth was invited and by this time Edward was far too ill to attend. He could not sleep for a harsh, racking cough, he was running a continuous high fever, he had broken out in ulcers and his whole body had begun to swell. He showed his approval, however, by sending gifts of 'rich ornaments and jewels' to the brides and kitted out the company in gold and silver tissue and rich fabrics from the royal wardrobe. Jane wore a gown of gold and silver brocade embroidered with diamonds and pearls.

After the wedding she was ill and thankfully – for once – returned home with her mother. Pembroke, meanwhile, warned his son not to consummate the marriage with Lady Catherine, so that it might more easily be annulled: it was only the beginning of the strange marital history of this unfortunate young woman, who, ironically, was to end up making a secret, controversial marriage with her sister Jane's cast-off fiancé, Lord Hertford, to become the distant ancestress of a twentieth-century queen regnant.

It was obvious to the Imperial ambassador that Northumberland was aiming at the crown and had decided to take up arms against Mary, using religion as an excuse. The matter was becoming international, because as Scheyfve warned the Emperor, Northumberland was prepared to barter Ireland to the French in exchange for their support. It was a short-term strategy, because, of course, the French King Henri II's only concern was to advance the claim to the English throne of his son's betrothed, Mary Stuart, Queen of Scots, granddaughter of Henry VIII's elder sister, Margaret.

Not approving of his sister's rackety marital history – a case of the pot calling the kettle black, if ever there was one – and angry at the Scots' reluctance to betroth the infant Mary to his son Edward, Henry in his will had relegated Margaret's descendants last in line of succession, after his own three children and the descendants of his younger sister, Mary, in the House of Suffolk. The Stuarts, after all, were foreigners, and he had no wish to see England become an appendage of their kingdom of Scotland. Indeed, it was this overturning of the natural order of succession by Henry VIII which probably put the idea of advancing the Suffolk line into Northumberland's head in the first place.

It was all the prompting Charles needed to increase the Imperial diplomatic presence in England, sending Jehan de Montmorency, Sieur de Courrières, Jacques de Marnix, Sieur de Thoulouse and the career civil servant Simon Renard, the real leader of the group. Ostensibly they were to enquire after the King's health, but in reality they were to do what they could, by tact, persuasion and propaganda, to ensure that Henri II was not given the means to turn England into a French province. They were to do all in their power to secure the crown for Mary Tudor, who could be relied on to uphold Habsburg interests. They were to remind Edward's Council that England's best interests had always been served by an Imperial alliance and that France was their ancient enemy. They were instructed to make contact with Mary, who was to make any necessary compromise concerning religion, even to keeping the status quo, and to promise to marry an Englishman of the Council's choice, if that's what it took to win the crown. In other words, she was to use political guile as a means to an end. It was not something which came naturally to her.

Northumberland had nearly everything in place for his intended takeover. The physicians had given up on Edward and rumours abounded that he was already dead, poisoned by Northumberland. To quell the rumours, Northumberland had the desperately sick boy with his shaven head held up at a window for the public to see. To buy the extra time needed to finalize his plans, he dismissed the physicians and brought in a female quack, who promised a quick cure. It seems that she was giving Edward potions containing arsenic, which prolonged life and greatly increased his suffering. His swollen body suddenly showed signs of gangrene at the extremities, his skin became discoloured, and his hair and nails fell out. It was agony for him to turn over in bed, as his body was covered in sores.

It remained to persuade Edward to sign the 'Device for the Succession' that Northumberland had drawn up. It was understandable that Edward would not want Mary to succeed him and overturn the Protestant state he had set his heart on, but Northumberland also had to persuade him to exclude the Protestant Elizabeth, his 'Sweet Sister Temperance'. If Northumberland ever considered including Elizabeth in his schemes, he had dismissed them. Elizabeth Tudor was far too clever and independent and he knew that he would never be able to control and manipulate her, as he hoped to do with the younger and seemingly more compliant Jane. He managed to convince Edward that he could not exclude one sister and not the other, that they were both unworthy to succeed him, being bastards and of the half blood. Besides, they might endanger the kingdom's independence by marrying foreign princes.

Lady Jane, on the other hand, was born in lawful wedlock, a good Protestant who shared Edward's vision for England, and she was already married to an Englishman. It seems that Edward shared his father's belief in the uselessness of women for sovereignty. The original idea was for him to leave the crown 'to the Lady Frances's heirs male if she hath any before my death' and otherwise to 'the Lady Jane's heirs male'. But time had run out and there were no male heirs. Northumberland had persuaded Frances to cede her claim to her eldest daughter, conveniently married to his son, so that now the wording was easily altered from 'the Lady Jane's heirs male' to 'the Lady Jane ['s deleted] *and her* [insert] heirs male'.

When summoned to the dying King's bedside to ratify the Device the Lord Chief Justice, Sir Edward Montague, the Solicitor-General and the Attorney General refused to do so. The Act of Succession of 1544, which gave Henry VIII the right to nominate his successors, made it treason to alter its provisions. As he was a minor, it was illegal for Edward VI, only sixteen at the time of his death, to make a will, while to allow the King a right to alter the succession without parliamentary approval was an unprecedented abuse of royal power. Edward expressed his extreme displeasure at the judges' refusal to do his bidding and Northumberland threatened them with death unless they complied. They gave in. The Council was next summoned to the King's bedside to swear to serve Queen Jane as their lawful sovereign. Archbishop Cranmer was one of the few who gave his consent to the Device willingly; most were bullied into doing so.

The final part of Northumberland's takeover plan was to lure both Mary and Elizabeth to Greenwich on the pretext of seeing their dying brother. Once there, he would seize and imprison them, perhaps even put them to death. Elizabeth was fond of her brother, but not so fond that she was prepared to place herself in Northumberland's power. She sent back an excuse that she was too ill to travel. Mary was torn. She wanted to go to her brother and offer what comfort she could. On 3 July, however, a friend at court warned her that it was a trap. She left her manor of Hunsdon in Hertfordshire next day, with the excuse that there was sickness in the household, but after travelling south as far as Hoddesdon, she suddenly turned tail and with a couple of ladies and a handful of gentlemen rode fast towards East Anglia with Northumberland's fourth son, Lord Robert Dudley, in hot pursuit.

The rebellion had begun.

On the night of the 5th, Mary took refuge with Sir John Huddlestone at Sawston Hall near Cambridge, where Mass was defiantly celebrated. Next morning after she left, her pursuers set fire to the house. Watching the blaze, she promised the dismayed Huddlestone that she would build him a new and grander house. She continued towards Thetford disguised as a serving maid, riding pillion behind one of Huddlestone's men. They covered the twenty-eight miles without stopping to Hengrave Hall, the home of the Earl of Bath near Bury St Edmunds. On 7 July she arrived at Euston Hall, near Thetford, the home of her friend, Lady Burgh. It was there that Robert Raynes, a City goldsmith apparently sent by Sir Nicholas Throckmorton at the instigation of William Cecil, caught up with her and advised her that her brother had died on the evening of 6 July. She found the gates of Norwich, the second city of the kingdom, closed to her, since the citizens had not had confirmation of the King's death. She pressed on to Kenninghall, which was sufficiently close to the coast to permit her escape to Flanders in the last extremity.

There was no official announcement of the King's death because Northumberland hoped to conceal it to gain more time; the only problem was what to do with the body, which was rapidly decomposing. There is a possibility that he had Edward buried hastily in some unmarked grave and a similar-looking boy substituted for the period of royal obsequies – interesting, in view of later 'sightings' of the boy-King, amid recurring rumours that he was not actually dead.

Before embarking on her flight, Mary had sent a message to Scheyfve informing him of her intentions. Showing a degree of resolution not apparent in her previous aborted escape, she was all for proclaiming herself Queen as soon as Edward's death was confirmed, but the Imperial diplomats considered this unwise. Right from the start, they were pessimistic about Mary's chances of success and thought that to declare herself Queen would be to provoke Northumberland. All the forces of the country, they believed, were in his hands and he would certainly send them against her if she gave him the excuse. It seemed that he held all the cards. 'The actual possession of power was a matter of great importance,' they maintained, 'especially among barbarians like the English.' Mary was unlikely to succeed, they told Charles, without help from abroad and they knew that the Emperor had no forces to spare. His overt interference would only draw in the French, making England a battlefield. Charles was quite resigned to her failure, indicating to his ambassadors that he would recognize Jane's regime, while urging them to obtain some guarantees for Mary's safety.

Meanwhile, the Duchess of Northumberland visited Lady Jane and told her that Edward had made her his heiress. It was the first indication the young woman had that her marriage was part of a nefarious scheme to wrest the crown from the rightful claimant. Later, she admitted to Mary that she was greatly disturbed and oppressed by the news. 'For whereas I might take upon me that of which I was not worthy, yet no one can ever say that I sought it as my own, or that I was pleased with it or ever accepted it.'

On the evening of 9 July she was brought to Syon House, the former priory at Isleworth on the Thames which Northumberland had appropriated, where she was greeted by him and other leading nobles. They did her 'such reverence as was not at all suitable to my state, kneeling down before me on the ground, and in many other ways making semblance of honouring me . . . acknowledging me as their sovereign lady'. She had a fit of hysterics, falling to the floor and bewailing the loss of Edward, then protesting that the crown was not hers by right. The company was just beginning to lose patience when she was persuaded to calm down and take her place under the canopy of estate.

The next day, Jane made her official entry into London to take up residence in the Tower, as was customary for a new sovereign. Pathetically, she had been made to wear wooden platform shoes, to make her look taller and more important. The Italian Baptisa Spinola watched her pass and, in lieu of an authenticated portrait, his description is the best we have of this ill-fated girl:

> Today I saw Lady Jane Grey walking in grand procession to the Tower. She is now called Queen, but is not popular, for the hearts of the people are with Mary, the Spanish Queen's daughter. This Jane is very short and thin, but prettily shaped and graceful. She has small features and a well-made nose, the mouth flexible and the lips red. The eyebrows are arched and darker than her hair, which is nearly red. Her eyes are sparkling and reddish brown in colour. I stood so near her grace that I noticed her colour was good but freckled. When she smiled she showed her teeth, which are white and sharp. In all a gracious and animated figure. She wore a dress of green velvet stamped with gold, with large sleeves. Her headdress was a white coif with many jewels. She walked under a canopy, her mother carrying her long train, and her husband Guildford walking by her, dressed all in white and gold, a very tall strong boy with light hair, who paid her much attention. The new Queen was mounted on very high chopines to make her look much taller, which were concealed beneath her robes, as she is very small and short. Many ladies followed, with noblemen, but this lady is very heretical and has never heard Mass, and some great people did not come into the procession for that reason.

Criers stood at the street corners declaring Mary's unworthiness to be Queen, as a bastard and a Catholic, but according to Scheyfve few showed any sign of rejoicing and no one cried 'Long live Queen Jane!' other than the herald and a few archers accompanying him, who did so without conviction.

For once Mary had ignored Imperial advice and followed her own instincts. They served her well. Her route from Hunsdon across a large sweep of East Anglia to Kenninghall had been deliberately charted – probably by the senior men of her household, Sir Robert Rochester, Sir Francis Englefield, Henry Jerningham and Edward Waldegrave, gentlemen with an 'affinity' in the area – to take her to sympathizers from whose lands she could raise forces. Kenninghall itself had belonged to the Duke of Norfolk before his attainder at the end of her father's reign and the many Howard retainers in the area were adherents of the old religion, so that they flocked to her support. On 9 July she received a second messenger at Kenninghall confirming Edward's death. Mary now summoned her household and announced the end of Edward's reign and the inauguration of her own. An East Anglian gentleman who witnessed the scene said that everyone present 'cheered her to the rafters'.

Mary wrote to the lords of the Council in London commanding them 'to cause our right and title to the crown and government of this realm to be proclaimed in our city of London' and throughout the kingdom. Her letter was delivered to Northumberland on the evening of 10 July, in the middle of a great banquet at the Tower. It was read out to Jane and the assembled company, who sat in stunned silence. They had considered Mary a lone woman, a fugitive, who could be discounted. But Mary was not a Tudor and the granddaughter of the great Isabella for nothing. She had evaded capture and defiantly thrown down the gauntlet.

Mary's proclamation was her first formal action as queen regnant. She now began to assemble her Council, consisting of the leading men of her household – Sir Robert Rochester, Henry Jerningham, Edward Waldegrave, Robert Strelly, Sir Thomas Wharton and others – loyal and devoted followers of long standing. For the conduct of the war she would need to enlarge the Council to include military advisers, peers and gentlemen, whose tenants and servants would form the nucleus of an army. Messengers went out to invite all the gentlemen of the surrounding countryside to come to Kenninghall to swear fealty to their sovereign lady. This produced the likes of Sir Henry Bedingfield of Oxburgh Hall, who eventually became Captain of the Queen's Guard. Sir Richard Southwell, who possessed thirty manors between Swaffham and Norwich, brought reinforcements of men, provisions and cash. Other gentlemen of substance followed suit and the city of Norwich declared for Mary as soon as it received confirmation of Edward's death and sent men and money. On 12 July the whole force moved to the great fortress of Framlingham in Suffolk.

Northumberland could not afford to ignore Mary's challenge. He wrote an insolent letter reminding her that Parliament had declared her a bastard and therefore not fit to wear the crown – a blatant disregard for the Act of Succession of 1544. He warned her to 'cease your pretence to vex and molest any of our sovereign lady Queen

Jane's subjects, drawing them from the true faith and allegiance due unto Her Grace'. He was aware that every day Mary remained at large, her following grew. Knowing that the Council's support was grudging and unreliable, Northumberland was reluctant to leave London. 'The Duke's difficulty is that he dares trust no one,' Charles's envoys reported, 'for he has never given anyone reason to love him.'

He was 'the best manne of warre in the realme', already so feared in East Anglia, owing to his savage repression of Kett's Rebellion in Norfolk in 1549, that it was believed 'none durst once lift up their weapon against him'. In the circumstances, however, he had decided to send the Duke of Suffolk in his stead to defeat Mary's forces. Hearing this, Jane started to cry, begging that her father stay with her in the Tower, and the Council joined her in urging Northumberland to lead the army he had mustered against Mary.

Meanwhile, Simon Renard was working behind the scenes to undermine Northumberland, exploiting the disaffection felt by many on the Council. Unknown to his colleagues, Northumberland had been in secret talks with the French ambassador, Antoine de Noailles, and was prepared to exchange Calais and the remaining English territory in France for the loan of French troops – ironic, since it was to be Mary who earned the opprobrium of losing Calais. On the 12th Renard warned two counsellors, Sir John Mason and Lord Cobham, that the only intention of the French was 'to stir up trouble and place Mary Stuart on the throne'. It must have given them pause for thought, because they started to collude with supporters of Mary on the Council. Next morning, even before Northumberland left London, they summoned Renard for talks; the revolution behind Northumberland's back had begun. Only Suffolk's threats and the fear of Northumberland's wrath if he returned in triumph kept the Imperialist party on the Council from proclaiming Mary Tudor Queen at once.

When Northumberland left London with his troops on the 14th, he was all too aware as he passed through the streets of Shoreditch that the crowds were silent. 'The people press to see us,' he observed, 'but not one sayeth God spede us.' Even so, the Imperial envoys were writing to Charles that day: 'We believe that my Lady will be in his hands in four days' time . . . he is strong on land and by sea.' Indeed,

Northumberland had sent five warships to the east coast to prevent Mary's escape, but he had reckoned without Henry Jerningham's going to Yarmouth and persuading the crews to mutiny in favour of Mary.

As he rode towards Cambridge, Northumberland found the land strangely empty of men to recruit, while gradually his troops began to desert. His son Robert, who had a small affinity in Norfolk as a result of his marriage to Amy Robsart of Syderstone and Wyndonham, had been captured by Mary's supporters at King's Lynn. News of spontaneous uprisings in other parts of the country began to reach Northumberland and depress morale. By the time he reached Bury St Edmunds, only thirty miles from Framlingham, he realized that he was so heavily outnumbered by Mary's forces – which were believed to number at least 15,000 – that he was forced to retreat to Cambridge.

On the 19th the Imperial envoys were writing to Charles that Mary's 'forces were reported to be increasing every day, for some helped with money, others with provisions, others with troops and others with ammunition'. That same day, Sir John Mason and Lord Shrewsbury came to tell them the extraordinary news that the majority of the Council had declared for Mary. The Lord Mayor and aldermen of London were commanded to have Mary proclaimed Queen throughout the City. 'There was such a shout of people that the style of the proclamation could not be heard,' the London citizen, Henry Machyn, recounted in his diary. An Italian reported that the news was all the more marvellous for being so unexpected. 'Men ran hither and thither, bonnets flew into the air, shouts rose higher than the stars, fires were lit on all sides, and all the bells were set a-pealing . . . The people went mad with joy, feasting and singing, and the streets were crowded all night long.' Northumberland's erstwhile ally, Lord Pembroke, threw capfuls of gold coins into the crowd, thinking it a good investment.

Lords Arundel and Paget left London that evening in order to deliver the Great Seal of England to Mary. They found her next day at Framlingham, reviewing her troops, having dismounted 'a frisky white charger' to walk among the men. Admitted to her presence, they threw themselves on their knees and begged her forgiveness for their disloyalty in supporting Jane, symbolically holding out their daggers with the points towards their stomachs. Mary was always inclined to be merciful to those who had committed offences against herself – as opposed to offences against God and His Holy Church – and readily forgave them. She then invited the household into the chapel, where a crucifix had defiantly been set up on the altar, for a *Te Deum*, giving thanks to God that the crown was hers without bloodshed. It was a miracle, she concluded, and God must have saved her for His own great purpose.

The coup d'état that brought Mary to power was the only successful rebellion of the Tudor period. It was a pity that she did not stop to appreciate that she had achieved this victory through her own initiative and courage, as well as the loyalty and support of her people. She owed little or nothing to the Emperor, but as the French ambassador shrewdly surmised, she was unwilling 'to recall that in all her own miseries, troubles and afflictions, as well as those of the Queen, her mother, the Emperor never came to their assistance, nor has he helped her now in her great need with a single man, ship, or penny'. She would continue to depend on Charles, even though she had shown that she had no need of him.

In London, Jane found herself almost deserted in the Tower. As she sat at supper, her father strode into her presence chamber and tore down the canopy of estate, muttering that such things were not for her. After declaring for Queen Mary on Tower Green, he and his wife went home, leaving their daughter locked in the Tower to face whatever fate their heedless actions had brought her to. William Cecil, secretary to Northumberland and the Council, had never agreed with the illegal usurpation of the crown, and now carefully altered the document before him to read 'Jana *non* Regina'.

What amazed the Imperial and French ambassadors was the role 'the people' had played in recent events. They were impressed by the fact that 'the English third estate seemed to have a mind of its own'. The English might be 'barbarians', but they had an innate sense of what was right and wrong. Legality mattered to them. They were not prepared to see the lawful succession overturned by a tyrant like Northumberland. Although she was half Spanish, a Catholic and known to identify strongly with Imperial interests, Mary was hailed with joy by patriots and Protestants alike, not least because everyone suspected something of how close Northumberland had come to selling his country to the French. Even a woman ruler – whatever handicaps her sex might bring – was preferable to a usurper. Mary was their rightful sovereign, the daughter of old King Henry VIII, and they had always held her in special affection.

'*Vox populi, vox Dei*': the voice of the people is the voice of God. It was something Queen Mary would do well to remember in the challenging times ahead.

4

Mary the Queen

O N 3 AUGUST 1553 Queen Mary I entered London in triumph. There is little evidence that she was imbued with a sense of destiny prior to her coming to the throne, but now she must have felt that God had preserved her for this moment. She was thirty-seven, not in the best of health, and had known very little happiness over the last twenty years. As queen she could undo all the wrongs of the past: she could bring England back to Rome, restore the true Church, and rescue her people from the tide of heresy that was imperilling their immortal souls.

Now she was Queen, Mary could indulge her passion for rich, elaborate clothing and jewels, but such ostentation did little to compliment a middle-aged woman whose prettiness had been marred by years of suffering. Her small figure was painfully thin. She was still described as being 'fresh coloured', but the lovely reddish-gold hair had long since faded. Typically, for the time, many of Mary's teeth were either missing or black. With her high forehead, large myopic grey eyes and pale eyebrows, and long, low nose flaring widely at the end, her face had a plain, naked look. Little artifice was applied either in real life or in her portraits to make her look more regal: what you saw was what you got with Mary. As the Venetian ambassador so diplomatically put it: 'she is a seemly woman, and never to be loathed for ugliness, even at her present age, without considering her degree of queen.'

Mary's wardrobe accounts show a preference for crimson, followed by black and purple. For her entry into London her diminutive figure was swathed in royal purple and weighed down by jewels: 'a gowne of purple velvet, hir kirtel purple satten all thicke sett with gouldsmithes work and great pearle, with her foresleves of the same sett with rich stones . . . a riche bowdricke of gould, pearl, and stones about her necke, and a riche billement of stones and great pearle on her hoode, her pallfray that she rode on richly trapped with gould embroidered to her horse feet.'

It was important on ceremonial entries into London for the monarch to appear powerful. What Mary lacked in personal presence she made up for in the size and splendour of the retinue that accompanied her. Apart from the royal trumpeters, heralds and sergeants at arms, she was preceded by more than 700 nobles, knights and gentlemen in velvet coats on horseback. One hundred and eighty ladies and gentlemen followed her, along with the foreign ambassadors – with the exception of the French ambassador, Antoine de Noailles, who was keeping a low profile – and their large companies. The Earl of Arundel rode before Mary bearing the Sword of State and Sir Anthony Browne followed, holding the long train of her gown over his shoulder. The Lady Elizabeth, who emerged perfectly fit and well just in time to join Mary in her triumphant entry into the capital, rode immediately after the Queen, presenting a striking contrast in age and looks. Fresh from their deliverance from Northumberland, the Tudor sisters were putting on a public display of unity and mutual affection. Thousands of horsemen brought up the rear.

All the splendour could not make up for the fact that Mary lacked charisma. She did not possess the sense of showmanship that her father and sister shared, nor her sister's quick wit and readiness with the right words of appreciation. For instance, before her entry into the City, Wriothesley recorded that 'The queen's grace stayed [stopped] at Allgate-Street before the stage where the poor children stood, and hard [heard] an oration that one of them made, but she sayd nothinge to them.' These were the children of Christ's Hospital, a post-Reformation charitable foundation formed after the dissolution of the monasteries. It was an example of Mary's failure, which she would repeat over and over again, to exploit a propaganda opportunity. Essentially passive, she seemed to have no idea that the monarch had to *work* the crowd. The love of the people had to be earned.

For the moment, however, they gave it willingly. A royal entry into the capital was more than an assertion of power and status. The notion persisted that monarchs ought to rule with their people's unforced obedience; their show of approval during the royal entry reinforced the aura of legitimacy. It was an opportunity for the two to bond. On such an occasion the crowd treated the monarch less as an awesome symbol of authority than as a popular hero. The obvious way in which it could do this was by making an enormous amount of noise; with the sounds of artillery and the pealing of all the parish church bells, the impression was one of pandemonium. The crowd's cheers were actually a blessing, expressed with great emotional intensity. Wriothesley noted that the streets were 'full of people shoutinge and cryinge Jesus save her Grace, with weepinge teares for joy'. The expression 'Jesus save her Grace', or 'God save the Queen', possessed a far deeper resonance in Tudor England than it does today.

The noise was indescribable, particularly as from the moment Mary entered the City the Tower guns had been firing off salvos 'which was like great thunder, so that yt had bene lyke to an earthquake'. In the Tower, Lady Jane must have been listening to the celebrations marking Mary's arrival with foreboding, but for other prisoners they signalled their imminent release. The elderly Duke of Norfolk and Stephen Gardiner, Bishop of Winchester, had been prisoners since the end of Henry VIII's reign, casualties of the factional strife that had seen these religious conservatives eclipsed by the rising reformists. Young Edward Courtenay, victim of Henry VIII's purge of the House of York, had grown to manhood in the Tower. After greeting the Queen, they were freed. Gardiner, one of Henry VIII's most prominent counsellors, was to be made Lord Chancellor, while Courtenay's hereditary title of Earl of Devonshire was restored to him.

Northumberland was already lodged in the Beauchamp Tower with three of his sons. Taken prisoner by Arundel at Cambridge on 20 July, he had had filth and insults hurled at him when he was brought back through the streets of London. He was to be tried and condemned for high treason, giving the new regime a propaganda boost when he asked to be reconciled with the Catholic Church before he went to the block. Other conspirators, including Thomas Cranmer,

Archbishop of Canterbury, had been rounded up, imprisoned and tried. Mary had a personal axe to grind against Cranmer, who had declared her mother's marriage invalid, making Mary a bastard; he would languish in prison until she could exact her full pound of flesh.

Mary treated most of the other conspirators with clemency. Knowing Lady Jane had been the victim of the adults' manipulation, she refused to agree to her death, even after she had been condemned at trial. She was to be kept in close custody in the Tower, as was Guildford Dudley. Husband and wife were lodged in separate quarters. Probably Jane experienced a freedom she had seldom enjoyed in her sixteen years. The Queen's mercy extended to the Duke of Suffolk, quite undeservedly, after his wife Frances – a favourite cousin of Mary's – had personally pleaded for his life. He walked free.

Several weeks after Mary's entry into London, on 27 September 1553, she arrived by water at the Tower, accompanied by Elizabeth, to take up residence in preparation for the coronation three days later. On the 29th the coronation procession set out from the Tower to wind through the City and on to the Palace of Westminster. In spite of its splendour, it was an oddly missed propaganda opportunity. Little effort had been made in the pageantry to define the nature and claims of the new regime, and nor was an account of it published afterwards. Mary was too complacent in relying on her own persona. She made little effort to create an image of herself with which the people could identify.

Adopting as her personal motto, 'Truth, the Daughter of Time', Mary thought it was enough that she was a known conservative after years of disturbing innovation. She assumed that the welcome she had received in August indicated that her people were of the same mind as herself. In reality, their enthusiasm reflected their relief that Henry's daughter, the rightful heir of the Tudor dynasty, had wrested back the crown from the usurper Northumberland and his greedy, unscrupulous gang. The rule of law and the legitimate line of succession had prevailed. The people were less sure about the Queen's evident drift back to Rome. Mary knew that the majority of her subjects outside London were still Catholic and that the Edwardian reforms had been too radical for them, but, having spent so many years in the country, she totally failed to appreciate how firmly rooted Protestantism had become in London.

Never a political animal, Mary was guided by her own moral compass, which was usually at odds with political pragmatism. Almost her first act on becoming Queen had been to write to Pope Julius III seeking absolution and inviting reconciliation with Rome. She apparently did this without reference to either Emperor Charles or the Council, neither of whom would have condoned such a rash move. Through his envoy, Simon Renard, Charles was anxious to convey to his cousin the importance of restraint in her religious policy. She was to tread carefully, to 'take great care, at the outset, not to be led by her zeal to be too hasty in reforming matters'. Mary must be guided by Parliament, when it met, and meanwhile restrict herself to observance of her religion privately in her chamber. 'Let her dissemble for the present, not to seek to order matters in a manner different from that now observed in England.'

The first sticking point came when Mary wished to bury her brother with full Catholic rites. It would 'violate her conscience' to do otherwise. Charles advised against it, telling her in no uncertain terms that 'if she inaugurates her reign in this fashion she will render herself odious and suspect'. Let the little heretic be buried as he had lived. Mary had to settle for a private Requiem Mass in the Tower and even this drew criticism.

Mary's first proclamation on religion took its inspiration from her father's last speech to Parliament. It forbade 'her subjects of all degrees, at their perils, to move seditions or stir unquietness in her people, by interrupting the laws of this realm after their brains and fancies'. It asked 'all her said good loving subjects to live together in quiet sort and Christian charity, leaving those new-found devilish terms of papist or heretic and such like' until a new religious settlement could be made. Mary's professed intention was to restore the Henrician settlement, although there must have been a suspicion that she would never be content with this alone. She had already put pressure on her sister to attend Mass and Elizabeth had thought it wise to concede.

It was a long time since Henry VIII's break with Rome; a whole generation had grown up in those years, and it was unrealistic to suppose that there could be revival of the Catholic England Mary fondly remembered – or thought she remembered – from her childhood. The royal supremacy was well established. The English liked the idea that the realm was an empire, owing allegiance to none but the monarch, and there was no particular desire to return to the papal fold. This independence was bolstered by growing nationalism. Pilgrimages, shrines, relics and indulgences were things of the past, and Mary showed no interest in restoring them. The focus of her personal worship had always been the Mass, which, despite its still being illegal, she immediately attended publicly, with the full panoply of Catholic ritual and the choir of the Chapel Royal. Soon it was being celebrated quite spontaneously in some of the London parishes, triggering disquiet among the diehard Protestants.

The relative coolness of the Londoners' response during the pre-coronation procession, compared with the wild frenzy that had greeted her arrival only a few weeks previously, should have given Mary pause for thought, but as ever she saw only what she wanted to see. God had protected her for His own purpose and she must not let Him down. 'If God be with us, who can be against us?' she was fond of saying.

The customary ritual of the pre-coronation procession was designed to display a male monarch who was a fighting leader. This was considered inappropriate for a queen regnant, even though Mary possessed manly courage and had successfully led an armed force in the recent rebellion. The solution was to draw on the iconography of a queen consort, as stipulated in the *Liber Regalis*, but to re-situate her in the procession as a ruler. Even though Mary was a fine horsewoman, she travelled in 'a litter decked by a canopy of gold, carried by two mules arrayed as well with gold', rather than on horseback. Significantly, she wore white cloth of gold and went 'in her hair' – the symbols of purity and fertility traditionally adopted by a queen consort – with a golden circlet studded with precious stones. Her long hair was reassurance that she intended to marry and hoped to prove fruitful. Of course, there was no precedent for a queen regnant to follow, but it is interesting that Mary readily accepted her presentation as a mere consort. After all, with marriage talks already under way, she did not intend to remain 'sole queen' for long.

Ideally, Mary would have liked Parliament to meet immediately after her accession to settle the religious question, but traditionally the coronation came first. This meant that her coronation would follow the pattern laid down by Archbishop Cranmer for Edward's in 1547, reflecting the monarch's new post-Reformation imperial status as Supreme Head of the Church. In no way did Mary want to be seen condoning the new religion and she wrote to her cousin, Cardinal Reginald Pole, to ask for absolution for herself and for all true Catholics taking part in the ceremony. Baulking at the idea of using the 'heretical' oil used by Cranmer for Edward's anointing, Mary had secretly sent to the Bishop of Arras in Brussels for some newly consecrated oil, which arrived in a silver gilt casket.

Shortly after ten in the morning, she entered Westminster Abbey, flanked by one spiritual peer, the Bishop of Durham, and one temporal peer, the Earl of Shrewsbury, according to the new rites of 1547. She was wearing a crimson velvet cape with a very long train carried by her chamberlain and the Duchess of Norfolk. Elizabeth followed close behind, her tall, regal figure with its stately glide in marked contrast to her elder sister with her low stature and indifferent gait. Anne of Cleves, the sole survivor of their father's six wives, preceded the peeresses, all wearing their coronets and cloaks and robes of crimson velvet lined with ermine. The peers carried their coronets and would not put them on until the Queen was crowned.

As Thomas Cranmer, Archbishop of Canterbury, and Robert Holgate, Archbishop of York, were obviously unwelcome and unavailable, Stephen Gardiner, Bishop of Winchester, did the honours. At the coronation, the approval of God had to be sought through prayer, but so too was the consent of the people. Mary stood on a dais under the lantern at the crossing of the transept of the abbey, while Gardiner turned her to the north, to the south, to the east and to the west, presenting her to the people as their rightful sovereign and asking them to do homage and service to her.

Like her predecessors, Mary almost certainly took the oath to preserve peace in the Church and among Christian people, to govern wisely and mercifully and to uphold the rightful customs of the land. The choir sang *Veni Creator Spiritus*. Mary withdrew to a private room to disrobe for the most solemn act of the ceremony, the anointing with holy oil, which was believed to give her sanctity and jurisdiction in spiritual matters. She emerged wearing 'a simple petticoat of purple velvet' and took her seat in front of the high altar. Dipping his fingers in the oil, Gardiner anointed her on the crown of the head, the breast, the shoulders and the palms of both hands, in the form of the cross.

Changing again into a white taffeta robe, Mary then underwent the same triple crowning as Edward, but with the crucial difference that the spiritual representative, Gardiner, alone placed them in turn upon her head, being handed them from the altar by the Duke of Norfolk. Lifting high the crown of St Edward the Confessor – its circular shape representing the eternity that would be the Queen's if she was virtuous – Gardiner placed it on Mary's head as the choir sang *Te Deum Laudamus*. Gardiner led the bishops and the Duke of Norfolk the lay peers in doing homage, each touching the crown and kissing the Queen on the left cheek.

The coronation ring was placed on the Queen's finger by Gardiner. As in 1547, the ornaments were presented by the great lay magnates, the Marquess of Winchester the orb, the Earl of Arundel the sceptre, the Earl of Bath St Edward's staff and the Earl of Pembroke the spurs. The French ambassador noted that during the sung Mass, 'the Queen kept kneeling, holding in her hands the two sceptres – the one of the King, the other bearing a dove which, by custom, is given to the Queen.' The sceptre with the cross symbolized kingly power and justice, and the sceptre with the dove, the prerogative of mercy. She appeared carrying only the orb, representing Christ's dominion over the whole world, as she left the abbey.

Meanwhile, another foreign observer described Mary as being, literally, elevated, as she took her place on the coronation chair: 'Her Majesty ascended upon a great platform, so high that it was mounted by twenty steps, and upon this another smaller one with ten steps to the chair, where she seated herself.' The Queen must have appeared like some floating deity, halfway between heaven and the groundlings below.

It was nearly five o'clock by the time Mary arrived at Westminster

Hall for the coronation banquet. She sat in solitary state on 'a stone chair covered with brocade' and 'rested her feet upon two of her ladies, which is also part of the prescribed ceremonial, and ate thus', served by her nobles. Elizabeth and Anne of Cleves sat at the same central table, but 'very far away'. The Knights of the Bath brought in the meats. The Imperial envoys had asked the Emperor's sister – Mary, the Regent of the Netherlands – to send wild boar from Bruges, which the Queen loved and could not obtain in England. More than 7,000 dishes were offered, of which nearly 5,000 were declared 'waste' and presumably given to the crowd outside.

Four days later Mary opened her first Parliament, after hearing the traditional Mass of the Holy Ghost. No time was wasted in passing an Act declaring the marriage of Henry VIII and Katherine of Aragon valid and the Queen legitimate. She was Queen anyway, by Act of Parliament and her father's will, but, ever anxious to eradicate the unhappy past, it was important to Mary to restore her mother's honour and her own status. She adopted her mother's badge of the pomegranate, redolent of Katherine's native Granada, as her own. Nothing was to be said in this Parliament about reconciliation with Rome, and she had to be content with the repeal of all Edward's religious legislation, including the Act of Uniformity and the use of the Prayer Book. Protestant services would cease to be legal on 20 December 1553.

A queen regnant was an anomaly, unprecedented in England. The Act Concerning Regal Power attempted to address the issue, but legislation worked only as far as the character concerned allowed it to. For instance, the sovereign was the fount of all honour, but there were certain roles that Mary, ever conscious of the deficiencies of her sex, was reluctant to fulfil. At the Knights of the Bath ceremony prior to her coronation, she sent Lord Arundel, the Great Master of the Household, to represent her. It was not a ceremony she could undergo herself, since the knights plunged naked into the bath and kissed the monarch's shoulder. But Mary also abrogated her sovereign right two days later, when she allowed Arundel to dub a larger group of knights who were fully dressed. It seems that Mary felt precluded by her sex from participating in these traditional displays of male chivalry or in any way trying to emulate a king who was *de facto* leader in the military field. She showed no interest in tournaments or in encouraging the nobles and gentlemen of her court in feats of chivalry – a pity, because they could so easily have been turned to her advantage, as Elizabeth was later to do with the Accession Day tilts.

The one indisputable duty of a queen was to marry and produce an heir. Mary had already made up her mind. If the people were worried about her religious intentions, they would like her choice of husband even less.

5

The Spanish Marriage

FOR THE FIRST time in her life free to make her own decisions, Mary might be forgiven for thinking that she was making her own choice of husband, but in this she was the dupe of her powerful Habsburg relative, the Emperor Charles.

From the moment Mary so unexpectedly won the crown, Charles was determined to marry her to his son, Prince Philip of Spain. He knew that the English would not swallow a Catholic revival *and* a Spanish marriage all at once, so he was prepared to stymie the first in order to advance the second. Whatever Mary might fondly imagine, Charles was essentially secular and pragmatic. The re-conversion of England could wait. The Pope must be persuaded that the time was not propitious for reconciliation and the papal legate, Cardinal Pole, physically restrained from crossing to England until Charles had accomplished his prior purpose. Nothing was more important than grasping this opportunity to bring England within the Habsburg fold. The perpetual enemy, France, would be encircled and there would be a clear sea route for the transportation of bullion and troops from Spain to the Low Countries.

Over the years, Mary the beleaguered princess had come to rely on Charles's ambassadors to offer her advice and support. They were often her only friends. It was not surprising, therefore, that she formed an immediate dependence on the Imperial envoy, Simon Renard, who was given secret, unofficial access, even smuggling himself into the palace in disguise at all hours. As she was Queen, Mary's natural advisers should have been her counsellors, but she did not feel comfortable with them. They were a large, unwieldy body, drawn from her household officers and the men who had rushed to support her against Northumberland, with the addition of twenty experienced men who had actually served in government. Mary never really liked or trusted the latter. Living very much in the past, she remembered how they had turned their coats in her father's and brother's reigns, or supported Northumberland in his recent takeover attempt, and she regarded most of them as traitors and heretics. Nevertheless, she recognized that she needed their expertise.

As the Council was so large and unwieldy, riddled with mutual resentment and divisions, all important business was transacted by an inner core, the key players being Stephen Gardiner, as Lord Chancellor, and William, Lord Paget – who hated each other – Arundel, and Sir William Petre, as principal secretary, but even then Mary had difficulty managing it.

What mattered was that the various members of the Council were loyal to the sovereign, whatever their personal differences, but Mary seems to have been unable to cope with even a normal level of argument. Having spent so many of her adult years in retirement, she suddenly found herself with the unaccustomed burden of office and it was onerous. She had had no training for the role of sole queen, nor had she any real political experience. She was intelligent and hardworking, a capable linguist who could communicate with foreign ambassadors in Latin or their native tongues, but she was not an original or incisive thinker and lacked imagination. A picture emerges of a conscientious and well-meaning woman, not really up to the task, and unable to prioritize.

The Venetian Soranzo reported that Mary was not strong, that she suffered from headaches and palpitations of the heart, and that she constantly had to take medicine and be blooded. She was probably anaemic. 'She is of very spare diet, and never eats until 1 or 2pm, although she rises at daybreak, when, after saying her prayers and hearing Mass in private, she transacts business incessantly, until after midnight, when she retires to rest.' It was a long day, 'for she chooses to give audience not only to all the members of her Privy Council, and to hear from them every detail of public business, but also to all other persons who ask it of her'.

Mary found it so much easier to decide policy on a one-to-one basis with Simon Renard, who was always so sympathetic, telling her what she wanted to hear. He began to behave as if he were the

Queen's natural and proper adviser, exploiting her trust and dependence on the Emperor to insinuate himself into her confidence,
skilfully playing on her fears and prejudices, and undermining the
mutual trust that should have existed between the Queen and her
Council, whose role Renard never really understood. Charles was
sensitive to the need for Mary to play down her Imperial connection,
recommending exactly the opposite course of action from the one
Renard was encouraging: 'Let her be in all things what she ought to
be; a good Englishwoman, and avoid giving the impression that she
desires to act on her own authority, letting it be seen that she wishes
to have the assistance and consent of the foremost men of the land
and, as far as it shall appear requisite, of Parliament itself.'

Renard's brief was to probe Mary's mind on the question of marriage and to implant the idea of Philip as the ideal candidate. He
obviously read her well, because he began by appealing to her sense of
helplessness as a woman:

> Your Majesty could but be mindful of the fact that a great part of the
> labour of government could with difficulty be undertaken by a
> woman, and was not within woman's province, and also that it was
> important that the Queen should be assisted, protected and comforted
> in the discharge of those duties. Your Majesty [Charles] therefore con-
> sidered that she would do well to entertain the idea of marriage, and to
> fix on some suitable match as soon as possible. If she wished to inform
> Your Majesty before coming to a definite decision, you would give
> your opinion, with the sincere and more than paternal affection you
> had always shown her, on that and on all other matters on which she
> might desire to consult you.

After a lifetime in which marriage had often been tantalizingly close,
yet elusive, it must have been pleasurable for Mary to contemplate that
it was hers for the asking, even though by the standards of the time she
was well into middle age. Her answer was suitably coy. 'As for the suggestion of marriage, she declared she had never thought of wedding
before she was Queen, and called God to witness that as a private individual she would never have desired it, but preferred to end her days in
chastity.' However, she was determined to follow the Emperor's advice
and 'choose whosoever you might recommend; for after God she
desired to obey none but your Majesty, whom she regarded as a father.'

She felt confident that the Emperor would remember she was 'thirty-seven years of age, and would not urge her to come to a decision before having seen the person and heard him speak, for as she was marrying against her private inclination she trusted your Majesty would give her a suitable match'. Of course, her request to inspect the candidate was no more practical than her father's had been when he asked Francis I to bring a batch of French princesses to Calais for him to make his choice.

In October Renard had a meeting with the Queen at Whitehall Palace, 'entering it by the gallery on the river Thames; and she came up so close to me that I was able to deliver your Majesty's letters to her without being seen by those who were in the same room'. Mary plied him with questions about her intended bridegroom. She was worried about his youth, as she was eleven years older. 'If he were disposed to be amorous, such was not her desire,' she confided, 'for she never harboured thoughts of love.' Renard hastened to assure her that Philip was already 'middle aged', and the father of a son; it was better that she should marry a younger man who would give her children and live long enough to see them grow up. He dispelled her doubts as to Philip's popularity with his subjects in the Low Countries, dismissing the rumour 'of his excessive pride and small wisdom' and emphasizing his virtues.

Mary had not completely lost her head. Perhaps recalling what her mother had told her about her grandmother, Queen Isabella, she indicated that she had no intention of yielding sovereignty to her husband. 'She would wholly love and obey him to whom she had given herself, following the divine commandment, and would do nothing against his will,' she assured Renard, 'but if he wished to encroach in the government of the kingdom she would be unable to permit it, nor if he attempted to fill posts and offices with strangers, for the country itself would never stand such interference.'

She ended the interview bemoaning the difficulty of reaching a decision, especially as she was doing so without the advice of her Council, yet by the end of the month Renard had his answer. He reported triumphantly to Charles that the Queen had sent for him to her chamber. There was no one else in the room but Susan Clarencieux, Mary's favourite attendant. The Queen confessed that she had been confined to her room feigning illness for two days while she tried to make up her mind. She had hardly slept, spending the time weeping and praying. As usual the Holy Sacrament was on an altar in the room and Mary asked Renard and Mrs Clarencieux to kneel with her and recite *Veni Creator Spiritus*.

Now Mary was sure that she was making the right decision. 'She felt inspired by God, who had performed so many miracles in her favour, to give me her promise to marry his Highness there before the Holy Sacrament, and her mind, once made up, would never change, but she would love him perfectly and never give him cause to be jealous.'

It had been inevitable that she would choose Philip. Other contenders for her hand – her old suitor Dom Luiz of Portugal and the Archduke Ferdinand of Austria, for instance – would have been less controversial, but Charles himself had played a duplicitous role in heading off these suits in favour of his son. The possession of England would strengthen Philip's hold on the Low Countries and perhaps advance his candidacy for the Imperial crown after Charles's retirement; the Spanish Habsburgs would thereby retain seniority over the Austrian branch of the family.

Then there were the English candidates: young Edward Courtenay, Earl of Devonshire, the 'last sprig of the White Rose', and Reginald Pole, who although a cardinal had only taken deacon's orders, leaving him free to marry. Like Mary, Courtenay was a great-grandchild of Edward IV, while Pole was Edward IV's great-nephew, the grandson of his brother Clarence. To Mary, there was no contest. Renard had shrewdly appealed to her pride in her Spanish royal blood, guessing that she would consider it beneath her to marry a mere subject. As heir to the Spanish crown, its colonies in the New World, the Low Countries, Naples and Sicily, Philip was, quite simply, the best match in Europe. It remained to convince her Council and the people.

Playing on Mary's pride again, Renard expressed surprise that she should concern herself with what the Council thought about her choice of husband. He knew he had the support of Paget, a career politician with no firm religious convictions, who believed that England needed the Imperial alliance. But the Lord Chancellor,

Gardiner, was vigorously opposed to the Spanish marriage. As a Catholic patriot he feared and hated the political influence of foreigners, believing that England should and could stand alone, without coming down on either the Imperialist or the French side. If England returned to Rome and re-established the old religion, Gardiner unrealistically believed, the country's ills would be solved. He immediately identified the weakest spot in Renard's argument: the Emperor's hypocrisy about his real motives in suggesting the marriage. By marrying Philip Mary would involve England in the Habsburgs' everlasting strife with France and invite the French to intrigue with English heretics. The Emperor would do better to be satisfied with England's good will, he maintained, without seeking an alliance through marriage.

Gardiner wanted Mary to marry the English candidate, Courtenay, whom he had grown fond of during the long years of imprisonment in the Tower. Mary tartly responded that she did not see why she should marry a man just because Gardiner had enjoyed his company in prison. Besides, although Courtenay's mother, Gertrude, Marchioness of Exeter, was a dear friend and the Queen's bedfellow, Mary did not like the young man. Outwardly charming and good-looking, he was already revealing himself to be dissolute, reckless and unreliable; he would be easy prey to the machinations of others.

That the Queen should rule alone, without a husband, was anathema. There was also the question of the succession. Validating Katherine of Aragon's marriage and her own legitimacy in Parliament had reopened in Mary all the wounds of the past. She had already admitted to Renard that 'it would burden her conscience too heavily' to allow that sly heretic Elizabeth, the daughter of the infamous whore Anne Boleyn, to succeed her. Was Elizabeth even her father's daughter, she asked, or had she been fathered by the musician Mark Smeaton, whom Mary in her bitterest moments fancied she resembled? It was imperative, therefore, that the Queen should marry and have a child of her own.

What she had not anticipated was that Parliament would send a delegation of twenty MPs to the palace to protest against her choice. When the Speaker argued against a foreign match Mary lost her temper, angrily shouting at them in her deep, masculine voice that

'Parliament was not accustomed to use such language to the kings of England.' She knew her duty to the country, but 'if she were married against her will she would not live three months, and would have no children, wherefore the Speaker would be defeating his own ends.' The delegation returned to Parliament empty-handed.

Never before had a Tudor ruler flouted popular opinion as expressed in Parliament so openly and at the same time so inexpertly. Powerless for so much of her life, Mary was now using her power unwisely, intent on having her own way. Successful sovereignty depends on the ability to listen and to conduct a dialogue with the people. No matter how autocratic her father had been, he had always been able to read the public mind and known when to give way, or appear to give way. National opposition to the Spanish match was not scotched by Mary's dismissal of Parliament's concerns, but driven underground and intensified.

The level of anti-Spanish sentiment ignited by news of the impending marriage took the Queen and the Imperialists by surprise. Spain, and more especially its territories in the Low Countries, had long been England's allies, but xenophobia was rife in Henry VIII's post-Reformation island empire. When the Emperor's ambassadors arrived to discuss the marriage treaty, the people made their disapproval felt. Small boys pelted them with snowballs and the crowd was sullen. Of course, the French ambassador, Antoine de Noailles, was playing a major role in fanning discontent, but the more militant Protestant propaganda machine was also at work, spreading alarmist rumours that the Spanish were coming to take over and that England would be forced back into subservience to the Pope.

The opponents of the marriage – Gardiner's faction in the Council and the parliamentary majority; a party of discontented nobles, including Lords Suffolk, Northampton, Pembroke, Clinton and the former adherents of Northumberland; and a handful of restless and adventurous knights and gentlemen – were motivated by patriotism rather than Protestantism. A series of popular risings was planned and organized, to be led by Sir Peter Carew and Edward Courtenay in the South-west, Sir James Crofts on the Welsh border, the Duke of Suffolk in the Midlands, and Sir Thomas Wyatt in Kent. Palm Sunday in mid March was set as the date for revolt, but leaks and the likelihood of discovery provoked the conspirators into premature action – rather as Renard, who had learned of the plot, intended.

The general aim of the conspirators seems to have been to depose Mary in favour of Elizabeth, who was to marry Courtenay. Renard, forever poisoning Mary's mind about Elizabeth – she was greatly to be feared, he warned, as she has power of enchantment – fuelled her suspicions that her sister was plotting against her. If Elizabeth knew about the plot, she was not necessarily implicated. There seems to be no doubt that the conspirators had been in touch, at least with senior members of her household, suggesting that she take up residence at her castle of Donnington. Elizabeth might well have been minded to do so, since Donnington could be more easily defended than Ashridge, where she was currently living. Mary fired her first shot across the bows by inviting Elizabeth to court for her own safety, rather than go to Donnington, 'whither, as we are informed, you are minded to remove'. Elizabeth declined the invitation, which convinced the sceptics that she must be guilty.

Only Wyatt's section of the planned revolt, in Kent, took off. The royal forces sent to defeat him joined him. Mary had no other army to interpose between Wyatt and his 3,000 followers as he approached the capital. As ever when personal courage was required, she rose to the occasion magnificently, riding with a train of lords and ladies from Westminster to Guildhall, to address the citizens with surprising eloquence. Her presence and oratory turned the tables on the rebels.

She began by appealing to the Londoners as their 'Queen and mother', 'not for having borne you as my children, but full of more than motherly love towards you since the day in which you chose me as your Queen and mistress.' They had chosen her as their queen, she continued, yet Wyatt was trying to depose her. Wyatt was not only going to take the Tower of London and the treasure of the kingdom, but he also had his eye on their personal wealth.

Her sole aim, she told them, was for the peace and tranquillity of the kingdom. Yes, a marriage was under discussion, but the matter was being decided by her counsellors, 'outstanding for their prudence and experience', and it would take place only if it was for England's good. 'I shall be pleased to submit the whole matter to Parliament, which should be called at an early date,' she promised. 'And should it not be recognized that the reasons which have induced myself and the Council to negotiate the marriage with the powerful Prince of Spain, are to the advantage of my kingdom and of the welfare of you all, I shall willingly refrain from pursuing it.'

She was not marrying for her own benefit, but for the good of her kingdom. She had spent most of her life unmarried, and would prefer to remain so, rather than provoke bloodshed in her kingdom. 'That being my mind and firm determination, I earnestly beg you, my beloved subjects, to openly state if I may expect from you loyalty and obedience, or if you will join the party of the nefarious traitor against me, your Queen.'

It was stirring stuff, if duplicitous. She was determined on the marriage, and nothing would dissuade her. Four days later she was telling Renard that she 'considered herself his Highness's wife, that she would never take another husband, and would rather lose her crown, her realm and her life'. The speech did the trick, however, inspiring London's trained bands to defend the City against the rebels.

When Wyatt and his force of 3,000 reached Southwark, he found London Bridge closed, with cannon pointed towards him. For three days he lingered on the south bank, before marching his troops west to Kingston, where he was able to cross the Thames and approach London through Knight's Bridge. As he neared St James's Park he made the fatal decision of splitting his force. The greater part continued north of St James's Palace and on to the City, while the rest made its way south of the royal hunting ground, to Westminster. The old leper hospital of St James's was Mary's favourite palace, but, refusing to take refuge in the Tower, she had stationed herself at Whitehall. As Wyatt's men approached, the royal guards in the outer defences panicked and retreated inside the gates. Mary remained undaunted, as palace officials and her ladies ran back and forth screaming. Her guards might be cowards, but Mary was prepared to stand her ground.

The rebels failed to take advantage of the disarray, continuing east, intent on taking the Tower. There were skirmishes at Temple Bar and along Fleet Street. Finally, Wyatt came to Ludgate, but could gain no admittance to the City. Realizing at last that he was beaten, he surrendered. Under torture, he refused to implicate Elizabeth, who was nevertheless brought to London for questioning. Wyatt was tried and executed, exonerating Elizabeth on the scaffold.

Renard was pressuring Mary to do away with Elizabeth, maintaining that she presented too much of a threat to Philip's safety to allow Philip to enter England. Whatever her personal inclination, Mary was insistent that her sister should be dealt with strictly according to law. Since no member of the Privy Council was willing to be responsible for Elizabeth, holding her in custody, she was taken to the Tower. By this time, it was clear that nothing could be proved against her. Later, John Foxe's emotive account of Elizabeth's arrival at the Tower – in which she prefers to sit outside in the rain rather than enter 'a worse place', where she is sure to meet her death – made good Protestant propaganda at a time when Mary's reputation was being blackened.

Fatally, Mary believed that her victory over Wyatt was a sign that God approved of her marriage. The rebellion reinforced the idea in her and Gardiner's minds that heresy, not patriotism, was the prime root of sedition in England. It gave Gardiner the motive to hurry forward the religious programme he had long been advocating, restoring the heresy laws in order to stamp it out. He believed that unless the old religion were firmly re-established before the marriage took place, the people would say that Catholicism was being reintroduced in the wake of Spanish domination. It was not a policy the secular Paget could condone and their quarrel spilled over on to the floor of the House of Lords – an unforgivable loss of control on the part of the executive, the Queen.

Treason was never condoned in Tudor England, but Wyatt had become something of a popular hero. The hundred-odd rebels who followed him to their deaths in the spring of 1554 were easily confused in the popular memory with the nearly 300 martyrs who were burned for their religious beliefs in succeeding years. Those who exhorted Bishop Latimer to courage at the stake and thrilled to his dying words perhaps remembered Wyatt's execution, when the onlookers had pushed forward to dip their handkerchiefs in his blood.

Henry VIII's breach with Rome had laid the foundation for that confusion of Protestantism with nationalism which would be such a prominent characteristic of Elizabeth's reign, but the process was greatly accelerated during the months following Wyatt's rebellion, when the clergy were talking about reviving the statutes against heresy and the executioners were exhibiting the severed heads and dismembered corpses of the rebels all over London – in the suburbs of Bermondsey and Southwark, at Leadenhall and Cheapside, Charing Cross and Tyburn. In the minds of many of Mary's subjects, Spain and Catholicism would soon be fused into a single symbol of horror.

6

Exit Jane

THE CHIEF VICTIM of Wyatt's rebellion was not Elizabeth, in whose name the rebels had acted, but Lady Jane Grey, the wife of Northumberland's son Guildford Dudley. A prisoner in the Tower, she was obviously innocent and had played no part in it. But she had been a Protestant figurehead once and might be again. She could not be allowed to live. It was only with the greatest reluctance and under pressure from the very members of the Council who had originally supported Northumberland's coup that Mary was forced to agree to her execution. It would elevate the girl to legendary status – that of Protestant Queen, heroine and martyr.

No trial was considered necessary, as Jane had already been tried and condemned for high treason in usurping the crown after Edward's death in 1553. With the executioner carrying the axe before them, Jane and those accused with her – her husband Guildford, his brothers Ambrose and Harry, and Thomas Cranmer, Archbishop of Canterbury – had walked from the Tower to Guildhall for the trial. Accompanied by her two ladies, Jane had dressed entirely in black lined with velvet, a black velvet book dangling from her waist and another book of devotions in her hand. They pleaded guilty and were duly sentenced to a traitor's death: the men to be hanged, drawn and quartered, Jane to be beheaded or burned at the Queen's pleasure. As was customary, the condemned returned to the Tower with the headsman's axe turned towards them.

Swept to power on a wave of popular enthusiasm, Mary was inclined to be merciful, at least to the young people. She was fond of Jane, despite her outspokenness; indeed, they were both inclined to speak their minds, and Mary probably respected this, whereas she felt she could never trust the sly and hypocritical Elizabeth. 'The Queen's majesty is a merciful Princess,' Jane commented appreciatively when she learned that her sentence was suspended. 'I beseech God she may long continue and send his bountiful grace upon her.'

Predictably, Jane was disgusted at Northumberland's conversion to Catholicism, especially if it was done to win a pardon: 'Woe worth him! he hath brought me and our stock in most miserable calamity and misery by his exceeding ambition,' she cried, adding:

> Like as his life was wicked and full of dissimulation, so was his end thereafter. I pray God, I, nor no friend of mine, die so. Should I, who am young and in my few years, forsake my faith for the love of life? Nay, God forbid! Much more should he not, whose fatal course, although he had lived his just number of years, could not have long continued. But life was sweet, it appeared; so he might have lived, you will say, he did not care how.

While her eldest daughter was a prisoner in the Tower, Frances Brandon was basking in the Queen's favour, often given precedence over Elizabeth at court. Places had been found as maids of honour for her younger daughters, Catherine – who had been sent home after Pembroke had had her marriage to his son annulled – and Mary. There is no evidence that Frances pleaded for her daughter's life, or even visited her in the Tower, nor would it have been in character, but she might have done.

Free at last from her dominating parents, Jane spent the intervening months quietly, devoting herself to her studies. She had 'the liberty of the Tower so she could walk in the Queen's garden and on the hill'. She was permitted a staff of four, including her old nurse, Mrs Ellen, and two gentlewomen, Mrs Tilney and Mrs Jacob, to wait on her. She had the Queen's assurance of her life and eventual liberty. Then events spiralled out of control and her thoughtless, selfish father – forgetting the Queen's clemency which had allowed him his life and liberty – became implicated in the plot against the Spanish marriage. Suffolk won little support when he tried to incite anti-Spanish sentiment in Leicestershire and with the failure of the uprising he was eventually found cowering in a tree on his estate.

Jane's execution was to take place on 9 February 1554, but there was a delay since Mary was determined to try to save her soul. She sent Dr Feckenham, the new Dean of St Paul's, to do his best to win over the strong-minded girl. Jane told Feckenham frankly that he was wasting his time, that 'she had taken leave from all earthly matters so that she did not even think of the fear of death and that she had prepared patiently to accept it in the way in which the Queen would be served to command; it was quite true that it would be painful to her flesh as a mortal thing, but her soul was happy to abandon this darkness and ascend to the eternal light, as she was confident, putting her trust in God's mercy alone.'

She was quite happy to dispute theology with him, however, defending her Protestant faith publicly in front of Tower officials. Their debate was published with her other writings in 1554, becoming the most powerful contemporary Protestant attack on the Marian regime. Her writings consisted of a letter to a friend newly fallen from the reformed faith – probably her first tutor, Dr Harding, whom she calls 'the deformed imp of the devil . . . the unshamefaced paramour of Antichrist . . . a cowardly runaway'; a prayer composed a few weeks before her death; letters to her father and sister Catherine written when she knew she was to die; and her speech from the scaffold. She would have been aware of their potentially wide distribution and shaped them accordingly, a public testimonial of her beliefs.

Her works reached the English exiles abroad – where she was already much admired by prominent European Protestants with whom she had been in correspondence – and nine years later were incorporated in the first edition of John Foxe's *Acts and Monuments*, which lauded her as a Protestant martyr, even though she was condemned for treason, not her religion.

In the prayer she wrote shortly before her death she falters slightly, describing herself as a 'poor and desolate woman'. She feared that she might succumb to despair, begging God, 'suffer me not to be tempted above my power'. The night before her death she wrote to her father. She did not gloss over the fact that it was his actions that had brought her to this end – 'Father, although it hath pleased God to hasten my death by you, by whom my life should rather have been lengthened' – yet she gave God 'more hearty thanks for shortening my woeful days'. As regards the coup, she had a clear conscience, although she would acknowledge in her scaffold speech her guilt for loving the world too much and for forgetting God.

Guildford Dudley was to die with his wife. According to one source, he had 'sent her word that before dying he wished to embrace and kiss her for the last time'. Jane replied that if it would have been 'a means of consolation to their souls, she would have been very glad to see him, but as their meeting would only tend to increase their misery and pain' it was better to wait, until they could meet in the next world. On the morning of his execution Jane positioned herself at the window, so that she could see him pass. She was still there when the cart bearing his corpse, the head wrapped in a bloody sheet, passed by on its return journey. Jane herself was to be beheaded within the precincts of the Tower, as befitted a lady of royal blood, so that she would have seen and heard the scaffold where she was to die being prepared over by the White Tower.

On the morning of her execution, Jane emerged leaning on the arm of Sir John Brydges, the Lieutenant of the Tower. She was wearing the same black dress she had worn to her trial. Mrs Tylney and her old nurse followed, weeping. Jane seemed to be quite composed, reading from the prayer book she held in her hand. She mounted the scaffold and turned to address the audience: 'Good people, I am come hither to die, and by the law I am condemned to the same. The fact, in deed, against the Queen's highness was unlawful, and the consenting thereunto by me: but touching the procurement and desire thereof by me or on my part, I do wash my hands thereof in innocence, before God, and the face of you, good Christian people, this day.'

As a Protestant, she did not believe in intercession for the dead, but exhorted them to pray for her only while she lived.

She shrank back from the executioner when he approached to take her outer garments, which were his perquisites of office. She turned to her ladies to help her undress. At last she was ready. The executioner knelt down and asked her forgiveness for what he was about to do, then directed her on to the straw.

For the first time, she saw the block and the axe nestling beside it. 'I pray you despatch me quickly!' she pleaded. She knelt down. 'Will you take it off before I lay me down?' she asked the executioner.

'No, Madam.'

She tied the handkerchief over her eyes, groping for the block. 'What shall I do? Where is it?' she panicked. Someone came over to help her. 'Lord, into thy hands I commend my spirit!' she whispered. The axe swung high and then plunged down into the innocent neck of the seventeen-year-old.

John Brydges was holding the prayer book Jane had given him. He opened it to find several inscriptions, ending with the words: 'Live still to die, that by death you may purchase eternal life . . . For, as the preacher sayeth, there is a time to be born and a time to die; and the day of death is better than the day of our birth. Yours, as the Lord knoweth as a friend, Jane Duddeley.'

Later that day, Lady Jane was laid to rest under the floor of St Peter ad Vincula between the remains of two headless queens, Anne Boleyn and Katherine Howard. Her nine days' reign had cost her dear.

7

The Phantom Pregnancy

TOWARDS THE END of July 1554 the Spanish fleet dropped anchor off the Isle of Wight and the Prince of Spain proceeded by barge to Southampton. His arrival had been keenly anticipated. The English fleet had been on patrol in the western approaches since May on the lookout for the great armada – Philip was bringing a personal train of 1,500, as well as 3,000 troops bound for the Low Countries, who were to remain on board discreetly out of sight – and his English household had been languishing in Hampshire for over a month. Always methodical, as ponderous as his great ships, Philip was not one to do anything in a hurry. Nor was he in any great rush to see his bride, the sad, middle-aged woman whom he had hitherto considered his maiden aunt.

It is tempting to ask why Mary was bothering to marry at all, especially given the amount of vociferous opposition to her choice of husband. At the outset of her reign, she had had her subjects' love; surely, given their detestation of the Spanish match, it would have been wise to reconsider? Perhaps, after all, it would be better to remain single, if only to win back some of that lost popularity. That was to reckon without Mary's personality, her habit of dependence, and the conventions of the time. It would take a very strong and original woman in the sixteenth century to flout the norm and choose not to marry. Mary was nothing if not conventional. Her whole upbringing had pointed to the need for a husband.

In spite of her undoubted courage and unexpected qualities of leadership in defeating Northumberland and quelling Wyatt's rebellion, Mary lacked the confidence to rule alone. She could not help comparing herself to her awe-inspiring father. She perceived him as strong, whereas she was weak and in need of a powerful figure to help her rule. For the enormous task of bringing England back to the true Church, no husband, she felt, would be more helpful than Philip; in fact, the reverse was true, as the unpopular marriage delayed the restoration of Catholicism and fixed that religion for ever in the popular mind as something foreign, alien.

The restoration of Catholicism could be secured, Mary felt, only by her founding a new, Catholic dynasty. It seems that she so desperately wanted to believe that she would have a child that she never permitted herself to consider the possibility that she would fail. But the chances of a woman of Mary's age, with her long history of menstrual disorder and the state of sixteenth-century obstetrics, conceiving and bearing a healthy child were remote. Her health problems were well known. The Venetian ambassador noted that she was

> often subject to a very deep melancholy, much greater than that to which she is constitutionally liable, from [menstrual] retention and suffocation of the matrix [infrequent or irregular periods] to which, for many years, she has been often subject, so that the remedy of tears and weeping, to which from childhood she has been accustomed, and still often used by her, is not sufficient; she requires to be blooded either from the foot or elsewhere, which keeps her always pale and emaciated.

The belief was that bleeding a patient would 'bring down the menses', the menstrual blood that had failed to flow, causing ill humours to remain in the body.

Perhaps it was in the knowledge that she was unlikely to bear a child that Charles was prepared to allow such favourable terms to the English when negotiating the marriage treaty. The position of king consort was unprecedented in England and unknown to English law. Charles, who negotiated the treaty for his son, was primarily concerned with strengthening Philip's hand in northern Europe, especially in the Low Countries. The English were deeply mistrustful of the whole business, especially given the Habsburg proclivity for 'conquest by marriage'.

A woman automatically ceded all her property to her husband on marriage. There was a school of thought that argued that a queen regnant had only a 'woman's estate' in the realm, meaning that the

kingdom would pass on her marriage to her husband in full owner-
ship and remain vested in him during his natural life, whether she was
alive or dead. The prevailing view, however, was rather more sophisticated. The royal office was unique, so that the laws of real property
did not apply. Just as medieval kings and, indeed, Henry VIII, sub-
scribed to the notion of the King's two bodies – the one mortal with
human frailties, the other the embodiment of the kingly office and
perpetual – so a queen regnant is two persons politically. She is a wife
who is subordinate to her husband in marital affairs, and a magistrate
who is superior to him and every one of her subjects in affairs of
state.

The marriage treaty of Mary and Philip preserves something of the
appearance of the relations of power in a traditional marriage, while
actually providing for the Queen's authority in matters of state. In
effect, she metaphorically emasculated her husband. She had the
precedent of her grandmother, Isabella of Castile, who had defined
her husband Ferdinand as a mere king consort, rather than a king regnant. Indeed, Isabella had gone ahead with her coronation without
him. Mary, like Isabella, was careful to maintain an appearance of
shared power. She conceded that Philip should take the title of King –
he started signing himself Philipus Rex before he was entitled to do
so – and allowed his title precedence over hers, for instance on official
documents and the coin of the realm. But the treaty explicitly prevented him from exercising any authority in England independent of
his wife.

The treaty contained a clear and unequivocal statement that, in the
case of there being no children of the marriage, Philip's interest in the
realm would cease with Mary's death. All offices were to be held by
English natives and Philip had no authority to appoint any foreigner
to office or benefice. Nor could he disturb the existing laws and customs. He would not be able to take the Queen or her children out of
the realm without parliamentary approval, nor the crown jewels, ships
or arms.

Charles envisaged that any child of Mary and Philip would inherit
England and the Low Countries, while Philip's son, Don Carlos,
would inherit Spain and the Habsburg lands in Italy. In other words,
the treaty as good as disinherited Philip's first-born from a valuable

slice of his inheritance. If Don Carlos – an inbred imbecile – did not survive, Philip and Mary's child would inherit everything.

The publication of the marriage treaty – which tried so hard to assuage English fears – was the only known attempt by Mary's government to mitigate English hostility to the Spanish match by means of the printing press. But if the English were appeased, Philip was not. When he read the treaty, he was so furious that he drew up a secret protest in the presence of his closest adviser, Ruy Gomez da Silva, and the Duke of Alva, absolving himself and his heirs from observing its terms. As an indication of his future intentions in England, he asked his father if the clause preventing him from involving England in his ongoing war with France could be amended. Charles knew the matter was far too sensitive even to broach with the English.

There was no enthusiasm on Philip's part for the marriage. It was simply duty. His father had to prompt him to make even the most basic gesture towards Mary. 'You will send to England a gentleman of position to take a present to be given to the Queen after her betrothal, a ring or some jewel of value, for it will be eagerly looked for,' he instructed. Mary hesitated to write to Philip, feeling that the man should initiate the correspondence. 'You have not privately written to me since our alliance has been negotiated,' she eventually hinted. It was not a hopeful sign.

Philip could hardly have complained about his welcome in England. The foremost noblemen had been sent to Southampton to greet him and they did so with all due courtesy. Lord Arundel presented him with the Order of the Garter and a white jennet harnessed in crimson velvet embroidered with gold, pearls and precious stones from the Queen. The next day the Lord Chancellor, Gardiner, arrived with Mary's gift of a large diamond, while Arundel in turn carried a diamond from Philip to Mary, 'but considerably smaller than the first one'.

On 21 July Mary issued a proclamation in London inviting all noblemen, gentlemen and ladies to 'repayre to the Cittie of Winchester, there to doe attendance at her graces marriage'. The wedding was to take place on St James's Day, 25 July, at Winchester Cathedral. On the 23rd Philip rode up from Southampton with a magnificent entourage, making his first acquaintance with an English summer. There was torrential rain and his fine clothes were soaked. 'He went straight to the cathedral, a fine building where there was such a crowd that they all were in danger of stifling, and then proceeded on foot to his quarters, not to the Queen's. He supped quietly with a small company and then went to visit the Queen.'

They were to marry in two days' time and this was their first meeting. At ten o'clock that night Philip was brought privately from the deanery through the gardens to the bishop's palace, where Mary was staying. Accompanied by her ladies and several counsellors, she was waiting at the door of her chamber to greet him. She was 'dressed in black velvet covered with stones and buttons and adorned with brocade in front' and many jewels. The couple kissed one another, according to the English custom, and 'went hand in hand to their chairs' under a canopy of state. As Philip was no linguist – he had not troubled to learn any English – and Mary understood but did not speak his native Castilian, their conversation, conducted in a mixture of French and Spanish, must have been limited to the general pleasantries. Mary taught Philip to say 'Good night, my lords all', which was to be the sum total of his communication with the English nobility in their own tongue. The next day he visited Mary again and 'they kissed and walked through two or three rooms, and then stood talking a long time.'

Mary was predisposed to love Philip because he came from her mother's family. The English had never treated her well and her mother's relatives had often seemed her only lifeline. As they were far away, she was oblivious of their imperfections. She was an idealist and might have imagined that she would receive from Philip something of the unconditional love her mother had given her as a child. After bitter years of loneliness, the once cherished child ached for love; she longed for someone to trust, to ease the strain of governing alone. She would also have found Philip's appearance reasonably pleasing. Like her, he was short and thin, but he had blue eyes and flaxen hair and the Habsburg jaw was not so marked as it was in his father.

Philip expected little so was unlikely to have been unduly disappointed by his bride. He was careful to mask his true feelings and at all times he treated her with the utmost respect and courtesy. His Spanish

attendants, however, did not trouble to conceal the truth in their correspondence.

'The Queen is a very good creature,' Ruy Gomez began tactfully in
a letter to the Emperor's Spanish secretary, Francisco de Eraso, 'though
rather older than we had been told. But His Highness is so tactful and
attentive to her that I am sure they will be very happy.' On further
reflection, he could not resist adding: 'To speak frankly with you, it
will take a great God to drink this cup . . . the best of it is that the
King fully realized that the marriage was concluded for no fleshly
consideration, but in order to remedy the disorders of the kingdom
and to preserve the Low Countries.'

Another of Philip's gentlemen wrote: 'The Queen, however, is not
at all beautiful: small, and rather flabby than fat, she is of white complexion and fair, and has no eyebrows. She is a perfect saint, and
dresses badly.' Gomez was of the opinion that 'if she dressed in our
fashions she would not look so old and flabby'. Nor was he impressed
by her abilities, commenting witheringly: 'The Queen is a good
soul, but not as able as we were led to suppose – I mean as a
stateswoman.'

She was already lavishing presents on her bridegroom. The day after
their meeting she sent 'her tailor with two suits, one of rich brocade
adorned with gold thread, pearls and diamond buttons, the other of
crimson brocade'. Mary was never overly generous, however, and it is
significant that she gave her husband no lands in England, as a king
always did his consort. Philip therefore had no personal patrimony in
the country and no English income. Perhaps Mary thought that he
was sufficiently rich without the need for English estates; on the other
hand, she might not have wanted him to establish an affinity – a following derived from landed property – as she had had when she was
a magnate in East Anglia during her brother's reign. Certainly, Philip's
interests in England could only be served by protecting his wife's
interests.

Whether it was an oversight or a calculated omission on Mary's
part, it meant that Philip had to finance the very considerable outlay
of pensions, rewards and bribes – to establish his influence and keep
the English nobility onside – from his Spanish revenues. As Ruy
Gomez ruefully remarked: 'Interest is a powerful motive in all

countries, but nowhere as powerful as it is here, where nothing is well done unless it brings money, a commodity of which we have so little that, if the English find out how hard up we are, I doubt whether we shall escape with our lives.' As Philip was to find, the English happily took his money, but would do little to repay him when he looked for their support.

Like a queen consort, Philip was provided with a household, which was paid for by Mary as an augmentation of the royal household. There was some ill feeling because Philip had brought his own complete household and ended up paying for his own and subsidizing the second. He used Spaniards almost exclusively in his Privy Chamber, and the English for the outer chamber and below stairs. An English secretary was provided to act as interpreter, but seems to have been largely ignored. Philip's Spanish attendants were affronted when they saw Englishmen standing behind Philip's chair when he dined in state. As Mary was already installed in the king's side, Philip was to be lodged in the queen consort's side at each of the royal palaces.

On his wedding day, Philip 'went forth with a brave following of grandees and gentlemen of his court, so magnificently attired that neither his Majesty's nor his Highness's court ever saw the like', one of them reported to the Emperor's secretary, 'such was the display of rich garments and chains, each one finer than the last'. Philip was wearing a doublet and hose of white leather embroidered with silver and a French mantle, of 'drawn and fluted gold, very richly bestrewn with precious stones and pearls and a very rich sword of gold, black velvet cap with white feathers and a necklace [which] was sent him by the Emperor'. Mary had provided Philip's mantle and wore a gown of matching material in the French style with a very long train, the sleeves elaborately worked with gold and enriched with pearls and diamonds, and a kirtle of white satin enriched with silver. A Spaniard noted approvingly that 'she had her hair dressed after our fashion with its chaperon of black velvet bestrewn with pearls which looked very pretty', while on her breast she wore the big table diamond that Philip sent at the time of their betrothal.

Just as her mother had done when she married Prince Arthur in 1501, Mary walked the whole distance from the cathedral's west door to the steps of the sanctuary on an elevated walkway. Perhaps now she would cement the alliance between England and Spain that her grandparents had so desired at that time. Symbolically, she was given away 'in the name of the whole realm' by the Marquis of Winchester and the Earls of Derby, Bedford and Pembroke. Although she was ablaze with jewels, she chose as her wedding ring a simple gold band, since 'her desire was to be married as maidens were married in the old time.' She would also promise 'to be bonny and buxom [willing], in bed and at board'.

Mary's Lord Chancellor, Stephen Gardiner, Bishop of Winchester, the chief of the five bishops present, confirmed that Philip had ratified the marriage treaty in Spain and held it up without reading it. The previous evening news had arrived that the Emperor had bestowed on his son the kingdom of Naples, so that Mary found to her delight that she was marrying a king rather than a mere prince. When the moment came for Philip to place the gold coins representing his worldly goods on the Bible, Mary scooped them up with a smile and handed them to her kinswoman Lady Margaret Clifford, who was holding her purse.

After the Mass, the 'King went up to the altar to receive the kiss of peace, which the Bishop gave him on his cheek, after the English custom, and then went to kiss the Queen, to whom he bowed low', one of his Spanish attendants observed. 'All the while, for an hour, she remained with her eyes fixed on the Sacrament. She is a saintly woman.'

The herald proclaimed Philip King of England and read out the couple's royal style and titles: 'Philip and Marie, by the grace of God king and queen of England, France, Naples, Jerusalem, and Ireland, defenders of the faith, princes of Spain and Sicily, archdukes of Austria, dukes of Milan, Burgundy and Brabant, counts of Habsburg, Flanders and Tyrol'. Then, 'to the sound of great rejoicing of the people, the blare of trumpets and other music', they walked hand in hand to the palace under a canopy of crimson velvet embroidered with gold, accompanied by their entourages. The Earl of Pembroke carried a second Sword of State before Philip as king.

At the wedding feast, the couple shared a table with Bishop Gardiner. It is significant that Mary sat on the right, in a superior chair to Philip's, and that she ate off gold, while her husband had to make do with silver plate. The ambassadors and grandees shared another table, while the various Spanish and English gentlemen took up several others. The Queen's ladies had their own table. Afterwards, the company proceeded to another hall, where Philip and Mary danced together 'after the German fashion'. It was an awkward gathering as the two nations did not know each other's dances and the Spaniards were not sure what to make of the English ladies. 'They are neither beautiful nor graceful when dancing, and their dances only consist in strutting or trotting about,' one complained. Neither understood the other's language, and only a few of the English ladies spoke Latin. The party was over by nine. Curiously, the bridal couple took supper separately in their own quarters.

Bishop Gardiner blessed the marriage bed and left the couple alone, still in their finery. A discreet veil has been drawn over the rest of the proceedings. 'What happened that night only they know,' one of the Spaniards recorded. 'If they give us a son, our joy will be complete.' Mary had been brought up to embrace chastity and had continued in that way of life; she was so innocent that she did not know the meaning of the word 'whore' or understand a risqué joke. Her apprehension at thirty-eight, having her first sexual experience with a younger man she barely knew, can be imagined.

The next morning when Philip's Spanish entourage noisily came to the bedchamber to congratulate the couple, they found the way barred by Mary's shocked ladies, who told them that it was not the custom for queens of England to be seen on the day following their marriage night, but to spend it alone in private. Philip was not there anyway, having risen at seven and been at his desk for hours. He would dine alone in public. 'This match will have been a fine business if the Queen does not have a child,' one of Philip's disgruntled attendants concluded, 'and I am sure she will not.'

Philip, it seemed, was handling the situation with some sensitivity, as his confidant Ruy Gomez was soon reporting: 'He treats the Queen very kindly, and well knows how to pass over the fact that she is no good from the point of view of fleshly sensuality. He makes her so happy that the other day when they were alone she almost talked love-talk to him, and he replied in the same vein.'

The couple slowly made their way to London, stopping at various great houses to hunt, until they arrived at Southwark, prior to Philip's official entry into the capital. The rotting body parts of the victims of Wyatt's defeat were hastily removed and much care had been taken with the pageantry. Gardiner was furious to see a tableau depicting Henry VIII holding a Bible with the words '*Verbum Dei*' prominently displayed. He ordered the painter to scratch them out and substitute a pair of gloves. Another tableau emphasized Philip's Lancastrian ancestry and his double descent from the legitimate off-spring of John of Gaunt, son of Edward III. Not only did Philip, with his fair colouring, look reassuringly English, but this tableau sought to impress upon the people that he was almost an English prince.

The first impression Philip made on the English was unexpectedly favourable, thanks to the careful coaching of his father and Renard. He was to make an honest effort to embrace English customs, even to dining in public – more often than Mary did – and drinking beer, which the English did to excess. Under the surface cordiality, how-ever, Philip was almost as unfitted for the task of governing England as his wife. His stiff dignity, notorious linguistic limitations, his distaste for the macho physical sports so dear to the English, and his narrow Spanish patriotism precluded his winning the hearts of the people, just as the same lack of warmth and engagement was alienating him from his subjects in the Low Countries.

Like Mary, Philip had no image of himself. He lacked charisma and a sense of showmanship. The official entry into London was his opportunity to bond with the crowd and he fluffed it. He remained mute and unresponsive; there was no repartee, no friendly badinage, no overt show of appreciation. The type of reciprocal gesture that the English expect of their sovereigns simply was not forthcoming. To make matters worse, English xenophobia was finding a ready target in his entourage. 'The English hate us Spaniards worse than they hate the Devil and treat us accordingly,' one of them wrote home. Brawls and robberies were frequent and the Spaniards found themselves given the worst lodgings and ripped off into the bargain.

In mid September, Mary's joy was complete when her physicians told her that she was pregnant. She had missed her period and was experiencing nausea in the mornings and changes in her breasts. Renard was one of the first to know, reporting to the Emperor: 'If it is true everything will calm down and go smoothly here . . . I have already caused a rumour to be started for the purpose of keeping the malcontents within bounds.' An heir would secure the regime and discourage its opponents. Perhaps Parliament would approve Philip's coronation and further religious legislation would be carried on a wave of sympathy for a queen who was to become a mother.

It seemed to Mary that God had wrought this miracle as a reward for her fidelity to the Catholic cause. She was not alone in this assumption. As one of Philip's nobles wrote to Charles's close adviser, the Bishop of Arras:

> The Queen is with child. I have personal reason to believe it, as I have noticed her feeling sick, besides which her doctor has given me positive assurance . . . The Queen was saved and preserved through many great dangers and raised to the throne almost by a miracle, and for the peace and good of the kingdom it was ardently to be hoped that she might bear children to establish and make safe the success of the undertaking to which she has set her hand, namely the restoration of the Catholic religion and faith.

Right on cue, Cardinal Reginald Pole wrote a long letter to Philip, begging for admittance in order to carry out his mission in England at last: 'A year has passed since I began to knock at the door of the royal house and none has opened to me . . . Now, what shall I say of Mary, the Queen? I know she rejoices, but I also know that she fears; for did she not, she would not so long have delayed to open.'

Renard had already warned the Emperor that the time was not ripe for a full restoration of Catholicism. 'Affairs are not settled here yet, and the King has only been a few days [six weeks] in the realm. The Spaniards are hated, as I have seen in the past and expect to see in the future . . . disagreeable incidents are of daily occurrence.' Renard, a native of the Franche-Comté, disliked Spanish hauteur just as much as the English did.

In the first week of November Renard was convinced that Mary's pregnancy was real. 'There is no doubt that the Queen is with child, for her stomach clearly shows it and her dresses no longer fit her.' One of Philip's nobles reported that 'she is fatter and has a better colour than when she was married, a sign that she is happier, and indeed she is said to be very happy.'

Weight gain and swelling of the abdomen are signs of a phantom pregnancy, just as much as a real one. Had Mary's physician had the knowledge or been allowed to examine her properly, he might have noted that the enlargement of her abdomen was not accompanied by the effacement of her umbilicus.

In spite of Renard's grim prognostications, on 24 November 1554 the aesthetic figure of Cardinal Pole, the papal legate, arrived at Whitehall by boat, dramatically holding the cross before him. He was greeted by Philip at the riverside. Inside, Mary welcomed her long-exiled cousin, kneeling for his blessing. Significantly, he addressed her in the opening words of the *Ave Maria*: 'Hail, Mary, thou art highly favoured, the Lord is with thee, blessed art thou among women.'

The suggestion was all it took for Mary to send him a message, after he had retired to Lambeth Palace later in the day, that she had felt the child in her womb quicken. There was an obvious parallel with St Elizabeth when she greeted her pregnant cousin: the child she was carrying, St John the Baptist, had leapt in recognition of the Christ Child in the Virgin Mary's womb. Mary the Queen's leapt in anticipation of her country's restoration to the faith.

It is not untypical for a woman to experience foetal movements during a phantom pregnancy, but of course there are no foetal heart sounds.

Pole took up the analogy four days later when, in the presence of Philip and Mary, he addressed Parliament, inviting it to annul the laws and statutes against the Pope's and the Church's authority as being unreasonable and contrary to established truth. The Pope and the apostolic see loved the kingdom of England, he told them, careful to play on the English nationalism so successfully awakened by Henry VIII. The people had been in error, but thanks to Mary and her marriage, all would now be well: 'And see how miraculously God of his goodness preserved her highness, contrary to the expectation of man, that when numbers conspired against her, and policies were devised to disinherit her, and armed power prepared to destroy her, yet she being a virgin, helpless, naked and unarmed, prevailed.'

In April 1555 a day of thanksgiving for the Queen's pregnancy was held, with the bells of St Paul's and London's forty-four parish churches ringing in celebration. Her confinement was expected in mid June. At Hampton Court she went through the formal ceremony of taking to her chamber, following the guidelines for the delivery of a queen laid down by her great-grandmother, Margaret Beaufort, in 1494:

> If it please the Queene to take her chamber, shee shall bee brought thither with the lords and ladies of estate, and brought into the chapel or church there . . . then to come into the great chamber and take spice and wine under the cloth of estate; then two of the greatest estates to lead her into her chamber where shee shall be delivered; and they then to take their leave of the Queene. Then all the ladies and gentlewomen to goe in with her; and after that noe man to come into the chamber where she shall bee delivered, save women.

While she awaited her confinement a queen would effectively be sealed off from the world, in a darkened chamber. But Mary, the first queen regnant, ignored protocol by appearing at the window on St George's Day, 23 April, to watch Philip lead the celebrations for the patron saint of the Knights of the Garter. So proud was she of her pregnancy that she positioned herself sideways at the window, so that eyewitnesses could see her swollen belly.

A vast gathering of ladies had converged on Hampton Court to await the birth, so that the palace was full to overflowing. The most important lady of all, however, after the Queen, was Elizabeth. Sure of her triumph over her bastard half-sister, Mary now freed Elizabeth from detention at Woodstock, where she had been sent after the Wyatt rebellion and a spell in the Tower, and brought her to court, to be present as a witness at the birth of the child who would supplant her as heir to the throne. Elizabeth arrived quietly, only being admitted to see her sister and brother-in-law once or twice 'by private stairs'. It was Philip's first glimpse of the red-headed Princess and he liked what he saw; she presented such a dazzling contrast to his thin-lipped, ageing wife. The Venetian ambassador, Giovanni

Michiel, was already speculating that if Mary died, Philip would marry her sister. Certainly, if Mary died, the possession of Elizabeth's person would guarantee Philip's safety until he could leave the country.

On the last day of April, a report was circulated in London that the Queen had been delivered of a son in the early hours. No matter how unpopular the regime was becoming now that persecution of Protestants had begun in earnest, the birth of a male heir to the throne threw the people into a frenzy of rejoicing. In London shops were shut, church bells rung, tables hauled out to the street and spread with wine and meats for all to enjoy, and bonfires lit. By afternoon, people returning from Hampton Court denied the report and the mood swiftly swung to disappointment.

A month later the child had still not arrived. 'Everything in this kingdom depends on the Queen's safe deliverance,' Renard wrote in agitation. Apparently, Mary's 'doctors and ladies have proved to be out in their calculations by about two months, and it now appears that she will not be delivered before eight or ten days from now,' he reported to Charles on 24 June. Philip's patience was wearing thin. Probably he already suspected that there was no baby. A child would have justified his presence; otherwise he regarded his sojourn in England as a distasteful and fruitless exile. He was so desperate to leave that, according to Michiel, 'one single hour's delay in this delivery seems to him a thousand years.' As ever, Renard imagined conspiracies: 'It is almost incredible how the delay in the Queen's deliverance encourages the heretics to slander and put about false rumours; some say that she is not with child at all, that a suppositious child is going to be presented as hers, and that if a suitable one had been found this would already have been done.'

And yet Mary continued to show every sign of being pregnant. Her girth had increased, consistent with a pregnancy of nine months, and her breasts were swollen and tender and secreting milk. She refused categorically, with characteristic stubbornness, to consider the possibility that she might not be pregnant or to undertake procedures that might clarify the situation. Pandering to her every whim, the doctors and her ladies baulked at telling her what they now suspected: that she was not pregnant at all. Only Frideswide Strelly, who had been a faithful attendant for many years, had had the courage to tell Mary all along that she was not pregnant, that there must be another explanation for her symptoms. The French ambassador was chortling with glee, because he had heard that Mary was able to drop down on a cushion and sit for hours with her knees pressed up against her chest, as no pregnant woman could do. Elizabeth, meanwhile, watched and waited, torn between pity for her sister and concern at the humiliating position into which the farce of her pregnancy was placing the monarchy.

As late as the third week in July the Venetian ambassador was reporting that the delivery 'is now unaccountably delayed'. A consultation had been held in which the physicians had cravenly suggested that they had miscalculated by two or three months. A woman who had given birth to live triplets at forty was brought to the palace to assure the Queen that she too could expect a happy delivery.

By now, Hampton Court stank. The unusually long occupancy of the royal household and the additional hangers-on who had taken up residence at the Queen's expense to be present at the birth, living in crowded conditions with sixteenth-century sanitary arrangements, had had the inevitable result. After one or two episodes of 'false labour', Mary's abdomen, which had had the appearance of full-term pregnancy, began to diminish. The signs of pregnancy disappeared and she was forced to concede that there would be no child after all. The baby's cradle which had stood in readiness with the rockers and layette were discreetly removed.

On 5 August Michiel reported that Philip and Mary had quietly slipped away from Hampton Court to Oatlands, where she had resumed her regal duties. No official announcement was made. Michiel was speculating that 'the pregnancy will end in wind rather than anything else', but in order to keep 'the populace in hope, and consequently in check', nothing would be said to disabuse them for the time being.

It was a classic case of pseudocyesis – false, phantom or hysterical pregnancy – the most public in history. The pain, the humiliation and embarrassment can only be imagined. Mary immediately plunged into depression, as was typical in the wake of a phantom pregnancy. Poor Mary, she had ended up in the same dynastic marriage trap as her mother, under intense pressure to bear a son. For all her show of defiance, she had re-enacted her father's chief obsessions, believing that she was valueless unless she could produce a male heir, and going to frantic lengths to convince herself and her people that she was capable of doing so. She shared her father's belief that her failure to have a son was a demonstration of deep inadequacy and suffered the same acute anguish. It seemed that God had withdrawn His favour from her, just as her father had imagined that He looked with disfavour on his incestuous marriage to Mary's mother.

A phantom pregnancy can be rooted in fear of pregnancy, but is more commonly encountered when the desire for pregnancy becomes an obsession. Some psychiatrists believe that it provides compensation for a real or imagined loss, that the condition stems from early unresolved loss of a parent. The sudden separation from a parent in childhood – such as Mary's from her mother when the latter was banished from court and sent to a place of confinement, and the abrupt termination of her father's love about the same time – can lead later to separation anxiety from a loved one and a desperate need to secure that source or object of affection. Perhaps Philip, a member of her mother's family, reawakened in Mary long-suppressed feelings of maternal loss, especially after they were sexually intimate. She probably believed that a child would bring her husband closer to her and, indeed, during her 'pregnancy' he had been most attentive.

Philip was all the more furious, therefore, when it proved false. His wife had made a laughing stock of him in front of all Europe. He knew now that there would never be a child by Mary and there was nothing to keep him in England. He left in disgust and irritation, adding to her loss of self-esteem. 'As may be imagined with regard to a person extraordinarily in love,' Michiel noted sympathetically, 'the Queen remains disconsolate, though she conceals it as much as she can, and from what I hear mourns the more when alone and supposing herself invisible to any of her attendants.'

On the day of his departure, the Queen saw Philip to the top of the stairs at Greenwich, where he kissed all her ladies and the Spanish noblemen kissed her hand. She maintained her dignity and gravity while in public, but on returning to her apartments overlooking the river, not thinking herself observed, 'she gave free vent to her grief by a flood of tears, nor did she once quit the window until she had not only seen the King embark and depart, but remained looking after him as long as he was in sight.'

8

The Burnings

WHILE THE QUEEN was preoccupied with her phantom pregnancy and depressed in its aftermath, the fires of Smithfield were burning fiercely. The intention had been to burn a few heretics to deter the rest, but it quickly became apparent that the burnings were having quite the opposite effect, stiffening Protestant resolve. A policy that was inviting defiance and creating revulsion was not working, but Mary was locked into it, showing that lack of imagination and flexibility that were to be so characteristic of her regime. The burnings took on a momentum of their own and Mary was too lethargic to stop them. Her name would be for ever tarnished.

The reconciliation of England to Rome was not achieved without compromise and a great deal of fancy footwork by Philip. Mary and Pole, being idealists, wanted nothing less than the return of all confiscated ecclesiastical property, namely the monastic lands now largely in the hands of the lay aristocracy and gentry, to the Church. Pole begrudged absolving the English for their sins while they still held on to Church land, while Mary – despite the depleted state of the treasury – was only too eager to return what lands were still in the crown's possession. The return of Church property was completely unrealistic and probably could not have been accomplished without the collapse of the regime.

It was Philip who broke the deadlock by convincing Pope Julius III to cut the Church's losses over ecclesiastical property in England and forcing a reluctant Pole to accept this and agree to issue a general dispensation. Philip spent much time with the English counsellors, preparing the strategy whereby the crucial legislation was steered through Parliament, and he appeared three times in the House of Lords with Mary, who always dreaded her parliaments. It was Philip who was probably responsible for the bull of 20 June 1555, finally settling the legal issue by canonically extinguishing the former religious houses. Outside England, the reconciliation with Rome was seen as a personal triumph for Philip.

In Westminster Hall, in a torch-lit ceremony designed to impress the Lords and Commons present with the full ritual glory of the Catholic Church, Pole received the submission of King Philip and Queen Mary and the realm of England to the authority of the Pope. He granted England absolution for twenty-one years of separation from Rome, and proclaimed that the anniversary of the ceremony, 30 November, should be celebrated as a great religious festival, the Feast of the Reconciliation, perpetually. He was loudly applauded.

It was not so much the restoration of papal supremacy as what followed that ignited the horror of Catholicism in the English psyche which would never be extinguished. In January 1555 the heresy laws, which had first been used against the Lollards in the fifteenth century and abolished under Edward VI, were revived. Heresy had always been considered a danger to the moral fabric of society, a disease to be eradicated before it contaminated the whole community. A heretic was tried before the ecclesiastical courts and put under great psychological pressure to recant. If he did so, he received the lesser sentence of imprisonment, was forced to wear a badge showing that he had been a heretic, and underwent a ritual known as 'burning the faggot'. He was taken to the place of execution holding a faggot, which he threw into the fire when it was lit, so that only the faggot was burned. A relapsed heretic was not given a second chance.

If the heretic proved unrepentant, the ecclesiastical court would ask the monarch to issue a warrant ordering the civil power to carry out the punishment. The law stipulated that a heretic be burned alive, just as he would writhe in the fires of hell for all eternity. Burning alive was not a punishment reserved for heretics alone; a queen could be burned alive for high treason – for committing adultery, for instance; a woman could be burned alive for murdering her husband or for witchcraft; and a man could be burned alive for committing sodomy or arson.

Later, the fires of Smithfield would be confused in the popular mind with the auto-da-fé in Spain, tales of whose cruelty were brought back by Elizabethan seamen. In fact, there was one important difference. In Spain, the heretic was strangled at the stake, so that he was already dead when the fire began to consume his body; in England, the death of a heretic was far more terrible, especially if it was prolonged because the faggots were damp and slow to burn. Many heretics were to suffer the fate of the former Bishop Ridley, who was tied to the same stake as Latimer. While the fire on Latimer's side quickly took hold and greedily consumed him, it lazily licked the flesh of Ridley's legs before fizzling out. He screamed in pain, shouting desperately, 'I cannot burn,' and begging God's help.

On 5 February 1555 Renard wrote an admonitory letter to Philip after the first execution:

> Sire: the people of this town of London are murmuring about the cruel enforcement of the recent acts of Parliament on heresy which has now begun, as shown publicly when a certain Rogers [a popular preacher] was burnt yesterday. Some of the onlookers wept, others prayed God to give them strength, perseverance, and patience to bear the pain and not to recant, others gathered the ashes and bones and wrapped them up in paper to preserve them, yet others threatening the bishops. The haste with which the bishops have proceeded in this matter may well cause a revolt. Although it may seem necessary to apply exemplary punishment during your Majesty's presence here and under your authority, and to do so before winter is over [spring being a popular time for rebellion in England] to intimidate others, I do not think it well that your Majesty should allow further executions to take place unless the reasons are overwhelmingly strong and the offence committed hath been so scandalous as to render this course justifiable in the eyes of the people.

It was good advice. Of course, the persecution of heretics was cruel and pointless, but Mary was acting in the light of her own times. Heresy was a sin and, as she saw it, the duty of the Church was to persuade those in error to recant, to save their immortal souls. If they refused to do so, then they must be punished according to law. It was a barbaric age. Hitherto, the people had accepted the punishment for heresy without question. Henry VIII had put to death Catholics and Protestants with impunity, on one occasion on the same day at Smithfield. The crowd had applauded when one of his Protestant victims had been held on a pike and playfully lifted up and down into the flames to prolong his agony.

But now the mood had changed. The people's attitude took the authorities by surprise and should have given them pause for thought. The large crowds of spectators came not to boo and heckle the heretic, but to sympathize and offer support, often building the fires higher so that the victim's agony would end sooner. Friends might bribe the executioner to allow a bag of gunpowder to be fastened round the victim's neck or waist, which would explode on contact with the flames, bringing a quick death.

The persecution of Protestants had become inextricably mixed up with resentment at foreign interference in English affairs. If the burnings continued, Renard warned, not only the future of the Church, but also the lives of Philip and Mary might be imperilled. It would give Elizabeth and other dangerous opponents the chance he imagined they wanted to overthrow the regime. Surely there were other means of chastising the obstinate, he urged.

The responsibility for the burnings has to rest with Mary, who as sovereign was head of the justice system that actually inflicted the punishment. She was initially supported by her Lord Chancellor, Gardiner, Bishop of Winchester. An intelligent man, he might have reconsidered when he saw the policy was not working, but he was mortally ill and died in November 1555. The greatest advocate was Bonner, Bishop of London, who, like that other enthusiastic persecutor of heretics, Sir Thomas More, would personally flog the victims in his garden. So great was the popular fear of Bonner that an invitation to visit him was enough to prompt the person to go into hasty, voluntary exile.

Although Philip enjoyed the auto-da-fé in his native Spain and once took his unstable young son to watch a day-long event, he was less than convinced of the wisdom of the burnings in England. He knew that he would be associated with them and that it would further exacerbate xenophobic sentiment against Spain. A few days after the execution of the first victim, one of Philip's Spanish monks gave a vigorous sermon at court condemning the burnings. He would not have done this without Philip's support, but still the burnings continued.

The more humanitarian Cardinal Pole was not in favour of the policy, focusing more on the Herculean task of reforming the Church from within and winning converts that way. Mary placed a unique confidence in Pole and he could have convinced her to stop the burnings, if he had troubled to exert his influence.

While many well-educated and articulate Protestants had fled the country, a strong core remained, including the most prominent, Archbishop Cranmer and the former Protestant Bishops Latimer and Ridley. Their policy of Christian obedience and non-resistance to their sovereign and the law of the realm encouraged others. They must hold firm to their religious convictions, refuse to recant, and submit to the flames if it was God's will. Many who followed their example were the men and women, old and young, of the artisan class, mainly in London and the South-east, who had embraced Protestantism and now stood firm.

What was shocking was the number of victims in such a short time span: between 4 February 1555 and 10 November 1558, 283 Protestants – 227 men and 56 women – were burned alive. About 100 others died in custody.

Mary drew special opprobrium for her treatment of Cranmer, who had already been condemned for treason for his part in usurping the crown for Jane Grey. She was determined to have her revenge on the man who had destroyed her mother's marriage by pronouncing the divorce, so that there was a large and ugly element of personal vindictiveness in this case, unworthy of a queen. Now Cranmer was also to be tried for heresy. When he wrote her a long letter and statement of his beliefs, she refused to read it, since it came from a heretic. The authorities toyed with Cranmer and treated him with gratuitous cruelty, forcing him to watch the double execution of Latimer and Ridley, leaving him in no doubt of the horror that awaited him. During his lengthy period of imprisonment harshness was alternated with leniency, diminishing his spirit of resistance. It would be a great propaganda coup to force Cranmer to recant, but so much more satisfactory to burn the Protestant Archbishop of Canterbury. Cranmer was only human and did recant, to the dismay of the Protestants, who claimed the recantation must be a forgery.

Mary now took the unprecedented step of announcing that even though Cranmer had recanted – and therefore should be reprieved from execution – he was to burn anyway. Through his last night, Cranmer wrestled with his conscience. He wrote out a very different statement than the one the authorities were going to make him read next day, this time condemning the Pope as the Antichrist and denying the Real Presence. He secreted the paper in his clothes before he was taken from his cell to sit out the long sermon which traditionally preceded a burning. At the church, he began his statement as the ecclesiastical and lay spectators expected. When he suddenly switched tack, he was silenced and dragged to the stake.

The morning of the execution, 21 March 1556, was wet, meaning that the fire would probably burn slowly, prolonging his agony. Cranmer took the paper containing his statement from his bosom and threw it into the crowd. As the flames reached him, he thrust his right hand – the one he had used to sign the recantation – into the fire and held it there. 'And forasmuch as my hand offended, writing contrary to my heart, my hand shall first be punished.'

It was a propaganda disaster for Mary, one from which she never recovered. The burnings continued, almost to the day of her death.

9

The Legacy

In the name of God, Amen. I Marye by the Grace of God Quene of England, Spayne, France, both Sicelles, Jerusalem and Ireland, Defender of the Faythe, Archduchesse of Austriche, Duchesse of Burgundy, Millayne and Brabant, Countess of Hapsburg, Flanders and Tyroll, and lawful wife to the most noble and virtuous Prince Philippe, by the same Grace of God Kynge of the said Realms and Domynions of England, Etc.

Thinking myself to be with child in lawful marriage between my said dearly beloved husband and Lord, altho' I be at this present (thankes be unto Almighty God) otherwise in good helthe, yet foreseeing the great danger which by God's ordynance remaine to all whomen in ther travel [travail, labour of childbirth], have thought good, both for discharge of my conscience and continewance of good order within my Realmes and Domynions to declare my last will and testament . . .

THEY WERE GRAND titles for a sad, lonely woman who was to face death knowing that she had failed in everything she had set out to do.

The will told its own story. There are affectionate references to 'my most dere and well-beloved mother, Quene Kateryn', whose body she asked to be brought from Peterborough to rest near her own, and only one to her father, asking that his debts be paid. She asked for Masses to be said for her soul, that of her mother and of their progenitors, and of Philip when he should die. Generous bequests were made to the religious houses she had re-founded: to the orders of the Carthusian monks and the Brigittine nuns at Syon and Sheen, to the Observant Friars at Greenwich and Southampton, to the monastery of Westminster, to the brothers at the Savoy Hospital, and to the black friars at St Bartholomew in Smithfield. A hospital was to be established in her name for poor, elderly soldiers, especially those injured 'in the warres and servys of this Realme'. Reflecting her interest in learning, money was left 'to the relefe of the pore scholars' at the universities of Oxford and Cambridge.

She asked that 'my saide most dearest lorde and husbande' keep the jewel the Emperor had sent her on their betrothal and 'also one other table dyamonde whiche his Majesty sent unto me . . . and the Coler of golde set with nyne diamonds, the whiche his Majestye gave me the Epiphanie after our Maryage, also the rubie now sett in a golde ryng which his Highnesses sent me by the Cont of Feria'. Many bequests were made to her attendants and she did not forget the ordinary servants.

The will was signed on 30 March 1558, when Mary fondly imagined a second time that she was pregnant. Pathetically, she refers to 'the Issewe of my bodye that shall succeed me in the Imperiall Crowne of this Realme'. On 28 October 1558, 'fealynge myself presently sicke and weake in bodye', she added a codicil. By this time, she had to admit that there was unlikely to be a child: 'Forasmuch as God hath hitherto sent me no frewte nor heire of my bodye, yt ys onlye in his most devyne providence whether I shall have onny or noo.'

She had only three weeks left to live. Much against her personal desire, but at the insistence of Philip, she knew now that the bastard Elizabeth, daughter of the whore Anne Boleyn who had ruined her mother's life and her own, would succeed her. The shameless girl seemed to have bewitched Philip and perhaps, Mary would have reflected sadly, he would marry her after she was gone. 'Yf yt shall please Almighty God to call me to his mercye owte of this transitory lyfe without issew and heire of my bodye lawfully begotten,' she continued, the crown would go to 'my next heire and Successour, by the Laws and Statutes of this Realme'.

She could not quite bring herself to name Elizabeth, the younger sister to whom she would always be compared so unfavourably, but in a final act of generosity she did beseech Philip, for the sake of the love she had borne him and the old friendship between England and the Low Countries, to take a special care of the realm: 'that yt may please his Majesty to shew himself as a Father in his care, as a Brother or member of this Realme in his love and favour, and as a most assured and undowted frend in his power and strengthe to my said heire and Successour, and to this my Country and the Subjects of the same'.

In October 1558 Mary had fallen victim to the influenza epidemic. No attempt had been made to go into quarantine – a precaution her father had always followed most assiduously. She seemed to rally, but then in November she deteriorated again. Mary might well have been suffering from an ovarian cyst, since she was in terrible pain, or even cancer of the uterus, but it was the influenza that undermined her ebbing strength and probably killed her. A few days prior to her death, she had sent her lady-in-waiting, Jane Dormer, to Hatfield, charged with handing over a case of her precious jewels to Elizabeth, and with asking for her assurance that she would continue to maintain the Catholic faith. Elizabeth returned an ambiguous answer.

Mary, meanwhile, drifted in and out of consciousness, at one point telling her attendants that she was experiencing visions of the heavenly joy that awaited her, seeing 'many little children like angels playing before her, singing pleasing notes, giving her more than earthly comfort'. At dawn on 17 November 1558, in pain but fully alert and able to voice the responses, she heard Mass in her chamber. The presiding doctor recalled that she slipped away quietly, almost imperceptibly, but Jane Dormer, writing years later, maintained that the Catholic Queen had died at the climax of the Mass, the elevation of the Host.

A few hours later, across the river at Lambeth Palace, Cardinal Pole died of influenza, having heard of the death of his cousin, whose life had been so entangled with his own. Ironically, the Pope had withdrawn Pole's legatine powers, after a quarrel with Philip, and demanded his return to Rome to answer charges of heresy. His life ended in frustration and failure, just as Mary's did.

When news of Mary's death reached Philip in Brussels, he paused in the letter he was writing. He had known she was mortally ill, but he had excused himself from being there through pressure of business. She had been too ill to read the letter he sent her. He picked up his quill and continued phlegmatically: 'The Calais question cannot be settled so soon, now that the Queen, my wife, is dead. May God have received her in His glory! I felt a reasonable regret for her death. I shall miss her, even on this account.'

The image posterity has of Mary is of a woman subservient to her husband, who was so in his thrall that she went to war for his sake and lost Calais, England's last possession in France. The truth is more complex. For all her professions of love and devotion and of needing Philip, Mary was never prepared to step aside and let him take over in her realm. She wanted him, but on her own terms.

If Mary was really determined about something, no amount of opposition would deter her. Yet she often flouted Philip's will. Before he left in August 1555, he complained that he had been excluded from the government in a way 'unbecoming to his dignity' and threatened 'never to return without sharing the government with her'. He sought a coronation in England, seeing it as the only way to gain any authority in the kingdom, or interest in it after her death. Mary replied to his constant pleas with excuses, saying that there was strenuous opposition she could not overcome in his absence. Parliament would never consent. They might give him the future shadow of a crown in the shape of a regent's rights, if he and Mary had a child, but were unwilling to give him its present substance for fear he might use it as an excuse to drag England into war with France.

Mary was trying to hold out the possibility of a coronation as an inducement to get him to return, while Philip expressed his unwillingness to do so without a guarantee. He would not contemplate the loss to his dignity of returning and then being refused.

Throughout 1556 Mary was more than ever incapable of giving the lead to her Council, left somewhat rudderless after the death of Gardiner. The long strain of ill health and emotional frustration were taking their toll. When one of Philip's emissaries came in July to say that Philip would be in England within six weeks she lost her temper. 'It was nothing but mere promises,' she shouted, with a resentment born of despair. Later, as rumours of Philip's womanizing filtered back to Mary's ears, the mischievous French ambassador, Gilles de Noailles, who had replaced his brother Antoine, reported that he had heard from some of her attendants 'that she has been seen scratching the portraits of her husband the King of Spain which she keeps in her rooms'. She would spend hours sitting on cushions on the floor of her bedchamber, moaning, and banging her head against the wall.

With Philip's departure, court life once more relapsed into the dull monotony only to be expected when the sovereign was an unhappy, middle-aged woman of uncertain health. Unlike her father or sister, Mary rarely went on progress. Even when she was not indisposed, she hesitated to travel far from her own palaces, conscious of the fact that a royal visit would lay an unnecessary burden on her subjects at a time of severe hardship.

Yet we catch glimpses of Mary at court conscientiously carrying out her ceremonial duties as queen. She touched for the Evil, rubbing her fingers on the swollen glands of the afflicted, just as her sainted fore-bear, King Edward the Confessor, had done. On Maundy Thursday she washed the feet of the poor and gave alms and hospitality, in memory of the Last Supper when Christ washed the feet of his disciples and of His commandment to them to love one another. As the choir chanted the Miserere and other psalms, Mary withdrew to change out of the gown she was wearing, one of fine purple cloth lined with marten's fur and sleeves that swept the ground, returning to give it to the oldest and poorest of the women.

By September 1556 Philip had still not returned to her and Mary was reduced to writing a pleading letter to her father-in-law, who was on the verge of retiring to a monastery in Spain, having ceded the Spanish crown to Philip. England had fallen into a deplorable state, she told him. 'I am not moved by my personal desire for his presence, although I confess I do unspeakably long to have him here, but by care for this kingdom.' The country needed a strong hand if it was not to fall into chaos.

When Philip did return in March 1557, the reason was blatantly obvious: it was to embroil England in his ongoing war with France. The worst fears of those who had opposed the Queen's foreign marriage were being realized. It seemed that despite the legislation designed to counteract it – the marriage treaty – a queen had no more power than any other woman to withstand a husband's pressure.

The Emperor's adviser, the Bishop of Arras, wrote confidently to

Philip the following month that he trusted England would be moved to declare war on France by 'the Queen's desire to please you in every way'. Hitherto Mary had resisted all Philip's entreaties to declare war, but now he told her categorically that unless she persuaded the Council, she would never see him again. Still passionately in love with him, she was reduced to summoning individual counsellors to her room and threatening them with dismissal if they did not do what she asked. They were prepared to offer Philip money and troops, but stopped short of a declaration of war. He would accept nothing less. In the end, it was the Protestant exile Thomas Stafford's French-sponsored attack on the east coast at Scarborough that thrust England into war.

The loss of Calais and Guisnes, the last of Edward III's conquests in France, was seen as a national humiliation. The chronic financial insolvency Mary had inherited from her predecessors meant that the string of forts in the Pale of Calais was run down; she was only too aware of this, while at the same time she was to work tirelessly to raise the money and men Philip demanded. The French took the opportunity to strike during the winter when the garrison was poorly manned and when weather in the Channel would prevent reinforcements being sent from England. It was a sure bet that the English garrison would be drunk over New Year, when the attack took place. Nevertheless, the English felt profoundly let down by Philip, whose duty as king was to provide military assistance to his wife.

Mary would have found some solace in the words of her far more capable cousin, Mary of Hungary, Regent of the Netherlands: 'A woman is never feared or respected as a man is, whatever her rank . . . in times of war . . . it is entirely impossible for a woman to govern satisfactorily. All she can do is shoulder the responsibility for the mistakes committed by others.'

Mary is said to have confided to Susan Clarencieux in the last months of her life that she had a secret sorrow which oppressed her. Was it the King's absence? Clarencieux asked, probably thinking of his philandering. 'Not that only,' Mary answered, 'but when I am dead and opened, you shall find Calais lying in my heart.' The story may be apocryphal.

Philip's brief visit triggered off Mary's second phantom pregnancy. She was now forty-one years old. Fearing that she might be mistaken again, she kept the knowledge to herself for several months. In January 1558, however, Philip wrote to Cardinal Pole, thanking him for his letters 'in which you send me news of the pregnancy of the Queen, my beloved wife, which has given me greater joy than I can express to you, as it is the one thing in the world I have most desired and which is of the greatest importance for the cause of religion and the welfare of the realm'.

Two months later, Philip's envoy, Count Feria, revealed that the Queen's confinement was expected in March: 'The one thing that matters to her is that your Majesty should come hither, and it seems to me she is making herself believe that she is with child, although she does not own up to it.' It was not until May that Feria was able to report that she 'now realized that her pregnancy has come to nothing'. Again, she was suffering from profound melancholy, but 'has taken patiently your Majesty's decision not to come for the present'.

As there would clearly be no heir, Philip's plan was to keep England in the Habsburg camp by marrying Elizabeth to Emmanuel Philibert, Duke of Savoy, who would be compensated with England for ceding what remained of his lands to Philip. For once, the two sisters were united in their opposition, although for different reasons. Mary was still having trouble coming to terms with the idea of Elizabeth succeeding her, while Elizabeth naturally had no intention of being her brother-in-law's pawn. Mary consistently opposed Philip's wishes on this question. Resentful of the pressure he was putting her under, she wrote him an angry letter, but decided against sending it. Instead, she snatched the opportunity to suggest he come to England so that they could discuss it properly.

If Mary had succeeded in bearing a child, there is reason to believe that England would have remained Catholic, benefiting from the Counter-Reformation which was under way in Europe. Cardinal Pole's reforms within the Church were slow, but they would eventually have had a positive result. Twenty years of schism and damage to the structure and the finances of the Church and a whole generation grown up in ignorance of its doctrine could not be undone in three or four years. It would take time to rebuild and train the priesthood. The latent strength of Catholicism in England at the end of Mary's reign can be gauged by how long and how difficult it was for her successor to eradicate it.

As it turned out, Mary's life and reign ended in sterility. She has been held responsible for putting the cause of Catholicism in England back 300 to 400 years. For all her mistakes, she cannot be blamed for prejudices which were inflamed by events that occurred after her death. Her reputation suffered retrospectively through growing anti-Spanish sentiment and hostility to Philip, who was to send the Armada against England thirty years after her death. In the context of the religious wars that afflicted France, the Netherlands and Germany in the sixteenth and seventeenth centuries, which were far more savage and claimed thousands of victims, the nearly 400 Protestants who died for their beliefs during Mary's reign in England were comparatively few. Their significance was magnified out of all proportion afterwards.

History is written by the victors. Mary's reputation has suffered almost irreparable damage owing to John Foxe's *Acts and Monuments*, popularly known as the *Book of Martyrs*, which became an anti-Catholic propaganda tool in the course of Elizabeth's reign. It is hard to judge the Marian persecution dispassionately because of the insidious power of this book. As one of 800 Protestant refugees who fled the country at the outset of Mary's reign, Foxe had begun by publishing at Strasbourg a book about the early Christian martyrs and the Lollards and Protestants in the fifteenth and sixteenth centuries who had suffered for their faith. Returning to England at Elizabeth's accession, undeterred by her placatory religious policy, he toured the country gathering material about those who had been burned under Mary, speaking to spectators and friends of the victims. He also took copies of the letters they had written and of the official records of their interrogations in the bishops' registers.

The book does not wilfully warp the truth, but it is skewed nevertheless by his often highly selective choice of material. 'Be of good comfort, Master Ridley and play the man. We shall this day light such a candle, by God's grace, in England, as I trust shall never be put out.' Did Latimer actually utter these heroic words? They might have been taken down by his servant, who later gathered Latimer's sermons together for publication, but we do not know. The quotation was not in the 1563 edition and one may legitimately question the veracity of an uncorroborated speech that entered the printed record fifteen years after the event. But it made good copy.

A battery of anecdotes, autobiographical memoirs, legal examinations, sermons, ballads, beast fables, letters, romanticized adventure narratives like the story of the hair's-breadth escape of the young Duchess of Suffolk, or the emotive description of Lady Jane Grey's execution, and, above all, of the final moments of Cranmer, Ridley and Latimer, and also of ordinary people, exclusively dedicated to one subject and taken out of context, obviously makes an overwhelming impression.

This monster edition, amounting to 1,721 pages, complete with propagandist woodcuts depicting the Marian bishops as beasts with their victims as slaughtered lambs piled at their feet, was published in 1563 and dedicated to the 'most Christian and renowned princess, Queen Elizabeth'. It celebrates the transition from 'the cruel practices and horrible persecutions of Queen Mary's reign' to that of her merciful and clement successor. Foxe conveniently overlooks the fact that Mary had stuck firmly to her religious principles during Edward's reign, whereas Protestant Elizabeth had conformed during her sister's reign.

A subsequent edition, including additional feedback he had received as a result of the previous one and judiciously omitting the excesses of Henry VIII, was published in 1570 and could not have been better timed. The international situation had deteriorated and Elizabeth and Philip were on a collision course. Mary, Queen of Scots, whom the Catholics recognized as the true heir to the English throne, was a prisoner in England. A papal bull excommunicated the heretic Queen, Elizabeth, and gave free licence to assassinate her. The gloves were off. In a calculated bid to arouse fear and hatred of Rome, the Pope and Catholics in the minds of the English people, Elizabeth's government was now prepared to give its official support to the *Book of Martyrs*.

Now the book was regarded as an expression of the national faith second in authority only to the Bible and as an unanswerable defence of England's ideological position in the contemporary struggle for national independence and power. It gave life to a body of legend which seemed to explain how and why England's current predicament had come about and to justify whatever course the Queen and the nation might take in its own defence and for the accomplishment of its destiny. The book was placed in every cathedral and many parish churches, for the people to read and absorb. A copy was placed on every ship, in conflict with the Spanish on the high seas and in the New World and, above all, on the ships that defeated the Spanish Armada in 1588. It was said to be as effective as Drake's drum.

It was reprinted in 1598 and four times during the seventeenth century. New editions appeared in England in the eighteenth and nineteenth centuries and in the United States in the twentieth century. The people were continuously reminded of what would happen if England was ever again ruled by a Catholic sovereign. By the seventeenth century, a period of intense religious conflict and civil war, the Protestants were calling Mary 'Bloody Mary', a term that Foxe did not specifically use, although the 1563 edition refers to the 'horrible and bloudy time of Quene Mary'.

It was certainly not a term that would have been used or approved by Elizabeth, who, whatever her private feelings about her sister, began her reign with a proclamation stating that it had pleased God to vest the crown in her 'by calling to his mercy out of this mortal life, to our great grief, our dearest sister of noble memory', the late Queen Mary. Mary was an anointed queen and Elizabeth would tolerate no criticism of her.

The legacy of childless queens was unease. Women's rule created a feeling of insecurity, especially at a time of religious upheaval. Everything that had brought comfort in previous centuries – the age-old traditions of the Church, which embraced kings, nobles and commoners in the whole body of Christendom from the cradle to the grave and beyond – was being stripped away, just as the familiar figure of the King was being replaced by a woman. It was no coincidence that when the people felt most insecure, rumours abounded that the King had returned. Queen Mary had failed to produce a male heir, but there were 'sightings' of Edward VI, who was supposed to have survived. It did not help that the last years of Mary's brief reign were also dogged by bad weather, failed harvests and epidemics.

The Protestant exile John Knox's polemic, *The First Blast of the Trumpet against the Monstrous Regiment of Women*, was a vicious attack on female rule, specifically Catholic female rule. It was a piece of sectarian political opportunism and Mary Tudor was one of his prime targets. 'It is a thinge most repugnant in nature that women rule and governe over men,' he expostulated, continuing: '. . . that a woman promoted to sit in the seate of God, that is, to teache, to judge or to reigne above man, is a monster in nature, contumelie to God, and a thing most repugnant to his will and ordinance.'

To Knox, Mary Tudor was just another Jezebel, Ahab's wife who tried to annihilate the preachers of God's word and ended her life wretchedly. She was a bastard and a vicious tyrant, 'unworthy by reason of her bloody tyranny of the name of a woman'. Her crimes were so monstrous that even the base name of woman was too good for her.

Knox's timing was unfortunate, since the book was published at Geneva in 1558, just as a Protestant queen was about to mount the English throne, and she sent him off with a flea in his ear for his presumption in criticizing queenship and her sex.

Female monarchy was regarded as a deviation from the 'natural' or proper order of things, in which a king sat on the throne and male supremacy was the social norm. Not that Mary or Elizabeth intended to do anything to change the lot of other women. As queens, they were set apart from the rest, chosen by God for His special purpose, divinely inspired. And yet Mary proved all too human, a prey to her unstable emotions and ill health, too conditioned by the bitterness of the past. The traditional preserves of a woman were marriage and childbirth, but they also made a queen regnant vulnerable. Mary failed at both.

Welcomed on a wave of good will, she squandered the people's love, because she was not sensitive enough to the popular mood, ignoring the vociferously expressed opposition to her choice of husband and the revulsion felt at the continuing persecution of Protestants. Her lifelong habit of dependence on foreign relatives raised the question of her national loyalty. To be the first queen regnant was not easy, especially in a time of religious turmoil. Her successor watched and learned. She noted the difficulty of being a queen and a wife and vowed not to commit the same mistakes.

Mary deserves sympathy and understanding, but, ultimately, she was ordinary, too ordinary to transcend the prejudice against female rule and prove it wrong.

ELIZABETH I

b. 1533, r. 1558–1603

10

The Little Bastard

On the afternoon of Sunday, 7 September 1533, Queen Anne Boleyn gave birth to a daughter, appropriately – for a future Virgin Queen – in a chamber hung with tapestries depicting the life of the Virgin at Greenwich Palace and on the eve of the Feast of the Nativity of the Blessed Virgin Mary. Her astrological sign was Virgo, the Virgin. The sex of the child was a grave disappointment and embarrassment, particularly to her father, King Henry VIII, who had broken with Rome and imperilled his immortal soul in order to cast off his previous queen and marry his mistress. It was not for another unwanted girl that Henry had risked so much. Anne had promised him a son and had failed to deliver. As the Imperial ambassador Eustace Chapuys gleefully reported to the Emperor, it was 'to the great disappointment and sorrow of the King, of the Lady herself, and of others of her party, and to the great shame and confusion of physicians, astrologers, wizards and witches, all of whom affirmed that it would be a boy'.

So sure had they been of the sex of the child that the Queen's letter to the courts of Europe announcing the birth of a prince had already been written, and there was scarcely room to insert an S. From this moment, Anne's star began to wane, but she loved her daughter with a fierce and protective passion, so much so that she wanted to take the unusual step – for a lady of high birth – of breastfeeding the child herself. Her wish was denied, not least because it was her duty to become pregnant again and produce a son with all possible haste. Queens consort were glorified breeding machines.

A splendid tournament to celebrate the birth of a son was hurriedly cancelled, but the royal couple was determined to put on a fine show for the christening. In lieu of a son, this child was to be the heir of

England, even though, in his heart, Henry could never accept a woman as his successor. How could a daughter, a visible sign of his inadequacy to sire sons, possibly embody the perfection of his regal identity? The Lord Mayor and aldermen and forty of London's chief citizens were commanded to be at the ceremony to be held on the Wednesday following the birth. They duly took barge for Greenwich at one o'clock on the appointed day, dressed in crimson velvet and scarlet and bristling with gold collars and chains of office.

The christening procession made its way from the palace to the Church of the Observant Friars through a specially erected passageway hung with rich arras and strewn with green rushes. The old Duchess of Norfolk carried the child, who wore a mantle of purple velvet, with a long train furred with ermine. The Duchess was flanked by the premier Dukes of Norfolk and Suffolk, while the Countess of Kent bore the long train of the child's mantle. Her grandfather, Thomas Boleyn, Earl of Wiltshire, and the Earl of Derby supported the train in the middle at either side, while her uncle, Lord Rochford, was among the four noblemen carrying the rich canopy of estate – denoting her royal status – over her head.

They were met at the church door by the Bishop of London, who named her Elizabeth, after her paternal grandmother, Elizabeth of York. Inside on a raised platform in the middle of the church, the silver font from Canterbury stood under a canopy of crimson satin fringed with gold. Several gentlemen with towels round their necks, 'that no filthe should come to the fonte', hovered round it. After the infant had been disrobed close to the warmth of a brazier, she was submerged in the water of the font three times. Her godparents were Thomas Cranmer, the new Archbishop of Canterbury, who had pronounced her father's previous marriage invalid and that to Anne Boleyn good and sound only a few short months previously, the old Duchess of Norfolk, and Margaret Grey, Marchioness of Dorset. As the devil was driven out, a lighted taper was placed in the child's hand and all the torches were lit. The Garter chief King of Arms then cried aloud: 'God of his infinite goodness send prosperous life and long to the high and mighty Princess of England Elizabeth!' There were many who wished the baby ill, but this wish would be granted.

The trumpets sounded and Elizabeth was taken up to the altar, where the Gospel was said over her. The godparents presented their gifts, then the company was treated to 'wafers, confects, and ipocrasse, in such plentie, that every man had as much as hee woulde desire'. The torch-lit procession returned to the palace in the same order, with the trumpets sounding and the christening gifts borne before the child by four persons. Elizabeth was brought to the door of the Queen's chamber and handed over to her attendants. The Lord Mayor and his companions were taken to the King's chamber, but they were not to be greeted by the great man in person. He sent Norfolk and Suffolk out to thank them. Then they were taken to the cellar for drinks and back to their barges.

Two months later Elizabeth made the first of many triumphal progresses in a long life as she was carried ostentatiously through the streets of London on the twenty-mile journey north to the former monastery of Hatfield in Hertfordshire, where according to tradition she was to have her own establishment in the charge of the royal governess, Margaret, Lady Bryan. Anne visited her daughter whenever she could, showering her with beautiful clothes – little caps of purple and white satin covered in gold net, kirtles of orange and russet velvet, of yellow satin edged with yellow velvet, green satin with green velvet and white damask with white velvet, and green satin for 'a little bed' – and occasionally, as at Eltham in the spring of 1534, Elizabeth received a visit from both parents. She might gradually have become aware of the brooding presence and resentment of her elder half-sister Mary, who had been sent to join her household when her own had been disbanded.

Elizabeth was at court in January 1536 when news came that the erstwhile Queen, Katherine of Aragon, was dead. Chapuys was shocked at the enthusiasm with which the news was greeted, noting that Henry sent for 'his little bastard' to join in the celebrations. She was a little over two, but it is just possible that she was aware of the excitement and her father's joy as he carried her into Mass to the sound of trumpets and later – clad in yellow from top to toe with a white feather in his cap – held her high in his arms and whirled her round, showing 'her first to one and then to another'. Elizabeth always loved to be the centre of attention and this might have been her first taste of it.

A few months later, she might have been conscious of a rather different scene, when her mother allegedly held her up in supplication to Henry as he stood looking down at them from an open window at Greenwich, barely suppressing his anger. Her mother was pleading with the King, but over what, we cannot be sure. The witness to this event – who recounted it to Elizabeth many years later – places it just prior to Anne's arrest, but this is unlikely to have been the case. Elizabeth was almost certainly at Hunsdon by the time of her mother's downfall.

On May Day 1536 Queen Anne was presiding over the traditional tournament at Greenwich when Henry quietly left, slipping out of her life as seamlessly as he had done Katherine's. The next day, she was arrested on trumped-up charges of adultery with four gentlemen of the Privy Chamber and a court musician, Mark Smeaton. She was also accused of incest with her brother, Lord Rochford. No crime was too monstrous to believe of a woman who was already held in suspicion for her heretical opinions and who, in some quarters, was branded a witch. Brother and sister, it was said, had been seen kissing, with their tongues in each other's mouth. More pertinently, if the foetus Anne had miscarried in January had been malformed, it would have been easy to persuade the King that such a monster was not his, but the product of an unnatural act.

Anne was also charged with despising her marriage, entertaining malice against the King and affirming that she would never love him in her heart. At the trial she acquitted herself well, but the verdict was a foregone conclusion. With her mocking laugh, she had touched the King on his most vulnerable spot, indiscreetly revealing that he was 'no good in bed with women, and had neither potency nor force'.

Henry was vicious in his revenge. Anne was condemned to be burned alive or beheaded at the King's pleasure. Her marriage was now judged unlawful, owing to his former relationship with her sister, Mary, and was dissolved. If Anne had not legally been a wife, she could not logically be condemned for adultery, but she was to die anyway. On the morning of 19 May Henry extended the mother of his child a modicum of mercy when on the green within the Tower of London the swordsman from Calais struck off her head with one swift, subtle slice. Her headless body was then pushed into an arrow box and unceremoniously buried beneath the flagstones of St Peter ad Vincula in the Tower.

We do not know when Elizabeth learned of her mother's terrible end and can only speculate as to what psychological effect the brutal truth that her father had judicially murdered her mother had on her young mind; she never spoke or wrote of it. While Elizabeth grew to adore and emulate her father, she certainly was not ashamed of her mother. She inherited many of her qualities: her love of learning and enquiring mind, her ability as an actress and linguistic skills, her elegance and love of dance and poetry, her independent spirit and her wit. As queen she surrounded herself with her mother's relatives and wore a ring with a portrait of Anne enclosed in a secret compartment.

Elizabeth had enjoyed the position of inheritrix of England for just over two and a half years. Now her fortunes changed abruptly. She was declared a bastard by the Act of Succession of July 1536. Like her elder sister Mary, she was no longer to be addressed as Princess, but as the Lady Elizabeth's Grace, the King's daughter. Mary and Elizabeth were both bastards now and Mary, basking again in her father's favour, began to show her little sister some sympathy and kindness. It was not the case with Henry.

While her mother was alive, Henry had appeared quite fond of Elizabeth, but now, just when she had reached the age when a girl-child relates to her father, he broke contact with her. Caught up in the excitement of his third marriage to Jane Seymour, which had taken place with indecent haste shortly after Anne's execution, Henry seems to have forgotten his little daughter. It was not altogether surprising that Henry did not want to see Elizabeth, the living reminder of a once passionate relationship which had descended into bitter humiliation. The child's red-gold hair and white skin were clearly his, but her dark, penetrating Boleyn eyes were there to remind him of an episode he would rather forget.

It was left to Lady Bryan to pen an exasperated letter to Cromwell, the King's secretary, to clarify the matter of her charge's status and to complain that she had outgrown all her clothes and had nothing to wear. 'Now it is so, my Lady Elizabeth is put from that degree she was afore, and what degree she is of now, I know not but by hearsay. Therefore I know not how to order her, or myself or her women or grooms,' she protested. She moved on quickly to the more practical problem of the clothes shortage: 'for she hath neither gown, nor kirtle, nor petticoat, nor no manner of linen, nor smocks, nor kerchiefs, nor rails [nightdresses], nor stitchets [corsets], nor handkerchiefs, nor sleeves, nor mufflers [mob caps], nor biggens [night caps]'. Once beautifully dressed by her mother and already keenly aware of her status, one can imagine the child's humiliation at having nothing to wear; it was a sharp contrast to the 2,000 or more dresses she left in her wardrobe at the end of her life.

Evidently, Sir John Shelton, the chief gentleman of the household, was still treating Elizabeth as a princess, because he had the three-year-old dining in state every day, much to the chagrin of her sensible lady mistress. 'Alas! my lord, it is not meet for a child of her age to keep such rule yet. I promise you, my lord, I dare not take it upon me to keep her Grace in health an' she keep that rule. For there she shall see divers meats, and fruits, and wine, which it would be hard for me to restrain her Grace from. Ye know, my lord, there is no place of correction there; and she is yet too young to correct greatly.' Lady Bryan, a stickler for discipline and good manners in her royal charges, was reluctant to chastise the child because 'she hath great pain with her great teeth, and they come very slowly forth, which causeth me to suffer her Grace to have her will more than I would.' Elizabeth already seems to have been showing signs of a formidable will.

When Henry's longed-for son, Prince Edward, was born in October 1537, the four-year-old Elizabeth made an official public appearance. She had been relegated to the shadows in the aftermath of her mother's disgrace, but it seems that she was to take her place with the rest of the family on ceremonial occasions. She was given a part to play at the christening, carrying the chrisom-cloth. She was so young that she had to be carried herself, in the arms of the Queen's brother, Edward Seymour, Viscount Beauchamp, while her elder sister Mary took her hand for the procession's return to the Queen's chamber, with Lady Kingston and Lady Herbert bearing their trains.

The sharp four-year-old might have drawn the conclusion from all the fuss being made over her baby brother that it was maleness, being a boy, that mattered. The birth of a brother also meant the loss of Lady Bryan, whose duty as royal governess meant that she had to turn her attention to the next child now. Only eighteen months after the loss of her own mother, Elizabeth lost her surrogate mother, but Cromwell made a wise choice in replacing her with Catherine, the daughter of Sir Philip Champernowne of Devon, who was to spend the rest of her life with Elizabeth.

Catherine, or Kat as she was usually known, was exceptionally well educated for a gentlewoman of her time and, recognizing that her small charge was extremely intelligent and, indeed, precocious, did everything she could to nurture her mental gifts. It was Kat who encouraged and oversaw Elizabeth's early education, and loved her as a mother. She was obviously doing a good job, because when Elizabeth was six Lord Chancellor Wriothesley visited her and reported: 'If she be no worse educated than she appears, she will be an honour to womanhood.' Elizabeth always responded to kindness – perhaps because she already suspected it was a rare commodity – and repaid Kat with her loyalty and devotion: 'we are more bound to those that bringeth us up well than to our parents,' she was later to write, 'for our parents do that which is natural for them – that is bringeth us into this world – but our bringers up are a cause to make us live well in it.'

The death from puerperal fever of Queen Jane Seymour only a few days after her great triumph and Henry's continuing turbulent marital history made little impact on Elizabeth, with the exception, perhaps, of the fate of his fifth wife, Katherine Howard. The flighty, flirtatious Katherine was Anne Boleyn's cousin and showed Elizabeth some kindness, giving the child little presents of jewellery of no great value. It is easy to imagine how eagerly the motherless Elizabeth must have responded to this show of affection from the new Queen, and how shattering the news of her brutal end – so reminiscent of her mother's – must have been to Elizabeth's young ears. When she was arrested, Katherine ran screaming along the gallery at Hampton Court, desperate to reach Henry. As with Anne Boleyn before her, he adamantly refused to see her. When Elizabeth later wrote to her sister Mary that she knew of many who had been brought to their death by being denied access to their prince, perhaps she had this scene in mind. More pertinently, according to her childhood companion Robert Dudley, it was from this time – when she was eight years old – that Elizabeth determined that she would never marry.

Within the security of her own household under Kat's care, Elizabeth was happy. Henry's three children spent much time together in the various royal residences at Hunsdon, Ashridge, Hatfield and Hertford Castle in Hertfordshire. Living with her little brother was a benefit. Not only did the two enjoy a close and affectionate relationship, but Elizabeth could share some of her brother's tutors and lessons. Edward's tutor John Cheke, of St John's College, Cambridge, happened to be Kat's brother-in-law; he introduced his star pupil Roger Ascham, who was to have a profound influence over Elizabeth's education. Ascham became a good friend of Kat and of her husband, John Ashley, a distant relative of the Boleyns, whom Kat married about this time, and he recommended as Elizabeth's tutor his own favourite pupil, William Grindal.

Grindal was to give Elizabeth a thorough grounding in Latin and Greek, while Ascham taught her to write in the distinctive italic hand, of which her signature on state documents is the prize example. With the aid of Jean Belmain and Battista Castiglione Elizabeth became so proficient at modern languages that as queen she could conduct a three-way conversation with, say, the French, Spanish and Venetian ambassadors each in his own language simultaneously. It was a skill, a sharpness of mind, perhaps facilitated by her mastery of Ascham's method of double translation: his pupil would translate from the Latin into English, then after a time translate back into Latin, attempting an exact reproduction of the original text.

There was no question of Elizabeth's tutors instilling in their female pupil the sort of passivity that was so inherent in Vives' education programme for her sister, Mary. These Cambridge men came with a reformist tinge and it was Ascham the supreme educator's goal to train Elizabeth to think for herself. Above all, he schooled her in rhetoric. The Pauline teaching so redolent in Vives' thinking, that a woman should be silent and by inference subservient to the male, had no place in Ascham's curriculum for *his* future queen.

When Henry married his sixth and last wife, Katherine Parr, in

July 1543 all three children were present at the wedding. Elizabeth's rehabilitation with her father had begun the previous year, when on a visit to Essex he invited his daughters to dine with him. It was almost certainly the first time that Elizabeth, then nine years old, had eaten with him. Henry, whose knowledge of his younger daughter had hitherto depended on the reports of carers and tutors, liked and approved of her. So much so that he proposed her as a suitable bride for the Earl of Arran, in line for the Scottish throne, although it came to nothing. Henry's children were already on amicable terms, but under Katherine's kindly influence all three began to spend more time at court, giving Elizabeth a chance to get to know her father.

Unlike Mary, who had pinned her colours firmly to her mother's mast and devoted much of her energy to defiance and rejection of her father, Elizabeth approached their relationship positively. She genuinely admired the mighty Henry and was proud to be his daughter. 'She prides herself on her father and glories in him,' the Venetian ambassador was later to observe. Elizabeth was said to resemble him far more than her sister did and she played on this family likeness, speaking of her father frequently in a way that caused people to associate father and daughter, even standing under his portrait when as queen she received foreign dignitaries at Whitehall Palace.

Henry, in turn, seems to have been impressed by Elizabeth, affectionately referring to her as his Bess. Her reward came in the spring of 1544 when she was restored to her place in the succession, after Edward and Mary. Henry did not go so far as to legitimize either of his daughters, but Elizabeth does not seem to have been too concerned about this. It seems to have been enough for her to be acknowledged as the King's daughter and as an heir to his crown. Later, she was particularly pleased to find that Henry had treated her and her sister as equals in his will. Henry made generous financial provision for them. As queen, Elizabeth made no effort – as Mary did – to have her parents' marriage declared valid and herself legitimate. She seems to have been content to leave the past where it belonged. In June that year Henry held a 'void' or reception at Whitehall, in which he presented his three heirs to the court.

Meanwhile, Queen Katherine Parr clearly saw Elizabeth's promise and took the girl under her wing, encouraging her in her studies – although Elizabeth was already streaks ahead of Katherine, who was a keen but late beginner – and gently inculcating her into the reformed religion. Elizabeth was already religiously devout and she had imbibed reformist ideas from her Cambridge tutors, but Katherine's influence on her at an impressionable age reinforced these ideas, which once implanted never left her. As a special tribute to her stepmother, Elizabeth translated Marguerite of Angoulême's religious poem, *Le miroir de l'âme pécheresse*, from the French and wrote it out in her own beautiful italic as her New Year's gift to the Queen in 1545. Like Katherine, Marguerite, sister of Francis I, had been the leading patroness of the reformed religion at the French court and, what's more, she had known Elizabeth's mother – another keen reformer, whose 1533 edition of the book Elizabeth might have used for her translation. The book seems to have represented Katherine and Elizabeth's joint religious belief, particularly the idea of justification by faith alone.

The translation and the prefatory letter which sums up the theme of the book were formidable intellectual achievements for an eleven-year-old, made all the more touching because from the evidence of the handwriting, which declined as the work progressed, and the standard of the stitching of the pansies that graced the cloth cover, she had left the endeavour too late and had to finish in a hurry – literally on New Year's Eve 1544 itself, leaving the messenger barely enough time to gallop from Ashridge to court with it. She apologized to Katherine for the writing, 'which I know in many places to be rude and nothing done as it should be', and pleaded with her not to show it to anyone else 'lest my faults be known of many'. Already, she was very mindful of her reputation.

The following year, Elizabeth complimented her stepmother by translating into French, Italian and Latin her book of devotions, *Prayers and Meditations*, and presenting the work to her father as his New Year's gift. The accompanying letter is the only one addressed directly from Elizabeth to Henry, the norm being to communicate with the King through an intermediary, such as the Queen. 'To the most illustrious and most mighty King Henry the Eighth, king of England, France, and Ireland, Defender of the Faith, and second to Christ, supreme head of the English and Irish Church, Elizabeth, his majesty's most humble daughter, wishes all happiness, and begs his blessing,' she begins. It is significant that Elizabeth alludes to the royal supremacy. Every day when Elizabeth opened her Bible (in English) she would have seen in the frontispiece her father enthroned, like God himself, or at least God's representative on earth. Elizabeth thoroughly approved this aggregation of the spiritual and temporal power in one person – the sovereign, 'whom philosophers regard as a god on earth'. There is no doubting Elizabeth's admiration for this exalted being, to whom she claimed to owe obedience as her 'greatest lord and matchless and most benevolent father by the divine law'.

Not only did Elizabeth admire and seek to emulate her father, she was enough of a flatterer of the male ego at twelve years of age to tell him so. 'May I . . . be indebted to you not as an imitator of your virtues but indeed as an inheritor of them,' she asked. Henry must have chuckled to think of a mere daughter following in his footsteps, but in fact it was by assimilating so many aspects of her father's identity that Elizabeth was able to buttress her own power as ruler. Eventually, she was to surpass him in achievement.

Elizabeth was left in the care of the Queen when Henry embarked on his last military campaign in France. Not only did she regard her father as a heroic leader in war – one of the prime functions of a king – but his absence gave Elizabeth the opportunity to experience female rule. Like Katherine of Aragon at the outset of Henry's reign, Katherine Parr ably fulfilled the role of regent, although unlike her predecessor she did not have to muster and supply an army to meet the Scottish threat on the northern border. Elizabeth saw a woman running the country, supported by the Privy Council, and it all seemed to work perfectly smoothly. Why should a woman not rule as well as a man? she might have asked herself.

When Henry died at Whitehall on 28 January 1547 his death was kept secret for several days while the new King's uncle made his bid for power, overturning Henry's express wishes that a council of equals should rule during his son's minority. Edward Seymour, who soon became Lord Protector and Duke of Somerset, secured the person of the young King and, in a surprising gesture of sympathy to the bereft children, brought him to Elizabeth at Enfield so that the two could be together when they learned of their father's death. They apparently fell into each other's arms, overcome by grief.

The happiest years of Elizabeth's childhood had been spent in the last years of her father's reign. At thirteen, the orphaned girl was all too vulnerable to the designs of the ambitious and unscrupulous men who hustled to fill the power vacuum.

11

The Affair

WHEN SHE WAS thirteen, Elizabeth had her portrait painted. The work, a companion piece to one of Edward, was intended for her father. It shows a serious young girl on the brink of womanhood. The small pointed breasts are visible under the gorgeous red damask of the gown. She is obviously studious, as one of her exquisite long white fingers is inserted at her place in the book she is holding, while another book – probably the Bible – is on a lectern behind her. The red-gold hair of the Tudors framing the white face is revealed under the fashionable French hood studded with pearls. Pearls, which were to become the trademark of the Virgin Queen because of their purity, encircle the slender neck and waist and embellish the top of the gown. The face still holds some of its childish roundness, but she has the high arched nose of her father; there is already a hint of the long, thin, oval face with high cheekbones and pointed chin she has inherited from her mother. The mouth is determined. The eyes are already wary.

In lieu of her father, Elizabeth presented the portrait to her brother in the late spring of 1549. Always conscious of and insecure about her looks but aware from an early age of her intellectual prowess, she wrote: 'For the face, I grant, I might well blush to offer, but the mind I shall never be ashamed to present.'

As Elizabeth had not yet come of age – fourteen for a girl – at her father's death, it was decided that she would continue in the household of the Queen Dowager, Katherine, with whom she enjoyed such a close and convivial relationship. Katherine, already a rich widow when she married Henry, had been left a generous legacy by the King; she now withdrew to her manor of Chelsea. Both Henry's daughters were taken aback by Katherine's remarriage, which took place with unseemly haste within three months, without waiting out the proper period of mourning for their father. Mary wrote to Elizabeth to suggest she leave their stepmother's household, but Elizabeth replied this would cause offence.

Thomas Seymour had been Katherine's sweetheart before her marriage to the King; he had tactfully withdrawn once the King's interest in Katherine, then Lady Latimer, had become apparent. It is salutary to know that the ambitious Seymour renewed his suit to the Queen Dowager only after he had asked his brother, Protector Somerset, for the hand of either Mary or Elizabeth – preferably the latter, who was by far the more nubile and attractive – and been refused. According to Henry VIII's will, neither of his daughters might marry without the Council's consent, and that would hardly have been forthcoming for a marriage between the Lady Elizabeth and this ambitious trouble-maker. Besides, there was the obstacle of consanguinity: Seymour was the brother of one of Elizabeth's stepmothers, whose marriage to the King her father had been made possible by the execution of her own mother, and he was the uncle of her brother; soon he would be the husband of another stepmother. It only shows how deluded Seymour was to have believed that such a match would ever have been considered.

Elizabeth seems to have learned of his interest from her governess, later admitting: 'Kat Aschylye tolde me, after that my Lord Admiralde was married to the Quene, that if my Lorde might have his own Wil, he wolde have had me, afore the Quene.' For her part, Katherine probably reasoned that she had nursed three ageing husbands – she had had to employ all her wits to survive Henry's capricious temperament – and now deserved some pleasure. She seems to have been in love with Seymour, a handsome rogue whose brazen charm and physique made him highly attractive to women.

Lord Admiral and newly created Baron Seymour of Sudeley, Thomas Seymour's ambition far outstripped his ability. He bitterly resented the fact that his elder brother had sole authority over their nephew and a monopoly of power, while he was merely allotted a place on the Council, a title, office and lands. Thomas sought to win the influence he felt was rightly his by other means. Quite unrealistically, he aimed to become the King's governor, leaving his elder brother to run the country. Already more popular with his nephew simply because he was more fun, he tried to subvert the King by slipping him extra pocket money. Katherine was appalled that her stepson, who had lacked for nothing when as regent she had charge of him, was being treated as a mere schoolboy and kept short of cash by Somerset. Since Henry VIII's will nominated the Suffolk family, the descendants of his younger sister Mary, as next in line of succession after his own three children, Thomas secured the Lady Jane Grey, the Suffolks' eldest daughter, as his ward, promising her ambitious parents that he would marry her to the King. Meanwhile, his own marriage to the Queen Dowager had given him control of the Lady Elizabeth, who effectively became his stepdaughter.

As stepfather and guardian, it was Seymour's duty to protect Elizabeth, an under-age girl living in his household. Instead, he abused his position of trust; it could be said that he sexually abused her. It was Elizabeth's first encounter with adult sexuality and was to mark her indelibly for life. All later favourites, particularly Leicester and Essex, bore some physical resemblance to Seymour. Tall and well built, with auburn hair and beard, he was dangerous, rash and impetuous, but even mature women found his charm irresistible. It is not altogether surprising therefore that Elizabeth fell for him; it was heady stuff, this delicious, forbidden entanglement with a man who made her feel desirable. And there was just that tinge of incest – taking 'Father' away from 'Mother', or accepting the sexual advances of 'Uncle' – to make it more piquant.

After Thomas Seymour was arrested for his treasonable activities and Kat Ashley was held in the Tower for questioning, she testified that

> he wold come many Mornyngs into the said Lady Elizabeth's Chamber, before she were redy, and sometime before she did rise. And if she were up, he wold bid hir good Morrow, an ax how she did, and strike hir upon the Bak or on the Buttockes famylearly, and so go forth through his Lodgings . . . And if she were in hir Bed, he wold put open the Curteyns, and bid hir good Morrow, and make as though he wold come at hir: and she wold go further in the Bed, so that he could not come at hir.

An invitation, if ever there was one, for him to do so. On another occasion, 'he strave to have kissed hir in hir Bed', at which Kat Ashley 'bad hym go away for shame'. When they were in residence at his town house, he possessed a key to the room and would sometimes enter in a state of undress, in his nightshirt and bare-legged. For Elizabeth, these visits must have been thrilling, exciting and frightening.

Although a sinister interpretation has always been placed on Seymour's actions, they might have been innocent horseplay. Even so, it was hardly appropriate behaviour for the King's unmarried sister, and Elizabeth must have appreciated this, because she took to rising very early, so that she was already at her books by the time Seymour entered her bedchamber. Katherine, pregnant and aware of her husband's frolics with her stepdaughter, does not seem to have known what to make of the situation or how to deal with it. After a word from a concerned Kat Ashley, she began to accompany Seymour when he came to tickle Elizabeth in bed, to ensure that it was just innocent play. On another occasion, however, Katherine laughingly held Elizabeth prisoner, while Seymour systematically tore her black mourning gown to shreds. The sexual innuendo is obvious, but Katherine seems to have been oblivious to it.

Any lingering doubts Katherine harboured as to her husband's probity were removed when she found Seymour and Elizabeth in an embrace. Angry recriminations took place behind locked doors. Probably Katherine did not hold her stepdaughter responsible, but she seems to have given Elizabeth a very stern lecture on the importance of guarding her virtue. The daughter of a queen who had been tried and executed for adultery and incest could not afford the slightest blemish on her reputation. Her enemies would be only too willing to believe that Anne Boleyn's daughter was as lascivious as her mother, or, indeed, as her aunt, Mary Boleyn, who had been King Henry's mistress.

The dual spectre of adultery and incest had overshadowed Elizabeth from birth and here she was, reliving the sins of her parents. A female without virtue would not be considered worthy of the crown or as a suitable bride for a prince. To preserve Elizabeth's reputation and to remove temptation from her grasping husband, Katherine decided it was best to send her to Cheshunt, the home of Sir Anthony Denny, a friend who had served the late King as chief gentleman of the privy chamber and who was married to Kat Ashley's sister, Joan.

It was a sobering experience for Elizabeth, who left the Queen Dowager's household uncharacteristically lost for words. On the journey she had time for reflection. She wrote to Katherine:

Although I could not be plentiful in giving thanks for the manifold kindness received at your highness's hand at my departure, yet I am something to be born withal, for truly I was replete with sorrow to depart from your highness, especially leaving you undoubtful of health [Katherine had been very sick in early pregnancy]. And albeit I answered little I weighed it more deeper when you said you would warn me of all evil that you should hear of me; for if your grace had not a good opinion of me, you would not have offered friendship to me that way that all men judge the contrary. But what may I more say than thank God for providing such friends to me . .

She signs the letter, 'Your highness' humble daughter, Elizabeth'.

Katherine moved to Sudeley Castle in Gloucestershire for her confinement and was soon missing Elizabeth's company. The two continued a loving correspondence. On 7 September 1548, Elizabeth's fifteenth birthday, Katherine gave birth to a daughter, and died of puerperal fever a few days later. In her delirium, she raved about those whom she loved betraying her. One of her attendants, Lady Tyrwhit, witnessed the scene, and would later hold it against Elizabeth.

Elizabeth's sorrow at the loss of such a true friend can be imagined; she must also have felt guilt, shame and remorse at her part in causing Katherine unhappiness during the last months of her life. The association between sex and death, first planted in the child's mind when she learned of her mother's execution, came back to haunt the adolescent. If Elizabeth had not already made up her mind at eight years of age never to marry, she might well have decided at fifteen that it led inevitably to death. It was perhaps no coincidence that she fell ill after the Queen Dowager's death.

None of this stopped Seymour from renewing his suit now that he was free. Elizabeth blushed at mention of his name. But while her governess, Kat Ashley, was urging her to consider him, Elizabeth kept a cool head. 'You may have him if you will,' Kat told her. Elizabeth had probably already decided against it, but she kept her own counsel. When her treasurer, Thomas Parry, pressed her to admit that she would be pleased to marry Seymour if the Council's consent was forthcoming, she answered carefully: 'When that comes to pass, I will do as God shall put in my mind.' She refused to write Seymour a consolatory letter on the death of his wife, 'for then she should be thought to woo him'. Nothing daunted, Seymour took it upon himself to hold discussions with Parry about the state of her finances – the normal prelude to any sixteenth-century aristocratic marriage.

The world might have been none the wiser about this sordid episode in Elizabeth's youth if Thomas Seymour had not been arrested for treason in January 1549. He had been plotting against his brother and tried to secure the person of the young King by breaking into his bedchamber, killing his spaniel in the process. The Council needed to establish whether or not he aimed at the crown through a marriage with Elizabeth. If Elizabeth had agreed to marry him without the Council's consent, she too could be indicted for treason. Kat Ashley and Thomas Parry were arrested and taken to the Tower for questioning. One sight of the instruments of torture for Parry and a night or two in a cold damp cell had them both spilling the beans on the goings-on in the late Queen Dowager's household.

At first badly shaken by the arrest of her servants and the appearance at Hatfield of Sir Robert Tyrwhit, who had been sent to interrogate her, Elizabeth quickly took control of herself and faced her interrogator with all the power of her formidable mind. 'She hath a very good wit, and nothing is gotten of her but by great polity,' he complained to Somerset. He was convinced that Elizabeth, Ashley and Parry had rehearsed their story beforehand – 'they all sing one song' – because there had been 'a secret promise between [them] never to confess to death'. There is probably some truth in this. When Sir Anthony Denny and William Paulet, Lord St John, came to Hatfield unannounced to take in Ashley and Parry for questioning, there seems to have been time to discuss tactics. Elizabeth might well have appealed to Denny, whose household she had left comparatively recently, and Paulet for advice, which was freely given.

Elizabeth quickly grasped the point that the only treasonable offence was if she had actually agreed to a marriage with Seymour without the Council's consent, and she had not done that. She knew the terms of her father's will and she would never disobey it. It was humiliating, of course, that thanks to the confessions of her servants over the following weeks the Council was to learn all the embarrassing details of her romps with Seymour, but none of that constituted treason, only the loss of her dignity.

'And as concerning Kat Ashley,' Elizabeth wrote to Somerset at the end of January 1549, 'she never advised me unto it but said always (when any talked of my marriage) that she would never have me marry – neither in England nor out of England – without the consent of the king's majesty, your grace's, and the Council's.' She ended her letter by declaring her innocence 'whereof my conscience beareth me witness, which I would not for all earthly things offend in anything, for I know I have a soul to save as well as other folks have'.

The clever fifteen-year-old now moved on to the offensive:

> Master Tyrwhit and others have told me that there goeth rumors abroad which be greatly both against mine honor and honesty, which above all other things I esteem, which be these: that I am in the Tower and with child by my lord admiral. My lord, these are shameful slanders, for the which, besides the great desire I have to see the king's majesty, I shall most heartily desire your lordship that I may come to the court after your first determination, that I may show myself there as I am.

What emerges in succeeding letters is Elizabeth's preoccupation with her reputation and, above all, how she is perceived by the people: her public image was to be a lifelong obsession and its manipulation the key to her success as sovereign. She is concerned that Somerset has not done anything to quell the rumours about her, but she declines to name the perpetrators, as he suggests, 'for it is mine own cause, and again that should be but a breeding of an evil name of me that I am glad to punish them, and so get the evil will of the people, which thing I would be loath to have'. She demanded a proclamation confirming her innocence and it was duly issued.

By early March Elizabeth had Protector Somerset sufficiently wrapped around her little finger to request the return of her governess, Kat Ashley. When Lady Tyrwhit had taken her place, Elizabeth had expressed her dissatisfaction in a storm of rage, tears and sulks. She had not so demeaned herself, she said, that the Council had to replace her lady mistress. Tyrwhit was of the opinion that the headstrong girl needed not one but two governesses, while Lady Somerset had severely castigated Kat Ashley, telling her she was not fit to have charge of a king's daughter. Now Elizabeth pleaded Kat's cause, not least 'because that she hath been with me a long time and many years, and hath taken great labor and pain in bringing of me up in learning and honesty'.

Shrewdly, Elizabeth realized that if Kat were not returned to her 'it shall and doth make men think that I am not clear of the deed myself, but that it is pardoned in me because of my youth, because that she I loved so well is in such a place.' But it was more than that. Elizabeth's servants were her 'family' in the true sense: they were the one fixed point in the insecure universe of her childhood and she would be loyal to them to the end. Even Parry, who it emerged in the course of the investigations had mismanaged Elizabeth's finances, was welcomed back, with the proviso that she would in future check her accounts herself.

No one who went to trial for treason in Tudor England escaped the scaffold, but, still, Thomas Seymour's execution on 20 March 1549 must have come as a shock to Elizabeth. She had been very fond of him. The comment she is supposed to have made – 'this day died a man of much wit and very little judgement' – is purely apocryphal. The whole affair marked Elizabeth's passage into adulthood. Her relationship with Seymour set a pattern for all her subsequent relationships with men: they ended in stalemate, frustration, even death. The experience threw into sharp relief what mattered to her, what defined her: her virtue which was integral to her royal status, her reputation, discretion, the good opinion of the people. Love, sex, marriage – they all came at a high price, perhaps one she was unwilling to pay, let alone risk.

Elizabeth had had a narrow escape and realized that she needed to repair her tarnished reputation. As she was always to do in difficult or stressful periods, she buried herself in her studies. Her tutor William Grindal had died of plague in early 1548 and immediately been replaced by Roger Ascham. Ascham was rare in that he did not believe in pressurizing his pupils – encouraging by his more kindly approach a love of learning – but Elizabeth had an extraordinarily brilliant mind, and he now had the opportunity to develop it to the height of its potential, rounding off the finest humanist education in England.

He had her begin each day reading the New Testament in Greek, after which 'she read the orations of Isocrates, and the tragedies of Sophocles, which I judged best adapted to supply her tongue with the purest diction, her mind with the most excellent precepts, and her exalted station with a defence against the utmost power of fortune.' She was steeped in 'almost the whole of Cicero' – to teach her oratorical skills – 'and a great part of Livy'. Ascham's goals were to inculcate in his pupil moral precepts or maxims, to fortify her mind against adversity, and to impart a model of style. For Elizabeth, style was everything, although in the convoluted sentences of her letters and speeches she did not always follow her tutor's precept to express herself plainly and directly.

She began to affect sobriety of dress, a calculated bid to persuade any sceptics that she was indeed a virtuous princess. Ascham noted that 'with respect to personal decoration, she greatly prefers simple elegance to show and splendour, so despising the outward adorning of plaiting the hair and wearing of gold.' John Aylmer, tutor to Lady Jane Grey, remarked that for the whole of Edward's reign Elizabeth declined to wear the rich clothes and jewels left her by her father, instead wearing the sort of plain apparel more suited to a Protestant maiden, making the ladies of the court 'ashamed to be dressed and painted like peacocks'. Indeed, when Mary of Guise made a state visit to Edward's court, Elizabeth refused to follow the rest of the ladies 'with their hair froused, curled, and double curled', but wore hers loose and straight.

Elizabeth's near disgrace does not seem to have damaged her warm relationship with her brother. When Somerset was toppled and subsequently executed, she ingratiated herself with John Dudley, Earl of Warwick, soon created Duke of Northumberland, who assumed power. Elizabeth, naturally acquisitive, now became a great landed magnate. According to her father's will, she was to receive an income of £3,000 a year. Under Somerset, she had received this sum, but in cash; by living in the households of first her stepmother and then Sir Anthony Denny, Elizabeth, who had her grandfather Henry VII's respect for money, was able to hoard a considerable stash of liquid capital. But it was land that counted, because with land came tenants and the ability to muster forces. Northumberland, whose interest was to keep Elizabeth onside and perhaps to use her for some dynastic marriage to a foreign prince, resolved the long-delayed question of what lands she should have with disarming speed. They would only be hers, of course, until marriage, when she would receive the £10,000 dowry stipulated in her father's will.

The lands lay in a great arc to the north-west of London, sweeping from Berkshire and Oxfordshire round to Buckinghamshire and Hertfordshire, up to Northamptonshire and into Lincolnshire. They included Ashridge, one of her favourite childhood homes, set in rich, wooded hunting country on the Buckinghamshire–Hertfordshire border. Soon she also acquired Hatfield, strategically situated in the middle of the county and only twenty miles to the north of the capital. To the east, her lands bordered her sister's large territory in East Anglia; it seemed that two over-mighty subjects had been created, but perhaps the intention was to make them rivals to each other rather than to the crown. In London she had Durham Place, but this was later exchanged for the much prized Somerset House, the splendid, Italianate river palace on which the fallen Somerset had lavished such attention.

While Mary remained stubborn in her outspoken opposition to the new regime's radical religious stance, Elizabeth basked in her new-found favour at court. Henry's three children had usually kept Christmas together and now Edward was King they maintained the tradition; that is, until Mary and Edward quarrelled over religion and Mary was reduced to tears. At Christmas 1551 the Imperial ambassador grudgingly noted Elizabeth's arrival, 'with a great suite of gentlemen and ladies, escorted by one hundred of the King's horse. She was most honourably received by the Council, who acted thus to show the people how much glory belongs to her who has embraced the new religion and is become a very great lady.'

By the spring of 1553 it was apparent that Elizabeth's relationship with Edward was under threat. It no longer suited Northumberland's purposes for them to be close and it soon became obvious to Elizabeth that they were being kept apart. Edward had already entered his final illness, the tuberculosis for which there was no cure. Elizabeth was naturally concerned for a brother whom she genuinely loved. She set out to visit him and was turned back, ostensibly in the King's name. She wrote to him of her disappointment that she was not to see him after all. She smelt conspiracy, but assured Edward that she had faith in him and in his affection for her: 'but the best is that whatsoever other folks will suspect, I intend not to fear your grace's goodwill, which as I know that I never deserved to faint, so I trust will still stick by me.'

Her trust was ill founded. As early as January 1553 Edward had begun to tamper with the succession, seeking to overturn his father's will, excluding his half-sisters in favour of the Suffolk line, namely Lady Jane Grey's male heirs. The ostensible reason was that both his sisters were bastards of the half-blood and unworthy to succeed, and that they might marry foreigners. It was also a typically chauvinistic reaction to the prospect of female rule. After Edward's death, Nicholas Ridley, Bishop of London, was to go so far as to declare in sermons at Paul's Cross on two successive Sundays that 'the Lady Mary and the Lady Elizabeth, sisters to the king's majesty departed, to be illegitimate and not lawfully begotten in the estate of true matrimony according to God's law' – an insult for which Elizabeth never forgave him or the bishops. So desperate was Edward to exclude Catholic Mary that he also allowed himself to be persuaded of Elizabeth's unsuitability, despite her Protestantism. Like Northumberland, Edward must have been all too aware of Elizabeth's loyalty to their father's memory and wishes, of her implacable belief in dynastic legitimacy.

By the spring it was apparent that there would be no male heirs of the House of Suffolk in the short period Edward had left to live, so that Northumberland pressured him to redraft his 'Device for the Succession', leaving the crown directly to Lady Jane Grey, who in May was forced into marriage with Northumberland's son. Northumberland's transparent motives, his greed for power, should have been obvious to Edward and given him pause for thought. However, in extreme pain and discomfort and dosed with opiates and other dubious concoctions, the dying boy acceded to all his demands; indeed, there is some suggestion that he drove them.

Elizabeth played no part in events following Edward's death, as Mary retreated into her East Anglian stronghold and led the rebellion against Northumberland and the new regime. She remained quietly at Hatfield awaiting the outcome, and then wrote Mary a prompt letter of congratulation. On 29 July Elizabeth entered London with an escort of 2,000, ostentatiously sporting the Tudor colours of green and white; it was a pointed reminder of her power as a great magnate, but also of her loyalty to the Tudor dynasty. She took up residence at Somerset House. A few days later, with her escort cut down to a less alarming half, she rode out to Wanstead to meet her sister as she prepared to make her triumphal entry into London. In the euphoria of victory, Mary welcomed her warmly. As heiress presumptive, Elizabeth rode into London just behind her sister.

Elizabeth had survived. The Tudor dynasty had survived. For the first time in English history a woman had succeeded to the crown and she had done so amid popular rejoicing. It seemed that all Elizabeth had to do was wait her turn.

12

The Suspect

ELIZABETH BELIEVED THE sovereign was an exalted being ordained by God. When she swore allegiance and obedience to Mary at her coronation, therefore, she sincerely meant it. Her loyalty was to be tested to the limit.

It did not take long for Mary's show of friendship towards Elizabeth to begin to cool and the old rivalry and jealousy between the sisters – at least on Mary's part – to reassert itself. Elizabeth found herself out of place in a court that was soon steeped in the Catholic revival. Sensing her sister's disapproval of her continuing apostasy, Elizabeth – ever the survivor and a pragmatist – decided to temporize. Unlike Mary under the previous Protestant regime, Elizabeth did not have a powerful relative like the Emperor to threaten war if she was not allowed to practise her religion. Elizabeth was essentially alone in what was rapidly becoming a hostile and menacing world.

She began by seeking audience with the Queen. Kneeling before her and in tears, she said she saw only too clearly that the Queen was not well disposed towards her, and she knew of no other cause except religion. She protested that she acted not from obstinacy but ignorance, that she had been brought up in the reformed faith and had never been taught the doctrine of the ancient religion. She asked for a priest to instruct her 'in the truth' or books so that 'having read them she might know if her conscience would allow her to be persuaded'. Somewhat mollified, Mary agreed and gave her a rosary of coral and gold. The test came on 8 September 1553, the Feast of the Nativity of the Blessed Virgin, when Elizabeth was expected to attend Mass. She turned up but, perhaps as a gesture to her supporters, complained 'all the way to the church that her stomach ached, and wearing a suffering air'.

Not surprisingly Mary taxed Elizabeth to tell her the truth: did she really believe the Catholic doctrine of transubstantiation, or did she attend Mass 'in order to dissimulate, out of fear or hypocrisy'. Elizabeth replied that she 'had considered making a public declaration that she went to Mass and did as she did because her own conscience prompted and moved her to it; that she went of her own free will and without fear, hypocrisy or dissimulation'. Mary noted that she trembled as she spoke and drew the conclusion that her sister was lying. The declaration, of course, was never forthcoming.

Mary was as eager to condemn her sister as a hypocrite as Elizabeth's critics among the Calvinists were later to do for conforming during her sister's reign, while others were going into exile for their Protestant faith. But this is to ignore and misunderstand Elizabeth's genuine evangelical piety. For her, true religion lay between the individual and God. The externals of worship which were dividing Christians were merely man-made and irrelevant. Elizabeth's personal book of prayers and devotions attests to her very real faith and close relationship with God.

Mary, whose inflexibility was always at odds with her sister's more fluid approach and ability to compromise, confided in the Imperial envoy Simon Renard that she did not trust her sister. The old vendetta seems to have been reawakened by the legislation passed in her first Parliament declaring the marriage of Henry VIII and Katherine of Aragon valid and herself legitimate. It bastardized Elizabeth all over again. By raising the ghosts of the past, Mary seems to have relived all the hurts and humiliations meted out to her mother and herself by Anne Boleyn. This time she was not powerless, however; she could right the wrongs of the past. By November 1553, she was telling Renard that 'it would burden her conscience too heavily to allow Elizabeth to succeed'. She was not a true believer and 'she had not a single servant or maid of honour who was not a heretic, she talked every day with heretics and lent an ear to all their evil designs.' Moreover, it would be 'a disgrace to the kingdom to allow a bastard to succeed'.

Mary's large and unwieldy Privy Council – an uneasy mix of conservative Catholic supporters with no experience of office and those who had served under Henry VIII and Edward – was far too divided to agree such a radical step as excluding Elizabeth from the succession. Even if they did, it would be difficult to persuade Parliament to enact the necessary legislation. Nor could public opinion, increasingly turning against Mary, be discounted. Elizabeth was very popular, especially in London. So Mary had to content herself by inflicting petty slights on her sister. At court, Elizabeth had to yield precedence to others in line of succession, notably the insufferable Lady Margaret Douglas, daughter of Margaret Tudor, Queen of Scotland, by her second marriage to the bigamous Earl of Angus. Lady Margaret, a Catholic, had married a Scottish exile at the English court, the Earl of Lennox. Elizabeth loathed her. Even Frances Brandon, Duchess of Suffolk, was given precedence, despite her family's treason in trying to usurp the crown.

Elizabeth had always been intensely proud of her royal lineage, especially as the daughter of Henry VIII, and now that pride was wounded. She was outraged. In December she asked permission to leave court for her house at Ashridge. The request was granted, with relief on both sides. Renard noted that 'she very courteously took leave of the Queen, who also dissembled well and gave her sister a rich coif of sable.' As a presage of things to come, she asked Mary 'not to believe anyone who spread evil reports of her without doing her the honour to let her know and give her a chance of proving the false and malicious nature of such slander, that were only designed to harm her'. Renard was already pouring venom into Mary's ear, feeding her suspicions: 'There is no persuading her that Elizabeth will not bring about some great evil until she is dealt with.'

At Ashridge, Elizabeth kept up the pretence of her conversion, sending for 'ornaments for her chapel', but she was not to be left in peace for long. Early in 1554 the rebellion that took its name from the key conspirator, Sir Thomas Wyatt – the son of the poet who had been her mother's admirer – broke out. It plunged Elizabeth into the most extreme danger, because – unknowingly or not – she was its intended beneficiary. It was triggered by dislike of the intended marriage between Mary and Philip of Spain. The plan was for simultaneous risings in Kent, the Midlands, Devon and the Welsh Marches. The leaders – Wyatt in Kent, Lady Jane Grey's father the Duke of Suffolk in the Midlands, Sir Peter Carew in the South-west and Sir James Croft on the Welsh border – would march on London and overthrow the government. The Spanish marriage would be blocked, Mary dethroned, and Elizabeth – married to Edward Courtenay, Earl of Devonshire, who had been alienated by Mary's rejection of him as the English candidate for her hand – made Queen in her place with Courtenay king consort.

The plot was leaked before the rebels could launch a co-ordinated attack. Wyatt and his Kentish army marched on London alone and were defeated, not least by Mary's courageous stand and by her rousing speech to the citizens, which reignited their loyalty to their rightful sovereign. Fresh from her triumph, she could now deal with her errant sister, for Mary was unwilling to believe her innocent. It looked bad for Elizabeth. At the outbreak of the rebellion Mary had written informing her of it and inviting her to court for her own safety, assuring her of a hearty welcome. Elizabeth had declined to come, fearing a trap and giving illness as her excuse. As it happened, she *was* ill. She was confined to bed, her face and limbs severely swollen. She was possibly suffering from acute nephritis, failing which some psychosomatic illness brought on by stress. Mary sent two of the royal physicians, Dr George Owen and Dr Thomas Wendy, to examine her. Having declared her fit to travel, Elizabeth dragged her swollen limbs to her litter and began the journey to London. She was so ill that she could be moved only in short stages. By the time she reached Highgate she had to stop and rest.

As ever with Elizabeth, she contrived to make a spectacle of her entry into London. Her litter was preceded and followed by a vast train of horsemen in scarlet, while she sat exposed to view, the pallor of her face and her white gown – the colour of innocence – presenting a dramatic contrast to her escort. The two rival ambassadors made their affiliations plain in their reports. Renard noted that 'her countenance was plain and stern, her mien proud, lofty and disdainful, by which she endeavoured to conceal her trouble.' The French ambassador, Antoine de Noailles, who had been encouraging the conspirators and had no qualms about involving Elizabeth in his constant plotting against the Habsburg alliance, was sympathetic, stating that 'she is so swollen and weakened that she is a pitiful sight.' He did not expect her to live long.

Elizabeth was not permitted an audience with the Queen, but lodged in an obscure part of Whitehall. The evidence against her was mounting. For some inexplicable reason, a copy of her letter to the Queen declining her invitation to court was found in a confiscated bag of the French ambassador's despatches. It was established that both Wyatt and Carew had been in contact with her – or at least with her servants – urging her to move from Ashridge to her more easily defended castle at Donnington. Elizabeth had been careful not to reply in writing. She had sent her servant William St Loe to Wyatt with a message 'that she did thank him for his good will, and she would do as she should see cause'.

From this it is clear that she had known conspiracy was afoot, but not necessarily what the objectives were. Arms and provisions had indeed been sent to Donnington, probably with Elizabeth's knowledge, as a defensive rather than offensive measure, in case the country descended into anarchy. At the least she was culpable of not coming forward to warn the government of impending trouble, but it was in character for her to look ahead and be prepared for any eventuality. If Mary was toppled, she had to be ready to protect her own position. She would have to make her bid for the crown against the rival claimants whose ambitions Mary had encouraged.

Wyatt could not be induced to implicate Elizabeth in the conspiracy and there was not enough evidence to condemn her. Nevertheless, Mary decided that she should be sent to the Tower, pending further investigation. She was informed of the decision by the Council, who came as a body to charge her with involvement in the plot. When the Marquis of Winchester and the Earl of Sussex came to escort her a few days later, Elizabeth, thinking with characteristic speed, begged to be allowed to write a letter to the Queen. Sussex, who was sympathetic and mindful of the fact that Elizabeth was heir to the throne, gave permission.

She began by recalling the old saying 'that a king's word was more than another man's oath', reminding Mary of her promise not to condemn her 'without answer and due proof'. She was innocent, yet being sent to the Tower, 'a place more wonted for a false traitor than a true subject'. She begged Mary to give her a hearing, so that she could answer the charges in person. Probably recalling her last critical encounter with danger during the Seymour investigation, she went on: 'I have heard in my time of many cast away for want of coming to the presence of their prince, and in late days I heard my lord of Somerset say that if his brother had been suffered to speak with him, he had never suffered. But the persuasions were made to him so great that he was brought in belief that he could not live safely if the admiral lived, and that made him give consent to his death.'

She quickly adds 'that these persons are not to be compared to your majesty, yet I pray God as evil persuasions persuade not one sister against the other and all for that they have heard false report and not hearken to the truth known'.

As for 'the traitor Wyatt', she continued, 'he might peradventure write me a letter, but on my faith I never received any from him. And as for the copy of my letter sent to the French king, I pray God confound me eternally if ever I sent him word, message, token, or letter by any means, and to this truth I will stand to my death.'

She ended the letter on the top quarter of the second sheet of parchment and took the precaution of scrawling diagonal lines down the rest of the blank page, so that insertions could not be made.

By the time she finished the letter, they had missed the tide, probably as she intended. It would be too dangerous to make the trip to the Tower at midnight, when the next high tide was due, so that the journey was delayed until morning. The exercise was futile, however, as the Queen stubbornly refused to grant an interview. The next day was Palm Sunday and Elizabeth was taken to the Tower while the rest of London was attending the re-established Palm Sunday service.

Much of the information about Elizabeth's arrival and imprisonment in the Tower comes from John Foxe's *The Miraculous Preservation of the Lady Elizabeth, now Queen of England* in his *Acts and Monuments*, which was first published in 1563. There is a substantial amount of truth in his narrative. One of his sources was likely to have been Elizabeth Sandes. She was with Elizabeth in the Tower and later accompanied her on the journey to Woodstock, after which she joined other English exiles in Geneva. Here she probably imparted the story to Elizabeth's kinswoman, Dorothy, Lady Stafford, who gave the details to Foxe. Foxe's narrative is factually based and full of accurate details, but is neither entirely factual nor entirely accurate. He was not writing a history, but a martyrology, so that he had to emphasize, if not exaggerate, his subject's suffering. His immediate goal was to depict Mary's Catholic government, particularly her Lord Chancellor, Stephen Gardiner, in the worst possible light.

Elizabeth protested her loyalty as she entered. 'Oh Lord! I never thought to have come in here as prisoner; and I praie you all, good frendes and fellows, bere me wytnes, that I come yn no traitour, but as true a woman to the queens majesty as any is now lyving.' Seeing the many guards on duty, she commented, 'yt needed not for me, being alas, but a weak woman.'

Foxe's version diverges from the reality in that Elizabeth did not enter by the Traitors' Gate, but landed at Tower Wharf and walked over the main drawbridge. The route took her past the menagerie of lions and within sight of the scaffold where Lady Jane Grey had recently died. During her incarceration, she would frequently ask if the scaffold was still standing, fearing that it was meant for her own execution.

Inside the Tower, Lord Sussex reminded the others that 'she was a kinges daughter, and she is the quenes sister . . . therefore go no further then your comyssyon.' Foxe leads us to believe that Elizabeth's lodgings were cold, dark and miserable, whereas they were some of the best in the royal apartments. They had an ominous significance for her, though, as they were the ones used by her mother before her coronation and during her trial for adultery. This is where her mother had spent her last night before her execution. No wonder Elizabeth believed she was to die, determining that she should follow her mother's example and ask to die by the sword rather than the axe.

Wyatt was offered his freedom in return for implicating Elizabeth in the plot, a fact the authorities were very eager to suppress when it leaked out, but he held firm. On the scaffold, he exonerated her. Unfortunately, he also exonerated Courtenay, who *was* implicated, throwing doubt again on Elizabeth. The only tangible evidence against her remained the fortifying of Donnington. At first Elizabeth feigned ignorance of having such a house – a transparent lie which reinforced the suspicion of her guilt. Eventually she was brought to admit to having a vague recollection of a conversation with her household officers in which it was decided to send arms and provisions to Donnington. But this was not a crime in itself. No treasonable activity could be proved against her.

Gradually, the conditions of her confinement relaxed. She was allowed to walk outside on the battlements and on the green. There is a pretty story that the son of one of the keepers gave her flowers, until he was forbidden to do so. In mid May she was informed that she was going to be moved to a place of detention, in the custody of Sir Henry Bedingfield, who would escort her under armed guard. She began her journey by barge up the Thames to Richmond, being cheered by the people on the banks, who assumed that she had been released. The rest of the journey turned into a triumphal progress – a reminder to Mary, if any were needed, of her sister's popularity. It was both a threat and a safeguard. It made Mary jealous and resentful, anxious to do away with her tiresome sister; yet it also forestalled her from making a move against her which would incur the anger of the people. Elizabeth seems to have believed that the threat against her life was real. Were they perhaps removing her to some obscure place so that they could do away with her? At Richmond she seemed to think the end had come, confiding in her attendants: 'This night I think to die.'

Crossing the Thames and passing into Berkshire and Buckinghamshire, she was fêted the whole way, with women loading her litter with gifts of cakes and wafers until she had to beg them to stop. At last she came to the old, dilapidated palace of Woodstock in Oxfordshire, where she was to live for the next few months under house arrest. Typically, Mary had chosen Elizabeth's gaoler, Sir Henry Bedingfield of Oxborough in Norfolk, for his Catholic credentials. Slow, methodical, conscientious and barely educated, he was no match for the sharp-witted Elizabeth, the best-educated princess in Europe. She teased and bullied him unmercifully and ran rings round him. His authority was further demeaned by the fact that although Elizabeth was a prisoner, she was still royal and Bedingfield had to address her kneeling. He was also financially dependent on her, as she was obliged to pay for his upkeep and that of his servants.

The absurdity of the situation is revealed by the fact that while Elizabeth was refused pen and parchment to write letters, her treasurer, Thomas Parry, had been allowed to set up quarters at the Bull Inn in Woodstock, giving the prisoner a ready channel to the outside world. Not only that, but Parry was receiving endless visitors whom Bedingfield suspected were conspiring against the government. Try as he might, however, he could make none of his suspicions stick.

Elizabeth did not wish to bring about her sister's dethronement or death. She had too much reverence for the monarchy to do that. Repeated usurpations would weaken it, undoing the life-work of her father and grandfather to enhance and strengthen it. With her own future in doubt, however, she wished to garner enough support among the disaffected – those of the reformed faith, who were her natural supporters, but also those who feared the implications of the Queen's Spanish marriage – to ensure her succession in the event of Mary's overthrow.

Her immediate concern was to get out of gaol. She wrote to Mary protesting her innocence. Mary's reply, addressed to Bedingfield to relay to the prisoner, made it clear that she did not believe her, that the conspirators would hardly have used her as a figurehead if they had not been sure of her approval. Elizabeth next sought to exploit the divisions in the Council. She was innocent, she told them, but if they did not believe her, then they should put her on trial. It was a daring strategy, typical of Elizabeth, who was never risk-averse if she felt the gamble would pay off. This time she was rebuffed in a direct reply from Mary. Elizabeth might be able to pull the wool over most eyes, but she had known her from childhood and had a good idea of what subterfuges she was capable of. In frustration, Elizabeth is said to have used a diamond to scratch on a window the words: 'Much suspected of me, nothing proved can be. Quoth Elizabeth Prisoner.'

Release came as a result of a most unexpected event. Mary's marriage to Philip of Spain had taken place in July 1554 and by the autumn she believed herself pregnant. In early April 1555 she and the King moved to Hampton Court in preparation for the ceremony of taking to her chamber. She could now afford to be magnanimous in what she saw as her final triumph over her sister. Elizabeth would be put in her place once and for all as the bastard she surely was. Mary's child, not Elizabeth, would rule England after her and ensure the continuation of a Catholic dynasty. On 17 April Elizabeth was released from Woodstock and summoned to London. She must be present in the lying-in chamber to witness the birth of the child who would supplant her as heir to the throne.

Elizabeth was not admitted to Mary's presence for another fortnight. Late one night, she was ushered by Susan Clarencieux into the Queen's bedchamber and knelt at her feet for the inevitable rebuke. According to Foxe, Elizabeth sensed someone else in the room, behind the arras. It seems that Philip was there, stealing his first glimpse of his sister-in-law and keen to hear how she would acquit herself. Mary's expansive mood of a few weeks ago had faltered as doubts began to creep in about her pregnancy. She was frustrated that Elizabeth had been brought back to court without admitting her guilt; once more the sly creature had got away with it and Mary had been baulked of her prey. Now she was under instructions from Philip to reconcile with her sister and he was there to see that she did it. Philip's agenda was different from hers: it was one of political expediency. It was already becoming clear to him that Mary's pregnancy was a fantasy and that the marriage would end in sterility and failure.

If the Habsburgs wished to retain England within their sphere of influence, then their best hope was Elizabeth. Until recently, they had wanted her dead. Now she had suddenly become valuable to them. She was quick to sense her advantage. The Venetian ambassador, Michiel, noted that Elizabeth 'has contrived to ingratiate herself with the King of Spain', who stopped his wife from punishing her. When Philip left England at the end of August, she was secure in the knowledge of his protection, so much so that when the Dudley–Ashton conspiracy to dethrone Mary was uncovered later that year, Philip ordered his wife to make no move against Elizabeth. Her servants' fingerprints were all over the plot, but not, of course, Elizabeth's. Mary was instructed to exonerate her from blame for her servants' misdeeds. She had to announce that she thought Elizabeth too wise and prudent ever to undertake anything against her sister and sovereign, although she could not resist letting Elizabeth know as an aside that her servants' confessions, extracted in the Tower, accused her of complicity. Always quick to sense her opponent's weakness, Elizabeth declined Mary's next invitation to court, something of a slap in the face for her sovereign.

Elizabeth was pleased enough, however, to be invited to court for Christmas 1556. When she arrived it was to discover, to her absolute fury, that she was to be pressured into marrying Emmanuel Philibert, Prince of Piedmont and Duke of Savoy, a Habsburg acolyte who had lost most of his lands to the French. Philip was proposing that if Elizabeth married the Prince, he would in turn guarantee that Mary would name her as her successor. Emmanuel Philibert would become King of England, in return for which he would cede his remaining continental lands to Philip. Elizabeth was incandescent with rage. The crown of England would be hers by hereditary right, her father's will and parliamentary statute. It was not in the gift of the King of Spain. Mary did her best to carry out her husband's instructions and put pressure on Elizabeth to comply. Finding the situation intolerable, Elizabeth promptly left London without waiting for the Christmas festivities.

For the first time in all the years she had lived under a cloud of suspicion, Elizabeth contemplated leaving the country. She communicated her fears to the French ambassador, Gilles de Noailles, who had replaced his brother Antoine, the inveterate plotter. It was so uncharacteristic of her to panic; she did not seem to be thinking with her usual clarity. If by escaping she meant to go to France, she would be leaving the frying pan for the fire. Mary Stuart, Queen of Scots, had an indisputable hereditary right to the English throne, as the granddaughter of Henry VIII's elder sister Margaret. Mary was betrothed to the Dauphin. Did Elizabeth seriously think she would be safe in France, in the very heart of this rival claimant's territory? The temptation for Mary's powerful maternal relatives, the Guises, to capture or do away with Elizabeth would have been overwhelming. Fortunately, de Noailles offered good and impartial advice. Elizabeth must not leave England, because if she did so, she could never hope to be Queen.

When Philip returned in the spring of 1557 he continued to press Emmanuel Philibert's suit. The implication was that if she did not comply, she would be disinherited. Elizabeth bitterly resented his attempt to bully and intimidate her. She remained adamant. She would not be forced into marriage, she told Mary's emissary, nor, indeed, was she minded to marry at all at the present time, 'though I were offered the greatest Prince in all Europe'. She found an unexpected ally in Mary. Far from thinking it reasonable to offer Elizabeth the crown in exchange for marrying a Habsburg nominee, Mary did not think her bastard heretic sister should wear the crown at all under any circumstances. Whether Elizabeth married or not, Philip realized that his only hope of retaining England in the Habsburg fold was by keeping Elizabeth onside. Far better that she should succeed than the Francophile Queen of Scots, now Dauphine of France. The only problem was convincing his wife of this and having her name Elizabeth her successor.

It looked as if Elizabeth might have to fight for the crown. When she moaned about poverty, it was because she had been devoting so much of her income to making preparations for such an eventuality. She would be able to raise an army if necessary. She had many friends and supporters, both in government and strategically based throughout the country. She had left nothing to chance. All allies and potential allies were assiduously courted.

At the end of October 1558 Mary, mortally ill, wrote a codicil to her will, conceding that in lieu of a child of her own, she would be succeeded by her next heir and successor according to law. But she was not content to leave it at that. She sent her lady-in-waiting Jane Dormer to Hatfield to extract from Elizabeth a promise that she would maintain the Catholic religion. Elizabeth, ever inscrutable, obliged by giving a placatory, somewhat ambiguous response, but of course she would follow her own conscience when the time came.

Philip sent the Count of Feria to England to give a letter to his dying wife and treat with Elizabeth. He found her at Brocket Hall, near Hatfield. It was a court and government-in-waiting. He enjoyed a convivial dinner with Elizabeth, where much wine was drunk and 'we laughed and enjoyed ourselves a great deal'. Elizabeth had a good sense of humour and would roar with laughter when she was amused. Now, she was at her most charming and obviously elated that the crown was finally within her grasp. After dinner, she dismissed everyone but a few of her ladies and settled down for a serious discussion with Feria in Spanish. All went well, with Elizabeth promising to maintain good relations with Philip, until Feria made a tactless blunder: 'I gave her to understand that it was your Majesty who had procured her recent recognition as the Queen's sister and successor, and not the Queen or the Council, and this was something your Majesty had been trying to secure for some time, as she no doubt realized.' Elizabeth's indignation can be imagined.

Feria took a long, shrewd look at Elizabeth and warned Philip what to expect. 'She is a very vain and clever woman. She must have been thoroughly schooled in the manner in which her father conducted his affairs, and I am very much afraid that she will not be well disposed in matters of religion.' The men he guessed would be appointed to office and with whom she surrounded herself, including Sir William Cecil, Sir Robert Dudley and traitors like Sir Peter Carew and Sir Nicholas Throckmorton, were all heretics. He realized that she bitterly resented what she saw as her mistreatment during her sister's reign and cautioned her against exacting vengeance.

Elizabeth herself had no doubt that God had protected her and preserved her from her earliest youth from many perils. It was to Him she owed her crown. But she also recognized the role of the people. 'She sets great store by the people and is very confident they are all on her side – which is certainly true,' Feria continued. 'She declares it was the people who put her in her present position and that she will not acknowledge that your Majesty or the nobility of this realm had any part in it.' She would be no cat's-paw of Spain. Unlike her brother or sister, 'She is determined to be governed by no one.' She was, after all, her father's daughter.

As Mary lay dying, a steady stream of courtiers drifted towards Hatfield, all intent on greeting the rising sun. It was something Elizabeth would never forget. After the troubles of her sister's reign when she had barely escaped with her life, nothing would ever induce her to name her successor, for she knew just how fickle men's loyalties were and how easy it was to become a figurehead of opposition, willingly or otherwise.

Fearing that she might be prompted to act by a false report of her sister's death, she charged Sir Nicholas Throckmorton with bringing her Mary's betrothal ring as proof. On the morning of 17 November 1558 she learned that she was Queen. 'My lords, the law of nature moveth me to sorrow for my sister,' she told the lords who came to greet their new sovereign, 'the burden that is fallen upon me maketh me amazed.' It was God's doing, she told them, and she prayed that He would help her in carrying out His work in the office He had entrusted to her.

13

Queen

THE QUEEN IS not Queen until the body of her predecessor has been laid to rest. The monarchy is continuous but the person of the sovereign is mortal. The first official act of any new reign is the burial of the dead sovereign. While Mary's funeral rites were taking place in London, Elizabeth remained at Hatfield. She would not enter Whitehall Palace until her sister had, as it were, vacated it.

There was plenty to do, although Elizabeth knew exactly how she was going to proceed. Indeed, on 17 November her chosen secretary and chief minister, Sir William Cecil, was already installed at his desk, where he was effectively to remain for the next forty years. Together, they were to use these few days, from 17 to 23 November when she left Hatfield to take up residence at the Charterhouse outside the City of London, to nominate the new government and lay the foundations for a mode of governing that was to serve Elizabeth well for the next forty-five years.

Unlike Mary's accession speech, which laid emphasis on her subjects' duty of obedience to her, in return for which 'they shall find us their benign and gracious sovereign lady', Elizabeth's typically stressed what she could do for them and her trust in them. She promised 'to all manner [of] people being natural subjects . . . no less love and care towards their preservation than hath been in any our progenitors, and not doubting on their part but they will observe the duty which belongeth to natural, good and true loving subjects'. When Elizabeth referred to her people, she almost always prefixed it with the word 'loving'. Hence, she began her Armada speech in 1588 with the words, 'My loving people', and in her Golden Speech of 1601 expressed her appreciation that 'no prince ever governed a more faithful, valiant, and loving people'. By offering the people her love and pledging them her life she was inviting their love and loyalty in return.

After the vicissitudes of her youth, the twenty-five-year-old Elizabeth was a shrewd judge of character. She and Sir William Cecil had had a long association. Cecil had been at St John's College, Cambridge, as a contemporary of Roger Ascham with Cheke as their tutor and he had married Cheke's sister as his first wife. Cecil shared Elizabeth's intellectual interests, therefore, and was of the reformed religion. He had been able to transfer seamlessly from academe to the cut and thrust of court politics, where he had proved an excellent administrator, first serving Somerset as secretary and then, after his fall, deftly moving on to become secretary to the Council, under Northumberland. He had the crucial experience of government which so many of Mary's counsellors lacked. During Mary's reign, he had quietly retreated into the background, not conforming exactly, but also not joining the exodus of Protestant exiles. While Elizabeth was in disgrace, Cecil had taken on the role of trustee, overseeing the management of her estates, which gave him the excuse to keep in contact with her. Now, she was able to honour him with a trust which was never misplaced:

> I give you this charge, that you shall be of my Privy Council and content yourself to take pains for me and my realm. This judgement I have of you: that you will not be corrupted with any manner of gift, and that you will be faithful to the state, and that without respect of my private will, you will give me that counsel that you think best, and if you shall know anything necessary to be declared to me of secrecy, you shall show it to myself only. And assure yourself I will not fail to keep taciturnity therein, and therefore I charge you.

Elizabeth was giving a clear indication that she would govern not as a tyrant, but by counsel. Unlike her sister, who had imposed her will in pursuit of her own narrow agenda, she would listen to the views of others. She was relying on Cecil to speak plainly and honestly, to give her the best and most impartial advice, no matter how unpalatable it might be to her.

Nor was Elizabeth prepared to continue with the over-large Council whose divisions and divergent interests had made it so difficult for Mary to govern or manage Parliament. It was a mess. Summoning her nobles, who were almost synonymous with Mary's Council, before her at Hatfield, she told them in the nicest possible way that she was dismissing most of them. The nobility, of course, were the monarch's 'family', or cousins. They were the natural supporters of the crown, having received their estates from 'my progenitors, kings of this realm'. They were honour bound, she reminded them, 'to have more natural care for maintaining of my estate and this commonwealth'. She promised to consult them as and when appropriate. As for those she did not appoint, 'let them not think the same for any disability in them.' She simply wanted a smaller, tighter Council, 'for that I do consider a multitude doth make rather discord and confusion than good counsel'.

Over the next few days, Elizabeth's Council of twenty-one hand-picked men took shape and the key appointments to her household were made. She rewarded many of those who had been loyal to her through her troubles, not least Thomas Parry, who became Treasurer of the Household and Master of the Court of Wards and a member of the Privy Council. Although she was present at the inaugural meeting of her Council, she was rarely to attend meetings. She was chairman rather than chief executive. Like all successful people, she was able to delegate, confident that those in whom she had placed her trust would show her an unswerving loyalty in return. In practice, a small inner core worked closely together and more often than not presented a united front, even if it was one advocating a policy the Queen disliked. Elizabeth wanted harmony, encouraging consensus; she was not a prince who sought to divide and rule.

She was to repeat the promise she had made in her short speech to Cecil in her first address to Parliament, which the Lord Keeper, Sir Nicholas Bacon, read out for her when it met in January. She would rule with 'counsel'. This did not mean that Elizabeth was willing to surrender the absolutist powers of the monarchy. Like her father, she believed her sovereignty was ordained by God alone and that her prerogative was unlimited by her counsellors' advice. She would not be ruled *by* her Council; she would rule *with* them and be advised by them. Elizabeth, only the second queen regnant, would be the last one to rule as well as reign. No one could ever mistake who was boss. She had a natural air of authority. As Feria reported, she 'seems to me incomparably more feared than her sister, and gives her orders and has her way as absolutely as her father did'.

Elizabeth also promised to do nothing to antagonize her people and drive them to rebellion. This was a radical departure from previous Tudor monarchs, who had demanded absolute obedience from their subjects. Rebellion against the monarch – God's anointed – was traditionally considered a sin. Elizabeth was prepared to admit that the misguided policies of her predecessors had provoked rebellion – Wyatt's revolt, for instance – but she would try to avoid such confrontation. She would not force her policies on an unwilling people. She would rule by consent.

To rule by consent, she must also be popular. Elizabeth never lacked popularity. She knew its importance and assiduously courted and bolstered it. She was an image-maker extraordinaire, a mistress of public relations and propaganda. She understood the power of the printed word. After composing and delivering her speeches, she would often edit them before releasing them for publication. She knew it was not just enough to be Queen: she must act the part, play the role for all it was worth. 'We princes are set on stages, in sight and view of all the world,' she commented. Nowhere is this consciousness of the need to perform more evident than in her pre-coronation procession through London, in which Elizabeth, the consummate actress, showed her star quality.

It was to take place in January, after the final ceremonies separating the late Queen's two bodies, the mortal and the immortal, were completed. Until then, Elizabeth remained low-key. She left the Charterhouse for the Tower on 28 November, accompanied by an entourage of 1,000. With the trumpeters heralding her arrival, she was preceded by the Earl of Pembroke, bearing the upright sword which was the symbol of sovereign power. Elizabeth, wearing a velvet gown of royal purple, was immediately followed by the dark, handsome figure of her Master of the Horse, Robert Dudley. The guns grew louder as she approached the Tower and disappeared inside. On 5 December she left the Tower for her London home, Somerset House in the Strand, which she reached by water.

Mary was still lying in state at St James's, and Elizabeth – inscrutable as ever – was delaying her entry into public life as long as possible. When she arrived at the palace, she would have to worship publicly in the Chapel Royal, and she was not yet ready to show her hand on the religious question. Sir Nicholas Throckmorton had advised her 'to succeed happily through a discreet beginning', but Elizabeth needed no such reminder. She was naturally cautious until she was sure of her ground. So far she had maintained a studied vagueness, while both sides, Catholic and Protestant, watched avidly for any clues. Although Elizabeth believed wholeheartedly in the royal supremacy, one of the central tenets of her father's monarchy, she was not yet in a position to assume the title. Like Mary on her accession, she followed the proclamation of her royal titles as Queen of England, Ireland and France, Defender of the Faith, with an Etc, Etc.

On 13 December Mary's funeral began, culminating in the burial in Westminster Abbey next day. Only after the regalia were offered up on the altar – symbolically returned to God from whom they had come – and Mary's household officers had broken their wands of office and thrown them on top of the coffin, and the heralds had torn off their tabards and hung them on the hearse, could Mary's sovereignty be said to have truly ended.

Only now could the heralds cry: 'The Queen is dead; long live the Queen!'

It was time for Elizabeth to proceed to Westminster, the seat of government, and take possession of her palace. On 23 December she arrived at Whitehall for Christmas. It was now that she gave the clearest indication yet of the religious position she would take, when she went to the Chapel Royal in procession with her ladies on Christmas morning, the holiest feast of the year and the most important on the court calendar. She had specifically asked Owen Oglethorpe, Bishop of Carlisle, *not* to elevate the Host in the Mass. As soon as he did so, the Queen stood up and swept out of the chapel.

Elizabeth consulted the astrologer-mathematician Dr John Dee to give her the most auspicious day for her coronation; not for her the leafing through a missal to find the most appropriate holy day. It was to take place on 15 January. A frenzy of preparations began, with a royal warrant demanding the holding of all imported silks, so that the Queen could take her pick of them; she chose a profusion of crimson damask and gold-striped crimson satin. The treasury might be empty, but Elizabeth, like Mary before her, was determined to put on a fine show. Sir Thomas Gresham was ordered to take out loans on the Antwerp money market, with the City of London providing bonds as security. As they were to be the main beneficiaries of the spectacle, they were probably happy to comply. The citizens were to bear the cost of staging the pageants and decorating the processional route with 'fyne payntynge and riche clothes of aras, sylver, and golde', while Elizabeth had the Master of the Revels lend them a number of costumes and props from the Great Wardrobe.

It is probable that Elizabeth spent some of the time leading up to the coronation vetting the script for her pre-coronation procession through the City. This had been a rite of passage for every monarch – his welcome and acceptance by the people, as he processed from the Tower in the east to Temple Bar on the westernmost edge of the City. Traditionally, the most important event was the actual coronation next day, when the monarch was imbued with the sacred powers lent by God. Realizing that the future of the monarchy no longer lay with the Church, Elizabeth sought to switch the emphasis from the religious to the secular. Sovereignty was still divinely ordained, but needed the support of the people. Knowing also that the religious compromise she intended would displease Catholics and Calvinists alike, Elizabeth would use her considerable theatrical skills to distract attention from problematic religious ritual at the coronation to the civic pageantry the day before. The civic progress, always more of a crowd pleaser, became the main event.

This was a job for a professional. The humanist scholar Richard Mulcaster, who had been trained in his craft by Nicholas Udall, who devised the pageantry for Anne Boleyn's coronation procession in 1533, was asked to script and arrange the various pageants, in liaison with the City authorities and with a large body of helpers. He was also to act as reporter, rushing his pamphlet, *The Quenes Maiesties Passage through the Citie of London to Westminster the Daye before her Coronacion*, into print within days. It was powerful propaganda, intended for the widest possible audience. Under this new Queen, secular ceremony and the printed word were to affirm royal authority more effectively than sacred ritual.

On the 12th, Elizabeth arrived by water at the Tower. Not only was this a royal palace, but part of the ancient city walls. By taking up residence there, the new monarch was in effect assuming command of the City defences. Wherever possible, processional routes moved from east to west. The east had a special significance: Christ the Redeemer had appeared in the East and altars in Christian churches were placed to the east. The traditional royal entry, which could be likened to a Roman triumph or Christ's entry into Jerusalem, took advantage of the sacral power of an east–west route and the geography of London lent itself perfectly.

Elizabeth left the Tower at two o'clock on 14 January. As she passed the lions, she stopped, ostentatiously offering up a prayer of thanks, reminding the onlookers of her incarceration during her sister's reign and the fact that God had delivered her, just as He had rescued Daniel from the lions' den. In this way, Elizabeth was contributing to the myth of her own suffering under Mary – a bond she shared with her people – and suggesting that she had divine sanction for her rule. It was duly recorded by Mulcaster. She was accompanied by a 1,000-strong cavalcade of officers, noblemen and -women, knights and foreign dignitaries, all splendidly attired in the richest fabric imaginable. 'The whole court so sparkled with jewels and gold collars,' reported the Italian, Il Schifanoya, 'that they cleared the air, though it snowed a little.' They left the Tower in ascending order of rank, culminating with the Queen at the apex of the social hierarchy and as the fount of all honour, with the guards bringing up the rear.

Like her sister before her, Elizabeth borrowed the iconography of a queen consort, as opposed to that of a male monarch who rode on horseback as a military leader. In time, her unmarried state was to become for the Virgin Queen what military virtue was for her male predecessors: the mysterious sign and source of her power to rule. Accordingly, she went 'in her hair' – the long, red-gold tresses hanging over her shoulders and down her back in token of her virtue – with a plain gold crown on her head. She was carried in an open litter covered in thick gold brocade and pulled by two mules swathed in the same material. In spite of the money being lavished on the spectacle, Elizabeth, in a characteristically careful piece of housekeeping, wore

Mary's rich mantle and kirtle of cloth of gold with silver tissue, with a new bodice to fit her slimmer figure and a new pair of sleeves. She was surrounded by footmen in jerkins of crimson velvet and yellow cloth of gold, with the Tudor rose and the letters ER embroidered in silver on their backs. Behind her rode the handsome figure of Robert Dudley, mounted on a fine charger and leading a white hackney covered with cloth of gold.

The procession was far more than a display of royal power and magnificence designed to impress the spectators lining the route. The ruler, the elite and the people were actors in a theatrical spectacle; the crowd, whose cries and actions were recorded in Mulcaster's pamphlet, acted as a dramatic chorus. Traditionally, it was an opportunity for subjects to counsel the new monarch through a series of didactic, edifying tableaux, with singing children, Latin orations, triumphal arches, and a frank expression of their hopes conveyed in rudimentary verse. On the day of Elizabeth's procession, the people had something they had never had before, however: a dialogue with the monarch. It was through this direct contact, maintained throughout her reign in the royal progresses, that Elizabeth cemented the relationship with her subjects, which was the core of her monarchy.

If not the first royal walkabout, Elizabeth interacted with the crowd as no previous monarch had done. There was no doubt she had the common touch. As Mulcaster noted: 'The people . . . were wonderfully ravished with welcoming answers and gestures of their princess.' Her genius was not only to show her love towards her people in general, but privately to particular individuals along the route in apparently unrehearsed stops. When an old woman stepped up to the litter to offer a sprig of rosemary, she insisted on pausing to receive it. She showed evident sympathy for the poor children of Christ's Hospital, almost patting their heads like some latter-day politician. When an old man shouted out, 'Remember old King Henry VIII?' she smiled broadly at this comparison between herself and her mighty father. Had the man perhaps been briefed?

And all along, Mulcaster was keeping pace with her, documenting her every word, expression and gesture, underscoring their significance, magnifying the Queen's rapport with her subjects, and ensuring that her exchanges with individuals were brought to the widest audience.

The tableaux were situated at five key points throughout the City. The first in Gracechurch Street depicted her grandparents, Henry VII and Elizabeth of York, and her parents, Henry VIII and Anne Boleyn. This was the first mention of the disgraced Queen since her execution, but Elizabeth's mother could hardly be airbrushed from the celebrations, as she had been from the public memory for the last twenty-odd years. It was not Anne, but Elizabeth of York – the female vessel who had transmitted her claim to the throne to Henry VIII – who was the crucial figure here. By her marriage, Elizabeth had brought an end to the Wars of the Roses; surely now her granddaughter and namesake would bring peace to a strife-torn England?

One of Elizabeth's greatest strengths was her ability to identify with her people. With her English parents and grandparents, the tableau was eager to remind them that Elizabeth had been born 'mere English here amongst us'. The criticism of the previous Queen, the half-Spanish Mary, was implicit. The loss of Calais was still raw, but this new, English Queen would not take England into a costly foreign war to please a Spanish husband. Moreover, Elizabeth was depicted in the tableau wearing an imperial crown – an arched, closed crown – reminding the audience that the Reformation Parliament had confirmed Henry VIII's imperial status in law. By inference, Elizabeth would embrace the royal supremacy and continue to adhere to true, or pure, religion. Unlike Mary, who had crawled back to the Roman allegiance, Elizabeth would be an imperial queen who would guarantee good government.

The flavour of the pageantry, as might be expected in strongly Protestant London, was anti-Catholic. The pageant at the Little Conduit in Cheapside was the most blatantly critical of the previous regime. It appropriated Mary's personal motto, *Veritas Filia Temporis*. 'Time!' Elizabeth exclaimed when the tableau was explained to her. 'And Time hath brought me hither.' On one side of Time was a tableau representing a decayed commonwealth, on the other a flourishing commonwealth – the first being Mary's, the second Elizabeth's. Time had a daughter, Truth, who carried a Bible in English, prominently labelled 'The Word of Truth'. Apparently impatient to possess the Bible, Elizabeth nudged an attendant forward to take it. But he was politely told to wait until a child had delivered a speech. The Bible was then lowered to the Queen on a silken thread. In raptures, she kissed it; she held it up for all to see, and then passionately clutched it to her breast, thanking the City. It was a brilliant piece of showmanship.

When the procession reached the end of Cheapside it was traditional for the Lord Mayor and aldermen to present the monarch with a purse of gold. Again, Elizabeth seized her chance to say something more memorable than mere thanks. 'I will be as good unto you, as ever quene was to her people,' she assured them. 'And perswade yourselves, that for the safetie and quietnes of you all, I will not spare, if nede be to spend my blood, God thanke you all.'

The biblical figure of Deborah, dressed as the Queen in her Parliament robes and sitting under a palm tree, was set up on a stage in Fleet Street. In the Bible, the Israelites were saved by Deborah; so England would be saved by Elizabeth. She would be an Anglicized Deborah, a ruling magistrate who took counsel from the three estates – the nobility, the clergy and the commons – who sat at Deborah's feet. Unlike Mary, whose parliamentary record was disastrous, it was the fondest hope of the organizers that Elizabeth would be a sort of Deborah-in-Parliament. There were to be ten Parliaments in her forty-five-year reign and it would indeed be the stage for some of her greatest triumphs.

At Temple Bar, her rite of passage was complete. Having been accepted by the people, she had now been integrated into the community as recognized, if still uncrowned, sovereign.

Elizabeth's passage through the City had been a triumph. It was to be less easy to win over Mary's bishops, who scented in Elizabeth's drift towards religious compromise rank heresy. Only one of them, Oglethorpe, of the minor see of Carlisle, could be prevailed on to anoint and crown her, but since he still proved intractable on the question of the elevation of the Host, the coronation Mass would be celebrated by the more compliant George Carew, Dean of the Chapel Royal, who could be relied on to refrain from any unwanted displays of clerical independence. Cardinal Pole, the Archbishop of

Canterbury, had conveniently died the same day as Mary, while Elizabeth herself explicitly excluded the Catholic primates, Heath of York and Bonner of London, from the service. She detested Bonner, whom she held largely responsible for the persecution of Protestants during her sister's reign – so much so that she would not suffer him to kiss her hand. The rest – their numbers depleted by ten owing to the flu epidemic – would attend the coronation, but other than swearing their allegiance play no part in the ceremony. Suspecting the worst after her behaviour at the Christmas Mass, Feria pointedly absented himself from the service at the abbey.

Coronations traditionally took place on a Sunday. On 15 January Elizabeth processed in solemn dignity from Westminster Hall to the abbey. Her tall, elegant figure with its superb posture and the slow glide she had perfected made her look truly regal. She wore her long red hair loose again and her crimson Parliament robes. Significantly, she was not escorted by a bishop and a layman, as her predecessors had been, but by the Earls of Pembroke and Shrewsbury, the emphasis again being placed on the secular. She was followed by the ladies of the nobility, also in crimson, wearing their coronets and dragging their long trains behind them.

The coronation was inadequately recorded – on purpose – and it is difficult to determine exactly what happened. It seems that Oglethorpe took Elizabeth up to the stage, or theatre, in the transept and presented her to the four points of the compass, asking those present each time if they would have her for their Queen. 'Yea, yea!' they cried, as the trumpets, drums, bells and organ all sounded together. After that, there is some confusion. Elizabeth took the oath, but whether it was the traditional one, or the one doctored by Archbishop Cranmer to fit the new circumstances of the post-Reformation monarchy and the implications of the royal supremacy is hard to determine.

There was a sung Mass, during which the Epistle and the Gospel were read not only in Latin but also in the vernacular. What happened at the moment of consecration is not clear. Elizabeth seems to have disappeared to the traverse behind the high altar next to St Edward's shrine, which was to serve for her frequent changes of clothes during the ceremony. Later, she told the French ambassador that she had not attended the Mass; at any rate, she seems not to have taken communion.

The rest of the ceremony proceeded according to form. She withdrew to the traverse again to strip down to her kirtle for the anointing. She leaned on cloth of gold cushions before the altar while a scarlet pall was held over her head, as the bishop anointed her on the shoulders, the breast, the inside of the arms, the hands and the head. Later, she complained to her ladies that the oil stank. Elizabeth seems to have been unusually sensitive to strong odours, so much so that she would use liberal quantities of rose water with cloves in the perfume pan in her private apartments, the council chamber and chapel and whenever she went out in her litter, but her turning her nose up at the oil might also have been prompted by her disdain for what she regarded as popish superstition. She took her place on St Edward's chair for the investiture with the ornaments: the sword, the bracelets, the mantle, the sceptre and the ruby ring, which she was to prize as symbolizing her marriage to England. As a woman, she did not actually wear the sword. The bishop then placed each of the three crowns on her head in succession.

Covered in gold robes from head to foot, with the imperial crown on her head, Elizabeth was once more led up to the stage to be hailed by the people – this time as their consecrated sovereign. Sitting on the throne with the golden sceptre in one hand and the orb in the other, she then received homage. In another break with tradition, the temporal peers went first, kissing her on the cheek, followed by the clergy.

The Italian, Il Schifanoya, noted that she left the abbey 'very cheerfully, with a most smiling countenance for every one, giving them all a thousand greetings, so that in my opinion she exceeded the bounds of gravity and decorum'. Elizabeth could well afford to be pleased. She had been crowned and anointed with full Catholic ritual without committing herself to the maintenance of her sister's Catholicism; indeed, leaving herself free to follow the course she thought best for her country.

The fourth part of the coronation ceremony was the feast held in Westminster Hall. Sitting in solitary splendour beneath a cloth of estate at a table set upon a dais, Elizabeth was served by Lord Howard of Effingham and the Earl of Sussex, the former carving and the latter placing and removing each dish, both of them on their knees. She was already feeling the onset of a cold and was so exhausted she could hardly speak. Each course was heralded by the sound of trumpets and its arrival preceded by Elizabeth's kinsman, the Duke of Norfolk, as Earl Marshal, and the Earl of Arundel on horseback. After the second course, Sir Edward Dymoke rode into the hall dressed as a knight in armour on 'a very handsome barbed charger', saluted the Queen, and threw down his gauntlet, challenging anyone who denied, disputed or contradicted that the Queen his Sovereign Lady was not the true and legitimate crowned Queen of England, France and Ireland. No one responded. Elizabeth drank the knight's health and, as was customary, gave him the silver gilt cup worth 200 crowns.

The coronation always took place before the opening of the monarch's first Parliament. On 25 January Elizabeth, wearing her crown and her crimson Parliament robes again, went in procession from Whitehall to Westminster Abbey, where traditionally the Mass of the Holy Ghost was said, to invoke divine inspiration for Parliament's proceedings. The Queen gave a hint of what was to come on her arrival at Westminster, when she was greeted by the abbot and the monks, swinging their censers and holding their lighted tapers. 'Away with those torches,' she cried, 'we can see very well.' Previous monarchs, with the exception of Edward VI, had always been censed by the clergy as they went in procession, associating the spiritual with the temporal powers. Like her father, Elizabeth was determined to subordinate her prelates to royal control. She believed that the clergy had no role in government and was impatient to relegate them to their proper place. The demise of ecclesiastical pageantry would heighten the importance of the secular ceremonial surrounding the monarchy.

The Queen moved on to the Lords' Chamber in the Palace of Westminster, where she took her place on the throne. The Commons were brought to the bar. The Lord Keeper, Sir Nicholas Bacon, read her accession speech, in which he emphasized the Queen's wish for unity among her people, which could be brought about only by a broad religious settlement. Her brother and sister had condoned extremism, opening the floodgates to discontent and rebellion, but Elizabeth wanted to steer a middle course. She reiterated her father's pleas in his last speech to Parliament, in which he had denounced the extremists of both kinds and urged his people to live together in Christian charity. As Supreme Head, the monarch's duty was to preside over an all-embracing, inclusive Church.

Elizabeth was aware that the country was still largely Catholic, but she was perhaps taken by surprise at the level of resistance put up by the Marian bishops and the conservative, Catholic lords in the Upper House. They watered down the proposed bill to restore the royal supremacy, indicating that it would not be conferred on her, but that she might assume it if she chose. A Uniformity Bill outlining the faith and liturgy of the proposed Elizabethan Church had been joined to the Supremacy Bill. The Upper House simply struck out its clauses and sent the mutilated bill back to the Commons, who were inclined to accept it, since otherwise they were stuck with the existing Catholic religion and the heresy laws.

Elizabeth had no intention of giving her assent. Instead of dissolving Parliament, she simply prorogued it for the Easter recess. On Easter Sunday she processed to the Chapel Royal, but instead of the Catholic Mass, the English communion service was used, as under Edward VI, with the laity receiving communion in both kinds – the bread and the wine. It was a blatant flouting of the law that was still in force.

The Queen's evident endorsement of the reformed religion was still not enough to move the Lords, however. Overt lobbying of the House when it was in session was not allowed, but now a more oblique tactic was applied. When Mary lay dying, Elizabeth had apparently promised that she would not change the Catholic religion, 'provided only that it can be proved by the word of God'. It was decided to test that proof by holding a great debate between the leading proponents of the Catholic and Protestant religions. The chairman was Lord Keeper Bacon and the judges the Privy Council. The Catholic prelates were outmanoeuvred, with two of them ending up in the Tower for contempt.

When Parliament reconvened the Supremacy Bill was brought in again and passed without a hitch. The only difference was to the

This Victorian painting of Mary I's triumphant entry into London in 1553 illustrates her love of gorgeous fabric – crimson and purple were her favourite colours – jewellery, and the rich furs required in a climate colder than today's. She inherited her passion for finery from her father. Lady Elizabeth accompanied her – the Tudor sisters making a rare show of unity in the wake of Northumberland's coup.

Mary I and her husband, Philip of Spain: eleven years her junior, he had hitherto regarded Mary, his father's cousin, as his maiden aunt. He had no enthusiasm for the marriage and, in the wake of her phantom pregnancy, left England in irritation and disgust, adding to her loss of self-esteem and plunging her into profound depression.

This fierce portrait of Mary I by Antonis Mor shows that she used no artifice in her personal appearance. Similarly, she failed to define or project her image or to understand the value of propaganda.

Contrast the happy, carefree childhood of Elizabeth II with that of Elizabeth I, opposite.
Cecil Beaton's engaging photograph depicts Princess Elizabeth soon after she had become
Honorary Colonel of the Grenadier Guards in 1942.

'For the face I grant I might well blush to offer, but the mind I shall never be ashamed to present,' Elizabeth wrote to her brother, Edward VI, when she presented him with this portrait. Elizabeth was always insecure about her looks, but she had an extraordinarily brilliant mind and during her troubled youth found solace in her studies. This dazzling portrait of the future Queen on the brink of womanhood captures a hint of her vulnerability; the dark Boleyn eyes are already wary.

Elizabeth II's coronation on 2 June 1953 was one of Byzantine splendour. Profoundly moved by the sacredness of the occasion, she was the first monarch to be crowned, literally, 'in the sight of the people', through the new medium of television.

At her coronation, Elizabeth I went 'in her hair', as medieval queens consort had done. It offered reassurance that the Queen Regnant intended to marry and prove fertile – even though Elizabeth was personally averse to marriage and would avoid it if possible.

Top left: Mary I and Elizabeth I were the first two female sovereigns to employ the monarch's healing touch, originally manifested by King Edward the Confessor. Mary I is seen here touching for the Evil, or bovine tuberculosis. It was taboo to touch while menstruating, and as Elizabeth's periods were irregular, there could be no set dates for healing ceremonies during her reign.

Top right: While discarding the more overtly Catholic ceremonies, Elizabeth I asserted her quasi-divine status by retaining those calculated to make the most dramatic impact. Here the Virgin Queen wears a blue gown, the colour associated with the Virgin Mary, for the Maundy ceremony, where the monarch traditionally washed the feet of the poor and gave alms and hospitality, in imitation of Christ.

Left: In a later revival of the traditional ceremony, Elizabeth II does not kneel down to wash the feet of the poor, as her Tudor predecessors did. The Maundy ceremony is held in a different cathedral each year, where she presents purses containing specially minted silver coins – based on the original Norman currency of sterling – to the same number of elderly men and women as her age.

Queen's title, which was altered from Supreme Head to Supreme Governor, a concession that answered concerns from both Catholics and Protestants about the appropriateness of a woman holding the former title. A separate Uniformity Bill imposed the 1552 Book of Common Prayer, with the communion text revised to reflect both the Catholic belief that the bread and wine contained the Real Presence of the body and blood of Christ and the Protestant belief that it was purely commemorative, as the liturgy of England. The bill passed by three votes – the crucial three being the two prelates still in the Tower and the Abbot of Westminster, who in the interests of harmony absented himself.

To the disgust of the Calvinist exiles returning from Geneva, the settlement left many aspects of the old religion intact. They were a small, vociferous minority, skilled in the art of propaganda, who felt that with the accession of a Protestant queen their time had come. Had she not been saved by God for this very purpose? Apart from the silver crucifix and candlesticks and sacred music in the royal chapel, they were disgusted that the Queen should dance and hunt on the Sabbath day and utter oaths – Elizabeth could swear like a trooper. Elizabeth's agenda was different from theirs. She denied the papal supremacy, rejected transubstantiation and asserted the supremacy of scriptural authority, but having spent much of her life steeped in Catholic ritual, she was comfortable with many of its externals. For her part, she was unhappy about clerical marriage and the Protestant inclination for sermonizing, but even she had to make concessions.

Overall, the religious settlement of 1559 was a qualified success for Elizabeth, a tribute to her determination to hold true to her principle, that compromise, a middle way, was the surest path to peace in her realm. She had adopted as her personal motto the words, *'Semper Eadem'* – 'Always one and the same'. In her religious settlement, at least, that was true. No amount of pressure would ever deflect her from it.

The motto belied a deeper truth about her: a fluidity of approach that made compromise possible. As she admitted, she had no desire to make windows into men's souls. There was only one Jesus Christ, she later told the French ambassador, and all the rest was a dispute over trifles. She simply asked for an outward conformity. This is not to detract from her very deep religious conviction. In her personal book of prayers and devotions, she exhibited no doubt that her cause was God's own, and that it was England's Church that held to His truth. When Elizabeth prayed, it was as if she had the sense of carrying the English people with her into God's presence. In this way, she fulfilled her queenly role as an intercessor.

14

For a Woman to Bear Rule

THE MONARCH WAS God's representative on earth and so, by definition, male. Elizabeth's challenge was to overcome the very considerable drawback of her sex and assert her authority over a rigidly patriarchal society.

It was not enough to be Queen. After the disaster of Mary, which had reinforced male prejudice against female rule, there was profound anxiety. Elizabeth knew that she had to address this. In order to function successfully in a man's world, she would have to present herself as an extraordinary woman – 'alone of all her sex'. The status of other women was not her concern. Thanks to her education, Elizabeth was able to function comfortably on a masculine level. She had been trained, as other women were not, in the use of rhetoric to assert her authority, and she was rigorously drilled in the language of men's privilege and power – Latin.

There is no doubt that Elizabeth genuinely believed that she had been chosen by God as His instrument, but she also recognized the propaganda value of adopting the persona of the divinely chosen ruler, to whom the people would give their unquestioning obedience. She did not bother to counter John Knox's polemic, *The First Blast of the Trumpet against the Monstrous Regiment of Women*, directed primarily against her sister, in which he equated authority with maleness and asserted that femaleness and rule were mutually contradictory. She simply reiterated her own divine sanction to rule, manifested by God's protection of her through the many perils of her youth.

In this she was aided by John Aylmer, formerly tutor to Lady Jane Grey, who in his *An Harborowe for Faithfull and Trewe Subjectes* advanced the doctrine that God's choice of a weak instrument such as a woman is evidence of His own miraculous strength. Unfortunately, he rather spoilt the case by adding that Elizabeth did not rule alone: she must rely on Parliament and the rule of law. England would triumph, he argued patronizingly, not simply because God would guide an untested young woman, but because the seasoned and wise men of Parliament would give her advice and counsel.

In her first speech to the nobility at Hatfield, Elizabeth had described herself as 'God's Creature, ordained to obey his appointment . . . the minister of His heavenly will'. Likewise, in the closing address to Parliament in 1576, she attributed the benefits England had enjoyed not to herself but to God: she was 'no better than His handmaid'. She could not take the glory which rightly belonged to God, she told them, adding in a nicely judged aside, 'My sex permits it not.' Similarly, in her Golden Speech in 1601 she reminds them that she has simply been the instrument of God's will. As a woman, she would not have the temerity to claim otherwise: 'Shall I ascribe anything to myself and my sexly weakness? I were not worthy to live then.'

Elizabeth could bolster her authority by assuming a dual sexual identity, as both king and queen. At the beginning of the reign Nicholas Heath, Archbishop of York, stated that by the 'appointment of God she [is] our soveraigne lord and ladie, our kinge and quene, our emperor and empresse'. He probably had in mind the Act Concerning Regal Power, passed at the beginning of Mary's reign, establishing that a woman could rule in her own right and had the same powers as a male monarch. The theory rested on the medieval concept of the king's two bodies, which Henry VIII had appropriated, and which lent itself perfectly to exploitation by Elizabeth.

The monarch's mortal body was subject to human frailties and imperfections, culminating in death; whereas his second body, incorporating the monarchy, was immortal. In this way, the king never died, he lived for ever. Elizabeth applied gender to the theory. Her 'natural body' was that of a woman, subject to the weaknesses of her sex; her 'body politic' was that of a king, carrying the strength and masculine spirit of the best of her male predecessors. She acknowledged this in her first speech to the nobility when she said, 'And as I am but one body naturally considered, though by His permission a body politic to govern'. It was for this reason that she was so keen to take on some of her father's male identity, frequently drawing attention to her resemblance to him and making comparisons with him in her speeches.

Hence in response to Parliament's petition in 1566 that she either marry or declare a successor, she tells them: 'And as for my own part, I care not for death, for all men are mortal; and though I be a woman, yet I have as good a courage answerable to my place as ever my father had.' She is at pains to remind them, however, that she is not just any woman, but an exceptional woman: 'I thank God that I am indeed endued with such qualities that if I were turned out of the realm in my petticoat, I were able to live in any place of Christendom.'

Elizabeth liked to show off her 'manly' brain – as, for instance, when she attended plays and disputations at the Inns of Court and Oxford and Cambridge and discoursed with the students in Latin – while at the same time calling attention to her womanly weakness when it suited her to do so. This was nearly always an implicit invitation to view her otherwise, though some of her male audience might have missed the cue.

She would make a point of referring to the 'defect' of her womanhood, a tactic to mask her hidden strength. She pandered to male discomfort at being commanded by a woman through her open acknowledgement of her weakness, while at the same time reminding them of her kingly status which transcends the deficiencies of her sex. There is no better example of this than in her Armada speech of 1588, where she seems to defy the law of nature itself by claiming to have 'the body but of a weak and feeble woman' but the 'heart and stomach of a king'.

Her frequent denigration of her sex reflected both her acceptance of contemporary mores and the need to emphasize the difference between her and 'ordinary' women. Again and again, Elizabeth through her oratory and speeches sets herself apart from other women, who never spoke in public. But at the same time, she was careful to 'disable' herself, as a concession to male notions of their supremacy over the inferior, weaker, female sex. It helped to be a great actress. 'The weight and greatness of this matter might cause in me some feare to speak, and bashfulness besides, a thing appropriate to my sex,' she soothes, before reminding them that she is different: 'But yet, the princely seate and kingly throne, wherin God hath constituted me, maketh these two causes to seme little in myne eyes, though grievous perhaps to your eares, and boldeneth me to say somewhat in this matter . . .' As, of course, she does.

Elizabeth seems to have believed that a woman in power needed to appropriate the language of kingship. As a young woman writing to her sister to protest her innocence, she vows that she does not share the 'rebellious hearts and devilish intents' of those who showed malice towards 'their anointed king'. The point was lost on Mary, however, as she had surrendered her 'kingship' to Philip. As queen, Elizabeth frequently referred to herself as 'prince', but this simply meant ruler in the sixteenth century; it did not have a gender, or if it did, it was assumed to be male. She uses 'princess' disparagingly, especially when writing to or about Mary, Queen of Scots, whom she felt had lost much of the respect due her as sovereign through her bad behaviour. Elizabeth had no objection to the term Queen in relation to herself, but tended to use phrases such as 'The Queen our Sovereign Lady' when it seemed apt, for instance, in time of plague, when she expressed a maternal concern for her stricken people. In her Golden Speech, she refers to herself as king and queen: 'To be a King and wear a crown is a thing more glorious to them that see it, than it is pleasant to them that bear it. For myself, I was never so much enticed with the glorious name of a King or royal authority of a Queen, as delighted that God hath made me His instrument to maintain His truth and glory, and to defend this Kingdom . . . from peril, dishonour, tyranny and oppression.'

It was important for Elizabeth as queen regnant to assert her authority over the court, which was very much a male club. One way to do this was through the royal progresses, which took place in the summer months when the roads were passable. The progresses inconvenienced every member of the court and cost her rather more than staying in the royal palaces, but as queen she found power in the turmoil of an itinerant court and in an ongoing dialogue with her subjects. For Elizabeth, going on progress reiterated her central position in the court and in the country. The progresses created a dislocating confusion that reminded ministers, courtiers, hosts and citizens of the Queen's centrality in their lives. Each day, whether the Queen was staying at a private house or visiting a town, began with everyone focusing on what she wanted: did she intend to stick to her schedule; did she intend to hunt; would she enjoy the ceremonies; would she grant a particular petition; what gift to give her? Elizabeth had found there were no prizes in being predictable.

Unlike her parents, Elizabeth never went abroad and even in her own country she was not adventurous in her choice of destination. Ever cautious, she restricted her travels to the more populated, prosperous and stable areas of her kingdom, validating royal authority, social stability and religious conformity where it already existed, rather than reaching out to new audiences. But the progresses fulfilled their function of taking her beyond the confines of the court to appear in public ceremonies, to consolidate her image and popularity, to strengthen royal authority in the towns and encourage civic pride and productivity, and to nourish social ties with the aristocracy and gentry – the women as well as the men.

At court, the dual existence of the Queen's two bodies – the one private and feminine, the other public and implicitly masculine – was reflected in the neutralization of the Privy Chamber as a political force. Under Elizabeth's father, his cronies in the Privy Chamber had derived political power and influence simply through being close to the monarch. It was no coincidence that the foremost among them, the Groom of the Stool, had the most intimate function of all – wiping the royal bottom. Gentlemen of the Privy Chamber were entrusted with diplomatic errands and were taken seriously by foreign potentates precisely because they were known to be in their sovereign's confidence. The dry stamp of the King's signature resided in the Privy Chamber, again lending power to those who had access to it.

As a woman, Elizabeth had to have an almost exclusively female household and, of course, these women could not play any part in political life. Their role was purely domestic and, by dint of that, the Privy Chamber became a sort of cocoon, an oasis for Elizabeth away from the political fray. She even tended to eat there privately, with very few attendants, dining in state only on special occasions. Elaborate court ceremony was still maintained, with the participants bowing to the empty throne as if the Queen were there in person:

When the Queen is served, a great table is set in the Presence Chamber, near the Queen's throne. The cloth being laid, a gentleman and a lady come in . . . and make three reverences, the one by the door, the next in the middle of the chamber, the third by the table. Then they set down the cover and the lady tries the food. The guards bring in the meat in the same manner; then the lady tries the food with a piece of bread and gives it to the guards; thence the meat, such as the Queen desires, is carried into the Privy Chamber where she dines.

At the outset, Elizabeth vested the secretarial and financial functions that had previously resided in the Privy Chamber in Sir William Cecil, who became both Secretary of State and her own personal secretary. There was no female equivalent of the Groom of the Stool. As Chief Gentlewoman of the Privy Chamber until her death in 1565, Kat Ashley performed the same tasks, being the receiver and keeper of the Queen's close-stools, but the office had been shorn of its political power, especially as it no longer entailed the keepership of the Privy Purse – which had sometimes been the predominant spending department – or the dry stamp of the royal signature. In the past, access to the sovereign had been everything, but again this no longer applied, although a hierarchy based on nearness to her prevailed among the women.

Elizabeth had tailored the Privy Chamber and the household to her own personal needs. As a woman, she needed a group of female attendants to wait on her in her chamber and run errands for her, while as a queen she needed an entourage of ladies to accompany her on formal occasions. Nearly all were derived from her milieu of relatives and loyal servants of long standing, as well as those families who had had an affinity to the Tudor court over several generations. Kat Ashley and Blanche Parry had been with her from childhood. Blanche, who was to be keeper of the Queen's jewels for forty years, had actually rocked her cradle, and Kat had been a second mother to her. Then there were her Boleyn relatives, particularly the descendants of her aunt, Mary Boleyn. The closest was probably Mary's daughter by her first marriage, Catherine Carey, wife of Sir Francis Knollys. Mary, Lady Sidney, sister of Robert Dudley, was also a very close friend, so devoted that she nursed Elizabeth through smallpox and caught the disease herself; her beauty was so marred that she did not appear at court again.

Under Henry VIII, the Privy Chamber had been a cockpit of faction, whereas under Elizabeth, faction had no place. The women's first loyalty was to the Queen. That was why she grew so angry when any of her maids of honour presumed to marry without her permission: it indicated a lack of trustworthiness. Some of her women might try to further a minor suit on behalf of a relative, but anything larger was frowned upon and discouraged. The only sense in which they might have acted as conduits was in relaying to the Queen gossip and information about the court, and in apprising Cecil and others of the Queen's mood, so that they could judge if it was an apt moment to raise a particular issue. They were not there to advance the interests of court factions. Nor did Elizabeth give her women any cause to think they could emulate her by flouting the conventions of the patriarchal society. *She* was exceptional – perhaps a part of God's inscrutable plan, certainly the token woman or honorary male – whereas *they* were ordinary women and must conform to type.

Elizabeth's dual existence was played out in two different arenas. In her capacity as queen and ruler she was, as it were, on the public stage. In her private capacity, as queen and woman, she retreated to the feminine confines of the Privy Chamber surrounded by her trusted *familia*. Here, behind the scenes, she could relax and be herself, although she was never alone. Outside she put on a performance. Like an actress, she dressed for the part, donning ever more fantastic clothes, jewels, wigs and cosmetics to perpetuate her goddess-like image. The magnitude of the Earl of Essex's offence in bursting into the Queen's bedchamber one morning while she was still in a state of undress, her red wig on its stand, her face bare of the elaborate make-up behind which it was in her later years habitually concealed and her grey hair in wisps about her temples, can be understood in this context. This was not just a case of *lèse-majesté*. It was an assault, an invasion of the Queen's privacy.

Perhaps because of the taint of her illegitimacy, Elizabeth was assiduous in treating fellow monarchs as part of her family. They were addressed variously as 'my very dear brother', 'my good brother and cousin' and 'my dear sister', as a reminder of the bond of sovereignty.

Her nobles were her 'right trusty and well-beloved cousins'. She might snip their power and relegate them to a secondary role in the governance of the country, but they were still part of her extended family, owing the monarchy a supra-familial loyalty. Elizabeth assiduously played her part, receiving them into the Privy Chamber for dancing and games, entertaining them at tournaments, providing them with London residences, attending their weddings, negotiating some of their marriages or acting as mediator in their quarrels, serving as godmother to their children. And like any family, the members exchanged gifts at New Year. There were perfumed gloves, gorgeous clothes, intricately designed jewellery rich in symbolism and purses of gold for the Queen, gifts of plate weighted according to the rank of the recipient from the Queen to them.

Whether there would be any room in this *familia* for a husband remained to be seen. The Scottish envoy Melville was shrewd enough to see the advantages of the Queen's dual persona, recognizing that if she married she would be but Queen of England, whereas now 'she was both king and queen'. The marriage question was the next challenge in Elizabeth's career as queen.

15

One Mistress and No Master

A S KING AND QUEEN both, it is hard to see how Elizabeth could accommodate a husband; yet as a queen and as a woman in post-Reformation England, it was unthinkable that she should not marry and produce an heir – preferably male. The Imperial ambassador echoed the universal male view when he said, 'For that she should wish to remain a maid and never marry is inconceivable.'

Elizabeth had already given several indications before she came to the throne that she was personally disinclined to marry. When her sister had sent Sir Thomas Pope to sound her out on a proposal from a foreign prince, she reminded him that when her brother had been king she had asked permission 'to remayne in that estate I was, which of all others best liked me or pleased me . . . I so well like this estate, as I perswade myselfe there is not anie kynde of liffe comparable unto it.' After she became queen, she confided to the Spanish ambassador, da Silva, that marriage 'is a thing for which I have never had any inclination', adding with almost modern insight: 'There is a strong idea in the world that a woman cannot live unless she is married, or at all events that if she refrains from marriage she does so for some bad reason.' Over the next twenty years or so, she was to say repeatedly that she preferred the virgin state. Men found this perplexing. Even taking into account the conventional protestation of maidenly modesty, it is likely that Elizabeth was expressing her true preference.

When her first Parliament petitioned her to marry in 1559 her response was probably the most honest revelation of her feelings on the subject she was ever to give publicly. As she came under increasing pressure to marry – for instance, in 1563 and 1566 Parliament's demands had turned from solicitous enquiry to outright hectoring and blackmail – subsequent statements probably reveal not so much what she felt about marriage, as what was politic to say about it.

She began by confirming that from her earliest years she 'happily chose this kind of life in which I yet live, which I assure you for mine own part hath hitherto best contented myself and I trust hath been most acceptable to God'. Neither ambition nor fear of death at the hands of her enemies had persuaded her otherwise. Her life is in God's hands to decide. She is confident that He who has 'preserved and led me by the hand, will not now of His goodness suffer me to go alone'. She promises that whenever it should please God to 'incline my heart to another kind of life', she will not choose a husband who will be displeasing to her people.

If it should please God that she remain unmarried, she assures them that He will not leave the realm destitute of 'an heir that may be a fit governor'. Indeed, the heir God provides might be 'more beneficial to the realm than such offspring as may come of me'. A child of her body might 'grow out of kind and become, perhaps, ungracious'. It was an uncannily accurate prediction of events and she even provided her own epitaph: 'And in the end this shall be for me sufficient: that a marble stone shall declare that a queen, having reigned such a time, lived and died a virgin.'

A second version of the speech, which appeared in Camden's *Annales* in 1615, contains a scene in which Elizabeth is described stretching out her hand to display her coronation ring, telling them: 'To conclude, I am already bound unto a husband, which is the kingdom of England, and that may suffice you . . . And reproach me no more that I have no children: for every one of you, and as many as are English, are my children and kinsfolks.' Camden probably picked up the anecdote from his patron, William Cecil, Lord Burghley, to whose papers he had access, but it does not necessarily belong here in Elizabeth's first response to the parliamentary petitioners in 1559, when the mood was conciliatory, less confrontational than it was to become. Elizabeth might well have made the gesture on some subsequent occasion, as she came under increasing pressure to marry or name an heir. Certainly she used the image in conversation with the Scottish ambassador, William Maitland of Lethington, when she told him: 'Once I am married already to the realm of

England when I was crowned with this ring, which I bear continually in token thereof.'

In this first answer to Parliament, Elizabeth was very careful to leave the door open. It was one thing to profess a preference for the virgin state as a private person, another as queen, when her person became the embodiment of the monarchy. Elizabeth probably tried to retain an open mind, prepared to do her duty to the state if necessary. As her father's daughter, she believed that it was her prerogative alone to decide the questions of marriage and the succession. While gently expressing her right as 'an absolute princess' to marry or not as she chose, she promised 'to do nothing to the prejudice of the commonwealth'. It was clever to assure them that she would only marry a husband who met with their approval, because, in the event, no candidate would satisfy everyone, leaving her unencumbered.

Many of Elizabeth's biographers have attributed her unwillingness to marry to some psychological barrier. Her mother and one stepmother were executed on her father's orders; two stepmothers had died in childbirth; her first foray into the world of adult sexuality had ended in the death of her would-be seducer. It would not be surprising, therefore, that somewhere in the recesses of her mind she associated marriage and sex with death.

It is more likely, however, that she had a well-founded aversion to the loss of power, to the loss of control over her person and sovereignty which marriage would inevitably entail. It was all very well for John Aylmer in his *An Harborowe for Trewe and Faithfull Subjectes* to try to reconcile the contradictions between being a queen and a wife – 'I graunte that, so farre as pertaining to the bandes of marriage, and the offices of a wife, she must be a subjecte: but as a Magistrate she maye be her husbandes heade' – but the theory was a long way from practice.

Her sister Mary's marriage treaty had been designed to give her autonomy as sovereign, leaving her husband in a subordinate position, but the treaty had provided few safeguards against human fallibility. A treaty only worked in so far as the characters concerned allowed it to. Mary had proved malleable, finally giving way to Philip's entreaties to bring England into a disastrous war. As a married woman, she had also lost control over her body, becoming physically, mentally and emotionally incapacitated for months by a phantom pregnancy, reducing her ability to govern effectively. If the example of her sister was not enough to warn Elizabeth off marriage, the subsequent marital adventures of Mary, Queen of Scots, in the 1560s would certainly serve to reinforce Elizabeth's very strong survivalist instincts that to remain single was the better option.

Elizabeth was intent on identifying with Tudor strengths – in particular, with her charismatic, powerful father – and realized that this would be fatally compromised by her participation in the institution that had revealed Tudor weakness. She had no wish to re-enact her father's and sister's desperation in trying to produce a male heir or make herself vulnerable to failure.

There has been speculation that Elizabeth knew she had some physical impediment that would prevent her having sexual relations, but this is unfounded. Foreign ambassadors would bribe her laundresses, Anne Twiste and Elizabeth Smithson, to discover whether she was 'normal'; she had an irregular menstrual cycle. Cecil, who made it his business to know the details of the Queen's 'bodily functions', was confident that if only she would marry, she would have no difficulty in having a child. The physicians were equally convinced of her childbearing capacity, although they were ignorant of the fact that the nephritis she might have suffered in her twenties would probably have caused miscarriage after miscarriage.

Elizabeth was a pragmatist. Just as she was wise enough to keep her options open in her response to Parliament's petitions that she marry, so she was quick to appreciate the diplomatic mileage that could be gained from protracted courtships with foreign suitors. She found her natural inclination to prevaricate and change her mind – which accorded with the prejudiced male view of 'womanly behaviour' – a useful tool in the marriage game. The unmarried twenty-five-year-old Queen was the greatest match in Europe. It satisfied her not inconsiderable ego to have kings and princes all vying for her hand. She enjoyed the whole ritual of courtship, so much so that it became an addiction. As the Spanish ambassador de Silva reported, 'She is vain, and would like all the world to be running after her.' No amount of flattery from her suitors would be too excessive. Endless talk of marriage became a substitute for the reality. Elizabeth was such a consummate actress that she could convince even the most sceptical that she was genuine, stringing out proposals for years, alternating between cool and eager, as diplomatic necessity prompted her.

Her former brother-in-law, Philip of Spain, was less inclined to take her at her word than most, cynically advising a Habsburg negotiator who believed the prize was within his grasp to 'get it in writing'. After her sister's death he had gone through the motions of proposing to her himself, but only out of duty, to keep England within the Habsburg alliance and to save it from heresy. Such lack of ardour would never have won Elizabeth, who expected her suitors to put on a convincing performance. His suit quickly foundered, but not before she had fully exploited it. Until she was crowned and anointed she had needed his support, although there was little chance at this stage of his backing the rival claimant, Mary, Queen of Scots. Conscious that she could not afford to alienate the powerful King of Spain, who was still England's ally pending the completion of negotiations ending the war with France, Elizabeth had moved cautiously, until the time was ripe for the pretence of courtship to be converted into more credible friendship. When he lost patience and married Elisabeth of France, Elizabeth – who had already acquired a taste for this game – teased the Spanish ambassador that Philip could not have loved her very much, since he had not waited even four months for her.

As queen, Elizabeth was careful not to let her heart rule her head. She was never a creature of impulse. As a woman she was passionate and emotionally needy, but suppressed her desires in the interests of her role as monarch. The cost to her private happiness might be measured in the outrage with which she greeted news of the less than queenly behaviour of Mary, Queen of Scots, in her sexual escapades with Bothwell, or in the foolish behaviour of her cousin, Lady Catherine Grey, who so far forgot herself as to marry without the Queen's permission and proceeded to give birth to two sons whose legitimacy was thrown into doubt by their mother's carelessness in losing the written proof of her marriage. Or of the youngest of the Grey sisters, the dwarf-like Mary, who made a preposterous misalliance with an enormously tall palace flunkey. In putting their emotions and lusts before their duty and failing to take account of the consequences of their actions, none of these women, in Elizabeth's opinion, was worthy to wear her crown.

Elizabeth was very good at compartmentalizing her life, but the wills of the Queen and the private woman were sometimes in conflict. Nowhere was this more evident than in her relationship with Robert Dudley, the love of her life. They had known each other since childhood and their friendship rested on a deep, long-standing affection. They had in common their experience of imprisonment in the Tower during Mary's reign, and they shared an interest in books and intellectual pursuits, dancing, riding and hunting. In the first heady months of her reign, Elizabeth's indiscreet passion for her Master of the Horse riveted, shocked and horrified onlookers and fed the reports of foreign ambassadors. So dark he earned the nickname 'The Gypsy', handsome, tall, with an excellent physique and that promise of sexual vigour, Dudley was the sort of swaggering charmer reminiscent of her first love, Thomas Seymour. He was equally unsuitable, since not only was he married, but he was the son and grandson of executed traitors.

As a married man, Dudley was 'safe'. Elizabeth might have felt she wanted to marry him, but she must have known in her innermost mind that it was not possible. And even if Dudley managed to divest himself of the encumbrance of his wife, Elizabeth knew that the Council would never agree to her marriage with a Dudley, the son of the usurper, the Duke of Northumberland, and the grandson of a mere lawyer and tax collector. Her cousin, the premier nobleman, Thomas Howard, Duke of Norfolk, looked down on him as an arrogant upstart who treated the Queen with unacceptable familiarity. Dudley was almost universally unpopular. Cecil disliked and distrusted him, but concealed his feelings behind a mask of amiability, until the opportunity presented itself to check his overweening ambition to marry the Queen.

Dudley's neglected wife, Amy Robsart, proved his Achilles heel. They had married for love when Dudley was still in his teens and she had remained loyal to him when he had lost everything – title, wealth and position – when his father had tried to usurp the crown in the name of another daughter-in-law, Lady Jane Grey, and ended up on the scaffold. As soon as Elizabeth came to the throne, Dudley rushed to court, determined to restore his family to its former rank and fortune. As Master of the Horse, he was constantly by the Queen's side whenever she rode out in public or to hunt. There can be no doubt that she was sexually attracted to him, so much so that at times it seemed she was in danger of losing her head.

Elizabeth was a striking-looking woman with a charismatic personality; she was a most engaging and lively companion and when she smiled, according to one of her godsons, it was pure sunshine. But her main attraction for Dudley lay in the fact that she was Queen. He must also have been drawn by her elusiveness – the fact that she was unobtainable – for there can be little doubt that despite the intensity of their relationship, she stopped short of consummation. Tempting as it might be, Elizabeth is unlikely to have surrendered her most valuable asset, her virginity, or given such an ambitious man as Dudley that hold over her. To keep his passion for her alive without ever allowing him to gain mastery over her was for Elizabeth a heady form of power. Controlling men was half the fun for her.

Damaging rumours of improper behaviour between the Queen and Dudley persisted, so much so that Kat Ashley begged Elizabeth on her knees to be more careful of her reputation. Elizabeth truculently argued that she lived surrounded by her ladies, so how could anything dishonourable occur between her and her Master of the Horse. Then, working herself up into a state of righteous indignation, she told Kat: 'If she had ever had the will or had found pleasure in such a dishonourable kind of life, from which may God preserve her, she did not know of anyone who could forbid her.'

The lovers' idyll was abruptly shattered by the death of Amy in mysterious circumstances. The Dudleys still had no home of their own and, shy and not invited to court to join the Queen's ladies, Amy had been forced to rely on the hospitality of others. It was while she was living with friends at Cumnor Place in Oxfordshire that the worst happened. There had been rumours at court about Amy's ill health and she seems to have been in the advanced stages of breast cancer. On 8 September 1560 – a day when her husband was absent as usual, hunting with the Queen at Windsor – she had urged the whole household to go to Abingdon to enjoy the fair, leaving her alone in the house. When two of the servants returned, it was to find Amy lying at the bottom of a short flight of stairs with her neck broken. Curiously, her headdress had not been dislodged by the fall, suggesting to contemporaries that she had been tidied up by an unknown assailant.

Modern medical knowledge, however, indicates that her death was an accident. Amy's spine was probably so brittle from metastasized cancer that even the act of stepping down a stair or two – especially if she stumbled – could have caused her neck to snap. The obvious inference – which Dudley's enemies eagerly seized upon – was that Amy had either been murdered, or had been driven to suicide by his neglect and the rumours that reached her that he was intent on marrying the Queen.

An inquest was ordered immediately, with Dudley understandably anxious to get to the truth of the matter and clear his name. Cecil's part in the whole business was suspect. He had recently drawn the Spanish ambassador, Bishop de Quadra, aside and told him that he was in such despair that the Queen was going to marry Dudley that he was about to tender his resignation. According to the ambassador, 'He ended by saying that Robert was thinking of killing his wife, who was publicly announced to be ill, although she was quite well, and would take very good care they did not poison her.' If it is true, it is a very odd remark for Cecil, whose spies must have kept him fully informed of Amy Dudley's state of health. It could only have been made with the intention of casting an irredeemable slur on Dudley's reputation, giving Elizabeth no option but to distance herself from her favourite, or the excuse to extricate herself from a relationship that was getting out of hand. Perhaps prompted by Cecil, Elizabeth also made an apparently ill-timed remark to de Quadra that Dudley's wife was at death's door, making it look as if she had prior knowledge of it before the news reached court.

It looked very bad for Dudley. At the very least, it reflected poorly on him that one of the witnesses at the inquest recalled hearing Amy praying to God to deliver her from desperation. Although he might have wished his wife dead, there is no proof whatsoever that he had sent someone to kill her. The inquest exonerated him, but he could never quite shake off the suspicion that he was somehow implicated in her death. 'The Queen of England is about to marry her horse keeper who has killed his wife to make room for her,' sneered Mary, Queen of Scots, at the French court, where the English ambassador, Sir

Nicholas Throckmorton, was mortified by the scandal. On the contrary, there could be no possibility now of Dudley ever marrying the Queen, although this did nothing to quench his ambition to do so. Unlike Mary in a similar situation a few years later, when she married the suspected murderer of her husband, Elizabeth kept her head and her distance. Dudley was banished from court until a thorough investigation could be carried out.

Elizabeth never ceased to love Dudley. He remained the favourite. The two would quarrel and make up like lovers and she would not be able to resist showing her affection for him publicly. When she created him Earl of Leicester, she tickled his neck familiarly while he knelt before her, which ambassadors felt was most unseemly behaviour. She knew she would never marry Dudley, caring more for her survival and the peace and unity of her realm than for him, dear as he was to her. His continuing devotion and attention gave her the emotional sustenance she needed, while withholding her commitment kept him keen.

Elizabeth did not hesitate to slap him down when necessary. On one occasion, he had an altercation with one of her servants who had, rightly, barred one of his men from access to the Privy Chamber. When the servant cleverly appealed to Elizabeth, asking her if she was still Queen, or whether Dudley was King, she had rounded on Dudley, reminding him that she could undo him as rapidly as she had made him: 'God's death, my Lord, I have wished you well, but my favour is not so locked up in you that others shall not participate thereof . . . and if you think to rule here, I will take a course to see you forthcoming. I will have here but one mistress, and no master.' It was not until the mid 1570s that Leicester finally gave up his pursuit. In the meantime, his presence was felt in Elizabeth's marriage negotiations as he intervened whenever he could to hinder them, pitting the French against the Habsburgs as he intrigued with their rival ambassadors.

In a bid to keep Philip of Spain and the Habsburgs onside, Elizabeth entered into a long period of negotiation to marry the Emperor Ferdinand's younger brother, Charles, who was also Philip's cousin. His Habsburg connections would guarantee England the friendship of Spain and security against France. As a second son, he would not have Philip's disadvantage when married to Mary, namely, that his attention was divided between England and his own territories. Charles was not even bad-looking. The stumbling block was always religion. There was no way that an ardent Catholic would consent to practise his religion in secret or attend the services of the English Church. For Elizabeth, there was a further consideration. Perhaps remembering the farce of her father's marriage to Anne of Cleves, based on his falling in love with Holbein's flattering portrait of her, she could never be induced to marry a man she had not met. Might not the archduke come to England in disguise, she suggested. It was to no avail. Habsburg princes did not offer themselves for inspection.

Parliament's patience was wearing thin with Elizabeth's prevarication. By 1563 the Lords had become so desperate that they were begging her to marry *anyone*: 'where it shall please you, with whom it shall please you, and as soon as it shall please you'. Some reasoned that she would be more likely to bear a child if she married a man to whom she was sexually attracted, such as Leicester, even though in one of his memoranda listing the pros and cons of Leicester versus the Archduke Charles, Cecil noted that 'Nothing is increased by Marriadg of hym either in Riches, Estimation, Power.'

Failing marriage, the Lords were urging Elizabeth to name her successor. It was something she categorically refused to do, even when she was dying in 1603. Indeed, she had nearly died of smallpox in 1562 and the incident had demonstrated the precariousness of the situation. Her counsellors could not agree who her successor should be. Some thought Lady Catherine Grey, others Henry, Lord Hastings, a descendant of Edward IV. No one suggested Mary, Queen of Scots, for the obvious reason that she was a Catholic and would undo the religious settlement, but also because she was a foreigner, born out of the realm.

There was no obvious successor, even if Elizabeth had been willing to name that person, which she was not. She was furious when a joint delegation of the Lords and Commons in 1566 had the presumption to press the succession question, which was her prerogative to decide when she judged the time was right. She resented their implication that her reluctance to settle the succession showed her careless of the safety of the realm. On the contrary, she told them, it was for precisely this reason that she declined to name a successor. None of them had been a 'second person', as she had in her sister's reign. 'I stood in danger of my life, my sister was so incensed against me . . . so shall never be my successor.'

Elizabeth was at pains to remind Parliament that 'I am your anointed queen. I will never be by violence constrained to do anything.' Yet she knew how to be gracious. She would not be forced to marry or declare her successor, but she could deflect their anger by turning a negative into a positive, for instance by voluntarily remitting a third of the Subsidy Bill which Parliament had been asked to vote. This was skilled management.

By 1569, Mary, Queen of Scots, was a prisoner in England and Spain was busy exploiting this Catholic threat to Elizabeth, supporting plots against her in England itself. A rapprochement with the French was in order. Elizabeth was now approaching her late thirties. She was physically fit. She could stand for hours, while those in audience with her wilted. Regular physical exertion, riding, hunting and dancing, and a careful diet meant that she had retained her trim figure, so that from a distance, with her fine posture and natural elegance, red wig and mask-like leaded make-up covering skin only slightly pitted by smallpox, she gave the illusion of a woman younger than her years. The Spanish ambassador might sneer that the game was up, that she could no longer maintain the fiction of her courtships, but the fact remained that she was still the most politically desirable match in Europe. Realizing that courtship could serve just as well as marriage in making alliances, Elizabeth played the game with aplomb for another ten years.

The degenerate brood of Catherine de Medici and Henri II of France had been too young to enter the lists as Elizabeth's suitors in the first decade of her reign. When Catherine's eldest surviving son, the immature, fourteen-year-old Charles IX, had first been raised as a possible suitor in 1565, Elizabeth had pretended interest but privately dismissed the suggestion as absurd. She had no wish to look a fool, an old woman leading a boy to the altar. But now the international situation had altered. The Pope had finally excommunicated Elizabeth and Spain had become a looming threat. The Habsburg negotiations with Archduke Charles had fizzled out in 1568 and England was looking increasingly isolated. Only by reviving discussions about a French match, holding out the tantalizing possibility of the English crown for one of Catherine de Medici's younger sons, could Elizabeth hope to prevent the alarming possibility of a Catholic, Franco-Spanish alliance against heretic England.

Catherine proposed her second and favourite son, Henri of Anjou. Eighteen years Elizabeth's junior, he was unpromising material. Dissolute, homosexual, unstable and sinisterly handsome, he was a pawn of the Catholic Guise relatives of the deposed Mary, Queen of Scots, who were now leading the pro-Spanish party in France. As Elizabeth's worst nightmare was of Mary, Queen of Scots, sprung from confinement, married to Anjou and sitting on her throne, she was willing to make a play for Anjou. Inevitably, the negotiations foundered on religion.

By 1572 Catherine's third son, Francis, Duke of Alençon – who was to take his elder brother's title of Anjou after the latter's accession to the French throne as Henri III in 1574 – had turned eighteen and was offered to Elizabeth as a more compliant candidate. She began reluctantly and the negotiations dragged, until in 1578 Anjou sent a gentleman of his household, Jean de Simier, to woo her by proxy. He overwhelmed her with French gallantry and they quickly established a rapport. It was Simier who turned the tables on Leicester when, as usual, he tried to scupper negotiations, by revealing that Leicester had married in secret. It was no coincidence that Elizabeth's rejected suitor chose as his second wife Lettice Knollys, the widowed Countess of Essex. Lettice was the daughter of Elizabeth's beloved cousin, Catherine Carey, and Sir Francis Knollys. The stiff Elizabethan portrait of her cannot conceal her vibrant sensuality; she had Elizabeth's red hair and the dark, mischievous Boleyn eyes. Elizabeth, who would brook no rivals, was absolutely furious. Leicester was banished from court, while she began to pursue her negotiations with Anjou with a vengeance.

The young Anjou had already championed the Huguenots' cause in France and had become involved in the Netherlands, which were in revolt against their ruler, Philip of Spain. It was this that piqued Elizabeth's interest. She could not possibly stand by and watch the

Flemish ports along the Channel – England's traditional trading partners – swallowed up by a French duke.

When Anjou came to England *incognito* in August 1579, Elizabeth entered on the performance of her life. He was the only one of her illustrious foreign suitors to court her in person and he came closest to winning her. The forty-six-year-old Queen and the French Prince twenty years her junior made an oddly assorted couple. Anjou was small of stature with a big nose and a skin badly pitted by smallpox, but it seems he had so much sex appeal that these imperfections were soon overlooked. He was the embodiment of charm and good manners. Elizabeth, who had never seen a relationship through to fulfilment, placed inordinate importance on the rituals of courtship and Anjou did not disappoint. During the thirteen days they spent together at Greenwich and Richmond, entertained by balls, parties and banquets, he played the game with conviction, showering her with praise and compliments, declaring his passion with all the appearance of sincerity. Elizabeth appeared enraptured and, with her penchant for giving nicknames, affectionately labelled him her Frog. For the middle-aged Elizabeth who had never surrendered to sexual passion, it was a delicious fantasy and she revelled in it.

The courtship was balm to Elizabeth's bruised feelings after Leicester's betrayal – all the more satisfactory as he was back at court and watching the very public courtship with mounting jealousy and agitation. He was so taken in by Elizabeth's adroit performance that he actually had the temerity to ask her if she was still a virgin. Having pressured Elizabeth unremittingly since she came to the throne to marry, loyal Englishmen began expressing reservations. Now that the candidate was actually here and Elizabeth was showing every sign of being in earnest, they decided they did not want a Frenchman and a Catholic for their king after all. They could not forget the French royal family's encouragement of the St Bartholomew's Day massacre of the Huguenots in Paris seven years before. Nor, now Elizabeth had reached the end of her childbearing years, was the game worth the candle any more.

Their anxieties found voice in a series of letters, ballads and pamphlets, of which the most notorious was John Stubbs's *The Discovery of a Gaping Gulf wherein England is like to be swallowed by another French marriage if the Lord forbid not the banns by letting Her Majesty see the sin and punishment thereof.* It was likely that the two arch-opponents of the match, Leicester and Sir Francis Walsingham, were behind this diatribe. Elizabeth was outraged at the insult to Anjou, a royal prince and a guest, and the criticism of her intentions. Stubbs and the publisher were condemned to suffer the full vigour of the law for the crime of seditious libel, having their right hands chopped off before a horrified crowd. Afterwards, Stubbs defiantly raised the other hand, crying 'God save her Majesty!' and fainted. It was a rare public relations disaster for Elizabeth.

Elizabeth's great strength as a ruler was her ability to listen, her sensitivity to public opinion, and an awareness of what was politically possible. Deciding that she would not go ahead with a match that bitterly divided her Council and was so displeasing to her people, she moved towards the grand finale of her last courtship. She had to extricate herself from the marriage carefully while leaving in its place friendship with France. When the French envoys arrived in London to ratify the marriage treaty, they were splendidly entertained, but found they could not get the Queen to discuss business. In July 1581 she wrote Anjou a loving letter, explaining that she could not marry him; she had already warned him that the match might founder on his insistence on practising his religion privately.

In rejecting Anjou's suit, she still needed to find a way of binding him to her. A second visit from her ardent suitor in November of that same year provided the opportunity. Confronted when she was walking with him in the gallery at Greenwich by the French ambassador with an ultimatum from the French King to declare her intentions regarding his brother, Elizabeth had no hesitation in telling him, 'You may write this to the French King, that the Duke shall be my husband.' With that she took off a ring and placed it on Anjou's finger, kissing him on the lips. In this way, she convinced Anjou of her personal good intentions, even if, as inevitably happened, she was prevented from realizing them by the disapproval of her Council, Parliament and people. Unlike her sister, Elizabeth was too wise to force the issue. Anjou was sent off with a consolation prize of £60,000 – a loan for his adventures in the Netherlands, where he was to be Elizabeth's champion.

When Anjou departed, Elizabeth put on a moving display of grief, although the Spanish ambassador's spies told him that in the privacy of the Privy Chamber 'she danced for very joy at getting rid of him'. Elizabeth might well have wept in the silent hours of the night, however. As a queen, she had played her role to perfection. She had strung out her courtships for over twenty years, as a brilliant ploy in the game of international diplomacy. She had given every appearance of acceding to demands to marry, while managing to avoid what was personally distasteful to her and possibly ruinous. But the cost to her personal happiness had been great. If she had ever harboured hopes of having a husband and children, those hopes were now irredeemably dashed. She was facing a lonely old age.

To the consternation of her Council, Elizabeth had actually broken down and wept when it had become clear that the marriage with Anjou could never proceed. Something of the strain of her divided personality, the dual role she was forced to play as queen and woman, is captured in her poem, 'On Monsieur's Departure':

> I grieve and dare not show my discontent;
> I love, and yet am forced to seem to hate;
> I do, yet dare not say I ever meant;
> I seem stark mute, but inwardly do prate.
> I am, and not; I freeze and yet am burned,
> Since from myself another self I turned.

There was nothing left but to re-invent herself as a Virgin Queen.

16

Two Queens in One Isle

Eᴌɪᴢᴀʙᴇᴛʜ'ꜱ ᴀᴄᴄᴇꜱꜱɪᴏɴ ᴡᴀꜱ quickly followed by the assertion of a rival claim to her throne. In France, Henri II encouraged his daughter-in-law, the sixteen-year-old Dauphine, Mary, Queen of Scots, and his son, François, to adopt the style of King and Queen of England and to quarter the royal arms of England on Mary's shield. It was a provocative gesture. In the eyes of Catholic Europe, Elizabeth, daughter of a bigamous marriage between Henry VIII and Anne Boleyn, conducted while his first wife was still alive, was a bastard. As such she had no right to the crown. In lieu of Elizabeth, Mary had the best claim to the English throne, as the granddaughter of Henry VIII's elder sister, Margaret, by her first marriage to James IV of Scotland. For the next three decades, Mary Stuart remained a thorn in Elizabeth's side.

Elizabeth and Mary, queens whose rivalry could end only in the destruction of one by the other, never met. By 1560, Mary – now the widowed Queen of France – decided to return to her own kingdom; Elizabeth refused to offer her safe passage through England, forcing Mary to take the more hazardous sea route. Elizabeth's favour was not forthcoming while Mary refused to ratify the Treaty of Edinburgh, which contained a clause renouncing her claim to the English throne. Mary, slightly modifying her position, refused to sign unless she was at least designated Elizabeth's successor.

Not content to be just Queen of Scotland – a paltry kingdom, in her view – Mary's gaze was forever fixed on England. In this, her attitude was in marked contrast to Elizabeth's, who loved her country and was fiercely patriotic. Mary, who had become Queen of Scotland when she was one week old and had been brought up as the spoilt darling of the French court, tended to take her good fortune for granted. Elizabeth, through the perils of her youth, had learned to take nothing for granted. It was because she herself had been placed in such danger during her sister's reign, the figurehead of conspiracy, that Elizabeth was reluctant to name anyone her successor, let alone the Catholic Queen of a neighbouring state.

As she told Mary's Secretary of State, William Maitland of Lethington: 'Howsoever it be, so long as I live, I shall be Queen of England; when I am dead, they shall succeed that has most right. If the queen your sovereign be that person, I shall never hurt her; if another have a better right, it were not reasonable to require me to do a manifest injury.' Naming Mary her successor, she explained, would not cement friendship between them; on the contrary. 'Think you that I could love my winding-sheet? Princes cannot like their own children, those that should succeed unto them.'

'I know the inconstancy of the people of England,' she continued, 'how they ever mislike the present government and have their eyes fixed upon that person that is next to succeed.' People naturally prefer the rising to the setting sun. 'I have good experience of myself in my sister's how desirous men were that I should be in place, and earnest to set me up. And if I would have consented, I know what enterprises would have been attempted to bring it to pass.' Men who bore her good will when she was Lady Elizabeth or thought they had her favour no doubt expected to be rewarded when she came to the crown. 'No prince's revenues be so great that they are able to satisfy the insatiable cupidity of men.' Elizabeth is sure her subjects love her, but some are bound to be discontented, and might they not in that case turn to her successor, if she should name that person? 'And what danger it were, she being a puissant princess and so near our neighbour, ye may judge; so that in assuring her of the succession we might put our present estate in doubt.'

It was likely that the Queen of Scots would remarry, complicating the issue. Elizabeth was as preoccupied by the question of Mary's marriage as her own. Having had the field to herself as 'the best match in her parish', suddenly Elizabeth had a rival. The Kings of Sweden and Denmark and Habsburg archdukes – even Don Carlos, the inbred, imbecilic son of Philip II – were now contenders for the hand of the Queen of Scots. She, too, had a crown to offer, perhaps eventually the crown of England as well. Her charms were already legendary.

No man could remain impervious to her seductive allure: those fascinating, slightly slanted hazel eyes, the luminous white complexion in a face framed by rich auburn hair, the melodious voice with its French-tinged Scottish accent, her infectious *joie de vivre*. The haunting Deuil Blanc portrait of Mary in white mourning, painted before her departure from France, had just come into Elizabeth's possession and she must have scrutinized it for clues. There was something crafty, enigmatic and beguiling about the woman in the portrait, a look that has prompted myriad interpretations of her character and left her vulnerable to the calumnies of her enemies.

Elizabeth and Mary were curious to see each other, but the intended meeting never came about. Instead, Elizabeth pressed the Scottish envoy, Sir James Melville, to describe his Queen. Who was the fairer? she asked him. 'She was the fairest Queen in England, and mine the fairest Queen in Scotland,' he answered diplomatically. 'They were both the fairest ladies in their countries; that her Majesty was whiter, but my Queen was very lovely.' Elizabeth asked which of them was taller, to which Melville replied that Mary was. 'Then,' she pounced triumphantly, 'she is too high; for I myself am neither too high nor too low.' She asked if Mary played well, to which he replied, 'reasonably, for a Queen', after which Elizabeth treated him to an impromptu performance on the virginals. He then watched her dance and had to admit that Mary 'danced not so high, and disposedly as she did'.

Elizabeth had no wish to see Mary married to a foreign, Catholic prince, undoing all her good work securing an Anglophile, Protestant government north of the border and posing a threat to England. Giving encouraging noises that if Mary would marry as she directed, she might see her way to recognizing her as her successor, failing any children of her own, Elizabeth put forward the extraordinary suggestion that Mary marry Robert Dudley. All too conscious throughout her life of her royal status, Mary was outraged at the very idea that she would stoop so low as to marry a mere commoner, a man suspected of complicity in his wife's death, and – if the rumours she had heard were true – the Queen of England's discarded lover. Knowing by now that she could not marry Dudley herself, Elizabeth probably felt that he was the one person she could trust to keep the Scottish Queen under her thumb. Mary was highly insulted by the suggestion, so much so that she veered off in another direction entirely.

Perhaps it had been Elizabeth's purpose all along to push Mary into the arms of the other candidate. For in the very act of creating Dudley Earl of Leicester, she asked Melville what he thought of 'yonder long lad, pointing to my lord Darnley'. Melville answered carefully that 'no woman of spirit would make choice of such a man, who more resembled a woman than a man. For he was handsome, beardless and lady-faced.' However, he added conspiratorially in his memoir, 'I had secret charge to deal with my Lady Lennox, to endeavour to procure liberty for him to go to Scotland . . . under pretext of seeing the country.'

Elizabeth loathed Margaret Lennox, the daughter of Margaret Tudor, with her pretensions to the English throne. The fact that she had been born in England gave her an advantage over Mary Stuart. On the other hand, there was some doubt about the validity of Margaret Tudor's marriage to the Earl of Angus, since it seems to have taken place while he was still married to his previous wife. It was a moot point, therefore, if Lady Lennox's pretensions were justified. Like her mother, she had made a similarly impetuous marriage to Matthew Stuart, Earl of Lennox, a Scottish exile at the English court. Lennox had now returned to Scotland and was requesting that his son, the English-born Henry, Lord Darnley, be allowed to visit him. Someone as shrewd as Elizabeth *must* have been aware of the machinations of Darnley's ambitious mother to marry him to the Queen of Scots, yet she gave Darnley leave to visit Scotland on a three-month passport.

For Mary, with her sights ever set on the English crown, a partnership with Darnley – one of her strongest rivals by blood for it – could only strengthen her claim and that of any children of the marriage. Of a similar height to her at around six foot, slim and graceful, the auburn-haired youth with the pretty if rather Pan-like features – those slanted eyes and pointed ears – made a favourable first impression on Mary, who thought him 'the lustiest and best proportioned long man that ever she had seen'.

Darnley had been carefully tutored by his mother in all aspects of courtly behaviour, but it was not long before the surface charm gave way to the vicious and debauched personality that was his natural bent, now that he had escaped his mother's tight leash. Mary, who seems to have fallen headlong in love, ascribed his nastiness to the illness that struck him in April. It was believed to be measles, but it is just possible that this was an early manifestation of the virulent syphilis which he was probably suffering from at the time of his death less than two years later.

It was now, with an exquisite sense of timing, that Elizabeth let it be known that she would not, after all, name her successor until such time as she herself had decided whether she would marry or not. Nor could she approve the Darnley match. In a fit of pique, Mary would be bound to marry Darnley now, and the question has to be asked whether this was Elizabeth's strategic goal. A shrewd judge of character, despising Lady Lennox and recognizing Darnley for a wastrel, had she sent him north to bring trouble and ruin to the Queen of Scots? Perhaps she had, although it is hard to see why she would have wanted these two strong claimants to her throne to unite. By July, when she recalled Lennox and Darnley from Scotland, they were sufficiently sure of themselves to defy her, so that Lady Lennox was treated to a spell in the Tower.

In Scotland opposition to the marriage of the Queen to this arrogant youth with his outbursts of temper and drunken loutishness was steadily mounting. In particular, Mary's bastard brother, James Stuart, Earl of Moray, who had hitherto been her chief counsellor, was jealous and resentful of the newcomer. With characteristic Stuart obstinacy, the more opposition to her marriage Mary encountered, the more determined she was to defy them all. On 29 July 1565 she married Darnley, according to Catholic rites, in the Chapel Royal at Holyroodhouse, proclaiming him titular King of Scots. Not even Elizabeth could have reckoned how quickly events would spiral out of control after this.

Love soon turned to disillusionment and hate. Humiliated by her husband's boorish behaviour and his nightly forays into Edinburgh to consort with the lowest prostitutes, Mary bitterly regretted her marriage. She had alienated Moray and the others for nothing. Her growing dislike for Darnley turned to revulsion after his part in the murder of her Piedmontese secretary, David Riccio. Darnley had held his wife's arms pinioned behind her back as one of his fellow con-spirators had pressed a loaded pistol against her heavily pregnant belly and another had thrust his dagger over her left shoulder – almost slic-ing her ear off in the process – into the victim, who had taken refuge behind her, clinging to her skirts. There followed an orgy of killing, as each of the conspirators plunged his dagger into the man whose only crime was to have been a foreigner who had crept too far into the Queen's confidence.

It had almost certainly been Darnley's intention that his wife should miscarry and die as a result of this experience, leaving him – as he foolishly imagined – to take the crown of Scotland. For this Mary would never forgive him, but before she could take revenge, she had to seduce him into betraying and abandoning his co-conspirators. Once Mary gave birth to Prince James, in June 1566, and the child had been acknowledged as his, Darnley had served his purpose. Mary's dilemma now was how to endure her miserable marriage, or how to be rid of him? She authorized her counsellors, including Moray and Maitland, to explore legal means of ending the marriage without jeopardizing the legitimacy of Prince James. Maitland assured her that a way would be found. Mary hastened to say, 'I will that you do nothing whereunto any spot may be laid to my honour or conscience.' Perhaps, after all, it would be better to leave things until 'God of His goodness put remedy thereto'. Darnley had made many enemies in Scotland who were only too happy to arrange his demise and Mary must have been aware of this. Either she was powerless to call a halt to plots to eliminate him, or she turned a blind eye.

It was Melville's unhappy duty to bring the news of Prince James's birth to the Queen of England. He found Elizabeth 'in great mirth, dancing after supper'. As Cecil whispered the news in her ear, 'all her mirth was laid aside . . . she did sit down, putting her hand under her cheek, bursting out to some of her ladies, that the Queen of Scots was lighter of a fair son, while she was but a barren stock.' Not particularly maternal herself, there is no reason to think that Elizabeth was any-thing more than momentarily nonplussed by the news. She always hinted in her speeches that even if she did not have any children of her own, God would provide an heir to her crown. Perhaps He had just done so. She gladly agreed to stand godmother to the Scottish Prince, sending a valuable gold font encrusted with jewels as his christening gift.

In January 1567 Mary suddenly decided to travel to Glasgow to visit Darnley, who had taken refuge with his father, and beguiled him into returning to Edinburgh with her. In view of subsequent events, her motives seem suspicious, because she must have known that he would be safer in Lennox territory than in Edinburgh, where so many of his enemies lurked. Later, her enemies implied that she was already involved with James Hepburn, Earl of Bothwell, and intended to lure her husband to his death in order to make way for Bothwell. Certainly Mary had come to rely increasingly on Bothwell's loyalty and strength. By now, Darnley was very ill, possibly with syphilis, as his whole body was covered in suppurating sores. Mary brought him to Kirk o'Field on the edge of the town. While he was there, Mary slept two nights at the house. Just before midnight on the third night, Maitland reminded her that she was due to attend a wedding party and she hurriedly said farewell to the protesting Darnley and left. As she left the house, she encountered a former servant of Bothwell's, French Paris, who was now in the royal service. He was so covered in what looked like soot, but was probably the gunpowder at that moment being laid in the cellar, that the Queen exclaimed, 'Jesu, Paris, how begrimed ye are!'

At two in the morning, Edinburgh was rocked by an enormous explosion. The house where Darnley had been lodged lay in total ruin, and according to a drawing of the scene immediately despatched to Cecil in London, Darnley himself lay dead in the garden wearing only his nightshirt, his semi-dressed valet lying near by with a chair, a quilt and a dagger. It was in the garden, as he escaped from the house, alerted perhaps by some untoward sound or the smell of burning, that Darnley met the party who were waiting to kill him by asphyxiation, almost certainly his Douglas cousins, bent on revenge for his betrayal of them after the Riccio murder. A neighbour allegedly heard a voice cry, 'Pity me, kinsmen, for the sake of Jesus Christ who pitied all the world . . .' It was only after this that the explosion occurred.

There is good reason to believe that Darnley's murder was the outcome of several plotters either working independently or in loose association. The consensus seems to have been to let Bothwell, the independent loner, take the blame; he was almost certainly implicated, but only as one among several parties to the murder. Whether or not Mary knew of the plot, or suspected it, or was already involved with Bothwell, the point was how she would behave now and what action she would take to bring the perpetrators to justice. She did nothing, withdrawing to Seton and sinking into a state of catatonic collapse, while in Edinburgh a cleverly orchestrated placard campaign was under way accusing Bothwell of the murder, but soon also the Queen, depicted as a crowned mermaid or prostitute, as his accomplice. Alarmed for her sister queen and the disrepute she was bringing to monarchy generally, Elizabeth wrote to Mary in the strongest terms:

> My ears have been so deafened and my understanding so grieved and my heart so affrighted to hear the dreadful news of the abominable murder . . . that I scarcely yet have the wits to write about it . . . O madam, I would not do the office of faithful cousin or affectionate friend if I studied rather to please your ears than employed myself in preserving your honour. However I will not at all dissemble what most people are talking about: which is that you will look through your fingers at the revenging of this deed, and that you do not take measures that touch those who have done as you wished, as if the thing had been entrusted in a way that the murderers felt assurance in doing it . . . I exhort you, I counsel you, and I beseech you to take this thing so much to heart that you will not fear to touch even him whom you have nearest to you [Bothwell] if the thing touches him, and that no persuasion will prevent you from making an example out of this to the world: that you are both a noble princess and a loyal wife. I do not write so vehemently out of doubt that I have, but out of the affection that I bear you in particular. For I am not ignorant that you have no wiser counsellors than myself.

Far from heeding her advice, Mary careered headlong down the path to her destruction. As she was returning from a visit to her son at Stirling in April, Mary's party was halted by Bothwell and several hundred troops; seizing the bridle of her horse, he demanded that she accompany him to Dunbar for her own safety. Here, apparently, he raped her. 'And' then the Queen could not but marry him, seeing he had ravished her and lain with her against her will.' As John Knox sarcastically remarked: 'It was true she was taken against her will, but, since her taking, she had no occasion to complain; yea, the courteous entertainment she had, made her forget all former offences.' It is unlikely that Mary colluded in her own abduction, but even if Bothwell had forced himself upon her, there was no need to marry him. Strangely apathetic, perhaps a willing party to what looked like a sado-masochistic relationship with the rough-and-ready border lord, Mary seemed to have lost her grip on reality.

Elizabeth was outraged. As queen, she had always placed her realm first, sacrificing her personal happiness with Leicester, while as the daughter of Anne Boleyn she had had to be especially careful of her honour. Now here was Mary Stuart – who had had the temerity to claim her crown and call her a bastard – behaving like a common whore. She had allowed her neediness for Bothwell and her own lusts to come before her duty as a queen and as the mother of a prince. Elizabeth fired off another letter, lambasting her:

> Madam, to be plain with you, our grief hath not been small that in this your marriage so slender consideration hath been had that . . . no good friend you have in the whole world can like thereof . . . For how could a worse choice be made for your honour than in such haste to marry such a subject, who besides other and notorious lacks, public fame has charged with the murder of your late husband, beside the touching of yourself also in some part, though we trust that in that behalf falsely. And with what peril have you married him that hath another lawful wife alive [Lady Jean Gordon, whom Bothwell had hurriedly divorced days before marrying Mary], whereby neither by God's law nor man's yourself can be his leeful [lawful] wife, nor any children betwixt you legitimate.

A month after the marriage, Mary and Bothwell met their enemies on the battlefield. After parlaying all day in the hot sun as their forces slipped away, Mary was persuaded to give herself up in exchange for Bothwell's freedom. It was in all their interests to allow Bothwell, the man who could point to all those implicated in Darnley's murder, to escape. He rode away and Mary was dragged into Edinburgh – her hair hanging wild and loose about her shoulders, her dress rent and her breasts exposed – before a howling mob. She had lost all the respect due to a queen. Lashed to a fury of Calvinist righteousness against a woman whom they believed to be a murderess and an adulteress, the crowd – especially the women – screamed, 'Burn the whore! Kill her, drown her!' Imprisoned on the island of Loch Leven, she gave birth to stillborn twins prematurely and, while laid low, was forced to abdicate.

As 'a good neighbour, a dear sister, and a faithful friend', Elizabeth could not stand by and do nothing:

> For which purpose we are determined to send with all speed one of our own trusty servants, not only to understand your state but also thereupon so to deal with your nobility and people as they shall find you not to lack our friendship and power for the preservation of your honour in quietness. And upon knowledge had what shall be further requisite to be done for your comfort and for the tranquillity of your realm, we will omit no time to further the same, as you shall well see.

In May 1568 Mary escaped her island prison and, defeated in battle, fled to England. Her supporters had begged her not to put her trust in the fair words of the Queen of England, but Mary would not listen. She was sure that she would find refuge there and that Elizabeth would restore her to her throne. Indeed, it was Elizabeth's first instinct to do so. She could not condone the behaviour of the Scottish rebels towards their anointed Queen. But Cecil and others persuaded her to change her mind. Mary confidently expected to be brought straight to Elizabeth, and was dismayed to learn that there could be no question of meeting the Queen until she was cleared of complicity in Darnley's murder. Moray produced the Casket Letters, purporting to be highly incriminating correspondence between the Queen and Bothwell. They may or may not have been doctored. No conclusion as to Mary's guilt or innocence was reached. The Scots did not want her back. She was to be Elizabeth's problem in England for the next nineteen years, disrupting the peace and forcing Elizabeth into extreme courses of action she would rather have avoided.

Elizabeth's dearest wish was for the peace and unity of her realm, which she felt would be best assured by outward conformity to an all-embracing state religion. A mark of the success of the Elizabethan Church settlement of 1559 was the fact that England did not suffer the religious wars tearing apart so many of its continental neighbours. With little active papal leadership to rally the Catholic cause, many Catholics were content to conform outwardly while practising their religion in secret, or drifted into conformity with the Established Church. If they were left unmolested, Elizabeth believed that in time Catholicism would die out, or operate on the margins as a harmless minority religion. Mary Stuart's arrival in England acted as a rallying cry, however, awakening Catholic opposition and giving it a focus. Having made her peace with the Pope and reinvented herself as a Catholic martyr, Mary was to be the willing figurehead of every Catholic plot to dethrone and kill Elizabeth. Why should she not plot for Elizabeth's crown, she would argue, since Elizabeth denied her her freedom?

In November 1569 Elizabeth faced the most serious rebellion of her reign, the Northern Rising, as the old, conservative Catholic nobility in the North, led by the Earls of Northumberland and Westmorland, took up Mary's cause. It was firmly suppressed. In 1571 a conspiracy was discovered which involved Elizabeth's kinsman, Thomas Howard, Duke of Norfolk, other disgruntled English noblemen, the Spanish ambassador, agents of Mary Stuart, and a Florentine banker, Roberto Ridolfi, who might have been a double agent working for Cecil. Norfolk, who had already spent some time in the Tower for entering into discussions about a possible marriage between him and Mary Stuart, had been contacted on his release by Ridolfi and persuaded to enter the conspiracy for the deposition of Elizabeth. Mary, married to Norfolk, would rule in her place. The Duke was found guilty of treason. After a long period of delay, Elizabeth signed his death warrant; she hated to spill blood. She firmly ignored demands that Mary be put on trial.

On 25 February 1570 Pope Pius V's bull, *Regnans in Excelsis*, excommunicated Elizabeth, declaring 'the pretended Queen of England' deposed and absolving her subjects from any oath of allegiance or fealty that they might have sworn. At the same time, the Catholic exile William Allen's English college at Douai was busy training priests, an army of missionaries who would infiltrate England in the 1570s, bringing Catholics back to the faith and strengthening their resolve. The number of recusants – from the Latin, *recusare*, to refuse – who declined to attend the Established Church, incurring increasing fines and running the risk of imprisonment, rose rapidly. As they became more vociferous, Parliament tightened legislation against them.

In 1580 the first Jesuits, including the Oxford scholar Edmund Campion, were unleashed, their aim being to bring about the return of England to the papal fold and mass conversion. The overthrow of Elizabeth was implicit. In retaliation, Parliament passed new legislation declaring that anyone who persuaded English subjects to abandon the Established Church for that of Rome would be guilty of high treason. Anyone reconciled with Rome would suffer the same fate. Protestantism was linked with patriotism, while Catholicism was increasingly seen as something alien, foreign and hostile. Most Catholics were loyal to Elizabeth, asking only to have the freedom to worship in peace. Now, they were being indelibly labelled as traitors. Campion's capture and his terrible suffering as he underwent the full punishment for treason – being hanged, brought down alive, dismembered, his bowels torn out and burned before his eyes, and quartered – in December 1581 demonstrated the government's new, more ruthless approach. Hundreds of priests, operating in fear of their lives as they slipped from one safe house to the next, suffered the same fate.

There was a very real danger that Elizabeth would be assassinated. On the Continent the Pope, Philip II in Spain, Mary's relatives the Guises, head of the Catholic party in strife-torn France, and the Duke of Alva in the Netherlands, waiting for the signal from Philip to invade England, all plotted her overthrow. Mary remained at the epicentre of all the conspiracies, at home and abroad, to depose Elizabeth. In 1584 an association was formed and sanctioned by Parliament to pursue to the death anyone plotting against the Queen, as well as any person on whose behalf they plotted. Such a person would be excluded from the English throne. Mary was not named as such, but the implication was clear. The association had *carte blanche* to act against her. Elizabeth intervened to insist that such a person would not be condemned without trial. Significantly, in the event of Elizabeth's assassination, Cecil formulated a plan whereby a Council of State would govern the country until such time as the Council and Parliament could decide on her successor. Naturally, Elizabeth did not approve of this attempt to encroach on the royal prerogative or alter the natural order of the succession.

Elizabeth had entrusted the task of detecting Catholic plotters to Sir Francis Walsingham. Clever, devious and utterly unscrupulous, he had built up a highly efficient spy network of agents and *agents provocateurs* both at home and abroad. He was determined to ensnare the Queen of Scots. He initiated false plots, such as the Parry plot in 1585, in the hope that Mary would become involved and condemn herself. For many years, Mary had enjoyed relative comfort under the kindly eye of her guardian, the Earl of Shrewsbury, and the companionship of his wife, Bess of Hardwick, in Derbyshire, but the conditions of her imprisonment became more severe when Shrewsbury was replaced by the unbending Puritan Sir Amyas Paulet, and she was removed to less salubrious surroundings. Paulet abruptly cut off her correspondence with the outside world.

By now, Mary was ill and depressed. Her son James, anxious to ingratiate himself with Elizabeth, had abandoned her. Frustrated by the years of confinement, she would condone any rash move to effect a change in her circumstances. Walsingham had infiltrated a spy, Gilbert Gifford, into her household and when a brewer who delivered beer offered to convey messages for her, Mary did not stop to think before plunging headlong into the trap.

Walsingham discovered that a group of young Catholic idealists, led by Sir Anthony Babington, were plotting to release Mary. It was easy to facilitate the correspondence between Mary and Babington, by smuggling the letters in and out of Chartley in the bottom of the brewer's beer-kegs. Rashly committing herself in writing, Mary gave her approval to all Babington's plans, in which the removal of Elizabeth was implicit. As soon as Walsingham's agent decoded the message, he saw that Mary had fallen into the trap. He drew a gallows on the letter and forwarded it to Walsingham. Walsingham forged a postscript, in which Mary asked for the names of the men involved in the conspiracy. He then re-sealed the letter and sent it to Babington. The trap snapped shut.

Babington and six fellow conspirators were arrested, hanged, drawn and quartered. At the end of September 1586 Mary was taken to Fotheringhay for trial. Always very insistent on her rights as a queen, if not so conscientious in fulfilling her responsibilities, Mary was still proclaiming her innocence. She told Paulet: 'As a sinner I am truly conscious of having offended my Creator, and I beg Him to forgive me, but as Queen and Sovereign I am aware of no fault or offence for which I have to render account to anyone below . . . As therefore I could not offend, I do not wish for pardon. I do not seek it, nor would I accept it from anyone living.'

There was no question that she was guilty and must die, but Elizabeth shrank from putting to death an anointed sovereign, a sister queen and kinswoman. The consequences did not bear thinking of. She was only too aware what the rest of the world would make of such a monstrous act. 'Princes, you know, stand upon stages so that their actions are viewed and beheld by all men; and I am sure my doings will come to the scanning of many fine wits, not only within the realm, but in foreign countries.'

She bemoaned the fact that

> since now it is resolved that my surety cannot be established without a princess's end, I have just cause to complain that I, who have in my time pardoned so many rebels, winked at so many treasons . . . should now be forced to this proceeding against such a person . . . What will they not now say when it shall be spread that for the safety of her life, a maiden queen could be content to spill the blood even of her own kinswoman?

Unlike her father and unusually for such a brutal age, Elizabeth possessed the quality of mercy. A king was 'scant well furnished', she said, 'if either he lacked justice, temperance, magnanimity, or judgement'. She was essentially humane. 'I may therefore full well complain that any man should think me given to cruelty . . . Yea, I protest I am so far from it that for mine own life, I would not touch her.'

As ever, she sought refuge in prevarication, telling a parliamentary delegation petitioning her to act: 'I shall pray you for this present to content yourselves with an answer without answer. Your judgement I condemn not, neither do I mistake your reasons, but pray you to accept my thankfulness, excuse my doubtfulness, and take in good part my answer answerless.'

The crisis of Mary Stuart's trial and execution put Elizabeth under enormous strain. She was as trapped as Mary, unable to find a way out. She hesitated and resisted pressure to sign the death warrant for many weeks. Yes, she wanted Mary dead; she wanted the nuisance dealt with, but not in such a way as to incur the opprobrium of her fellow sovereigns. In desperation, she suggested that Paulet find the means of shortening Mary's life; after all, he had been quick enough to sign up to the association. He was outraged: 'God forbid that I should make so foul a shipwreck of my conscience!'

Finally, on 1 February 1587 Elizabeth's secretary, William Davison, handed her a pile of papers for signature. She signed each one with barely a glance, pretending she did not know what they contained. Later, she protested that although she had signed the warrant, she had told Davison she did not want it to be executed until further notice. Burghley, Walsingham, Leicester and other members of the Council appended their signatures and decided that the warrant should be rushed to Fotheringhay without further delay, so that the execution could be carried out before the Queen changed her mind.

When she discovered that Mary was dead, Elizabeth was furious that her orders, as she saw them, had been countermanded. The Council, acting together, had seized the initiative and proceeded to carry out this terrible deed without her express permission. As a woman, Elizabeth's greatest fear was that her male counsellors would unite against her and overrule her wishes. This was the most flagrant example of it. They had plotted together to bring a queen down. They had exposed the limits of monarchy and, in executing an anointed sovereign, set a dangerous precedent for the future. It was incipient republicanism. She wrote to James of Scotland telling him how much she deplored 'the miserable accident, which far contrary to my meaning hath befallen'. She was innocent. Burghley was banished from her sight for four months and Davison sent to the Tower. Elizabeth collapsed in genuine grief. Authorizing her cousin's execution had been one of the severest tests of her queenship.

Never to meet in life, both queens would perhaps have been surprised to find themselves brought together in death, lying close to each other in Westminster Abbey. In spite of the long, destructive course of their relationship, something positive had come out of it. Mary's son, James VI of Scotland, would succeed the childless Elizabeth as James I of England, uniting the two realms under the crown, although they would not be politically integrated as Great Britain until the reign of James's great-granddaughter, Queen Anne, in 1707. Elizabeth and Mary had, after all, produced something far greater than themselves.

17

The Image of the Queen

WHEN ELIZABETH ASCENDED the throne, everyone confidently expected her to fulfil the first duty of a queen and the normal function of her sex by becoming a wife and mother. Since she declined to do this, she had to become something else. As a ruler, she had already been absorbed into the patriarchal system, de-sexed, elevated and hence transformed into a figure above and distinct from other women. If she was to continue to hold sway over recalcitrant men who resented female rule and over a far from united country, she could not allow her image to slip into that of ageing, childless spinster. Something else was needed to bolster her authority. Consciously or otherwise, she found she could rely on her sex to tap into the emotional power behind the image of wife-mother, particularly the most sacred mother of all, the Virgin Mary.

From the outset, Elizabeth affirmed her marriage to the kingdom and her fictional motherhood of the people. These were not novel concepts. Monarchs had always, in a mystic sense, been 'married' to their realms. The first queen regnant, Mary I, had used the mother image. Elizabeth assured her Parliament in 1563 that 'though after my death you may have many stepdames, yet shall you never have any a more mother [a more natural mother] than I mean to be unto you all'. Isaiah 49: 23 reads: 'And kings shall be thy nursing fathers and their queens shall be thy nursing mothers.' Elizabeth was often eulogized as the nursing mother of the English Church. When she made a progress to Norwich in 1578 the city's farewell oration addressed her as 'the mother and nurse of this whole common welth, and countrie', and said of the people's distress at her departure: 'How lamentable a thing it is, to pul away sucking babes from the breastes and bosomes of their most loving mothers.'

The need for a mother figure probably goes back to the beginning of human history. In replacing the Virgin Mary, or the mother figure once represented by the Goddess, Elizabeth was fulfilling the same universal psychological need.

A belief had developed since the Middle Ages that the anointed sovereign was God's earthly representative. Elizabeth's dual role as head of state and Supreme Governor of the Church placed her in a unique position, as the symbolic personification of the English Church and guardian of the 'true' faith. She united Church and state through herself in a spiritual marriage both with God and the nation. As a consecrated virgin, she was also – nun-like – a bride of Christ and, like the Virgin Mary, an intercessor with the supreme Deity for her people.

The idea of associating the Queen with the Virgin Mary was not new. The association of the feminine ideal, the sacred and the regal already existed long before Elizabeth came to the throne. Mary I's reign had seen extensive use of Marian iconography, which had traditionally been associated with that of queens consort, and highlighted the parallels between the two. Just as Catholics prayed to the Virgin Mary to intercede for them with God and her son, Jesus Christ, so queens consort were seen as loving mediators between the King and his people. Their coronation pageantry included the same paradox as existed in the Virgin's life: they were praised for their virginal chastity and for their fertility.

John Aylmer was the first to associate Elizabeth with the Virgin Mary, albeit for Protestant purposes. He did this by transforming the medieval figure of the Virgin as Mother of the Church into 'Mother England', who gave birth to the English Reformation. He invested Elizabeth with the qualities of Mother England, linking love of England and obedience to the Queen in strongly nationalistic terms.

It was not until the 1570s, however, that the cult of Elizabeth as the Virgin Queen began to take hold. She was in her late thirties and, although marriage negotiations would continue for another decade, it was generally recognized that she was nearing the menopause and was unlikely to have a child of her own. To elevate her virginity to a cult was to make a virtue out of necessity, and it grew in intensity with succeeding years as the ageing, mortal body became increasingly divorced from the youthful, goddess-like image. The papal bull of 1570, *Regnans in Excelsis*, excommunicating Elizabeth and giving Catholic assassins licence to kill her, transformed her into a Protestant saint virtually overnight. Suddenly faced with the alarming prospect of the Catholic Mary Stuart on the English throne, English Protestants began to appreciate the Queen they had, and the person of Elizabeth became very precious to them. In Parliament, they stopped haranguing her to get married; at court and in public – but only to some extent, since the country was far from united in religious belief – she became an object of worship.

It was no coincidence, then, that Elizabeth's Accession Day, 17 November, began to be celebrated as a sort of Protestant holy day. The first Accession Day began spontaneously in Oxford in 1570, but by 1576 it was recognized officially as a Church holiday with a specific service and liturgy. It was a day of public thanksgiving, sermons, bell ringing, bonfires, elaborate pageants and tournaments. Over time, the celebrations were extended to 19 November – St Elizabeth's Day in the Catholic calendar. The Queen's birthday, which fell on 7 September, became another occasion for public rejoicing with religious overtones. One prayer asked God to bless Elizabeth and curse her enemies. Some considered it a divine omen that Elizabeth shared the Virgin's birthday, the eve of the Feast of the Nativity of the Blessed Virgin Mary. This belief was intensified when her death – 24 March – coincided with the eve of the Annunciation of the Virgin Mary.

It may well be that with the demise of the Catholic calendar of holy days, the chief of which had coincided with the major festivals at court, Elizabeth's government had felt obliged to inaugurate some secular holidays. However, the appropriation of the former feast day of the Virgin for the Queen's birthday celebration, implying that Elizabeth was either a rival or a replacement for the Virgin Mary, offended Catholics and extreme Protestants alike.

While Protestant England banned religious images as idolatrous – falsifying, seductive distractions from the direct worship of God – images of the monarch were accorded the ceremonial deference formerly reserved for the holy. This was permissible, because the ruler was secular. The elevation of Elizabeth to the status once held by the

Virgin Mary followed a period of intense iconoclasm, when religious paintings and statues had been systematically destroyed and smashed. In pre-Reformation England the Virgin Mary had been held in profound esteem. Her image had been ubiquitous; many shrines and churches had been devoted to her and public spectacles and ceremonies held in her honour. Her demise must have left many people bereft, suffering from a deep sense of deprivation.

Fortuitously, the accession of a virgin queen suggested a means of filling the void by re-channelling the loyalty – and the emotional power that accompanied it – formerly given the Queen of Heaven to the Queen of England. The jewel-encrusted statue of the Virgin which had been cast out of the churches and monasteries and wayside shrines was replaced by the gorgeously arrayed, bejewelled figure of the Queen at court. She was carried on progress much as the Virgin had been carried in procession, so that her subjects could adore her. 'Hail Mary!' gave way to 'Long live Eliza!' To be visited by the Queen on progress was tantamount to having one's house or town blessed.

It is impossible to say for certain how much of this was orchestrated by the Queen and the court, and how much of it was a natural, spontaneous refocusing of the people's energies. Elizabeth had a powerful charisma and well understood how this was reinforced by magnificent displays of dress and elaborate jewellery. The royal wardrobe was a sort of props department to bolster the Queen's majestic image. Always careful with money, she treated it almost as a state treasure. A large number of people were employed making, maintaining, replenishing, repairing and recycling its contents.

Elizabeth used only two tailors between her accession and her death; they would make a toile and send it to a tailor in Paris, who used a woman Elizabeth's size to fit the gown exactly. Not only were the Queen's gowns superbly cut and styled, but she often copied the fashions of France and Spain, keeping up with the fashion news by having dolls or finished gowns sent from abroad. Others were employed acquiring the cloth of gold and silver tissue, the velvets, silks and satins denoting the Queen's status and embroidering them with the flowers she favoured – sometimes copied from those in her gardens, or else from illustrated herbals – or with motifs such as the letter S for 'Soverayne' in gold. The robes were too heavily embroidered to wash, so that Elizabeth, ever fastidious about personal cleanliness, would have them scented with rose water. When she had finished with them, they were often handed down to the ladies and gentlewomen of the Privy Chamber and the maids of honour as the perquisites of office.

For someone so conscious of her image, it is surprising that Elizabeth herself was slow to manipulate it in her portraiture. Unlike her father, whose image as a larger-than-life macho ruler was forged through his patronage of Hans Holbein, or even her sister Mary who employed Antonis Mor who painted her with the sort of guileless, transparent honesty that was one of her chief characteristics, Elizabeth appointed no official court painter. She had inherited an empty treasury and the money-saving instincts of her grandfather, Henry VII, so was probably chary of spending money on having herself painted. The nearest she came to official sponsorship was by commissioning Nicholas Hilliard to paint dozens of miniatures of her during the last two decades, giving them to courtiers and servants as tokens of her favour – to be worn rather as Catholics wore medals. She found she could rely on others, such as the favourites, Lord Leicester and Sir Christopher Hatton, as well as Sir William Cecil and Sir Henry Lee, to commission major portraits on her behalf. Her non-employment of a court painter meant that she had less control over how she was portrayed, while those who commissioned the portraits had their own agenda.

In order to exert some control over her image, a modicum of censorship was applied to the ordinary portrait. In 1563 and 1596 Cecil drafted proclamations ordering the destruction of non-authorized portraits of the Queen, while the later proclamation stipulated that all new images must be approved by George Gower, the Queen's Sergeant Painter. Gower's role also involved managing a large body of temporarily employed artists, reproducing portraits of the Queen from patterns based on some of the key images. Few portraits were made directly from life, especially as Elizabeth was not prepared to spare the time for sittings. One of her ladies would arrange for the props – some of the hundreds of gowns from the royal wardrobe, jewels and accessories – to be placed in a studio for the artist to copy, or she might even take the Queen's place for the pose.

The demand for the Queen's portrait was apparently very high from subjects 'both noble and mean'. To display her portrait in the home was a sign of unswerving loyalty, especially after the papal bull of 1570. The lowliest members of society are likely to have seen her image only on the coin of the realm.

With the exception of Federico Zuccaro's Darnley portrait of Elizabeth, commissioned by Leicester in 1575, which captures the full penetrating power of her black-eyed gaze from the life, no attempt was made to produce a true resemblance of the Queen in her portraits. Elizabeth the woman was irrelevant. What was being portrayed was the Queen's Majesty, her authority, wealth and greatness – the qualities that require absolute obedience. The portrayal of the face was less important than the detailed rendering of items of dress, jewellery and accessories, all of which were richly symbolic. Her preference for certain colours is well recorded. As she once remarked to the French ambassador, her colours were white and black, the first for virginity or virtue, the second for constancy. She was also portrayed in gold, silver, russet and crimson. After she fell ill with smallpox in 1562, Elizabeth seems to have begun to lose her hair and no portrait was complete without the red wig – the hair colour of the royal house.

The portraits had to demonstrate Elizabeth's right to rule, in spite of her sex. Her representation developed according to her status as an unmarried virgin queen. Initially, she was a virgin queen who might get married, so still nubile. Eventually, she was a virgin queen whose body was a static emblem of female virtue, the very embodiment of stable monarchy. The portraits subdue her sexuality in order to proclaim her power and in the process place her outside the realm of nature. This was imperative as she grew older when, goddess-like, she had to be seen to escape the constraints of time and space and appear immortal.

Elizabeth told her best artist, Nicholas Hilliard, that she disliked artful shadowing on the face, which was anyway coated with a concoction of lead, powder and egg white, giving it a mask-like appearance. Hilliard's jewel-like miniatures show an impossibly young Elizabeth with the flowing hair and uncovered bosom of the virgin and the unlined face and skin of youth, implying that her sexual intactness had brought with it resistance to bodily decay. Elizabeth's motto, *Semper Eadem*, came to signify not just constancy, integrity and singularity, but also a miraculous physical purity and immutability. However, the idea that the Queen's triumph over the flesh would ensure the same over time and death concealed an underlying anxiety about the future beyond her death.

Virginity was not the exclusive preserve of the Virgin Mary. Christianity had inherited from the classical world an assumption that virginity was powerful magic and conferred strength. The virgin body equated with wholeness, or holiness, and was charmed. Virginity was symbolic of political integrity and independence, making Elizabeth's virtue synonymous with the good and security of England. By devoting herself to God and keeping herself pure, Elizabeth would argue, she won His favour for her realm. In the 1580s, when England was feeling isolated and beleaguered as a Protestant nation under threat from more powerful Catholic neighbours, the Queen's virginity became emblematic of the defiant impregnability of the body politic.

This was the theme of the series of eight Sieve portraits, painted between 1579 and 1583. Accused of breaking her vow of chastity, Tuccia, the Vestal Virgin, had refuted the slander by filling a sieve with water from the Tiber and carrying it back to the Temple of Vesta without spilling a drop. The Queen holding a sieve invokes the magic power of chastity, demonstrated by Tuccia, to seal the leaky orifices of the female body, to make it impenetrable and, by inference, invulnerable. Elizabeth-Tuccia's virginity shows her more than a woman, more than human. She transcends the body of a weak and feeble woman, until she becomes the personification of mystical sovereignty. Similarly, in the Ermine portrait, the ermine on the Queen's arm symbolizes virginity, since according to legend it died if its white coat became soiled. The creature's gold collar in the painting is in the form of an open crown and, together with the sword of justice on the table close to the ermine, this insignia of royalty implies that the body politic, like the Queen's natural body, is pure, uncorrupted and strong.

The more precarious the Queen's power, the more extravagant were the claims of the royal portraits. They were weapons in an ideological and cultural struggle. Many portraits of Elizabeth were devised principally by her courtiers and involved complex allegorical and emblematic themes; as such they were the preserve of a small, ruling, male elite, whose privileged classical education enabled them to read their meaning. While ostensibly championing the Queen's virtues, their main purpose was to advance their patron's agenda or signal his indispensability. For instance, the Queen's old favourite, Sir Christopher Hatton, commissioned the Sieve portrait of 1583 to commemorate the success of his counsel in warning against the Anjou marriage, of which he had strongly disapproved. Sir Henry Lee commissioned the Ditchley portrait in 1592, depicting the Queen standing like the Queen of the Heavens, literally, on the top of the world – with the royal feet firmly planted on his home at Ditchley in Oxfordshire – perhaps as part of a general policy held by certain courtiers to encourage her to look outward, towards global expansion.

In the Rainbow portrait, the Queen is portrayed in masque costume as a goddess, her fingers touching a rainbow, on which the words 'No rainbow without the sun' are inscribed. A serpent embroidered on her left sleeve has a ruby in its mouth, denoting wise counsel. The dominant motif of counsel is continued in the eyes, ears and mouths dotted on the golden mantle. The portrait could only have been commissioned by one of the Cecils – William, or his son Robert, who succeeded him. As royal secretary, they both had sight of all official documents and controlled much of the intelligence system and they were advocating a policy of peace with Spain in the 1590s.

Portraiture was not the only expression of the cult of the Virgin Queen. Simultaneously, the discourse of courtly love was permeating the English court in poetry and pageantry. The Queen was addressed either as a saint or a goddess. Quasi-religious devotion to Elizabeth is used as a metaphor for erotic desire for her, which in turn is a metaphor for political loyalty to her. The Kenilworth entertainment of July 1575, staged by Leicester in his final bid to win the Queen, was the first hint of the idealization of Elizabeth's unmarried state which would become the central element in the courtly and popular expression of her cult.

As in other entertainments of this kind, Leicester's three-day extravaganza had an ulterior motive. He was hoping to further his military ambition by soliciting the Queen's support for England's participation in the revolt against Philip of Spain in the Netherlands. Unlike the

Queen and Cecil, Leicester and other militant Protestants wanted a foreign policy in which they could play heroic roles, incidentally defining a sphere of male action beyond the boundaries of Elizabeth's, who could not follow her father as an active leader on the battlefield. She was being put on a pedestal, leaving Leicester to play questing knight. But Elizabeth was not so easily manipulated. Not only did she refuse to play the marriage game at Kenilworth, but it was to be another ten years before she would change her foreign policy and agree to active military involvement in the Netherlands.

How far the cult of Elizabeth permeated society beyond the rarefied world of the court is open to speculation. Beneath the veneer of adulation were less savoury undertones. As an autonomous woman with political authority, Elizabeth was inevitably unsettling. Many of her subjects had ambiguous feelings about being ruled by a woman. She had come to the throne amid controversy about female rule, and then remained unmarried, contravening Protestant ideology and royal precedent and leaving the succession in doubt. Together with the love and respect Elizabeth undoubtedly inspired, there was antagonism towards a queen who refused to secure her people's future by providing a successor.

This manifested itself in malicious rumours. Elizabeth's government took adverse criticism of her extremely seriously and many people were brought before the courts for spreading slander about the Queen. The obvious target was her sexuality. Her indiscreet behaviour with Leicester quickly led to speculation that they were lovers. There were even rumours that she had children by him, that she went away on progress every summer in order to have those children. In 1587 a young man, Arthur Dudley, turned up in Spain, claiming to be the illegitimate son of the Queen and Leicester. Just as in Mary's reign after the disappointment of her false pregnancy, the longing for a king led to renewed 'sightings' of Edward VI in the 1580s and 1590s. To some extent, these rumours reflected a wish to imagine Elizabeth fulfilling her womanly function, but they also revealed a tendency to denigrate her as a whore, an incompetent female, unfit to rule.

In 1597 Simon Forman the astrologer recorded a dream in which Elizabeth was leaning over him, about to kiss him, when he awoke. It is not unusual to 'dream the Queen' in any century, but Forman's dream, in which Elizabeth has become both mother and sex object, indicates how deeply her image as Virgin Queen, quasi-divine goddess and mother of her people had penetrated the nation's psyche. It is testimony to the power of her personality and to her success as a ruler.

18

Eliza Triumphans

ELIZABETH REACHED HER apogee as queen with the defeat of the Spanish Armada in 1588. Like so much of Elizabeth's queenship, her role was pure theatre, it was inspirational, but it was one that was carefully orchestrated and built into mythic proportions after the event. Elizabeth herself had always believed in the wheel of fortune, which rose and dipped, bringing her from the depths of despair in her sister's reign to the throne, and which now, in the face of invasion, threatened to dip again, before rising miraculously. 'God blew and they were scattered,' proclaimed one of the medals struck in the wake of victory. But fate was not so random. The defeat of the Armada was largely attributable to the superior technology of the English ships and guns and the brilliant tactics deployed by Hawkins, Drake and the other English naval commanders – and all this in spite of the fact that the parsimonious Elizabeth kept her navy dangerously short of powder, shot and provisions.

By 1588 the struggle in the Netherlands, where English troops and money had been expended since 1585 in the rebels' cause after many years' surreptitious aid, and the undeclared war in the Indies between Spain and the English sea dogs, had driven Philip II to the limits of his very considerable patience. Drake's constant provocation and plundering of the Spanish treasure fleet on the way from the Indies was imperilling a major source of revenue to the perennially insolvent Spanish crown. It did not help that when Spanish ships bound for the Netherlands, laden with Genoese gold to pay Alva's troops, took shelter from a storm in an English port, Elizabeth seized the gold. Far from discouraging these piratical activities, Elizabeth herself was taking a share of the booty. The execution of Mary, Queen of Scots – who had bequeathed her claim to the English throne to Philip, as if it were in her gift to do so – provided a further incentive for Philip, backed by the Pope, to defeat and overthrow England's heretic Queen.

The legend of Elizabeth owes a great deal to the speech she is said to have made on the second day of her visit to the army camped at Tilbury. The idea for the Queen's visit emanated from the Earl of Leicester, the Lieutenant and Captain-General of her land forces. The favourite's public relations stunts were better than his military skills, which fortunately were not put to the test. The arrangement for Elizabeth's appearance at Tilbury was made *before* news of the English engagement of the Spanish fleet could reach her, but she made the speech knowing that the Armada was as good as defeated. For days, the navy, led by Lord Howard of Effingham, with Hawkins, Drake, Frobisher and the other skilled seamen under his command, had been using their intimate knowledge of the winds and tides off the south coast of England to provoke, harass and attack the cumbersome great ships of the Armada, advancing towards the Channel in stately formation. Their tactics prevented the Armada from anchoring off the Isle of Wight, as planned, or making any landfall along the south coast, driving it ever onwards towards Calais Roads, the only shelter to be found on the hostile French coast.

Here the Spanish commander, the Duke of Medina Sidonia, was forced to drop anchor, while he waited for word that Parma's army further up the coast at Dunkirk was ready, in its under-provisioned and leaky barges, to make the Channel crossing, theoretically at least under the protection of the Armada. Parma was dismayed that Medina Sidonia had brought the entire English fleet with him, rather than defeating it en route. Whether or not he would have embarked under these hazardous conditions is questionable, but the decision was taken from him when the English sent in fireships to break up the Armada and drive it from its anchorage. The plan succeeded beyond all expectation, since the terrified Spaniards, panicking at the sight of the hell-burners set loose among them, cut their cables, leaving at least 200 anchors behind as they fled. There was no possibility of a rendezvous with Parma now. The great Armada was at the mercy of the winds, as it was buffeted towards the dangerous shoals off the Dutch coast – where the rebels had removed all the markers –

and then pushed and tossed north towards the inhospitable coast of Scotland.

On the morning of Thursday, 8 August, as the battered remnants of the Armada were struggling through mountainous seas near the Shetlands and the Queen's victorious ships were returning to port, Elizabeth took barge at Whitehall for Tilbury, amid a cacophony of trumpets and the ringing of all the London church bells. No one in the capital could have been left in ignorance that she was going to review her troops. Reaching Tilbury at noon, she was greeted by the boom of cannon. Mounted on a white gelding, with the ageing and portly Leicester on one side and his stepson and the Queen's kinsman, the handsome young Robert Devereux, Earl of Essex on the other, Elizabeth rode through the camp. She had purposely come with a modest escort, the Earl of Ormonde carrying the Sword of State before her, and two pages in white velvet, one leading her horse, and the other ceremoniously carrying a silver helmet on a velvet cushion. The helmet, had she worn it, would have looked very strange atop her red wig and it is debatable whether Elizabeth, in a white velvet gown dripping with pearls and diamonds, really did wear a breastplate or carry a silver truncheon, as the myth-makers would have us believe. If she did, it was the only occasion that she ever donned something approximate to male dress.

It was during the first day at Tilbury that the Earl of Cumberland brought word of the Armada's fate. While the Queen was dining in state with Leicester in his pavilion, as all the army captains queued to kiss her hand, she received word that there was a possibility that Parma's army of 40,000 men would arrive with the day's tide. English intelligence was already well informed as to the unsuitability of the barges for the Channel crossing and, in the event, the report of Parma's imminent invasion proved false. If Parma did come, common sense and intelligence, if it could be gleaned, indicated that he would make the shortest crossing, landing on the east coast of Kent, near Margate. It is to be wondered, therefore, that Leicester had placed his army of 7,000 men north of the Thames at Tilbury. The spectacle of the Queen's visit to Tilbury was a distraction from the reality that the English were ill prepared to meet the invaders, that their forces were inadequately trained, armed and deployed and would have been no match for Parma's professional army of seasoned troops.

On the second day, the Queen made a formal review of her troops. Someone with Elizabeth's supreme command of oratory and the English language would not have missed the opportunity to address them:

> My loving people, I have been persuaded by some that are careful of my safety to take heed how I committed myself to armed multitudes, for fear of treachery. But I tell you that I would not desire to live to distrust my faithful and loving people. Let tyrants fear: I have so behaved myself that under God I have placed my chiefest strength and safeguard in the loyal hearts and goodwill of my subjects. Wherefore I am come among you at this time but for my recreation and pleasure, being resolved in the midst and heat of the battle to live and die amongst you all, to lay down for my God and for my kingdom and for my people mine honour and my blood even in the dust. I know I have the body but of a weak and feeble woman, but I have the heart and stomach of a king and of a king of England too – and take foul scorn that Parma or any prince of Europe should dare to invade the borders of my realm. To which rather than any dishonour shall grow by me, I myself will venter my royal blood; I myself will be your general, judge, and rewarder of your virtue in the field. I know that already for your forwardness you have deserved rewards and crowns, and I assure you in the word of a prince you shall not fail of them. In the meantime, my lieutenant general shall be in my stead, than whom never prince commanded a more noble or worthy subject. Not doubting but by your concord in the camp and valour in the field and your obedience to myself and my general, we shall shortly have a famous victory over these enemies of my God and of my kingdom.

Marvellous, rousing words, but did she say them? There has been some doubt. Certainly the speech sounds very like Elizabeth and deploys her known expertise with language. She disliked long harangues and this one, comprising 250 words, takes two and a half minutes to deliver. Elizabeth tended to use two chief contemporary styles in writing and speeches – one complex, often ambiguous, the other simple and direct – as the need served. In the Tilbury speech she uses the succinct, English mode to convey the royal will and message. It follows the general plan of Elizabeth's orations. She opens graciously, turns at once to business, presents her position, and then concludes with a brief but effective peroration that reiterates the main idea.

Elizabeth was delivering the speech in the open air on a flat field on a windy day and tailored it accordingly. The speech is full of doublets and triplets, a device well suited to the outdoors with its noise and distractions. If the listeners missed a few words, they could still get the sense of the whole by the constant use of repetitions such as 'faithful and loving people', 'loyal hearts and goodwill of my subjects', 'weak and feeble woman', 'heart and stomach of a king', 'chiefest strength and safeguard' and 'for my God and for my kingdom and for my people'.

It is reasonable to assume that the speech was Elizabeth's own composition; if she did not give the exact version that has come down to posterity then it was probably something very similar. Most unusually for Elizabeth, the speech does not appear to have been printed and disseminated afterwards, or, if it was, no copy survives. The only explanation for this rare failure to grasp a propaganda opportunity was that she was distracted in the weeks following the defeat of the Armada. Her beloved Leicester died and she was grieving for him.

The first printed version of the Tilbury speech, as we know it, emerged in *Cabala, Mysteries of State, in Letters of the Great Ministers of King James and King Charles*, published in 1654, where it forms part of an ingratiating letter from Dr Lionel Sharp to the first Duke of Buckingham. The letter was probably written after Buckingham's first expedition to Spain in 1623, when he was trying to arrange a marriage between Prince Charles and the Infanta. Sharp, who had been at Tilbury with Leicester as chaplain, comments that Elizabeth made an excellent oration at the camp. According to Sharp, who tended to exaggerate his own role at the centre of affairs and cannot be wholly relied upon, he was asked to read the speech to the army again next day, after the Queen's departure for St James's. He kept the text. 'No man hath it but myself, and such as I have given it to.'

Other versions of the speech emerged, probably based on copies of the original text rather than the speech itself. Of course, only a few of those actually present at Tilbury would have caught the Queen's words, or been able to repeat them with any accuracy.

During the autumn thanksgiving services were held throughout the country, culminating on 4 December 1588 in the warrior-queen's triumphal procession in a mock-Roman chariot decorated with golden lions and dragons and topped with an imperial crown to St Paul's. She knelt on the cathedral steps to give thanks to God, in full view of the people, for her great victory, before entering the great west door for the service. Captured Spanish flags, banners and other booty from the Armada were paraded down the aisle and draped round the altar.

It is salutary to know that beyond the spectacle was an uglier reality. Far from giving her soldiers and seamen the 'rewards and crowns' she had promised them 'in the word of a prince', they had been discharged shortly after Tilbury without pay. Seamen of Devon and Cornwall were left to make their own way home as best they could, although Howard of Effingham, Hawkins and Drake dug deep into their own pockets to make sure that their men had a few pence at least for risking their lives and saving the country from foreign occupation. The treasury was all but empty, but by the time Elizabeth rode to St Paul's in triumph many of the brave men she had lauded at Tilbury and who had harried the Spanish ships to their destruction were dying in the streets of their wounds, hunger and disease.

Naturally, Protestant England's victory over the Catholic-inspired Armada was seen as the miraculous sign of God's intervention to protect His chosen people from the Antichrist. The ruling elite at court sought to emphasize Elizabeth's personal role in the victory and to build it to mythic proportions for its own purposes. The Queen was to be symbolic of an emergent militant England, an imperial power, and, by extension, a unified political power she did not actually command. In reality, she ruled over a country divided in religion and in severe financial straits, as it embarked on more than a decade of warfare with Spain.

Elizabeth herself loathed war, regarding it as a waste of money. Unable to take the field herself as a woman, it was an area where she lacked control – as Leicester's campaign in the Netherlands after 1585 had shown all too clearly. Against her express wishes, he had accepted the governorship offered by the rebels, bestowed countless knight-hoods, and squandered her carefully hoarded treasure without rendering the proper accounting that she repeatedly requested. Nor was she altogether convinced of the value of imperialist expansion. Tilbury provided the ideal occasion to link the Queen with the Armada's defeat, incidentally disguising the fact that her prevarication and cheeseparing attitude to her navy had almost jeopardized the victory.

Elizabeth's chastity, or virtue, was closely associated with England's impregnability and welfare. Elizabeth the Queen represented the body politic, but she was also a woman: hence, the defeat of the Armada could be expressed in sexual terms. The attack on England could be seen as an assault, or a rape. Nowhere is this idea more perfectly illus-trated than in the three extant Armada portraits. Just as Elizabeth had compared herself with her father in the Tilbury speech, so the portrait depicts her in a bodice shaped like a breastplate and enormous padded sleeves reminiscent of Holbein's macho depiction of Henry VIII. In the place where the muscular and masculine Henry has his codpiece, Elizabeth displays a white ribbon from which hangs a giant pearl, symbolic of her chastity. Indeed, she is bestrewn with pearls, many of them probably looted from Spanish treasure ships. The triangular composition of the portrait, drawing the eye from the two sea scenes on either side of the background down the length of the ropes of pearls in a V to the pearl placed at the Queen's pudendum, insists on the pearl's emblematic significance.

Behind the Queen's head to the right of the portrait is the storm-tossed Armada in dark seas; Elizabeth stands resolutely with her back to the turmoil and darkness, confident in the power of the Protestant wind which God has used to destroy the enemy of His Church and people. On the other side, to which her luminous face is turned reflecting the light, is her own navy on calm seas, bathed in light. On the arm of the Queen's chair, behind her, is the carved figure of a mermaid, representing the dangerous and destructive possibilities of uncontrolled female sexuality – the obverse of Elizabeth's chastity. Her right hand rests delicately but decidedly on the globe, caressing that portion of it that represents America; by 1588 the colony of

Virginia had been established as the foundation of the British Empire in the New World, although the English hold was still far from secure. The imperial crown, hers by hereditary right, is confidently placed at her right elbow, so that Elizabeth appears not only as the ruler of a victorious realm, but also as an aspiring empress of the world.

19

The Setting Sun

MANY OF POSTERITY'S most enduring images of Elizabeth and her era derive from the last decade of her reign. It was seen as a time of dashing chivalric adventurers and of the greatest flowering of English literature, most notably in the works of William Shakespeare, which still dominate the world stage today. At the centre of this golden age – its inspiration and patroness – was Elizabeth, hailed as Gloriana, Cynthia, Astraea and the Faerie Queene. She was the Virgin Queen, the goddess, who with her eternal youth and ageless beauty ruled over men's hearts.

There was a dark underside to all this. The assertion that Elizabeth ruled as a goddess among men, eternally virginal and ageless, became more strident in the 1590s, as she entered her sixties and her death inevitably drew closer. The more decrepit the reality, the more excessive was the adulation. It was a sign of desperate insecurity, as the childless Queen was still refusing to name her successor. Either men wanted the Queen to live for ever, or they were impatient for the coming of a king. Isaac Oliver was one of the few artists privileged to draw the Queen from life and had been so rash as to depict her in 1592 as she really was: the red hair, obviously false; the long thin face, gaunt and wrinkled, with its sunken cheeks; the hooded, watchful eyes, so like those of her grandfather, Henry VII; the thin lips carefully closed to conceal discoloured teeth and toothless gums.

Perhaps stemming from insecurity about her looks as a young woman, and encouraged by years of flattery from aspiring suitors and fawning courtiers, Elizabeth was inordinately vain. The French ambassador, André Hurault de Maisse, noticed how she would constantly speak of her beauty, fishing for compliments. It was not altogether unfounded. The Venetian ambassador reported that he could still see the traces of beauty in her. She would proudly draw attention to her exquisite white hands with their long, thin fingers, by drawing her gloves on and off. Thanks to her natural gracefulness, fine posture, spare diet and lifelong habit of exercise, she had retained her youthful figure, so that from a distance, according to one observer, she looked 'no more than twenty years of age'.

Elizabeth was extremely sensitive about her age. When one of her bishops was tactless enough to preach a sermon in which he referred to a time of life 'wherein men begin to carry a calendar in their bones, the sense begins to fail, the strength to diminish, yea all the powers of the body daily to decay', Elizabeth impatiently pushed open the window of the royal closet, where she sat during services in her chapel, and shouted that 'he should have kept his arithmetic to himself'. Her temper was not improved by careless young maids of honour who could not be bothered to do their job properly. Lady Mary Howard had failed to bring her cloak at the hour when the Queen liked to walk in the garden and answered back rudely when reprimanded. Elizabeth was furious: 'Out with such ungracious, flouting wenches!' she fulminated. She had always had a fiery temper and a tendency to lash out at those closest to her, but her older female attendants, such as Lady Dorothy Stafford, Lady Mary Scudamore and Mrs Mary Ratcliffe, who had been with her for years, understood her many cares and preoccupations and made allowances.

The Queen still possessed a powerful aura and the ability to charm. De Maisse noticed that 'she preserves a great gravity amidst her people' and that 'she walks in a manner marvellous haughty'. Paul von Hentzer watched her process to chapel at Greenwich in 1598:

> Her air was stately, her manner of speaking mild and obliging . . . as she went along in this state and magnificence, she spoke very graciously, first to one, then to another . . . in English, French and Italian . . . Whoever speaks to her, it is kneeling; now and then she raises some with her hand . . . Wherever she turned her face as she was going along, everybody fell down on their knees . . . In the ante-chapel where we were, petitions were presented to her, and she received them, most graciously, which occasioned the acclamation of 'God save Queen Elizabeth!' She answered it with 'I thank you my good people.'

Foreigners remarked on the curious custom of the Virgin Queen leaving her breasts uncovered, 'as all the English ladies have it, till they marry'. A German visitor in 1595 noted that 'over her breast, which was bare, she wore a long filigree lace shawl, on which sat a hideous large black spider that looked as if it were natural and alive.' When de Maisse first entered the royal presence, Elizabeth was recovering from some minor illness and she received him in her undress. His description is of a curiously eccentric figure:

> She was strangely attired in a dress of silver cloth, white and crimson, or silver 'gauze', as they call it. This dress had slashed sleeves lined with red taffeta, and was girt about with other little sleeves that hung down to the ground, which she was for ever twisting and untwisting. She kept the front of her dress open, and one could see the whole of her bosom . . . and often she would open the front of this robe with her hands as if she was too hot . . . On her head she wore a garland of the same material and beneath it a great reddish-coloured wig, with a great number of spangles of gold and silver, and hanging down over her forehead some pearls, of no great worth . . . Her bosom is somewhat wrinkled . . . but lower down her flesh is exceeding white and delicate.

In conversation with de Maisse, Elizabeth would call herself 'old and foolish', but in reality she was as sharp as ever. He concluded that 'she is a very great princess who knows everything' – as indeed she should, she reminded him, as she had reigned for forty years. She had once commented sagely that 'Men do adore the rising than the setting sun.' James of Scotland was tacitly considered to be her most likely successor and Elizabeth cannot have remained ignorant that many of her leading ministers and courtiers, from Sir Robert Cecil and the Earl of Essex downwards, were in correspondence with him. Men were showing her less reverence now her life and reign were drawing to a close. She was not so vain or foolish that she did not know what was happening.

Now, when she made her summer progresses, the voices of reluctant hosts grew louder and uglier as they warned the Queen away from their homes. Times were hard. They had done their sums and there was nothing to be gained any more from offering the Queen hospitality. Even Sir Henry Lee, who had commissioned the Ditchley portrait after Elizabeth's visit to his home in Oxfordshire in

1592, did not scruple to write to Sir Robert Cecil eight years later, excusing himself from receiving his sovereign. All his efforts to court royal favour had been a waste. He had not been rewarded with high office. He was not prepared to spend any more: 'my estate without my undoing cannot bear it, my continuance in her court has been long, my charge great, my land sold and debts not small: how this will agree with entertaining of such a prince your wisdom can best judge.'

After the glory of the Armada, the last decade of Elizabeth's reign was full of troubles, a time of prolonged war with Spain, high taxation, inflation, failed harvests and epidemics. Vagrants were a scourge, their ranks swelled by deserters from the army and navy, so that it was said that 'the Queen is troubled wherever she takes the air with these miserable creatures.' At court, self-interest, greed and venality were rife. Bribery had become endemic, even among the judges, and there was a 'black market' in court offices, which were overtly traded. When Elizabeth had first appointed Sir William Cecil, now Lord Burghley, to office, she trusted that he would 'not be corrupted with any manner of gift'. Burghley – first, always and last the Queen's servant – might not have been corrupted, but as Master of the Court of Wards he was pocketing considerable sums in 'arrangement' fees. Many blamed Elizabeth for not paying her servants properly, but she in turn was being systematically fleeced, especially by corruption among the commanders of her sea and land forces.

Not surprisingly, Elizabeth cultivated more than ever a public image of quasi-divinity, as the fissures in her government started to widen. Dissatisfaction often took the form of revived doubts as to the efficacy and validity of female sovereignty. There was a re-emergence of misogyny – even an increase in witchcraft trials. De Maisse observed that although Elizabeth was still greatly loved by the people, 'if by chance she should die, it is certain that the English would never again submit to the rule of a woman.'

Elizabeth's grip seemed to be slackening. Long-standing counsellors were dying and she was not replacing them; the Council, which had consisted of twenty-one members at the outset of her reign, was down to eleven. She was reluctant to create new peers and mean with her knighthoods. The rewards of royal service were much diminished; no wonder it was degenerating into a free-for-all. Some of the angriest scenes of the reign took place in Parliament over the crown's flagrant abuse of monopolies. Poverty forced the Queen, as the fount of all patronage, to reward her favoured courtiers with these monopolies – taxes on the import of commodities or domestic manufactures – rather than with much depleted crown lands, so shifting the cost of royal largesse from the crown to the commonwealth.

In this way, she financed her favourite, Robert Devereux, Earl of Essex, by granting him the lucrative 'farm of sweet wine' for a ten-year period. The monopoly would revert to the crown on Michaelmas Day 1600; it must have seemed an unimaginable length of time to the twenty-three-year-old. It suited Elizabeth admirably that young Essex was one of the poorest noblemen in the kingdom, since she liked to bestow her largesse on men who had no fortune of their own, who therefore found themselves entirely beholden to her. By the time the lease expired, Essex was in disgrace and Elizabeth declined to renew it. Essex, encumbered by an extràvagant lifestyle and debt, was ruined. It tipped the mercurial and unstable courtier over the edge into rebellion.

But before that, Essex was Elizabeth's last love. Tall, auburn-haired, gracefully athletic, cultured and chivalrous, he was very much Elizabeth's ideal man. It helped that he was Leicester's stepson. Elizabeth might even have seen in the young man the son they had never had together. Essex's mother was Elizabeth's kinswoman, Lettice Knollys, who had long ago incurred her jealousy and banishment from court for her secret and underhand marriage to Leicester. His natural father, the first Earl of Essex, boasted among an array of noble ancestors Edward III and the Plantagenets; he had died of disease in Ireland, losing his fortune in the Queen's cause.

The charming youth was able to make Elizabeth feel young again. 'When she is abroad, nobody near her but my Lord of Essex, and at night my Lord is at cards, or one game or another with her, that he cometh not to his lodgings till birds sing in the morning.' He filled an emotional void in Elizabeth's life when she was lonely and vulnerable. Her beloved Leicester was dead and soon she would lose her old friend and admirer, Sir Christopher Hatton. Essex's rival for the Queen's favour, Sir Walter Raleigh, was banished from court in 1592 for conducting a secret affair with her maid of honour, Elizabeth Throckmorton, and marrying without the Queen's consent. It was not so much a case of sexual jealousy; after all, when Essex married Sir Philip Sidney's widow, Frances Walsingham, she dismissed it as unimportant, something far less than the love they shared. In Raleigh's case, she was angry that a favoured courtier and one of her maids of honour should deceive her in this way. It would be five years before Raleigh could find his way back into royal favour, leaving the field clear for his young rival.

Courtiers who wanted to win the Queen's favour had to speak the language of love to her. Essex was able to carry off the absurdity of playing lovesick suitor to a woman thirty years his senior with apparent ease, writing her passionate love letters. It might have been Essex who commissioned Hilliard to paint him as the *Young Man among the Roses*. Certainly, the miniature depicted someone very like him, apparently pining for his love, symbolically wearing the Queen's colours of black and white and surrounded by her favourite flower and emblem, the white eglantine. It was the sort of gracious compliment Elizabeth relished.

The charismatic Essex was a disruptive and ultimately destructive influence. Harmony, which Elizabeth had always encouraged among counsellors who operated in friendly rivalry, gave way to factionalism, as Essex, representing the old aristocratic values of natural law and martial valour, vied with Sir Robert Cecil, the modern, professional administrator, to influence the direction of royal policy. Lord Burghley had been one of Essex's guardians as a boy and he retained a modicum of respect for the old man, but he bitterly resented the fact that he was quietly grooming his son, Sir Robert Cecil, as his successor. Surely he, Essex, as a leading member of the old nobility, had a natural right to be the Queen's chief counsellor; more than that, he wanted total domination of the Queen's government.

For forty years Elizabeth had governed by consensus; she was hardly likely to change now. Nor was she so besotted as to give in to Essex's pleas for the post of Secretary of State, vacant after the death of Sir Francis Walsingham, especially when there was a better man for the job. Sir Robert Cecil was the antithesis of Essex. Crippled by a spinal injury when his nurse dropped him as a baby, he was clever, cool and calculating, where Essex was rash, impulsive, a man of action. Pressed for a decision, Elizabeth, as ever, took refuge in prevarication. The post remained unfilled for the time being.

If Essex could not win political advancement for himself, he was determined to promote the cause of his 'clients', Anthony and Francis Bacon. The Bacons were Burghley's nephews, but he was not prepared to further their ambitions to the detriment of his own son. They switched their allegiance to Essex, who showed his lack of judgement by putting Francis forward for the post of Attorney General. He was hardly qualified, but Essex pestered the Queen remorselessly, until she was 'heard to mutter that she would 'seek all England for a solicitor', rather than give the job to Bacon.

Essex's failure to impose his will on the Queen badly damaged his standing at court but, undeterred, he sought to upstage the Cecils by setting up an independent foreign-intelligence-gathering department as a rival to Burghley's, under the aegis of Anthony Bacon. The upshot of this was the 'discovery' of a Spanish-inspired plot to kill the Queen. 'I have discovered a most dangerous and desperate treason,' Essex wrote self-importantly to a friend. 'The point of conspiracy was her Majesty's death. The executioner should have been Dr Lopez; the manner poison.'

Under torture, various so-called conspirators pointed the finger at the Queen's physician, Dr Roderigo Lopez, a Portuguese Jew. In vain, Lopez explained that Walsingham had encouraged his correspondence with the Spanish court to pass false information to the enemy; unfortunately, Walsingham was no longer around to verify Lopez's version of events. In Essex's excitable mind, it was essential to prove the existence of the plot and the efficacy of his intelligence service by making the Queen believe her life was really in danger. Elizabeth was less than convinced but, inevitably, the plot took on a momentum of its own. Lopez was duly found guilty and, after three months' delay in which Elizabeth hesitated to sign the warrant, he was executed.

Elizabeth's susceptibility to flattery had encouraged Essex to believe he would be able to manipulate her, but this was proving far from the case. He failed to appreciate the power of her intellect or her strength of character. Rash and impulsive himself, he could not understand the Queen's cautious approach or her tendency to prevaricate, which had always served her well. Elizabeth knew her own mind, even when she procrastinated, but Essex dismissed it as womanly weakness. He began to treat her dismissively as a typically unpredictable, wilful and irrational woman – and an old one at that. In a court riddled with resentment at the lack of royal largesse and tired of the old Queen's regime, Essex became the most vociferous voice of dissent, telling the French ambassador that 'they laboured under two things at this Court, delay and inconstancy, which proceeded chiefly from the sex of the Queen.'

Nowhere was this more apparent than when the two clashed over war. The Queen and the Cecils, conscious of the depleted state of the treasury, were united on a cautious and largely defensive maritime strategy, whereas Essex – who had espoused Leicester's stance as defender of the beleaguered Protestant cause in Europe – advocated military engagement on the Continent to quell the power of Catholic Spain and prevent an attack on England. Left to herself, Elizabeth would have liked to restrict military activity to the artificial world of the tournament and joust, the Accession Day tilts, of which Essex had made himself the undisputed hero.

Given a command and let off the leash, Essex soon realized all Elizabeth's worst fears. At Cadiz, the Queen's instructions were to make a quick, pre-emptive strike; instead, Essex showed every sign of hijacking the whole expedition to suit his own view of how England should fight the war. He quarrelled with his fellow commander, the Lord Admiral, Howard of Effingham. He took the town, but he was so intent on plundering and laying it waste that he failed to take account of a merchant fleet, laden with £3 million worth of goods, moored in the harbour. Similarly, when he was sent to destroy Philip's new Armada in Spanish ports, he disobeyed instructions and dashed off to the Azores on a useless quest to intercept the Spanish treasure fleet. It was Elizabeth's nightmare scenario: England left unprotected with Spanish ships roaming freely in the Channel, while her own fleet had been taken off on Essex's mad quest. By the time he did return to England, much of the booty he had taken at Cadiz seemed to have gone astray. Elizabeth was absolutely furious at this poor return on her investment and ordered an investigation into the disappearance of the prize goods.

Essex had flouted his sovereign's explicit commands and she was not slow to retaliate. Sir Robert Cecil was given the coveted post of Secretary of State. Howard of Effingham was created Earl of Nottingham, with the letters patent mentioning his distinguished service at Cadiz, a glory Essex felt belonged to him alone. When he tried to publish a pamphlet emphasizing his heroic role in the Cadiz expedition, Elizabeth had it suppressed. Victory belonged to the Queen, not the subject. It seemed that Essex – whose militant policy accorded well with the prevalent mood of nationalistic Protestantism – was trying to subvert the Queen's power and cultivating public popularity in opposition, or as an alternative focus, to her.

The increasingly strained relationship between the Queen and her favourite finally exploded in a Council meeting in 1598 over the question of whom to appoint as Lord Deputy in Ireland. Essex belligerently suggested Sir George Carew, a supporter of the Cecils. Elizabeth, well aware of the intensification of factionalism at her court since Essex's return from Cadiz, spurned his suggestion. With studied insolence, the Earl turned his back on the Queen. Infuriated, she boxed his ears, bidding him go and be hanged. Essex then did the unthinkable. He reached for his sword, at which Nottingham stepped forward to interpose himself between the Queen and the madman. Shouting that he would not have put up with such an affront to his dignity even at the hands of Henry VIII, Essex stormed out of the Council chamber. That was surely the point: he would never have dared behave so disrespectfully to a king.

Essex genuinely believed that the Queen owed him an apology. Lord Keeper Egerton tried to give him some friendly advice. It was not for monarchs to apologize. Even if the Queen had given cause for offence, it was Essex's duty to 'sue, yield and submit to your sovereign'. Essex was unable to contain his fury, returning a reply that was revolutionary in its doctrine: 'What, cannot princes err? Cannot subjects receive wrong? Is an earthly power or authority infinite?'

He would have sulked in the country indefinitely, but for the fact of Lord Burghley's death in August 1598. It was imperative for Essex to return to court if he wanted to be a beneficiary of the general reshuffle. Much to his amazement, the Queen at first refused to receive him. He confidently expected to obtain Burghley's lucrative office, the Mastership of the Court of Wards, and wrote indignantly to protest when he did not. The only way he could think of to win back the Queen's favour was to offer his services as her commander in Ireland, to quell the rebellion of Hugh O'Neill, Earl of Tyrone. Having plenty of experience by now of Essex's reckless behaviour on military expeditions and his disregard for orders, Elizabeth seriously doubted his ability for the task, but no one else could be found to do the job.

Ireland was to be Essex's nemesis. No effort was spared to give him all he needed in terms of men, money and provisions. All he had to do was carry out the Queen's instructions by seeking an immediate confrontation with the rebel Tyrone in his Ulster stronghold. Four months later, Essex still had not done so, and his fine army was being depleted by disease. He began to talk of deferring the invasion of Ulster until the following year. Elizabeth, as ever impotent in the military field owing to her sex, could only watch the unfolding disaster in mounting fury. Nothing could have prepared her, however, for his next stunt. He wrote that he had agreed a truce with Tyrone, but failed to apprise the Queen of its terms. 'You have prospered so ill for us by your warfare as we cannot but be very jealous lest you should be as well overtaken by the treaty,' she wrote. Her indignation was justified: the terms as good as gave Ireland back to the Roman allegiance and the Irish people, showing Essex to be a man of the most spectacular misjudgement.

In late September 1599, the Queen was at Nonsuch when Essex suddenly burst without warning into her bedchamber. He had ridden post-haste from Ireland, having impetuously decided that the only way to explain his conduct was to the Queen in person. Without even bothering to stop to clean the mud of the journey off him or announce himself properly, he strode resolutely towards her apartments. He found Elizabeth 'newly up', still in her undress, her wig on its stand, her face not made up. But she had her wits about her. Realizing that Essex might have brought what was left of the army with him, she was careful to conceal her outrage. She talked to him calmly and then suggested he go to change, before they met again.

Having ascertained that the Earl's arrival did not herald a coup d'état, the Queen's attitude was markedly cooler when she received him later in the day. Why had he deserted his post without a warrant? How could he justify his conduct in Ireland? Without listening to his excuses, she lambasted him for his disobedience and for disregarding her wishes, especially in bestowing countless knighthoods. Why, she mocked him, the Irish were laughing that he never lifted a sword except to dub a knight!

Guilty of gross contempt and disobedience, Essex had lost the Queen's favour and could not hope to return to court. He had badly underestimated her. By unhappy coincidence, his monopoly on the importation of sweet wines was just about to expire. He wrote begging to 'kiss her fair correcting hand', but she knew what he was about. If she did not renew the monopoly he would be ruined. She decided that the revenues should return to the crown. He had already contemplated rebellion, fantasizing about a situation where Elizabeth would be forced to listen to his demands and grant them. Now he embarked on a treasonable correspondence with James of Scotland, inviting his support. Whether he imagined that he would dethrone Elizabeth and hold the regency or that James of Scotland would succeed straight away with Essex the kingmaker his right-hand man is open to conjecture.

By the beginning of 1601, Essex House on the Strand was a hot-bed of anti-court activity. A group of conspirators were meeting at the lodgings of Essex's friend, the Earl of Southampton, to discuss Essex's proposals for seizing the court, the Tower, and the City to force the Queen to change her advisers, namely, to replace Robert Cecil with Robert Devereux. Violence against the Queen's person was not ruled out. There was great unease at court. Elizabeth's godson, Sir John Harington, who was regretting that he had accepted a knighthood from Essex in Ireland, wrote to a friend: 'The madcaps are all in a riot, and much evil threatened.' The Queen

is quite disfavoured, and much unattird, and these troubles waste her muche . . . Each new message from the City doth disturb her, and she frowns on all the ladies. I had a sharp message from her brought by my Lord Buckhurst, namely thus, 'Go tell that witty fellow, my godson, to get home; it is no season now to foole it here.' . . . I must not say much, even by this trustie and sure messenger; but the many evil plots and designs have overcome her Highness' sweet temper. She walks much in her privy chamber, and stamps with her feet at ill news, and thrusts her rusty sword at times into the arras in great rage.

On Saturday, 7 February, Essex's followers ostentatiously attended a special performance at the Globe of William Shakespeare's *Richard II* with its politically contentious deposition scene. As Elizabeth wearily told William Lambarde, Keeper of the Records at the Tower, 'I am Richard II. Know ye not that?' She must have been aware that it was only one of a number of plays in the last decade of her reign in which the problems of kingship and of a state in crisis were explored and developed. That evening, Essex was summoned to appear before the Council, but refused. All hope of taking the court by surprise was lost.

The next morning, 8 February 1601, he and about 200 young noblemen and gentlemen made their way into the City, with Essex shouting, 'For the Queen! For the Queen! A plot is laid for my life!' Cecil had hurriedly sent a message to the Lord Mayor and a herald was proclaiming Essex a traitor in the streets of London. Essex had been immensely popular while he was the Queen's favourite, but now he found his support melting away. The citizens of London remained mute and unresponsive and at the word 'traitor' many of his followers slipped away. The Earl returned to Essex House by water. That evening, after burning incriminating correspondence, he surrendered and was put under arrest. Less than two weeks later, he and his fellow conspirators were brought to trial. The guilty verdict was inevitable and he was condemned to death. This time, Elizabeth behaved with uncharacteristic haste, signing Essex's death warrant within twenty-four hours. He was beheaded within the confines of the Tower.

It is a wonder that Elizabeth tolerated the antics of this deranged young man so long. Normally such a shrewd judge of character, she had been foolishly fond and over-indulgent of him. Her crown had been in jeopardy, perhaps even her life, but in the final resort the establishment had rallied round.

In the aftermath of Essex's insurrection, she was depressed. She would still weep for Lord Burghley, who had been dead three years now. She continued to keep a sword by her side. Sir Robert Sydney wrote to Sir John Harington: 'I do see the Queen often; she doth wax weak since the late troubles . . . she walketh out but little, meditates much alone, and sometimes writes in private to her best friends.' With a slight limp now, Elizabeth no longer danced, but had always enjoyed watching others. 'The Queen smiled at the ladies,' Sydney continued, describing Elizabeth's visit to his home, 'who in their dances often came up to the steps on which the seat was fixed to make their obeisance, and so fell back into their order again.' She ate little and 'at going upstairs she called for a staff, and was much wearied in walking about the house.'

She rallied herself to address a delegation of Parliament, assembled in the Council chamber at Whitehall, for the last time. She had taken note of parliamentary opposition to monopolies and promised to look into the matter. Little had been done to address the issue, but now she deftly met their criticism with a gracious response, which quite disarmed them. The speech has come to be known as her Golden Speech and it was effectively her farewell:

> There is no jewel, be it never so rich a price, which I set before this jewel – I mean your loves. For I do more esteem it than any treasure or riches . . . and though God has raised me high, yet this I count the glory of my crown: that I have reigned with your loves. This makes me that I do not so much rejoice that God hath made me to be a queen, as to be a queen over so thankful a people. Therefore I have cause to wish nothing more than to content the subjects, and that is a duty which I owe. Neither do I desire to live longer days than that I may see your prosperity . . . My heart never was set on worldly goods, but only for my subjects' good. What you bestow on me, I will not hoard it up, but receive it to bestow on you again . . . There will never queen sit in my seat with more zeal to my country, care to my subjects, and that will sooner with willingness venture her life for your good and safety, than myself. For it is not my desire to live nor reign longer than my life and reign shall be for your good. And though you have had and may have many princes more mighty and wise sitting in this seat, yet you never had or shall have any that will be more careful and loving.

When she finished, she commanded the Speaker, 'before these gentlemen depart into their countries, you bring them all to kiss my hand.'

Elizabeth spent her last Christmas at Whitehall. It was particularly jolly, with the Queen in good spirits. In January she moved to Richmond, in foul weather, and was able to give audience to the Venetian ambassador, who was impressed by her 'lively wit'. At the end of that month, decline set in. Her dear cousin, Lady Nottingham, died, plunging her into depression. Her coronation ring, which had become embedded in her flesh, had to be sawn off. The ring had been the symbol of Elizabeth's marriage to her kingdom; now it seemed that she and her beloved people were being torn asunder. Her godson Harington came to court and 'found her in most pitiable state'. He tried to cheer her up, reading her one or two of his rhyming epigrams. 'When thou dost feel creeping time at thy gate,' she told him, 'these fooleries will please thee less; I am past my relish for such matters.' Next her young kinsman, Robert Carey, tried to cheer her by saying how well she looked. 'Nay, Robin,' she told him, 'I am not well.'

Elizabeth was refusing to eat or take physic. She might have been suffering from a septic throat, for at some point an abscess burst and she felt a little better, but, in reality, she had lost the will to live. She sank down on the cushions strewn about her chamber and lay for hours, staring at nothing, sucking her finger. Sir Robert Cecil ventured boldly, 'Your Majesty, to content the people, you must go to bed.'

'Little man, little man,' she roused herself to reprove him, 'the word *must* is not used to princes.'

Eventually, Nottingham persuaded her to go to bed. Her dear William Whitgift, Archbishop of Canterbury, knelt beside her, holding her hand and praying aloud. She had lost the power of speech and frowned when the archbishop prayed for her longer life, but when he spoke of heaven and its joys, she would press his hand. Whenever he stopped, she nudged him to continue. In the early hours of 24 March 1603, in her seventieth year, Elizabeth slipped away 'mildly like a lamb, easily like a ripe apple from the tree'.

Towards evening the bells were ringing. 'We have a King! We have a King!' the people rejoiced. Right to the end, Elizabeth had refused to name her successor, but she had tacitly trusted Sir Robert Cecil to arrange the smooth transfer of power to James of Scotland – 'they that have most right'. As Robert Carey was galloping north with the ring, which was to be token of James's accession to the crown of England, Elizabeth's body was being carelessly wrapped in cerecloth. No longer king and queen both, just the carcase of a mortal old woman, she was disgracefully neglected in death. Only her friend, Anne, Lady Warwick, sat with the body until the black-draped coffin was taken by river to Whitehall to lie in state. She was buried with appropriate pomp in her grandfather's splendid chapel at Westminster Abbey on 25 April.

'The Queen is dead. Long live the King!'

Before long, those who were celebrating the coming of a king were looking back with nostalgia to the golden days of Elizabeth. Her reputation grew through the first half of the seventeenth century as disillusion with the Stuarts set in and, closely identified as she was with her country's greatness, continued to rise through succeeding centuries. Four hundred years after her death, the subject of plays, films, operas and novels, she has been hailed as perhaps the greatest English woman who ever lived, certainly England's greatest sovereign.

PART TWO: *House of Stuart*

MARY II

b. 1662, r. 1689–1694

20

Princess of Orange

WHEN PRINCESS MARY was born at St James's Palace on 30 April 1662 very few of the nobility bothered to visit her mother in her lying-in chamber to offer their compliments, which they surely would have done if the child had been a boy or if they had known that the new occupant of the royal cradle would one day be queen.

The unwanted Princess was baptized a few days later in the Chapel Royal at St James's, her parents' official residence, according to the rites of the Church of England. Her godparents included the valiant old Cavalier, Prince Rupert of the Rhine, her father's friend and cousin. She was named after her great-great-grandmother, Mary, Queen of Scots, whom, as a young girl, she was to resemble closely in looks. She inherited the lustrous, almond-shaped eyes, the alabaster skin and the rich brown locks so typical of the Stuart women, as well as the exceptional height of the Scottish Queen, which made both women stand out among their contemporaries.

As a girl and the offspring of King Charles II's younger brother, James, Duke of York, Mary was of little account. This may have saved her from the ministrations of the royal physicians, whose well-meaning but ignorant practices had already killed off her elder brother, Charles, Duke of Cambridge. It was perhaps as well the boy had died, since the circumstances of his birth meant that his legitimacy would always have been called into question.

By the time Mary was born the strains were already showing in her parents' marriage, as they were bound to do when the man felt that he had been trapped. Anne Hyde was a commoner, the daughter of Sir Edward Hyde, a Wiltshire lawyer who had become Charles II's Lord Chancellor during his long exile on the Continent. As a reward for her father's loyalty, Anne had been appointed maid of honour to

Charles's sister, the widowed Mary, Princess of Orange, at her court at The Hague. Clever and witty, Mistress Hyde was good company. No great beauty, she was handsome and voluptuous and soon attracted the attention of the philandering James.

What no one had foreseen was that James would be foolish enough to enter into a clandestine marriage with her – the two exchanged vows before witnesses and then consummated the union, which amounted to a marriage in the eyes of the Church – at Breda in the Dutch Republic, just a few months prior to the Restoration of the monarchy in England in May 1660. After years of penurious exile, James had not foreseen that his brother's fortunes would change so rapidly and that he would return to his throne by over-whelming popular demand; he could then have married any princess in Europe, but he was so besotted with Anne it probably made no difference. For a royal duke and the heir to the throne to marry a commoner was a huge misalliance. When the secret began to leak out and Anne's first pregnancy became glaringly obvious back in London in the autumn of 1660, it embarrassed the royal family and scandalized society.

Anne's father was so appalled that he said he would rather she was the Duke's whore than his wife and urged the King to punish her presumption by sending her to the Tower. The Stuarts' royal relatives were shocked and disgusted that James should make such a base marriage. His aunt and godmother, Elizabeth, Queen of Bohemia, was incredulous. She was living at The Hague when Anne Hyde was resident there, so that she was in a position to know that the girl had taken physick to try to induce an abortion. Surely she would not have done such a thing, she claimed in a letter to her son, if she had been legally married when she became pregnant?

Irritated with his brother, Charles had not the heart to disgrace the daughter of the man who had served him so faithfully and upon whom he was more than ever dependent to carry out the tedious business of government. The couple underwent a second, secret marriage ceremony in England and the union was subsequently recognized. The new Duchess was rather a stately figure and stepped into her role as second lady of the kingdom with ease. She had the knack of attracting people of merit and her court at

St James's was far more brilliant than that of Queen Catherine at Whitehall. She was a formidable character and it was noted that while she was not able to control the Duke's rampant womanizing – according to Pepys's sources, the Duke's pimps brought women to his closet, so that 'he hath come out of his wife's bed, and gone to others laid in bed for him' – she dominated him in every other respect.

Like many upper-class women who did not breastfeed, the Duchess embarked on a series of annual pregnancies, bearing a son, James, Duke of Cambridge, a year or so after Mary, and a daughter, Anne, the year after that. Two more boys and a girl followed. She was not particularly maternal: Princess Mary retained only the vaguest memory of her mother, but she was to be her father's favourite. When she was just over two years old, Samuel Pepys was charmed by the sight of the Duke playing with her 'just like an ordinary private father of a child'. James liked to think of himself as a fond father, but in reality he was more taken up with his work as Lord High Admiral, the court, his hunting and his women than his children. If he made a fuss of Mary on the few occasions she was brought to St James's from her nursery at Richmond or her maternal grandfather, the Earl of Clarendon's house at Twickenham, where she spent some of her early childhood, such an event was rare.

The York children were housed at Richmond Palace under the care of their governess, Lady Frances Villiers, and Mary's nurse – 'my mam' – the gossiping Mrs Frances Langford. It was a licentious age; the fact that women were held in low esteem, as sexual objects, meant that their education was not a high priority. James's own education had been interrupted by the outbreak of the civil war, when the royal family began its peripatetic existence. Not very well educated himself, he was not the kind of man to have a high opinion of the female mind, and probably thought that a good education would be wasted on his daughters. He did not draw up a programme of studies for them as he later did for the Prince of Wales, which was a pity as his elder daughter was highly intelligent.

Unlike the Tudor princesses, there was no question of these girls learning Latin or Greek, or even history, geography, or law. Mary's command of English spelling, grammar and punctuation remained execrable, and judging by the chaotic state of her account books later in life her grasp of arithmetic was slender. She made good progress in French under Peter de Laine, who found her diligent. She proved a talented pupil of Mr Gibson, her dwarf drawing master, a fine miniaturist who taught her to paint on ivory. Above all, she had a good ear for music and learned to dance under the direction of the elderly Frenchman, M. Gorey, who had taught all the royal family and earned a princely £400 a year. Just short of Mary's seventh birthday, Pepys noticed her at Whitehall: 'I did see the young Duchess, a little child in hanging sleeves, dance most finely, so as almost to ravish me, her ears were so good.'

In 1667 both Mary's little brothers died within a month of each other, leaving Mary and her sister Anne second and third in line to the throne, after their father. High infant mortality was all too common, but, with the exception of Mary, all the York children were born weak and sickly. Gilbert Burnet, an enemy of the Duke, maintained that James had passed a venereal disease on to his wife and that their children were nothing but 'the dregs of a tainted original'.

The deaths of so many of her siblings – five of them during her childhood – must have left an indelible impression on Mary, perhaps sowing the seeds of the morbidity that would be such a striking facet of her adult personality. As a child in the nursery she must have been aware of the anxious whispers and panic of the nurses and rockers every time one of the children fell sick, perhaps frightened by the presence of the black-clad physicians with their doomed expressions and desperate remedies. Then there were the suddenly empty cradles, the little waxen corpses laid out in dark candlelit chambers swathed in black, and the burials with all the pomp of royal mourning.

As it became ever more apparent that King Charles's Portuguese Queen would remain childless, the York children grew in importance. The question of their upbringing took on added impetus at the beginning of 1669, when their father made the most momentous and politically damaging decision of his life. He abandoned the High Anglicanism of his youth and embraced Roman Catholicism. Knowing what anathema the Church of Rome was to Englishmen, Charles begged his brother to reconsider, or at least keep his conversion a close secret. When the Duchess followed suit, her father

Clarendon, a staunch Anglican, was horrified and wrote to warn her of the inevitable consequence: 'That she would bring all possible ruin upon her children, of whose company and conversation she must expect to be deprived; for, God forbid, that, after such an apostasy, she should have any power in the education of her children.'

The question did not arise, because the Duchess was already entering upon her final illness. Constant childbearing had destroyed whatever pretensions she had to a good figure, and she had alleviated her unhappiness at James's womanizing by overeating. A courtier wrote that it was an edifying sight to watch the Duchess at table, where she indulged her hearty appetite. The memory of her corpulence probably accounted for Mary's later terror of becoming fat. Even as the Duchess gave birth to her eighth child, however, she was dying of cancer. Mary must have known her mother was desperately ill, but there is no evidence that she was brought to say a final goodbye on her deathbed, perhaps because of the hushed-up scandal over the Duchess's change of faith. 'Truth, truth,' Anne replied when a well-meaning Anglican chaplain approached to ask if she remained true to the faith, 'what is truth?' Then, turning to her husband, she muttered, 'Duke, Duke! Death is terrible – death is very terrible,' and died.

The immediate impact of their mother's death and James's conversion was that Mary and Anne were removed from their father's care, lest he contaminate them with his Catholicism. They became children of state. Nobody minded that their education was being badly neglected, as long as they became good little Protestants. Dr Edward Lake and Dr Doughty gave them religious instruction and, later, Charles chose as their preceptor Henry Compton, Bishop of London. A fierce Anglican, he was a vigorous opponent of Catholicism. He instilled in the Duke's daughters an unshakeable conviction that the Church of Rome was in grave error, scarred by centuries of abuse and deviation from pure truth.

James loathed him and, when the time came, sulkily refused to give his permission for Mary's confirmation. He protested that 'it was much against his will that his daughters went to church and were bred Protestants; and that the reason he had not endeavour'd to have them instructed in his own religion, was because he knew if he should have attempted it, they would have immediately been quite taken from him.' Compton simply went over his head and gained the King's permission to proceed.

It was about the time of her mother's death in 1671, when Mary was nine years old, that she developed a schoolgirl infatuation with a young lady of the court, Frances Apsley, who was a few years older. In her letters to Frances, Mary, the rather neglected child, assumes an air of world-weary sophistication. 'If I had any nuse to tel you I wold, but hear there is none worth a chip,' she wrote, adding, 'Tho St Jeames is so dul as to afford no news dear husban now Windsor may shake hands with it.' It is interesting that Mary, playing the role of wife, wrote these letters in a language that not only expressed heterosexual husband/wife conflict, tension and desire, but also positions of dom-ination and submission, authority and obedience – terms that corresponded to the patriarchal world around her.

Mary lived mainly apart from her uncle's dissolute court, but at Christmas 1674 she made her debut in John Crowne's masque, *Calisto, or the Chaste Nymph,* in which she appeared 'all covered in jewels'. After this exciting glimpse of the grown-up world, when the young ladies waiting in the wings were able to cast surreptitious glances at dashing young gallants, such as Mary's cousin, the bastard Duke of Monmouth, in the audience, Mary's letters to Frances became more passionate. She started to address her as Aurelia, the part she had played in the masque, signing herself Mary Clorine. The letters were replete with protestations and vows of eternal love, outbursts of jeal-ousy and accusations of infidelity, lamentations over her lover's indifference, enticements and threats. She spoke of 'violent love', 'rude longing', being carried away 'in ecstasy'. 'I love you with a love that was never known by man,' she assured Aurelia. Although she used quires of paper dashing off letters written with a 'new crow quil pen', they were invariably full of excuses for her tardiness in writing:

Why dear cruel loved blest husban do you think I do neglect my wrighting you your self know I could not Monday senat [sennight, in other words, seven night or a week ago] was the King's beirth day so tusday I slept till eleven a cloke Thursday morning I was so busie trying on mantos and a gown that I did not see Mr Gipson [Gibson, her dwarf drawing master, who carried her letters to Frances] nor had

I time to wright Saturday you know I could not wright Tusday last I took fisike [physick – it was a regular practice to take a laxative] so pray judg yourself when I could wright I confese dear Aurelia I am in fault if my dear dear dear husban think so.

It was two years after his first wife's death before James remarried, choosing as his bride the beautiful fifteen-year-old Princess Mary Beatrice D'Este of Modena. 'I have brought you a new playfellow' was how he broke the news to his elder daughter, who was only four years younger. The prospect of the heir to the throne marrying a Catholic, a relative of the Pope no less, caused riots and Mary and her sister, watching from the mullioned windows of St James's Palace, might have seen the angry bonfires lit in protest. However, Mary found a new friend in her stepmother, who grew to love her as her own daughter. Just as Mary admired the older and very pretty Frances Apsley, she must have admired the new Duchess and basked in the attention she gave her.

Four months into the marriage, Mary Beatrice joined the Duke's daughters at Richmond when she discovered that James had a mistress in Arabella Churchill. Far from looking disdainfully on her step-mother's tears like her stoical sister Anne, the emotional Mary would have sympathized with her distress at her husband's betrayal. Her feel-ings found expression in a letter to Frances: 'Who can imagin that my dear husban can be so love sike for fear I dont love her but I have more reson to think that she is sike of being wery of me for in tow or three years men are always wery [weary] of their wifes and looke for a Mrs. [mistress] as sone as they can get them.'

Endearingly innocent for her age, the romantic girl who had only known life in palaces and worn the richest silks and finest lawns next to her skin swore that she would live with Frances and 'be content with a cottage in the contre [country] & cow a stufe peticot & wast-cot in summer & cloth in winter a litel garden to live upon the fruit & herbs it yields or if I could not have you so to myself I would go a beging be pore but content what greater hapynes is there in the world then to have the company of them on [one] loves to make your hapynes compleat.'

Her idyll was about to be rudely shattered by the arrival of a real husband.

Towards the end of October 1677, Mary and her sister were at St James's when they heard of the return of the court from Newmarket several days earlier than expected. An informal meeting had been arranged between Mary and her cousin, Prince William of Orange, who had joined his uncles at the races and accompanied them back to London. As the only child of the royal brothers' eldest sister, Mary, Princess Royal and Princess of Orange, William was in the line of succession after James and his daughters. It is not certain whether Mary had encountered William on a previous visit when she was a child, but the impression she would have formed of him now, through the romantic eyes of a girl of fifteen, is unlikely to have been favourable.

The Dutch Prince was old – nearly twenty-seven – and seemed older because his slight frame was hunched and stooped. At five feet six and a half inches, he was of average height for a man of his time, but small compared with his Stuart uncles, who were just over six feet tall, and he would have had to look up at Mary, who as a grown woman was five feet eleven. In the damp, fog-thickened London air and the dark candlelit rooms, he wheezed as if unable to breathe. There was no court repartee in the few words he did utter in a thick Dutch accent. Unlike the fashion-conscious fops of the court with their periwigs and gaudy clothes, this Prince wore his own dark hair loose and a black suit, so plain as to look like one of the despised Dissenters. His features were aquiline, with a nose 'curved like the beak of an eagle'. Only his dark eyes made an impression, lighting up with a brilliant lustre when he saw something he admired. And he admired the beauty, the gentle disposition, the charm and the good manners of the tall girl standing before him. So much so that he instantly went to his uncle the King and asked for her hand in marriage.

Rumours of a marriage between William and Mary had occurred intermittently, but until now he had not been in a position to think of it. He had been too busy fighting for his country's survival in the face of French aggression. When he had opened negotiations with his uncles at Newmarket, he had shocked them by saying that he must meet the young lady before any proposal could be made. James was outraged. Naturally, he considered Mary a great prize. Not only was she the first daughter of the crown, heir to the throne after himself, but she was a beauty. For some time, James had been strung along by the French ambassador, Barillon, who on instructions from Louis XIV had led him to believe that a marriage between Mary and the Dauphin was in the offing. Such a marriage would have the additional advantage, in James's eyes, of necessitating her conversion to Catholicism. He had no wish to see Mary wed to this stern Dutch Calvinist, who drew his title from a small principality in the South of France and was merely the elected Stadholder of the Dutch Republic. He neither liked nor trusted his nephew.

The King was ruled by other considerations. Perhaps if he married his niece to her Protestant cousin some of the heat would be taken off him, whose nefarious dealings with Catholic France had long been suspected. James's blatant Catholicism had caused Charles endless trouble with Parliament and he recognized that some concession had to be made to Protestant sentiments. He had promised his brother he would not dispose of Mary's hand without first obtaining his consent. Of course, being Charles, this promise was ignored. "Od's fish,' he declared, when reminded of it, 'I know I promised, but he *must* give his consent.' Ever obedient to the King's wishes, James gave in, but with an ill grace.

Something of James's disapproval must have communicated itself to his highly strung daughter when, after dinner at Whitehall on 21 October, he came to St James's and led her into her closet to break the news of her impending marriage. Mary promptly burst into tears. Her chaplain, Dr Lake, noted that 'she wept all that afternoon and all the following day.' Louis XIV never seriously entertained the idea of marrying Mary to his son; how could a prince of the blood royal marry the daughter of a commoner, someone of the half-blood? But when he heard the news, he protested to James that he had given his daughter to his mortal enemy. While commenting publicly that William and Mary were nothing but a couple of beggars who were well matched, in private he conceded that their marriage was the equivalent to him of the loss of an army.

The country was ecstatic about the forthcoming union of two Protestant heirs to the throne. In the succeeding days the members of the Privy Council, the Lord Mayor and aldermen and the judges trooped to St James's to congratulate the couple. On Lord Mayor's

Day, the whole royal family attended the show in the City, followed by a lavish banquet. The City noted with approval William's serious dress and demeanour, one City wife commenting, 'What a nice young man he looked, not like those popinjays at the court!'

The marriage ceremony at which Bishop Compton officiated took place on William's birthday, Sunday, 4 November 1677, between eight and nine o'clock at night. It was a small private family affair held in the bride's apartments at St James's. A slightly inebriated Charles gave his tearful niece away and his quips were the only mark of joviality in the otherwise subdued atmosphere. When William laid the coins symbolic of his worldly goods on the prayer book, Charles urged Mary to 'Gather it up, gather it up and put it in your pocket, for 'tis all clear gain.' The solemn couple must have looked a strange sight before the clergyman, the red-eyed statuesque Mary being so much taller than her wheezing bridegroom. A heavily pregnant Duchess of York looked on, no doubt with pity for her young stepdaughter, whom she would miss terribly. The bride's sister, Anne, was absent, as she was unwell.

The following day, William's closest friend, Hans Willem Bentinck, came to present the new Princess of Orange with William's magnificent wedding present to her: £40,000 worth of jewels, including the huge pearls she wore in all her subsequent portraits and the ruby ring 'she came to value above her kingdom'. Mary was also to have the Little Sancy, a great diamond which her late mother-in-law had pawned to raise funds for the exiled Charles II, and a huge single pearl drop earring which her grandfather, Charles I, had worn to the scaffold. The value of the jewellery was equivalent to Mary's dowry, which was paid late by her chronically insolvent uncle, in tiny grudging instalments, or not at all. After the ceremony, Mary's tears continued and she proved obdurate when William urged her to move out of St James's, where her sister Anne and others now lay sick of the smallpox, and into the apartment that had been placed at his disposal at Whitehall. She was adamant that she would not leave her home until the very last minute.

They could not depart from London until after Queen Catherine's birthday ball on 15 November, when Mary appeared wearing all her jewels. By this time, William had completely run out of patience with his tearful adolescent bride and was anxious to leave his uncle's dissolute court and return to business at home. His coolness towards Mary at the ball, where he danced with her only once, was noticed with indignation. This was the moment when he acquired the names 'Caliban' and the 'Dutch Abortion', and when the belief took root that William treated his wife badly. It was quite unfounded.

The crossing to Holland was rough, and, as the couple travelled in separate yachts, William had to watch his wife's being tossed in the water. She was the only person on board who was not seasick. Their arrival found the port of Rotterdam iced up. They embarked on sloops that took them to a fishing village further along the coast and William carried his exhausted wife up the beach. There were no coaches to meet them and the party walked three miles along the icy lanes before being picked up and driven to the palace of Honselaersdijck. Here, Mary's mother, as plain Anne Hyde, maid of honour to the previous Princess of Orange, had played games of ninepins with young English gallants in the gallery. Now it was one of several splendid houses of which William's fifteen-year-old wife would be mistress.

To Mary's surprise and delight, she liked her new country, and the Dutch people immediately took her to their hearts. When she made her state entry into The Hague, her regal bearing was evident, but she gave the impression of being pleased and wanting to please. All her life, she had heard nothing but jokes and sneers about the hated Dutch republicans – who had fought three naval wars with England in the last quarter-century – but she was curious and intelligent enough to make up her own mind about her new people. She won the Dutch over with her easy charm, her gaiety and conversation, while the good housewife in her admired their order, neatness and cleanliness, the antithesis of what she had been used to in London.

The couple spent the first weeks of their marriage quietly ensconced at Honselaersdijck, getting to know each other. Soon the impressionable young girl, so hungry for affection, had fallen in love with her solemn husband, admitting in a letter to Aurelia that 'she had played the whore a little'. She saw a new side to William. In the Dutch Republic he was a hero, who would fight to the last ditch rather than surrender his country to the French. With his male friends, loyal, long-term companions of the hunting field and his military campaigns, William was relaxed and at his most jovial, sharing animated conversation. The intensely feminine Mary had no intention of intruding into this male world and showed no jealousy of his preference for their company. After the stresses of public life, she would offer William peace and tranquillity. When he came to join her in her rooms, they spoke English together, and she would entertain him with light chatter, a delightful distraction from the cares of state.

Life at William's court was more sedate than at Whitehall, but it obviously agreed with Mary. Its sobriety calmed her over-excitable temperament. There would be the occasional ball when she would indulge her love of dancing, sometimes until dawn, but otherwise social life consisted of private dinner parties with friends such as the Bentincks, tea parties in which the expensive new drink was imbibed, and endless games of cards. While regretting that she had taken to card playing on Sundays, her former chaplain Dr Lake heard that 'the princess was grown somewhat fat, and very beautiful withal'. Mary quickly learned Dutch and made friends among the Dutch ladies, while the people would be treated to the sight of the Princess and her attendants passing along the canals in her barge, embroidering while Mary's chaplain read to them. The Dutch approved of a princess whose hands were never idle and with such domestic virtues.

The couple shared an appreciation of fine painting, inherited from their grandfather, Charles I; Mary had exquisite taste and soon William entrusted her with the embellishment and furnishing of their homes at Honselaersdijck, Soestdijck, Dieren and, in due course, Het Loo. She would build up a fine collection of blue and white Chinese porcelain, brought from the East by Dutch traders as ballast for their ships. Together they were interested in the design and planning of the gardens, with their smart box topiary and hedging, and in the introduction of new plants from more exotic climes. In the gardens of Het Loo, Mary, who loved birds, would have an aviary.

When the time came for William to return to the army, Mary accompanied him as far as Rotterdam, where her uncle, Laurence Hyde, Earl of Rochester, was pleased to note 'a very tender parting on both sides'. Mary wrote to Frances expressing a sorrow she had never known, even worse than her sadness at leaving her country, her family and friends:

> I suppose you know the prince is gone to the Army but I am sure you can guese at the troble I am in . . . I never knew sorrow for what can be more cruall in the world then parting but parting so as may be never to meet again to be perpetually in fear . . . for god knows when I may see him or wether he is nott now at this instant in a batell . . . I recon him now never in safety ever in danger . . . oh miserable live that I lead now.

The partings and Mary's anxiety for William's safety were to be the pattern of their married life.

Mary was already pregnant, but nevertheless she set off in a bone-jolting coach in the harsh conditions of a Dutch winter to join William first at Antwerp then at his castle at Breda. The result was disastrous. She had a miscarriage and probably one with consequences. If she had been at home at The Hague, she would have been able to call on the services of Dr Drelincourt, the brilliant gynaecologist and embryologist, or Cornelis Solingen, a renowned surgeon and obstetrician. Neither was available at Breda, and it is possible, in view of Mary's subsequent gynaecological history, that an infection set in that rendered her sterile. Meanwhile, it was clearly not advisable for a young woman in a delicate condition to be gadding about after her soldier husband. Her father wrote anxiously from London, expressing his sorrow at the miscarriage and urging 'pray let her be carefuller of herself another time'.

Mary's health remained poor, but then in the summer of 1678 she was overjoyed to experience the symptoms of pregnancy again. While the King and the Duke were at Newmarket, Mary Beatrice decided to pay a visit to her stepdaughter, whom she had dubbed her 'dear Lemon' in compliment to her husband's title of Orange, bringing her sister Anne and a small party to The Hague to cheer her up. They found Mary in good spirits and her pregnancy seemed to be progressing well. On the party's return to England, James was unusually effusive in a letter to William. The Duchess, he wrote, was 'so satisfied with her journey and with you, as I never saw anybody; and I must give you a thousand thanks from her and from myself, for her kind usage by you: I should say more on this subject, but I am very ill at compliments, and you care not for them.'

By the spring of 1679, anti-Catholic hysteria in England and the Whigs' determination to exclude James, Duke of York, from the throne had left the King with no alternative than to send his brother and sister-in-law into exile. Brussels in the Spanish Netherlands was their chosen destination. Its proximity gave Mary Beatrice the opportunity to visit Mary again. She was indignant to find that she 'had spent the nine months since her pregnancy in great loneliness', taking away an impression of William's coolness towards his wife which coloured James's view of him in the future. It was clear by now that something was wrong. As Mary's delivery date came and went, it became apparent that she was not pregnant at all. The sickness and malaise and lack of periods which had been taken for pregnancy, the intermittent fevers she had been experiencing which were so similar to the ague, or malaria, common in the Low Countries, were possibly symptoms of an ongoing gynaecological infection.

The disappointment was profound, leaving Mary low and depressed. Although she never ceased to hope for children, and was generous enough to rejoice at others' good fortune in having them, she and the Prince were to remain childless. She began to spend a lot of time alone, praying and meditating, and steeping herself in books on divinity and history, making up for the defects in her education. Deep introspection and sadness were an increasingly prevalent aspect of Mary's mentality, not helped, as she became more absorbed in religious devotion, by her belief in her unworthiness before an exacting God.

21

Unnatural Daughter

IT WAS INEVITABLE THAT Mary's father and husband would end up on opposite sides of the political and religious divide and, when it came to it, there was no question which side Mary, the loyal and malleable wife, would choose. The Glorious Revolution of 1688 could not have taken place as smoothly and bloodlessly as it did without her compliance, but the ousting of her father meant that she was castigated as an unnatural daughter.

When Charles II died in 1685, James II succeeded peacefully, against all the odds. With his accession, Mary, as the elder of his two surviving children, became heiress presumptive to the three kingdoms of England, Ireland and Scotland, and she was served at table on bended knee. This was a privilege that came automatically. Where it was in his power to do more, as he should have done, James did nothing. He gave Mary no extra allowance and sent her no jewels or gifts in recognition of her new dignity. Indeed, Mary's dowry had never been fully paid and she had a mere £4,000 a year for her own spending money. Out of this, she would ask Frances Apsley, now Lady Bathurst, to buy her the latest fashions in London, although as the leader of society in The Hague she was careful not to 'bring up such a fashion heer which the purses could not bear'. She gave generously to charity, not least to the thousands of Huguenot refugees fleeing religious persecution and terrible cruelties in Louis XIV's France.

Paranoid about William's intentions, James always maintained that he could not be sure that any money he sent for his daughter would not be used against him. After all, had not her husband plotted with the Duke of Monmouth to usurp the crown? It was not true, but James stubbornly clung to the notion of his two Protestant nephews conspiring against him, until Monmouth's rebellion gave James the chance to end his troublesome life. Mary was not a greedy or acquisitive person, but her father's meanness, neglecting to give her some token of her new status, must have saddened her.

James had gradually alienated her affections in other ways. He tried to break up her marriage by encouraging English members of her household to spy on William's nocturnal activities and apprise Mary of his supposed affair with Elizabeth Villiers. Confronted by Mary as he emerged from Elizabeth's room in the early hours, William hotly denied that anything improper had transpired; it is just possible that the clever and witty Elizabeth, very much in demand on the diplomatic social circuit at The Hague, was an agent for William, and their late-night trysts were debriefing sessions rather than sexual encounters. Wanting to believe him, a weeping Mary threw her arms round her husband and begged his forgiveness. Her malicious, gossiping staff, including her old nurse Mrs Langford, were sent back to England in disgrace.

When Louis XIV took possession of William's principality of Orange, torturing and killing the Huguenots who had taken refuge there, Mary turned to her father for help. His protests to the French were half-hearted and he excused himself by saying it was not a matter worth going to war over. 'The only thing I ever asked the King, my father, to do was to use his influence with the King of France to prevent the seizure of the Principality of Orange,' she recalled sadly. 'But my father preferred to join with the King of France against my husband.'

Hitherto, Mary had not interfered in politics, but now she began to take an interest. Above all, she was concerned for the Anglican Church in the face of her father's evident determination to undermine it. She protested to James when Henry Compton, Bishop of London, was brought before the hated Ecclesiastical Commission and suspended when he refused to dismiss Dr Sharp for preaching an anti-Catholic sermon. James rebuked her for meddling in such matters. William and Mary were in favour of religious toleration and, therefore, of the suspension of the penal laws against Catholics and Dissenters. But they could never approve James's wish to abolish the Test Act, which deprived from office anyone not of the Anglican faith, as they felt it guaranteed the supremacy of the Established

Church. When James misused his prerogative and arrested seven bishops for refusing to read his Declaration of Indulgence from the pulpit, Mary had her chaplain write to the Archbishop of Canterbury to express her sympathy, assuring him that she could never condone illegal actions of this kind, since they devalued the monarchy.

James hoped to convert one or both of his daughters to the Catholic faith. Mary promised to read some of the books he sent her, together with the devotional papers of Charles II and her mother. 'I have found nothing in all this reading but an effort to seduce feeble spirits,' she wrote, 'no solid reasoning, and nothing that could disturb me the least in the world, so much that the more I hear of this religion the more pleased I am with my own, and more and more thanks I have to render to my God for His mercy in preserving me in His true faith.'

Gilbert Burnet, a Scottish clergyman who had taken refuge at William and Mary's court when James came to the throne, read Mary's responses to her father. 'It gave me an astonishing joy to see so young a person all of the sudden, without consulting any one person, to be able to write so solid and learned a letter, in which she mixed with the respect that she paid a father so great a firmness, that by it she cut off all further treaty,' he wrote. 'And her repulsing the attack, that the King made upon her, with so much resolution and force, did let the popish party see, that she understood her religion as well as she loved it.'

William had always encouraged his wife to play a subservient, frivolous role. He did not invite her to discuss weighty affairs with him, perhaps taking her gay chatter at face value. Burnet was the first to recognize that she possessed a formidable intelligence and he could not praise her too highly. Burnet claims to have raised a matter with Mary that William had never been able to bring himself to discuss with her in all the years of their marriage. Whether Burnet had the audacity to do this of his own volition, was prompted to do so by William whose ambitions it served, or just invented the scene when writing his *History of His Own Time* after the Revolution to put himself in a good light, is a moot point.

He asked Mary what her intentions towards her husband were when she became Queen. Mary did not understand. Burnet explained that as queen regnant she would have the superior role, while William would merely be her consort. Since he knew their marriage had been 'a little embroiled' of late, owing to the Elizabeth Villiers business, he had the temerity to suggest that she should have the real authority vested in her husband, while she should be content to play the lesser role.

It is hard to believe that Mary was so ignorant of English royal custom, but, according to Burnet, the next day she asked him to be present at a meeting with William. She stated that 'she did not know that the laws of England were so contrary to the laws of God, as I had informed her: she did not think that the husband was ever to be obedient to the wife: she promised him he should always bear rule; and she asked only, that he would obey the command of "husbands love your wives", as she should do that, "wives be obedient to your husbands in all things."' True or not, the incident perfectly describes the role Mary was to embrace in the dual monarchy with William.

Any thoughts of Mary inheriting her father's crown were thrown into jeopardy by the announcement of Queen Mary Beatrice's pregnancy, which, coming so many years after her other pregnancies, seems to have taken everyone by surprise. Mary's initial response to the news was pleasure. There is no evidence to suppose that she was annoyed because a brother would oust her from the succession. 'I rendered thanks to God that this news did not trouble me in any fashion,' she wrote in her journal, 'God having given me a contented spirit and no ambition but to serve my Creator and conserve my honour without stain.'

Mary had no wish to leave her adopted country, where she was loved and happy. She knew that she had a far better life as Princess of Orange than she would as Queen of England. 'This it has pleased the Lord to make of me contents me and, in the state where I am, I am better able to serve Him than I should have been in a post more eminent.' All members of the King's family should rejoice in the fact that he might have a son, she wrote, except that 'one cannot do so without being necessarily alarmed by the thought of a papist successor.'

If Mary did not want the crown for herself, she recognized that she should feel obliged to want it to please the Prince and to protect her beloved Church of England. 'Besides the interest of the Church,' she wrote, 'the love that I have for the Prince made me wish him all that he merits, and though I regret not to have more than three crowns to bring him it is not my love that blinds me; no, I can see his faults, but I say this because I know also his merits.'

From the evidence of her journal, Mary at first had no thoughts of discrediting the Queen's pregnancy or of doubting its veracity. In March 1688 all that changed when she received the first of her sister Anne's letters implying that foul play was intended. The Queen was not pregnant at all, but pretending, presumably with the intention of passing off a changeling as the heir to the throne, so stealing Mary's birthright and perpetuating the Catholic dynasty. Anne was at pains to warn her sister and brother-in-law not to think of visiting England, implying that their lives would be in danger. Possibly Anne feared that the Princess of Orange would be able to witness for herself the true state of the Queen's pregnancy, for surely she would permit her dear Lemon to feel her belly?

Unsure what to believe, Mary decided to place her trust in God and wait upon events. Her sister's presence as a witness at the Queen's confinement would surely reveal the truth. What Mary probably did not appreciate was that there was a concerted Protestant plot to discredit the pregnancy and throw doubt on the child's legitimacy from the first and that her sister Anne was very much part of this plot. Throughout her life Anne gave or withheld her presence to great political effect, so that well before her stepmother went into labour Anne had purposefully left for Bath, too far from London to return in time. The truth, however, was important to Mary. Exasperated by her sister's absence, she compiled an extensive questionnaire for Anne to complete with the details of the birth gleaned from those who had been there. Naturally, Anne's vague, biased and muddled answers did nothing to assure Mary that the new Prince was indeed her brother.

Three weeks after the birth of James Francis Edward, Prince of Wales, on 10 June 1688, seven prominent Englishmen sent an invitation to the Prince of Orange, inviting him to England to restore liberty and the rule of law. In the letter, they reprimanded him for his public recognition of the Prince. William had gone through the proper formalities, ordering prayers to be said for the child in the

Princess's chapel and sending his cousin, Count Zuylestein, to the English court, ostensibly to offer congratulations, but, more pertinently, to report to William on the state of affairs.

'We must presume to inform Your Highness, that your compliment on the birth of the child (which not one in a thousand here believes to be the Queen's) hath done you some injury,' the seven conspirators wrote. They advised him that this 'false imposing' of a fictitious heir, to the injury of the Princess Mary and the nation, must be listed in William's forthcoming manifesto as one of the chief causes of his 'entering the kingdom in a hostile manner'.

It is unlikely that William had entertained any idea of armed intervention in England until the pregnancy of the Queen was announced on Christmas Eve, 1687. Now revolution became a real possibility, as Protestant Englishmen looked into the abyss and saw James's regime perpetuated as a Catholic tyranny on the French model. Whether William believed the hoax theory or not, he could not stand by any longer and watch Mary's inheritance put in jeopardy. If James were allowed to continue, he would destroy the monarchy. England might even swing back to a republic. Only by having his own hand on the tiller could William bring about the Anglo-Dutch alliance Europe so desperately needed to quell the French. If the English conspirators fondly thought he would go home after he had served their purposes, William at least was never in any doubt that his goal was the crown.

For the moment, William determined to salvage what he could of Mary's rights and to secure the best out of the situation for his own country. It remained to convince Mary of what was at stake. She had to know what was going on, because if her father were dethroned it would be in her name, as she, not William, was the heir to the throne.

Far away in the Netherlands and dependent on her sister's reports, surrounded by James's enemies, Mary was already inclined to believe that the Prince of Wales was a changeling. She recorded in her journal that the eventual return of Zuylestein from England 'brought only the confirmation of the suspicions that we already had'. She seems to have been genuinely convinced that the child was not her brother, the true heir to her father's throne. From now on, she never betrayed the slightest doubt that a dreadful 'trickery' had been perpetrated on her and the English people.

Queen Mary Beatrice, who had always been so good to Mary, was hurt that in her letters she had 'never once . . . taken the least notice of my son, no more than if he had never been born'. James refused to believe that his daughter was acquainted with William's plans for invasion, writing to her early in October:

> This evening I had yours of the 4th, from Dieren, by which I find you were then to go to The Hague, being sent for by the Prince. I suppose it is to inform you of his design of coming to England, which he has been so long a contriving. I hope it will have been as great a surprise to you as it was to me, when I first heard it, being sure it is not in your nature to approve of so unjust an undertaking. I have been all this day so busy, to endeavour to be in some condition to defend myself from so unjust and unexpected an attempt, that I am almost tired, and so I shall say no more but that I shall always have as much kindness for you as you will give me leave to have.

On this same day, Mary heard from her stepmother:

> I am much put to it what to say, at a time when nothing is talked of here but the Prince of Orange coming over with an army. This has been said a long time and believed by a great many, but I do protest to you I never did believe it till now very lately, that I have no possibility left of doubting it. The second part of this news I will never believe, that is that you are to come over with him; for I know you to be too good, that I don't believe you could have such a thought against the worst of fathers, much less perform it against the best, that has always been kind to you, and I believe has loved you better than all the rest of his children.

Convinced that her father was the perpetrator of a Catholic conspiracy to subvert the Protestant succession, Mary had no doubt where her loyalties lay. James would have been cut to the heart had he been able to read her journal, where she admitted that she was an accessory to her husband's intention to take her father's crown: 'The consideration of all this and the thought that my father was capable of a crime so horrible and that, humanly speaking, there was not any other means to save the Church and the State than that my husband should go to dethrone him by force, are the most afflicting reflections and would not be supportable without the assistance of God and a firm and unshakeable confidence in Him.'

Mary's inner turmoil seemed to derive more from shame at her father's perceived crime than pity for his impending downfall. As ever, she relied on God to sustain her. Careful not to betray her emotions, Mary assumed an untroubled countenance to the world, 'for I cannot talk with liberty to anyone except to the Prince, who has seen my tears and has pitied me'.

Later, James's supporters, the Jacobites, accused Mary of being an unnatural daughter. Her first loyalty, they claimed, should have been to her father. Disobedience to a father was deemed a fundamental breach of both natural and divine law. Mary's violation of the fifth commandment, 'Honour thy father and thy mother', was to become one of the major themes of Jacobite propaganda. But this was to ignore the fact that on marriage a woman's obedience was transferred from father to husband. Did St Paul not say, 'Wives, submit yourselves unto your own husbands as unto the Lord'?

James wrote Mary one last pathetic letter before the invasion, deepening her dilemma:

> And though I know you are a good wife, and ought to be so, yet for the same reason I must believe you will be still as good a daughter to a father that has always loved you so tenderly, and that has never done the least thing to make you doubt it. I shall say no more, and believe you very uneasy all this time, for the concern you must have for a husband and a father. You shall still find me kind to you, if you desire it.

There was no question of William taking his wife with him on this dangerous venture. The evening before his departure, the couple had an emotional meeting. He advised her that in the event of his death, she should remarry. Mary was so horrified by the thought of his death that it was 'as if someone had torn my heart out'. She refused to contemplate remarriage. 'I assured him that I had never loved any except himself and that I should never love another; besides that, having been married so many years without it having pleased God to bless me with a child, I believed that alone sufficient to prevent me from ever thinking of this that he proposed.'

William had already made his will and the following day he addressed the States-General, thanking them for their loyalty and the support they were offering in his invasion of England. 'What God intends for me I do not know,' he told them, 'but if I should fall, have a care of my beloved wife who always loved this country as her own.'

That afternoon, he and Mary dined together at Honselaersdijck for the last time and she bid him a tearful farewell. A week later, when the mighty fleet was thrown back on Dutch shores by a westerly, 'popish', wind, William invited her to Brill. Their meeting was short and, for Mary, the second separation was even more painful than the first. The following day she attended public prayers in the town for the success of the expedition; her husband's enemies noted that the King of England's daughter had publicly given her prayers and good wishes to a task force setting out to ruin him.

It was some time before William wrote to her, leaving Mary to hear of his success from others. Disconcertingly, James fled the country and weeks of wrangling followed between William and the English. There was no consensus as to what to do about the vacant throne. Mary spent Christmas and New Year alone in Holland in an agonized frame of mind. She had given up cards and dancing, 'which had been to me one of the prettiest pleasures in the world'. Her delight at William's success was blighted by concern for her father. She was glad to hear that he had escaped with his life. Any guilt she felt was outweighed by her steadfast belief that she was acting for God and His Church.

When William eventually summoned her, she was grieved to leave Holland, the country that had become so dear to her, where she had been happy: 'Yet when I saw England, my native country, which long absence had made me a stranger to, I felt a secret joy, which doubtless proceeded from a natural sympathy, but that was soon checked with the consideration of my father's misfortunes, which came immediately to mind.' She was filled with happiness at the prospect of seeing William again, and 'the thought that I should see my husband owned as the deliverer of my country, made me vain; but, alas, poor mortal! thought I then, from whom has he delivered it but from my father!'

22

Sovereign and Consort

O N 13 FEBRUARY 1689 William and Mary, hand in hand, entered the Banqueting House at Whitehall, where almost exactly forty years previously their grandfather, Charles I, had lost his head for upholding the divine right of kings, and took their places on chairs beneath the canopy of estate. Both Houses of Parliament were present as the Declaration of Rights, outlining the conditions on which they were to be offered the crown, was read aloud to the Prince and Princess, who remained holding hands, a posture surely designed to placate those who had wanted to vest the crown in Mary alone and to underscore the dual nature of the new monarchy. The Speaker advanced and asked if they would accept the crown as joint sovereigns. Illustrating Mary's subordinate status, William answered for both of them; Mary's contribution was merely 'her looks and a little curtsey'.

It was the first time since her arrival in London the previous day that she had shown what was considered to be the correct demeanour. Courtiers who already resented the Dutch usurper had looked forward to Mary's coming. Their latent xenophobia had been roused by his obvious preference for his Dutch cronies. At least she was an English princess, a Stuart born and bred in England, and would know how royalty should behave. Unlike her dour, inaccessible husband, they knew Mary to be gracious, charming, lively and gregarious. They thronged to Whitehall to see her, only to be shocked by the manner in which she entered her father's palace. 'She came into Whitehall, jolly as to a wedding, seeming quite transported with joy,' noted the diarist John Evelyn reprovingly. Surely this was not how the daughter of a dethroned king should act when taking possession of his palace?

Not only had Mary been deliberately installed in the same apartment, but also slept in the same bed Queen Mary Beatrice had shared with James. 'She ran about it, looking into every closet and conveniency, and turning up the quilts of the beds, just as people do at an inn, with no sort of concern in her appearance,' Sarah Churchill commented scathingly in her *Conduct*, written many years after the event. 'I thought this strange and unbecoming conduct; for whatever necessity there was of deposing of King James, he was still her father, who had been lately driven from that very chamber, and from that bed; and if she felt no tenderness, I thought, at least, she might have felt grave, or even pensively sad, at so melancholy a reverse of fortune.'

Mary's affected gaiety, verging on hysteria, continued the next day, the day of the ceremony at the Banqueting House. 'She rose early in the morning,' Evelyn heard from a relative who was waiting on her, 'and in her undress, before her women were up, went about from room to room, to see the convenience of Whitehall.'

Admiring Mary as he did, Gilbert Burnet was perplexed by her inappropriate behaviour. William had written ordering her to 'put on a cheerfulness', she admitted, adding that she was aware of the raised eyebrows and frowns of disapproval. She had clearly gone too far, as it was not a part that came naturally to her. William was adamant that they would not be apologetic for the overthrow of James's regime, but his instructions to his ever obedient wife had struck the wrong note and she knew it.

A glance at Mary's journal, which presents her side of the story and was written up at the end of each year perhaps with her historical reputation in mind, reveals that she felt anything but cheerful at the prospect of assuming her father's crown. She did not want it. She wrote that 'I had been only for a Regency, and wished for nothing else', but she was bound to play her part in William's plans. She dreaded the prospect of being Queen, 'knowing my heart is not made for a kingdom and my inclination leads me to a retired quiet life', but the fact that William would now be King 'lessened the pain, but not the trouble of what I am like to endure'.

There was a feeling among the English that events had somehow moved too fast and that matters had not turned out as expected. They had believed William's manifesto, which stated he came only to guarantee the calling of a free Parliament, which everyone agreed was the only remedy for the ills that had arisen under James's rule. As far as most people were concerned, James was still their rightful sovereign, even if he had been a disaster. For them, there had never been any question of deposing him, only of forcing him to rule according to the laws of the land. When William ended up with the crown, many felt they had been duped.

In lieu of James, who had taken refuge with his wife and son at the French court, someone had to fill the void. In January 1689 a convention was elected to settle the question, but the debate only intensified. One solution was to place Mary on the throne alone. In theory, there was nothing to prevent her elevation as queen by right of inheritance: the only drawbacks were William's vociferously expressed opposition; her own diffidence about her abilities, a reflection of her limited education and adherence to conventional ideas about women's place in society; and the prevailing patriarchal ideas about female rule and the relationship of husband and wife.

A century after Elizabeth I's Armada triumph, and only forty years after the civil war era when women had been unusually active in politics and religion, the English were once again debating a woman's capacity to rule. It is significant that the issue had been given an airing only a year after Mary's marriage in 1677, when François Poulain de la Barre's essay, translated into English as 'The Woman as good as the man, or the equality of both sexes', argued that women were capable of leading armies, holding ecclesiastical office and acquitting themselves as ministers, governors and advisers to monarchs.

The Exclusion Crisis had focused attention on Princess Mary as one of several possible claimants to the throne. Perhaps it is no coincidence that books about Queen Elizabeth appeared in 1675, 1680, 1683, 1688 and 1689, which provided specific illustration of the capacity of a woman to govern England. When James Crouch, whose vignettes of great women in the past purported to show that 'women can equal, if not exceed, the deeds of man', published his *Female Excellency, or the Ladies' Glory* in 1688, he surely had it in mind that Mary was heiress presumptive.

As early as 26 December 1688 a small group of Tories led by Lord

Danby sought to make Mary queen regnant, with William her consort. Their purpose was to preserve a façade of legitimacy and to further their own political interests. As queen, Mary would obscure, or at least soften, the violations to the principles of legitimacy and direct hereditary succession that were necessary to achieve a Protestant monarchy. The deliberately circulated rumour that James's son was suppositious had served its purpose; the Tories wanted no further disruption to the principle of divinely inspired, hereditary monarchy.

Throughout January 1689 arguments for and against Mary becoming sole queen were aired in the convention and in the press. Members of the Commons insisted that the English monarchy was hereditary, but that James's son suffered a natural and legal incapacity; since the child was no longer in the country, it was further argued, his legitimacy could not be determined either way. They stressed that Queen Elizabeth had proved a woman could rule 'gloriously' and asserted that 'there is no other way to have peace and quiet, but by recognizing the Princess'. They suggested that to promote William in place of his wife would 'sully' his glory.

The publication of Robert Filmer's *Patriarcha* in 1680 had reinforced the patriarchal ideology of the time. Men opposed to Mary becoming sole queen fell back on traditional views of women's place in society and marriage. In the convention an MP stressed the danger England faced from France and urged members to 'chuse a King to go before us and fight our battells . . . [which] a Woman cannot so well do'. Another pointed out that it was against the law of nature to expect William to be subject to his wife.

The idea of making Mary queen regnant and William her consort appalled the Prince, his friends and Mary herself. Burnet even argued that since Mary, as William's wife, was a *femme covert*, it could be said the crown, hers by inheritance, already belonged to her husband. This betrayed his ignorance of the sixteenth-century Act Concerning Regal Power, which had been passed to safeguard the kingdom when Mary Tudor was in a similar situation. As a magistrate, it declared, the Queen was the equivalent of a man; to all intents and purposes, she was a man. Only as a woman should she defer to her husband. Even if William were to accept the role of consort, what would happen to him in the event of her death? After everything he had risked and invested, he wanted a life tenancy at least.

William realized that if he did not force a decision, the English would talk and argue for ever. He declared that he had no intention of being his wife's 'gentleman usher' or of holding 'anything by the apron strings'. He would accept nothing dependent on the life of another or on 'the will of a woman'. He let it be known that unless he was offered the crown 'he would go back to Holland, and meddle no more in their affairs'. Very grudgingly he conceded that he would accept a joint monarchy with his wife, but only if the 'sole and full exercise of the regal power' was vested in him. Mary would have the title of Queen only. She would not have the Sword of State carried before her as her sovereign predecessors had done.

The coronation ceremony on 11 April 1689 contained subtle details which indicated that Mary's status was subordinate to her husband's. Although a second orb, sceptre, Sword of State, and a special chair were made for Mary, and although the couple replied simultaneously to each proposition put to them as the ceremony unfolded, kissed the Bible together, and received homage jointly, the symbols of sovereignty were reserved for William. He was anointed first. The spurs were touched to his heels alone; he received the ring first and he was crowned before Mary. The significance of these distinctions was obvious.

Official documents and all prayers and litanies of the Church ran in the names of both monarchs, but in conformity with William's assumed superiority, his name always preceded Mary's. Most medals cast to commemorate the coronation showed William and Mary as joint monarchs, their busts facing each other within wreaths of roses and oranges. In one, however, William is depicted as the Belgic Lion crowned. The lion drives away James II and his Jesuit adviser, Petre, who is holding the baby boy. Serpents underfoot indicate discord and evil. On the reverse of the medal are two female figures, representing Mary and Anne, as suppliants before the throne of Jupiter (William), while Saturn (James), Jupiter's father, who had conspired against his son's interests, is shown in flight, devouring the infant. There could be no doubt here of Mary's feminine, subordinate role.

The Jacobites deliberately misinterpreted the official coronation medal, which depicted Jove thundering against Phaeton, who was driving a chariot over a burning world, conveying the idea that James had nearly destroyed the government of England and was displaced so that it could be saved. His supporters likened Mary to the Roman matron, Tullia, who had urged her husband to kill her father so that they could inherit the crown. Like Phaeton in his chariot, Mary-Tullia had driven over the remains of her dethroned father.

Even before Mary reached England, men who knew she had declined the opportunity to be sole queen disparaged her as either very good or very stupid. For the first year or so of the dual monarchy, she was portrayed as a politically naïve woman with the essentially feminine characteristics of a queen consort. Her beauty was only fitting in a queen, however, and inspired much comment. A young lady of the Russell family wrote:

> At night, I went to court with my lady Devonshire, and kissed the Queen's hands, and the King's also . . . He is a man of no presence, but looks very homely at first sight: yet, if one looks long at him, he has something in his face both wise and good. As for the Queen, she is really altogether very handsome; her face is agreeable, and her motions extremely graceful and fine. She is tall, but not so tall as the last Queen. Her room is mighty full of company, as you may guess.

Aphra Behn, the first Englishwoman to earn a living by her pen, found in Mary's beautiful face the 'God-like' attributes of monarchy, which she identified as gracious sweetness, affability, tender mercy, and true piety – but these were also the ideal womanly virtues.

Mary had not just the looks, but all the charm and social skills her husband lacked. 'She smiled upon all, and talked to everybody,' Evelyn noted. If the nobility could not easily resort to William, they felt that they could approach the Queen for favours. But it soon became apparent that she would do nothing without referring to her husband. What was the point of a queen who could grant no favours? Gradually, they drifted away and left her alone.

It came as something of a relief to Mary. In her journal she complains that 'I was come into a noisy world full of vanity.' It was not the peaceful life she was used to, when she would attend prayers four times a day. In England she had 'hardly leisure to go twice, and that in such a crowd, with so much formality and little devotion'. A loyal daughter of the Anglican Church, Mary craved the blessing of William Sancroft, Archbishop of Canterbury, and the approval of the clergy, but they were not forthcoming. The archbishop might have had his differences with James, but he was his anointed sovereign to whom he had given his oath of allegiance. 'Tell your princess first to ask her father's blessing; without that mine would be useless,' Sancroft told Mary's messengers.

Increasingly, Mary found herself lonely and isolated. 'I found myself here very much neglected, little respected, censured by all, commended by none,' she wrote. At court and elsewhere she was subjected to insult for her disloyalty to her father. When her father's ex-mistress Catherine Sedley, Countess of Dorchester, told friends that she was going to court, she was warned that Mary, with her strict ideas about morality, would treat her 'on no higher foot than her father's daughter', to which the witty Catherine replied, 'Then I will treat her like her mother's.' When Mary duly acknowledged her coolly, Catherine retorted, 'Why so proud, Madam? For if I broke one commandment with your father, you broke another in coming here.'

The Revolution had been a violent disruption of the patriarchal ideal. James, the King, father of his people, had been ejected from his kingdom, while as father he had been overthrown by his children. As the daughter who had perpetrated the deed and been set up as sovereign in his place, Mary was the butt of Jacobite propaganda.

When not identified with Tullia, the Jacobites referred to her as 'Moll'. A 'Moll', in the colloquial usage of the time, was a woman of ill repute. By calling her Moll, they identified her as a thief, who had stolen the crown, and as a whore, who had lusted for power and sold her soul as well as her body for three kingdoms. They represented the sexual relationship between her and William as either perverse or perversely non-existent and transformed her into 'the whore', unsatisfied, lusting for the phallus as she had lusted for power, the masculine domain. William, the homosexual who had failed to satisfy his youthful wife's sexual appetite or to provide an heir, was accused of impotence. An impotent king symbolized a dysfunctional body politic.

Even at the theatre Mary was insulted. When she went to a performance of Dryden's *Spanish Friar*, the whole audience turned to watch her reaction to the words:

> *Very good: she usurps the throne: keeps the old King*
> *In prison; and at the same time is praying for a blessing:*
> *O religion and roguery, how they go together!*

It was worse in the fourth act:

> *A crown usurped, a distaff on the throne . . .*
> *What title has this Queen but lawless force?*

She could only bury her face in her fan.

In 1690 a Jacobite poem entitled 'Female Parricide' ran:

> *Oft I have heard of impious sons before*
> *Rebelled for crowns their royal parents wore*
> *But of unnatural daughters rarely hear*
> *'Till those of hapless James and old King Lear.*

Controversial plays such as *King Lear* and *Richard III* were banned.

In William's absence at the wars, Mary was lonely and isolated. Her natural confidante should have been her sister, Anne, but relations between them had soured very quickly. Anne was aggrieved that Mary's husband had usurped Anne's place in the succession and, what's more, he treated her husband, the kindly but ineffectual George, with scant respect. Petty quarrels about Anne's allowance and lodgings were magnified out of all proportion, with Anne's friend Sarah Churchill fanning the flames of Anne's jealousy of her sister and resentment of her brother-in-law. Soon the sisters were not speaking to each other and Anne had ostentatiously removed herself from court.

'In all this I see the hand of God, and look on our disagreeing as a punishment upon us for the irregularity by us committed upon the revolution,' Mary confided sadly in her journal. Soon she suspected that Anne was in correspondence with their father and that Sarah's husband, John Churchill, Earl of Marlborough, hedging his bets, was engaged in treasonable activity with the exiled court. When he was dismissed in 1693, Mary advised Anne that Sarah could no longer remain in her service. Defiantly, Anne came to court, bringing her friend. The wife of a disgraced man should not appear at court and Anne, who was a stickler for etiquette, knew this. It was a deliberate insult to William and Mary.

'I must tell you I know what is due to me,' Mary wrote to her sister, 'and expect to have it from you.' Anne refused to dismiss her favourite. 'My sister has not mistaken me,' Mary told Anne's emissary. 'I never will see her upon any other terms than parting with Lady Marlborough – not for a time, but for ever! I am the Queen,' she exclaimed, 'I will be obeyed!' The sisters remained unreconciled.

The perception of Mary began to change in 1690 when William decided that he would personally lead England's army against James in Ireland, who, with French help, was attempting to reclaim the throne. Although it was a dual monarchy, the administrative power rested in William's hands alone and therefore the question arose of who would rule in his absence. At first he was inclined to leave the Privy Council in charge but subsequently, probably because he felt he could trust Mary implicitly to follow his lead, he proposed that she should rule as regent. He could not have made a better choice. She was entirely devoted to him and without personal ambition.

Although Mary was fully conscious of her public position and political value, she was a firm believer that 'women should not meddle in government'. Diffident and untried, she confided to William her concern that she 'should not make a foolish figure in the world'. She so underestimated her own abilities that she later told Sophie of Hanover: 'a woman is but a very useless and helpless creature at all times, especially in times of war and difficulty. I find by my own sad experience, that an old English inclination to the love and honour of the nation signifies nothing in a woman's heart and without a man's head and hands.'

The Regency Act of May 1690 enabled Mary to exercise regal power in her name and William's during his absence, but gave William authority to override her acts and specified that upon his return all powers reverted to him. The Act inspired new public respect for Mary, who developed her own style of queenship. Like Queen Elizabeth before her she understood the importance of symbolic gestures. A naturally majestic figure with presence, she used the trappings of sovereignty to inspire reverence and loyalty. She would dress in royal robes and, seated on a throne in the Banqueting House, receive the London citizens.

Reluctant she might have been, presenting the image expected of her as the loyal, deferential wife, but she was not unwilling or ineffective. During her four regencies, she issued thirty-seven proclamations, ordered fasts, heard petitions, reviewed troops, censored the press, called and prorogued Parliament, made appointments to the Church, navy and administration, and pardoned, transported, imprisoned and executed criminal and treasonous subjects. It was no mean achievement.

She had a Council of Whigs and Tories of varying degrees of loyalty, who thought that they would be able to take advantage of the inexperienced woman. They soon learned otherwise. Recognizing her lack of knowledge and experience, her initial silence at Council meetings enabled her to conceal her ignorance, listen to all the arguments, and form judgements on the nine members, some of whom tried to dominate or circumvent her. She proved an astute judge of character and adept at composing differences and reconciling members to courses of action they had not originally intended. She referred all major decisions to William, sitting up late into the night straining her eyesight in the candlelight to write him long letters. 'I ever fear not doing well, and trust to what nobody says but you,' she told him.

In an emergency there was no time to consult William and here Mary acted courageously and decisively. There was treason and suspicion of treason in the higher reaches of government, all the more serious in that the country was at war. There was a traitor in the Council and Mary suspected it was Lord Mordaunt, betraying secrets to France. When treachery was exposed, she did not hesitate to act. In 1690 she insisted that her uncle, Henry Hyde, Earl of Clarendon, be arrested for corresponding with her father. Later that year a planned uprising of some of James's supporters was discovered. The conspirators were seized, tried and sentenced to death. Mary signed the warrant of one of them, whom she had known since childhood, in great distress, but showed no sign of weakness.

Soon the French fleet was in the Channel and Admiral Herbert was showing a marked reluctance to engage it, but 'lay drinking and treating his friends'. Mary was about to relieve him of his command when he engaged the French off Beachy Head. But he let the Dutch do all the fighting, keeping the English fleet to the rear and then retreating into the Thames. After the inevitable defeat, Mary was mortified, writing to the Dutch government to give her personal apology.

Although she was rapidly gaining the love of her people through her dedication, piety and goodness, Mary's health was suffering under the strain of it all. Her day began at six, when she was awoken with tea – one of her expensive indulgences – and she spent two hours reading and writing. Prayers were at eight, followed by business for four or five hours until dinner. There were cards and public receptions from four until seven. Evening prayers and supper over, she would attend to her private correspondence until midnight or the early hours of the morning. She went to sleep in the knowledge that she might be woken at any hour to deal with a national emergency. Through all this she had to cultivate a serene manner and an inscrutable countenance, to mask her feelings so that no one would guess the condition of affairs by her expression. 'I must grin when my heart is ready to break,' she told William, 'and talk when my heart is so oppress'd I can scarcely breathe.'

On top of all this, she had to contend with the very real threat of assassination and was distraught with worry about William. Contrary to the belief of her critics, she did feel a sense of guilt over her father and fear for his safety. She confessed her anxieties to Daniel Finch, Earl of Nottingham, during the Irish campaign. After William's victory at the Battle of the Boyne in 1690, believing her father to be a prisoner – he had actually fled to Dublin and then to France – she wrote to William: 'I know I need not beg you to let him be taken care of, for I am confident you will for your own sake. Yet add that to all your kindness, and, for my sake, let people know you would have no hurt come to his person.' Her attitude changed in 1692 when she learned that James was party to a scheme to assassinate William. She was ashamed that 'he who I dare no more name father was consenting to the barbarous murder of my husband . . . I fancied I should be pointed at as the daughter of one who was capable of such things, and the people would believe I might by nature have as ill inclinations.'

James's defeat in Ireland did nothing to reduce the Jacobite threat. In the New Year of 1692 a French force of 20,000 men gathered at La Hogue, on the Cherbourg peninsula, where James joined them with a contingent of Irish soldiers. A new invasion scare swept England, putting fresh heart into the Jacobites. There was a plot to seize Mary on her father's landing. She was sure that she would be murdered. There were fears of disloyalty in the navy, which Mary addressed by appealing directly to her officers, expressing her complete confidence in them. The Queen's appeal led the men to sign a statement promising their support. At the same time, she went to Hyde Park to review the few troops – those whom William had not taken to Europe – who were left to defend the country.

At this moment, James unwittingly came to her aid. He issued a declaration, promising that on his restoration he would continue much as before, and listing hundreds of names on whom his vengeance would fall. It was so ludicrous that the Jacobites hurriedly sought to publish a toned-down version, but Mary was too quick for them. Showing that she had learned a great deal from William about the value of propaganda, she promptly had James's declaration printed and distributed, with her own comments on it.

When an Anglo-Dutch fleet under Admiral Russell and Lieutenant-Admiral Van Almonde won a great victory at La Hogue, a grateful Mary immediately despatched £38,000 for distribution among her seamen. This was a rare instance of royal generosity. Normally rewards promised before battle fail to materialize after victory. As a further mark of her appreciation, Mary promised that the unfinished royal palace at Greenwich would be transformed into a hospital for sick and disabled seamen. Her popularity among her people soared. She should have ordered a public thanksgiving for La Hogue, but typically wanted to make it a joint thanksgiving for the victory that she was sure would be William's at Steinkirk. Instead, he was defeated with terrible losses. 'Will should have knotted,' was the English people's verdict – referring to Mary's new hobby of tying linen threads into knots to keep her agitated hands occupied – 'and Moll gone to Flanders.'

In 1692 *A Present for the Ladies* went so far as to compare her with Queen Elizabeth, not least because her actions preceding La Hogue evoked comparison with Elizabeth's at Tilbury, and the following year a medal commemorating her regency shows her holding a palm branch in one hand and a mirror in the other. The hand holding the mirror rests on a rudder, signifying that the Queen guides the ship of state with mildness and prudence.

Mary's handling of affairs won her the gratitude of William and of many in the government. When Parliament presented her with an address of thanks for her 'prudent care in the administration of government' Mary made a response characteristic of her deep-seated view of the position of women. Curtseying to her husband and the assembly, she replied, 'I thank you, gentlemen, for your address. I am glad I have done everything to your satisfaction.' Nothing could have been further from the way Elizabeth would have reacted, but Mary's modest demeanour was more typical. Her femininity was effective.

Her diffidence accorded well with patriarchal sentiments. The Whig propagandists were able to present her as the good wife, confidently, if only temporarily, managing the kingdom. In deference to patriarchal anxieties about female rule, she did not 'reign' – a masculine performance – but 'managed', as 'became a wife'. Her power was not to be feared, for it was merely that of a wife executing a husband's commands. When Bishop Burnet later praised her talent for government, he was at pains to assure his audience that she 'never affected to be masculine'.

Not only did she win applause for the efficient discharge of her duties, but she was praised for the graceful way in which she surrendered her powers whenever William returned. *A Dialogue Concerning Women* compared her with the Roman general Cincinnatus, who had left his private duties to take on public responsibilities, but willingly returned to private life at the end of the crisis. It was an apt comparison, for Mary liked nothing better than to resume the consort's role, looking after her husband, carrying out her social and charitable duties, looking out for the moral welfare of the nation, and redesigning her palaces and gardens at Kensington and Hampton Court.

The royal couple decided to leave Whitehall, with its grim reminder of Charles I's execution, associations with Stuart corruption, and the smoke-filled atmosphere of London, which played havoc with William's asthma. Lord Nottingham's 'sweet villa' at Kensington was acquired for 18,000 guineas and Sir Christopher Wren was engaged to transform it into something resembling a palace. Wren found the Queen an exacting employer but a lady of exquisite taste. Several times a week she would walk from Whitehall to Kensington, her tall figure striding across the parks with her architect at her side, to check progress.

At Hampton Court the idea was to pull down Cardinal Wolsey's old palace and build a magnificent new European palace on the model of Versailles, but an outcry at the extravagance of it all meant that the plans had to be modified. A new building, which resembled Het Loo in many respects, was added to the old, leaving large sections of the Tudor building, including the clock tower and kitchens, intact. Pending the completion of the works, Wren transformed an old Tudor gatehouse on the river into a Water Gallery for the Queen, providing temporary accommodation for her, complete with her own marble bathroom with hot and cold running water – a great novelty.

In the homes she created, Mary rediscovered something of the serenity of the domesticated existence she had enjoyed in Holland. The Queen's subjects could admire her talent for embroidery in her bed curtains, the new printed calicoes imported from the East, and the large collection of blue and white Delftware and porcelain from China she had heaped on Grinling Gibbons's elaborately carved oak chimney-pieces and tiered shelves. Together with her introduction of pug dogs and the concept of keeping a goldfish as a pet, Mary set an enduring national trend for chintz and blue and white china and inspired her people's love of gardening.

Gardens were a passion for Mary, providing respite from other cares. Daniel Defoe had once seen her walk past him in the park looking truly animated as she discussed with Wren the laying of the foundations of the gardens at Kensington; it was as if, he said, she was conscious that she would only have a few years to enjoy them. It was no coincidence that the layout of the gardens at Kensington and Hampton Court were French-inspired, since the designers William and Mary employed were Huguenots. At Hampton Court long gravel walks and avenues of trees were complemented by canals and fountains, which William planned with the Huguenot Daniel Marot, their principal garden designer, while the Dutch influence was seen in the divisions of the garden into sections devoted to specific purposes.

The tight geometrical patterns owed less to art than to the science of mathematics, explaining why Daniel Marot was referred to as the 'royal mathematician'. Plants and flowers were cultivated in tubs – a new concept in England – neatly outlining the courtyards and punctuating the walkways, while rows of neat box marked the boundaries. The couple brought their own orange trees from Holland and Mary had glasshouses built for a large collection of tropical plants and flowers despatched from Virginia, the Canaries and the West Indies. Her botanist, Leonard Plunkenet, looked after a rare collection of over 400 exotic plants. Gardening was Mary's greatest extravagance, but she comforted herself with the fact that 'it employed many hands'.

As queen, Mary championed moral, social and religious reforms – a forerunner of the modern monarchy's obligation to lead by moral example and play an active philanthropic role. She was appalled at the immorality, pugnacity, rough manners, swearing and drunkenness, and lack of religious devotion she found among her people on her return to England. This behaviour was endemic in all classes. In an age that still believed that a nation's sins could bring down God's wrath, Mary was surprised 'to see so little devotion in a people so lately in such eminent danger'. She issued numerous proclamations to reform manners and discredit drinking, but her good intentions made little headway.

A loyal daughter of the Anglican Church, she used her influence in ecclesiastical appointment to moderate the extremism of right-wing Anglicans. After his victory at the Boyne, she urged William to strengthen the Anglican Church in Ireland and to use some of the confiscated estates to endow schools. She was tolerant both of the non jurors – the bishops and clergy who had refused to swear allegiance to William and Mary because they had taken a prior oath to James – and the Dissenters, who had won only modest religious toleration in the Revolution settlement and whose condition she sought to ameliorate. She continued to support the Society of the French Gentlewomen at The Hague and gave generously to their fellow Huguenot refugees in England. She supported Thomas Bray, the founder of the Society for Promoting Christian Knowledge. In 1693 in support of the petition of

James Blair, a clergyman from New England, she arranged for an endowment of £600 a year for the College of William and Mary in Virginia to train missionaries.

Nor did she neglect charity to individuals. Her account books show that she gave sums to 'a poor woman at Hampton Court' and 'for Mrs Miller a blind woman', and many others. She had made herself responsible for the upkeep of a little boy and girl boarded with a woman in Kensington. Some of the last entries in the accounts show that these orphans received 'for cutting the boys hair & new combs 5s 6d', 'apothecarys bill when the boy was sick 8s', '2 pair of gloves & new ribin for the girls cap 7s', 'a cosy winter coat twelve shillings'. As she entered her final illness, she was concerned that her few debts be paid, her charities be continued, and that her servants should be looked after, obligations that her husband, in his profound grief at her death, would honour.

On the night of 21 December 1694 Mary, suspecting that she had contracted smallpox and was likely to die, sat up all night in her closet, going through her papers, preserving some and burning others. She was sufficiently conscious of her image to destroy anything discreditable. It is significant that her journal remained virtually intact. These memoirs abound with traditional notions of the proper place of women, according very much with the way the Whigs presented her and which would remain the standard view of her over succeeding centuries. Fortunately, enough of her letters to Frances Apsley, discovered in an attic 300 years later, and to William survived to provide insights into her lively, engaging personality and her acute political sense.

Her untimely death on 28 December 1694 at the age of thirty-two provoked an extraordinary outpouring of public grief. William was utterly distraught, surprising the many who had always considered him cold. His attachment for Mary evidently went much deeper than anyone had ever guessed. 'He said, during the whole course of their marriage, he had never known a single fault in her,' Burnet wrote, 'there was a worth in her that nobody knew besides himself.'

James refused to mourn a daughter who had long been dead to him. He forbade his court at St Germain to go into mourning and asked Louis XIV to issue the same instruction at Versailles. The

Jacobites saw her early death as divine retribution. The Modenese ambassador summed up their feelings when he reported:

> The news will have reached you of the death of the Princess of Orange [as she was still referred to by those who did not recognize the regime] of putrid smallpox after three days' illness . . . That Princess, young, beautiful, and reputed the delight of a rebellious people, is suddenly become a frightful spectacle, and a subject for their bitter tears. She was a daughter who sinned against the commonest and most indispensable law of Nature ordained by God – that of honouring her parents . . .

If James and the Jacobites thought the demise of Mary would weaken William's hold on the throne, they were sadly mistaken. The English drew together in grief, rallying round William in his terrible loss. The most elaborate funeral ever accorded a sovereign was planned. The court and the country were plunged into the deepest mourning. The embalmed body of the Queen was taken from Kensington to Whitehall, hung with yard after yard of black cloth, where it was to lie in her bedchamber until the route to the Banqueting House could be made ready with black-covered walkways. Here, where less than six short years previously she had accepted the crown, she was to lie in state for three months. From 21 February, members of the public were admitted to pay their last respects. Even though it was so cold that the Thames had frozen, they took up their positions in the snow from six in the morning, being admitted only from noon until five.

They found the inside of the Banqueting House ablaze with candles. Twelve gentlemen-at-arms stood on either side of the empty throne. The Queen lay with her hands crossed over her breast on draperies of purple velvet fringed with gold. At her head were the crown of state, the sceptre and the orb, at her feet the sword and the shield. At each corner of the open coffin stood one of her ladies swathed in deepest mourning, relieved by others every half an hour. In an alcove behind curtains of purple velvet inscribed with the Orange family motto, *Je Maintiendrai*, William mourned in private, his deep grief concealed from the curiosity of his subjects.

The state funeral took place on 5 March, when the bells of the parish churches tolled all over England. The honour of chief mourner went to the Percy heiress, Elizabeth, Duchess of Somerset, the highest lady in the land after Princess Anne, who was pregnant. Women were conspicuous in the funeral procession. Three hundred poor women led the funeral cortège, followed by the officers of Mary's household, her chaplains, the Lord Mayor and aldermen of London, and Sir Christopher Wren, Surveyor-General of the Works. It was appropriate he was here. As a public tribute to Mary, William had decided to press on with Wren's building of the Greenwich Hospital for Sick and Disabled Seamen, a project dear to her heart. For the first time ever, members of both Houses of Parliament, all 500 of them, attended a royal funeral. The Great Seal of William and Mary had been broken on her death although, since this was a dual monarchy, Parliament continued to sit.

Preceded by the banners of England, Wales, Scotland, Ireland, France and Chester, Mary's Master of the Horse, Lord Villiers, led her favourite mount. The Queen's coffin was carried in an open chariot drawn by eight horses, a man leading each of them. Six peers acted as pallbearers. One of the Queen's bedchamber women rode at each end of the chariot, guarding the body. The Duchess of Somerset, as chief mourner, followed behind, flanked by the Lord Privy Seal and the Lord President of the Council. The Duchess's long mourning train was carried by two duchesses. Eighteen peeresses, six ladies of the bedchamber, six maids of honour and six women of the bedchamber brought up the rear. As they wound their way from the Banqueting House by way of Whitehall Palace to Westminster Abbey, the ladies' trains dragged in the snow and remained wet while they sat in the chilly stone edifice through the long funeral service.

Henry Purcell, who had been employed as singer and organist in the Chapel Royal and at Westminster Abbey for most of his life and who had composed many celebratory odes for Mary on happier occasions, had composed the music. The Queen's Funeral March with its repeated muffled strokes was followed by the Canzona and then his new choral setting of 'Thou knowest, Lord, the secrets of our hearts, shut not thy merciful ears unto our prayers, but spare us, Lord most holy . . .', before the measured tones of the Funeral March were resumed.

The Archbishop of Canterbury, Tennison, took the opportunity in his funeral sermon to reprimand the congregation for their sinful lives. The Queen's untimely death was a sign of God's anger because her people had ignored her many proclamations urging them to reform and show more devotion to God. They had not been sufficiently grateful for their recent delivery from popish tyranny and had lost a good and pious queen through their failure to heed her advice and follow her example. He praised her for discharging both roles as wife and queen in exemplary fashion; she was commended for the piety and purity of her court, her skill in governing and her avowed desire to heal religious divisions.

After the service, the Duchess of Somerset and a few of the female mourners accompanied the coffin and a small party into the vault for the interment. Their duty to their royal mistress severed by death, Mary's household officers broke their white staves and threw them and their keys of office into the vault. Then Mary was shut into the impenetrable darkness as it was sealed.

There is no doubt that Mary's death was a severe blow to the Revolution. She had not only been the more legitimate half of the dual monarchy, but also the more popular. The Williamite press responded by producing a deluge of literature in praise of the late Queen, which also further glorified the King and justified the Revolution again. The numerous essays, elegies and sermons that poured forth reiterated the familiar themes – Mary as virtuous, pious, beautiful, industrious and charitable – an excellent queen and a devoted, loving and obedient wife. Burnet's *Essay on the Memory of the Late Queen*, portraying her as a woman with no appetite for government, its burdens unwillingly assumed and modestly managed, in complete union with William, dominated the Whig-Liberal vision of Mary through succeeding centuries.

The effective exercise of political power exalted Mary in the eyes of her contemporaries, even though she emphatically denied wishing to exercise that power. As ever, the challenge was to reconcile the political leadership of a woman with patriarchal ideas of female inferiority, complicated by the fact that Mary was a wife as well as a queen, in a dual monarchy which was unique in English history. There is no need now to defer to those patriarchal assumptions that have defined her. Mary proved both a stronger and more competent ruler than either she realized or posterity has understood.

ANNE

b. 1665, r. 1702–1714

23

Lady Anne

ANNE STUART WAS born on 6 February 1665, the year of the plague. Her mother's labour was so fast that it is doubtful if King Charles II and his Queen and many of those who usually crowded into the lying-in chamber at a royal birth arrived at St James's on time. As she was the fourth child and second daughter of the King's brother, James, Duke of York, and his wife Anne, she was not considered likely to come to the throne. Besides, she was a weak little thing and looked likely to follow her elder brother to the grave.

On the birth of a second daughter to the Duchess of York, Charles II wrote to his sister the Duchess of Orléans in France, showing how undervalued a princess was:

> I am very glad to hear that your indisposition of health is turned into a great belly. I hope you will have better luck with it than the Duchess here had, who was brought to bed Monday last of a girl. One part I shall wish you to have, which is that you may have an easy labour, for she despatched her business in little more than an hour. I am afraid your shape is not so advantageously made for that convenience as hers is; however, a boy will recompense two grunts more.

Lady Anne, as the younger daughter of the heir apparent was known throughout her childhood, was named in honour of her mother, Anne Hyde, the commoner who had lured a royal duke into marriage. Her christening took place in the Chapel Royal at St James's Palace a few days later. Her godparents included her three-year-old sister, Mary, who was held up at the font by her governess. Edward Hyde, the Lord Chancellor, created Earl of Clarendon in the wake of his daughter's marriage, seemed particularly pleased with this new granddaughter, perhaps because she resembled the Hydes and had such a placid temperament. But she was delicate and would need to survive the perils of infancy, the attentions of the royal physicians, and the plague which raged in London and then in the provinces through the first two years of her life.

The Duke and Duchess spent the summer of 1665 in York with their three children, Mary, James, Duke of Cambridge, and Anne, and in the autumn the family took up residence in the Oxford colleges with the rest of the court, avoiding the plague-ridden capital. When the court returned to London in the spring of 1666, the York children were sent to the healthier environment of Richmond Palace further up the Thames. A new baby, Charles, Duke of Kendal, soon joined them. Here they had their own 'family' or household. The world Lady Anne was most familiar with consisted of her siblings, her wet nurse Mrs Martha Farthing, her governess Lady Frances Villiers, the under-governess Mrs Mary Kilbert, and other servants including nurses, rockers, a dresser, a seamstress, a necessary woman, a laundress and a page of the backstairs. Mrs Dawson, an attendant of the Duchess's who later joined Anne's household, would be with her when she died forty-nine years later. As she grew up, her 'family' came to mean more to Lady Anne than her blood relatives, with whom her relations were increasingly political and fraught.

The Duchess of York was a handsome, rather magisterial figure, too preoccupied with the affairs of the court and keeping her errant, womanizing husband in check to take much notice of her children, although she did make something of a pet of Anne, inviting her to sip chocolate and feeding her titbits so that she became as round as a ball. When she was three, Anne was sent to live with her grandmother, the Dowager Queen Henrietta Maria, the widow of Charles I, in France. The purpose of the visit was to find a treatment for Anne's 'sore eyes', which could not stand bright light and would not stop watering. Although there is no evidence of it in her portraits, according to contemporary accounts the disability made her squint, lending her face a sour, petulant expression. It added to her natural shyness. As she grew up, she preferred the closet to the drawing room, and would rather move in a small circle of known acquaintances than large gatherings where she would be unable to see people. Using poor eyesight as an excuse, she would rarely pick up a book, although she was able to manage an expansive correspondence.

A portrait of her during her sojourn in France shows a child with serious grey eyes in a stubborn little face under a halo of light auburn curls. There is already a hint of the self-protective survivor in the set of the vulnerable bare shoulders. Having been separated from her mother so young, the child now lost her grandmother to consumption. She was sent to live with her aunt, the charming Minette, Duchess of Orléans, who placed the chubby little girl in the nursery with her own two. Anne became fluent in French and seems to have been happy there, because in her will she fondly remembered the younger of these two cousins as her closest living relative. However, the security and comfort of the nursery world was abruptly shattered by the sudden death of Minette, and it was decided that it was time for the English Princess to go home. The Sun King, Louis XIV, gave the five-year-old a very handsome leaving present, 'two braceletts of pearle besett with diamante valued at 10,000 crowns'. He could not have anticipated that this small girl, who was so shy and taciturn and had to screw up her eyes to look at a person, would grow up to be his great adversary.

When Anne returned to England, her life changed dramatically. During her absence, her parents had taken a step that was to have enormous and far-reaching consequences for James, his children and the nation. They had converted to Roman Catholicism. Before the secret leaked out, the Duchess died. Anne had just passed her sixth birthday and she had lost three crucial maternal figures – her grand-mother, her aunt and her mother – all within two years of her short life. Inured to loss at such a young age, it was fortunate that she was a stoical character and not surprising that she would become very self-sufficient. She was brought up to accept God's will, which, as a deeply religious person, gave her enough inner strength to survive the disap-pointments and sadness to come.

As the sole survivors of the eight children born to the Duke of York and his English commoner wife, after the death of their infant siblings, Mary and Anne rose in importance as second and third in line to the throne after their father. It was crucial that they should be removed from their father's Catholic influence and brought up as good Protestants to appease the nation, and so they were made children of state, living apart from their father in their own household at Richmond. Their chaplains, Dr Edward Lake and Dr Doughty, indoctrinated them in the tenets of the Anglican Church. Every year without fail the anniversary of King Charles I's execution on 30 January was held as a day of mourning, fast and prayer. Clad in black, Anne and her sister observed the occasion with the strictest solemnity. It was a timely reminder that their grandfather had died a martyr for the Anglican faith, even if their father appeared to have forgotten this, and of what happened to kings when they crossed the will of the people.

Later, their preceptor, Henry Compton, Bishop of London, left them in no doubt that Catholicism, their father's faith, was the most dangerous evil in the world. They were lessons Anne took to heart. 'I must tell you I abhor the principles of the Church of Rome as much as it is possible for any to do, and I as much value the doctrine of the Church of England,' she assured her sister a few years later. 'And certainly there is the greatest reason in the world to do so, for the doctrine of the Church of Rome is wicked and dangerous, and directly contrary to the Scriptures, and their ceremonies – most of them – plain, downright idolatry.'

Showing that she had absorbed all Compton's teaching to the letter, she continued: 'But God be thanked we were not bred up in that communion, but are of the Church that is pious and sincere, and conformable in all its principles to the Scriptures. Our Church teaches no doctrine but what is just, holy and good.'

Her devoted adherence to the Church of England provided Anne with a much needed rock of stability from her insecure youth.

Unfortunately, in the Richmond household little attention was being paid to the York princesses' other studies. Their education was woefully neglected. Even though one or both of these girls might later be Queen, it was assumed they would have husbands. The emphasis was placed on wifely accomplishments, although, noticing his niece's mellifluous voice, Charles II had the celebrated actress Elizabeth Barry train her in public speaking. Later, after she had fallen out with Anne, Sarah Churchill was to complain that she was 'ignorant of everything but what the parsons had taught her as a child' and this might well have been true. Sarah's vicious comments about Anne are largely responsible for the widespread belief that she was slow and dull-witted. Certainly she lacked her sister's high intelligence, curiosity and infectious vivacity, but Anne was bright enough. Naturally reserved, she was quiet, an observer; later, as queen, this ability to watch and listen would prove useful. She also had a large modicum of common sense.

In the intense friendships that pervaded the girls' school atmosphere of Richmond Palace, Anne was emotionally cautious, writing to her sister's friend Frances Apsley: 'I am not one of those who can express a great deale & therefore it may be thought I do not love so well but whoever thinks so is much mistaken for tho I have not may be so good a way of expressing my self as some people have yet I assure you I love you as well as those that do & perhaps more than some.' It is interesting that where Mary, in her excessive protestations of love for Frances, was to play the 'wife' to Frances's 'husband' Anne took the male lead in their playful correspondence.

Already imperceptibly alienated from their father because of his religion, the sisters' relationship with him took a new twist when he married an Italian princess, Maria Beatrice D'Este of Modena, who was only a little older than themselves. The angry bonfires lit by the Londoners to protest at the marriage of the heir to the throne to a Roman Catholic must have made an impression on eight-year-old Anne, perhaps sowing the seeds of her future suspicion of her step-mother. Not possessing her sister's Latin temperament, the more phlegmatic Anne never seems to have warmed to Mary Beatrice, although at first the relationship was at least superficially amicable.

The consequence of the Duke's Catholicism was a series of hyster-ical anti-popish plots, scares and rumours, and a vigorous Whig campaign to exclude him from the throne. The King bowed to pres-sure to send the Duke and Duchess into exile, first in Brussels and then in Edinburgh. Apart from making brief visits to them in each place, Anne was not permitted to accompany them. By the time they returned from exile in May 1682, she was seventeen, already well past the age when a princess might expect to be married. There had been talk of her marrying her second cousin, George of Hanover, but their meeting seems to have been a stilted affair, conducted in French. Later, Anne's critics maintained that his failure to propose accounted for her lifelong enmity, but there is no reason to think that she was anything but indifferent to the German prince.

George was short, blond, with bulging blue eyes, and rather dull, whereas Anne was at the height of her looks. With her rich dark brown auburn-tinted curls, the lovely arms and hands that contemporaries considered such an asset to a woman's beauty, and a generous, sensual mouth, she soon attracted an unwanted suitor in John Sheffield, Lord Mulgrave, one of the King's favourite courtiers who shared his eye for the ladies. Although he protested that his crime was 'only ogling', the scandal of the mild flirtation was enough to get him sent to Tangiers in a leaky boat.

A more suitable husband for the King's niece was found in Prince George of Denmark. He was twelve years older than his bride, a distant cousin, and the fact that he was a Protestant pleased Anne and the nation. John Evelyn noted that he 'had the Danish countenance, blond; a young gentleman of few words, spake French but ill, seemed somewhat heavy; but reported valiant'. He had had a military career and shown courage in the field, but he was neither clever nor witty, as Charles soon discovered: 'I have tried him drunk and I have tried him sober and there is nothing in him.' Mulgrave quipped that the asthmatic Prince was forced to breathe hard, lest people think he was dead. But he was kind and considerate to Anne, prepared to take second place in her household and later as her consort, and she was delighted with him.

The wedding took place at ten o'clock at night on 28 July 1683 in the Chapel Royal at St James's. Although henceforth she was to be known as the Princess of Denmark, Anne was to reside in England. Her generous dowry would enable her to live in some style, while the King gave her as an outright gift the Cockpit in Whitehall, approximately where Downing Street stands today, as her official London residence. The Denmarks were to spend their time in the idle pursuits of the aristocracy. Any activity at all seems to have been an effort for George. 'We talk here of going to tea, of going to Winchester, and everything else except sitting still all summer which was the height of my ambition,' he complained. Apart from endless games of cards and gambling for high stakes, Anne loved to hunt. She would join the King and her father at Newmarket, where she enjoyed both the racing and cock fighting. Just as Charles was responsible for Newmarket, Anne would later launch Royal Ascot.

Just prior to her marriage, she had the added joy of persuading her father to allow her friend, Sarah, Lady Churchill, to transfer from the Duchess's household to her own. 'The Duke of York came in just as you were gone, and made no difficulties, but has promised me that I shall have you, which I assure you is a great joy to me,' she wrote excitedly. 'I should say a great deal for your kindness in offering it, but I am not good at compliments. I will only say that I do take it extreme kindly, and shall be ready to do you all the service in my power.'

A little older than herself and a friend from her Richmond childhood, the vibrant Sarah provided all the passion and excitement that Anne lacked in her relationship with her cosy nonentity of a husband. During Sarah's absences from court, Anne suggested they correspond as Mrs Morley and Mrs Freeman. In her *Conduct* Sarah recalled: 'My frank, open temper naturally led me to pitch upon Freeman, and so the Princess took the other, and from this time Mrs Morley and Mrs Freeman began to converse as equals, made so by affection and friendship.'

As a royal princess third in line to the throne, Anne's duty was to provide heirs for the House of Stuart. Three months after her marriage, she embarked on the first of seventeen pregnancies which were to break her heart and wreck her health. In May 1684 she gave birth to a stillborn daughter. 'I believe you will be sorry to hear of my daughter, the Princess of Denmark, being delivered of a dead child,' James informed the Prince of Orange, 'they say it had been dead some days before, so that it is a great mercy it come as it did, and that she is so well after it.' By the end of the year she was pregnant again, which might have accounted for the fact that she does not seem to have been present when her uncle, King Charles II, died on 6 February 1685.

It was Anne's twentieth birthday, and so intense was her dislike of Catholicism that she gave some credence to the ridiculous rumour that the Jesuits had poisoned her uncle to make way for her father, who became the first Roman Catholic king in over a century.

24

The Conspirator

THE ACCESSION OF King James II triggered the gradual awakening of Anne's political conscience. With Charles dead and her married sister Mary in the Dutch Republic, she had become the sole member of the royal family participating in Anglican services in the Chapel Royal at Whitehall. Conscious of her political significance as second in line to the throne, she became ostentatious in her support of the Established Church. As her father's policies increasingly threatened its supremacy, Anne, the assiduous churchgoer, also attended sermons given by some of the more vociferous anti-Catholic preachers. Seeing herself as a Protestant heroine, she became a magnet to the silent opposition.

The personal antipathy in which Anne now held her stepmother could not be divorced from the religious question. While Anne was increasingly seen as the representative of Anglicanism, Mary Beatrice was regarded by many as the leader of the opposing Catholic party. Anne felt that she influenced the King to be more bigoted than he would otherwise have been, although she also blamed Lord Sunderland and the priests for her father's extremism. Her greatest fear was that James would try to enforce her conversion. 'I am of your opinion that it is more likely he will use fair means rather than force,' she wrote to Princess Mary in Holland, 'and I am in as great expectation of being tormented if he had not some hopes that in time he may gain either you or me.' When Mary exhorted her sister to stay firm to her religion, Anne assured her that she would 'rather beg my bread than ever change'.

The birth of her child, Lady Mary, on 1 June 1685 at Whitehall increased Anne's political importance. Her sister's marriage to Prince William of Orange had produced no children, so that the future of the dynasty seemed to rest with Anne. Anne might never, so far, have been ambitious of the crown for herself, but the arrival of children undoubtedly gave her a stake in it. Lady Mary, named for her aunt, was a poor scrap of a child. A second daughter, Lady Anne Sophia, was born prematurely on 12 May 1686. When the King visited her lying-in chamber with a Catholic priest in tow, Anne promptly burst into tears. She spent the summer convalescing at Tunbridge Wells and by the end of the year she was pregnant for the fourth time in her four-year marriage.

Early in the New Year of 1687 Anne wrote a letter to her sister that, as things turned out, was unbelievably poignant: 'I have always forgot to thank you for the plaything you sent my girl. It is the prettiest thing I ever saw, and too good for her yet, so I keep it locked up and only let her look on it when she comes to see me. She is most delighted with it in the world and in her language gives you abundance of thanks.'

A few days later Anne suffered a miscarriage, brought on, she suspected, by a new dance called the rigadoon. 'I have no reason to like it now,' she concluded sadly, 'for I believe it was the dance that made me miscarry for there is a great deal of jumping in it.' She was still recovering when Prince George and their two infant daughters fell sick with the smallpox. Anne nursed her family devotedly, but first Anne Sophia and then Mary died within days of each other. A few days later the bereaved couple withdrew to Richmond to mourn their children. 'The good Princess has taken her chastisement very heavily,' Rachel Russell wrote, observing of the grieving parents: 'Sometimes they wept, sometimes they mourned in words; then sat silent, hand in hand; he sick in bed, and she the carefullest nurse to him that can be imagined.'

Childless again, Anne asked her father's permission to visit her sister, which was refused. He already had spies in Anne's household and, clearly, he did not think it a good idea to have the two Protestant heirs to the throne colluding. Furious, Anne now indicated her intention of communicating with Everard van Weede van Dijkvelt, the agent William had sent to England to sound out the nobility about his plans to bring James to heel. As Anne knew she was being watched, she sent John Churchill to speak to Dijkvelt on her behalf. Two months later Churchill was writing to William to assure him that the Princess was prepared 'to suffer all extremities, even to death itself, rather than be brought to change her religion'.

Anne knew she had made an irrevocable step in joining the opposition to her father. 'Pray don't let anybody see this,' she urged Mary in a letter of 13 March 1687, 'nor speak of it: pray let me desire you not to take notice of what I have said to anybody except the Prince of Orange, for it is all treason that I have spoke.' She warned 'one dares not write anything by the post', so that, henceforth, the sisters used trusted messengers to carry their letters. When Dijkvelt returned to Holland in June 1687, he brought a secret code for the sisters to use. Their father became 'Mansell' in their increasingly disrespectful and dangerous correspondence.

From the discovery of her pregnancy in the spring of 1687, Anne absented herself from court as much as she decently could, dividing her time between Richmond and Hampton Court. On 22 October, two months before her time, Anne gave birth to a stillborn son who had apparently lain dead inside her for a month. It was shortly after this latest disappointment that she heard the disquieting rumour that her stepmother, after a gap of several years, was pregnant. Perhaps this child would survive where the others had all died. Worried for her religion, still grieving for the loss of her own children, her body and emotions in turmoil from repeated pregnancies that came to nothing, Anne now turned all her furious jealousy and pent-up anger on her hated stepmother, whose child – if a boy – would continue the Catholic tyranny.

Far from there being a Catholic plot to perpetrate a false pregnancy and smuggle a changeling into the Queen's bed, it seems much more likely that there was a Protestant plot to discredit the pregnancy and throw doubt on the child's legitimacy from the first. The chief perpetrator was Princess Anne, whose support lent the malicious rumours credibility. Princess Mary's side of the correspondence no longer exists, but it seems that it was Anne who first implied that the pregnancy was a hoax and persuaded her sister to believe it. On 14 March 1688 she wrote a highly seditious and damaging letter to Mary:

I must tell you I can't help thinking Mansell's wife's great belly is a little suspicious. It is true indeed she is very big, but she looks better than she ever did, which is not usual: for people when they are so far gone, for the most part, look very ill. Besides, it is very odd that the Bath, that all the best doctors thought would do her a great deal of harm, should have had so very good effect so soon, as that she should prove with child from the first minute she and Mansell met, after her coming from thence. Her being so positive it will be a son, and the principles of that religion being such that they will stick at nothing, be it never so wicked, if it will promote their interest, give some cause to fear there may be foul play intended. I will do all I can to find it out, if it be so: and if I should make any discovery, you shall be sure to have an account of it.

The following month, Anne was reported to be so ill her life was in danger. In the early hours of the morning of 16 April she apparently suffered another miscarriage. Her uncle, Lord Clarendon, went to visit her and found the King at her bedside. In his diary entry, Clarendon made an interesting comment, namely that 'the rumour among the women was, that she had only had a false conception.' It is possible that Anne was so overwrought by events and so desperate to bear a child after the failure of so many pregnancies that she had been experiencing a false pregnancy. Given that she was so busy implying that the Queen's pregnancy was false, it would be ironic if it were true.

She needed to convalesce. The advice of the royal physicians was sought as to whether or not it was a good idea for her to attend a spa. They gave different opinions, perhaps prompted by conflicting interests, Anne's Sir John Lowther thinking it was a good idea, the Queen's Sir Charles Scarborough being against it for the time being. In his *History* Gilbert Burnet claimed that Anne's friends urged her to stay in London. According to his account, it was James who 'pressed her to go to the Bath, since that had so good an effect on the Queen', the implication being that there was some conspiracy to get Anne out of the way just when the Queen's confinement was due.

Far from wanting his daughter away from court at this time, James had everything to gain from her attendance at the birth. But he was concerned for her health. Even Burnet, one of his severest critics, had to agree that James was a kind and indulgent father. It is most unlikely that James ever succeeded in making his obstinate daughter do anything she did not want to do, so that it was probably *he* who acceded to *her* wishes to leave London for a period of recuperation. He might well have hoped that she would return in time for the birth, but Anne had no intention of being a witness or offering her word as proof of its authenticity. She had nothing whatsoever to gain from the perpetuation of a Catholic dynasty and possibly something to gain from its overthrow. It must have been with a great deal of satisfaction, therefore, that she took her leave of the heavily pregnant Queen in the third week of May, offering as her parting shot the meaningful words: 'Madam, I think you will be brought to bed before I return.'

With the Queen's confinement safely out of the way on 10 June 1688, Anne lost no time in returning to London, all thoughts of convalescence apparently forgotten. Soon after her arrival, she dashed off a letter to her sister, full of hypocrisy and malice:

> My dear sister can't imagine the concern and vexation I have been in, that I should be so unfortunate to be out of town when the Queen was brought to bed, for I shall never now be satisfied whether the child be true or false. It may be it is our brother, but God only knows, for she never took care to satisfy the world, or give people any demonstration of it. It is wonderful, if she had really been with child, that nobody was suffered to feel [it] stir but Madam Mazarin and Lady Sunderland, who are people that nobody will give credit to. If out of pride she would not have let me touch [her] methinks it would have been very natural for her sometimes, when she has been undressing, to have let Mrs Robarts . . . see her belly . . . But that which to me seems the plainest thing in the world, is her being brought to bed two days after she heard of my coming to town [my being about to come back to town], and saying that the child was come at the full time, when everybody knows, by her own reckoning, that she should have gone a month longer. After all this, 'tis possible it may be her child; but where one believes it, a thousand do not. For my part, except they do give very plain demonstrations, which is almost impossible now, I shall ever be of the number of unbelievers.

James was slow to react to the persistent rumours surrounding the birth of his son and heir. At first he had been incredulous that anything so public as a royal birth should be called into question, or that he should be considered so wicked as to contrive to alter the hereditary succession. How could anyone, he asked, think him so unnatural a father that 'he would debar his own daughters from the right of succeeding him, to give his kingdoms to a suppositious son?'

At a special meeting of the Privy Council on 22 October, James called forty witnesses who were present at the Queen's confinement to swear on oath as to what they had seen. No gynaecological detail was spared. There was one notable absence from the meeting. James was anxious that Princess Anne should be present to hear what the witnesses had to say and to 'depose her own knowledge, which (before so many witnesses of her being privy to the Queen's being with child) she durst not have disown'd'. Had she not, after all, been present several times at the Queen's dressing and handed her her shift? She declined to attend, on the pretext that she was pregnant and not strong enough to leave her chamber.

The next day Lord Clarendon found his niece with her ladies, making jokes about what had transpired at the meeting. He was appalled and asked to speak to her in private, but she made an excuse that it was late and she had to go to prayers. When he finally managed to pin her down, he told her he was 'extremely surprised and troubled the other day, to find Her Royal Highness speak so slightingly of the Prince of Wales's affairs, and to suffer her women to make their jests upon it'. She replied that surely he had heard the common rumours about him. 'Is it not strange,' she mused, 'that the Queen should never (as often as I am with her, mornings and evenings) speak to me to feel her belly?' He asked if she had been invited to do so during the Queen's other pregnancies, and when she replied that she had not, her uncle asked why, then, she should have expected to do so on this occasion. 'I cannot but wonder there was no more care taken to satisfy the world,' she persisted.

James sent the Privy Counsellors to Anne with copies of the depositions. She did not even glance at them. 'My lords, this was not necessary,' she told them ingenuously, 'for I have so much duty for the King, that his word must be more to me than these depositions.'

It was not until 17 November, nearly two weeks after his son-in-law Prince William of Orange had landed in the West Country with a massive armed force, that James left London to join his army assembled on Salisbury Plain. It was now that his leading officers, notably John, Lord Churchill, but also the Prince of Denmark, deserted him in the face of the invader. The effect of their disloyalty on James's morale was so devastating that he refused to engage the enemy but retreated to the capital, so losing the military advantage. Any lingering hope he retained that his younger daughter was loyal, despite her husband's desertion, was shattered when he returned to Whitehall to find she too had defected. She had stolen out of the Cockpit in the early hours of 27 November with her friends Lady Churchill and Mrs Berkeley, leaving a note of explanation for the Queen. 'Never was anyone in such an unhappy condition, so divided between duty and affection to a father and husband,' she moaned:

> and therefore I know not what I must do, but to follow one to preserve the other. I see the general feeling of the nobility and gentry who avow to have no other end than to prevail with the King to secure their religion, which they saw so much in danger by the violent counsels of the priests, who to promote their own religion, did not care to what dangers they exposed the King. I am fully persuaded that the Prince of Orange designs the King's safety and preservation, and hope all things may be composed without more bloodshed, by calling a Parliament.

The letter never reached the Queen, but was leaked to the *London Gazette*.

In her *Conduct* Sarah Churchill denied that there had been any pre-arranged plan for the Princess to abscond from her father's court, or, indeed, that there had been any conspiracy at all. 'It was a thing sudden and unconcerted,' she claimed, 'nor had I any share in it, farther than obeying my mistress's orders.' According to Sarah, news of the Prince of Denmark's going over to the Prince of Orange and the King's imminent return 'put the Princess into a great fright. She sent for me, told me her distress, and declared that rather than see her father she would jump out at window. This was her very expression.'

If Sarah was trying to imply that the news of the Prince of Denmark's defection came as a surprise to Anne, the evidence suggests otherwise. The Denmarks had been planning their defection for about three months, in concert with the Churchills. Churchill had written to William as early as 4 August to assure him of his support. Then there is the undeniable fact of Anne's letter of 18 November to her brother-in-law, leaving no doubt where her loyalties lay:

> I shall not trouble you with many compliments, only in short assure that you have my wishes for your good success in this so just an under-taking, and I hope the Prince [of Denmark] will soon be with you to let you see his readiness to join with you . . . He went yesterday with the King towards Salisbury, intending to go from there to you as soon as his friends thought it proper. I am not yet certain if I shall continue here or remove into the City; that shall depend on the advice my friends will give me, but wherever I am I shall be ready to show you how much I am your humble servant.

It might well have been a shock to Anne that no battle had taken place and that her father was returning to London so soon. She might even have expected him to have been killed or captured. No wonder she panicked at the prospect of his imminent return and made her hasty get-away. It is significant that the backstairs she used had only recently been constructed, almost certainly with the purpose of escape in mind. It is interesting to note that just a week later, with her father on the brink of losing his throne and rioting in the streets of London, Anne could coolly write to her household treasurer, Sir Benjamin Bathurst: 'I have nothing to say only to desire you to give order that the back stairs at the Cockpit may be painted that they may be dry against I come home.'

Met by Charles, Lord Sackville, outside the Cockpit, the party made their way through the darkness to Charing Cross, laughing hysterically after Anne lost one of her high-heeled shoes in the mud. Bishop Compton, the mastermind behind the operation, was waiting in a hackney coach to drive them to his house in the City. From there, they were taken in slow stages to Nottingham, the bishop wearing military attire and brandishing a pistol to protect his Protestant Princess. 'Nor did she think herself safe,' recalled Sarah, 'till she saw that she was surrounded by the Prince of Orange's friends.'

Pretending 'that her father the King did persecute and use her ill for her religion, she being a Protestant and he a Papist', Anne joined the old Protestant Association, whose original purpose had been to bring her great-great-grandmother, Mary, Queen of Scots, to justice. Now the association was pledged 'to destroy all the papists in England, in case the Prince of Orange should be killed or murdered by any of them'.

The realization of Anne's defection left James so distraught that he lost his mind. 'God help me!' he cried. 'My own children have deserted me.' His only thought now was to send the Queen and the Prince of Wales to safety and to quit the country himself. The Prince and Princess of Denmark returned to town the day after her father departed. She showed no remorse for his misfortune. William immediately went to the Cockpit to pay them his respects. Even though they had served his purpose and his use for them was almost at an end, he was careful to observe the polite formalities. Anne greeted him wearing orange ribbons like a party badge.

An eyewitness was horrified to observe: 'King James was carried down the river in a most tempestuous evening, not without actual danger; and while her poor father was thus exposed to danger, an actual prisoner under a guard of Dutchmen, at that very moment his daughter, the Princess Anne of Denmark, with her great favourite, Lady Churchill, both covered in orange ribbons, went in one of his coaches, attended by his guards, triumphant to the playhouse.'

No sooner was their father dethroned and cast out than the protagonists began to quarrel among themselves. Probably Anne had not envisaged that William would take the crown. Her own place in the succession slipped a notch, as in the event of her sister Mary's death William was to reign alone, followed by Anne. William refused to give Prince George the honours which Anne, as a loving wife, felt he deserved. Mary was angry that Anne failed to pay sufficient respect to her and William. Soon, the sisters were not speaking to each other at all and, after Mary demanded that she dismiss Sarah from her service as the wife of a suspected traitor, Anne ostentatiously left the court, determined to appear as the injured party. She spent the next few years, until Mary's premature death in 1694, nursing an exaggerated sense of grievance for imagined wrongs inflicted on her by the 'Dutch Abortion', as she called her brother-in-law, and her proud sister.

Nothing would induce her to part from her favourite. She was even prepared to forgo some of her revenue rather than lose Sarah, and Prince George was in agreement with her. 'Can you think either of us so wretched that for the sake of twenty thousand pound, and to be tormented from morning to night with flattering knaves and fools, we would forsake those we have such obligations to? . . . No, my dear Mrs Freeman, never believe your faithful Mrs Morley will ever submit. She can wait with patience for a sunshine day, and if she does not live to see it, yet she hopes England will flourish again.'

If on a visit to Bath the Lord Mayor and corporation did not show Princess Anne 'the same respect and ceremony as has been usually paid to the royal family' and if she found that the minister of St James's Piccadilly, where she now worshipped since she was living privately at Berkeley House, had been forbidden to place the text of his sermon on her cushion, the normal courtesy afforded royalty, what did it matter? Anne had a highly developed sense of her own importance in the scheme of things. She could bide her time.

William could never trust John Churchill, a man who had deserted his King and commander in the field. He was right to suspect his treachery. Feeling cheated of the rewards and responsibility he felt were owed him, in spite of receiving the earldom of Marlborough, Churchill decided to take out an insurance policy with the exiled Jacobite court at St Germain-en-Laye. He might also have been seeking to allay the Jacobite threat by pretending that Anne would restore her brother's rights when it was in her power to do so. At any rate, he persuaded her to write a letter of penitence to her father:

> I have been very desirous of some safe opportunity to make you a sincere and humble offer of my duty and submission to you and to beg that you will be assured that I am both truly concerned for the misfortune of your condition and sensible, as I ought to be, of my own unhappiness. As to what you may think I have contributed to it, if wishes could recall what is past, I had long since redeemed my fault.

James rightly decided that Anne's plea for forgiveness was not sincere. Why should she want to restore her brother, James Francis Edward, to the throne, when she herself was now the mother of a son? On 24 July 1689 her political importance soared with the birth of a son, William, Duke of Gloucester. At his birth, he was described as a 'brave lively-like boy', but within six weeks he suffered convulsion fits so severe that the physicians despaired of his life. It is just possible that this acute infection – perhaps meningitis, or an infection of the middle ear – interfered with the normal process of absorption of cerebral fluid, which accumulated in excessive amounts in the brain. This would account for the subsequent hydrocephalus, which would give the otherwise diminutive boy such an enlarged head that only a man's hat would fit. With an impaired sense of balance, he would find it difficult to manage stairs or get to his feet if he were lying down.

'My poor boy' was the way Anne always referred to her son. He remained her only hope. Over the succeeding eleven years she had ten further pregnancies. Some, including one set of twins, ended in miscarriage, some were stillborn or died within hours of birth, and in at least two cases she gave birth to a baby who had been dead in the womb for up to a month. Even by the standards of the time, this was a poor return, begging an explanation. In the initial phase of her childbearing, two of her early children were born alive and survived for up to three years, dying of infection. In the second phase, of four foetuses that reached viability, only one survived, two died almost immediately and one succumbed several weeks before it was born. In the third phase, involving eight pregnancies, no child was born alive.

Three conditions could account for this pattern: the mother is rhesus negative; diabetes; or intra-uterine growth retardation due to placental insufficiency. In the first, if the mother is rhesus negative and the child rhesus positive, the mother responds by forming antibodies. These react on the baby's blood, destroying the corpuscles, so that the child becomes increasingly anaemic. The antibodies do not normally develop in the first pregnancy, but in a subsequent one, perhaps the second or third pregnancy. If a rhesus negative mother develops antibodies in, say, her third pregnancy, her next one may show a foetus moderately affected, and each subsequent one progressively more so. The more severely affected the child the more likely it is to die in the womb before term and as pregnancy follows pregnancy, as in Anne's case, these deaths may occur earlier and earlier.

What is not typical is the death in uterus of her fifth child and the later survival of William. If rhesus incompatibility caused the death of the fifth child it is unlikely that the child of the seventh pregnancy would have survived. However, there are occasional variations in the degree to which a foetus can be affected and such a sequence of events is not impossible.

More likely, in Anne's case, than rhesus incompatibility or diabetes is insufficiency of the placenta causing intra-uterine growth retardation. The placenta is a rich vascular organ which allows the foetus to take oxygen and nutrient substances from its mother and to pass carbon dioxide and waste products back to her. If the placenta is poorly formed or if some of its blood vessels become thrombosed and unable to permit this essential exchange, growth of the foetus may be limited, and if the oxygen supply is very poor, it may die in the uterus before the end of the pregnancy, or be born very small with a serious risk of dying in the first few days or weeks of life. This is precisely the pattern of Anne's pregnancies after the first three.

Tragically, the year of Anne's last pregnancy, when she gave birth to a son who had been dead in the womb for a month, brought the death of her precious only son. On 24 July 1700 William, Duke of Gloucester, celebrated his eleventh birthday at Windsor Castle. There was an elaborate banquet followed by dancing, at which the child 'overheated' himself, before watching a spectacular firework display from the ramparts. That night he was put to bed complaining of a sore throat and chills, while his devoted mother tended him anxiously. Possibly he had scarlet fever. A week later, he was dead. Anne never recovered from the loss of her only son. Henceforth, she would always sign her letters to Sarah, 'Your poor unfortunate faithful Morley'.

The eyes of Europe were now locked on the English succession. At Het Loo for the summer, William III was stunned by the death of the heir. Even though he had had his differences with the mother, he had been very fond of the boy. Something had to be done, and soon, to declare the order of the English succession in statute. The 1689 Bill of Rights had already declared that no Roman Catholic could succeed to the throne, ruling out the exiled Prince of Wales and the Catholic heirs of Charles I and his sister, Elizabeth of the Palatinate, Queen of Bohemia. However, the twelfth of her thirteen children, Sophie, widow of Ernst August of Brunswig-Lüneburg, Elector of Hanover, happened to be Protestant. In 1700 she was a sprightly seventy years of age and still had four sons living, of whom the eldest, George Ludwig, erstwhile suitor to Princess Anne, was undoubtedly Protestant. It was agreed that after Anne, Sophie and her heirs 'being Protestant' were to succeed to the English throne.

In September 1701 James II died in exile. His widow, Mary Beatrice, wrote to Anne: 'Some days before his death, he bid me find means to let you know that he forgave you from the bottom of his heart, and prayed God to do so too, that he gave you his last blessing, and prayed God to convert your heart, and confirm you in the resolution of repairing to his son the wrongs done to himself.'

Had Anne ever promised her father that she would restore her brother's rights? If she did, it is unlikely that she meant it. Any recognition of her brother would be to admit the lie she had perpetrated at his birth. Only by denying his right could she ensure that the monarchy would remain Protestant. No one knew better than Anne how to dissemble. All that is certain is that when William died in the early hours of 8 March 1702 and the crown at last fell within her grasp, ambition won. She was greeted in a huge wave of popularity.

25

Good Queen Anne

ANNE WAS A VERY ordinary woman who presided over an extraordinary period of the island's history. It has been too easy to dismiss her as a dull, overweight matron, deemed unfit to rule through the deficiencies of her health, education, intelligence and experience, and under the baleful influence of her favourites. Such a view may coincide with prejudices about a woman's ability to do the job. While lacking the brilliance of Elizabeth I, she was no fool. She had a clear-eyed view of what was right and the determination to pursue it, a shrewd political nose and impeccable sense of timing, and an ability to choose good men. She gave her name to an age of phenomenal military, diplomatic, economic and cultural success.

When Anne's 'Sunshine Day', as she had called her eagerly antici-pated accession, arrived on Sunday, 8 March 1702, the triumvirate of her advisers – John Churchill, Earl of Marlborough, Sidney, Lord Godolphin, and Robert Harley – had everything in place to effect a smooth transition of power. In consultation with the Princess, they decided that a continuity of William III's policies, particularly the war against Louis XIV's France, should be stressed, but that Anne should make a decisive break with her unpopular foreign brother-in-law in other respects.

In her first speech to Parliament, written by her uncle the Tory Earl of Rochester, Anne drew a parallel between herself and Queen Elizabeth. She played on the fact that, like Elizabeth, she was born in England of an English mother and had grown up in England. 'As I know my heart to be entirely English, I can very sincerely assure you there is not anything you can expect or desire from me which I shall not be ready to do for the happiness and prosperity of England,' she told the assembly in her melodious speaking voice. 'Never any woman spoke more audibly or with better grace,' one member noted approvingly.

The English sentiment was not one to win the hearts of her Scottish subjects, whose traditional loyalty to the House of Stuart and desire for independence inclined them towards Jacobitism. As long as the Scottish Parliament refused to endorse the Hanoverian succession, encapsulated in the Act of Settlement of 1701, there was a real possibility that the northern kingdom would go its separate way after the death of the new Queen. It was for this reason that William III had recommended union with Scotland in his last speech to Parliament, a policy Anne approved and would bring to fruition.

Like Elizabeth, Anne was a Protestant queen faced with the formidable task of rallying a divided nation against the most powerful Catholic king on earth. Elizabeth had shown that an image of feminine vulnerability, properly exploited, could arouse the gallantry and loyalty of the gentlemen of England. Less artfully, but just as effectively, Anne's shyness manifested itself in blushing as she spoke, which some considered very becoming in a woman.

She continued the analogy with Queen Elizabeth when she adopted her motto: *Semper Eadem*, Always One and the Same. It was appropriate for a woman who was steadfast and loyal both to her principles and to her friends, although it would be a mistake to take that loyalty for granted. Sarah Churchill, Lady Marlborough, might be forgiven for thinking she was invulnerable and irreplaceable when the Queen wrote to her: 'As for your poor unfortunate faithful Morley . . . if you should ever forsake me, I would have nothing more to do with the world, but make another abdication, for what is a crown when ye support of it is gone, I never will forsake your dear self, Mr Freeman nor Mr Montgomery, but always be your constant faithful servant, & we four must never part, till death mows us down with his impartial hand.'

Her dearest Sarah, or Mrs Freeman, was given the most prized offices of the court: Groom of the Stole, Mistress of the Robes and Keeper of the Privy Purse. Mr Freeman – Marlborough – immediately received the Garter William had denied him and, after his great victory at Blenheim two years later, was elevated to a dukedom, while Mr Montgomery – Sidney, Lord Godolphin – became Lord Treasurer or First Lord of the Treasury, effectively her chief minister. Convention dictated that Anne could not lead her armies in combat, the traditional arena of kingship, as William had done. Nor had she been able to have her husband named Commander-in-Chief of the allied forces. But her close friendship with the Churchills and William's recognition of Marlborough's abilities made his selection as her Captain-General inevitable. It was an excellent choice. With the addition of Robert Harley, this group were the brains and the energy behind Anne's regime for the first eight years, but her own part should not be underestimated.

The Queen, who had ruined her health in a forlorn attempt to give England an heir, would now channel her maternal instincts into her role as monarch. She would be the mother of her people. Her coronation sermon was preached on Isaiah 49: 23: 'And kings shall be thy nursing fathers and their queens thy nursing mothers.'

The contrast between Anne and her Dutch predecessor was equally marked by her revival and exploitation of royal ritual and ceremony. If at thirty-seven she was almost an invalid, being carried to her coronation in an open chair, Anne still had something of majesty about her and, resplendent in full regalia, could rise to the occasion. Again, she identified herself with Elizabeth by reviving two activities closely associated with her: the royal progress and the public thanksgiving for military victory. In the early autumn of 1702, ostensibly for Prince George's health, there was a progress to Bath, via Oxford and Cirencester, and in December that year she became the first sovereign since Elizabeth to attend a service of public thanksgiving in St Paul's, for the naval victory at Vigo Bay. It is appropriate that Queen Anne's statue now stands before St Paul's, where she so often had occasion to give thanks over succeeding years.

Where under James II the nobility had skulked on its estates, avoiding the Catholic monarch both at court and when he travelled in their vicinity, and where under William III they had sulked over his obvious preference for his Dutch cronies, now under Anne they were to be drawn back into the monarch's orbit. Thanksgiving days began with the Queen receiving the compliments of the nobility at St James's, followed by a procession of the great officers of state and the law, the members of both Houses of Parliament, the foreign ministers and, finally, the monarch herself, her consort, and their respective retinues. The spectacle of the Queen, her court and the officers of state in full panoply, uniting with the people in celebration of the benefits of her reign, was purposely designed to impress and therefore the procession extended over several hours from St James along the Strand and up Ludgate Hill to the cathedral, so as to reach the widest possible audience.

The relationship between the monarchy and the City of London was reinforced by the procession's pausing at Temple Bar, where the Queen was greeted by the Lord Mayor, who surrendered the City sword and made a short speech of welcome, inviting her to enter. Provincial progresses equally served to inspire civic expressions of loyalty to the monarch, as communities spared no expense to prove they were as loyal as the capital. Like Elizabeth, Anne would bestow her company on various country houses, being careful to divide her favour equally between Whigs and Tories. When the Whigs hijacked the progresses for their own political purposes, Anne ceased to make them, only resuming them after the fall of the Whigs in 1710 and the rise to power of Harley and the Tories on a platform of moderation and national unity. It was a clear example of Anne's refusal to be used.

For a regime embroiled in a costly and unpopular war, the enthusiasm generated by the Queen's first progress to Bath could be seen as setting the seal of popular approval on its policies. Anne was able to boast to Parliament of her reception in the Tory West Country, in spite of the fact that the Tories were opposed to a land war in Europe and advocates of a naval war in which France and Spain would be attacked on the high seas and in their colonial empires, before promptly asking for supply for the next year, specifically for Marlborough's next land campaign.

A queen who would be a mother wanted to give expression to her motherly instincts by touching her people. Convinced that they were God's representatives on earth and imbued with a strong mystical sense of their sovereignty, the first four Stuart monarchs in England had all touched for the King's Evil, or scrofula, following Christ's example of healing by touch. Anne knew very well that her power derived from Parliament, that she was an elected monarch, albeit hereditary, but nevertheless, motivated by sincere religious conviction as well as a desire to court popularity, she revived the practice which her Calvinist brother-in-law had discounted as papist superstition. She was the last English monarch to do so, inspiring devotion and reverence for the monarchy. As a child, Samuel Johnson had received Queen Anne's touch and all his life retained a solemn memory of the lady in diamonds.

'There are now in London several thousands of people, some of them ready to perish, come out of the country waiting for her healing,' Archbishop Sharp noted early in the reign. Fasting beforehand, Anne regularly touched up to 200 sufferers at a time, twice weekly, during the court season. 'I desire you would order 200 pieces more of Healing Gold, for I intend (if it please God) when I come from Windsor to touch as many poor people as I can before the hot weather comes,' she wrote to Sarah, referring to the medals she gave the afflicted. 'I do that business now in the Banqueting House, which I like very well, that being a very cool room, and the doing of it there keeps my own house sweet and free from crowds.'

Nothing was more liable to upset the Queen than division and strife among her people. 'As long as I live,' she told Godolphin, 'it shall be my endeavour to make my country and my friends easy.' As the symbol of national unity, Anne saw the monarchy as being above politics, harking back to Elizabeth's day before the advent of party, when the sovereign was the sole focus of loyalty, and at the same time anticipating the constitutional monarchy of the future. It was a time of transition, of bitter party rivalry, yet a time when political affiliation was still fluid. Anne, doggedly holding on to the crown's prerogatives, found the whole idea of party politics anathema.

Respecting the Revolution settlement as she did, Anne's reign was free from the kind of constitutional strife between crown and Parliament or the politically motivated violence that characterized those of her predecessors. The Queen's reputation for mercy and clemency meant there were no political beheadings, even of captured Jacobites, and her womanly compassion meant that she personally mitigated the sentences of certain criminals condemned to death or transportation. She 'rules a willing people, not by the terror of rods and axes, but with the indulgent tenderness of a common parent', one sermonizer commented, reiterating the maternal theme. Anne's benevolence was consistent with her avowed desire to 'be Queen of all her subjects . . . who would have all the parties and distinctions of former reigns ended and buried in hers'.

As party warfare between Whigs and Tories reached a new intensity, fanned by a burgeoning press newly liberated from the restraints of censorship, Anne valiantly tried to steer a middle course. Like William before her, she believed it was her prerogative to choose whichever ministers she pleased, regardless of their party affiliation. Her natural inclination, as a Stuart and the granddaughter of Clarendon, was towards the Tories, who had been such firm supporters of the monarchy and of her beloved Anglican Church. But she could not condone the extreme High Church Tories, men such as Lord Nottingham, or her uncle, Lord Rochester, any more than she could the extremists of the other party, the Whig Junto.

Anne, whose goal was 'to keep me out of ye power of ye Mercyless men of both partys', determined to form a 'mixed ministry' of moderates, with her dear friends Marlborough and Godolphin, who were loosely Tory, and Robert Harley, who with his Nonconformist, parliamentarian background had come from the Whigs. They all agreed that the continuation of the war was essential. With Lord Marlborough leader of the Grand Alliance and Captain-General of the allied forces, it was Godolphin's job at the treasury to ensure that the army received its pay and supplies, while Harley was to use his considerable political skills to manage Parliament.

In spite of Marlborough's great victories at Blenheim, Ramillies, Oudenarde and Malplaquet, accomplished in the Queen's name, the country became increasingly divided between those who wanted to continue the war, among them those Whigs making money from it, and those who wanted peace. Tired of the bloodshed and the expense of it all, Anne yearned for peace, the more since her relationship with the Marlboroughs began to deteriorate and she looked to the Tories to provide a get-out from the war, which would release her from them.

It seems that her friendship with Sarah had been under strain right from the beginning of the reign, Anne later telling her erstwhile favourite: 'it has not been my fault that we have lived in ye manner we

have done ever since I came to the crown.' Sarah was impatient with
the idea of sovereignty and the awe and respect it should be accorded,
having witnessed at first hand royalty's all-too-human faults and weaknesses. Gaining in confidence all the time, Anne was only too aware
of what was due to her as queen. Sarah failed to see that frank, open
discussion which had been encouraged between a princess and a
friend was inappropriate between a queen and a subject. She took at
face value Anne's polite insistence:

> I beg my dear Mrs Freeman would banish the hard thought out of her
> head that I can ever be displeased at anything that comes from you, for
> sure I must be void of all reason if I were not sensible that there can not
> be a greater mark of kindness than telling one every thing freely, it is
> what has always been my request to you to do, & I do again beg you
> would continue that goodness to your poor unfortunate faithful
> Morley.

Contrary to what people thought and came to believe, largely thanks
to Sarah's biased account in her *Conduct* in which she claimed that
Anne 'wou'd not go to take the air unless somebody advised her to it',
Sarah knew that Anne had always been her own person. She was
tenacious and independent, with her own ideas and all her father's
obstinacy. If she lacked Sarah's volubility, her silence was a useful
attribute at times when it was necessary to keep her position ambiguous or flexible and her leading politicians off-balance. With the
impatience of a quick-witted person at someone reflective and stubborn, Sarah became increasingly frustrated by Anne's dogged refusal to
fall in with her wishes in the matter of party politics.

No one knew better than Sarah how greatly Anne feared her half-
brother, James Francis Edward, whom she had not seen since his infancy.
Not only did he have a better claim to the throne than she did, as their
late father's only legitimate son, but he was a living reminder of Anne's
betrayal of her father, and of the lies and duplicity she had used to oust
them both from the throne. Sarah tried to convince Anne that the Tories
were all secret Jacobites at heart, but Anne was too level-headed to
accept such a generalization:

> I own I can not have that good opinion of some sort of people that you
> have, nor that ill one of others, & let the Whigs brag never so much of

their great services to the country & of their numbers, I believe the revolution had never been, nor the succession settl'd as it is now, if the Church party had not joyned with them, & why those people that agreed with them in these two things should all now be branded with ye name of Jacobites I can't imagine.

Sarah bombarded the Queen with letters, lecturing her endlessly on the merits of the Whigs, and as good as told her that she was too stupid to make her own decisions. 'I must own I have ye same opinion of Whig & Tory that ever I had, I know their principles very well, & when I know my self to be in ye right, nothing can make me alter mine,' Anne replied. As Marlborough warned his wife: 'You know that I have often disputes with you concerning the Queen, and by what I have always observed that when she thinks herself in the right, she needs no advice to help her to be very firm and positive.'

When the High Church Tories introduced the Occasional Conformity Bill, targeting those who attended communion at the Anglican Church only occasionally so as to qualify for public office, as a means to undermine the Toleration Act of 1689, suppress the Dissenters and snub the Whigs, Sarah rushed to the defence of the Whigs and to press her arguments on the Queen, who replied: 'I can't forbear saying that I see nothing like persecution in this Bill, you may think this is a notion Lord Nottingham put in my head, but upon my word it is my own thought.'

Just as she resisted the Whig extremists, Anne had no intention of being intimidated by the High Church Tories. No one was a more loyal daughter of the Church than Anne, but in the final resort she could not support their Occasional Conformity Bill. This infuriated them, but she still showed her preference for the Established Church over her Nonconformist subjects by yielding her income from first fruits and tenths – Queen Anne's Bounty – to support the poor parish clergy. Later she would have Nicholas Hawksmoor build new churches in London's sprawling suburbs, so that her people would not be won over to dissent. She did not need Tories such as Lord Nottingham, or, indeed, Whigs such as the Duchess of Marlborough, to tell her where her duty lay.

Matters took a turn for the worse when a Whig majority was returned to the Commons in the election of 1705. Now the Whig extremists, the Junto, demanded that one of their own have a ministerial position. Thinking that as the Marlboroughs' son-in-law he would have the best chance of being accepted, their chosen candidate was Charles Spencer, Earl of Sunderland. Anne, whose weakness was to let her personal likes and dislikes of people influence her decisions, loathed him. She bitterly resented Whig attempts to foist him on her, and, more particularly, she resented the fact that the once moderate Marlborough and Godolphin were pressuring her to fall in with the plan. The war could not be continued, they argued, without Whig support, so that some concessions had to be made to the extremists. Godolphin even threatened to resign if the Queen refused to accede to their demands. While she retaliated that 'he should do as he pleas'd, with all she cou'd find enough glad of that staff', in reality, the prospect alarmed her, as she was not yet ready to dispense with his services. When she was, three years later, she dismissed this dedicated minister as perfunctorily as Charles II had done her grandfather Clarendon.

'Whoever of the Whigs thinks I am to be hectored or frightened into a compliance, though I am a woman, is mightily mistaken in me,' she warned Godolphin in 1705. 'I thank God I have a soul above that, and am too much concerned for my reputation to do anything to forfeit it.'

It went against all Anne's instincts to give in, telling Godolphin in exasperation:

All I desire is my liberty in encouraging & employing all those that concur faithfully in my service whether they are call'd Whigs or Torys, not to be tyed to one, not to ye other, for if I should be so unfortunate as to fall into ye hands of either, I shall look upon my self tho I have the name of Queen, to be in reality but their slave, which as it will be my personal ruin, so it will be ye destroying of all government ... Why for God's sake, must I who have no interest, no end, no thought but for ye good of my country, be made so miserable as to be brought into ye power of one set of men, & why may I not be trusted, since I mean nothing but what is equally for ye good of all my subjects?

Anne had to back down in the matter of Sunderland in order to secure the necessary supplies for the war which had yet to be concluded, but it meant that Marlborough and Godolphin had forfeited her trust. They had failed to protect her from the extreme Whigs.

Anne tried to find a way out of the impasse and build a bridge with the Tories through her bedchamber attendants, who had constant access to her when she was incapacitated by illness. As Marlborough and Godolphin moved inexorably towards the Whigs, their former colleague Robert Harley was moving towards the Tories. Anne's patronage was evenly distributed, so that the members of her household were both Whigs and Tories, but her favourite physician, Dr John Arbuthnot, was a High Tory and the bedchamber woman, Abigail Hill, was also a Tory. Ironically, she was a poor relation of Sarah's, but equally closely related to Harley on her father's side. Harley took the trouble to court Abigail's favour, as a channel to the Queen, but could not muster enough support to defeat the Whigs, so that Anne was forced to dismiss him. Marlborough did not endear himself when he wrote advising her 'to have no more resentments to any particular person or party [meaning Sunderland and the Whigs], but to make of such as will carry on this just war with vigour, which is the only way to preserve our religion and liberties, and the crown upon your head'.

It was not the first occasion Anne had to exercise patience. She would bide her time.

Anne's health had been impaired for a while. In the summer of 1703 she was virtually an invalid, so lame that she could hardly cross the room except on two sticks. The physicians diagnosed gout, but this is unusual in a woman, especially a pre-menopausal woman, and unlikely.

In 1707 Sir John Clerk of Penicuik, a Scot who had come to England to discuss the union of the two kingdoms, found her in a pitiable condition. If the Queen had 'two bodies' – the one symbolic of the power of the crown, the body politic, the other her mortal body – it was decidedly the mortal one he was seeing:

> Her Majesty was labouring under a fit of the gout, and in extreme pain and agony, and on this occasion everything about her was much in the same disorder as about the meanest of her subjects. Her face, which was red and spotted, was rendered something frightful by her negligent

dress, and the foot affected was tied up with a pultis and some nasty bandages.

What are you, poor mean mortal, thought I, who talks in the style of a sovereign. Nature seems to be inverted when a poor infirm woman becomes one of the rulers of the world.

When he visited her again, the 'despicable' situation had not improved, and he was struck by her isolation:

> The poor lady, as I saw her twice before, was again under a severe fit of the gout, ill dressed, blotted in her countenance, and surrounded with plaisters, cataplasisms, and dirty-like rags . . . I believe she was not displeased to see any body, for no court attenders ever came near her. All the . . . adoration offered at courts were to her ministers . . . her palace of Kensington, where she commonly resided, was a perfect solitude, as I had occasion to observe several times. I never saw anybody attending there but some of her guards in the outer rooms, with one at most of the gentlemen of her bedchamber. Her frequent fits of sickness, and the distance of the place from London, did not admit of what are commonly called drawing-room nights, so that I had many occasions to think that few houses in England belonging to a person of quality were kept in a more private way than the Queen's royal palace of Kensington.

Even when Anne was not ill, court life was not what it was under her scandalous, profligate uncle. Burnet's verdict was that 'she laid down the splendour of the court too much'. Anne's virtues of frugality and good management were practically middle class – if such a class had existed at the time – but were also dictated by the fact that England was engaged in a prolonged and costly war. Outlawing the sale of office as corrupt, her court offered few of the material, political, social or cultural opportunities that had made attendance at previous Tudor and Stuart courts so attractive. Her poor eyesight meant that she had little interest in the visual arts or in literature, although she did love music and patronized Handel, who wrote his only birthday ode in her honour. Her shyness and poor conversational abilities made the drawing rooms, which she held twice weekly during the season if she was well enough, a trial. For wit and debate, in the age of Swift, Defoe, Addison, Steele and Pope, people turned to the coffee-houses. To make their fortunes, there was the City and the ever wider world beyond St James.

There were intervals when Anne was blessedly free of pain, such as when Jonathan Swift described her at Windsor 'hunting the stag till four this afternoon . . . she drove in her chaise above forty miles.' Anne could no longer ride, but she was not deterred from hunting 'in a chaise with one horse, which she drives herself, and drives furiously, like Jehu, and is a mighty hunter, like Nimrod'.

Neglected by Sarah, whose official duties, if not gratitude for the Queen's boundless generosity to her and her family, should have brought her to court, Anne found the comfort she needed in the soothing presence of Abigail Hill, now Lady Masham. When she was in pain and discomfort, Abigail was always there with a kind word, a dish of tea, and a pleasant tune on the harpsichord, quiet and unassuming, in contrast to the strident, volatile Duchess.

Jealous of the bedchamber woman who she felt had usurped her place as the Queen's confidante, Sarah made a rare appearance at court at the end of July 1708, bringing with her a scurrilous verse, probably written by Arthur Maynwaring, an unsavoury associate of the Whigs:

> When as Queen Anne of great Renown
> Great Britain's Sceptre sway'd,
> Besides the Church, she dearly love'd
> A Dirty Chamber-Maid.
>
> O! Abigail that was her Name
> She stitch'd and starch'd full well,
> But how she pierced this Royal Heart,
> No Mortal Man can tell.
>
> However, for sweet service done
> And Causes of great Weight,
> Her Royal Mistress made her, Oh!
> A Minister of State.
>
> Her Secretary she was not
> Because she could not write
> But had the Conduct and the Care
> Of some dark Deeds at Night.

Not content to leave it at that, Sarah followed it up with a letter in which she accused the Queen of lesbianism:

I remember you said . . . of all things in this world, you valued most your reputation, which I confess surpris'd me very much, that Your Majesty should so soon mention that word after having discover'd so great a passion for such a woman, for sure there can be no great reputation in a thing so strange & unaccountable . . . nor can I think the having no inclination for any but of one's own sex is enough to maintain such a character as I wish may still be yours.

It was outrageous. It is impossible to imagine anyone having the audacity to speak to Queen Elizabeth or Queen Victoria in this way and get away with it. There was, of course, no truth in the accusation. The passionate friendship Anne and Sarah had once enjoyed had no sexual dimension, and there is no reason to suppose that Anne Stuart, even if she had been that way inclined, would have had a relationship with a servant. She was far too conscious of her rank and dignity. The Queen could not dismiss Sarah from office while her husband was deemed essential to the war, but their friendship was now beyond repair.

'I believe no body was ever so used by a friend as I have been by her ever since my coming to ye crown,' Anne wrote sadly to Marlborough. 'I desire nothing but that she would leave off teasing & tormenting me & behave herself with the decency she ought both to her friend & Queen, & this I hope you will make her do.'

The death of Prince George, her dearest husband and best friend, in November 1708, prompted Anne to retreat almost as fully as Queen Victoria was to do after the death of Albert over a century and a half later. Poor health and mourning gave her the excuse not to go to St Paul's to give thanks for the victories of a Whig general in a war she and her subjects had now grown tired of.

The impeachment by the Whigs of Dr Henry Sacheverell, the crypto-Jacobite who had preached an incendiary sermon attacking the Revolution Settlement and the Hanoverian succession – indeed, questioning by what right Anne sat on the throne – united the fragmented Tory Party against the government. Anne was sufficiently interested in the outcome of Sacheverell's trial to attend it, just as, like Charles II, she attended debates in the House of Lords. By 1710 Marlborough, who was so full of his own power that he was demanding to be made Captain-General for life, was being accused of prolonging the war for private profit.

The opposition was in agreement that the Queen should be rescued from the tyranny of the Marlborough family and that England should get out of the war, but this is not to say that she was a passive victim of events. Her manipulation of the situation, using her backstairs link with Harley and the Tories, was subtle and effective. She chose her moment well, when more might be gained from diplomacy than arms and when the tide of public opinion swung decisively in the opposition's favour.

The Tories saw the Queen's desire for peace as consistent with her concern for her people. It was conveniently overlooked that Anne had supported the Whig war for so long, but, on the other hand, 'perfidious Albion' was going to do very well out of opening separate peace talks with France, gaining Gibraltar, parts of the West Indies, and uninhibited access to the lucrative slave trade, which would provide the financial underpinning for the wars of the eighteenth century.

The Marlboroughs did not go quietly. 'I can't help but think the nation wou'd be of opinion that I have deserv'd better than to be made a sacrifice to the unreasonable passion of a bedchamber woman,' Marlborough complained. Sunderland, meanwhile, raised the question of Abigail Masham in Parliament, demanding her dismissal. Anne was incandescent with rage. She was no more inclined to bow to pressure to dismiss one of her servants now than she had been in the late Queen her sister's time, when Lady Marlborough's dismissal was being demanded.

Sarah was threatening that 'such things are in my power . . . that might lose a crown'. She would publish the Queen's letters to her, letters containing such protestations as 'I wish I may never see the face of Heaven if ever I consent to part with you' and 'I wish I may never enjoy happiness in this world or the next, for Christ Jesus sake do not leave me.' Obviously, they would cause an international sensation. As Anne told Sir David Hamilton: 'when people are fond of one another, they say many things . . . they would not desire the world to know.' Sarah was finally dissuaded from publishing the letters, but she did not leave her apartments at St James's without ripping out the fixtures and fittings. In retaliation, Anne ordered a temporary halt to the construction of Blenheim Palace, her gift to the Duke for his first great victory, angrily saying 'that she would not build the Duke a house when the Duchess was pulling hers to pieces'.

Elizabeth, Duchess of Somerset, replaced Sarah as Mistress of the Robes and Groom of the Stole, while Masham took charge of the Privy Purse. Sir David Hamilton was pleased to note that this Duchess 'is of the first quality and in that respect suitable to you. She seems to converse with a courteous calmness which makes her the more suitable to Your Majesty's temper.' The Queen could only agree and so soothing did she find the Duchess's company that she insisted on retaining her despite her husband's being a fierce Whig.

The 'Jacobite peace' with France fuelled speculation that Anne was secretly in favour of her half-brother succeeding her. Not only did James Francis Edward receive this impression, but also he was convinced that Anne had made such a promise to their father. Knowing the threat from the Jacobite quarter was real, it served her purpose to keep their hopes of the succession alive, while having no intention of sanctioning it. When Hamilton repeated the rumours to her in the autumn of 1712 that 'things looked as though the Pretender was designed and all in places who are for him', Anne replied, 'O fye, there is no such thing. Do you think I am a child, and to be imposed upon?' She assured the bishops that her zeal for the Church of England and the liberties of the nation was unimpaired.

Both Whigs and Tories in opposition had flirted with the House of Hanover, insisting that the Electress Sophie, Anne's designated successor by the terms of the 1701 Act of Settlement, or her son or grandson should take up residence in England. Soon Sophie and her son George were demanding not just the invitation, but also a civil list allowance. Like Elizabeth, Anne had no intention of tolerating a rival court which would become the focus of opposition. She fired off letters to Sophie, her son and grandson, telling them in no uncertain terms that their presence would not be welcome, that it would lead to disturbances among her subjects and put the succession of their family in jeopardy. The harshness of her letter came as such a disagreeable shock to the eighty-four-year-old Sophie – who might otherwise have been England's fifth queen regnant – that she died within days.

Only two months later, Anne too was slipping out of the world.

On 30 July 1714 she suffered a stroke. Speechless, one of her last acts before her death two days later was to hand the treasurer's staff of office to the moderate Whig, Lord Shrewsbury, who would ensure the smooth accession of George I. She had worked tirelessly for her country and acquitted herself well. 'I believe sleep was never more welcome to a weary traveller,' Dr Hamilton told Jonathan Swift, 'than death was to her.'

After the arrival of German George, there was nostalgia for the days of 'Good Queen Anne', the last properly English monarch for a very long time. The last of her dynasty, Anne had also proved the most successful of the Stuart sovereigns. She prosecuted a successful war, won a favourable peace, defended the Church and ensured the monarchy would remain Protestant, while maintaining the toleration the Nonconformists had won at the Revolution, respected the constitutional proprieties, and finally accomplished the union of her great-grandfather's two kingdoms of England and Scotland. It was no small thanks to Queen Anne that the new kingdom of Great Britain emerged as a power in the world.

PART THREE: *House of Hanover*

VICTORIA

b. 1819, r. 1837–1901

26

Kensington Girl

ON 24 JUNE 1819, at three o'clock, a christening ceremony took place in the Cupola Room at Kensington Palace. A gilded font stood in the centre and the walls had been specially hung with crimson velvet. A christening is usually a solemn, yet joyous occasion, but at this one the tension was palpable. The Prince Regent did not like his brother, the father of the baby, and perhaps he resented the fact that she was in some sense replacing his own dead daughter, Charlotte. The Duke and Duchess of Kent had chosen the names for their infant – Victoire Georgiana Alexandrina Charlotte Augusta – and out of courtesy had informed the Prince Regent of their intention. Only the night before, they were surprised to receive a messenger with the Regent's objections. The name Georgiana could not be used, since he did not choose to place his name before that of the Emperor Alexander of Russia – one of the godparents – and he could not allow it to follow. As for the other names, he would indicate his wishes at the christening.

So now when it came to pronouncing the child's name, the Archbishop of Canterbury turned expectantly to the parents, who looked helplessly at the bloated, perfumed figure of the Prince Regent. Eventually, he spoke. Charlotte – the name of his mother and the child's grandmother, Queen Charlotte, but also of the dead Princess his daughter – would not do. Nor did he approve of Augusta, after the child's maternal grandmother, the Dowager Duchess of Saxe-Coburg-Saalfeld. It was too magisterial. 'Alexandrina,' he ventured, for the Tsar.

The Duke of Kent urged a second name: Elizabeth, perhaps?

The suggestion was too audacious. Ever prickly with his brother and knowing now that no child of his would inherit the throne, the

Regent bridled at the thought of Kent's brat bearing the name of England's great queen. 'Give her her mother's name also then, but it cannot precede that of the Emperor.' But the Duchess of Kent's name, Victoire, was French. It must be anglicized to Victoria, a name hitherto unknown in England. Little Alexandrina Victoria spent the first years of her life as 'Drina' and her first language, imbibed from her mother who spoke very little English, was German.

Drina, or Victoria as she would later be known, was born at Kensington Palace on 24 May 1819, 'a pretty little Princess, as plump as a partridge'. That she was born in England at all was purely fortuitous. Her parents' marriage had been the result of an unseemly rush on the part of three of the seven surviving sons of the still living but mentally incapacitated King George III to marry and produce a legitimate heir to the throne after the death of Princess Charlotte.

Of the remaining sons, the bigamous Prince Regent – he had married Mrs Maria Fitzherbert, a Catholic, in secret, so the marriage was considered invalid – had little hope of divorcing his estranged wife, Caroline of Brunswick, no matter how many lovers she took in exile. The philandering Frederick, Duke of York, was married to an eccentric Prussian princess who was unlikely to bear him a child. The universally loathed Ernest Augustus, Duke of Cumberland, was married and living in his father's kingdom of Hanover, and so far childless. Augustus, Duke of Sussex, had fallen foul of the Royal Marriages Act by marrying a commoner, Lady Augusta Murray, without the King's permission, so that their children were excluded from the succession. That left the Dukes of Clarence, Kent and Cambridge to do the deed. The betting fraternity had its money on Cambridge, who had already found a suitable bride, to win the royal sweepstakes.

Licentious, scandalous, gluttonous, idle and spendthrift, the sons of George III had brought the monarchy into dangerous disrepute, just at a time when a massive groundswell of agitation for electoral reform was gathering force. Republicanism was in the air. Public sympathy was with the women: the rejected Caroline, unkempt, even smelly, so that the fastidious Regent could not bear her, but wronged and all the more tragic for that. Above all, it was with their daughter. Charlotte, young, gracious and feminine – the antithesis of the corrupt old wicked uncles – and married to a respectable and sensible prince,

Leopold of Saxe-Coburg, had offered hope for the monarchy. But she had died after a forty-six-hour labour and the birth of a stillborn son in November 1817; the doctor subsequently committed suicide. With her death, hope for the British monarchy seemed to be extinguished. It was not until the advent of another young woman as heir to the throne that it revived. Public sympathy for Charlotte carried over to the next royal female, Victoria, who benefited from her popularity.

Lured more by the incentive of parliamentary funds than the glory of having his progeny sit on the British throne, William, Duke of Clarence, trawled the pool of plain and homely German princesses – virtually the only royal brides in Europe who, as Protestants, would satisfy the criteria of the Act of Settlement – and eventually found one willing to accept him. The kindly Adelaide of Saxe-Meiningen was half his age and likely to bear children. The actress Dora Jordan, his devoted companion of twenty years and the mother of his ten bastards, was pensioned off, but died in debt shortly afterwards.

Encouraged by Princess Charlotte and Leopold, Edward, Duke of Kent, had already begun his suit to Leopold's sister, Victoire, Dowager Princess of Leiningen, an attractive thirty-year-old widow with two children. She was initially reluctant to give up her independence for the impecunious Duke, but the death of Charlotte and the prospect of a child of theirs being heir to the British throne seems to have increased the Duke's ardour and changed her opinion. It was only when she read of the likely match in the newspaper that Edward's loyal companion of twenty-seven years, Mme Julie de St Laurent, discovered that she was about to be discarded by her royal lover.

On 11 July 1818, in the presence of Queen Charlotte and the Prince Regent at Kew Palace, Clarence and Kent married their German princesses in a double wedding. Before the end of the year, the Duchesses of Clarence, Kent, Cumberland and Cambridge were pregnant. It looked as if the royal succession would be secured. Marriage had hardly improved the Duke of Kent's finances, in spite of the £6,000 annual allowance Parliament voted him now that he was doing his duty. Kent accepted it as no less than his due after the great sacrifice he was making: 'As for the payment of my debts, I don't call them great. The nation, on the contrary, is greatly my debtor.'

He seemed perennially incapable of living within his means. He had lavished sumptuous wedding presents on his bride which was all very commendable, but even when he returned to live at her home at Amorbach near Darmstadt to save on living expenses, he needlessly frittered money away aggrandizing the old castle. Before long, the Duchess was pregnant. Convinced that his child would inherit the throne, Kent was determined that the birth should take place in England. Ignoring the fact that Clarence's child would take precedence over his, he invited the most prominent men of the kingdom – the Archbishop of Canterbury, the Bishop of London, the Duke of Wellington, the Chancellor of the Exchequer and others – to be present as witnesses.

Once more he was broke – too broke to afford the journey. He set down his requirements to the Regent – money for the journey, a yacht to cross the Channel, an apartment at Kensington Palace, and perhaps a seaside house for after the confinement – confidently expecting them to be met. The Regent flatly refused. Kent's friends then clubbed together for the Duke and Duchess to return to England, although in much reduced style. To save the expense of a coachman, the Duke drove his own phaeton across several hundred miles of bumpy roads to Calais, with the seven months' pregnant Duchess travelling beside him, followed by a shabby procession of assorted vehicles carrying the Duchess's daughter – her son staying behind in Germany – her lady-in-waiting, her midwife, the governess, servants and baggage. The Regent had been shamed into providing a yacht to bring the party across the Channel and one month before the birth the Kents were installed in rooms at Kensington Palace.

Kent never expressed any doubt that his daughter would inherit the throne, despite the fact that when she was born she was only fifth in the line of succession and there was every possibility that the Clarences would produce an heir and, indeed, her own parents might yet have a son. 'Look at her well,' he would tell his friends, as he showed her off, 'for she will be Queen of England.'

He did not have long to enjoy the child, or the connubial happiness he had found with Victoire. Christmas 1819 found the Kents in a rented house at Sidmouth on the Devon coast, ostensibly for the baby's health, but in reality because it was cheaper to live in obscurity. Tall, sturdy, although with the Hanoverian proclivity for being over-weight, a former serving officer in the army – he had been forcibly retired from his command 'on a charge of disciplinary fanaticism amounting to brutality' – Kent had always prided himself on his robust physique, predicting that he would outlive his dissolute broth-ers. The house was cold and no doubt damp and the weather was foul. Little Drina was suffering from a sore throat and the Duke caught a cold which turned to pneumonia. Proper nursing would probably have saved his life, but, in the fashion of the day, the doctors killed him with their bleeding and cupping of an already weakened constitution.

He died on 23 January 1820, only one week after his father, old King George III. So now the Prince Regent was King George IV and Victoria took her place as third in line of succession. The Clarences had lost their baby – a girl named Charlotte Augusta – and they were to lose two more, but at the time everyone confidently expected them to produce the heir. Consequently, little account was taken of the eight-month-old Princess at Sidmouth who had just lost her father. In a will hurriedly signed by the dying man, his widow had been appointed sole guardian of their child. The Duchess of Kent, a foreigner who spoke little English, was left stranded without funds. She was also homeless, as rooms at Kensington Palace depended on the new King's favour. It was not readily forthcoming, no doubt because he hoped that she would disappear with her child abroad. Her brother Leopold, Princess Charlotte's widower, came to the rescue.

He dissuaded his sister from her first instinct, to return home to Amorbach, taking Victoria away from England and perhaps her des-tiny, and he urged the King's favourite sister to persuade him to allow the Duchess to live in his late brother's apartment at Kensington. Leopold had been voted £50,000 a year for life on his marriage to Princess Charlotte; it had not been envisaged that she would die, and there was a certain amount of resentment that the parliamentary grant had failed to include a get-out clause and that Leopold continued to accept these funds when he no longer had any reason to stay in England. Certainly, George IV's opinion was that his former son-in-law should dip into his own pocket to support his sister and her offspring.

Leopold offered to pay Victoire an allowance of £3,000 a year, which, added to the late Duke's allowance of £6,000, which reverted to his widow, would be sufficient for the Duchess and her child to live in genteel, if not royal, comfort; later, Parliament voted an increase in the allowance for the Princess's education and upbringing. As Queen Victoria later told Disraeli, she was brought up very simply: 'I never had a room to myself; I never had a sofa, nor an easy chair; and there was not a single carpet that was not threadbare.' Regular, simple meal-times when the small child sat beside her mother at table and ate her bread and milk out of a silver basin were punctuated by play, lessons, fresh air and outdoor exercise.

Leopold's contribution was hardly generous and he could have afforded far more, but it was enough to give him enormous leverage. With Charlotte's death, he had been disappointed of his ambition to rule England, or at least wield influence over the monarchy. But now he saw his chance to mould the mind of a new heir to the throne, his niece, who looked on him as a father figure. The impact of the Duke of Kent's premature death on Victoria cannot be underestimated. Years later, writing to her eldest daughter, she referred to herself as the poor fatherless child of eight months. The naturally passionate Victoria had not found a focus for her love in childhood, nor had she felt the benefit of a father's love. 'I had led a very unhappy life as a child,' she wrote, 'had no scope for my very violent feelings of affection – had no brothers and sisters to live with – never had had a father – was not on a comfortable or at all intimate or confidential footing with my mother . . . and did not know what a happy domestic life was!'

She thought of her father as a soldier and had an exaggerated notion of male strength. All her life she looked for a father figure, a strong man to lean on. Brought up in an almost exclusively female environment, she imagined that men were somehow superior and she always sought male approbation. Dependence on male mentors became a habit. First, Leopold, of whom she confided in her journal: 'I love him so very very much. He is *Il mio secondo padre* or rather *sole padre*! for he is indeed my real father, as I have none!' Then her first

Prime Minister, Lord Melbourne, an elderly, benevolent, fatherly figure, for whom she conceived a possessive love; her husband Prince Albert – 'he was my father, my protector, my guide and adviser in all and everything, my mother (I might almost say) as well as my husband' – and after his death, her Highland servant, the rough, dependable, ever loyal John Brown.

The Duchess of Kent was a good mother, if not a very wise woman. Unusually, she breastfed her child, a practice Queen Victoria herself thought disgusting. She strongly discouraged it in her own daughters. 'No lady, and still less a Princess, is fit for her husband or her position, if she does that,' she was to warn her eldest, Vicky. It was not long before Victoria's strong character, wilfulness and stubbornness were manifest. At only a few months, her mother fondly admitted that she was showing 'symptoms of wanting to get her own little way'. She was soon displaying the violent outbursts of temper so characteristic of the Hanoverians – a trait that she would never manage to control, and which would later send her grown-up sons and officials running for cover – but offsetting this was a transparent honesty, a directness and strict adherence to the truth. When her mother admonished her for a fit of temper, saying she made them both unhappy by such behaviour, Victoria typically replied, 'No Mama, not me, not myself, but *you*.'

Victoria's childhood, spent mainly at Kensington Palace, was solitary. Her first memory is of crawling on a yellow carpet and being told that if she cried and was naughty her 'Uncle Sussex', who lived below, would hear her and punish her. On the other hand, another of her 'wicked uncles', the Duke of York, was always very kind to his little niece and gave her 'beautiful presents'. Her aunt, the Duchess of Clarence, who must have grieved for her own dead infants, adored her. 'My dear little heart,' she wrote to the three-year-old, 'I hope you are well and don't forget Aunt Adelaide, who loves you fondly.' Instead of building bridges with the royal family, the Duchess of Kent kept them all at bay, increasing her daughter's loneliness and isolation. Visits to her Uncle Leopold at Claremont, his country seat near Esher, were the high points in her existence.

Apart from her half-sister Feodore, to whom she was close, there were no childhood companions. She was kept well away from her cousins, the sons of her father's younger brothers, Princes George of Cumberland and George of Cambridge, and increasingly disliked the daughters of her mother's adviser, Sir John Conroy, whose company was forced upon her. Instead, she lived in a world of dolls, dozens of them, all beautifully dressed. Later, a King Charles spaniel, Dash, would become a beloved companion. Always very proprietary about her possessions – ranging from childhood toys to an empire in later life – the Princess once told a child who was brought to play with her in her clear, piping voice, 'You must not touch those, they are mine; and I may call you Jane, but you must not call me Victoria.' It was a hint of the imperious, autocratic tone that she would make peculiarly her own. Lord Albemarle remembered glancing out of a window at Kensington Palace and seeing a small, fair girl wearing a big straw hat to protect her from the sun tending her garden with intense concentration, impartially sharing the contents of the water-pot between the flowers and her little feet. It was a sunny picture, but belied the reality of what she later came to call a melancholy childhood. There was certainly a darker undertone.

Cold-shouldered by her brother-in-law the King, the Duchess of Kent made a virtue out of necessity, living in semi-isolation from the royal family, ensuring that Victoria would not be tarnished with the same brush as the unpopular Hanoverians. It was not until 1826 that George IV deigned to take notice of his fatherless niece, inviting the Duchess and her daughters to Windsor. The visit and her first sight of the King obviously made a great impression on the child. 'When we arrived at the Royal Lodge the King took me by the hand, saying: "Give me your little paw." He was large and gouty but with a wonderful dignity and charm of manner,' she wrote. He presented her with 'his picture set in diamonds, which was worn by the princesses as an order'. The King's mistress, Lady Conyningham, pinned the blue ribbon holding the picture on to her shoulder. 'I was very proud of this,' she recalled.

She was taken on a drive and met the King with his sister Mary in a phaeton. 'Pop her in!' he ordered, before speeding away. The Duchess of Kent's terror may be imagined, because she had a real fear that the King would try to kidnap Victoria to bring her up under his own unsavoury influence. Whatever her mother thought of her uncles, Victoria at seven was willing to please. When the King told her that the orchestra would play any tune she liked, she tactfully requested 'God Save the King', and she was quite prepared to sit on the royal knee and kiss the flabby face coated with cosmetics.

Victoria's education began when she was not quite four. Lessons were taken with the Reverend Davys, later Bishop of Peterborough. He recalled teaching her to read by writing some short words on cards and having her bring them to him from a distant part of the room as he named them. By the age of six she had grasped the rudiments of reading, writing and arithmetic – she would always have a good head for figures – and Davys also gave her religious instruction. When she was five, she came under the care of her sister's governess. The strong-minded Louisa Lehzen, whom George IV made a Hanoverian baroness, was the daughter of a Lutheran pastor from Hanover and was to be one of the most important formative influences on the young Princess. Every minute of her day was prescribed in her educational timetable for six days a week. Idleness was not an option. Lehzen would read to her while she was having her hair brushed morning and evening. In this way, she instilled in her pupil the keen sense of duty and rigid work discipline which served the Queen well throughout her life, compensating for her lack of imagination.

The Princess received the sort of education that would have been thought admirable for an upper-class girl of the time, but was hardly good enough for a future ruler. Unlike the Tudor queens regnant and despite her future destiny, she was not given the classical education that was the shared intellectual heritage of the men of the political classes. As an adult, she felt her intellectual inferiority, but was smart enough to keep silent when she knew she was out of her depth in a conversation. Perhaps if she had been an intellectual, she would have been less successful as a monarch. Certainly her devoted subjects among the expanding middle class were to find the very ordinariness of their Queen both appealing and oddly reassuring.

Davys had managed to eradicate her German accent. Now she proved a good linguist, studying French and German; later, her love of opera prompted her to learn Italian. With Lehzen and Davys she also studied history, geography, natural history and some Latin. She had to learn poetry by heart and the art of letter writing; as a result, she displayed a formidable memory as queen and was a fluent and prodigious writer – so much so, in fact, that she would only communicate with her private secretary by memoranda and in the third person.

She loved history, encouraged by Leopold to read widely and learn from the past. 'I am much obliged to you, dear Uncle, for the extract about Queen Anne,' she wrote, 'but must beg you, as you have sent me to show what a Queen *ought not* to be, that you will send me what a Queen *ought to be*.' It was supposedly while perusing a history book, with a genealogical table which had been temporarily removed re-inserted, that the eleven-year-old Victoria realized for the first time that she would be Queen. 'I see I am nearer the throne than I thought,' she commented. 'I *will* be good.' It is a pretty story, but we only have Lehzen's word for it.

In 1830, when Victoria was almost eleven, the Duchess called in the Bishops of London and Lincoln to test her daughter's progress. They reported that she displayed 'an accurate knowledge of the most important features of Scripture, History and the leading truths and precepts of the Christian Religion as taught by the Church of England', as well as 'an acquaintance with the chronology and principal facts of English History remarkable in so young a person'.

The emphasis of Victoria's education was on the feminine accomplishments. Dancing, music and drawing were important parts of the curriculum. In spite of her short stature and tendency to plumpness, she was a graceful and tireless dancer. She made her court debut when she was ten, dancing at the Juvenile Ball given by the King in honour of her contemporary, the Queen of Portugal. Charles Greville, the Clerk to the Privy Council, sighed at the plainness of the English Princess. It might have been at this time, too, that her cousin George of Cambridge, disgusted to discover that Victoria was to inherit the throne – 'Good heavens!' he exclaimed. 'A woman on the throne of so great a country, how ridiculous!' – described her as 'a fat, ugly, wilful and stupid child'. It is true that she had inherited the protruding dark blue eyes, arched nose, receding chin and heavy jowls of the Hanoverians – she was very like her grandfather, George III – and a habit of keeping her mouth open, but she had a natural dignity, almost an aura, which impressed more discerning observers.

She was an excellent horsewoman, rejoicing when she was able to gallop off and escape the surveillance that she was constantly subjected to at home. So over-protective was her mother that Victoria slept in the same bedroom as her until the day of her accession and someone always sat with her in the evening until her mother was ready to go to bed, so that the child was never alone. She was not even allowed to descend the stairs without someone holding her hand. The constraints must have been oppressive for a girl with such natural energy and zest for life.

When Victoria was eleven her life suddenly became more fraught. Her Uncle Leopold became King of the Belgians and left England and although the two began a steady correspondence, she missed him sorely. King George IV died, to be succeeded by the Duke of Clarence as William IV. Although there was still no guarantee that Queen Adelaide would not have a child of her own, Victoria was now second in line to the throne. Thinking that William would be more malleable than his brother, the Duchess of Kent now started making loud demands to be placed on the same footing as a Dowager Princess of Wales; she also wanted Victoria to receive an allowance befitting the heiress presumptive – an allowance to be controlled by her mother. Above all, she wanted to be appointed regent in the event of Victoria succeeding before her majority at eighteen.

Both William and Adelaide were fond of their niece and wanted to see her take her proper place at court and, indeed, nearly all the Duchess's demands were met. Instead of taking the olive branch, however, the Duchess set herself up in opposition, restricting Victoria's visits to the King and Queen and being as difficult and quarrelsome as possible. To Victoria's intense disappointment, her mother decided at the last minute that neither she nor Victoria would attend the coronation. Ambitious, possessive, and ill advised, she was determined to keep Victoria isolated from influences other than her own.

The Duchess not only misjudged William IV, but also her daughter, who was already far too strong a character to manipulate. The Duchess's poor judgement was matched only by that of her *éminence grise*, Captain Conroy. Sir John Conroy had been equerry to the Duke of Kent and continued in the Duchess's service after his death. Anglo-Irish, with the gift of the gab and a way with women, the married Conroy had assumed such ascendancy over the Duchess that the assumption was that they were lovers. The Duke of Wellington attributed Victoria's loathing of Conroy to her witnessing 'familiarities' between him and her mother, but this is too facile an explanation.

Conroy was supposed to be managing the Duchess's financial affairs – in due course it emerged that she was desperately in debt, which suggests that Conroy was siphoning off funds for himself – but was consumed with the ambition to rule the future queen through her mother. There is no reason to think that the Duchess was not fully in accord with his ambition to rule through her daughter, but she was driven more by stupidity than anything else. Together, they devised the 'Kensington system', the aim being to ensure that Victoria would be totally dependent on them when she came to the throne and subject to no other influences. It was hopelessly naïve.

While keeping Victoria in isolation from the court, the plan also involved promoting her publicly. In 1830 the Duchess underwent the first in a series of summer 'progresses', to show Victoria to the people; in fact, the tall Duchess with her large hats took centre stage and the diminutive Princess was relegated to the back. Over succeeding summers, visits were paid to the great country houses of the nobility, but Victoria also caught her first glimpses of industrial Britain, the dark satanic mills in which so many of her future subjects now slaved for a bare subsistence. Everywhere the young Princess was received with great enthusiasm.

Although the Duchess maintained that her only purpose was to show Victoria her country with its historic sites, the King rightly took exception to the tours, especially when the Duchess refused to accede to his request that the Royal Navy desist from giving her a royal salute. In 1835 the King wrote to Victoria personally asking her not to undertake a summer progress that year. She was fully in sympathy with his request, but after a showdown with her mother, she had to concede defeat. The Duchess was never slow to employ emotional blackmail: 'I must tell you dearest love, if your conversation with me could be known, that you had not the energy to undertake the journeys or that your views were not enlarged enough to grasp the benefits arising from it, then you would fall in the estimation of the people of this country.' It was a blatant flouting of the King's wishes – *lèse-majesté*. And what did the Duchess – regarded by many as 'a stupid foreigner' – understand of 'the people of this country'?

All this quarrelling within the family caused Victoria emotional distress. As she later told her eldest daughter, she spent her childhood 'always on pins and needles, with the whole family hardly on speaking terms. I (a mere child) between the two fires – trying to be civil and then scolded at home! Oh! It was dreadful.' Her confirmation service had been marred by the King's angrily ordering Conroy out of the Chapel Royal. Now, on the progress of 1835, Victoria's state of mind manifested itself in tiredness, lethargy, headaches and backache. By October she was very ill indeed. Whether it was a case of typhoid or simply collapse from nervous strain cannot be determined.

With the full agreement of her mother, Sir John Conroy took the opportunity of Victoria's debility to attempt to force her to agree to make him her private secretary when she became Queen. It is to her credit that the sixteen-year-old Princess resisted the pressure. Her resolve stiffened by her dear Lehzen, her only support in the household, she stubbornly refused. How different her response might have been had Conroy and her mother treated her with respect. A show of deference and a touch of flattery went a long way with Victoria and she was always loyal and generous to those who served her well.

Matters came to a head in August 1836 when the King and Queen invited the Duchess and her daughter to Windsor for a week to celebrate their birthdays. William IV remained kindly and genial towards Victoria, despite all the provocation he received from her mother, and she in turn was fond of her uncle. 'I know the interest which the public feel about her,' he told the guests when toasting her at the wedding of one of his illegitimate daughters, 'and although I have not seen so much of her as I could have wished, I take no less interest in her, and the more I do see of her, both in public and in private, the greater pleasure it will give me.' Now the Duchess replied to his kind invitation with studied insolence. Ignoring the Queen's birthday on the 13th altogether, the Duchess wrote that she would spend her own birthday on the 15th at Claremont, but would come to Windsor on the 20th.

At his birthday dinner on the 21st, the King rose and once and for all repaid the Duchess, who was placed next to him, for her insulting behaviour and disrespect.

> I trust God that my life may be spared for nine months longer, after which period, in the event of my death no regency would take place. I should then have the satisfaction of leaving the royal authority to the personal exercise of that young lady (pointing to the Princess), the heiress presumptive of the Crown, and not in the hands of a person now near me, who is surrounded by evil advisers and who is herself incompetent to act with propriety in the station in which she would be placed.

The Queen looked embarrassed, the company of one hundred guests were aghast, and Victoria burst into tears. The Duchess immediately called for her carriage, but was persuaded to delay her departure until morning.

Through sheer willpower, the ailing William IV managed to cling to life long enough to see Victoria reach her majority. A week before her birthday, he wrote her a letter to be placed in her hands alone. First Conroy, then the Duchess tried to take the letter, but the Lord Chamberlain, Conyngham, insisted on handing it directly to Victoria. The King told her that he intended to ask Parliament for an allowance of £10,000 a year for her, so that she would be independent. It was a generous and thoughtful gesture. The Duchess and Conroy dictated Victoria's reply. She was ordered to write that she accepted the allowance but, because of her youth, asked that it be paid directly to her mother – who claimed the bulk of it for herself – who would administer it. That evening, she recorded in her journal that she was too upset to go down to dinner. 'Victoria has not written this letter,' the King concluded.

On 24 May Victoria celebrated her eighteenth birthday and attained her legal majority, according to royal rules, although her mother was pressing for her majority to be augmented to twenty-one, which was the legal milestone for the rest of the population. Conroy might also have been responsible for a scurrilous rumour that Victoria was backward and unfit to rule, which was far from the case. Awed but not daunted by the prospect before her, Victoria made a vow, in her journal, to study with renewed assiduity and prepare herself for the task ahead. That night she attended a ball in St James's, before returning to Kensington Palace. 'The courtyards and the street were crammed when we went to the ball,' she wrote in her journal, 'and the anxiety of the people to see poor stupid me was very great, and I must say I am very touched by it, and feel proud, which I always have done of my country and the English nation.'

Less than one month later she became Queen.

27

Victoria Regina

JUST BEFORE DAWN on the morning of 20 June 1837, William Howley, Archbishop of Canterbury, and the Lord Chamberlain ordered a carriage and drove post-haste from Windsor to Kensington Palace. They gained admittance to the sleeping household only with difficulty, the Duchess eventually conceding to wake Victoria. The Princess, still in her nightclothes and with her fair hair loose about her shoulders, entered her sitting room alone – she stresses this being '*alone*' in her journal with relish. The two men greeted her with the words 'Your Majesty', knelt and kissed her hand. Lord Conyngham told her that the King had died just after two and 'consequently that I am Queen'.

'Since it has pleased Providence to place me in this station,' she confided in her journal, 'I shall do my utmost to fulfil my duty towards my country; I am very young and perhaps in many, though not in all things, inexperienced, but I am sure, that very few have more real good will and more real desire to do what is fit and right than I have.'

Although Victoria might sometimes act misguidedly during a reign of over sixty years, her good intentions could never be called into question.

The proclamation of accession declared that 'the High and Mighty Princess Alexandrina Victoria is now, by the death of our late Sovereign William the Fourth, of happy memory, become our only lawful and rightful liege Lady Alexandrina Victoria I, Queen of Great Britain and Ireland . . .'. On her first day as queen, Victoria settled the name problem once and for all. One of her first acts was to write to Uncle Leopold, signing herself 'Your devoted and attached Niece, Victoria R'. Later in the day, she signed the Privy Council register as 'Victoria'. 'Alexandrina' was quietly dropped.

She breakfasted with Baron Stockmar, Leopold's long-standing friend and adviser, whom he had sent to England to guide her. A native of Coburg, Stockmar was a man of no personal ambition and had won general respect as a man of quiet common sense. The Prime Minister, William Lamb, Viscount Melbourne, sent the Queen a note to advise her that he would wait on her after breakfast in order to brief her for the Privy Council meeting at eleven. It was fortunate for Victoria that, unlike her uncles who were strict Tories, her mother had always been associated with the Whigs and that a Whig government was currently in power. Leopold had already advised her of her part:

> The moment you get official communication of it [William IV's death], you will entrust Lord Melbourne with the office of retaining the present Administration as your Ministers . . . The fact is that the present Ministers are those who will serve you, personally with the greatest sincerity and, I trust, attachment. For them, as well as for the Liberals at large, you are the *only* Sovereign that offers them *des chances d'existence et de durée*.

She followed his advice to the letter, receiving Melbourne at nine 'in my room, and of *course quite alone*, as I shall *always* do all my Ministers'. Aristocratic, urbane, and, as she was soon to discover, harbouring a romantic and tragic past, Melbourne endeared himself to Victoria and immediately won her confidence. 'He is a very honest, good and kind hearted, as well as very clever man,' she reported. A childless widower in his fifties – his late wife Lady Caroline Lamb had fallen in love with Byron and gone mad, while none of Melbourne's three children by her had reached maturity – he easily assumed the role of mentor to the young Queen, spending far more time with her than is usual for a Prime Minister. 'It is become his province to educate, instruct and form the most interesting mind and character in the world,' Charles Greville commented. Melbourne was charming and Victoria, always a woman of fierce loyalties, soon came to adore and rely on him. While he probably looked upon her as fondly as he would a daughter, Greville believed that her feelings for Melbourne were sexual 'though she does not know it, and are probably not very well defined to herself'.

At eleven the doors of the red saloon were thrown open and

Victoria entered alone. A painting of the occasion by Sir David Wilkie highlights the small, female figure, radiant in a dress of shining white, although in fact Victoria was plainly dressed in a simple black gown, in mourning for her uncle. The most powerful men in the nation gaze raptly at the young woman, their faces shining in the light she exudes. They are grouped together as a distinct entity, their age and gravitas accentuating Victoria's youth and femininity. Although she is undoubtedly the focal point of the painting, there can be no doubt that real power has shifted to Parliament, represented by the men in the room. Melbourne holds out the pen for her to sign her document of accession, a reminder that she is a constitutional monarch and that her sovereignty is only possible by the validation of Lords and Commons.

Kept in 'such jealous seclusion' by her mother, no one quite knew what to expect of the eighteen-year-old Queen, whose 'character, disposition, and capacity' was a mystery. The diarist Charles Greville, Clerk to the Council, records the impact she made at that Privy Council meeting:

> There never was anything like the first impression she produced, or the chorus of praise and admiration which is raised about her manner and behaviour . . . It was very extraordinary, and something far beyond what was looked for. Her extreme youth and inexperience, and the ignorance of the world concerning her, naturally excited intense curiosity to see how she would act on this trying occasion . . . the Queen entered, accompanied by her two uncles, who advanced to meet her. She bowed to the Lords, took her seat, and then read her speech in a clear, distinct, and audible voice, and without any appearance of fear or embarrassment.

She had a clear, melodious speaking voice which carried far. The speech had been prepared for her by Melbourne and Victoria thought it 'very fine'. The old question of whether the power of the state resided in the crown or in Parliament had been irrevocably settled in favour of Parliament, whose power now rested on a more broad-based electorate. 'I place my firm reliance upon the wisdom of Parliament and upon the loyalty and affection of My People,' she assured those present. She praised her predecessor under whom the Great Reform Act of 1832, giving parliamentary representation to new industrial towns such as Birmingham, Manchester, Leeds and Sheffield, and extending the franchise, had been passed. Leopold had advised her to show attachment to the Church of England as 'you are particularly where you are, because you are a Protestant.' Now she declared that 'it will be my unceasing study to maintain the reformed religion as by law established, securing at the same time to all the full enjoyment of religious liberty.' In a society rent by class division and poverty on a massive scale she promised to 'promote to the utmost of my power the happiness and welfare of all classes of my subjects'.

Leopold had taught her that as queen she was to be above party. As the 220 Privy Counsellors present advanced, she was careful not to betray any preference for Whig or Tory. She occasionally looked towards Melbourne for guidance, but otherwise impressed everyone with her 'perfect calmness and self-possession . . . graceful modesty and propriety'. The eldest of Victoria's surviving uncles, Ernest, Duke of Cumberland, was absent. Since the reign of George I, the sovereign of Great Britain had also been Elector, latterly King, of Hanover, but the Salic law, whereby a woman might not succeed to the crown, applied in Hanover. Cumberland now succeeded as King of Hanover; the old reactionary was apparently highly resentful that Victoria should succeed to the throne of Great Britain and Ireland. He was not popular with the English, especially the Whigs. As Leopold had already explained to Victoria, 'your immediate successor with the moustaches is enough to frighten them into the most violent attachment to you.' The other royal dukes, Cambridge and Sussex, were the first to swear allegiance, kneeling before her. Greville noticed that she blushed as they did so and seemed 'rather bewildered at the multitude of men who were sworn and came one after another to kiss her hand'.

Victoria came to the throne in a period of social, political and economic turbulence, one in which the monarchy was at a particularly low ebb. The nation welcomed the advent of a new, young monarch who contrasted in every way – age, gender and political loyalty – with her unpopular predecessors, George III, George IV and William IV: 'an imbecile, a profligate and a buffoon'. Everyone seemed to have forgotten that the young George III, like Victoria born in England and fiercely patriotic, had begun his reign with similar optimism; like him she was also to be a model of domestic propriety.

Even more, perhaps, than was the case with Queen Anne, it was not a disadvantage to be a female sovereign in 1837. Both Victoria's youth and her sex were disarming. She invited the sentiment previously roused by Queen Caroline and Princess Charlotte, receiving such saturation coverage that the press was accused of suffering from 'Reginamania', and a chivalric protectiveness from the men who were bound to serve her. An anonymous pamphlet written by Lord Brougham in the form of an open *Letter to the Queen on the State of the Monarchy* summed up this patriarchal attitude, incidentally highlighting the contradiction between Victoria's state body and her private body:

> I am an experienced man, well stricken in years. I hold myself before *you*, a girl of eighteen, who, in my own or any other family in Europe, would be treated as a child, ordered to do as was most agreeable or convenient to others – whose inclinations would never be consulted – whose opinion would never be thought of – whose consent would never be asked upon any one thing appertaining to any other human being but yourself, beyond the choice of gown or cap, nor always upon that: yet before you I humble myself . . .

Victoria's political innocence meant that she was not associated with the oppressive power of the monarchy and, indeed, her assumed Whig sympathies linked her with the impulse for political reform. As a fetching young woman in a sentimental age, she appeared less politically threatening to the opponents of monarchy and more amenable to constitutional control in the eyes of those who supported a limited monarchy than her grandfather and uncles, who made no secret of their political partisanship. A female monarch must always have appeared less 'political' in an age in which public political action was exclusively a male preserve. In contrast to her debauched uncles, Victoria was a virgin queen and had decorative appeal.

But while she excited the protective feelings of the male counsellors who caught their first glimpse of her that morning, Victoria was no ingénue. For some time she had been quietly coached for her role by Leopold. 'My object,' he told her, 'is that you should be no one's *tool*, and though young, and naturally not yet experienced, your good natural sense and the *truth* of your character will, with faithful and proper advice get you very well through the difficulties of your future position.' The 'irksome position' in which she had lived, he knew, would have taught her '*discretion* and *prudence*, as in your position you never can have *too much* of either'. He advised her to stress the fact that she had been born in England and that she could never sing the praises of her country and its inhabitants too loudly.

A year before her accession she read avidly his 'Directions and Advices', outlining the rules of sovereignty in general, which Leopold had prepared for his nephew and Victoria's cousin, Ferdinand, upon his marriage to the Queen of Portugal. Leopold liked to think of himself as a 'constitutional' monarch, but that is not to be confused with the modern, post-Bagehot understanding of the term in which the monarch's role is merely to be consulted, to encourage and to warn. Leopold left Victoria in no doubt that the monarchy should be strong and that she should vigorously guard her prerogatives and seek to augment the power of the crown lost by her predecessors:

> Monarchy to be carried on requires certain elements, and the occupa-
> tion of the Sovereign must be constantly to *preserve these elements*, or
> should they have been too much weakened by untoward circum-
> stances, to contrive by every means to *strengthen them again*. You are far
> too clever not to know, that it is not the being *called* Queen or King,
> which can be of the *least consequence*, when to the title there is not also
> annexed the power indispensable for the exercise of those functions. All
> trades must be learned, and nowadays, the trade of a *constitutional*
> *Sovereign, to do it well, is a very difficult one.*

When Leopold advised Victoria that the crown should be above party he did not mean that she should be a sovereign with no governing power. Party was anathema to royal thinking, giving too much scope for self-seeking politicians to place their individual interests before the good of the nation as a whole; it made it impossible to form an administration of the best men, loyal and obedient to the sovereign; and it meant that the power of the monarch to be centrally, creatively and actively involved in the governing process was fatally circum-scribed. Constitutional monarchy, as Leopold and Stockmar saw it, implied a ruler who was emancipated from the politicians, rather than fettered by them; a crown that was influentially, not impotently, above the battle; a sovereign who ruled as well as reigned. Indoctrinated with these views, Victoria was to be no cipher, vigorously defending monarchical power, until in the course of time that power was quietly exchanged for influence.

Leopold 'conceptualized' monarchy for the nineteenth century in bourgeois terms, imagining the monarch to be 'in trade'; the notion anticipated King George VI's labelling of the royal family as 'The Firm' in the twentieth century. Just as Lehzen had instilled the work ethic in her pupil, now Leopold wrote to advise the new Queen on 'the habits of business' the role entailed. 'The best plan is to devote certain hours to it; if you do that, you will get through it with ease.' Nor was she to decide on any question of importance, no matter how urgent, until she had had a chance to sleep on it. Even Melbourne was to find that she would never give him an immediate answer, but would keep the papers to consider overnight. 'Good habits formed *now* may for ever afterwards be kept up, and will become so natural to you that you will not find them at all fatiguing,' Leopold continued. He advocated firmness: 'People must come to the opinion *it is of no use intriguing, because when her mind is once made up, and she thinks a thing is right*, no earthly power will make her change.' Victoria's Prime Ministers would often have cause to complain of her stubbornness and immovability. They were lessons that Victoria faithfully followed for a lifetime.

Before long, Leopold must have been thinking that his niece had absorbed his teaching a little too thoroughly. He was in the habit of writing to Victoria about foreign affairs. Belgium was in dispute with France and Holland and, instead of siding with Belgium, the British government was being frustratingly neutral. Within a year of her coming to the throne Leopold tried to exert pressure on Victoria to persuade her government to declare outright support for Belgium.

'All I want from your kind Majesty,' he wrote, 'is that you will *occasionally* express to your Ministers, and particularly to good Lord Melbourne, that, as far as it is *compatible* with the interests of *your own* dominions, you do not wish that your Government should take the lead in such measures as might in a short time bring on the *destruction* of this country, as well as that of your uncle and his family.'

A week later, after consulting Melbourne on the subject, she gently rebuffed him. While expressing her affection for her uncle, she informed him that although her government would not be party to any measure prejudicial to Belgium, it would not intervene to alter existing treaty arrangements. Victoria was fiercely patriotic. She and her ministers would decide Britain's foreign policy and do what was best for Britain. Faced with his niece's forthright determination not to be swayed by family pressure, Leopold retreated.

Victoria embraced her new role with enthusiasm, delighting in the work and relishing her new-found independence. Her pleasure in the latter can be gauged by her proud use of the word '*alone*' in her journal in describing her first acts as queen. On the morning of her accession she wrote a kind letter to Queen Adelaide, inviting her to reside at Windsor for as long as she liked. She wasted no time in asserting her independence from her mother by ordering that her bed be removed from her room that very day. The poor Duchess was now to be made to pay for her championship of Conroy against her own daughter. She resented her displacement as Victoria's manager and the growing influence of Melbourne. 'Take care Victoria, you know your Prerogative! Take care that Lord Melbourne is not King,' she wrote waspishly. Conroy himself was summoned to Victoria's presence and invited to name his price for the services he had rendered her parents; she was prepared to pay any amount just to see the back of him. A baronetcy and a pension of £3,000 a year was agreed upon and Victoria made it clear that, although he remained for the time being in her mother's household, he would never be admitted to her presence again.

Three weeks after her accession, the Queen moved into Buckingham Palace, the first British sovereign to take up residence there. As she was unmarried, she had to bring her mother with her as chaperone, but she was careful to place the Duchess in an apartment as far away from her own as possible. A public appearance of cordiality between mother and daughter was maintained, but the Duchess was soon bemoaning the fact to Princess Lieven that she had to make an appointment to see Victoria, who often sent back a note that she was too busy. Dear Lehzen was placed in the bedroom next to the Queen's with a communicating door between them. She would remain with Victoria as a friend, but would 'take no situation about me'; in effect, she assumed an unspecified responsibility for Victoria's household. Ministers noted that Lehzen would discreetly leave the room when they arrived for an audience with the Queen and slip back in again as they left.

'She has great animal spirits,' Greville wrote, 'and enters into the magnificent novelties of her position with the zest and curiosity of a child.' As a young unmarried woman, she loved to be in London and heartily embraced its pleasures. She enjoyed the opera and the theatre and liked nothing better than to dance until dawn. 'I can assure you all this dissipation does me a great deal of good,' she told Leopold. She had 'no pretension to beauty', Greville decided, but 'the gracefulness of her manner and the good expression of her countenance give her on the whole a very agreeable appearance'. Charles Creevey noted her *joie de vivre*: 'A more homely little being you never beheld, *when she is at her ease*, and she is evidently dying to be always more so. She laughs in real earnest, opening her mouth as wide as it can go, showing not very pretty gums . . . She eats quite as heartily as she laughs, I think I may say she gobbles . . . She blushes and laughs every instant in so natural a way as to disarm anybody.'

Victoria was always hungry and had a lifelong habit of eating her food too fast, to the consternation of the slow eaters at her table whose plates were whisked away as soon as the Queen had finished. One of her biographers suggested that her passionate, vibrant nature foreshadowed her sexual liveliness.

Carefully managed by Melbourne, Victoria would ride out regularly in Hyde Park with her Prime Minister and other Whig ministers beside her. She was distancing herself from the 'old royal family' with its disreputable ways. That summer, she reviewed her troops in the park, wearing a version of the Windsor uniform, a dark blue habit with red collar and cuffs. Priding herself on being a soldier's daughter, Victoria always enjoyed military display, although as a female sovereign she could only play at soldiers. 'The whole went off beautifully,' she wrote on this first occasion, 'and I felt for the first time like a man, as if I could fight myself at the head of my Troops.' She was less enthusiastic about addressing the members of both Houses of Parliament, when she went to the Lords to prorogue Parliament that July. Even with Lord Melbourne carrying the Sword of State before her and standing beside her while she read her speech, she confessed in her journal that she was extremely shy and nervous. It was something that she was never able to overcome, made worse in middle age after her widowhood, when she just could not bring herself to do it.

Compared to the superbly orchestrated royal ceremonies in the latter part of her reign, Victoria's coronation, on Thursday, 28 June 1838, was an ill-managed affair. *Figaro in London*, the predecessor of *Punch*, called it 'the shabby Coronation' and depicted Victoria being carried in a wooden chair by two footmen, a parasol in one hand, the orb and sceptre in the other, with the crown hung negligently on the back of the chair. The Tories saw the pared-down coronation as yet another example of the Whigs' relentless drive to diminish the constitutional role of the crown. Public enthusiasm for the event seemed strong in London, but was less fulsome in the industrial North, particularly in Manchester, the cotton manufacturing centre whose sudden growth made it the 'shock city' of the age. Chartists, pressing for *all* adult males to be given the vote, and working-class radicals were critical of the coronation's medieval flummery and expense; as far as they could see, the new reign had changed nothing.

Nothing could mar the day for Victoria. Having been awoken at four by the noise of the people and the bands in the park, she left Buckingham Palace at ten in the state coach. 'It was a fine day, and the crowds of people exceeded what I have ever seen,' she wrote in her journal, 'many as there were the day I went to the City [for the Lord Mayor's dinner], it was nothing, nothing to the multitudes of my loyal subjects, who were assembled in every spot to witness the Procession. Their good humour and excessive loyalty was beyond everything, and I really cannot say how proud I feel to be the Queen of such a Nation.'

The processional route no longer encompassed the old, sacred route from the Tower in the east through the City but centred on Westminster and was much longer than hitherto, to allow the maximum number of people – perhaps as many as 1 million – to glimpse the new monarch. Only six years after the Great Reform Act, this was, after all, the dawn of the democratic age. At Westminster Abbey, there had been no rehearsal and Victoria looked in vain for guidance from the officiating clergy, while some of her eight train-bearers, dressed in white satin and silver tissue with pink roses, chattered throughout the ceremony. The ruby ring had been measured for the wrong finger, but the archbishop insisted on forcing it on to the fourth finger; it was only with the greatest difficulty that Victoria managed to ease it off in the robing room afterwards. When it came to the peers swearing allegiance, eighty-two-year-old Lord Rolle lived up to his name by failing to make it up the steps to the seated Queen and rolling down again. 'May I not get up to meet him?' a concerned Victoria asked, before descending the steps to help him.

The existing crown, made for George IV, was far too heavy for a young woman and a new one, including the Black Prince's ruby, which Henry V reputedly wore at Agincourt, and other precious gems and pearls, was fashioned for Victoria. Even so, its weight was considerable.

It was not until six that she returned to the palace through the cheering crowds. Not at all tired, she ran upstairs to give her spaniel Dash his bath. In a break with tradition, there was to be no coronation banquet for the nobility, no Queen's champion throwing down his gauntlet to any who challenged her title, just a small family dinner. In another nod to populism, theatres and places of popular entertainment were free that night and there was a three-day fair in Hyde Park, while in provincial towns and rural parishes celebratory dinners were provided for the poor, aged and infirm. Victoria enjoyed the fireworks standing on her mother's balcony. 'You did it beautifully – every part of it,' Lord Melbourne assured her at the end of the day, 'with so much taste; it's a thing that you can't give a person advice upon; it must be left to a person.'

Early in 1839 the new Queen began to lose some of her gloss. Prompted by her old hatred of Sir John Conroy, she became mired in a court scandal. Her mother's lady-in-waiting, Lady Flora Hastings, daughter of the Marquess of Hastings, began to display a suspiciously enlarged abdomen. Before long, the gossips had it that she was pregnant. Who was the father? Had she not travelled down from Scotland after Christmas with Sir John Conroy? Willing to believe any misdeed of Conroy and encouraged by his old nemesis, Lehzen, Victoria lent an ear to the rumours, when what she should have done as queen and head of society was to investigate, discover the truth, and act decisively, either clearing the unfortunate lady's reputation or asking her to leave court.

'Lady Flora had not been above two days in the house before Lehzen and I discovered how exceedingly suspicious her figure looked – more have since observed this and we have no doubt that she is – to use the plain words – with child!!!' Victoria wrote in her journal: 'the horrid cause of all this is the Monster and Demon Incarnate whose name I forbear to mention [Conroy].' Having worked herself into a state of righteous indignation, she ended with the words: 'this disgraceful subject . . . makes one loathe one's own sex. When they are bad how disgracefully and disgustingly servile and low women are! I don't wonder at men considering the sex despicable.'

In the Flora Hastings affair Victoria was not well served by Melbourne, who with his laissez-faire inclinations advised her to wait and see, nor by the royal physician, Sir James Clark, who examined the lady. Although handicapped by the convention of examining a female patient fully dressed, Sir James failed to consider the other possible explanations for Lady Flora's enlarged abdomen. He was inclined to believe that she was pregnant, until a second examination with another physician – this time with the lady having removed her stays – confirmed that she was a virgin. The outraged Hastings family demanded the dismissal of Clark; Victoria failed to comply. Not only was this unwise – Clark, after all, was expendable – but it would come back to haunt her many years later when he failed to diagnose Prince Albert's typhoid. Embarrassed now, she was induced to visit Lady Flora:

> I found Lady Flora stretched on a couch looking as thin as anybody can be who is still alive; literally a skeleton, but the body very much swollen like a person who is with child; a searching look in her eyes, a look rather like a person who is dying . . . she was friendly, said she was very comfortable, and was very grateful for all I had done for her . . . I said to her, I hoped to see her again when she was better, upon which she grasped my hand as if to say 'I shall not see you again'.

Lady Flora died on 5 July 1839 and a post-mortem revealed she had been suffering from a growth on the liver. Although the public at large was not much concerned with this court scandal, society was scathing of Victoria's behaviour in the affair. The Hastings family were Tories and were determined to make political capital out of Melbourne's failure. It reflected badly on Victoria. 'Nobody cares for the Queen,' Greville concluded, 'her popularity has sunk to zero, and loyalty is a dead letter.' Two aristocratic ladies hissed as the Queen passed at Ascot, although they claimed their target was Melbourne who accompanied her.

Meanwhile, it looked as if Melbourne's government, facing defeat on a colonial issue, would have to resign. Victoria dreaded losing the man on whom she was so dependent, politically and personally. 'The state of agony, grief and despair into which this placed me may be easier imagined than described! All all my happiness gone! That happy peaceful life destroyed, that dearest kind Lord Melbourne no more my minister,' she wrote melodramatically. When Melbourne came to offer his resignation on 7 May 1839 she sobbed and grasped his hand and could not bear to let go, pleading that he not forsake her. Although the sovereign no longer had the power enjoyed by Queen Anne to choose between Whig and Tory, she could exercise the option to choose between one man and another of the incoming party to lead the government, as well as appoint the ministry. Melbourne advised her to send for the Duke of Wellington. While negotiations with the Tories were under way, it would not be proper for Melbourne and the Queen to meet, but she wrote begging him: 'The Queen ventures to maintain one thing, which she thinks is possible; which is, that if she rode out tomorrow afternoon, she might just get a glimpse of Lord Melbourne in the Park; if he knew where she rode, she would meet him and it would be such a comfort; there surely could be no earthly harm in this.' No wonder the public had taken to shouting 'Mrs Melbourne' at her.

Wellington explained that he would not be the best man to lead the government; he was too old and he had no influence in the House of Commons. He advised the Queen to send for Sir Robert Peel. Prone to make hasty judgements about people and very decided in her likes and dislikes, Victoria did not care for Peel. A clever, plain-speaking man of middle-class origin with none of Melbourne's romantic appeal or suavity, he and Victoria had an awkward meeting, his stiffness and abruptness no doubt exacerbated by the fact that it was obvious that she did not want him to be there. Ministers were always at a disadvantage when there was antipathy or controversy, because in an audience with the sovereign a minister had to stand and must always show respect and restraint. He was unable to argue or employ the frankness he would with an equal. This was especially the case when the sovereign was a woman.

Unwittingly, Melbourne had already put the idea into Victoria's head that Peel would demand some changes among her ladies. At the outset of the reign, when the Queen knew no one, all the ladies Melbourne had placed about her, from the Mistress of the Robes downwards, happened to be Whigs. 'Your Majesty better express your hope that none of Your Majesty's Household, except those who are engaged in Politics, may be removed. I think you can ask him for that.' Obviously no women were engaged in politics, but took their political affiliations from fathers and husbands.

Forewarned, Victoria was adamant when Peel raised the subject. He probably would have been content with a gesture, but in her frenzied state of mind she chose to believe that he meant her to get rid of all her ladies. 'I cannot give up *any* of my Ladies,' she told him at their second meeting. 'What, Ma'am!' Peel queried. 'Does your Majesty mean to retain them *all*?' '*All*,' she replied. Perhaps she saw a means of getting Lord Melbourne back. She fired off a letter to him:

> The Queen writes one line to prepare Lord Melbourne for what may happen in a very few hours. Sir Robert Peel has behaved very ill, and has insisted on my giving up my Ladies, to which I replied that I never would consent, and I never saw a man so frightened. He said he must go to the Duke of Wellington and consult with him . . . He was quite perturbed . . . I was calm but very decided, and I think you would have been pleased to see my composure and great firmness; the Queen of England will not submit to such trickery. Keep yourself in readiness, for you may soon be wanted.

Later that day, she wrote again:

> Lord Melbourne must not think the Queen rash in her conduct; she saw both the Duke and Sir Robert again, and declared to them she could not change her opinion . . . The Queen felt this was an attempt to see whether she could be led and managed like a child; if it should lead to Sir Robert Peel's refusing to undertake the formation of the Government, which would be absurd, the Queen will feel satisfied that she has only been defending her own rights, on a point which so

nearly concerned her person, and which, if they had succeeded in, would have led to every sort of unfair attempt at power.

The principal male officers of the household, including the Lord Chamberlain, the Lord Steward, the Master of the Horse and the eight Lords-in-Waiting, were always political; usually members of the House of Lords, they changed with the government of the day. Victoria had no quarrel with that. The protocol governing a queen regnant was ill defined, but the convention for a queen consort since the Hanoverian succession had been to replace some of the Ladies of the Bedchamber with those of the same political persuasion as the incoming government, and this seemed a good enough precedent for a queen regnant to follow. The key appointment was the Mistress of the Robes, always a duchess. She was not in attendance on a daily basis, only on state occasions. The rest comprised the Ladies and Women of the Bedchamber – known as ladies-in-waiting when on duty – and the Maids of Honour.

Their function was to keep the Queen company when she needed it, to go driving or sketching or walking with her, dine with her, sit with her, and undertake a certain amount of correspondence. They were expected, therefore, to have a working knowledge of French or German, preferably both, to be able to sing and play the piano and ride. Below them, a dresser such as Marianne Skerrett, who had been in the Queen's service since her accession, acted as a personal secretary, writing letters on her behalf to tradespeople.

Peel's argument was that the Queen's household was a public and state, not a private, institution, so that she must make changes among her ladies. Her refusal to co-operate indicated to the outside world that she had no confidence in Peel, making it impossible for him to accept the reins of government. 'Was Sir Robert so weak that *even* the ladies must be of his opinion?' she asked. Actually Victoria might well have played into Peel's hands; he cannot have relished the task of forming a minority government. There was a feeling that the Queen had overstepped the thin line of constitutional propriety.

'It is a high trial of our institutions when the caprice of a girl of nineteen can overturn a great Ministerial combination,' Greville wrote in exasperation, 'and when the most momentous matters of Government and legislation are influenced by her pleasure about her Ladies of the Bedchamber.' It was ironic that the Tories, traditionally the upholders of the royal prerogative, were effectively prevented from taking office by an assertion of that prerogative and the Whigs, one of whose salient principles was the curtailment of the prerogative, found themselves kept in power by it. What were the Whigs thinking of, Greville asked, to pander to her private gratifications rather than the public good? Nor had Wellington succeeded in persuading her. 'There is something which shocks one's sense of fitness and propriety in the spectacle of this mere baby of a Queen setting herself in opposition to this great man,' Greville continued, 'to whom her Predecessors had ever been accustomed to look up with unlimited confidence as their surest and wisest Councillor in all times of difficulty and danger.'

Victoria had given Melbourne and the Whigs the impression that Peel had been unreasonable and they naturally rushed to her defence, without taking time to ascertain the truth of the matter. They acted unconstitutionally in communicating with the Queen while negotiations were still in hand with the Tories. '*She* might be excused for her ignorance of the exact limits of constitutional propriety, and for her too precipitate recurrence to the Counsels to which she had been accustomed,' Greville mused, 'but *they* ought to have explained to her, that until Sir Robert Peel had formally and finally resigned his commission into her hands, they could tender her no advice, and that her replies to him, and her resolutions with regard to his proposals must emanate solely and spontaneously from herself.'

In the 'bedchamber crisis' Victoria had acted emotionally, but she was also testing the limits of her power. Her behaviour raised a larger question: that of whether Parliament or the sovereign should have the decisive say in the formation of the government. Victoria's fierce partisanship and meddling in politics had interrupted the natural course of parliamentary government, but, ironically, her interference made her less of a sovereign than if she had been above it all; she was seen as 'Queen of the Whigs' rather than Queen of the nation. She was spared the reprimand she deserved because, as Greville put it, 'it would be to impair the authority, the dignity, the sanctity of the Crown she wears . . . it is necessary to spare the individual for the sake of the institution.'

She had won Lord Melbourne back for another two years, but her behaviour had awakened doubts in some minds about the suitability of a woman, especially one so headstrong, on the throne. All the old arguments about female weakness resurfaced. It was time for the Queen to take a husband; it was hoped that a dominant male partner would be able to mend her ways.

28

Wife, Mother and Queen

THERE HAD BEEN an understanding in the family that Victoria and
her cousin, Prince Albert of Saxe-Coburg and Gotha, the second
son of the reigning duke, would marry. Born only a month apart, the
two had been brought into the world by the same midwife. Once it
became apparent, in the mid 1830s, that Victoria would inherit the
throne, Leopold had decided that his nephew Albert would be the
ideal husband for her and began grooming him for the role. Studious
and intellectually curious, Albert had received the sort of first-class
education of which Victoria was deprived because of her sex. The
Prime Minister Benjamin Disraeli later commented that the Prince
was one of the best-educated men he knew. Leopold and Stockmar
had seen to it that the young man was also well versed in politics and
foreign affairs. Whether he would be able to handle Victoria, of
course, remained to be seen.

King William IV had desperately tried to scotch Coburg ambitions
by promoting an alternative suitor from the House of Orange; failing
that, he would have liked to see either of his nephews, George of
Hanover or George of Cambridge, married to his heir. In spite of the
King's vehemently expressed disapproval, Victoria entertained her
Coburg cousins, Ernest and Albert, in England in 1836. She knew
what was expected of her, writing to Leopold:

> I must thank you, my beloved Uncle, for the prospect of great happi-
> ness you have contributed to give me, in the person of dear Albert.
> Allow me, then, my dearest Uncle, to tell you how delighted I am with
> him, and how much I like him in every way. He possesses every qual-
> ity that could be desired to render me perfectly happy. He is so sensible,
> so kind, and so good, and so amiable too. He has, besides, the most
> pleasing and delightful exterior and appearance you can possibly see.

Since that visit, however, her ardour had cooled. As queen she was relishing her independence and liked nothing better than to have her own way. She confided in Melbourne. 'I said, why need I marry at all for 3 or 4 years? Did he see the necessity? I said I dreaded the thought of marrying; that I was so accustomed to having my own way that I thought it was 10 to 1 that I shouldn't agree with any body. Lord M. said, "Oh! But you would have it still" (my own way).' Underlying Victoria's sudden nervousness about marriage, of course, was her dread of childbirth. Princess Charlotte had died; might she not die too?

Melbourne felt the couple were too closely related. 'Cousins are not very good things,' he cautioned. Victoria brushed this aside. 'I don't think a foreigner would be popular,' he tried. Victoria baulked at marrying a subject: 'I observed that marrying a subject was making yourself so much their equal, and brought you so in contact with the whole family. Lord M. quite agreed in this and said, "I don't think it would be liked; there would be such jealousy."'

Victoria's nervous uncertainty can be gauged in a letter to Leopold, prior to Albert's proposed second visit to England in the autumn of 1839:

> First of all, I wish to know if Albert is aware of the wish of his Father and you relative to me? Secondly, if he knows that there is no engagement between us? I am anxious that you should acquaint Uncle Ernest, that if I should like Albert, that I can make no final promise this year, for, at the very earliest, any such event could not take place till two or three years hence. Though all the reports of Albert are most favourable, and though I have little doubt I shall like him, still one can never answer beforehand for feelings, and I may not have the feeling for him which is requisite to ensure happiness . . . and should this be the case (which is not likely), I am very anxious that it should be understood that I am not guilty of any breach of promise, for I never gave any.

Leopold must have been concerned that his carefully laid plans were unravelling, while Albert, apprised of Victoria's reluctance, left his beloved home confident that he would soon be back. He had already decided, after Victoria had sent him a haughty response to his letter of congratulation on her accession, that she was an uppity miss and declared frankly that if she intended to delay their marriage, he would not wait for her.

The Queen was at Windsor when news of the arrival of Albert and

As Elizabeth aged, she was depicted more as a goddess than a mortal woman. In the Armada portrait she wears a bodice shaped like a breastplate and enormous padded sleeves reminiscent of Holbein's macho depiction of Henry VIII. In the place where the muscular and masculine Henry had his codpiece, Elizabeth displays a giant pearl, symbolic of her chastity, equated with England's impregnability. With the dark forces of the defeated Armada behind her, she rests her hand tentatively on the portion of the globe that represents the colony of Virginia. Not only is she the ruler of a victorious realm, but also an aspiring empress of the world.

This portrait of the eighteen-year-old Mary, Queen of Scots, in white mourning depicts a woman at once fascinating and beguiling, crafty and enigmatic. The 'daughter of debate', as Elizabeth called her cousin, was to remain a thorn in her side until Mary's execution in 1587. The rival queens now rest together in Westminster Abbey.

Princess Mary, the future Mary II, painted on the eve of her marriage to her cousin, Prince William of Orange, in 1677. As a young girl, Mary showed a marked resemblance to her great-great-grandmother and namesake, the ill-fated Queen of Scots, opposite. Apart from sharing the slightly slanted hazel eyes, luminous complexion and rich auburn hair of the Stuart women, at just under six feet they were both exceptionally tall for their time.

The dual monarchy of William III and Mary II is unique in English history. Mary II was both more than a consort and less than a queen regnant. She was a gentle, charming and intelligent woman who was happiest looking after her husband, her houses and her gardens. However, during William's frequent absences on the Continent, she proved a most able and sympathetic ruler and was greatly loved.

Queen Anne was a very ordinary woman who presided over a period of extraordinary achievement in the island's history. 'As long as I live it shall be my endeavour to make my country and my friends easy,' she vowed.

'There never was anything like the first impression she produced . . .' The most powerful men in the nation gaze raptly at the small, feminine figure of the eighteen-year-old Queen Victoria, presiding over her first Council, their faces reflected in the light she exudes. In Victoria's case, her sex was a definite asset.

Victoria, the subservient wife, looks adoringly at her husband, Prince Albert, purposely portrayed as the central character, while their first-born, Vicky, plays nearby. Albert had moulded Victoria's image into one of becoming womanhood – so reassuring to her male subjects. Deliberate emphasis on the domestic virtues belied the fact that Victoria was a fierce protector of her prerogatives and constantly interfered in ministerial decisions.

At the end of her reign, Victoria the Queen-Empress presided over the largest empire the world has ever seen, while she was known to most of the crowned heads of Europe simply as 'Grandmama'. This official photograph, taken to mark her Diamond Jubilee in 1897, was deliberately not registered for copyright, ensuring that it would be widely distributed throughout the empire and used on thousands of commemorative souvenirs.

The most photographed woman in the world at eighty. At twenty-one the future Elizabeth II made a vow 'that my whole life, whether it be long or short, shall be devoted to your service' and she has remained true to that promise.

his brother, after a storm-tossed Channel crossing, reached her. Albert had been a boy of seventeen when they last met, shy and a little gauche; now he was a young man of twenty, handsome, sensitive and refined. 'It was with some emotion that I beheld Albert,' she confided in her journal, 'who is *beautiful*.' Always susceptible to good looks in a man, she waxed lyrical about his 'beautiful blue eyes, an exquisite nose, and such a pretty mouth with delicate moustachios and slight but very slight whiskers; a beautiful figure, broad in the shoulders and a fine waist; my heart is quite going . . .'. Later, she was equally enraptured by his long legs in 'tight cazimere pantaloons (nothing under them) and high boots'.

Victoria discussed her marriage plans with Melbourne before broaching the subject with Albert. 'I think it is a very good thing,' Melbourne assured her, 'and you'll be much more comfortable; for a woman cannot stand alone for long, in whatever situation she is.' As sovereign, it was up to Victoria not only to choose a consort but also to propose – a notion that intrigued and sent shudders through the average Victorian male, who baulked at this unnatural show of female independence. Might this 'sexual deviancy' not set a dangerous example to the rest of the female population? A street ballad encapsulated the underlying concern:

Since the Queen did herself for husband 'propose,'
The ladies will all do the same I suppose;
Their days of subservience now will be past,
For all will speak first*, as they always did* last!

Albert accepted immediately. It is unlikely that he was in love with her, but clearly, since they immediately fell into each other's arms and showered each other with kisses, he felt affection and tenderness for her. Small and very feminine with huge blue eyes conveying an endearing innocence, she aroused his chivalrous, protective instincts. Soon afterwards, he wrote expressing his happiness that he would 'be always near you, always your protector'. For a girl ever in search of a father figure, someone to lean on, it was irresistible. There can be no doubt of Victoria's passionate feelings, so long pent up through what she chose to see as a sad, lonely and loveless childhood, which were now channelled into an all-consuming love for Albert:

Oh! To feel I was, and am, loved by such an Angel as Albert was too great a delight to describe! He is perfection; perfection in every way – in beauty – in everything! I told him I was quite unworthy of him and kissed his dear hand – he said he would be very happy [to share his life with her] and was so kind and seemed so happy, that I really felt it was the happiest brightest moment in my life, which made up for all I had suffered and endured. Oh! How I adore and love him, I cannot say!! How I will strive to make him feel as little as possible the great sacrifice he has made; I told him it was a great sacrifice, – which he wouldn't allow . . . I feel the happiest of human beings.

Given the strength of her feelings, it was fortunate for Victoria that Albert seemed uninterested in other women and was to remain faithful to her for life. The idea of marital fidelity seemed quaint to the raffish aristocracy – 'Ought to pay attention to the ladies,' Melbourne muttered – but from the outset Victoria and Albert were determined to break with the recent royal past. The debauchery of George III's sons had undermined the standing of the monarchy. After her marriage, Victoria completely identified herself with the slightly prudish virtue of her husband's family. Victoria and Albert's court, if rather dull, was to be renowned for its high moral tone, while their happy marriage and family life were to be an inspiring example to the nation.

Meanwhile, there were plenty of teething problems. For all her professions of devotion and gratitude to Albert, Victoria remained as imperious as ever. 'I signed some papers and warrants etc. and he was so kind as to dry them with blotting paper for me,' she noted complacently in her journal. Once Albert returned to Coburg, the strain of separation and pre-wedding nerves led to many misunderstandings. Without consulting him, Victoria informed Albert that Lord Melbourne's secretary, George Anson, was to be appointed his private secretary. As it happened, the two were to become firm friends, but Albert felt it was an affront not to be able to make his own choice.

'Think of my position, dear Victoria,' he pleaded. 'I am leaving my home with all its old associations, all my bosom friends and going to a country in which everything is new and strange to me . . . Is it not to be conceded that the two or three persons who are to have the charge of my private affairs should be persons who already command my confidence?' Victoria was adamant, replying in a letter in which virtually every word was underlined: 'It is, as you rightly suppose, my greatest, my most anxious wish to do everything most agreeable to you, but I must differ with you respecting Mr Anson . . .'

His household, exclusively Whig, was also appointed without consultation. Albert's precise, analytical German mind could not comprehend the obtuseness and intricacies of English party politics. Coached by Uncle Leopold and Stockmar, he was convinced that the crown's strength lay in being above party politics, which surely meant that his household should be made up of both Whigs and Tories as evidence of royal neutrality. It was out of the question, Melbourne explained. Victoria, who was anything but impartial in the political arena, brushed aside his qualms, so that it seemed as if she cared more for Melbourne's advice than Albert's wishes. 'As to your wish about your gentlemen, my dear Albert, I must tell you quite honestly that it will not do.'

Then there was the question of rank. There were few precedents to follow among previous queens regnant. Only the husband of Mary I, of unhappy memory, had been allowed the courtesy title of King. Queen Anne's husband, Prince George of Denmark, had received no new title on her accession, although by virtue of the fact that there were no other royal princes, he took precedence in rank straight after his wife. Leopold wanted his nephew to be given an English peerage, but again Victoria disagreed, informing Albert somewhat tactlessly that the English would never tolerate a foreigner interfering in the political life of the country. 'Now, though I know you never would, still, if you were a peer they would all say the Prince meant to play a political part.'

Albert, a Serene Highness, would have to be content with being made a British Prince and a Royal Highness after his marriage and naturalization as a British subject. Victoria, who secretly cherished the idea of making her husband king consort, asked Melbourne if perhaps it could be done by Act of Parliament. 'For God's sake, Ma'am,' he replied, 'let's have no more of that. If you get the English people into the way of making kings, you will get them into the way of un-making them.'

The 'old royal family' bitterly resented the Coburg interloper and treated him with studied insolence. After all, the Hanoverian dynasty would have to give way to the new, as Victoria and Albert's children would be of the House of Saxe-Coburg-Gotha. It seemed reasonable that the husband of the Queen should take precedence after her, at least until the birth of a Prince of Wales. The elderly royal dukes vigorously protested and there were some unseemly scuffles as they rushed to elbow Albert out of the way at every opportunity, even though Victoria had exercised her right as sovereign to declare the order of precedence she desired by the issue of Letters Patent.

When the question of Albert's allowance was discussed in Parliament, the princes lent their weight to those who protested that the proposed £50,000 was too much. Leopold had been in receipt of that amount, as had Prince George of Denmark over two centuries earlier, but a combination of Tories, a few Whigs and the ultra radicals defeated Melbourne on the issue. Broadsheets galore repeated jibes about Germans, sausages and Albert who 'comes to take, "for better or worse", England's fat queen and England's fatter purse'.

'Party spirit runs high, commerce suffers, the working classes are much distressed,' Melbourne apologized to Leopold. It was the first indication that the new monarchy was going to be held closely accountable to Parliament in financial matters. In exchange for surrendering her hereditary revenues to the state for her lifetime, Victoria had been voted a civil list of £385,000 a year – considerably less than her predecessor – which included provision of £60,000 for the Privy Purse. In addition, she had the revenues from the duchies of Lancaster and Cornwall; hitherto exempt as the sovereign's private property, the duchies' accounts were now to be submitted to parliamentary scrutiny.

At Victoria's accession the crown was impoverished, but her upbringing had made her thrifty. In the first year of her reign she was able to devote £50,000 from her Privy Purse to paying off her father's debts. After that, she had the whole sum – paid in monthly installments of £5,000 by the treasury into her private account at Coutts – at her disposal to use as she liked. Few saw why, at a time of economic hardship, the Queen's consort should be in receipt of an additional £50,000. After heated debate, Albert's allowance was reduced to £30,000. It was considered a slap in the face and the Queen blamed the Tories, especially her old nemesis, Sir Robert Peel. 'Monsters!' she cried. 'You Tories shall be punished. Revenge! Revenge!'

It was not surprising, then, that in her current mood Victoria decided that she would not invite any Tories to her wedding on 10 February 1840. Only at the last minute did she make a concession and invite the Duke of Wellington and Lord Liverpool. The wedding, too, was something of a departure from royal tradition. Hitherto, royal weddings had taken place privately, often in the evening, and with no great ceremony. The wedding of the first queen regnant in living memory – an attractive young woman marrying the prince of her choice, a love match no less – naturally evoked popular interest. The burgeoning newspaper industry loved it. Victoria, who also broke with tradition in sleeping under the same roof as her bridegroom and seeing him that morning before the ceremony, went in procession the short distance from Buckingham Palace to St James's, where the wedding was to take place at one o'clock in the Chapel Royal. She was given away by her father's brother, the Duke of Sussex.

> I wore a white satin gown with a very deep flounce of Honiton lace, imitation of old. I wore my Turkish diamond necklace and earrings, and Albert's beautiful sapphire brooch. Mamma and the Duchess of Sutherland [Mistress of the Robes] rode in the carriage with me. I never saw such crowds of people as there were in the Park, and they cheered most enthusiastically. When I arrived at St James's, I went into the dressing-room where my 12 young Train-bearers were, dressed all in white with white roses, which had a beautiful effect.

Typically, the ceremony had not been rehearsed and the bridesmaids formed an ungainly gaggle as they stumbled over each other as each tried to hold on to too short a train. Victoria, who had obviously been crying with happiness, was too wrapped up in her bridegroom to notice. 'I felt so happy when the ring was put on, and by Albert,' she wrote simply in her journal. Those who had not been invited consoled themselves by denigrating everything about the wedding, describing the wedding breakfast as 'a mere Whig party'. But Victoria recorded that the crowd was immense and that 'they cheered us most warmly and heartily'. Tories such as Charles Greville sneered that the couple left for their honeymoon at Windsor in 'very shabby style'.

The honeymoon was another bone of contention. Albert was surprised and disappointed that he and his bride were to have only three days together at Windsor, before returning to Buckingham Palace and business. Even though she promised to obey her husband in the marriage ceremony, Victoria was unyielding: 'You forget, dearest Love, that I am the Sovereign, and that business can stop and wait for nothing. Parliament is sitting, and something occurs almost every day, for which I may be required, and it is quite impossible for me to be absent from London; therefore two or three days is already a long time to be absent.' How very different from the later days of her reign when nothing her ministers could say or do would induce the Queen to return to London.

The high-profile nature of Victoria's wedding and the brevity of her honeymoon further provoked male suspicions about her brazen female independence. She had refused to play the blushing bride, but had put herself wantonly on display; nor had she hidden herself away on honeymoon, the sexual rite of passage which traditionally required the couple to stay out of circulation for a month. Not only that but she actually *entertained* at Windsor during those three days.

Misunderstandings between the couple were forgotten on the wedding night. They dined in their sitting room, but Victoria 'had such a sick headache that I could eat nothing, and was obliged to lie down in the middle blue room for the remainder of the evening, on the sofa, but, ill or not, I never, never spent such an evening . . . He called me names of tenderness, I have never yet heard used to me before – was bliss beyond belief! Oh! This was the happiest day of my life!'

The section of Victoria's journal devoted to her wedding night – which it is not permitted to quote from – leaves the reader in no doubt that she enjoyed it. 'When day dawned (for we did not sleep much),' she continues, 'and I beheld that beautiful angelic face by my side, it was more than I can express! He does look so beautiful in his shirt only . . .'

Marriage altered the way the Queen was perceived. She was no longer a maiden but a wife, and soon she would be a mother; all this served to downplay her regal and sexual independence. But there was no defined role for the husband of a queen regnant. While certain sections of the press congratulated Albert for winning 'the grey mare' – a common metaphor for a highly spirited woman – and the *Satirist* portrayed him as a fecund German stud brought in to sire an heir to ensure the continuation of the monarchy, the constitution did not recognize his existence. Victoria made it plain that politics were to be her preserve, not his. Albert chafed at his enforced idleness. Nor was he finding his relationship with Victoria easy. She was his wife, but also his sovereign.

The terms of Victorian masculinity were measured in part by the management of one's wife. Albert was determined to be the master in his own home, but also to mould Victoria's public image. He believed that there were many advantages to being a female sovereign; qualities associated with true womanhood – domesticity, motherhood and sympathy – transmitted in images of Victoria and her happy home life were to prove useful in securing the powers of a strong constitutional sovereign. His idea of exploiting Victoria's womanhood depended for its success on a strong husband manager who did not compete for attention with his wife. In order to work, this formula 'requires that the husband should entirely sink his own individual existence into that of his wife – that he should aim at no power by himself or for himself . . . but make his position entirely part of hers . . . continually and anxiously watch every part of business in order to be able to advise and assist her'.

Albert's programme entailed the considerable task of making an already strong, independent woman follow his lead and as a consequence change her assumptions and behaviour. By sinking his existence into hers, Albert did not mean that he would accept Victoria as he found her. Being an only child with no father to observe as head of the household, Victoria did not immediately appreciate her subservient status as a Victorian wife. Moreover, she had enjoyed three independent years as an unmarried queen. Albert needed to make his will master of hers. It was not easy.

There were frequent scenes. Albert had been warned about Victoria's violent temper; Stockmar feared that she took after her grandfather, George III, and that the outbursts indicated that she had inherited his 'madness'. Guarding Victoria's mind – ensuring that its precarious balance was never upset – became one of Albert's abiding concerns. While his wife screamed and threw things, Albert tended to take refuge in chilly rationality, which enraged her all the more. He would leave the room and the corridors would echo to his wife's fury and slammed doors. He would compose his response in writing, admonishing her as if she were a recalcitrant child. Victoria, once so blithe and buoyant a spirit, became accustomed to finding herself in the wrong, blaming herself for disputing with her husband and not showing him the obedience that was his due.

Fortunately for Albert's plans, Victoria embraced wholeheartedly the prevalent view of the correct relationship between the sexes: women were by nature inferior and dependent. She would have no truck with female emancipation, not hesitating when the issue arose to express her hostility to women's entry into the professions, never mind political life. She successfully concealed the extent of her own participation, by allowing an image of her to be presented that was almost entirely domestic. Like the previous queens regnant, she thought of herself as an exceptional woman, separated from others by the peculiarity of her anomalous position. Victoria was indeed exceptional, a complex character, a woman trying to do a man's job as well as her own as wife and mother, always torn between her duty to her office and the lure of a private, domestic existence.

Seen in due course as a matriarchal figure, the mother of her people and the empire, the grandmother of Europe, no less, her example just might have strengthened the moral authority of women in the family. If the presence of a woman as the head of state worked at a deeper level to make that of women in public life more acceptable, or nudge the legal processes forward, change was a long time in coming. When Victoria died in 1901 her obituary in *Reynolds's Newspaper* acknowledged:

> Her life has had one great use. It has taught us the power we are wilfully allowing to go to waste in the womanhood of the nation. If Victoria has been all her flatterers say, then there are many thousands of possible Victorias in the kingdom. No longer can it be argued . . . that women are unfitted for public duties. The feature of the twentieth century probably will be the utilization of this rich reserve of force. If it be so, that will be the greatest result of the reign of Victoria.

Victoria readily admitted that marriage was a lottery. She was unique among married women, however, in never having been subject to the law of coverture, by which a woman was compelled to hand over her property to her husband on marriage. Unlike other British women, she was not prevented by marriage from entering into independent contracts or disposing freely of her own property. It was not until the late 1870s that the laws governing married women's property began to be liberalized and it was the end of the century before women saw their legal status improved in a number of ways. Divorce became available, at least to the wealthy, through the law courts, instead of only through private Acts of Parliament, while legal separation offered some refuge for poor women from brutal and disastrous marriages.

To gain total domination over his wife, Albert saw that the influences of the past had to be broken. He had come to terms with Lord Melbourne, who receded gradually into the background, but Lezhen's departure was more problematic. Albert thought her scheming and manipulative. He had been shocked at how much the Duchess of Kent, his aunt, had been marginalized, blaming Lehzen for coming between mother and daughter, and he suspected that she was trying to drive a similar wedge between Victoria and him. Certainly he did not seem to have Victoria's entire confidence, whereas her old governess seemed to know all her secrets. Lehzen had to go. Albert systematically plotted her departure, which ultimately was brought about after a furious row between husband and wife about her former governess's damaging influence in the royal nursery. Inevitably defeated, Lehzen packed her bags and returned to Hanover.

Only when she appreciated her feminine place could Albert disappear behind the newly subordinated Victoria. Nature came to his aid. A queen is as subject to the biological imperative as any other woman. Nine months after her honeymoon, Victoria gave birth to her first child, Victoria, the Princess Royal, known affectionately as Pussy and later as Vicky. The following year the Prince of Wales, Albert Edward or 'Bertie', was born. They were followed by Alice in 1843, Alfred or 'Affie' in 1844, Helena or 'Lenchen' in 1846, Louise or 'Louischen' in 1848, Arthur in 1850, Leopold in 1853 and Beatrice or 'Baby' in 1857. It was rare at the time, even for a well-to-do family, to lose no children in infancy, but all Victoria's survived. Only the health of Leopold, who had inherited haemophilia through his mother, gave cause for concern.

Victoria had a strong constitution and there were no complications in any of her confinements. Superstitiously perhaps, she wore the same night shift for each confinement. Transferring from her bed to a sofa in her dressing room after a few days, she was soon up and about, but she was increasingly subject to post-natal depression. 'One becomes so worn out and one's nerves so miserable,' she complained. As early as her second pregnancy, her *accoucheur*, Dr Locock, decided that 'she will be very ugly and enormously fat . . . her figure now is most extraordinary. She goes without stays or anything that keeps her shape within bounds . . . she is more like a barrel than anything else.' She bitterly regretted becoming pregnant so quickly after marriage, leaving her little time alone with Albert and, with no knowledge of or access to contraception, loathed the fact that she was so frequently pregnant. Could not she just have fun in bed, she asked her doctor after the birth of her last child, without the consequences?

Locock had been taken aback by what he called the Queen's 'indelicacy'. Victoria was modern enough to regard childbirth not as an illness, which was still the prevalent view, but as a natural process; always plain speaking, she did not see why she should not be frank with the doctor. This is not to say that she did not find the whole business of procreation – what she later described to her eldest daughter as 'the shadow side' of marriage – disgusting and degrading. 'What you say of the pride of giving life to an immortal soul is very fine, dear, but I own I cannot enter into that,' she wrote to Vicky. 'I think much more of our being like a cow or a dog at such moments.' To have children one after the other, she warned her daughter, was to be avoided. 'I positively think those ladies who are always *enceinte* quite disgusting; it is more like a rabbit or a guinea pig than anything else and really it is not very nice.'

As for the agony of childbirth, she told her daughter, 'those very selfish men would not bear for a minute what we poor slaves have to endure.' The birth of her last two children was eased by the administration of 'the blessed chloroform', which Sir James Clark obtained through his contact with the Scottish doctors, Simpson and Snow. It was a revolutionary step, since traditionally in Christian society it was considered a woman's lot to endure the pains of childbirth to atone for Eve's sin in the Garden of Eden. The Queen's approval of the new panacea made it respectable for other women to follow suit.

Victoria's fertility meant that Albert's role was transformed from wielding the blotting paper to dictating the despatches. Given the keys to the boxes of confidential state documents, he would read and summarize papers for her, drafting replies for her to copy in her own hand. As he admitted to Lord Wellington, he had become her sole confidential adviser, her private secretary and her permanent minister. Soon ministers noticed that when they had an audience with the Queen, her husband would always be present. It was now a question of 'We' not 'I'. Greville remarked that while Victoria had the title, Albert was discharging the functions of the sovereign.

In spite of a succession of babies, Victoria conscientiously fulfilled her ceremonial duties with the grace and dignity that the public had come to expect of her. She would attend the State Opening of Parliament, receive foreign royalty and review her troops. During the London season, between February and July, she would hold monthly court levees – afternoon assemblies at which only men were received – and about four drawing rooms, where debutantes and young married women were presented. Sometimes there were as many as 3,000 at these events. She attended balls, the opera, concerts and plays; she loved the circus, and invited the American performer Tom Thumb to Buckingham Palace.

Even so, Victoria seemed to collude in her own diminishment. 'I am every day more convinced that *we women*, if we are to be good women, *feminine* and *amiable* and *domestic*, are not *fitted to reign*,' she pronounced, after she had been sovereign for fifteen years. 'If we are good women, we must dislike masculine occupations,' she wrote to Leopold. She had become dangerously dependent on Albert.

Victoria was so much in thrall to her husband that she never put on a bonnet or a gown he did not approve. She dressed to please her man and obeyed him in this as in everything else. When the milliner came from Paris, Albert would be in the room making all the decisions. This was the beginning of Victoria's lifelong love affair with the bonnet, which became almost the trademark of the Queen-Empress, but, according to Charlotte Canning, a lady of the bedchamber,

Albert's choice of bonnet made his wife look more like 'an old woman of seventy'. Albert's own taste in dress was questionable. To an English gentleman in his sombre, classically cut tailoring, there was something just a bit too foreign about Albert's high leather boots, velvet coats and lace cuffs. It was the same sort of raffish eccentricity that marked the Jewish Disraeli as alien. Victoria would have been better advised by her good friend the Mistress of the Robes, the beautiful Harriet, Duchess of Sutherland, whose taste was impeccable, but she never sought it.

From her appearance, Victoria's subjects could be forgiven for thinking that she was not interested in clothes. The despair of her dressers, she confessed that she had neither the time nor the inclination to concentrate on her appearance, although her journal reveals that she took a lively interest in what other women wore. She was careless enough to appear on a state visit to Belgium with a pink petticoat showing beneath the hem of her muslin gown. Like many women who are not beautiful, do not have a fashionable physique, and have not had a thorough grounding in the art of dressing well, Victoria got her image wrong more often than right.

The Court Circular, which she corrected in her own hand, dutifully recorded what she wore. At official receptions she would wear a tiara sometimes including the Koh-i-noor diamond, which could be detached to form a brooch, and the crown diamonds. She had good shoulders and showed them to advantage in low-cut gowns. She would always wear the blue ribbon of the Order of the Garter across her chest. At court functions she wore a diadem – a coronet of opals and diamonds or a diamond circlet – and a court train, perhaps of white and gold moiré watered silk trimmed with gold blonde lace and red velvet bows, with a gown of white satin with trim to match the train. At the christenings of her children she wore her wedding lace and a white dress, in a way that celebrated the connection between the sacrament of marriage and the offering of this new life to the service of God.

Posterity thinks of Victoria as a black-clad widow, but as a young queen, wife and mother her cupboards were filled with gowns of softest white or lilac silk, rich brocaded court trains of red or gold or silver, riding habits of dove grey, ball dresses of pink or blue tulle over silk, worn with diamonds nestling in the roses, lilac or jasmine that adorned them, Honiton lace and gold and silver lace, and ribbons of all hues. Unfortunately, she had a propensity for draping herself in shawls, wearing over-decorated dresses cluttered with lace, ribbons, bows and flounces and, prompted by Albert, who would often be in her dressing room as she changed, had taken to swathing her dresses in huge floral trimmings. Sometimes at dinner she would wear fresh flowers in her hair. She also wore too great an array of jewellery, smothering her hands with rings in an attempt to hide their ugliness.

Nothing illustrates the clutter of Victoria's appearance more than the descriptions of her during the reciprocal visits between the English royal family and the Emperor Napoleon III of France and his wife Eugénie in the mid 1850s. Entering Paris – the city of *haute couture* with the English couturier, Worth, at its pinnacle – Queen Victoria amazed and amused the sophisticated Parisians with her bizarre appearance. In the summer heat she was swamped by a massive white silk bonnet with streamers behind and a tuft of marabou feathers on top, weighted down by a mantle of crude green over a flounced white dress, and she carried a green parasol and a large silk reticule embroidered with a gold poodle – a hand-made gift from one of her daughters.

This was the age of the crinoline, that imprisoning garment which inhibited a woman's mobility and yet whose sheer size indicated her growing centrality – not in entering a man's world, but perhaps in occupying more symbolic importance in it. Its broad tiered skirts were most unflattering to a small, rotund woman like Victoria, while the tall, elegant Empress Eugénie carried the style superbly. A fervent admirer of beauty in either sex, Victoria showed no jealousy of Eugénie. The Queen of England did not have anything to prove.

The nation found the homely figure of the Queen and her subservience as a wife reassuring. Motherhood served to increase her status. Not that Victoria was particularly maternal. She found small babies most unappealing. 'I have no *tendre* for them till they have become a little human,' she confessed to Vicky, 'an ugly baby is a very nasty object – and the prettiest is frightful when undressed – till about four months; in short as long as they have their big body and little limbs and that terrible frog-like action.' Small children were more tolerable, as long as they were pretty and well-mannered. In spite of the royal family's cosy domestic image, Victoria's children saw as little of their parents as any other upper-class children, confined to the nursery with their tutors, governesses and nursemaids. Albert, credited – wrongly, as it happens – with introducing the Christmas tree to England, and as a kindly and benevolent paterfamilias prepared to get down on the floor and play with his children, was in reality a stern, unbending and dictatorial father. He expected too much of his children. Only the eldest, Vicky, who had inherited his good brain and shared his intellectual interests, came anywhere near his exacting standards. The Prince of Wales, whom Albert expected to mould into the ideal prince, just as he had moulded Victoria, was a grave disappointment to both parents.

From the moment of his birth, a rigid educational programme was mapped out for Bertie, which took no account of his mental abilities or predilections. Victoria feared her son was a caricature of herself. He seemed to have inherited all the worst Hanoverian traits. She complained of his idleness, his laziness, the fact that he showed an interest in nothing but clothes, and his violent outbursts of temper – no doubt the result of his frustration at the over-strict regime imposed on him – and, in due course, the certainty that he would be as devoted to pleasure and debauchery as her wicked uncles. Neither Victoria nor Albert was prepared to acknowledge or encourage their eldest son's merits, which later manifested themselves in a real talent for friendship and for communicating with men from many different walks of life and shades of political opinion.

Even Vicky, the paragon, was not exempt from Victoria's criticism. She was only fourteen when she fell in with her parents' known wishes and accepted the proposal of Prince Frederick William 'Fritz' of Prussia. It was a cruel sacrifice of a young girl to Albert's impossible dream of a peaceful, liberal Prussia presiding over a united Germany in friendship with England. As a young married woman trying to get to grips with a difficult new family and political situation in Berlin, Vicky was bombarded by pestering and reproachful letters from her mother and then attacked for becoming pregnant far too soon and far too young.

As the younger children were unlikely to inherit, less was demanded of them, but Victoria, always jealous of anyone or anything that took Albert's attention from her or intruded into their intimacy, often resented their presence. She had little patience with them. She seemed to think that being a mother meant being a scold. 'It is indeed a pity that you find no consolation in the company of your children,' Albert admonished her.

The distinction between private and public life was drawn more firmly than in previous reigns. Albert taught Victoria to appreciate the countryside. Soon the search was on for a home of their own, where they could bring up their children in more salubrious surroundings than smoke-infested London with its stinking, sewage-filled river. With the memory of seaside holidays in her childhood, Victoria chose Osborne House near Cowes on the Isle of Wight as a summer retreat. The original house was pulled down and Albert designed a new one in the Italianate style. Government ministers now had all the bother of taking one of the new trains from London and crossing the Solent to see the Queen.

But Osborne was still not private enough for the royal couple. A visit to the Duke and Duchess of Atholl at Blair Castle in Perthshire opened their eyes to the beauty of Scotland, so like Albert's 'dear little Germany'. Learning that the climate on the east coast, Deeside in particular, was more temperate, the couple rented Balmoral in Aberdeenshire with its relatively small estate of 17,000 acres. A good businessman who had restored the royal finances, Albert eventually persuaded the owner to sell for £30,000 in 1852. After the profligacy of Victoria's predecessors, it was impressive that Victoria and Albert could buy both these private homes out of their savings. They were exhibiting the sort of good financial management their middle-class subjects thoroughly approved of. The original house was demolished and Albert designed a new castle; wholeheartedly embracing all things Scottish, they decorated the rooms in wall-to-wall tartan which made visiting ministers wince.

Years later, Victoria reinforced the idea of the royal family's domestic idyll with the publication of her book, *Leaves from the Journal of Our Life in the Highlands*, which describes family picnics, walks, Albert's deer stalking and her sketching, building a cairn and dancing round a hillside fire to celebrate the fall of Sebastopol while imbibing copious quantities of whisky, the gillies' ball, good faithful servants such as John Brown, and many other Highland delights. Written in the most mundane style, the public lapped it up. Why, the Queen was just like an ordinary person. It was so reassuring to have such an exemplary figurehead, a monarch who left politics to the politicians. Few realized just how busy the Queen was behind the bland façade and how involved she still was in the political process.

29

The Dual Monarchy

'WHY, WHEN ONE is so happy and blessed in one's home life, as I am, Politics (provided my country is safe) must take only second place,' Victoria wrote. It belied the fact that the Victorian monarchy was very hands-on. Far from being above politics, as the press and the public liked to imagine, Victoria and Albert demanded to be consulted on every aspect of policy and constantly intervened. Albert tackled a mountain of paperwork and wrote long memoranda to government on every conceivable subject of public importance, from foreign affairs to the arts and sciences to the amelioration of housing for the poor. Both he and the Queen routinely dealt with a vast correspondence.

Victoria was a determined upholder of her prerogatives and Albert stiffened her resolve. Indoctrinated by Leopold and Stockmar, he refused to contemplate a new and impotent monarchy. It should be his and Victoria's task to revive a more energetic crown on an older model. Albert's theories rested on some shaky assumptions. Stockmar had mistakenly dismissed the House of Commons as a talking shop which had usurped too much influence since the Reform Act of 1832. Prime Ministers came and went. The monarchy was the only fixed and disinterested part of government, which should reclaim supreme power and reassert itself as the 'permanent premier who takes rank above the temporary head of the cabinet'.

This ran contrary to the theory, later articulated by Walter Bagehot in his *The English Constitution* in 1867, that the constitution was divided into two parts: the 'dignified' and the 'efficient'. The sovereign and the House of Lords represented the dignified, or decorative, part, whose function was to feature in imposing spectacles designed to serve as reminders of a glorious past and to impress the uneducated populace with the authority of the state. The word 'ceremonial' increasingly came to mean powerless or empty. Behind the façade, the Cabinet and the House of Commons were the efficient part, doing the real work, transacting the affairs of state. The sovereign's exact role and power were vague; there was 'no authentic blue book to say what she does', no written constitution, but the 'mystique' of the monarchy was part of its power. Albert was determined that it should be part of the efficient, rather than the decorative, side of the constitution. He believed that the sovereign had to watch and control ministers and be centrally active in the governing process. Throughout the 1840s and 1850s he and Victoria worked tirelessly to assert the authority of the crown.

Albert's cool temperament contrasted with the headstrong, emotional and impetuous Victoria's. This advantage immediately came into play when Lord Melbourne's government was finally about to fall in 1841. Through the mediation of Albert and his private secretary George Anson, who conducted preliminary discussions with Peel, another 'bedchamber crisis' was averted. Albert arranged for some of the Queen's Whig ladies to resign and be replaced by ladies with less overt political sympathies. In this way, both sides saved face. The Queen was not seen to be bowing to the demands of her Prime Minister in the choice of her ladies and it looked as if the Prime Minister had her confidence. Before long, Albert had also succeeded in convincing Victoria of Peel's worth. He was a man after Albert's own heart: hard-working, earnest, reserved, dedicated. The royal couple's preference was always for a Prime Minister who placed country above party, what they termed 'a safe pair of hands'; by the time of Peel's resignation after the Repeal of the Corn Laws in 1846, Victoria was bemoaning the loss of 'our worthy Peel . . . a man of unbounded loyalty, courage, patriotism, and high-mindedness'.

Albert regarded foreign affairs as the crown's special preserve and conducted private correspondence with other crowned heads, independent of the Foreign Office, in which he did not hesitate to criticize his own government. It was inevitable that he would clash with the Foreign Secretary, Lord Palmerston, whose 'gun-boat' diplomacy and marked show of favour towards foreign radicals advocating the overthrow of their absolutist rulers – many of them their relations – horrified Victoria and Albert. They were particularly incensed by Palmerston's refusal to submit diplomatic despatches to Buckingham Palace for clearance before they were sent off, which was discourteous, if not unconstitutional. Palmerston, who took the traditional Whig view of the relationship between crown and Parliament, did not see why he should acquiesce in this royal meddling in government affairs.

In 1851, however, he overstepped the mark. The Prime Minister, Lord John Russell, who had hitherto ignored the Queen's frequent pleas to get rid of him, only just pre-empted her in dismissing Palmerston over his unauthorized approval of Louis Napoleon's 'coup' in France, in contravention of Britain's declared neutrality. It is significant, however, that although the sovereign's prerogative of appointing ministers had not yet fallen into abeyance, and Albert in particular was active in negotiating the formation of cabinets, the royal couple proved powerless to stop Palmerston's return to Cabinet office in 1852. If he could not be kept out of the Cabinet, Victoria could at least exercise her influence by suggesting an individual was inappropriate for a particular office. Palmerston had to accept the Home rather than the Foreign Office. There was a backlash after the outbreak of the Crimean War, when Palmerston was temporarily out of office, and a scapegoat had to be found for the mismanagement of the war. Albert, a foreigner, was viciously attacked in the press for being in cahoots with the Russian enemy.

Victoria was inclined to change her mind about Palmerston in the course of the war, especially after he became Prime Minister in 1855 and his belligerent stance matched her own. Never much interested in domestic policy, Victoria was deeply concerned with Britain's place in the world. Like Palmerston, she was fiercely patriotic and a determined advocate of British interests. With the outbreak of war, Victoria the soldier's daughter assumed a thoroughly martial spirit. Her cousin, the Duke of Cambridge, was Commander-in-Chief, but Victoria played a prominent role. She reviewed her troops on horseback at Aldershot, wearing a scarlet and gold military-style tunic, navy riding skirt and small felt hat with plumes. She insisted on going in person to watch her soldiers and sailors depart and became engrossed in the distant war, seizing on despatches and news, writing directly to her generals, and sending personal letters of condolence to officers' widows.

'You will understand it when I assure you that I regret exceedingly not to be a man and to be able to fight in the war,' she wrote to Princess Augusta of Prussia. 'My heart bleeds for the many fallen, but I consider that there is no finer death for a man than on the battle-field!' Far removed from the horror and the squalor of it all, someone of Victoria's romantic bent might well think so.

She helped to design the Victoria Cross, suggesting its famous motto, For Valour, and instigated the casting of the Crimean campaign medal, bestowing it personally on hundreds of returning soldiers: 'From the highest Prince of the Blood to the lowest Private, all received the same distinction for the bravest conduct in the severest actions, and the rough hand of the brave and honest private soldier came for the first time in contact with that of their Sovereign and their Queen!' she wrote exultantly to Leopold. 'Noble fellows! I own I feel as if they were my own children; my heart beats for them as for my nearest and dearest. They were so touched, so pleased; many, I hear, cried – and they won't hear of giving up their Medals, to have their names engraved upon them, for fear they should not receive the iden-tical one put into their hands by me, which is quite touching. Several came by in a sadly mutilated state.'

The Queen visited countless wounded soldiers, urging the gov-ernment to provide adequate hospital facilities for them and laying the foundation stone of the military hospital at Netley, in which she con-tinued to take a keen interest all her life. As the *Illustrated London News*'s engraving, 'Queen Victoria Inspecting the Wounded at Buckingham Palace', demonstrates, these were scenes charged with sentiment. Here was a compassionate and patriotic Queen, her femi-nine sympathy aroused by the heroism of her soldiers, still wearing the clothes in which they had fought. In contrast, *Reynolds's Newspaper* with its republican sympathies deplored the fact that demands for jus-tice on behalf of the mismanaged soldiers should have been 'swallowed in torrents of flunkey adulation which has been evoked by what has been termed the kindness and condescension of the Queen in visiting the sick and wounded'.

She wrote to Florence Nightingale to express her warm admiration for her services, 'which are fully equal to those of my dear and brave soldiers, whose sufferings you have had the privilege of alleviating in so merciful a manner'. She sent Miss Nightingale a brooch 'as a mark of the high approbation of your Sovereign!' with her assurance that she looked forward to meeting 'one who has set so bright an example to our sex'.

The Crimean War was scarcely over when news reached London of a mutiny by sepoys in the Bengal army of the East India Company at Meerut in May 1857. They had seized Delhi and other nearby towns and a month later the revolt spread to the Ganges valley. Victoria was shocked by the accounts of the massacres. Always sympathetic to the natives, she wrote to the Governor General's wife, her former lady-in-waiting, Charlotte Canning: 'I think that the greatest care ought to be taken not to interfere with their religion – as once a cry of that kind is raised amongst a fanatical people – very strictly attached to their religion – there is no knowing what it may lead to and where it may end.' She hoped that the conduct of her own officers and men would 'show the difference between Christian and Mussulmen and Hindoo – by sparing the old men, women and children,' adding, 'Any retribution on these I should deeply deprecate for then indeed how could we expect any respect or esteem for us in future?' When India was brought under direct British rule in 1858, Victoria insisted that the proclamation included an assurance of religious toleration.

At home, a new sense of order and endeavour was brought to the conduct of royal business. The Hanoverians had never touched on the lives of ordinary subjects, nor sought to align the monarchy so emphatically with the major developments of the day. Under Albert's direction, this changed dramatically. The sovereign and her consort went out among the people, to the centres of industry and new concentrations of population, such as Manchester, Birmingham, Leeds and Liverpool. Their presence was an acknowledgement of the economic and social power of manufacturing and reinforced the monarchy's centrality at a time of disorientating change. Always scornful of what they called the 'Foxhunters' – the old landed, reactionary aristocracy, with its idleness and extravagance – Victoria and Albert identified themselves with the new, burgeoning middle classes, embracing the same ethics of hard work, thrift, domestic probity and the belief in progress. In doing so, they satisfied the demand for a more utilitarian monarchy, one that was at least being put to work for its handsome remuneration.

Victoria had at first been reluctant to participate in civic pageantry. In September 1842, on her first visit to Scotland, she revealed an indifference to public relations that would have had later royal managers and spin doctors reeling. After a rough voyage the royal party arrived unexpectedly early in the morning. Understandably, Victoria's only thought was to get off the heaving ship. They passed quickly through the empty streets, making straight for their temporary residence at Dalkeith House. The people of Edinburgh were dismayed that their elaborate preparations had been bypassed in this way. Members of the town council went to see Sir Robert Peel, who was travelling with the Queen, and a reluctant Victoria was persuaded to progress through the streets two days later. Similar incidents occurred on a marine tour of the south coast in 1843, when the mayors of Weymouth, Falmouth, Penryn and Truro had themselves rowed out to the royal yacht to give loyal addresses and ask 'if it was the royal pleasure to land?' It was not and they were dismissed.

The public desire for the royal presence was strong enough to survive Victoria's 'courteous' refusals and soon the situation took a new turn. A visit to the Midlands in 1843 included an excursion to Birmingham for Albert, which was really a fact-finding mission, prompted by his interest in industry. Albert had sent a list of the places he wished to visit, but the mayor persuaded him to broaden his programme. After this, fact-finding visits to the provinces were quickly transformed by eager civic authorities into crowd-pleasing spectacles.

The Midlands visit, coincidentally, was one of the first occasions the royal couple travelled by train, although at 30mph Albert considered the new mode of transport dangerously fast. The number of subsequent tours and the range of places they were able to visit was, in part, a product of the railways' ability to transport the Queen with relative rapidity. The royal railway carriage had a crown on top and crowds lined every station and the tracks along the route to cheer her as she passed.

The first twenty years or so of Victoria's reign coincided with a tremendous expansion of the newspaper industry, made possible by the mechanization of production, the creation of large urban markets, and the transport infrastructure provided by the new railways. Technological advances, particularly in the field of graphic news, and the reduction and finally the abolition of stamp duty and the paper tax made printed matter more affordable to an increasingly literate readership. The development of the electronic telegraph meant that reports of the Queen's engagements could be transmitted back to London, where newspaper offices eagerly awaited the latest royal bulletins.

The revolution in print culture became inextricably linked with the new style of monarchy inaugurated by Victoria and Albert. They undertook a vast number of regional tours, reciprocal state visits, military reviews and civic engagements, setting the precedent for future constitutional monarchs. Philanthropic activities included hospital openings, prison visits and Albert's ceaseless drive for better housing for the working classes. What, after all, is a monarch to do, once he or she is removed from the political sphere? Much of the impact of these tours was owing to their novelty. A young couple touring different parts of the country without the traditional trappings of royalty, frequently accompanied by their infant family, meant that articles could be invested with a heady mixture of romantic sentiment, family propriety, royal patronage and local civic pride. The cumulative effect of all the media attention ensured that the monarchy continued to dominate the public sphere. As most of the coverage focused on the 'apolitical' side of the Queen's activities, it reinforced the idea that the monarchy had become politically neutralized, or inactive, rather sooner than was the case.

Reading about the Queen in a newspaper or periodical, looking at the engraving of the scene described, became an everyday practice of collective identification with the Queen a national figurehead and her family everyone's family. Most of the coverage was supportive of the monarchy; the thousands of spectators in attendance, which tended to dominate the diminutive figure of the Queen in the engravings, were seen as confirmation of the Queen's centrality in the life of the nation and of her reliance on her people's support. Royal visits were made to signify a popular constitutionalism, with the Queen willingly placing herself before the people; in theory at least, her position was validated not by ceremony but by the approval of her subjects. The very ordinariness of Victoria's appearance, in bonnet and shawl, helped reinforce this notion of 'democratic' monarchy.

The contrast between Victoria's reception by her people and the fate of other European monarchs in the year of revolutions, 1848, could not have been more marked. The benefits of constitutional monarchy as opposed to absolutism were there for all to see in the press reports and illustrations of the orderly crowds, the banners and cheers greeting a visit from the Queen, as opposed to the barricades, chaos and insurrection on the Continent. Only Britain escaped the upheaval, although the Queen and her family did secretly leave the capital for Osborne just before a large Chartist demonstration, which turned out to be a damp squib.

'Our little humbug of a queen is more endurable than the rest of her race because she calls forth a chivalrous feeling,' George Eliot noted a little acerbically. Later, in 1851, *Reynolds's Newspaper* made the same point, claiming that the 'sex of the Sovereign, more than her virtues, has closed many a quiver full of arrows that might have been discharged with fatal accuracy'. Gender might have had something to do with it, although it had not saved the heads of other queens in history who had fallen foul of the people. Nor did the Queen's sex protect her from seven assassination attempts in the course of her reign, although most of these were not politically motivated. The royal couple's diligence in being seen carrying out their public duties, as well as the power of a largely supportive press, undoubtedly contributed to the stability of the Victorian monarchy at this time.

The Hungry Forties were followed by a period of stability and expansion. Britain was becoming the workshop of the world; optimism was possible even outside the ranks of the increasingly prosperous middle class. The era was ushered in by the Great Exhibition of the Industries of All Nations at the Crystal Palace in Hyde Park, the brainchild of Albert. It was to be an international celebration of work and peace, as each nation was invited to exhibit its wares. 'The Earth is the Lord's and all that therein is' were the words chosen by Albert as the exhibition's motto and printed at the head of the catalogue. To work is to pray. It was a wholesome concept after the fury of war and revolution.

Needless to say, there was plenty of opposition, not least from the London residents who did not want to see their park spoilt. Albert held on to his vision. Years before, he had admired Joseph Paxton's splendid glass conservatory at Chatsworth. Might Paxton be able to build something similar on the grand scale in Hyde Park, incorporating the centuries-old trees, so that they need not be felled? The result was a triumph for Albert, one of Victoria's proudest days. On 1 May 1851 she recorded in her journal:

> This day is one of the greatest and most glorious days of our lives, with which, to my pride and joy the name of my dearly beloved Albert is forever associated! It is a day which makes my heart swell with thankfulness . . . At half past 11, the whole procession in 9 state carriages was set in motion. Vicky and Bertie were in our carriage. Vicky was dressed in lace over white satin, with a small wreath of pink wild roses, in her hair, and looked very nice. Bertie was in full Highland dress. The Green Park and Hyde Park were one mass of densely crowded human beings, in the highest good humour and most enthusiastic . . . before we neared the Crystal Palace, the sun shone and gleamed upon the gigantic edifice, upon which the flags of every nation were flying . . . The tremendous cheering, the joy expressed in every face, the vastness of the building, with all its decorations and exhibits, the sound of the organ (with 200 instruments and 600 voices, which seemed nothing), and my beloved Husband the creator of the great 'Peace Festival', uniting the industry and art of all nations of the earth, all this, was indeed moving, and a day to live forever. God bless my dearest Albert, and my dear Country which has shown itself so great today.

Victoria visited the exhibition many times, systematically combing through the exhibits, fascinated by the glimpses they offered of foreign lands. Before it closed in October, 6 million visitors had passed through and the substantial profit was to be devoted to the creation of four museums dedicated to the arts, natural history and science, built on a four-acre site in South Kensington. It was a fitting legacy of Albert's bold vision.

Victoria's perceived intimacy with her subjects was accentuated by the ubiquity of her image. Previous sovereigns had to rely mainly on the coinage for the circulation of their image; Victoria had the postage stamp. In May 1840 the Penny Black was released. There had been no plan to use the Queen's head, but the design was the result of a national competition and Benjamin Cheverton's winning entry happened to be the only one to use it. In due course, Victoria's image would adorn a whole plethora of artefacts, from plates to biscuit tins, which could now be produced cheaply and plentifully.

The waning of traditional court portraiture has to be seen in the context of the creation of a more populist monarchy. The growth of the print trade created a demand for more informal royal portraits. The accession of a personable young queen in 1837 had been manna from heaven for the Books of Beauty, which fed their female readers with a diet of glamorous, heavily idealized femininity. Their influence was such that their style of portraiture permeated the entire market. A prettified Victoria was depicted as softly feminine, sweet and vulnerable, decorative rather than majestic.

After she was married, Victoria's contradictory dual role as queen and wife was captured by her court artist Sir Edwin Landseer in his *Windsor Castle in Modern Times*. In this romantic and fanciful domestic scene, Albert the husband is the centre of attention, as the Queen looks down demurely at him, his dog Eos gazes at him adoringly and the Queen's Skye terrier sits up to lick his hand. He is wearing his hunting clothes, his bag of game improbably strewn about the floor, the manly sport being in sharp contrast to the Queen's womanly delicacy, as she stands in evening dress, posy in hand. Reinforcing this vision of the family virtues, a tiny Princess Royal plays near by, while in the park outside, the Queen's mother is being wheeled about in a bath chair. The only concession to Victoria's regal status is that she is standing, enhancing the authority of a small woman who would otherwise be overshadowed by her husband.

Similarly, in Landseer's painting of the royal couple dressed as Edward III and Queen Philippa at the fancy dress ball Victoria gave in support of the hard-pressed Spitalfields silk weavers, the irregularity of their relationship is again addressed. Clad in their Plantagenet costumes, the Prince no longer seems to be subservient to his wife. Standing on the steps of the throne, he is looking up at her, but he holds his lady's hand, honouring yet ruling her. He wears the crown and the sword at his side replicates the jewelled Sword of State. Carl Haag in his *Balmoral, Bringing Home the Stag* emphasizes the Prince's virility as he displays a recently slain stag for his wife's admiration. Typically, Victoria is in evening dress, the princes are in their tartans, and the other men in the painting are appropriately in awe of Albert's achievement.

The advent of photography, which the royal couple eagerly embraced, helped extend the popular character of the monarchy. Victoria was the first British monarch to be subject to the camera lens. Photographs of the royal family were first put on public display at the Manchester Art Treasures exhibition, which Albert opened in May 1857. The following year, Leonida Caldesi's photograph of Victoria and Albert and their completed family of nine children taken at Osborne was displayed in the London Photographic Society's fifth annual exhibition. Photographs provided a new and more accessible means of participating in the life of the royal family. Now the image of the Queen could be placed, literally, in the homes of her subjects, extending her intimacy with them. The ordinariness of her appearance – the camera did not lie, but the photographic studios took the initiative in retouching – devoid of the trappings of sovereignty symbolized the shift towards a more inclusive style of monarchy. As the mystique of monarchy began to unravel before a merciless camera lens, so the promotion of a homely royal family came to the fore.

'A *family* on the throne is an interesting idea . . . It brings down the pride of sovereignty to the level of petty life,' Bagehot was to write in 1867. 'Just so a royal family sweetens politics by the seasonable addition of nice and pretty events. It introduces irrelevant facts into the business of government.' The press and the public had become insatiable in their demand for royal coverage; the growth of women's periodicals meant that there was also a large female readership to satisfy. 'The women – one half of the human race at least – care fifty times more for a marriage than a ministry,' Bagehot shrewdly noted. Weddings, christenings, birthdays could no longer be considered the private preserve of the Queen and her family; they were now media events, the bigger the better. Whether they liked it or not, royalty was now locked into a pattern of mutual benefit and antagonism with the press. A court newsman was appointed to act as the interface between the royal household and the press; he was the official source, offering necessary but bland information. Henceforth, the royal family was required to perform.

By the late 1850s the novelty of Victoria and Albert's frequent public appearances had worn off and the focus was moving gradually to their children, who had the appeal of youth. The first to be married was Vicky, the Princess Royal, in January 1858. Irked by the fact that Albert was so often outranked at events involving foreign royalty and anxious to establish his precedence after her so that he would not find himself relegated to an inferior place to his own children once they grew up, Victoria conferred the title of Prince Consort on him by Letters Patent in June 1857.

'It is a strange omission in our Constitution that while the wife of a King has the highest rank and dignity in the realm after her husband assigned to her by law, the husband of a queen regnant is entirely ignored by the law,' she wrote in a memorandum. 'This is the more extraordinary, as a husband has in this country such particular rights and such great power over his wife, and as the queen is married just as any other woman is, and swears to obey her lord and master, as such, while by law he has no rank or defined position. This is a strange anomaly.'

Vicky was making a dynastic marriage to Prince Frederick William, eldest grandson of the King of Prussia. The Prussians were demanding that the marriage of the Hohenzollern heir should take place in Berlin. With characteristic aplomb, Victoria squashed any such idea. 'Whatever may be the usual practice of Prussian Princes,' she wrote in a note to Lord Clarendon, the Foreign Secretary, to pass on to the Prussian ambassador, 'it is not every day that one marries the eldest daughter of the Queen of England. The question therefore must be considered as settled and closed.' She was less successful when she demanded a dowry of £80,000 and an annuity of £10,000 from Parliament for her daughter; the amounts were reduced to £40,000 and £8,000 respectively. The press, meanwhile, was demanding value for money. *The Times* argued that the expense of the wedding would be justified provided Londoners were given a decent glimpse of the couple.

With the exception of the loss of her father, the Queen had hitherto been untouched by death. In March 1861, however, her mother died and Victoria suffered what seems to have been a nervous breakdown. Thanks to Albert's mediation, relations between mother and daughter had been close for many years, but now profound feelings of guilt about her earlier estrangement from her mother surfaced. She filled pages of her diary with obsessive details about her mother's last hours, her corpse, and reflections on the past. 'I had never been near a coffin before,' she kept repeating, sitting for hours in her mother's room. 'My head has been tiresome and troubles me and I can still bear little or no noise. The relief of tears is great – they come again and again every day,' she wrote to Vicky. 'I love to dwell on her, and to be quiet and not to be roused out of my grief.'

With Victoria indulging in an excessive display of grief and remorse and refusing even to come to meals, it was left to Albert to carry on the business of the monarchy and care of the family. He was already exhausted, worn down by the unremitting work he had taken, or rather inflicted, upon himself. Years spent labouring at his desk into the small hours meant that his once splendid figure had become flabby; he looked older than forty-two and he had gone bald. Victoria had occasionally mentioned in her letters to Vicky that Albert was suffering from his 'old complaint'; he might have had stomach or colonic cancer for some time.

In November, feeling depressed and far from well, he pushed himself to visit the Prince of Wales in Cambridge. Bertie had already got himself into a scrape when, during a spell in the army in Ireland, his comrades had taken pity on him and smuggled an actress, Nellie Clifden, into his bed. Others would have shrugged off the incident as a natural right of passage for a young man, but Albert was heartbroken that his son had eschewed his example and advice to remain pure. Victoria, when she heard the 'disgusting details', was sickened. At Cambridge father and son went for a walk, which was unfortunately extended in the extreme cold as Bertie lost his way. In the carriage home, Albert began shivering; he seemed to have caught a chill. At Windsor, he took to his bed. His last service to Victoria and his adopted country was to amend the wording of a telegram to the United States government just as that country descended into civil war; his intervention probably prevented war between Britain and America.

'I do not cling to life,' he had once told Victoria. 'You do; but I set no store by it.' And then he added, 'I am sure, if I had a severe illness, I should give up at once, I should not struggle for life. I have no tenacity for life.' Indeed, 'he died for want of pluck,' Victoria later accused him. 'The Queen alone is enough to kill any man,' William Ewart Gladstone complained in another context. Nevertheless, the notion persists that like the spider who eats her mate, Victoria had killed her man. Albert had worked himself to death in her service.

As Lord Clarendon scathingly noted, Prince Albert's medical attendants were 'not fit to nurse a sick cat'. Sir James Clark, the principal physician in attendance, failed to diagnose typhoid or to invite a second opinion until it was too late. If and when he did suspect typhoid, he hesitated to name the disease for fear of upsetting Victoria, whom he considered incapable of bearing anxiety. It might have helped if Albert had received professional nursing, but it was left largely to his daughter, Princess Alice, and his valet to care for him. Victoria refused to believe the illness was fatal, until the morning of 14 December. As she entered the sickroom, 'never can I forget how beautiful my darling looked lying there with his face lit up by the rising sun, his eyes unusually bright gazing as it were on unseen objects and not taking notice of me.' '*Es ist kleines Frauchen*,' she whispered to him, as he slipped in and out of consciousness that day. Towards evening, she briefly left the room and was hastily called back by Princess Alice, who recognized the death rattle.

'Oh, this is death,' Victoria cried, taking his cold hand, 'I know it. I have seen *this* before.' With Victoria kneeling beside him and the Prince of Wales and other members of the family and the doctors gathered in the room, Albert died just before eleven that night. 'Oh! my dear Darling!' she cried in despair, kissing him on the forehead.

At first she appeared calm, in shock. 'You will not desert me? You will all help me?' she enquired anxiously of everyone there.

'We have buried our sovereign,' Benjamin Disraeli commented after Albert's funeral. 'This German prince has governed England for twenty one years with a wisdom and energy such as none of our kings has ever shown.' Disraeli exaggerated, although the sentiments were genuine enough. Albert had never really been popular in England; he was considered too German, too earnest, too prim.

The dual monarchy was over. Victoria confidently expected to follow her 'beloved angel' to the grave shortly. Given the severity of her grief, she would have been dismayed to know that her life span had just entered its second half and that she would reign alone for another forty years.

30

The Widow

VICTORIAN WOMEN WERE expected to mourn their husbands publicly, wearing widow's weeds of deepest black for one year and half mourning for at least six months after that. Remarriage was frowned upon in certain quarters, not least by the Queen, who believed that she would be reunited with her beloved Albert in the afterlife. As a woman, it was considered only right and proper that Victoria should grieve and be incapacitated following her husband's death. As sovereign, however, she was expected to resume her political and ceremonial duties after a decent interval. Always torn between her private and public lives, prostrate with grief, Victoria resented and resisted pressure to perform. The chivalry of her ministers did much to protect her from the inevitable backlash.

At first Victoria thought she was 'going mad' with grief. She kept tapping her forehead and repeating, 'My reason! My reason!' She had always feared and dreaded madness. It was hardly surprising, then, that some believed that hereditary eccentricities, perhaps even George III's madness, were reasserting themselves, although there is no evidence that she had inherited the porphyria gene from her grandfather. For a time she refused to meet her ministers face to face, using Princess Alice or her equerry, General Charles Grey, as go-betweens. When the Privy Council met, the Queen sat in one room, the counsellors in another, with the door open but Victoria hidden from view, as the secretary to the Council, Arthur Helps, communicated her wishes.

Sir James Clark denied Victoria was 'mad', but acknowledged her to be highly strung and conceded her duty to pay attention to her 'nerves'. Sir William Jenner, who succeeded Clark as physician-in-ordinary, inclined more to Stockmar's belief in Victoria's mental instability. Victoria was not mad, but she positively wallowed in her grief and, with Albert gone, there was no one to gainsay her. She shamelessly used her doctors to keep her ministers at bay. Jenner would write snippets in the *Lancet* emphasizing the Queen's imperative need for 'repose and rest', but many of his communications were composed and dictated by Victoria herself.

'I will do all I can to follow out all his wishes – to live for you all and for my duties,' she promised her eldest daughter in the immediate aftermath of Albert's death.

> But how I, who leant on him for all and everything – without whom I did nothing, moved not a finger, arranged not a print or photograph, didn't put on a gown or bonnet if he didn't approve it shall be able to go on, to live, to move, to help myself in difficult moments? How I shall long to ask his advice! . . . The day – the night (above all the night) is too sad and weary . . . I try to feel and think I am living on with him, and that his pure and perfect spirit is guiding and leading me and inspiring me!

To Uncle Leopold she wrote:

> The poor fatherless baby of eight months is now the utterly broken-hearted and crushed widow of forty-two! My life as a happy one is ended! The world is gone for me! If I must live on . . . it is henceforth for our poor fatherless children – for my unhappy country, which has lost all in losing him – and in only doing what I know and feel he would wish . . . But oh! To be cut off in the prime of life – to see our pure, happy, quiet domestic life, which alone enabled me to bear my much disliked position, cut off at forty-two – is too awful, too cruel!

A few days later she assured him that Albert's 'views about everything are to be my law! And no human power will make me swerve from what he decided and wished.'

As someone who had hitherto formed a habit of dependence on men, she would now have to find within herself qualities of independence and self-reliance previously unknown to her. She was determined, she told Leopold, 'that no one person, may he be ever so good, ever so devoted among my servants – is to lead or guide or dictate to me . . . And I live on with him, for him; in fact I am only outwardly separated from him, and only for a time.'

More than a year after Albert's death, Lord Clarendon had a meeting with the Queen in which she constantly referred to the Prince Consort 'as if he was in the next room, indeed it was difficult not to think that he was so for everything was set out on his table, the blotting book open with a pen upon it, his watch going, fresh flowers in the glass'. 'She believes that his eye is now constantly upon her,' Clarendon continued, 'that he watches every action of hers and that in fact she never ceases to be in communion with his spirit.' There were rumours that she took part in séances to summon up his spirit, but they seem to be unfounded. After the deaths of her mother and husband, ceremonies for the dead – above and beyond even the elaborate mourning customs of the age – became part of a way of life for Victoria. Her only happiness was in dwelling on her departed loved ones.

At Windsor she dedicated the Blue Room as a shrine to Albert. Rather than following the German custom of the *Sterbezimmer*, where time stands still and the only change is measured in the accumulation of dust, Victoria had the room redecorated, laid wreaths on both beds, and ordered new china. The sculptor William Theed fashioned a marble bust of the Prince, to be placed between the two beds. Albert's dressing case stood open and ready, fresh towels and hot water were replenished daily and his clothes laid out ready to wear. Every day Victoria would place fresh flowers on the bed. She slept clutching his nightshirt. A marble model of his dead hand stood on the table beside her bed for her to clutch, while a photograph of Albert taken *after* his death lay on his pillow in every bed she slept in.

Whatever Albert had liked, touched or designed became preserved as sacred relics. Accordingly, Victoria spent much of her time at Osborne and Balmoral. When the upholstery at either home wore out, it had to be removed silently, reproduced exactly and the furniture replaced precisely where it had always stood. At Windsor, of course, she could visit Albert's resting place in the mausoleum she had built for them both at Frogmore; she went every day. She brought the family there to visit him, feel his presence, even to receive his judgements.

Victoria, who believed so strongly in mourning that she insisted that even babies and nurseries should be swathed in it, had decided to wear full mourning for the rest of her life. The undemanding simplicity of a widow's black dresses and caps suited her admirably; it was one less worry, as she grappled with the work of government and the affairs of her large fatherless family. All correspondence was conducted on paper with one-inch black borders, so that her large loopy handwriting had to be squeezed into the remaining space. Eventually she abandoned the heavy black crape of first mourning for lighter silks and plain black cloth, adorned with lace or jet, silver, gold and ermine, and copious quantities of jewellery. It was Victoria's adherence to strict mourning that made her so reluctant to don her red Parliament robes, which lay draped over the throne during the State Opening of Parliament, whether the Queen was present or not. The widow's white cap with the long streamers was worn more frequently than the crown.

It was not until 1864 that she decreed that although her ladies-in-waiting must continue to wear black when in attendance on her at court, the other ladies of her household might wear lilac, grey or white, the colours of half mourning. There was always the chance, however, that one of the Queen's numerous royal relations would die, plunging them all back into full mourning. A young maid of honour who despaired of ever getting out of black was once tempted to ask, 'Ma'am, how many more relations do you have?'

Victoria's acute loneliness was exacerbated by the isolation of her unique position as queen. She had friends among her ladies, notably the Duchesses of Sutherland and Atholl, Lady Ely and Lady Augusta Bruce, but she had never been able to forget she was Queen and confide in them, woman to woman. Albert had been best friend as well as lover. She missed him physically. 'What a dreadful going to bed! What a contrast to that tender lover's love! All alone!' she confided in her journal. 'I am alas! not old – my feelings are strong and warm; my love is ardent,' she confessed to Vicky. Only the baby of the family, four-year-old Princess Beatrice, could offer some solace. 'Sweet little Beatrice comes to lie in my bed every morning which is a comfort,' she told Vicky. 'I long so to cling to and clasp a loving being.'

It was unfortunate for Victoria that, coinciding with her double bereavement, she was approaching the change of life – a partial death in itself. The Victorians believed that forty-two was a dangerous age for a woman. In an intermittent fertile state, the 'dodging time', women in their forties were entering the phase the Victorian medical profession called 'the climacteric'. The label denotes danger, a crisis when virtually anything in a woman's physical or mental constitution could go awry. She was likely to be peevish, irritable, morose and passionate on the slightest provocation; she found it difficult to concentrate and could not tolerate noise. Much of Victoria's behaviour during her early widowhood fits this description. As she wrote to her eldest daughter in February 1863, prior to her visit: 'I wish you would say in your affectionate letters that you will do all to help me in checking noise, and joyousness in my presence for I fear you always think that I am not ill, that I can bear it, and I cannot and it makes me wretched and miserable beforehand if I think I shall be excited. I cannot join you at dinner; I must keep very, very quiet.'

Not only was Victoria going through the peri-menopause, but the doctors believed that the melancholia at the loss of the person she most depended on, coming only a few months after the death of her mother, could intensify the malady. In June 1863 she told Leopold:

> I have been so unwell, the result of over-exertion this last week, that I can hardly hold my pen for shaking, and hardly know what I am about. I was so unwell on Sunday, from violent nervous headache and complete prostration, that I nearly fainted, and Clark and Jenner both say that, with the extreme state of weakness which I am in, if I did faint I might not come back to life. My weakness has increased to that extent within the last two months, as to make all my good doctors anxious. It is all the result of overwork, over-anxiety, and the weight of responsibility and constant sorrow and craving and yearning for the one absorbing object of my love, and the one only Being who could quiet and calm me; I feel like a poor hunted hare, like a child that has lost its mother, and so lost, so frightened and helpless.

According to Victorian doctors, the climacteric could be brought on by emotional shock. 'Wherever widowhood or separation takes place at the change of life, all the distressing symptoms and the ovario-uterine excitement, are considerably aggravated,' one of them wrote. Without the regular monthly bleed, it was believed that the menopausal female body was left victim of its own undisciplined devices. There was a curious notion that blood not expelled during menstruation turned to fat in the menopausal woman. Within a decade of Albert's death, Victoria's waist was forty-eight inches, making her only ten inches less wide in the middle than she was tall.

In spite of the sympathy she deserves going through the menopause at a time of immense sorrow and upheaval, it cannot be denied that Victoria was indulging in a selfish and self-centred grief of which Albert would not have approved. Blaming Bertie, unfairly, for his father's death, Victoria confessed that she could not look at her eldest son 'without a shudder'. When Princess Alice, who had been her constant companion since Albert's death, married in the summer of 1862, Victoria had to admit that it was 'more like a funeral than a wedding'. There was to be no relaxation in mourning and the wedding was a subdued affair. Victoria could think only of herself and her own loss; she envied her children their prospects of happy married life.

When the Prince of Wales married the beautiful and gentle Princess Alexandra of Denmark in March 1863, Victoria behaved like the spectre at the feast. When they arrived at Windsor, the Queen took her new daughter-in-law and Bertie straight to Albert's tomb at Frogmore. 'He gives you his blessing,' she assured them after this morbid greeting, joining their hands together and kissing them. Just as she had with Princess Alice, she had her photograph taken with Bertie and his bride, with Theed's bust of Albert in the middle. Victoria gazes up at her dead spouse, making it clear that she was pledged to the past and death, rather than to the future through the young couple. Similarly, photographs of Victoria the widow looking sadly at a bust of Albert, distributed in the form of *cartes de visite*, were public demonstrations of the depths of her grief; the viewer became a voyeur of the Queen's suffering.

At the wedding in St George's Chapel, Windsor, her black-clad figure watched the proceedings taking place below from the obscurity of Katherine of Aragon's closet, exciting the curiosity of Disraeli who was caught raising his monocle to get a better look at her, so long had it been since she had been seen in public. She refused to join the rest of the family at the luncheon that followed, dining alone with 'Baby'. As soon as Bertie and his bride left on their honeymoon Victoria returned to the mausoleum with her daughter Lenchen and 'prayed by that beloved resting-place, feeling soothed and calmed'.

Leopold advised her that she would find consolation in work. Sitting very straight to ease the pressure on the back, Victoria had always been a dutiful desk worker, preferring it to her ceremonial role, but she was simply unused to the sheer volume and complexity of the paperwork, a burden that Albert had carried for her for so long. 'I must work and work, and can't rest and the amount of work which comes upon me is more than I can bear!' she complained to Vicky. 'I who always hated business, have now nothing but that! Public and private, it falls upon me! He, my own darling, lightened all and every thing, spared every trouble and anxiety and now I must labour alone!'

In spite of a formidable memory and grasp of detail, Victoria was never to exhibit Albert's capacity for work. Whether she liked it or not, she would inevitably be less of a hands-on monarch than Albert had intended. Domestic policy, including social reform, did not much interest her, although when she embraced a cause – such as opposition to vivisection or cruelty to animals – she did so wholeheartedly. She remained as opposed as ever to women's rights, denouncing the agitation for their advancement as 'dangerous, unchristian and unnatural'.

'The Queen is a woman herself – and knows what an anomaly her *own* position is . . . But to tear away all the barriers which surround a woman, and to propose that they should study with *men* – things which could not be named before them – certainly not *in a mixed* audience – would be to introduce a total disregard of what must be considered as belonging to the rules and principles of morality,' she commented on the proposal to admit women to the study of medicine. 'Let woman be what God intended; a helpmate for a man – but with totally different duties and vocations,' she wrote to Gladstone in 1870.

On no account were women to be given any political recognition. 'The Queen is most anxious to enlist every one who can speak or write to join in checking this mad, wicked folly of "Women's Rights", with all its attendant horrors, on which her poor feeble sex is bent, forgetting every sense of womanly feeling and propriety. Lady —— ought to get a *good whipping*.'

'It is a subject which makes the Queen so furious that she cannot contain herself,' she continued. 'God created men and women different – then let them remain each in their own position . . . Woman would become the most hateful, heathen, and disgusting of human beings were she allowed to unsex herself; and where would be the protection which man was intended to give the weaker sex?'

Even in mourning, Victoria could still summon the will to oppose and obstruct her ministers and did not hesitate to do so; she was a shrewd, persistent and opinionated adviser of her governments. Given her tendency to see politics in personal terms, she was only really roused by foreign affairs, in which many of her own relatives were the key players. Here she insisted that no step was to be taken without her previous sanction and she exercised close control over the content of despatches. Ideally, she would have liked the Foreign Secretary to report directly to her without reference to the Cabinet. Bagehot was to dismiss the Queen as 'a retired widow'; not having read her letters, published after her death, he could not know the extent of her interference.

In the Schleswig-Holstein dispute, which blew up in 1864, her views were directly opposed to those of her chief ministers, Lords Palmerston and Russell. Should the duchies belong to Denmark or be part of the German confederacy? The question was complicated and was said to be understood by only three people: a German professor who had gone mad, the Prince Consort who was dead, and Lord Palmerston, who had long since forgotten what it was all about. Following Albert's known wish to see a united Germany under a strong, liberal Prussia and her own German bias, Victoria was considered a partisan. It is difficult to determine how far she really was responsible for British neutrality and the abandonment of Denmark to its fate. She expressed her wishes, which ran contrary to those of the Prince and Princess of Wales, of course, and a large section of public opinion, most vociferously to Palmerston:

The Queen has read with the greatest alarm and astonishment the draft of a despatch . . . in which Lord Russell . . . stated that, in the event of the occupation of Schleswig by Prussia . . . Denmark would resist such an occupation and that Great Britain would aid her in that resistance. The Queen has never given her sanction to any such threat, nor does it appear to agree with the decision arrived at by the Cabinet upon this question . . . England cannot be committed to assist Denmark in such a collision. The Queen has declared that she will not sanction the infliction upon her subjects of all the horrors of war, for the purpose of becoming a partisan in a quarrel in which both parties are much in the wrong.

Not only did she express her wishes, she insisted on them prevailing.

On numerous occasions Victoria's knowledge of and contacts with foreign rulers proved to be of immense value. Although she was pro-German, she was not necessarily pro-Prussian and was often at pains to curb Prussian arrogance. In 1864 she offered to intervene to smooth the peace process, writing to Vicky's father-in-law, the King of Prussia: 'I should deeply regret if the prospect of Peace were to be marred by too great demands of Prussia. Your arms have been victorious, and it now depends on the use you make of your victory, whether the public opinion which now inclines to the weaker side be rallied on your side or not.' And in 1870, at the end of the Franco-Prussian War, she wrote to him again: 'The Queen asks the King of Prussia as a friend whether, in the interests of suffering humanity, he could so shape his demands as to enable the French to accept them.'

She could expect to make less headway with Bismarck, although he considered her a worthy and formidable adversary. When she had a meeting with the Iron Chancellor in Berlin in 1888, after the accession of her grandson, Kaiser Wilhelm II, her private secretary Arthur Bigge noted that Bismarck emerged mopping his brow. 'That was a woman,' he said. 'One could do business with her.'

In spite of all this activity in international relations, at home ministers were frustrated by the Queen's lack of visibility. In 1864 a notice was pinned to the railings of Buckingham Palace in the manner of an advertisement: 'These commanding premises to be let or sold, in consequence of the late occupant's declining business.' 'To be invisible is to be forgotten . . . To be a symbol, and an effective symbol, you must be visibly and often seen,' Bagehot admonished three years later. Victoria was adamant that she would remain in seclusion. By 1863 a decent period of mourning had elapsed, but she refused to perform one of her foremost ceremonial duties: the State Opening of Parliament, where her presence symbolized her wholehearted confidence in the government of the day. At the end of the following year, she excused herself again, writing a memorandum to Lord Russell:

> The Queen would wish to say with reference to what Lord Russell said to her this morning about the opening of Parliament, that she would be thankful if he would take any opportunity that might offer to undeceive people upon that head. The Queen was always terribly nervous on all public occasions, but especially at the opening of Parliament, which was what she dreaded for days before, and hardly ever went through without suffering from headache before or after the ceremony; but then she had the support of her dear husband, whose presence alone seemed a tower of strength . . . Now this is gone, and no child can feel more shrinking and nervous than the poor Queen does, when she has to do anything, which approaches to representation; she dreads a Council even.
>
> Her nerves are so shattered that any emotion, any discussion, any exertion causes much disturbance and suffering to her whole frame. The constant anxieties inseparable from her difficult and unenviable position as Queen, and as mother of a large family (and that, a Royal family), without a husband to guide, assist, soothe, comfort, and cheer her, are so great that her nervous system has no power of recovery, but on the contrary becomes weaker and weaker. This being the case, Lord Russell . . . will at once see that any great exertion which would entail a succession of moral shocks as well as very great fatigue, which the Queen must avoid as much as possible, would be totally out of the question.
>
> She has no wish to shut herself up from her loyal people, and has and will at any time seize any occasion which might offer to appear amongst them (painful as it ever is now), provided she could do so without the fatigue and exertion of any State ceremony entailing full dress, etc.

The situation had scarcely altered two years later, when she wrote to Russell comparing the opening of Parliament to an execution, so great an ordeal was it for her:

> The Queen must say that she does feel very bitterly the want of feeling of those who ask the Queen to go to open Parliament. That the public should wish to see her she fully understands, and has no wish to prevent – quite the contrary; but why this wish should be of so unreasonable and unfeeling a nature, as to long to witness the spectacle of a

poor, broken-hearted widow, nervous and shrinking, dragged in deep mourning, alone in State as a Show, where she used to go supported by her husband, to be gazed at, without delicacy of feeling, is a thing she cannot understand, and she never could wish her bitterest foe to be exposed to!

A king would not have got away with it or expected to, but allowances had to be made for a female ruler – a unique and unfathomable element in public life. To be fair, since her widowhood Victoria had developed trouble with her legs, so that at times she could not actually walk. The doctors associated this incapacity with hysteria. It might be assumed that she had now passed from the peri-menopause to the menopause proper. Seven years after Albert's death, Vicky was to write to her mother: 'I fear you are already approaching a stage in your health, which is said to be the most trying and unpleasant in a woman's life, and at which the strongest constitutions suffer as well as the most delicate.'

When it suited her, Victoria was an astute manipulator of the perceived weakness of her sex. She knew that she could rely on the chivalry of her ministers and, of course, they were far too reticent or embarrassed to recognize the real cause of the Queen's contradictory behaviour. As one of Gladstone's private secretaries wrote: 'Many were the times when, if Mr G. had chosen to cross her and take his own line on the threat of resigning, she would have had to give way to him or have run the risk of bringing the crown into odium. But sooner than this, he would give way – he attached such great importance to the maintenance of the monarchy as a popular institution, and he felt that much was due to [the throne's being occupied by] a *woman.*'

What baffled and infuriated the ministers was the fact that Victoria seemed perfectly capable of attending any number of opening ceremonies for Albert memorials; she could dance with abandon at the gillies' ball at Balmoral, ride up in the hills all day long whatever the weather, or 'nip' over to Germany; but she refused point blank to open Parliament or defer her departure for Balmoral or Osborne on occasions when it would have helped the government. In June 1867, for instance, she was asked to delay her journey to Osborne for three or four days in order to greet the Sultan of Turkey. It turned into the usual tussle with Victoria writing to Lord Derby: 'The word distasteful is hardly applicable to the subject; it would be rather nearer the mark to say extremely inconvenient and disadvantageous for the Queen's health.' While conceding grudgingly that she *would* change her schedule to meet the Sultan, she suggested that he change his own plans and arrive a day earlier. 'Still, whatever the poor Queen can do she will; but she will not be dictated to, or teased by public clamour into doing what she physically cannot, and she expects her Ministers to protect her from such attempt.'

'Eliza is roaring well and can do everything she likes and nothing she doesn't,' Clarendon remarked. Her wilfulness impaired the monarchy's credibility, to the despair of its supporters, and gave rise to fears that it might have outlived its usefulness.

She did open Parliament in 1866 and afterwards told Russell that she hoped that he would 'in future trust to her doing what she believes to be necessary for the good of the country, without her movements being dictated to her.' Only by preserving her health, she argued, could she continue to serve. The following year brought in the Second Reform Bill, adding nearly 1 million more voters to the electorate, and the Tory Lord Derby persuaded the Queen that she should show her support for the proposed legislation by opening Parliament in person. The Reform Bill was very much the work of the Chancellor of the Exchequer, Benjamin Disraeli, who had taken the trouble to ingratiate himself with her, and so she agreed, but with the proviso that 'the Queen must have it clearly understood that she is not to be expected to do it as a matter of course, year after year.'

'Yesterday was a wretched day,' she complained to Vicky after the opening, 'and altogether I regret I went – for that stupid Reform agitation has excited and irritated people, and there was a good deal of hissing, some groans and calls for Reform, which I – in my present forlorn position – ought not to be exposed to. There were many, nasty faces – and I felt it painfully. At such times the Sovereign should not be there.'

Victoria was largely sympathetic to electoral reform, although not universal suffrage. 'The higher classes – especially the aristocracy . . . are so frivolous, pleasure-seeking, heartless, selfish, immoral and gambling that it makes one think . . . of the days before the French

Revolution. The young men are so ignorant, luxurious and self-indulgent – and the young women so fast, frivolous and imprudent that the danger really is very great, and they ought to be warned,' she wrote to Vicky, no doubt recalling that the Prince of Wales was very much part of the 'fast set' she so deplored. 'The lower classes are becoming so well-informed, are so intelligent and earn their bread and riches so deservedly – that they cannot and ought not to be kept back – to be abused by the wretched, ignorant, high-born beings who live only to kill time.'

William Gladstone, the Liberal who became Prime Minister in November 1868, was highly critical of Victoria's reluctance to perform her ceremonial duties and of her long absences from the capital. 'To speak in rude and general terms, the Queen is invisible and the Prince of Wales is not respected,' he complained. Others joined the chorus of disapproval.

The mid 1860s were a time of acute political tension, economic difficulties and social dislocation; pauperism and unemployment reached levels unknown since 1848. If the monarchy at the apex of society were allowed to decay through inanition, surely the whole social fabric would collapse? The exacting standards set by Albert were those the public had now come to expect of the monarchy, and it seemed that Victoria was no longer meeting them. It was asserted that the middle classes were disaffected because their feelings of loyalty were not constantly 'nourished by fantastic ceremonies and spectacles' and the 'outward signs and symbols' by which they were 'unconsciously swayed'. Walter Bagehot argued that by her prolonged absence from public life, 'the Queen has done almost as much to injure the popularity of the monarchy . . . as the most unworthy of her predecessors did by his profligacy and frivolity.'

But Bagehot was a political journalist writing in *The Economist* and tended to view the monarchy in narrow political terms. This was to ignore the whole gamut of philanthropic and civic activities that Albert had initiated and encouraged in the 1840s and 1850s and which Victoria quietly continued after his death. As queen and head of a hierarchical society in which it was the Christian duty of the better off to help those beneath them, Victoria had always taken her charitable duties seriously and set a good example to others. Attention to

benevolent causes and the encouragement of public-spirited endeavour reflected well on the monarchy, as well as the civic institutions and
individuals who participated.

Victoria contributed to hundreds of charities, including schools,
hospitals, churches and asylums; she would far rather open a hospital –
she laid the foundation stone of the new St Thomas's Hospital in May
1868, for instance – than Parliament and, while 'politically invisible',
was busy enough visiting hospitals, prisons and workhouses and doing
what she could to ameliorate the conditions of the poor. She gave
donations to the relief of victims of earthquakes and storms, fires and
shipwrecks, famines and colliery disasters. About 15 per cent of her
Privy Purse income, or 10 per cent of her personal wealth, was
donated to good causes, while the value of royal patronage was
incalculable.

Gladstone had his own agenda in urging the Queen to be more visible. By being seen to associate with royalty in public, politicians hope
a little of the magic will rub off on them. It was important to be seen
to have royal endorsement for their policies. Victoria, who had begun
life as a Whig, had become a Conservative. She distrusted the Liberals
and her dislike of Gladstone – 'I cannot find him very agreeable, and
he talks very much,' she told Vicky – would soon turn to loathing.
Treat the Queen as a woman, his wife urged, to no avail. Gladstone
addressed the Queen like a public meeting, writing long, tedious,
indigestible memos she could not understand.

Reform had been the work of the Conservatives, but no one
knew how reliable the new electorate would be. While it alarmed the
upper classes, there was disillusionment at the limited scope of
the Second Reform Act. Gladstone wanted the Queen to open
Parliament in February 1869 to give the new legislation her seal of
approval. Her refusal to do so was a political act, as she was vigorously
opposed to Gladstone's Irish policy. Ironically, her reversion to her old
tactic of publicly withholding royal endorsement for a political
agenda mattered less as the electorate became broader-based.
Increasingly, politicians drew their authority from the people, not
the crown.

The first real break in Victoria's seclusion came in November 1869,
when Gladstone persuaded her to go in public procession in an open

carriage for the opening ceremony of Blackfriars Bridge and Holborn Viaduct. One million people waited in the cold to see her pass. 'Nothing could have been more gratifying,' she wrote in her journal that evening. Through the long years of seclusion, Victoria had never doubted her popularity or the loyalty of the people. Ministers despaired at the amount of time she spent in the Highlands – it was hardly conducive to the work of government for the monarch to be 600 miles away from Westminster, Disraeli had commented – but Victoria had deftly turned this to advantage with the publication early in 1868 of her *Leaves from the Journal of Our Life in the Highlands*, which was a runaway success.

'From all and every side, high and low, the feeling is the same, the letters flow in, saying how much more than ever I shall be loved, now that I am known and understood, and clamouring for the cheap edition for the poor – which will be ordered at once. 18,000 copies were sold in a week,' Victoria gushed in a letter to Vicky, who like her siblings was embarrassed by her mother's public revelations about the family's private life. 'It is very gratifying to see how people appreciate what is simple and right and how especially my truest friends – the people – feel it.'

Leaves from the Journal is an idealized portrait of Victoria's life in the Highlands while Albert was still alive. She offers selected glimpses of family activities among close family retainers – one of them being the gillie, John Brown. It was a happy coincidence that the book presents the late lamented Albert as the paterfamilias, the central figure, at a time of growing rumours of an illicit connection between the Queen and Brown, whose rugged handsomeness, aggressive masculinity and familiar manner towards the Queen had fed the scandal. Albert had warmly approved of Brown, which was enough to recommend him to Victoria, and early in 1865 he was brought south as her outdoor servant, leading her out on her pony or in her carriage, where his sharp observation and quick response foiled more than one assassination attempt. He was quickly promoted to 'an upper servant, and my permanent personal attendant' – the Queen's Highland servant. 'It is a real comfort, for he is so devoted to me – so simple, so intelligent, so unlike an ordinary servant, and so cheerful and attentive,' she had enthused to Leopold. To Vicky she wrote: 'He comes to my room after breakfast and luncheon to get his orders – and everything is always right; he is so quiet, has such an excellent head and memory, and is besides so devoted, and attached and clever and so wonderfully able to interpret one's wishes. He is a real treasure to me now, and I only wish higher people had his sense and discretion, and that I had as good a maid.'

She is describing a servant, not a lover, but ugly rumours persisted. Some maintained that the Queen had gone mad and Brown was her keeper, others that he was the Queen's stallion. It is an illustration of the double standard that a man could take a mistress, but for a woman, even if unencumbered with a husband, to engage in an irregular sexual relationship was considered so outrageous as to be unthinkable. Respectable women, never mind queens, were not supposed to have sexual impulses. Doubts were reawakened about the efficacy of female rule. A pamphlet entitled *Brown on the Throne* compared the monarchy to a greengrocer's shop; it suggested that others could run the business better than the 'widow woman' in nominal charge: 'A woman can't attend to it like a man.' Victoria had fulfilled her role as wife and mother; perhaps now she should step aside and let her son take over.

The best that can be said of Brown is that, unlike numerous royal mistresses and favourites in the past, he was not personally ambitious or greedy and did not meddle in politics. Disraeli, who treated him with kid gloves nevertheless, had quite a lot of respect for him. But Brown, with his brusque manner, offended many. The Queen's children were affronted by the familiarity with which he treated their mother – 'Can yer no' hold yer head up, wumman?' was his typical manner of speaking to her – when everyone else including themselves approached her with awe. The Prince of Wales, who was already humiliated by his mother's reluctance to give him any responsibility, bitterly resented Brown's closeness to her. Soon, Brown's wishes were given priority over theirs. The men of the royal family, all of whom smoked like chimneys, were informed that the smoking room would be closed at midnight, as it was inconvenient for Brown. Brown was allotted the best shooting and fishing. Brown had the ear of the Queen. They did not.

No one could deny that the relationship between Victoria and

Brown was intense. It grew into one of mutual devotion. She described them as being best friends and she addressed him in a letter as 'Darling One'. They liked a nip of whisky together. They were intimate, but it is unlikely that they were sexually intimate. Victoria believed in the class structure, but she was no snob; she was willing to flout the conventions to enjoy a close friendship with Brown. But how could Victoria, who believed she would be reunited with Albert in the afterlife, give herself to another man? Three hundred letters, many of them supposedly 'most compromising', written by the Queen to Brown were bought by Bertie after his mother's death and destroyed. Perhaps a clue is to be found in her reaction to Brown's death eighteen years after he had come to England to serve her.

The entry in her journal invites no suspicion of a relationship beyond that of employer and servant: 'Leopold came to my dressing-room, and broke the dreadful news to me that my good, faithful Brown had passed away early this morning. Am terribly upset by the loss, which removes one who was so devoted and attached to my service and who did so much for my personal comfort. It is the loss not only of a servant, but of a real friend.'

The language lacks the usual drama and, indeed, the journal was doctored by Princess Beatrice after her mother's death and some of it burned. However, the Queen's letter to her daughter Vicky also refers to Brown in the same vein:

> The terrible blow which has fallen so unexpectedly on me – and has crushed me – by tearing away from me not only the most devoted, faithful, intelligent and confidential servant who lived and, I may say (as he overworked himself) died for me – but my dearest best friend has so shaken me . . . The shock – the blow, the blank, the constant missing at every turn of the one strong, powerful reliable arm and head almost stunned me and I am truly overwhelmed.

She confided to Sir Henry Ponsonby, who had been equerry to the Prince Consort and was to serve her devotedly as private secretary and Keeper of the Privy Purse for twenty-five years: 'The Queen is trying hard to occupy herself but she is utterly crushed and her life has again sustained one of those shocks like in 1861 when every link has been shaken and torn . . . the loss of the strong arm and the wise advice, warm heart and cheery original way of saying things and the sympathy . . . is most cruelly missed.'

Significantly, with the 'loss of the strong arm', the man she had depended on for nearly twenty years, she temporarily lost the use of her legs, just as she had when Albert died. 'The Queen can't walk the least and the shock she has sustained has made her very weak – so that she can't stand,' she told Ponsonby. Certainly, her private secretary did not believe that the Queen and Brown were lovers, or so his son Frederick believed.

After Brown's death, she published a second volume of her Highland journal, *More Leaves from the Journal of Our Life in the Highlands*, dedicated to her 'devoted personal attendant and faithful friend John Brown'; later she decided to compose a memoir of the former gillie for publication. Her friend, Randall Davidson, Dean of Windsor, advised her to desist from this folly. Surely Victoria's very artlessness in being so open and sincere about her affection for Brown shows that there was nothing 'shameful' to hide. She was transparently honest, without guile; deceit was not in her nature.

Meanwhile, in July 1866 *Punch* published a spoof of the Court Circular:

Balmoral, Tuesday
Mr John Brown walked on the slopes. He subsequently partook of a haggis. In the evening, Mr John Brown was pleased to listen to the bagpipe. Mr John Brown retired early.

The following year the *Tomahawk* published the cartoon 'Where is Britannia?' showing the throne empty, the royal robes draped over it, the crown insecurely balanced on top and the British lion dozing on the floor. This was followed by 'A Brown study', which shows the same scene, except that the crown is at the side, under a glass case, and leaning negligently against the throne is the dour figure of John Brown in Highland dress, pipe in hand, the British lion roaring at him.

The Brown scandal was unhelpful at a time when the public's patience with Victoria's seclusion was wearing thin. Republican agitation had been reawakened in the 1860s, fuelled by the Queen's perceived failure to fulfil her duties and the Prince of Wales's reputation as a womanizer and a gambler. John Bright, the radical MP for Durham and Manchester, was one of the few who refused to condemn the Queen, when he declared at a Reform meeting:

> I am not accustomed to stand up in defence of those who are possessors of crowns; but I could not sit here and hear that observation without a sensation of wonder and of pain. I think there has been by many persons a great injustice done to the Queen in reference to her desolate and widowed position. And I venture to say this, that a woman – be she the Queen of a great realm, or be she the wife of one of your labouring men – who can keep alive in her heart a great sorrow for the lost object of her life and affection, is not at all likely to be wanting in a great and generous sympathy with you.

For the most part, however, radical politicians saw the monarchy as irrational and unnecessary and it was beginning to look as if they were right. Bagehot attributed the appeal of monarchy to the fact that it 'is a government in which the attention of the nation is concentrated on one person doing interesting actions', whereas a republic was faceless and therefore of less appeal to the masses. As Charles Bradlaugh, the republican journalist and politician, wrote in 1870: 'The experience of the last nine years proves that the country can do quite well without a monarch and may therefore save the extra expense of monarchy.'

He had unwittingly put his finger on the real issue. The threat to Victoria's monarchy came not from republicanism, but from the call for accountability in mundane matters of money and behaviour. Was the public getting value for money? It seemed not. The assumed partiality of the court to Prussia, the aggressor in the Franco-Prussian War of 1870, highlighted the fact that Britain was saddled with a lacklustre and expensive royal family allied to unpopular foreign royalty. The overthrow of Napoleon III and the Second Empire in 1871 and the establishment of the Third Republic in France fuelled republican agitation in Britain.

It was at this juncture that Victoria agreed to open Parliament and, in a spectacular piece of misjudgement, brought her begging bowl. She wanted a dowry and an annuity for Princess Louise, who was to marry the son of Scotland's richest aristocrat, and an allowance for Prince Arthur, who was coming of age. The radicals swung into action. Why could the Queen not provide for her children herself?

Was she not in receipt of a civil list amounting to £385,000 annually? There was little sign that she was applying it to her ceremonial role and there was no court to speak of, so what was she doing with it?

Charles Bradlaugh, as President of the London Republican Club, was lecturing on 'The Impeachment of the House of Brunswick', later published as a bestselling pamphlet. In September 1871 an anonymous pamphlet entitled *What Does She Do with It?* claimed that public funds to uphold the dignity of the crown were being misappropriated to the Privy Purse. The author, who might have been the Scottish MP G.O. Trevelyan acting on inside information from the treasury, argued that the civil list voted by Parliament gave Parliament the right to enquire into its administration. Sir Charles Dilke, independent radical MP for Chelsea, made the biggest impression with a speech to working men at Newcastle, where he reviewed Trevelyan's evidence and called for a republic. Trevelyan, meanwhile, demanded a public enquiry.

'When there is a select committee on the Queen, the charm of royalty will be gone,' Bagehot had warned in 1867. 'Its mystery is its life. We must not let in daylight upon magic.' Gladstone found that regular savings were being made on the civil list and transferred to the Privy Purse, which was not exactly illegal, just against the spirit of the agreement. The principal source of these savings was not the Queen's retirement from public life, as the royal household had to be maintained whether or not she engaged in public duties, but reforms of the household carried out by Prince Albert in the 1840s and better management of the business affairs of the Duchies of Cornwall and Lancaster, which were yielding increasingly substantial returns. In addition, the Queen had been paying income tax since its introduction by Peel in 1842, but there was an anomaly in that tax, not payable on the actual civil list for household expenses, should have been paid on the savings transferred to the Privy Purse.

It was the most serious crisis of Victoria's reign. Hitherto, the crown had accepted money in return for turning over its hereditary revenues to Parliament. The sovereign and royal family had not been expected to do anything for the money. They had given up their own hereditary estate and relied on the generosity of Parliament to maintain the dignity of the crown. By the 1860s, however, there was an expectation that the monarchy was to be visibly active, to prove that it was giving value for money. More was expected of it than in previous eras. It was the beginning of public accounting for royal services rendered, which by the reign of Victoria's great-great-granddaughter, Elizabeth II, progressed to a running tally of public engagements kept by each member of the royal family as demonstrated evidence of public worth.

Victoria, meanwhile, became so wary of parliamentary intrusion into her financial affairs that she grew more frugal than ever. In later years, rather than risk asking Parliament for extra funds, she would meet deficits in the household budget from her own private fortune – she was, after all, the richest person in England by the 1880s. When her bed broke, she refused to incur the expense of having it mended, while visitors to Windsor found newspaper squares rather than lavatory paper in the loos.

At the end of 1871 the monarchy was overwhelmed by a tidal wave of public sympathy for the Prince of Wales, who nearly died of typhoid. That summer Victoria had had a major contretemps with Gladstone when she refused to delay her departure for Balmoral until Parliament was prorogued. 'The conduct of the Queen . . . weighs upon me like a nightmare,' he told his wife. As a constitutional sovereign, Victoria was supposed to act on ministerial advice, but instead the ministers were embarrassed by her refusal to take that advice. 'We have done all we can. She will decide,' Gladstone told Sir Henry Ponsonby. 'Of course, if challenged, I shall take responsibility. But this shield will not wear very long.' When the Prime Minister visited the Queen at Balmoral, she kept him waiting for several days before receiving him and when he was admitted into the presence he found 'the repellent power which she so well knows how to use . . . put into action against me'.

Ironically, Victoria had become truly ill at Balmoral. In September she reported: 'My foot much swollen, and I could hardly walk a step. The doctors . . . pronounced it to be severe rheumatic gout, and I was not to walk, indeed I could not.' The following month, she complained of 'A most dreadful night of agonising pain. No sedative did any good. I only got some sleep between five and eight this morning. Felt much exhausted on awaking, but there was no fever, and the pain was much less.' She seems to have lost the use of her hands, as well as her legs. 'My utter helplessness is a bitter trial, not even being able to feed myself . . . Was unable all day to eat anything. Dictated my Journal to Beatrice, which I have done most days lately.' A few days later, she was feeling much better and 'was able to sign, which is a great thing'.

By the end of November she was well enough to get up and have breakfast with her children, when she received the news of Bertie's illness. Given her antipathy to her son, the family hesitated to tell her at first. As soon as she heard, she rushed to his side. 'How very kind of you to visit,' the genial Bertie told her in a rare moment of lucidity. The Queen stayed at his bedside. The crisis came on 14 December, the tenth anniversary of Albert's death. Bertie survived.

While Victoria fervently hoped that the close brush with death would persuade her eldest son to mend his ways, Gladstone saw the opportunity to put the Prince of Wales's recovery to good use. Republicanism had been checked, but only the Queen could unite the divided nation. When the idea of a public thanksgiving was put to Victoria, she was predictably reluctant. Gladstone stressed the precedent of the public thanksgiving held after George III's recovery in 1789. He had to coax her along, making it look as if the idea had been hers; to claim ministerial control over royal ceremonial would have been to invite disaster.

Persuading the Queen to act took up an inordinate amount of Gladstone's time, when the Cabinet had other very important business to attend to. Victoria's preference was for a more low-key affair. Gladstone's vision was for something spectacular. He prevailed, although he could not persuade the Queen into regal mode. 'Went to dress, and wore a black silk dress and jacket, trimmed with miniver, and a bonnet with white flowers and a white feather,' she recorded in her journal when the great day came. She refused to pay for the event out of the civil list, so that, to keep the peace, Gladstone had to persuade Parliament to vote funds for it.

On 27 February 1872, 13,000 dignitaries, including 50 selected workmen, crowded into St Paul's Cathedral. 'The deafening cheers never ceased the whole way,' Victoria wrote in her journal, describing her procession to St Paul's with the Prince and Princess of Wales, their eldest son Albert Victor, and Princess Beatrice in an open landau. Parliament's supremacy over the crown was signified by the Speaker in his gold coach at the head of the procession. At Temple Bar the Lord Mayor, in a crimson velvet and ermine robe, went up to the Queen to present the sword, which she touched and returned to him, before passing into the City. Military bands along the route played 'God Save the Queen' and 'God Bless the Prince of Wales', evoking fresh outbursts of cheering from the thousands of spectators. As the royal party emerged from St Paul's, Victoria kissed her son's hand. The crowd applauded delightedly. Back at Buckingham Palace, the Queen and members of her family were cheered on the balcony. 'Could think and talk of little else, but today's wonderful demonstration of loyalty and affection, from the very highest to the lowest,' she recalled in her journal. 'Felt tired by all the emotion, but it is a day that can never be forgotten!'

Victoria was out of seclusion and it had been a day of healing and national reconciliation.

31

The Great White Empress

FOR THE LAST quarter-century of her reign Queen Victoria was revered; she became the awe-inspiring, almost mythical Queen-Empress, a fittingly imperious and venerable monarch of a global empire on which the sun never set.

Much of the credit for Victoria's coming out of retirement is due to two men: John Brown and Benjamin Disraeli. Brown with his stead-fast devotion and common sense had forced her to start living again. Disraeli brought romance back into her life. He inspired her with the possibilities of her position. Instead of remaining in seclusion, becoming more lethargic and unpopular by the year, Victoria emerged with new energy and zest for life. For the first time since Melbourne's day, politics became fun again.

Victoria had a taste for the exotic. Disraeli, whom Albert had dismissed as 'no gentleman', was exotic and, more, he shared Victoria's fascination with the exotic. 'India should belong to *me* . . .' she had stated emphatically when the India Bill was passed in 1858, transferring India from East India Company rule to governance under the British crown. Disraeli quite agreed. The people of the East, he surmised, needed a monarch to relate to, a mother figure, not a chartered company. At the time, Disraeli had reassured Victoria that the India Bill was 'only the ante-chamber to an imperial palace'. Eighteen years later he made her Empress of India.

For years Disraeli had been feeding the Queen with colourful missives from the House of Commons. Parliamentary debates were made to sound as compelling as his novels. But what really endeared Disraeli to Victoria was his unsparing praise of the late Prince Consort. Mr Disraeli, she said, was the only person who appreciated her beloved Albert, the only one who could understand the depth of her loss. By happy coincidence, just as Victoria was coming out of the worst decade of her life, Disraeli became Prime Minister for the first time, in February 1868. All he could offer her was devotion, he wrote on the first day of his premiership. It would be 'his delight and duty, to render the transaction of affairs as easy to your Majesty, as possible'.

'He is full of poetry, romance and chivalry,' she enthused to Vicky. 'When he knelt down to kiss my hand which he took in both of his he said "in loving loyalty and faith".' He was so attentive, so considerate, so obliging. He never seemed to disagree with her; only put his head on one side and had a way of saying 'Ma'am . . .' He knew how to amuse and interest her; she relaxed in his presence. Unlike others, he never lectured, badgered or pressured her. He had no need to. Treating her as a woman first, he had only to invite her to comply, to flatter and charm her, and he won her round.

Disraeli's letters and reports of proceedings in the House which, as Leader, he was constitutionally bound to submit to the Queen, continued to be written in the vivid, dramatic, even racy, style of a novelist. 'Dizzy writes daily letters to the Queen in his best novel style,' Lady Augusta Stanley reported to Clarendon, 'telling her every scrap of political news dressed up to serve his own purpose, and every scrap of social gossip cooked to amuse her.' He was treating the Queen as a human recipient of gossipy letters. Victoria, who admitted that she had never before known *everything*, relished the correspondence.

Victoria had always been inhibited by what she saw as her intellectual shortcomings. Albert – so dominant, so controlling, so superior – had not encouraged her to think otherwise. But Disraeli had the happy knack of drawing Victoria out. He appeared interested in everything she had to say. One of the Queen's granddaughters later put it succinctly when she said, 'When I left the dining room after sitting next to Mr Gladstone, I thought he was the cleverest man in England. But after sitting next to Mr Disraeli, I thought I was the cleverest woman in England.' It was just the sort of confidence booster that Victoria needed at this low point in her life. Although she would not be able to bring herself to open the book of piano duets she had played with Albert until 1876, with Disraeli's encouragement she began to trust and rely on her own intuition; instead of slavishly following the traditions established by Albert, Victoria branched out, taking holidays in the sun-drenched Mediterranean.

Disraeli sent the Queen a complete set of his novels, and she returned the compliment by giving him a copy of her recently published *Leaves from the Journal of Our Life in the Highlands*. As part of his charm offensive, the Prime Minister experienced Balmoral for himself, braving the freezing, fireless rooms, which Victoria so relished, to everyone else's discomfort, and the hideously dull evenings. Never again! he promised himself. 'There is a freshness and fragrance about the book like the heather amid which it was written,' he told her unashamedly. Flattery never came amiss, he told Matthew Arnold, 'and when you come to royalty, you should lay it on with a trowel'. Victoria basked in his praise. 'We authors, Ma'am,' he would say conspiratorially.

Unhappily, Disraeli's first ministry lasted only a few months and in November the Queen had to send for Mr Gladstone to form a government. She had been thoroughly in accord with Disraeli's politics. His popular Conservatism recognized the importance of social reform and, indeed, there was to be more legislation passed during Disraeli's two premierships to ameliorate the lot of the working classes than in the whole of the rest of Victoria's reign. More to the point, however, as far as Victoria was concerned, was that he stood for 'a spirited foreign policy', the greatness of Britain and the consolidation of empire, as opposed to Gladstone's 'Little England' policy. Even Gladstone had to recognize that imperialism offered a distraction from problems at home. The cultivation of national patriotic feeling that accompanied the promotion of imperialism could heal or disguise class divisions. All would be enriched by the expansion of overseas empire, or at least that was the theory.

Albert had approved of Gladstone but, even so, Victoria never took to him and was predictably disgusted when she heard of Gladstone's sexual predilections and his obsession with 'saving' fallen women. Nor could she summon up any enthusiasm for his agenda for domestic reforms. Years later, she was gratified that he seemed to agree with her on the subject of education: 'it being carried too far . . . it entirely ruined the health of the higher classes uselessly, and rendered the working classes unfitted for good servants and labourers.' This is not to

say that she did not have the interests of the poor at heart. In April
1871 she objected to his proposed new match tax, 'which is said to be
the sole means of support of a vast number of the very poorest people
and little children, especially in London, so that this tax, which it is
intended should press on all equally, will in fact be only severely felt by
the poor, which would be very wrong and most impolitic at the present moment'. The idea was dropped.

Gladstone was much preoccupied with 'the royalty question'. His
awe of the institution of monarchy led him to set too exacting a standard for the individual who represented it. His mistake was to treat
Victoria not as a woman, not even as Queen Victoria, but always as
the crown. The only way to mend the malaise currently affecting the
monarchy, he decided, was for the Queen to come out of seclusion
and the Prince of Wales to be given useful employment. Encouraged
by the success of the St Paul's thanksgiving in February 1872, the following year Gladstone presented Victoria with his master plan. Ireland
might be pacified if the Prince were to become her Viceroy there.

Apart from the attractions of the racing, Dublin had no more appeal
for Bertie than the troublesome country had for Victoria. Her love
and loyalty had always been reserved for Scotland, to Ireland's detriment. More concerned than anyone about the Queen's invisibility,
since he had a personal stake in the future of the monarchy, Bertie had
worked hard to fill the vacuum left by his mother's abdication of her
duties in society. He and the Princess of Wales stood in for the Queen
at levees and drawing rooms and, as the leaders of the fashionable
Marlborough House set, entertained in style.

Jealous of any attention being diverted from her, Victoria looked
askance at her son's extravagant pursuit of pleasure and had no higher
opinion of his abilities than she ever had. He had never been allowed
access to the despatch boxes and she had no intention of trusting him
in any official capacity. She pretty much told Gladstone to mind his
own business. Disraeli would have known when to retreat, but
Gladstone doggedly wrote her a series of letters – the dry memoranda
that she loathed – in which he set out to prove under separate head-
ings that her objections to his plan were unfounded. Victoria was
incredulous. 'The Queen therefore trusts . . . that this plan may now
be considered as *definitely* abandoned,' she concluded hopefully after

his third attempt. When he wrote a fourth time, she told him emphatically that it was 'useless to prolong the discussion'.

In February 1874 Gladstone lost his majority and Victoria sent for Disraeli with relief. True to form, the sixty-nine-year-old premier fell to his knees before her. 'I plight my troth to the kindest of mistresses.' The idyll had begun in earnest. Relations between the two were suffused with a rich halo of romance. Soon he was calling her Queen Titania or the Faery Queen, after Edmund Spenser's poem for Elizabeth I. When she took to sending him primroses from Windsor and violets from Osborne, his response was that 'your Majesty's sceptre has touched the enchanted isle.'

Disraeli's promise to do whatever the Queen wished was soon put to the test when Archibald Tait, Archbishop of Canterbury, introduced the Public Worship Regulation Bill, to purge the Anglican Church of the Romish practices that had been creeping in. Disraeli, a Jew who had been brought up Christian, was not remotely interested, until he saw that Gladstone was vigorously opposed to it. The bill had the Queen's wholehearted approval. Her preference was for the simple, plain service of the Church of Scotland, which she enjoyed at Crathie Church whenever she was at Balmoral. 'But here [in England] flowers, crosses, vestments, all mean something most dangerous!' she moaned to Vicky. 'Thank God the Scotch Church is a stronghold of Protestantism, most precious in these realms.'

Taking seriously her responsibility as Supreme Governor of the Church, Victoria wrote to Disraeli: 'The Queen is deeply grieved to see the want of Protestant feeling in the Cabinet.' He 'should state . . . how strongly the Queen feels and how faithful she is to the Protestant faith, to defend and maintain which, her family was placed upon the Throne! She owns she often asks herself what has become of the Protestant feeling of Englishmen.'

Disraeli did not disappoint and afterwards travelled down to Osborne to convey the good news, allowing her the impression that it was her personal intervention that had saved the day. 'I can only describe my reception by telling you that I really thought she was going to embrace me,' he told his friend Lady Bradford. 'She was wreathed with smiles and, as she talked, glided about like a bird.'

Ever solicitous of his comfort, the Queen took the unprecedented step of inviting Disraeli to sit down. He did not at this stage avail himself of the invitation, but was gratified that he had been asked. It was a singular mark of royal favour. When Lord Derby had been recovering from a severe illness, Victoria had commiserated and apologized that etiquette forbade her from asking him to sit. 'She says I am never to stand,' Disraeli confided to Lady Bradford. Later in their relationship, Disraeli did indeed sit down, as by then his conversations with the Queen were running way beyond the allotted time. On one occasion, they were so engrossed in conversation that Disraeli nearly missed his train back to London. 'Run away, run away directly,' the Queen urged him, prompting Disraeli to report gleefully to Lady Bradford, 'and so at an audience instead of being dismissed, I dismissed my Sovereign.'

The Queen and her Prime Minister were soon enjoying such a cosy relationship that some worried about the constitutional propriety of it. Disraeli offered Victoria friendship, as well as a compatible and fulfilling political partnership. He found her female wiles endearing: 'there came a most perplexing, but most agreeable telegram from Balmoral, giving me a great deal of trouble; but in so feminine a manner that it was delightful,' he wrote to Lady Bradford. 'I must say that I feel fortunate in having a female Sovereign. I owe everything to woman; and if in the sunset of life I have still a young heart, it is due to that influence.'

Within a few months of taking office, he managed something Gladstone had never, in his wildest dreams, been able to do. He actually persuaded the Queen to defer her departure for Balmoral for two days, so as to welcome Tsar Alexander II. 'My head is still on my shoulders. The great lady has absolutely postponed her departure!' he told Lady Bradford. 'Everybody had failed, even the Prince of Wales . . . Salisbury says I have saved an Afghan war, and Derby compliments me on my unrivalled triumph.'

'Nobody can have managed the lady better than you have; but is there not just a risk of encouraging her in too large ideas of her personal power, and too great indifference to what the public expects?' the more prosaic Derby cautioned him. 'I only ask; it is for you to judge.'

Disraeli had an instinct for showmanship which appealed to Victoria. His first great opportunity came in 1875 when he heard that the debt-ridden Khedive of Egypt was looking to sell his shares in the Suez Canal. Built by the French and largely owned by them, the canal meant more to the British, since it was the gateway to India. Neither the Queen nor Disraeli wanted to see the canal wholly owned by the French. Disraeli urgently needed £4 million to buy the Khedive's shares, but how to get the money when Parliament was not sitting? Having persuaded a reluctant Cabinet of the wisdom of the enterprise, he sent his secretary, Montagu Corry, round to Baron Lionel de Rothschild.

The Prime Minister, Corry told him, needed £4 million.

'When?' Rothschild asked.

'Tomorrow,' came the reply.

'What is your security?' he asked.

'The British Government,' Corry answered.

'You shall have it,' Rothschild pronounced.

'It is just settled,' Disraeli wrote triumphantly to the Queen at Osborne, 'you have it, Madam.'

It was as if Disraeli had bought the entire canal and laid it as a gift at the Queen's feet. In fact, he had acquired less than a half share, but it showed him to be a master of the grand gesture and it was a brilliant move.

It was the prelude to an even more magnificent coup. Victoria had long been affronted that while other rulers were emperors, she was merely a queen. Her old friend, Emperor Napoleon III, had, alas, been ejected, but the Habsburgs were still Emperors of Austria, the Tsar of Russia called himself an emperor and, since he had been made Emperor of Germany in 1871, the King of Prussia was also an emperor. This meant that when her son-in-law Fritz inherited, her eldest daughter Vicky would also be an empress and take precedence over her mother. Victoria's son Alfred had married the Tsar's daughter, Marie Alexandrovna; did she take precedence over Victoria's other children as a grand duchess? The question of rank had already caused ill feeling when the Tsar had refused to allow his daughter to present herself at Balmoral for Victoria's inspection; the Empress of Russia suggested that Victoria might see Marie in Germany if she cared to travel there. Victoria was apoplectic, writing to her daughter Alice, Grand Duchess of Hesse, who was liaising with the Russian court:

I *do not* think, dear Child, that *you* should tell *me* who have been nearly 20 years *longer* on the throne than the Emperor of Russia and am the Doyenne of Sovereigns and who am a *Reigning* Sovereign, which the Empress is *not – what I ought to do*. *I* think *I* know *that*. The proposal received on *Wednesday* for me to be at *Cologne* . . . tomorrow, was one of the *coolest* things *I* ever heard . . . I *own everyone* was shocked.

It was all very irksome. Naturally, Victoria wanted to be an empress too, and what was more appropriate than that she should be Empress of India – the jewel in her crown?

In 1875 the Prince of Wales, who was itching to experience the opulence of India and shoot some tigers, went on an exploratory tour, representing the British crown. Predictably, Victoria had been reluctant to let him go. Disraeli had had to tread a diplomatic tightrope, playing down the importance of it to Victoria and fending off the Princess of Wales, who was desperate to accompany her husband. At least if she was not there, there would be an excuse for Bertie's amatory escapades. Too many of Bertie's disreputable friends were going with him, in Victoria's view, and it fell to Disraeli to convince them to behave themselves. Victoria refused to finance the trip, and Disraeli had to squeeze the funds out of a reluctant Parliament.

As it happened, the tour was a great success. The Prince of Wales was welcomed by maharajahs and people alike as the symbol of the British monarchy, suggesting that Victoria was as much the sovereign of India – and not just of India's conquerors – as she was of Great Britain and Ireland.

The year 1876 was one occasion when the Queen was only too happy to open Parliament. When the Royal Titles Bill was introduced, however, Parliament was reluctant. There were sound reasons for making Victoria Empress of India: the assumption of the title would give an air of stability and permanence to British rule in India, and the presence of the British Queen-Empress across the North-West Frontier, metaphorically speaking, would sound a warning note to the Tsar of Russia in his drift east. It took all of Disraeli's energy and skill to shepherd the bill through Parliament and on 1 May 1876 it was passed, with the proviso that the imperial title was to be used only in the context of India and in correspondence relating to the subcontinent. Victoria paid no attention, blithely sending Disraeli a Christmas card that year signed VRI – Victoria *Regina et Imperatrix* – the title she used at every opportunity forever after. In 1880 she insisted that Ind. Imp. – Empress of India – be engraved on the new coinage.

On 1 January 1877, at a durbar on the great Plain of Delhi, Victoria was officially proclaimed Empress of India by the Viceroy, Lord Lytton. How gratifying to know that she had been hailed, apparently with unfeigned joy, by her millions of Indian subjects as Shah-in-Shah Padshah – Monarch of Monarchs. At a sumptuous celebratory banquet at Windsor that night, Victoria appeared weighed down by her Indian jewellery. The huge, multicoloured gems would have suited some dark beauty; they were entirely inappropriate for a white-haired, fair-skinned, little old lady. Disraeli, newly created Earl of Beaconsfield, gave one of his most florid speeches, followed by the toast: 'Your Imperial Majesty'. It was their finest hour.

India was not the last of Disraeli's offerings to his queen. In the summer of 1876 the story broke of atrocities carried out by the Turks on their Bulgarian subjects. Twenty-five thousand had been slaughtered. Disraeli was predisposed to prefer the Ottoman rulers to their subject peoples and made light of the reports, but Gladstone saw this as an opportunity to strike. His inflammatory pamphlet, *The Bulgarian Horrors and the Question of the East*, reflected the sympathies of the majority of the British people, which were with the oppressed subjects of the decaying Ottoman Empire. If the 'Sick Man of Europe' was to be carved up, who was going to benefit? While denouncing Gladstone as a mischief-maker and firebrand, Victoria was not about to sit back and give her old *bête noire* the Tsar of Russia, who had ostensibly come to the aid of his fellow Serbs in the Balkans, a free passage to Constantinople.

'You say you hope we shall keep out of the war and God knows I hope and pray and think we shall – as to fighting,' Victoria told her eldest daughter. 'But I am sure you would not wish Great Britain to eat humble pie to these horrible, deceitful, cruel Russians? I will not be the Sovereign to submit to that!'

Disraeli was looking for a diplomatic solution, while trying to tamp down the Queen's belligerence and at the same time using her bellicosity to coax his divided Cabinet into a more warlike frame of mind.

It was not easy to quell Victoria's impatience. While they prevaricated, Britain was losing its prestige and position abroad, she nagged, bombarding Disraeli with telegrams. The Russian Tsar would be before Constantinople in no time. 'Then the Government will be fearfully blamed and the Queen so humiliated that she thinks she would abdicate at once. Be bold!' she urged.

'Oh, if the Queen were a man,' Victoria cried, 'she would like to go and give those horrid Russians, whose word one cannot trust, such a beating.'

It did not quite come to war. Disraeli had hoped that a show of British force would be enough to persuade Russia to climb down. He judged correctly. Bismarck's Prussia put itself forward as the unlikely mediator. In June 1878 Disraeli represented Britain at the Congress of Berlin and stood up to and triumphed over Russian demands. '*Der alte Jude, das ist der Mann*,' an admiring Iron Chancellor remarked of Disraeli's sangfroid. He did not come home empty-handed: Britain had gained control of Cyprus, a base in the eastern Mediterranean from which to check any Russian advances in the area.

'If *we are* to *maintain* our position as a *first-rate* Power . . . we must with our Indian Empire and large Colonies, be *Prepared* for *attacks* and *wars, somewhere* or *other*, CONTINUALLY, and the true economy will be to be *always ready*,' Victoria sought to impress on her Prime Minister. 'Lord Beaconsfield can do his country the greatest service by repeating that again and again, and by *seeing it carried out*.' She was right, of course. In 1878 and 1879 alone, Britain was involved in wars in Afghanistan and South Africa, where the Zulus won a victory over British troops at Isandhlwana. Fierce criticism of these military engagements offered a splendid opportunity for Gladstone to speak of the poor, suffering Afghans and Zulus, the victims of Disraeli's imperialist policy, those 'false phantoms of glory', in his election campaign. There was also a feeling that Disraeli's close relationship with the Queen had allowed her too much power to influence events. The House of Commons debated the motion 'that the influence of the Crown has increased, is increasing, and ought to be diminished'.

In the spring of 1880 Disraeli's government was defeated and the Queen was confronted with the unwelcome prospect of Mr Gladstone's return. As she told Ponsonby, 'she would sooner abdicate than send for or have any communication with that half-mad firebrand who would soon ruin everything and be a Dictator. Others but herself may submit to his democratic rule, but not the Queen.' She sent first for Lord Hartington, leader of the Liberals in the House of Commons, then for Lord Granville. Neither 'Harty-Tarty' nor 'Puss' Granville felt he could form a government, however, and Gladstone, at seventy the Grand Old Man, was certainly not prepared to serve under either of them.

Victoria, who prided herself on her prerogative of choosing her Prime Minister, found she was powerless. She had no option but to send for Gladstone. She obstructed some of the appointments he wished to make and strenuously objected to both Joseph Chamberlain and Sir Charles Dilke, because of their radicalism. It was to no avail. The growing size and importance of the electorate, especially after the passing of the Third Reform Act in 1884, combined with increased party consciousness, meant that she would have even less room for manoeuvre in future.

She had already conceded to Hartington and Granville that she would be prepared to give the new government her support, 'but that this must entirely depend on their conduct. There must be no democratic leaning, no attempt to change the Foreign policy . . . no change in India, no hasty retreat from Afghanistan, and no cutting down of estimates. In short *no lowering* of the *high position* this country holds, and *ought always* to hold.'

It was a tall order, and Gladstone was bound to disappoint. In January 1881 there was a major rumpus when the government sent Victoria the Queen's Speech to be read out from the throne at the State Opening of Parliament, leaving it too late to amend. The speech was written for the monarch and outlined the government's policy; she merely had to read it. Victoria felt that as it purported to be *her* speech, she should have some say over its content. The Afghan War of 1878–80 had resulted in the temporary occupation of Kandahar by British troops. The intention of the Liberal government was to quit the volatile country as quickly as possible, but Victoria strongly objected to the inclusion of a passage in the speech announcing 'the abandonment of Kandahar, without my having heard a word about it':

The war in Afghanistan has been brought to a close, and, with the exception of the Kandahar force, my troops have been recalled within the Indian frontier. It is not my intention that the occupation of Kandahar shall be permanently maintained; but the still unsettled condition of the country, and the consequent difficulty of establishing a native government, have delayed for a time the withdrawal of the army from that position.

When Lord Spencer, Lord President of the Council, was told that the Queen objected to the passage concerning Kandahar, his response was that it could not be changed. The Queen then refused to approve the speech. She complained to Ponsonby that 'she was treated as a child by being kept in ignorance and then forced at the last moment to assent.'

The Home Secretary, Sir William Harcourt, said 'it should be explained that this was really the Cabinet's speech. It was their policy, and any change was an interference with their policy.' He was saying, in effect, that she was obliged to make it, whether she approved it or not. Sir William's opinion, Victoria told Ponsonby, had 'no weight whatsoever with *her*, for he has never been in office before and she thinks her experience of forty-three years more likely to enable her to know what is her position and standing than he does'.

It was too late by this time to call a Cabinet to discuss the matter, as the Leader of the Opposition had to have the speech by seven in the evening. Victoria complained to Ponsonby: 'The Queen has never before been treated with such want of respect and consideration in the forty-three and a half years she has worn her thorny crown . . . she is kept (purposefully) in the dark and then expected simply to agree . . . Sir Henry must tell Mr Gladstone . . . that she will not *stand* such treatment.'

Solicited by the Queen for his view, Disraeli told her what she wanted to hear:

Madam, and Most Beloved Sovereign, The principle of Sir W. Harcourt, that the Speech of the Sovereign is only the Speech of the Ministers, is a principle not known to the British Constitution. It is only a piece of Parliamentary gossip. The Speech from the Throne must be approved in Council by the Sovereign, but to be so approved, it should be previously considered by the Sovereign. Ample time ought to be secured to the Sovereign for this purpose, so that suggestions may be made and explanations required and given . . . The unfortunate state of parties at this moment limits the power of the Throne, but that is no reason why the constitutional prerogative of the Crown should be treated as non-existing. Even under the present circumstances, Your Majesty has a right which it would be wise always to exercise, to express your Majesty's opinion on every point of the policy of your Ministers and to require and receive explanations.

Put in its starkest terms, Disraeli's summary was a denial of the principle of ministerial responsibility, but the point about the English constitution was that it was opaque – it could not be seen in terms of black and white. It depended on compromise and mutual trust. Was it not the sovereign's right 'to be consulted, to encourage, and to warn'? Courtesy, surely, and deference to Victoria's long experience, demanded that she be consulted. The letter was the last service Disraeli paid to his sovereign. Before he died, in April 1881, someone asked if he would like to see the Queen to say goodbye. 'Better not,' came the witty response. 'She will only ask me to take a message to Albert.'

The problem was that while Victoria had been almost totally in accord with Disraeli's Conservative policies, she had no sympathy whatsoever with Liberal governments. When the Liberals were in power, she never regarded herself as bound to behave impartially or even constitutionally. She felt shut out. While Disraeli had informed her of everything that went on in the Cabinet and of the views of each individual, Gladstone informed her only of what had been decided. She hated not to be kept fully informed. It made her overreact and increase her vigilance. As Sir Charles Dilke complained:

The Queen does interfere constantly; more, however, when Liberal Ministers are in power than when she has a Conservative Cabinet, because on the whole the Conservatives do what she likes, as she is a Conservative; whereas the Liberals are continually doing, and indeed exist for the purpose of doing, the things she does not like. But it is very doubtful how far her interference is unconstitutional, and it would be quite impossible to prove it, unless Mr Gladstone, for example, were to publish her letters – a not very likely supposition. The Queen is a woman of great ability . . . She writes to her Prime Minister about everything she does not like, which, when he is a Liberal, means almost everything that he says or does. She complains of his colleagues' speeches. She complains, with less violence, of his own. She protests against Bills. She insists that administrative acts should not be done without delay, for the purpose of consulting . . . persons whose opinions she knows will be unfavourable. This is not unconstitutional, however.

Victoria did not trouble herself with constitutional rectitude in trying to defeat Gladstone's policy of Home Rule for Ireland. Surreptitiously and without the advice of her Prime Minister, she tried to promote a 'loyal' and 'constitutional' 'national government, in order to defeat the Liberal Party'. None of this was reconcilable with the functions of constitutional monarchy, but Victoria excused herself by claiming Home Rule was not a party question. Never sympathetic to the Irish problem, she refused to contemplate the diminution of her sovereignty that Home Rule would entail.

As late as 1893, Victoria was still insisting on her right to amend the Queen's Speech and a strict adherence to the truth, writing to Gladstone: 'I cannot say that his measure [his Second Home Rule Bill] will be for the *better* government of Ireland. Can you leave out "better"?'

Victoria's condemnation of Gladstone was most emphatic on the occasion of the death of General Gordon. Gordon had advanced to Khartoum in the Sudan and found himself besieged by the mystic prophet, the Mahdi, and a host of thousands. Egypt must *not* be allowed to fall to the Mahdi, she warned Gladstone. 'It would be a disgrace to the British name, and the country will not stand it. The Queen trembles for General Gordon's safety. If anything befalls him, the result will be awful.'

Gladstone was slow to act. 'Gordon is in danger: you are bound to try and save him,' Victoria pressed. 'Surely Indian troops might go from Aden: they could bear the climate. You have incurred fearful responsibility.'

The following month, March 1884, she wrote again, protesting that the relief forces Gordon requested five weeks ago had still not been forthcoming. 'If only for humanity's sake, for the honour of the Government and the nation, he must not be abandoned!'

She wrote to Vicky deploring her powerlessness. To be a constitutional sovereign and 'unable to prevent grievous mistakes is a very hard and ungrateful task. This Government is the worst I have ever had to do with. They never listen to anything I say and commit grievous errors.' She was justifiably angry, therefore, when in February 1885, after months of cajoling Gladstone to do something, the worst happened: 'Khartoum fallen, Gordon's fate uncertain! All greatly distressed. Sent for Sir H. Ponsonby, who was horrified. It is too fearful. The Government is alone to blame, by refusing to send the expedition till it was too late. Telegraphed *en clair* to Mr Gladstone, Lord Granville, and Lord Hartington, expressing how dreadfully shocked I was at the news, all the more so when one felt it might have been prevented.'

To telegraph the Prime Minister *en clair* was tantamount to a public announcement of the sovereign's lack of confidence in him. Gladstone had to consider whether to resign or not. He was deeply wounded when after a lifetime of public service Victoria accepted his resignation in 1894, ostensibly on the grounds of failing health, after the defeat of Home Rule, without a word of appreciation, sympathy or gratitude. After his final interview, in which as ever she was scrupulously courteous but cold, he received a curt note from her, ending: 'The Queen would gladly have conferred a peerage on Mr Gladstone, but she knows he would not accept it.' He confided in his diary that he had asked her that the details of his painful relationship with her be kept secret and, of course, he chivalrously shielded her from the consequences of her prejudices against him and his party.

Four years later when Gladstone died, she felt no more kindly disposed towards him: 'I am sorry for Mrs Gladstone,' she said, when pressed to make some comment, 'as for him, I never liked him, and I will say nothing about him!' Gladstone had always respected Victoria's adherence to the truth.

32

Matriarch

ON THE EVENING of 20 June 1887 Queen Victoria sat in the garden of Buckingham Palace, writing in her journal: 'Fifty years to-day since I came to the Throne! God has mercifully sustained me through many great trials and sorrows.' She regretted that she was 'alone, though surrounded by many dear children', but far from feeling that she wanted to die, as she had for years after the death of her beloved husband, a reinvigorated Victoria was praying that she might be spared a while longer, to serve her country and her empire.

The magic of monarchy seemed to be increasing as its political power declined. As Victoria entered her last decade and Britain enjoyed a period of stability, prosperity and self-congratulation, she basked in the glow of revivified royalism. The Queen-Empress was the unifying symbol of the empire and the nation, the focus of patriotic fervour. While in other parts of Europe countries such as Hungary were asserting their nationality and independence against the imperial control of an alien ruler, in Britain nationalism asserted itself through attachment to a hereditary monarchy, in particular to the reassuringly familiar figure of Victoria.

Whenever she appeared in public, she received an overwhelming ovation. In 1886 she attended the opening of the Colonial and Indian Exhibition at the Imperial Institute in South Kensington. 'The crowds were enormous and most good humoured and enthusiastic,' she wrote. The following May she opened the People's Palace in the East End of London. 'From the moment we emerged from the station the crowds were immense and very enthusiastic with a great deal of cheering; in the City especially, it was quite deafening.' On this occasion, she also had to admit to hearing 'a horrid noise *quite* new to the Queen's ears': 'the booing and hooting, of perhaps only two or three, now and again, all along the route, evidently sent there on purpose, and frequently the same people, probably Socialists and the worst Irish'.

For the Imperial Institute event, the Foreign Secretary, Lord Rosebery, urged that she should come wearing the crown and the robes of state, in order to impress the colonial representatives who would be present. 'The symbol that unites this vast Empire is a Crown not a bonnet,' he told Ponsonby. As usual, Victoria had her way. On this occasion and at both her jubilees, despite the pleas of the Princess of Wales to don all her regal splendour, the bonnet triumphed. 'Then dressed, wearing a dress and bonnet trimmed with white point d'Alençon, diamond ornaments in my bonnet, and pearls round my neck, with all my orders,' she recorded in her journal on the day of her Golden Jubilee parade. Long used to the sight of the little black-clad figure of their queen, the public found Victoria's appearance endearing. Rotund as she was, she had so much natural grace and dignity that what she wore simply did not matter.

Since she had so recently been unpopular, Victoria was surprised at the level of public enthusiasm for her Golden Jubilee. What began as a restricted entry service at the abbey and a family reunion of 'all the Royalties' at the palace – at the Queen's own expense – resulted in an orgy of national rejoicing that raised the monarchy to new heights of popularity.

'It is impossible for me to say how deeply, immensely touched and gratified I have been and am by the wonderful and so universal enthusiasm displayed by my people, and by high and low, rich and poor, on this remarkable occasion, as well as by the respect shown by Foreign Rulers and their peoples,' Victoria wrote to Rosebery a month later. 'It is very gratifying and very encouraging for the future, and it shows that fifty years' hard work, anxiety, and care have been appreciated.'

In her personal life, Victoria was probably happier than at any time since Albert's death. Marie Mallet, appointed a maid of honour in 1887, loved the Queen dearly, describing her as a lively, warm, humane person, with a good sense of humour. In her photographs, Victoria felt it was her regal duty to look stern, but in reality she had a ready smile and laughed with real gusto. Her health was better too. Dr James Reid, a Scot and a German scholar, became physician-in-ordinary in 1883, when her 'nerves' were no longer a problem. Of all her doctors, he was the least encouraging of any neuroses. He would see her every morning at nine-thirty, but until she lay dying he never saw her in bed.

Victoria rewarded her doctors well, but believed that at table they should sit 'below the salt'. Reid took to giving alternative dinner parties, to which members of the household gravitated, lured by his witty conversation, a welcome contrast to the rather dull monotony of the royal table. Once she heard about Reid's dinner parties, Victoria readily invited the rival attraction to join her at table. Not only did she value his advice on medical matters, but she relied on him for his excellent judgement on matters outside his profession.

Even Reid, however, was unable to prevail on Victoria to curb her hearty Hanoverian appetite and watch her weight. In despair, Marie Mallet was to note in 1900:

> The Queen is certainly less vigorous and her digestion is becoming defective after so many years of hard labour! If she would follow a diet and live on Benger's Food and chicken all would be well but she clings to roast beef and ices! . . . Sir James has at last persuaded her to try Benger's and she likes it and now to his horror, instead of substituting it for other foods, she adds it to her already copious meals.

The widowed Queen had kept her youngest child, Princess Beatrice, with her after her marriage to Prince Henry of Battenberg and lived happily with Beatrice, 'Liko' and their children. Her numerous grandchildren were getting married and having children of their own. While half deploring the fact that her family were breeding like the rabbits in Windsor Park, she thought her grandchildren dear little things and liked to have one or two of them always around her.

After the death from diphtheria of her daughter Princess Alice, Grand Duchess of Hesse, in December 1878, the Queen had assumed special responsibility for Alice's motherless children. The eldest, Victoria, had married Prince Louis of Battenberg and the Queen presided at her first confinement, when she gave birth to a daughter in the same bed in which her mother had been born. The child was called Alice after her grandmother and would in turn become the mother of Prince Philip of Greece, who would marry another of Victoria's great-great-grandchildren, Queen Elizabeth II. Victoria was less than happy about the impending marriage of the youngest of her Hesse granddaughters, Alix, to the future Tsar Nicholas II of Russia.

'My blood runs cold when I think of her so young most likely placed on that very unsafe throne, her dear life and above all her husband's constantly threatened and unable to see her but rarely. It is a great additional anxiety in my declining years!' she wrote to Victoria, Princess Louis of Battenberg.

She was right to be concerned. Two of Victoria's daughters, Alice and Beatrice, had inherited the haemophilia gene from her and Alice passed it on to Alix, whose son the Tsarevich Alexis was to suffer very severely from haemophilia. The Tsarina's dependence on Gregory Rasputin, the disreputable 'mad monk' who seemed to be able to soothe the Tsarevich during his worst bleeding episodes, was a major contributory factor in the fall of the Romanov dynasty. Victoria was right in her forebodings. Tsar Nicholas, her granddaughter Alix, and all five of their children were murdered by their Soviet guards in the cellar of their Ekaterinburg prison in 1918.

In March 1884 the Queen's haemophiliac son, Leopold, Duke of Albany, died as a result of a fall while he was staying in the South of France for his health. The cleverest of Victoria's sons, he had ably fulfilled a secretarial role for the Queen, being given access to papers never allowed his eldest brother, the Prince of Wales. Against all the odds, Leopold had married and fathered two children. The haemophilia gene, which could have been the result of a spontaneous mutation in Victoria, cannot be passed on by the male. Although Victoria understood her son's disease, little care was taken when arranging the marriages of the daughters of Alice and Beatrice, who were carriers of the disease and passed it on to the next generation.

The celebrations for Victoria's Golden Jubilee in 1887 were overshadowed for her by worry over the declining health of her dear son-in-law Fritz. The following year, he died of throat cancer. He had reigned as Emperor of Germany for only ninety days. For some time Victoria had been concerned at the ascendancy of the militarists in Prussia and their antagonism towards England. Fritz's death was the final blow to the Prince Consort's vision of a peaceful, united, liberal Germany, allied in friendship to England. Victoria was saddened for her daughter Vicky, who was treated none too kindly by her son, the new Kaiser Wilhelm II.

Although the rest of the family considered Willy a pain in the neck, Victoria still tended to view her first grandson as the 'dear little boy' who had been such a favourite of his grandfather Albert. She did not hesitate to slap down his pretensions, however. No sooner did he become Emperor than he was complaining that he was not being shown sufficient respect – treated as 'his Imperial Majesty' in private as well as in public – by his uncle the Prince of Wales. 'He has been treated just as we should have treated his beloved father and even grandfather,' Victoria protested. 'If he has such notions, he [had] better never come here. The Queen will not swallow this affront.'

The two jubilees and the catalogue of royal weddings, births and christenings kept the royal pageant well to the fore and served to fan the flames of royalist fervour. In 1893 her grandson Georgie, the Duke of York, married Princess May of Teck, daughter of Victoria's cousin Mary of Cambridge and a great-granddaughter of George III, so uniting a scion of the 'old royal family' with the new Coburg dynasty.

'To describe this day fully would be impossible,' Victoria wrote. 'It was really (on a smaller scale) like the Jubilee; and the crowds, the loyalty and enthusiasm were immense. Telegrams began pouring in from an early hour. Was rolled to our usual dining-room, to see from the window all that was going on. Troops, Infantry, Cavalry, Volunteers, crowds, bands, all presented a most brilliant animated appearance. Already, whilst I was still in bed, I heard the distant hum of the people.'

True to her tradition, Victoria wore her 'wedding lace over a light black stuff, and my wedding veil surmounted by a small coronet'. She travelled with the bride's mother 'in the new State glass coach' amid cheering crowds and later stepped out on to the balcony at Buckingham Palace holding the hands of the bride and groom to resounding cheers.

In June 1894 the Duchess of York gave birth to a son, christened Edward but known in the family as David, the future Edward VIII and Duke of Windsor, closely followed in December 1895 by another

Albert, born on the thirty-fourth anniversary of the Prince Consort's death. 'Georgie's first feeling was regret that this dear child should be born on such a sad day,' Victoria confided in her journal. 'I have a feeling it may be a blessing for the dear little boy, and may be looked upon as a gift from God!' Albert, or Bertie, was the future King George VI.

Before long Victoria posed for a formal photograph which combined the intimacy of family photography with the iconography of state portraiture. It was a group photograph of the Queen, the Prince of Wales, the Duke of York and the little Prince Edward of York – three future kings. The photograph stresses primogeniture, the continuity of the royal succession in the male line – after the aberration of a woman's rule – and promotes the monarchy as a source of stability in a time of rapid, disorienting change.

The Queen was also entering a happier period politically. She confessed to Marie Mallet that she had always disliked politics, that the Prince Consort had forced her to take an interest in them and that since he died she had tried to keep up the interest for his sake. Certainly she did not hesitate to enter the fray, even beyond the requirements of a constitutional sovereign; the level of her activity would indicate, if not genuine enthusiasm, at least a very strong sense of duty and a determination to uphold and exploit her prerogatives.

Victoria's longevity gave her an immense advantage in later years. It suited the politicians that she should be surrounded by an aura of moral certainty. While those projecting a popular royal image deliberately accentuated the non-political nature of the Queen, Victoria herself was never slow to assert her superior experience over that of her ministers. Until her letters were published after her death, most people did not realize her extensive knowledge of and participation in state affairs, especially in the realm of foreign policy. Just as she insisted that as sovereign she was head of the army and must sign all commissions personally and that as Supreme Governor she should have the last word on ecclesiastic appointments, so she exercised much influence in foreign affairs by vetting the personnel of British representatives abroad. Whatever the constitutional proprieties of her interference, with her broad knowledge of world politics, her superb memory and attention to detail, matched with common sense and a decisive temperament, no minister could afford to ignore the Queen's opinion.

When Lord Rosebery became Foreign Secretary in 1886, she had been at pains to remind him: 'The Queen is delighted to be able to assist Lord Rosebery in his very difficult task. She has nearly fifty years' experience, and has always watched particularly and personally over foreign affairs, and therefore knows them well . . . All the Powers are very suspicious of a Government at the head of which Mr Gladstone's name appears,' she added witheringly. 'But Lord Rosebery has done much to dispel this already.'

Nor did she reserve her ire for Gladstone alone. Guarding the vested interests of rank and privilege, she was strongly opposed to Lord Rosebery's plan to reform the House of Lords, after he succeeded Gladstone as Prime Minister: 'The House of Lords might possibly be improved, but it is part and parcel of the much vaunted and admired British Constitution and cannot be abolished. It is the only really independent House, for it is not bound as the House of Commons is, where they are constantly made to say what they would not otherwise do by their constituents, whom they try to please in order to be elected.'

Perhaps because of her genuine devotion to duty, her will to do what was right and her apparent simplicity, Victoria gained the reputation of being a model sovereign, while sometimes straining the constitution almost to breaking point. Fortuitously, her convictions and prejudices so exactly mirrored those of her era, in particular the sentiments of the middle classes, that she was exonerated. 'I have always felt that when I knew what the Queen thought, I knew pretty certainly what views her subjects would take, and especially the middle classes of her subjects,' Lord Salisbury declared. The middle-class image of the Queen which was assiduously cultivated bore little relation to the reality of her life. When she travelled abroad, staying on the Riviera, she did so with an immense retinue of servants and ate off solid gold plates; at home the increased opulence of the age meant that her household budget had to stretch to champagne rather than wine and hothouse flowers and fruit. As ever, her ugly fingers were so weighted with jewels that on occasion she could barely lift a knife and fork.

Victoria's fascination with her Indian empire and her predilection for the exotic led her in 1887 to engage some Indian servants. Two of them, Abdul Karim and Mahomet, were soon singled out for special favour. The Queen 'cannot say what a comfort she finds *hers*', she enthused about the novelty of having Indian servants who, incidentally, kissed her feet. 'Abdul is most handy in helping when she *signs* by drying the signatures. He learns with extraordinary assiduity & Mahomet is wonderfully quick and intelligent and understands everything.'

The following year Abdul Karim was relieved of his domestic duties. He declared that he did not belong to the servant class and held aloof from his fellow servants, sulking or throwing a tantrum if anyone questioned his pretensions. Victoria wrote innocently in her journal:

> Am making arrangements to appoint Abdul a *munshi*, as I think it was a mistake to bring him over as a servant to wait at table, a thing he had never done, having been a clerk or *munshi* in his own country and being of rather a different class to the others. I had made this change, as he was anxious to return to India, not feeling happy under the existing circumstances. On the other hand, I particularly wish to retain his services, as he helps me in studying Hindustani, which interests me very much, and he is very intelligent and useful.

At last Abdul Karim became the Munshi Hafiz Abdul Karim, the Queen's Indian secretary, and, in deference to his sensitivity on the subject, all photographs of him handing dishes to the Queen were destroyed. He was given a bungalow at Osborne, where he housed his harem of wives or mistresses – no one was ever sure which. The British doctor who attended the munshi's 'wife' claimed that a different tongue was put out every time. When the Queen's son Arthur, Duke of Connaught, took exception to the munshi standing conspicuously among the gentry at the Braemar Games in 1890, he took his complaint to Sir Henry Ponsonby, not daring to approach the Queen herself. Fortunately, Ponsonby's sense of the absurd fitted him well for his role. 'I replied that Abdul stood where he was by the Queen's order,' he recalled, 'and that if it was wrong, as I did not understand Indian Etiquette and HRH did, would it not be better for him to mention it to the Queen. This entirely shut him up.'

Enquiries in Agra revealed that Abdul Karim's pretensions were quite unfounded. His father was not a surgeon-general, as he claimed, but an apothecary in a prison hospital. Not only was the munshi a phoney, but the Prince of Wales and members of the royal family and then government ministers began to suspect that he was leaking confidential information to undesirable contacts in India. He became a target for press attacks. In 1894 Victoria, perceiving in the criticism of the munshi the racial and social prejudices she so deplored, fired off a memorandum to Ponsonby:

> The Queen wrote rather in a hurry when she mentioned to him the stupid ill-natured article or rather letter about the poor good Munshi & she wd wish to observe that to make out that he is so *low* is really *outrageous* & in a country like England quite out of place as anyone can [see] this. She has known 2 Archbishops who were the sons respectively of a Butcher & a Grocer, a Chancellor whose father was a poor sort of Scotch Minister, Sir D. Stewart & Ld Mount Stephen both who ran about barefoot as children and whose parents were very humble and the tradesmen M. and J.P. were made baronets! . . . The Queen is so sorry for the poor Munshi's sensitive feelings.

Only after the Secretary of State for India threatened to stop sending the Queen confidential papers relating to India did she agree to prevent the munshi having access to them.

By September 1896 Victoria had reigned longer than any other English sovereign. On the fifty-ninth anniversary of her accession that year, she had written: 'God has guided me in the midst of terrible trials, sorrows, and anxieties, and has wonderfully protected me. I have lived to see my dear country and vast Empire prosper and expand, and be wonderfully loyal!'

For the first time she was photographed by Downey 'by the new cinematograph process'. Her enthusiasm for photography remained undimmed. 'It is a very wonderful process,' she wrote of the new technique, 'representing people, their movements and actions, as if they were alive.' In May 1897 she was seventy-eight. Incipient cataracts meant that she could barely see and she walked with a stick, or was wheeled in her chair, but her energy remained impressive. 'Seventy-eight is a good age,' she wrote, 'but I pray yet to be spared a little longer for the sake of my country and my dear ones.' The following month, June 1897, she reached the apogee of her reign, the sixtieth anniversary of her coming to the throne.

'A never-to-be-forgotten day,' she wrote. 'No one ever, I believe, has met with such an ovation as was given to me, passing through those six miles of streets . . . The crowds were quite indescribable, and their enthusiasm truly marvellous and deeply touching. The cheering was quite deafening, and every face seemed to be filled with real joy.' Prevented from travelling with her eldest daughter Vicky, since as an Empress etiquette prevented Vicky from sitting with her back to the horses, the Queen-Empress travelled in an open state landau, drawn by eight cream horses, a solitary figure, with the Princess of Wales dressed in lilac and her daughter Lenchen sitting opposite her. 'I felt a good deal agitated,' Victoria confessed touchingly, 'and had been so all these days, for fear anything might be forgotten or go wrong.'

This was the high noon of empire and imperial splendour: Victoria ruled over one-quarter of the population of the entire world. Her gender was an asset. Her image as a mother and grandmother, exhibiting the feminine qualities of maternal devotion and disinterested family loyalty, meant that she could be raised to mythic status, as the mother of them all, bringing together many different nations and races under her benevolent protection. Between 1877 when Disraeli made her Empress of India and the Diamond Jubilee in 1897, when Joseph Chamberlain brought the colonial premiers and troops to parade in the Diamond Jubilee procession, every great royal occasion was also an imperial occasion. 'Before leaving I touched an electric button, by which I started a message which was telegraphed throughout the whole Empire,' Victoria wrote. 'It was the following: "From my heart I thank my beloved people, May God Bless them!"'

With Elgar's 'Imperial March' the hit music of the year, the Diamond Jubilee was one of the first major ceremonial occasions to be filmed – a key event in the development of the British film industry. An official photographic portrait of the Jubilee Queen was deliberately not registered for copyright. Consequently, it appeared on thousands of commemorative plates, biscuit tins and souvenirs of all kinds, and was distributed throughout the empire.

In the 1860s Bagehot had predicted: 'The more democratic we get, the more we shall get to like state and show, which have ever pleased the vulgar.' The jubilees in 1887 and 1897 benefited from concurrent developments in the media. Newspapers became increasingly nationalized; the *Daily Mail*, launched by Harmsworth in 1896 and with a circulation of 700,000 in four years, was typical of the new London-based and Conservative press. Criticism of the British monarchy might be found in foreign newspapers, but at home the royal family had become virtually sacrosanct. New techniques in photography and printing meant that illustrations were no longer confined to the expensive, middle-class weeklies. The great royal ceremonies were described and illustrated with unprecedented vividness in a sentimental, emotional, admiring way, which reached a broader section of the public than ever before.

By the end of the Queen's reign, there was almost no one left who could remember her at the beginning. Victoria's longevity gave a unifying impression to the era and imbued the monarchy and the history of Britain with a monolithic identity and spurious unity which belied and denied the many changes that had actually taken place in both. If Victoria had died a quarter of a century sooner, her reign would not have been regarded a success and the British monarchy might not have survived. As it was, it became possible to depict the jubilees, those supreme moments of apotheosis, as the natural and appropriate reward for long service and consistently good conduct. It was easy to believe that the Queen had intended to be good from the outset, that there had been no ripples on the smooth surface of relations between Victoria and her ministers, Parliament and people, that there had been no dips in the popularity of the monarchy bringing it almost to the brink of collapse: in other words, that Victoria had succeeded in being good, just as she had promised. She left the monarchy vastly stronger and more important than she had found it.

The outbreak of the Boer War in 1899 marred the sunset of the reign. The eighty-year-old Queen was belligerent as ever: 'We are not interested in the possibilities of defeat,' she announced, 'they do not exist.' She inspected the Gordon Highlanders before their embarkation for South Africa. Just as during the Crimean War she had knitted balaclavas for the men, now she took to crocheting shawls for them. At Christmas she sent out a box of chocolate to every man at the front with a coloured print of herself on it. The chocolate melted long before it reached the men, but many treasured the tin. She fired off a note to Lord Salisbury: 'I sincerely hope that the increased taxation, necessary to meet the expenses of the war, will not fall upon the working classes; but I fear they will be most affected by the extra six-pence on beer.'

By the end of 1900 the Queen's health was failing. She had lost her appetite and was unable to sleep. The will was as indomitable as ever, but her physical strength was ebbing inexorably. She missed going to church, 'which annoyed me very much'. The last entry in her journal, first given her by Mama when she was a girl to record one of the summer progresses that so irritated William IV, was on 12 January 1901.

'The news from Osborne is as sad as it can be,' Lord Esher wrote on 20 January, 'but what a comfort that the end of this long and splendid reign should come so rapidly. No lingering illness. The Queen drove out on Tuesday. To-day she is at the point of death.'

Family and ministers began to congregate at Osborne. Arthur Balfour, who was to succeed Lord Salisbury as Prime Minister in 1902, was astounded at the accumulation of official boxes in only a few days, since it showed the mass of routine work the Queen had to do. The Duke of Argyll told Sir Frederick Ponsonby, one of the Queen's equerries, that observing Victoria's last moments was like watching a great three-decker ship sinking. She would sink, then rally, then relapse. Briefly regaining consciousness and recognizing her eldest son, Victoria held out her arms, crying, 'Bertie.' She died at half past six on the evening of 22 January 1901, with her grandson the Kaiser supporting her on one side, and Dr Reid on the other, sur-rounded by her children and grandchildren.

The raucous and disrespectful behaviour of the British and foreign press who congregated outside the gates of Osborne disgusted wit-nesses. As soon as they were given word of her demise, they stampeded in a frenzied mass towards the post office in East Cowes, shouting, 'Queen dead!' The telegraph network made her death one of the first truly global media events.

The new King, Edward VII, and Prince Arthur lifted their mother into her coffin. As soon as the family had retired, Dr Reid set to work following the instructions she had left with one of her dressers. Victoria wore her widow's cap on her head and her wedding veil over her face. The coffin contained Albert's dressing gown, locks of her children's hair and other mementoes, and, in her folded hands, the doctor placed a photograph of John Brown and his mother's wedding ring, as she had requested. He carefully concealed them behind the Princess of Wales's flowers; Alexandra was so upset by the Queen's passing that she refused to assume the title of Queen or allow anyone to kiss her hand until after the funeral. Bertie, who stripped, burned and destroyed every vestige of John Brown's existence as soon as he possibly could, would never have allowed it, had he known. Victoria must have loved Brown very much.

Mourning at Queen Victoria's death was widespread and universal. If the values of her age already seemed to the young to be outdated, narrow, philistine, moralistic and prudish, the more prescient must already have regretted the passing of an era, a twinge of nostalgia for its implications of moral certainty, and a faint foreboding about the future. Britain's ascendancy was already under threat.

As befitted a soldier's daughter and a sovereign in time of war, she was given a military funeral, the tiny coffin being carried on a gun carriage through the streets of London and, when the traces of the horses snapped, being pulled by sailors at Windsor. Half the crowned heads of Europe followed the coffin of the woman known to them simply as 'Grandmama'. It was appropriate that a film of the funeral procession of the great Queen-Empress, Victoria *Regina et Imperatrix*, the Shah-in-Shah Padshah, the Doyenne of Sovereigns, should be shown around the world in cities as far apart as New York, Melbourne, Cape Town and Delhi. She was laid to rest in the mausoleum she had built at Frogmore, entombed under a marble statue modelled at the time of Albert's demise forty years previously, the adoring wife lying beside her beloved husband, united at last in death.

ELIZABETH II

b. 1926, r. 1952–

33

Lilibet

PRINCESS ELIZABETH ALEXANDRA Mary of York was born on 21 April 1926 at 17 Bruton Street, Mayfair, in central London, the home of her maternal grandparents, the Earl and Countess of Strathmore and Kinghorne. It was a Caesarean delivery. Later that day Queen Mary came to visit her first granddaughter and reported that she was 'a little darling with lovely complexion & very pretty fair hair'. A month later the christening took place at Buckingham Palace. She was named after her mother and two queens, her grandmother Mary and her great-grandmother Alexandra, who had recently died. She wore the christening robe used by the children of her great-great-grandmother, Queen Victoria, and howled loudly. It was the only occasion in a long life when her behaviour was less than perfect.

Princess Elizabeth was to be profoundly influenced by her parents. Her father, Albert or 'Bertie' as he was known in the family, was the second son of George V and Queen Mary. Only eighteen months younger than his brother, Edward, Prince of Wales – the golden boy idolized by the public – Bertie lived uncomfortably in his shadow nearly all his life. As a child he had developed a nervous stammer, made worse by his father's impatient barking of 'Spit it out, boy!' and had had to wear iron splints on his legs because of his knock-knees. He had found brief refuge in the Royal Navy, being present at the Battle of Jutland in 1916, but had been invalided out owing to a stomach ulcer. After the war, a role was found for him as President of the Industrial Welfare Association, dedicated to improving industrial relations through social welfare and improved amenities for the workers. Conscientious, tenacious and hard-working, Bertie went to work with a will; a little later, his achievement on the domestic front was augmented by his active involvement in the Duke of York's camps, an idealistic enterprise whereby public school boys were brought together with boys from poor and disadvantaged backgrounds in an attempt to improve understanding between the classes. Personal happiness remained elusive, until he met and fell in love with Lady Elizabeth Bowes-Lyon at a London ball in June 1920 and determined to marry her.

Lady Elizabeth's childhood, as the ninth and second last child of her parents, had been immensely happy. The Strathmores were wealthy aristocrats. Her father Claude, 14th Earl of Strathmore, could trace his descent from Robert the Bruce, King of Scotland; her mother, Cecilia Cavendish-Bentinck, was a descendant of Henry VII through the unfortunate Lady Catherine Grey, but also of the redoubtable Bess of Hardwick, matriarch of the Cavendish dynasty, and connected to many of the great Whig families. Her father was a countryman through and through and a keen sportsman; her mother a gracious hostess and homemaker. The family spent its time at Glamis Castle in Scotland, St Paul's Walden Bury in Hertfordshire, and, before the First World War, a large town house in St James's Square, London, which they used during the season.

With her cornflower-blue eyes, petite figure and engaging charm, Elizabeth Bowes-Lyon was one of the most popular debutantes of her year. Unlike the shy, stammering Bertie, she had a ready wit and a talent for mimicry, but she was also kind and sympathetic, with the ability to make the person she was talking to feel he was the most important in the room. 'You'll be a lucky fellow if she accepts you,' George V told his son and, indeed, when Bertie proposed Elizabeth turned him down. There was a suggestion that she was in love with the dashing Lord James Stuart, but she herself admitted to Lady Airlie that she was reluctant to embrace the restrictions on her freedom that the royal role would entail. Both mothers were sorry. 'I like him so much,' Cecilia told Mabell Airlie, Queen Mary's lady-in-waiting and confidante, 'and he is a man who will be made or marred by his wife.' Whether it was because James had been conveniently removed from the scene to Canada or because Elizabeth, who was genuinely fond of Bertie, felt the pull of duty, she accepted Bertie's second proposal. They were married in April 1923 and three years later their first child was born.

Even though it seemed likely that the Prince of Wales would marry and have children of his own, or that her parents would yet have a son who would take precedence over her in the line of succession, there was a huge amount of public interest in Princess Elizabeth from the outset. When she was only two her mother wrote to Queen Mary: 'It almost frightens me that the people should love her so much. I suppose that it is a good thing, and I hope that she will be worthy of it, poor little darling.' At about this time Elizabeth's future Prime Minister, Winston Churchill, observed in her 'an air of authority and reflectiveness astonishing in an infant'.

The Yorks' duties had already separated them from their baby daughter for six months while they made a tour of Australia and New Zealand, rather as Elizabeth would be separated from her own children soon after she became Queen, but, as a naturally serene character, she seems to have been unfazed by it. She was secure in the care of her nanny, Clara Knight, affectionately known as Allah, who had looked after her mother before her, and had two sets of doting grandparents. George V, who had been such a forbidding parent to his own children, absolutely adored her and soon the two would forge a very close bond. When he became seriously ill in 1929 and went to convalesce at Bognor, he took Elizabeth, not quite three, as his companion to cheer him up.

Elizabeth spent the first ten years of her life at 145 Piccadilly, overlooking Green Park and just across the road from the Duke of Wellington's residence, No. 1 London. The house was obliterated by bombing during the Second World War. Elizabeth's nursery was on the top floor, which she shared with her nanny and the nursemaid, a Scottish girl whose father was a railway worker, Margaret Macdonald. 'Bobo', as she was called, would remain Elizabeth's close personal attendant – and the scourge of the couturiers who tried to address the Queen's staid image – for more than sixty years. When she was four, Elizabeth was joined in the nursery by a sister, Margaret Rose, born at Glamis in August 1930. It seemed increasingly unlikely that there would be a son.

The Duchess of York's education had been undertaken by her mother, who saw no need for a girl of her station to acquire any academic qualifications. What had worked for her, the Duchess reasoned, should work for Elizabeth. She was genuinely bemused when Queen Mary suggested that her granddaughters should be given a rather more challenging education. After all, the Duchess told a friend, all the girls in her family had married well, one of them – herself – very well.

A young Scottish governess, Miss Marion Crawford, who had graduated from the Moray House Training College in Edinburgh with the intention of becoming a child psychologist, was engaged by the Duchess as governess to five-year-old Elizabeth. In her saccharine account entitled *The Little Princesses*, for which she was ostracized by the royal family when it was published in 1950, Crawfie, as Elizabeth was to call her, described their first meeting.

Arriving at 145 Piccadilly and being admitted to the nursery, she found a small figure with a mop of golden curls sitting up in bed wearing a nightie with little pink roses on it. She had tied the cords of her dressing gown to the knobs of the bed and was busy driving her team of horses.

"'Do you usually drive in bed?" I asked.

"'I mostly go once or twice round the park before I go to sleep, you know," she said. "It exercises my horses." She navigated a dangerous and difficult corner, and went on, "Are you going to stay with us?"'

Elizabeth was already horse mad, a love encouraged by her grandfather the King. So besotted was he by Lilibet, as he called her after her first attempts to pronounce her name, that he was sometimes to be found down on the floor on hands and knees pretending to be a horse, while she led him by the beard. He gave her her first pony, a Shetland named Peggy, for her fourth birthday, and at Sandringham he would take her to see his favourite horses and the stud, awakening a lifelong interest in blood lines, breeding and racing. At home in London the York children had a whole stable of toy horses, all of which had to be exercised, fed and watered.

Crawfie found Elizabeth highly intelligent and an interesting child to teach, although she might have been concerned at her obsession with orderliness – to the extent that she would sometimes jump out of bed and line up her shoes, making sure they were exactly straight. She had already been taught her letters by her mother, who would read her Bible stories; as an adult, she was to display an impressive knowledge of the Bible. *Peter Pan, Alice, Winnie the Pooh*, the classics – usually gifts from Queen Mary – and anything about horses or dogs were to become favourite reading. Queen Mary was concerned that Crawfie's curriculum contained far too much arithmetic and not enough history. After all, the princesses would never have to do their own accounts – royalty did not even carry money. But they should have a sound knowledge of the British Empire, geography, and of British and European history and culture. The latter was subsequently addressed by the engagement of Mrs Montaudon-Smith, known as 'Monty', who laid the foundations of Elizabeth's excellent French.

A dash of current affairs was added with a subscription to the *Children's Newspaper* and, later, *Punch*, while Queen Mary insisted on educational outings to such places as the Tower of London, the Mint and Hampton Court. An expedition arranged by Crawfie, by which Elizabeth was granted her wish for a ride on the Underground to Tottenham Court Road, calling in at the YMCA for tea, proved less successful. Elizabeth did not realize that it was self-service. 'If you want it, you must come and fetch it yourself!' the woman at the counter bawled at her. Two smartly dressed children, accompanied by a governess and a detective, were all too conspicuous and a car had to be summoned to take them home.

Artists who have painted Queen Elizabeth II often describe her staring almost wistfully out of the window of Buckingham Palace during the sittings, keenly observing the life going on outside. So it was in her childhood, when she and her sister would stare out of the nursery windows of 145 Piccadilly at the passers-by, particularly at the poor tired dray horses which returned in the evening. It was the same after she moved into Buckingham Palace. 'They all seemed so busy,' she later recalled to Pietro Annigoni when he was painting her portrait, 'I used to wonder what they were doing and where they were all going, and what they thought about outside the Palace.' She would be forever on the inside looking out, separated by an impenetrable screen. Sometimes the children of their parents' friends and courtiers would be brought to play or share dancing lessons or the princesses, beautifully dressed in their party frocks by Allah, would be taken to children's parties. In the park, they would stare shyly at other children, eager to be friendly, but never quite crossing the gulf. For a short time Elizabeth did have a friend, the daughter of a doctor who lived near by, until the girl was sent to boarding school.

Elizabeth was essentially cocooned. Her constant companion was her younger sister, Margaret, of whom she was always very protective. Serious and unbelievably well-behaved herself, she was amused and exasperated by the naughty child's pranks. 'What are we going to do with Margaret, Crawfie?' she would say. In spite of the four-year age difference, the Duchess insisted on dressing her daughters in identical outfits, which looked increasingly inappropriate as Elizabeth entered her teens.

In the gilded cage of their childhood, the princesses saw a good deal more of their parents than other upper-class children tended to do. Theirs was a happy and devoted family. Every morning they would race down to their parents' room for a romp before they got up. At night the Yorks would go up to the nursery for bath-time and bedtime stories, returning downstairs with the children calling after them, 'Goodnight, Mummy, goodnight, Papa!' Elizabeth's father later described their close-knit family group as 'Us four'.

The Duke of York had always looked up to his brother, the Prince of Wales, who in turn was fond of his nieces. Uncle David, as the Prince of Wales was known to them, would often call in at 145 Piccadilly for tea and games of Snap and Happy Families with his nieces – that is, until he took up with Mrs Wallis Simpson in 1933.

In May 1935 the King-Emperor celebrated his Silver Jubilee, overwhelmed by the outpouring of love from his people. Elizabeth and her sister, dressed in pink with little flowered bonnets, drove with their parents in an open carriage to St Paul's Cathedral for the thanksgiving service. It was Elizabeth's first experience of royal pomp and ceremony. George V had done more than any other monarch in the twentieth century to maintain the power and dignity of the British crown and save the dynasty; unlike those of his cousins, the Kaiser in Germany, the Tsar in Russia, and others, the British crown had not toppled at the end of the First World War. George had been prepared to sacrifice the lives of the Tsar and his family by refusing them refuge in England to save his own dynasty. He had dissociated himself from his German relatives – 'I'll be buggered if I'm an alien,' he had said –

and, at the suggestion of his private secretary Lord Stamfordham, had re-named his dynasty the House of Windsor. It was reassuringly English. George's happy marriage to an exemplary consort, Queen Mary, had re-emphasized the family values of which Victoria and Albert had been such great proponents and for which the British monarchy, in its role as moral arbiter, stood as the prime example.

Elizabeth's beloved grandfather had been ailing for some time, however. The old King had come to recognize that of all his sons Bertie, in his very ordinariness, was most like himself; thanks largely to the confidence he derived from his wife, Bertie was steady and reliable, a safe pair of hands. Restless, erratic, selfish, impatient with tradition and exhibiting dangerous modernizing tendencies, the Prince of Wales had been at loggerheads with his father for years. Fully aware of his entanglement with a twice-married American, the King despaired that he would ever make a suitable marriage. 'I pray to God that nothing will come between Bertie and Lilibet and the throne,' he confided in his friend Cosmo Lang, Archbishop of Canterbury, predicting, 'After I've gone, the boy will ruin himself within six months.'

The royal family spent Christmas 1935 at Sandringham as usual. A few days later a household official recalled: 'Out of the mist came the King, mounted on his white pony, Jock. Walking at the head of the pony, as if leading it along, was the little figure of Princess Elizabeth. She was taking her grandfather back to the house.' It was a touching sight: the one a king who had been born in the nineteenth century and known his grandmother Queen Victoria well, the other Victoria's nine-year-old great-great-granddaughter, who would steer the monarchy into the twenty-first century. On 20 January, two days after Elizabeth returned to London, King George V died. When Elizabeth was taken to Westminster by her mother to see him lying in state, she was struck by the stillness of his four sons keeping vigil by the coffin – just as her own sons and Margaret's would keep vigil by the coffin of their grandmother over sixty years later.

Edward VIII fulfilled his father's prophecy: 1936 was the Year of Three Kings. Before the year was out, Elizabeth's uncle had abdicated in order to marry Mrs Simpson and was living abroad as Duke of Windsor and her father had become King George VI. At the time, Elizabeth was probably protected from much of the anguish her parents felt at what they saw as David's betrayal of the family, his dereliction of duty, and his thrusting the unwelcome responsibility on his ill-prepared brother. Elizabeth's mother never forgave him or Mrs Simpson, believing that the undue strain, particularly during the war years, shortened her husband's life. Relations between the brothers quickly deteriorated into an acrimonious dispute over money – Elizabeth's father, never having enjoyed the Duchy of Cornwall revenues Edward had accrued as Prince of Wales, yet obliged to pay his brother a substantial allowance, was left rather badly off – and unceasing bitterness on the Duke's part at George VI's withholding the HRH title from his wife.

The new Queen did not care to dwell on the unpleasant so that, ostrich-like, the family never spoke of the matter – a trait Elizabeth tended to adopt when crises arose in her own family – but the bitterness of the abdication, the disgrace of it and the danger in which it had placed the dynasty, went deep. Elizabeth, who was to keep her own strong emotions under iron control, would have deduced from Uncle David's fate that this is what happened when a sovereign allowed the indulgence of personal feelings to come before duty. It was an unpardonable loss of control.

In the aftermath of the abdication crisis, George VI felt a need to provide reassurance. There must be no more rocking the boat. Partly because of what had happened, partly because of his personality, the acceptance of a cipher-monarchy, cautious of political interference, began in 1936. To know George VI is to understand Elizabeth; she was to admire and emulate her father, to model herself on him. In many ways, he was the ideal constitutional sovereign; not too imaginative, prepared to put in the hours on the paperwork that his brother had found so tedious, dogged in his devotion to duty, and an exemplary family man. Knowing what her father's accession meant, Elizabeth, according to her grandmother Strathmore, was earnestly praying for a baby brother, but there was really no question now that she would one day be Queen.

At ten she was young enough to take it in her stride. Had she had a choice, as she once told her riding instructor, she would like when she grew up to be a lady living in the country with lots of horses and dogs. A straightforward, almost phlegmatic character, with a wry sense of humour, conformist and amenable, she accepted her destiny with equanimity. Unlike any of his predecessors from George I to Victoria, who were always at war with their heirs, Elizabeth's father began to inculcate her in her future role. He was immensely proud of her and Crawfie noticed that he spoke to her as to an equal – not least, perhaps, because she had always shown a maturity beyond her years.

Her studies were augmented to include constitutional history. Twice a week Elizabeth would go to the Vice-Provost, Sir Henry Marten, at Eton College for a tutorial. Like her grandfather and father before her, she methodically worked through Bagehot; her copy of *The English Constitution* is heavily underlined and annotated. Like her, Marten was an admirer of Queen Victoria, whom Elizabeth was to resemble in some ways. He taught her that the secret of the British monarchy's survival was its ability to adapt – a lesson she obviously took to heart. The Vicomtesse de Bellaigue was engaged to take her for French, French literature and European history. She was invited to join her parents when they entertained, being encouraged to sit beside visiting foreign dignitaries, politicians and diplomats and converse intelligently with them.

Shy and introverted like her father, this cannot have been easy for Elizabeth. Sir John Colville, private secretary to Churchill and then to Princess Elizabeth between 1947 and 1949, recalled that she 'has the sweetest of characters, but she is not easy to talk to, except when one sits next to her at dinner, and her worth, which I take to be very real, is not on the surface'. At first he found her uninterested in politics. No intellectual and shying away from those of academic achievement, clever enough to know the limits of her education, Elizabeth, like Victoria before her, never wanted to get into a conversation too deep, but as she grew older she became extremely well informed about political and world affairs and could rely on a retentive memory. Like Victoria, too, she was endowed with considerable common sense.

Elizabeth was only thirteen when she met the man she was going to marry. By her own admission to her father's best biographer, she fell in love with him at their first meeting. Always reserved and quiet about her feelings, according to Crawfie, if 'you once gained her love and affection you had it for ever, but she never gave it easily'. Young as she was, Elizabeth seems to have had a clear-eyed view of her future; there was never to be anyone but Philip for her.

Like her, Prince Philip of Greece and Denmark was a great-great-grandchild of Queen Victoria. His mother, Princess Alice, was the daughter of Victoria of Hesse, whose husband Louis of Battenberg was First Sea Lord before he was compelled to resign, owing to his German background, during the First World War. Philip's father was Prince Andrew of Greece, whose grandfather Willy, the Danish Prince who had been given the throne of Greece in 1863, was Queen Alexandra's favourite brother. There was also Romanov blood through his grandmother. Royal on both sides of his family, unlike Elizabeth, Philip was never going to be overawed by her status, but he had not had the benefit of a happy, secure childhood. Much of it had been spent in exile and in relative poverty. His family had been forced to flee Greece and later, after his mother suffered a breakdown, his parents had separated. Homeless, Philip found refuge with his mother's brothers, first the Marquis of Milford Haven, then with Lord Louis Mountbatten, but the insecurity of his childhood would have a profound effect on him and on his relationships with his own children.

Only five years older than Lilibet, Philip was already a young cadet at the Royal Naval College at Dartmouth. When the King and Queen and their daughters visited the college in July 1939, Philip's uncle, Louis Mountbatten, ever ambitious for his family, made sure that it was Philip who entertained the two princesses. First they played with a train set and then they went to the tennis court to see who could jump the nets highest. Crawfie, while applauding Philip's blond Viking good looks, decided he was a bit of a show-off. Elizabeth thought he was wonderful. Gradually they began a correspondence, so that in the course of the war, as Philip served in the Royal Navy with gallantry, Elizabeth had a sweetheart in the armed forces to write to, just like other girls. She kept a photograph of a bearded Philip on her mantelpiece. He was also invited to Windsor when on leave.

At the outbreak of war a couple of months later, the King would not hear of his daughters being sent to Canada, like other privileged children. The children will not leave me, said the Queen, and I will not leave the King. The family would stay together, emphasizing the values for which Britain was fighting. If politicians and people were a little unsure of George VI's suitability when he came to the throne, he emerged a hero. His quiet stoicism and courage and determination to share the fate of his people won their hearts. Elizabeth and her sister spent almost the entire war at Windsor; as Princess Margaret later put it: 'We went for the weekend and stayed for five years.' Once again, they were comparatively isolated. At Buckingham Palace they had mixed with other children, albeit those from exclusive families, in the Girl Guides and Brownies, but at Windsor they were once more thrown on each other's company. For the first time the family was spending time apart, with the King and Queen braving the bombs in London during the week.

By October 1940 Britain stood alone and Princess Elizabeth made her first radio broadcast, ostensibly directed at British children who had been evacuated, not least those who had been sent overseas. It was actually a propaganda exercise to influence adult opinion in the United States, as American help was desperately needed. Elizabeth was fourteen and a half when she made the broadcast and some winced at the sentimental tone and content of the speech that had been created for her, but the broadcast was considered a triumph, attracting wide-spread media attention and public sympathy in the States for the plight of Britain's children.

The war gave Elizabeth the only chance in her young life to fulfil a role outside the palace. As a royal princess, she was already Honorary Colonel of the Grenadier Guards, but now she did what every eight-een-year-old girl in wartime Britain was bound to do: she signed up, joining the ATS as a second subaltern early in 1945. She began train-ing in driving and vehicle maintenance at Aldershot but, unlike the other recruits, returned home to sleep at Windsor Castle every night. On VE Day, 8 May 1945, she appeared in her uniform on the balcony at Buckingham Palace when the royal family and Mr Churchill were loudly cheered by the crowd below. That night after dinner the princesses, together with their uncle David Bowes-Lyon and a group of young Guards officers including Lord Porchester, who shared Elizabeth's passion for horses and was to become a lifelong friend, ventured out into the streets and celebrated victory along with every-one else. It was a rare moment. Generally speaking, and to Queen

Mary's concern, Elizabeth was not interested in broadening her social circle beyond the narrow confines of her class.

Having chosen Prince Philip and remained single-minded in her intention to marry him, Elizabeth never seriously looked at another man, despite her mother's best attempts to introduce her to the most eligible scions of the great noble families. The King liked Philip; the Queen, not overly keen on Germans, less so. They were not actually opposed to the marriage, but they worried that she was too young, had too little experience of life to make such a decision. It was decided that Elizabeth and her sister would accompany the King and Queen on a tour of South Africa in 1947, which would give her time for reflection. It was the first time she had left British shores and she felt guilty that she was not sharing the post-war discomforts of her countrymen in the severest of winters. Worst of all, she was leaving Philip behind. Anticipating an engagement, the American press had already made Princess Elizabeth their idol, their pin-up girl; around the world the heiress presumptive to the British crown was seen as a beautiful young woman of exemplary character who represented hope for the future, particularly among young people.

It was only fitting, then, that she should take the opportunity of her twenty-first birthday to make a broadcast to the British Empire and Commonwealth, in which she made a solemn vow to dedicate her life to the service of her people. The speech, written by the courtier Sir Alan 'Tommy' Lascelles, brought tears to Elizabeth's eyes when she first read it and to those of many of her listeners.

'Although there is none of my father's subjects . . . whom I do not wish to greet, I am thinking especially today of all the young men and women who were born about the same time as myself and have grown up like me in the terrible and glorious years of the Second World War. Will you, the youth of the British family of nations, let me speak as your representative?' She spoke of the British Empire which had saved the world, and 'has now to save itself', and of making the Commonwealth more full, prosperous and happy. She then made her dedication:

> There is a motto which has been borne by many of my ancestors – a noble motto, 'I serve'. Those words were an inspiration to many bygone heirs to the throne when they made their knightly dedication

as they came to manhood. I cannot do quite as they did, but through the inventions of science I can do what was not possible for any of them. I can make my solemn act of dedication with a whole Empire listening. I should like to make that dedication now. It is very simple.

I declare before you all that my whole life, whether it be long or short, shall be devoted to your service and the service of our great Imperial family to which we all belong, but I shall not have the strength to carry out this resolution alone unless you join in with me, as I now invite you to do. I know that your support will be unfailingly given. God help me to make good my vow and God bless all of you who are willing to share in it.

The South African tour had shone the beam on empire. One of the reasons Britain had fought the war was to preserve the British Empire. Minds were briefly distracted from Britain's near-bankruptcy and post-war depression and the imminent loss of India — whose independence Lord Louis Mountbatten was negotiating in Delhi — by the royal tour and Elizabeth's professed hopes for the future. Her first overseas tour made a tremendous impression on her. It highlighted for her the significance of the British imperial family of nations; like her father, she could not agree with the Smuts's government's segregation of the black population of South Africa. George VI was King of all the people, not just the whites. During the long tour she spent a great deal of time with her father and thoroughly absorbed his vision for a new Commonwealth, in which the ties linking the countries of the former empire to the crown and kinship to each other would be maintained. Loyalty to the Commonwealth and its preservation would be a consistent theme of her reign.

Princess Elizabeth's wedding to Lieutenant Philip Mountbatten, RN, as the newly naturalized Prince was known before the King created him Duke of Edinburgh, Earl of Merrioneth and Baron Greenwich, on 20 November 1947, injected what Churchill described as 'a splash of colour' into the post-war gloom. The Labour government made a conscious decision to make the wedding a full-blown state occasion. People were tired of rationing and shortages, which were worse than they had been in wartime, and they saw no end in sight. There was some resentment that Elizabeth was to have the splendid white wedding that was denied so many others. Her pearl-studded silk dress alone would cost £1,200 and 300 coupons, not to speak of the trousseau with its calf-length hemlines. On the other hand, thousands queued along the Mall for hours just to have a chance to view the 1,500 wedding presents and, later, the dress on display. In retrospect, the Westminster Abbey wedding, broadcast on the wireless by the BBC in the tones of reverence and awe it then reserved for royalty, was seen to be the moment when Britain's fortunes began to rise again. It was considered a good omen.

The fairytale wedding of the Princess and the handsome war hero, in which being a traditional girl she promised to 'obey' her husband, was a reminder of the crown's representation of the sanctity of marriage and the virtues of family life. The monarchy was a mirror in which the people could see their own ideals of life. They were ideals that Elizabeth, with the shining example of her own parents ever before her, held dear. Harking back to pre-war ceremonial, the extravagant wedding was a reminder to a world just entering the Cold War of the value of tradition, of the stability of Britain's constitutional monarchy and institutions, and the underlying strength of a nation drawn together by loyalty to the crown.

Following the wedding, Elizabeth was even more of an international celebrity, if that were possible. She was the most publicized young woman in the world. Small, at only five feet four inches, she had the regal carriage and natural dignity that observers had remarked in Queen Victoria, while Annigoni, when he painted her, admired the lovely poise of her head. With her vivid blue eyes, delicious cream and roses complexion, and graceful figure, finely complemented by her couture clothes, Elizabeth was not just a figure of glamour, but seen as an ambassador both for her country and her generation.

Ever the perfect princess, Elizabeth fulfilled her duty as heir presumptive by giving birth to a son and heir, Prince Charles, at Buckingham Palace on 14 November 1948. A daughter, Princess Anne, followed in August 1950. For a short time, Elizabeth was able to live a comparatively normal existence as a naval officer's wife in Malta, although not so normal that it meant bringing her children, who were left in England in the care of their grandparents. Supremely happy in her marriage, she would always be a woman who would place husband before offspring. Elizabeth undoubtedly loved her children and there are home movies taken of her and Charles which touchingly capture her delight and joy in him, but even before she took up the burden of queenship, she was not particularly maternal. Already the calls of duty seemed to be taking precedence over those of mother. The King's deteriorating health was a nagging worry. Elizabeth, a Counsellor of State since she had turned eighteen, took on an increasing number of her father's duties, especially during the Festival of Britain in 1951 when there were increased demands for a royal presence.

That year, the King was too ill to attend the Trooping the Colour ceremony and Elizabeth took his place – 'a woman alone', as *The Times* described her, at the centre of an all-male military event. Like Victoria, Elizabeth rode side-saddle, a fine, erect figure in the scarlet tunic of a colonel of the Grenadiers; subsequently, she would diet vigorously in the weeks leading up to the ceremony and put in hours of dedicated practice. Her superb horsemanship was put to the test years later when an attention-seeker fired several blank bullets from a replica pistol and her horse Burmese, startled not by the shots but by two officers of the Household Cavalry spurring their horses forward to protect their sovereign, became agitated. Although irritated with the cavalrymen for upsetting her horse, Elizabeth remained calm and in control.

On 31 January 1952 George VI, old beyond his years and in the grip of lung cancer, whatever the doctors would have him believe, braved the foggy chill at London airport to see Elizabeth and his son-in-law off on the first leg of an Antipodean tour they were undertaking on his behalf. He must have known that he had not long to live as he took leave of his beloved daughter – one sovereign to the next – staring after her with that fixed, strained look that betrayed his deep emotion at their final parting.

34

Elizabeth Our Queen

Her majesty queen Elizabeth II, the thirty-eighth sovereign of England since William the Conqueror, and the sixth queen regnant, succeeded her father at an unknown moment in the early hours of 6 February 1952. She was far away at Sangana Lodge in Nyeri, Kenya, waiting for the dawn to come up from a lookout point at the top of a tree, which gave an unrivalled view of the animals at the watering hole below. She was accompanied by Lieutenant-Commander Michael Parker, private secretary to the Duke of Edinburgh, who recalled that as they looked at the iridescent light that preceded the sunrise, an eagle hovered over their heads. It was about this time that the King died alone in his sleep at Sandringham and that Elizabeth succeeded to the throne.

Queen Elizabeth II was the first sovereign to be proclaimed *in absentia* since the accession of her German forebear, George I, in 1714. In Kenya, Martin Charteris, who was to serve her as assistant private secretary and private secretary for twenty-seven years, asked her what she wanted to be called as queen. 'My own name, Elizabeth, of course,' she replied. Strictly speaking, north of the border in Scotland she is Elizabeth I. Touching down in London after a twenty-four-hour journey, the slight, graceful figure of the twenty-five-year-old Queen, dressed in black mourning, walked alone down the aircraft steps to greet the Prime Minister, Sir Winston Churchill, and the officials gathered for her arrival.

At the Accession Council held at St James's Palace on 8 February Elizabeth appeared, like Victoria, a solitary young woman among 'hundreds of old men in black clothes with long faces'. Her femininity inspired the same male protectiveness – and the urge to place her on a pedestal. Churchill, whose first response on hearing of George

VI's death had been to say that the new Queen was a mere child and that he hardly knew her, was soon besotted. 'All the film people in the world,' he told Lord Moran, 'if they had scoured the globe, could not have found anyone so suited to the part.' Queen and Prime Minister presented an interesting contrast in age and experience. He greatly looked forward to their audiences and she was to reward him with the highest honour in her personal gift, the Garter.

Elizabeth was the first British monarch since Victoria who did not hold the imperial title, Empress of India. She was proclaimed as 'Elizabeth the Second, by the Grace of God of the United Kingdom of Great Britain and Northern Ireland and of Her Other Realms and Territories, Queen, Head of the Commonwealth, Defender of the Faith'. In 1952 she was Queen of Canada, Australia, New Zealand, the Union of South Africa, Pakistan and Ceylon. India had become a republic during her father's reign, but acknowledged her as Head of the Commonwealth. She was also head of colonies, territories, protectorates and protected states ranging from Hong Kong to Kenya, Cyprus to Brunei, Barbados and Jamaica to the Falkland Islands, Gibraltar to Malaya, Brunei and Sarawak to Trinidad and Tobago, Nigeria to Mauritius, Singapore to Sierra Leone, and many more. Across the globe, 539 million subjects and citizens owed her allegiance. She was a declared Protestant and Supreme Governor of the Church of England and yet Queen to millions who professed a different religion.

The monarchy was the magic link that united the loosely bound Commonwealth, embracing people of many races, colours and faiths. Perhaps conscious that the decline in the imperial role of the monarchy had already diminished its grandeur, and that the disappearance of empire would weaken its hold on the popular imagination, Elizabeth was to make it her life's work to keep the Commonwealth together. What she had inherited from her father, she saw it as her sacred duty to hand on to her successor, although her heir will not automatically be Head of the Commonwealth.

If Elizabeth's accession proceeded seamlessly, the vexed question of the name of her family and dynasty did not. The Duke of Edinburgh's life had changed profoundly with the accession of his wife to the throne. He had already given up his immensely satisfying and promising naval career in order to support her in her royal duties, but now he found himself in the unwelcome position of nearly all the male consorts who preceded him. He had no wish to play a political role, participating in a dual monarchy, as his great-great-grandfather Albert had done with Victoria. But like Albert he was resented by the tightly closed circle of austere and hidebound courtiers as a foreign interloper with suspect modernizing tendencies. They were hostile and obstructive.

Their worst fears were realized when Lord Mountbatten boasted at a dinner party that the House of Mountbatten now reigned. In fact, Jock Colville maintained that Philip would have been just as happy if his children and dynasty took the name of Edinburgh, but his uncle's inflammatory comment was a reminder to the old guard, if any were needed, of the ambitions of the 'upstart' Mountbattens. When it reached the ears of those two formidable matriarchs of the House of Windsor, Queen Mary and Queen Elizabeth the Queen Mother, there was uproar. Sir Winston Churchill, who had no liking for the man who had given away India and was a friend of the Labour Party, eagerly espoused their cause. Cabinet and courtiers followed suit.

The young and inexperienced Queen was reputedly overawed by Churchill, the world statesman, and readily acceded to his proposal that the name of the royal house would remain Windsor. If the Prime Minister offered advice, she might have reasoned, she was constitutionally bound to take it. Indeed, taking advice was to be the passive option she generally adopted through a long reign. Lacking imagination, she rarely if ever took the initiative; she expected others to make suggestions, then she would react with caution. Nor did she ever like to gainsay her mother. She was already guilty enough that her mother had had to move out of Buckingham Palace; smarting from the fact that she was no longer Queen, she was feeling marginalized. A favourite tactic of Queen Elizabeth the Queen Mother if she did not approve of something was to state that 'the King' – as she continued to call her late husband – would not like it. Elizabeth and the family would instantly fall into line.

Indulging her mother – which became a lifelong habit – and giving in on the question of the name meant that Elizabeth deeply wounded her husband. Had she realized how hurt he would be, she would almost certainly have acted differently. It caused a *froideur* in the marriage for a time. Prince Albert had had the satisfaction of knowing that his son and heirs would be of the House of Saxe-Coburg-Gotha; Philip was denied that. 'I am the only man in the country not allowed to give his name to his children,' he fulminated, no better than 'an amoeba'. Although the Queen decreed in 1952 that her husband would take 'Place, Pre-eminence and Precedence' directly after herself, it was not until 1957 that she gave him the style and titular dignity of a Prince of the United Kingdom of Great Britain and Northern Ireland by Letters Patent under the Great Seal and, in due course, their younger children took the name Mountbatten-Windsor.

Unlike Elizabeth's mother and other queens consort, who were crowned alongside their husbands, male consorts were not crowned. At her coronation on 2 June 1953 Elizabeth processed up the aisle and sat alone throughout the proceedings. Philip merely took his place in the procession as the premier royal duke, the first to swear fealty to her. She had given Philip a role in the committee organizing the event. This was the first coronation where television cameras filmed the actual ceremony, the first time a whole nation and, indeed, a considerable part of the world's population saw a crown being placed on the head of a queen. Elizabeth, shy of the new medium, was initially opposed to the idea of the ceremony being filmed, but eventually responded to the groundswell of public opinion in favour of it. Churchmen had worried that television would detract from the sanctity of the occasion, but on the day Elizabeth's concentration was so intense that she appeared to have forgotten the presence of the cameras. When Elizabeth says, 'With God's help . . .' she means it. She truly believes her sovereignty is God-given, appealing to her people in her Christmas broadcast in 1952 about the coming event: 'I want to ask you all, whatever your religion may be, to pray for me on that day – to pray that God may give me wisdom and strength to carry out the solemn promises I shall be making and that I may faithfully serve Him and you, all the days of my life.'

At the coronation only the anointing took place out of the view of the television cameras. When she received the Sword of State, with Geoffrey Fisher, Archbishop of Canterbury, exhorting her 'to do justice, stop the growth of iniquity, protect the holy Church of God, help and defend widows and orphans . . . punish and reform what is amiss, and confirm what is in good order,' and she solemnly placed the sword upon God's altar, one of the officiating bishops observed: 'She never thought of the crowds of people. She was completely taken up in her Act of Dedication. The most wonderful thing I ever saw in my life was the moment when she lifted the Sword and laid it on the altar . . . She was putting her whole heart and soul to the service of her People.'

'She has a great sense of vocation,' another added. 'She is a woman not only graceful in her humanity, but full of the grace of God.'

Ritual and ceremony, linking Britain to its historic past, masked the fact that the British Empire was fragmenting and Britain's future was uncertain. Yet at the same time there was an exceptional degree of moral consensus, a habitual unity left over from the war. It was easy to focus the nation's hopes on the young Queen. The age often takes its identity from the monarch – Victoria's certainly did – and this was optimistically called the New Elizabethan Age. That it turned out to be nothing of the sort, with Britain's status in the world in decline and decades of social disintegration, industrial unrest and economic reversals at home, cannot be blamed on the Queen. She merely reigns and leads by moral example; it is her governments who have the power to effect change.

The televised coronation heralded a new kind of mass participation in national events, which changed for ever the way in which royalty would be perceived. Television created an illusion of intimacy between the royal family and the public, whetting an appetite for more. Deference was still the order of the day, however. Newspaper proprietors, eager to uphold the British establishment's respectability, had no wish to destabilize the monarchy; besides, during the war the press had developed habits of self-censorship that still held good. For the first few years of her reign, Elizabeth II was the subject of unparalleled adulation, young, beautiful, with a dream family and the adoration of her people around the globe. There was an inherent danger in the fact that the monarchy appeared to accept such uncritical approbation as its due, without taking the opportunity to modernize or slim down, so as to be able to weather the changing times ahead.

The Queen was the embodiment of the nation, the universal representative of society, and it was in her that people saw their better selves ideally reflected. Since part of the popular ideal was family life, it followed that the Queen's family, including her sister, played a part in this process of reflection. The first intimation of a relationship between Princess Margaret and the older, divorced Group Captain Peter Townsend revealed itself to the public when a camera caught the Princess, in an unguarded gesture, picking a piece of fluff off his coat. It was the first ripple on the smooth surface of the monarchy's unblemished reputation.

Bereft after the sudden death of her beloved father, whose spoilt darling she was, it was understandable that Margaret should seek solace in Townsend, a former RAF hero and equerry of the late King, who treated him almost as a son. The affair had been going on for some time, but Margaret was persuaded to keep it under wraps until after the coronation. The whole business was badly handled, with Sir Alan 'Tommy' Lascelles misleading the couple into believing that they might marry when she reached the age of twenty-five, when she would no longer be subject to the terms of the Royal Marriages Act. Only then, two years later, did it transpire that she could not marry Townsend without giving up her royal status.

The Queen was determined that her sister should make up her own mind. With extraordinary care, Elizabeth managed to remain outside the argument – neither alienating her sister, nor seeking to force her hand. She accepted that nothing could be done to sanction the marriage without the approval of Parliament, the Cabinet and the Commonwealth, but she could have let it be known that, unadvised, she would have accepted the marriage. She gave not an inkling of her opinion and it remains a matter of speculation. 'Mindful of the Church's teaching that Christian marriage is indissoluble', Margaret chose duty over love. It was a pointless sacrifice in view of the later shenanigans of Elizabeth's children.

The Townsend affair was the first of importance that required the Queen to exercise her independent judgement. Her handling of it signalled a future pattern. On delicate matters, especially involving the family, she would let events unfold, not take sides, and – if a decision was unavoidable – make scrupulously certain that any blame for a mistake would be taken by 'advisers', if not in Downing Street, then at the palace. She was nothing if not a cool-headed professional, never letting emotions get in the way. After all, she had been entrusted with a sacred duty: the monarchy must come first.

Those same advisers found the Queen a joy to work with – accessible, disciplined and efficient. The little girl who slipped out of bed to straighten her shoes had grown into an orderly woman who liked the predictability of the royal year. Christmas and New Year were always to be spent at Sandringham, with the Queen leaving before 6 February, the anniversary of her father's death at the house; Easter and most weekends at Windsor; part of August and September at Balmoral, and much of the rest of the time, when she was not on overseas visits, at Buckingham Palace. As she enters her ninth decade she has indicated that she will be spending more time at Windsor.

Recurring events included the Royal Maundy service on the Thursday before Easter, a 'reinvention of tradition' by George V, which is now held at a different cathedral each year; the monarch no longer washes the feet of the poor, as the first two queens regnant did, but she distributes special Maundy money, based on the old Norman currency of sterling, to as many of the deserving elderly as the years of her life; the ceremony of the Trooping the Colour, on her official birthday in June; investitures at Buckingham Palace; receiving ambassadors and their wives; garden parties at Buckingham Palace and at Holyroodhouse in Edinburgh; attendance at the Cenotaph Memorial Service on Remembrance Day in November; and also in November, the State Opening of Parliament, when Elizabeth wears the imperial crown and the scarlet velvet robe she wore at her coronation. She has missed it only twice, when she was expecting Andrew and Edward. No monarch in recent times has fulfilled her ceremonial role so graciously.

It helped that she loved being Queen, positively relished the job, just as the young Victoria had done. Nothing deflects her from her duty and she has never been heard to complain about having to perform it. Like her father, Elizabeth is hard-working and conscientious, a stickler for detail, but, unlike him, she rarely loses her temper. His famous 'gnashes' were to bypass Elizabeth, but reappear in her son Charles. George VI taught her that a rebuke from the monarch was far worse than a rebuke from anyone else, so that she has become a mistress of gentle admonishment and understatement. 'Are you sure?' 'How would that help?' 'Is that wise?' are Queen's-speak for 'That's a ridiculous idea', 'Forget it!' and 'Not likely!' She is also conscious that when people are introduced to her they are in a terrifically overexcited state, so that it is virtually impossible to have a normal conversation. It does not help that she has no small talk. She avoids making even the smallest off-the-cuff speech and her public jokes, like her speeches, are always scripted.

The Queen feels the monarchy must keep a certain distance if it is to retain any sense of magic. Even people who know her well have to be careful not to step over the boundary between informality and familiarity. Harold Wilson had an excellent relationship with her as Prime Minister, so much so that there was a widely publicized episode at the time of the Queen and Mrs Wilson doing the washing up together. After he retired, however, the Queen wanted to take the relationship no further. When Wilson was seen to be edging too close to her at a Buckingham Palace garden party an equerry was sent to ward him off. 'No further,' was the message. On the other hand, her natural humility means that she has never had any wish to be the centre of attention, unlike her late daughter-in-law, Diana, Princess of Wales. She is utterly straight and, like Victoria, a strict adherent of the truth: 'I am pleased to be at Kingston,' she corrected an early script writer. 'Not *very* pleased to be at Kingston.' A shrewd judge of character and acute observer, the Queen has a gift for mimicry on a par with Rory Bremner's. Exercised strictly behind the scenes, it is a natural outlet to the formality that surrounds her.

Even those who have known and worked with her for years find the Queen something of an enigma. To the outside world she seems opaque, still the girl behind the glass. Cautious and conservative by nature and upbringing, she has always guarded her tongue, even in her own home, where she is rarely alone. She gives away little of what she thinks and offers no hostages to fortune. To express feelings in public, as her son Charles has regrettably done, is to reveal one's weaknesses, opinions and prejudices – something she believes no royal, and certainly not a constitutional monarch, should do. Ultimately, she has gained more respect by not wearing her heart on her sleeve. Even courtiers who have worked for her for years admit they have no idea of her opinions on a vast range of subjects. In the words of one commentator, 'she remains impenetrably Delphic'. Prince Philip is the only person with whom she can be absolutely frank. To the horror of observers, he does not hesitate to shout, 'Don't talk rubbish, Lilibet!' and 'Don't be a bloody fool!' when called for, but she gives as good as she gets and has been known to tell him to shut up.

Her love for horses and dogs perhaps derives from the fact that she is not a queen, just a person to them, and she can be completely herself, at ease, in their company. She has owned and bred horses for years and knows all there is to know about equine pedigree. It has been an interest and a passion offering diversion and relaxation in a life otherwise devoted to duty. Her late racing manager Lord Carnarvon – 'Porchey' – and trainers could always get through to her on her private number. When President Bush appointed William 'Will' Farish, the Texan racehorse owner and breeder, US ambassador to the Court of St James it was an inspired choice, as the Queen has often stayed on his Kentucky stud farm on her unofficial visits to the States to inspect world-class stallions and arrange matings between her own horses and theirs. When matters, particularly family matters, are fraught, she takes refuge behind the covers of *Sporting Life*.

The Queen can look forbidding, but is naturally kind. Her face is either animated by a wonderful smile which reaches her eyes, or serious, almost sulky, in repose. There is no expression in between. She is very good at conveying by the merest gesture – a cool stare or the raising of an eyebrow – her disapproval if she has been placed in an undignified or embarrassing position. When Prime Minister Blair's wife refuses to curtsey, there is a hint of wry amusement behind the cool blue Windsor stare. Recently, word has got out that when the Queen enters a room she can almost hear Cherie Blair's knees locking. But a queen who performs her own duties so punctiliously is not always prepared to ignore discourtesy or disrespect in others. When the King of Morocco kept her waiting, she betrayed her irritation by tapping her foot and switching her handbag from one arm to the other, but she received him with immaculate courtesy when he did show up. The rebuke came when he left *Britannia*. The Queen accompanied her guest to the top of the gangplank. When he reached

the bottom and turned for a final wave he found himself waving foolishly at nothing. She had gone.

The Queen derives satisfaction from the expert way she carries out
her duties, attributing her success to early training. This is evident in
the professionalism with which she tackles her boxes. The contents of
the despatch boxes – from the Cabinet, the Church and the Foreign
Office, not to mention the Commonwealth papers which come to
her directly as its head – are initially sorted by her private secretary,
before going up for her perusal and signature. Edward VIII had
returned the boxes late, often unread and bearing the marks of cock-
tail glasses, and today there is similar frustration at the Prince of
Wales's erratic approach to paperwork. This has never been the case
with the Queen. If she receives her boxes on Friday, they are invariably returned read, annotated and signed first thing Monday
morning. She would ask for the boxes within a day or two of giving
birth. Unlike her father, who would often delay a decision until he
could solicit his wife's opinion, Elizabeth has never held up decisions
pending Philip's input. She has always been very clear in her own
opinions.

Over the years the contents of the boxes have given her an extraordinary overview of events, especially as, unlike political leaders, she has
never spent any time out of office and has seen the whole unfold
without interruption. She needs to be well informed in order to deal
intelligently with her own ministers and officials and also those from
foreign and Commonwealth countries. Her knowledge of what is
going on is also bolstered by reading Hansard, the official verbatim
accounts of proceedings in Parliament, newspapers and periodicals, a
large postbag from members of the public – many petitioning her for
help, just as the people have always done the monarch – and meeting
people from all walks of life. Overseas visits involve her spending
many hours reading up on the place, the personalities, the policies and
the problems – as well as putting aside time for the fittings of the
clothes she will take with her. She also enjoys television documen-
taries and glimpses of the lives of ordinary people that television
affords. Rather as Albert did for Victoria, Philip has gone out and
brought information back for her, especially in the fields that interest
him, from science and industry to conservation.

The depth of her experience and knowledge acquired over half a century give the Queen an enormous advantage in her weekly audiences with the Prime Minister. Tony Blair, her tenth Prime Minister, was not even born when she came to the throne. The Queen is the only person to whom the Prime Minister can talk frankly, knowing that the meeting is totally secure. The private secretaries liaise before an audience about the subjects for discussion, but neither the agenda nor a strict time limit is always adhered to. Tony Blair, who reputedly in his early days could not find time for the Tuesday audiences, latterly has had audiences lasting as long as an hour and a half. Although no Prime Minister has ever revealed what has transpired at his weekly audiences with the Queen, out of respect to her and the constitution, James Callaghan has described the techniques she would employ. She would often express or hint at her own opinion by asking a leading question, or referring to someone else who held an alternative view. If she approved of a measure, she would say so, positively. Disapproval was indicated by a significant failure to comment.

She is there to be consulted, to encourage and to warn. She has the right to know all the Cabinet's decisions, although not necessarily their differences. She can draw the Prime Minister's attention to a past event that has parallels with something he is proposing to do and which may have similar consequences. The monarchy acts as a fail-safe mechanism, an important safeguard. As a former Foreign Secretary has put it, the Prime Minister's weekly visits to the palace are a deterrent from shabby or sordid actions. He will have to explain, and justify, his actions to the Queen, who represents moral rectitude in terms of public behaviour and the sanctity of the constitution. In extremis, she can appeal over the head of a government if she feels it is acting contrary to the will or interests of the people; for example, if it turns totalitarian. At least, that it the theory.

The monarchy's prestige comes from being above politics, non-partisan. It offers a reassuring link with the past, when a government's progressive legislation might otherwise seem alarming. Free from political pressure, the Queen can take a longer view than a politician dependent on votes. However, Elizabeth II has been so punctilious at keeping out of politics that it would seem that she has reduced the monarchy to a position where it hardly seems to matter. Characteristically, she has taken no risks and played it absolutely safe.

Perhaps she has not been assertive enough. In a recent interview Tony Blair referred to himself, with reference to the Iraq War, as Commander-in-Chief. No one picked up on it. It is the Queen, not the Prime Minister, who is head of the armed forces. They are, literally, the soldiers of the Queen and owe their loyalty to her as their sovereign lady. When war is declared it is by 'The Queen's Most Excellent Majesty in Council', but she is powerless to prevent war if the government decides on it. In much the same way, even though all justice derives from the crown and is dispensed in the Queen's name, the prerogative of mercy is now exercised by the sovereign on the advice of her ministers, namely the Home Secretary.

As to war, when Anthony Eden provoked the Suez crisis in 1956 the Queen was better informed of his plans than many members of the Cabinet, but even she might not have been given the full picture. According to Martin Charteris, she did not trust Eden and thought him mad, but she could only warn him. She might have ventured something like, 'Are you sure this is wise?' After the debacle, she apparently sighed with relief at his departure in mid term, owing to ill health.

In the case of a mid-term appointment of a Prime Minister, the Queen's prerogative was to act as arbiter, to decide on his successor. After Eden's resignation she asked Churchill and Lord Salisbury for advice and having asked for it was constitutionally bound to take it. They recommended Harold Macmillan rather than R.A. Butler. The Queen had failed to use her prerogative but handed it over to the Tory old guard, which set its own precedent, signalling that the royal prerogative had become a doubtful instrument. Nor did she exercise her prerogative when Macmillan in turn was resigning owing to ill health. He duped her into accepting his nominee as his successor. Again, the best candidate was the deputy Prime Minister, R.A. Butler, but Macmillan was determined to scotch that.

As it happened, the man he recommended was none other than Alec Douglas-Home, an old friend of the Bowes-Lyons in Scotland and someone the Queen felt socially at ease with, whereas Butler was too remote and complex for her taste. Her personal preferences aside,

Elizabeth had allowed the monarchy to become the pawn of a faction in the Conservative Party. Her passivity and unwitting collusion with Macmillan's scheme is probably the biggest political misjudgement of her reign.

By the time the Labour Prime Minister, Harold Wilson, made the decision to resign, she was only peripherally involved in the choice of his successor. To save face, Charteris came up with a formula in which Wilson resigned only as Leader of the Labour Party, leaving the party to elect a new leader, and a variation of this was adopted. Wilson informed the palace that James Callaghan had received the most votes and went to tender his resignation as Prime Minister. He was careful *not* to advise the Queen whom to choose, so preserving the notion of her constitutional right of choice, when in reality she had had none.

The Queen's discretionary power in the choice of a Prime Minister had, for all practical purposes, ceased to exist.

Because of the nature of her job, the Queen has spent her working life almost exclusively with men. She has a calculating mind like a man and tends to relate better to men than to women. Yet she does not hesitate to use her feminine charms discreetly on susceptible males. It was interesting to see, therefore, how she would get along with her first woman Prime Minister, Margaret Thatcher, when she came to power in 1979. Thatcher had as little time for inherited privilege as she had for the feckless malingerers at the bottom of the social heap, but she was apparently in awe of the Queen. 'Her curtsey almost reached Australia,' a courtier observed sardonically. However, at the weekly audiences the Queen was hardly ever able to get a word in edgeways. According to one of her former private secretaries, audiences 'tended to be a one-sided rehearsal of what the Prime Minister intended to do'.

The Queen is part of the system of checks and balances, but what if the 'wayward' leader came from the right, as Margaret Thatcher did? The style and priorities of the uncompromising premier apparently raised questions at the palace. The 'welfare monarchy' dedicated to charitable patronage, of which all British sovereigns since Victoria have been such eager proponents, did not find it easy to embrace a leader and an administration that treated welfare policies as soft. Thatcher also had little time for the Commonwealth. When the

Americans sent troops into Grenada, a Caribbean island with a population of less than 100,000, in 1983, the Queen was furious. She happened to be Grenada's head of state and no one had bothered to consult her.

Apart from the weekly audiences and the official functions they both attended, and the Prime Minister's annual weekend at Balmoral – which Thatcher, inappropriately dressed and tottering around on high heels, could not wait to escape – the two women did not impinge on each other. They were discreet about their differences, until in 1986 the editor of *Today* was given a scoop by the Queen's press secretary, Michael Shea, about her dismay at the divisive policies of her Prime Minister. No one picked up on it until a few weeks later when Andrew Neil splattered the story all over the *Sunday Times*. Shea was the Queen's official mouthpiece, but as ever she was able to distance herself. Even though there was much public sympathy with the palace's viewpoint, the *Guardian* expressed concern that the monarchy was seeking to rally public opinion against an elected government. The Queen was advised to ring up Thatcher and the two commiserated with each other.

There remained a competitive edge in their relationship. At the victory parade after the Falklands War, it was the Prime Minister, not the Queen, who took the salute as the troops marched past in the City. When Thatcher through sheer exhaustion had to sit down at the annual diplomatic reception two years running, the Queen, who has inherited her mother's iron constitution and stamina, quipped to Robert Runcie, 'Oh look! She's keeled over again.' Nevertheless, the Queen recognized Thatcher's achievement by making her the first non-royal Lady of the Garter on her retirement from the Commons in 1992.

Long before women came to the workplace in force, Queen Elizabeth faced the eternal dilemma of the career woman: how to juggle the job and the family so that neither is neglected. Queen Victoria felt that it was an impossible task, frustrated as she was by the conflicting demands of queenship and motherhood, but she remained very hands-on as a mother. It has to be said that while Elizabeth II has been an excellent queen, she has placed her duty to the country before her children and perhaps fallen short as a mother. She is not a tactile person and, after a separation, she was more likely to be seen shaking the hand of her small son Charles than giving him a big hug and kisses, as Diana did her sons. By the time that Prince Andrew was born in 1959 and Prince Edward in 1963, the Queen was able to afford them more time, but still not enough. Theirs was an old-fashioned upper-class upbringing, surrounded by servants, with Mummy holding them emotionally at arm's length. They needed more than she was able to give.

Perhaps to assuage her guilt at the secondary role her husband was forced to play, Elizabeth allowed Philip to become the dominant force in the family, but he had no model of happy family life to go on. How could he be a father, when his own had deserted him? He expected the children to be self-sufficient, to fend for themselves, as he had had to do. With the exception of Anne, who stood up to him, Philip tended to bully his children, particularly Charles, a shy, sensitive boy who was the antithesis of himself. Philip simply could not abide his whingeing and his diffidence. Charles found the sympathy and under-standing his parents denied him in his grandmother, Queen Elizabeth the Queen Mother, and in Lord Louis Mountbatten, whose influence proved a mixed blessing.

The Queen's failure to forge a special relationship with her son and heir, as George VI did with her, has arguably made the future of the monarchy less secure. Perhaps she felt a boy should be left to his father. Never having been to school herself, she entrusted his educa-tion to Philip. The Queen Mother protested about the choice of Gordonstoun, when Eton or Westminster would have been more apt choices for someone of Charles's character. The Queen briefly con-sidered the alternatives, but deferred to Philip's judgement that the rough and tumble of Gordonstoun would toughen Charles up. The years he spent at the school, where he was bullied unmercifully, were sheer misery. Apparently, he has never forgiven Philip.

In June 1969 the film *Royal Family*, released in the run-up to the televised investiture of the Prince of Wales in a mock medieval cere-mony at Carnarvon Castle, was an attempt to win some popularity for the monarchy and boost the image of the 'model family'. Needless to say, the Queen did not initiate it; she knows she is an icon and has no need to sell herself. It was Philip who had these 'modernizing' bursts.

In his biography of the Queen, Ben Pimlott states that 'The idea of the film was to shatter the iconography as conclusively as a brick heaved through a stained-glass window.' It was naïve to think that public appetite would be satisfied with this behind-the-scenes glimpse, which was very much on the monarchy's own terms. If the royal family was going to exploit the opportunities the media provided, they were fair game for the media. The film gave licence, in due course, to a level of media intrusion that the bemused dynasty was ill equipped to meet.

At her silver wedding in 1972 the Queen remarked how fortunate she had been to grow up in a happy and united family and how fortunate she was in her children. She reiterated the social value of a strong marriage. Her own marriage has proved strong. At their golden wedding anniversary in 1997 she paid a public tribute to Philip: 'He is someone who doesn't take kindly to compliments, but he has, quite simply, been my strength and stay all these years.' Philip enjoys the company of beautiful women, but if his friendships have been more than platonic, he has been discreet. No hint of scandal has ever touched him or the Queen. Sadly, that was not to be the case with their children. As they grew up, the children were given far too much licence, with their own apartments, secretaries and programmes while they were still in their teens. It was indeed more like 'the Firm' than a family. If there were problems, they did not talk about them. The Queen, who hated confrontation, would rather busy herself with her boxes than deal with something unpleasant, such as disciplining her children or having a family row. All of them respected her authority; unfortunately, she did not exercise it enough.

Since the First World War, the royal family has looked for its brides beyond the princely courts of Europe, first among the British aristocracy, then, in the case of three of Elizabeth's children, to the upper and middle classes. Again, the Queen seems to have offered her children no guidance in their choice of partners. By the time he was thirty, the heir to the throne had still to find a bride. True to Mountbatten's advice, he had been sowing his wild oats. As early as 1973 Sir Martin Charteris told the Queen that the Prince of Wales was having an affair with Camilla Parker Bowles, the wife of a fellow officer, and 'the Regiment don't like it, Ma'am.' Genuinely believing in the sanctity of marriage, the Queen considered her son's affair with a married woman deplorable, yet at the same time 'safe', since the woman was unavailable. Knowing that Camilla was not the only one – Charles was promiscuous – she probably thought it would blow over, but Charles had found the mother-figure he had never had in Camilla and would never let her go.

In 1977 the Queen had had 'a love affair' with the country during her Silver Jubilee, when she repeated the vow she had made at twenty-one to serve her people all the days of her life. Four years later, the wedding of the Prince of Wales to Lady Diana Spencer – a descendant of two Stuart kings, Charles II and James II – at St Paul's Cathedral was greeted with ecstatic enthusiasm. The birth of two sons, William and Harry, followed in quick succession. It was still possible to identify the monarchy with the model family rather than the dysfunctional family. Behind the façade, however, the war of the Waleses was well into its stride.

The Queen was perplexed by Diana. Neurotic, wilful, no country lover, she was simply not her type of girl. Nevertheless, she was prepared to listen to Diana's troubles, and later was anxious to do what she could to keep the unstable girl onside. Charles, meanwhile, was complaining that he had been pushed into the marriage by his father, and bitterly resented the fact that his parents seemed to hold him largely to blame for its breakdown. In about 1986 Charles resumed his affair with Camilla, smuggling her into Highgrove after Diana and their sons had left for London each week. It is significant that the Queen visited Highgrove only twice in fourteen years, no doubt wanting to keep out of the war zone. Not surprisingly, William and Harry enjoyed being with the Queen – an oasis of calm and stability away from their unhappy parents.

All four of the Queen's children, according to those who know them, are arrogant, spoilt and selfish, which is probably why three of their marriages have failed. Perhaps to compensate for not giving them enough time, the Queen has been hugely generous in providing expensive homes for Anne, Andrew and Edward. She is unable to deny her children anything. So indulgent was she of her youngest son Edward that she agreed to his proposal for members of the family to take part in *It's a Royal Knockout*, although she knew it was a bad idea.

It was such a disaster that even the tabloids were left speechless and Edward flounced out of the media tent in disgust. If the royals make fools of themselves, an article in *The Times* argued, what is the point of the monarchy continuing?

The Queen's sister had broken the royal taboo about divorce. Princess Anne and Mark Phillips separated in 1989 and divorced in 1992. Prince Andrew and Sarah Ferguson separated in 1992 and, after the revelation of Sarah's toe-sucking episode in the South of France, divorce was inevitable. A courtier who observed the Queen on the day Sarah quit Balmoral with her daughters said she looked completely drained. That same year, Andrew Morton's book, *Diana: Her True Story*, with its intimate and shocking revelations of the true state of the Waleses' marriage, stripped away the last vestige of royal mystique, at least from the younger generation. Deference had no place in a world where the royal family washed its dirty linen in public. Worse was to come. A tape of a conversation Charles had made on his mobile phone to Camilla – its exact source never quite established – brought the monarchy to a new nadir, when the heir to the throne told his mistress that he wanted to be a Tampax so that he could stay inside her.

The behaviour of the Queen's family, for which she must be held partly responsible, damaged the standing of the monarchy, undermining all her good work. The younger generation, particularly her daughters-in-law, had confused royal fame with celebrity, playing a dangerous game of collusion, revelation and counter-revelation with the media. But celebrity is fleeting and those who live by the press die by the press. In the words of *Guardian* columnist Julie Burchill, the once revered family had descended to 'Life imitating soap imitating life'. If it no longer represented the 'model family', what did the Windsor monarchy have to rest on?

At a Guildhall lunch at the end of 1992 the Queen described the year as her 'annus horribilis'. All institutions must be subject to scrutiny, she agreed, while appealing for tolerance and understanding. Apart from the misfortunes of her children, she had received another blow when Windsor Castle, which she regards as her real home, was badly damaged by fire. In a further shock, there was a public outcry when a government minister blithely announced that the taxpayer would pick up the tab for the repairs. It was a salient reminder of how low esteem for the monarchy had sunk. Although the matter had been set in motion months before, the Queen announced her decision to pay income tax. The frivolity of the younger royals was partly responsible for this *volte face* but, even so, she drove a hard bargain.

Her troubles were by no means over. In Jonathan Dimbleby's authorized biography, Charles publicly rebuked Elizabeth and Philip for their deficiencies as parents. 'We did our best,' Philip later told a biographer. Charles was the only one of the four to point the finger of accusation and his siblings were outraged, coming to their parents' defence; they appreciated that their mother's duties as queen meant that she had had less time to give them, but denied that she had been remiss as a mother. Charles's admission of adultery with Camilla Parker Bowles in the Dimbleby television interview in front of millions of viewers in 1994 – the Prince's need to unburden his conscience in public left Camilla and the cuckolded Parker Bowles with no option but to divorce – was followed by Diana's tit-for-tat *Panorama* interview the following year, in which she threw doubt on the Prince of Wales's suitability for 'the top job'.

Enough was enough. In neither case was the Queen warned of what was coming, an unpardonable breach of etiquette on the part of her son and heir. For all her great gifts, Diana had proved utterly untrustworthy, a loose cannon. The behaviour of her children and the unresolved state of the Waleses' marriage were undermining the Queen's good work and her devoted service over forty years. For a long time she and Philip had dithered, unsure what to do for the best. 'Where did we go wrong?' they plaintively asked friends whose children were also divorcing. It was the Queen's private secretary, Sir Robert Fellowes, Diana's brother-in-law, who finally persuaded the Queen to write to Charles and Diana separately, demanding that they divorce. The marriage was dissolved on 28 August 1996.

One year and three days later, Diana was dead and the Queen faced the worst crisis of her reign.

35

After Diana

IN THE EARLY hours of Sunday, 31 August 1997, the Queen was at Balmoral when she was awoken by a telephone call from her deputy private secretary, Sir Robert Janvrin, with the news that Diana, Princess of Wales, had been involved in a car crash in Paris. Just before four confirmation came through from the British Embassy that Diana had died. The Queen's first thought was for her grandsons, William and Harry, who she insisted should be allowed to sleep undisturbed for what remained of the night.

Charles was shattered, but, typically, his main concern was what it would mean for him. 'They're all going to blame me, aren't they? What do I do? What does this mean?' Certainly any steps towards public acceptance of Camilla Parker Bowles would now have to be put on hold. A little after seven, still red-eyed but a little calmer, he went in to tell his sons that their mother was dead.

Although the royal family was as shocked and distressed as anyone by the news, it was typical that they concealed their emotions later that morning when they attended the usual service at Crathie Church, where the Princess's name was not even mentioned in the prayers. Elizabeth II had never been in the habit of revealing her feelings and did not intend to start now, but to the public it seemed so uncaring. Tony Blair captured the mood of the moment when on the way to church in his constituency he made what was apparently an improvised speech, calling Diana 'the People's Princess'.

It had been the century of the Windsor women: Queen Mary, Queen Elizabeth the Queen Mother, Elizabeth II and Diana, whom large sections of the British public and the world had elevated almost to goddess status. The Queen and Prince Philip had realized immediately that the public grief at Diana's death would be immense and that this called for something more than the private family funeral the Spencers wanted. While the Queen and Philip were anxious to stay at Balmoral where they could comfort their grandsons, Charles was despatched to Paris with Diana's two sisters to bring back the body, which after a detour to the mortuary in Fulham would be taken to the Chapel Royal at St James's Palace, where it would lie surrounded by candles and covered in white flowers.

The Lord Chamberlain, Lord Airlie, and his team joined forces with the Prime Minister's appointees, including Alastair Campbell, to plan the funeral. There was no precedent for the burial of an ex-Princess of Wales who was divorced and no longer an HRH, so they would have to improvise. All week, as the flowers piled up outside the palaces and the files of mourners queued to sign the condolence books, the phone lines between London and Balmoral were busy as the two teams liaised.

It is impossible for anyone who was not in London that week to fathom the mood: overwhelming grief that slipped into anger at the lack of a royal presence, which finally turned ugly. Balmoral is the place where the Queen truly relaxes, so much so that she slips into what they call 'Balmoral time'. Even though television coverage was showing that something very strange was unfolding in the capital, the royals at Balmoral were slow to grasp it. At one stage during the week, an exasperated Charles complained to Mark Bolland, his deputy private secretary in London, that the whole family were locked in their rooms drinking.

Ever faithful to tradition and protocol, the Queen was adamant that she was not going to give in to demands to let the royal standard fly at half mast at Buckingham Palace. It had become an inflammatory issue with the media and the people and soon the Queen's advisers were unanimously advising her to compromise. Usually so amenable to advice, they were surprised by the strength of her resistance and there were some bruising exchanges spoken in the heat of the moment. Finally, a compromise was reached whereby the Union flag would fly at half mast at Buckingham Palace, in lieu of the royal standard, which according to form would not be raised on the palace flagpole until the Queen's return at the end of the week.

With newspaper headlines screaming, 'Where is our Queen?' and dark muttering in the streets growing ever louder, there was a real fear that the Queen and her family might be lynched when they returned to the capital. On the Thursday, Princes Andrew and Edward were sent out on a test run, walking down the Mall among the crowds. The gesture was welcomed and they were treated courteously. On Friday afternoon the car carrying the Queen and Prince Philip stopped outside the gates of Buckingham Palace, where they stepped out to inspect the messages on the flowers piled up there. Plainclothes officers merged with the crowd, ready to spring if the people turned on their monarch. The tension was broken by a little girl presenting the Queen with a bouquet. 'Do you want me to place them for you?' she asked. 'No, Your Majesty, they are for you.' The people began to clap. The relief was palpable.

At the eleventh hour, Elizabeth II had rescued the tottering monarchy from the brink. That she did so was thanks to advisers both in the palace and in Downing Street, but also to the residual affection and respect in which the people had always held her, conscious of her dedication and long service. As ever, the short speech that was televised live that evening was scripted for her, including the words 'as a grandmother', a nice touch which Alastair Campbell had thought to insert. It was one of the television crew's ideas to film her against the open window, uniting her visually with the grieving crowd outside, although later a journalist commented that the piece looked like a hostage video with the speaker reading the words in front of her in order to save her neck. There was an air of compulsion about it.

Back now in full professional mode, she agreed that she and the whole royal family would walk to the palace gates next morning to be there as the funeral cortège passed on its way to Westminster Abbey. As the gun carriage carrying Diana's coffin, with the poignant word 'Mummy' prominent on a card amid a wreath of white flowers, drew close, Elizabeth II bowed her head in respect. The sovereign had done everything expected of her.

It was only after the event that the Queen and Prince Philip realized that in Earl Spencer's brilliant and emotive funeral oration at the abbey they had been thoroughly insulted. Still, it was over.

There remained the problem of what to do about Charles and Camilla Parker Bowles. When the Queen had taken her son to task during the melt-down of his marriage to Diana, Charles had denied that he was having an affair with Camilla. The Queen was justifiably cross that she had been lied to and angry about the mess that Charles's selfish behaviour had left, which reflected so badly on the monarchy. Unlike the divorces of the Queen's other children, there was a constitutional implication to the end of Charles's marriage and his continuing liaison with a married woman. Was he fit to be King? Could a divorcee be head of the Church if he did become King? Should the succession bypass Charles in favour of William? These were all reasonable questions.

After Charles's divorce from Diana, Philip wrote to his son advising him to drop Camilla. The advice was ignored, with Charles subsequently stating categorically that Camilla was 'non negotiable'. He was prepared neither to give up the throne, when the time came, nor to give up his mistress. Nothing he did, however, could persuade the Queen to acknowledge Camilla. 'Never mention that wicked woman's name to me again,' she is said to have expostulated when he tried to arrange for the two to meet at his fiftieth birthday party. Determined to get his own way, Charles was prepared to encourage criticism of the Queen in the media if she did not accept Camilla.

Certainly while the Queen Mother was alive, there was no chance of Charles marrying Camilla, but after her death in 2002 there was a wind of change at the palace. Having been under her mother's influence all her life, the Queen at seventy-six, in her Golden Jubilee year, was her own woman at last. Her natural conservatism and resistance to change had been reinforced by her mother, who was vigorously opposed to attempts to reform or modernize the monarchy. Opening Buckingham Palace to the public to raise funds for the restoration work at Windsor had provoked a major row with the Queen Mother. She was no less angry at the Queen's agreement to pay tax, as well she might be, since in the course of her fifty-year widowhood she had been hugely subsidized by her daughter. Living in pre-war regal splendour with no idea of the cost of anything, the Queen Mother's extravagance knew no bounds. So frugal that she has been known to go round turning off the lights in her palaces, scrutinize her dressmakers' bills and have her breakfast cereals brought to the table in Tupperware containers, the Queen was prepared to indulge her mother, but she was irritated that she had indoctrinated Charles in the same habits.

The Queen is a pragmatist. She may not like Camilla and she certainly does not approve of marital infidelity, but if the country was prepared to accept it, she would not stand in the way of Charles's marriage. He was, after all, well into his fifties. Ever cautious, the Queen would only ever act on advice. Prime Minister Blair is a Christian, an advocate of marriage. It is reasonable to assume that he would have advised in favour of regularizing the union. The Queen, who had spent so much of her life under the shadow of the abdication of 1936, gave her cautious approval. A registry office and a finger buffet, rather than the organic extravaganza Charles had planned, were the order of the day. There is time for Charles and his wife to win public acceptance during the Queen's lifetime, ensuring his smooth succession when the time comes. The idea is for them to take on more of her duties, although she must worry about her son's frequent voicing of his opinions.

Entering her eighties, the Queen is seen to smile more and she has plenty to smile about. Family affairs seem more settled than they have for twenty years and she has enormous pleasure in her grandchildren. Her health is good, apart from the occasional headaches and sinusitis she treats with homeopathic remedies, and she remains as indefatigable as ever. In her eightieth year she undertook nearly 400 engagements. On one day alone she attended the State Opening of Parliament, flew to Canada and attended an evening function there, with the wilting press in tow. She continues to travel widely, a source of pride to accompanying British ministers and diplomats, who value her practised ability to show interest in everything and disguise exhaustion and boredom.

By assiduous hard work and her people skills – showing almost a mothering instinct where it is concerned – she has preserved the idea and reality of the Commonwealth, when many British politicians might have consigned it to history. Australia, which has long been close to becoming a republic, has hesitated to do so while Elizabeth is its Queen. By her uncompromising majesty, she has conveyed no sense at all of Britain's decline, or, in the context of the tightening European Union, of any loss of sovereignty.

At the time of Diana's death, the message given out was that lessons had been learned. Now when the Queen visits a school, she will come in and sit down with the children, rather than stand at the door. But she has never been one for the spontaneous gesture, nor is she the touchy-feely type. Sitting on the bed of a sick patient during a hospital visit or hugging a child are simply not her. Nor, thankfully, does she exploit press opportunities. She is all the more respected for that.

Whenever the Queen travels, she personally packs a photograph of her father, George VI. Ever her father's daughter, she has remained faithful to the past and slow to change the monarchy. She inherited a secure throne at a time when popularity for the monarchy did not need to be actively cultivated. The standing of the monarchy is lower now than when she came to the throne and no doubt she is partly responsible. The behaviour of her children and changing times are equally to blame. No previous monarch or royal family has been so visible or subject to such scrutiny. Contrary to the myth, the royal family is not perfect, but we can accept that if it is matched by the unfailing dedication to duty that this queen has shown.

The sixth queen regnant could become our longest-reigning monarch, if she exceeds her great-great-grandmother Victoria's sixty-four years on the throne. At twenty-one Elizabeth made a vow 'that my whole life, whether it be long or short, shall be devoted to your service', and she has remained true to that promise. Perhaps one of the greatest yardsticks of her success is that there can be no question of Britain becoming a republic while she lives. For many of us she has always been there – the Queen – ubiquitous. She exists somewhere deep in our collective consciousness, a sole fixed point in a world that has changed beyond all recognition. It is impossible to imagine life without her.

Epilogue

'I will be as good unto you, as ever queen was to her people'

Elizabeth I

'I declare before you all that my whole life, whether it be long or short, shall be devoted to your service'

Elizabeth II

MONARCHY IS A contract between sovereign and people, but neither Elizabeth would have been able to carry the burden of queenship – symbolized by the sheer weight of the crown – without a profound belief that she was chosen by God and accountable to Him.

'My lords, the burden that is fallen upon me maketh me amazed,' the first Elizabeth told the lords on her accession, 'and yet, considering I am God's creature, ordained to obey His appointment, I will thereto yield, desiring from the bottom of my heart that I may have assistance of His grace to be the minister of His heavenly will in this office now committed to me.'

She appeals to the lords, her natural advisers, to assist her, 'that I with my ruling and you with your service may make a good account to almighty God and leave some comfort to our posterity in earth.'

Four hundred years later, the young Elizabeth II, making her first Christmas broadcast, echoed the words of the dedication she had made on her twenty-first birthday. Then, she had pledged her whole life to the service of her people: 'I shall not have the strength to carry out this resolution alone unless you join in with me, as I now invite you to do. I know that your support will be unfailingly given. God help me to make good my vow.' Now, she declared: 'At my Coronation next June, I shall dedicate myself anew to your service.'

She asked her listeners to pray that she might faithfully serve God 'and you all the days of my life'.

'Sirs, I present unto you Queen Elizabeth, your undoubted Queen.' The Archbishop of Canterbury's opening words at the coronation in 1953 echoed those of 1559. The sacred ceremony of the coronation emphasizes the sovereign's other-worldly status by bringing her 'into the presence of the living God'. She is recognized by the people, makes a special, sacrificial pact with God, and takes an oath to govern according to the laws and customs of the land. It is the bond uniting all sovereigns, going back to the beginnings of England's monarchy in the tenth century, while at the same time it is a reminder to the people of their historic past, of the evolution of the Anglo-Saxon political tradition into the modern state.

In 1953 it was apt that the most solemn part of the ceremony, the anointing with holy oil, took place out of view of the television cameras. Like her predecessors, Elizabeth II divested herself of her robes and donned a simple, white garment, before taking her place on the coronation chair, concealed under a canopy held by Knights of the Garter. Dipping his fingers in the holy oil, the archbishop made the sign of the cross on her hands, chest and head, intoning the words of the ancient text: 'Be thy Head anointed with holy Oil: as kings, priests, and prophets were anointed. And as Solomon was anointed King by Zadok the priest and Nathan the prophet, so be thou anointed, blessed and consecrated Queen over the Peoples, whom the Lord thy God hath given thee to rule and govern . . .'

The sacred ritual – elevating her into the realm of mystical sovereignty – is said to have profoundly affected her.

With the demise of the Church in the sixteenth century, there was an increase in secular ceremony focusing on the monarch, who had aggregated the powers of the former Church to himself. As a woman, Elizabeth I deferred to male sensitivity, calling herself Supreme Governor rather than Supreme Head of the Church, but it amounted to the same thing. All subsequent queens have taken seriously their responsibility towards the Church of England, including Elizabeth II, who is Queen of a multi-faith society.

At the Reformation, the images of the saints were deliberately devalued, to be replaced by the symbols of monarchy. But the sovereign had always been considered holy, being possessed of an aura or 'mana', creating an awe or dread of their person and authority in the minds of their subjects. There is a sense in which this feeling survives today. When people meet the Queen, they either freeze or begin a stream of mindless chatter. She understands. She smiles graciously, nods, and moves on.

In the past, the symbolism of the office was centred on the human body of the monarch. Those who touched the King drew off some of his aura or holiness to themselves. It was no accident that his closest body servants were often those sent on the most delicate diplomatic missions to fellow sovereigns; they understood that someone in such close attendance, so close they actually touched their sovereign, could be trusted with confidential information. Significantly, the body servant accorded the most public power and influence was the Groom of the Stool, who fulfilled the most intimate role of all – wiping the royal bottom. Queens seem to have dispensed with this service; certainly Kat Ashley, who held the office of Groom of the Stool to Elizabeth I and was keeper of the royal close-stools, had no political power. It was merely a ceremonial duty. Now, the monarch's relieving herself is 'such an awesomely private affair' that one of the usual preparations for a royal visit is the construction of a special WC, dedicated to the Queen's sole use.

As a Catholic monarch who saw the Reformation as a tragic aberration, Mary I continued to use her God-given power to carry out the sovereign's traditional role in imitation of Christ. On Maundy Thursday she would kneel down and wash the feet of the poor; then she would give the most deserving of the women – usually the oldest – the gown she was wearing. Similarly, she would touch for the Evil – scrofula or bovine tuberculosis – rubbing the swellings of the afflicted, just as she would touch 'cramp rings', as a healing weapon. On Good Friday she underwent the creeping to the cross ceremony, going on her knees through the various stages of Christ's journey with the cross. Elizabeth, in turn, asserted her quasi-divine status by appropriating those pre-Reformation ceremonies – the Maundy ceremony, for instance – that would make the most dramatic impact.

Mary II fulfilled none of these functions, since her husband poohpoohed them as popish superstition, but Anne revived them. 'I desire you would order 200 pieces more of Healing Gold,' she wrote to her Mistress of the Robes, the Duchess of Marlborough, for her forthcoming healing ceremony in the Banqueting House. Elizabeth II continues to hold the Maundy ceremony, but she does not wash the feet of the poor; she hands out the specially minted money with gloved hands. In the eighteenth century, Samuel Johnson and other sufferers of the King's Evil treasured their 'healing gold' – the medals they received from the monarch. Today, Maundy money is on sale on eBay the next day.

Only the first two of the six queens regnant ruled as well as reigned. While recognizing that Parliament had its uses, Elizabeth I intended to rule as absolutely as her father had done. It helped that the Tudor queens, unlike their female successors, were superbly educated, but then the role of an absolute monarch is so much more challenging than the role of a constitutional one. Mary I might not have been a success as a monarch, but the speech she gave at the Guildhall during Wyatt's rebellion – composed by herself and delivered with rousing aplomb – was every bit as good as her sister's brilliant oratory over a forty-five-year reign. In a fiercely media-driven age, Elizabeth II is not a natural communicator and she cannot ad lib. Unlike the first Elizabeth, she relies on others to write her speeches. Even the short speech she read out from the television autocue after the Princess of Wales's death was the work of her advisers in liaison with Downing Street and it was the Prime Minister's spin doctor, Alastair Campbell, who thought to include the crucial, affecting phrase 'as a grand-mother'.

The evolution from absolute to constitutional monarchy over four centuries has diminished the sovereign's political power to the point where it is exerted so subtly it might as well not exist. The growth of government business and the ever expanding state meant that as early as the eighteenth century Anne could not hope to see every document and know every facet of policy as Elizabeth I had done. Although an assiduous desk worker, Victoria was unable to cover the workload that Albert had mastered, while coincidentally, in the course of Victoria's reign, the drive towards universal suffrage – albeit male – meant that politicians increasingly drew their authority from the people, not the sovereign. Once the electorate had spoken in 1880, for example, the Queen could no more keep Disraeli in than Gladstone out. In the same way, in 1940 George VI would have liked Halifax for

Prime Minister rather than Churchill, but he was powerless to achieve it. His daughter, Elizabeth II, would in effect surrender the sovereign's last remaining prerogative to choose a successor to a Prime Minister leaving office while a government was still in power. The process of royal political disempowerment was complete.

A monarch who no longer ruled had to do something. Elizabeth I had found power in an itinerant court and ongoing dialogue with her subjects; Victoria and Albert would take this to new heights. They embarked on an unprecedented number of regional tours, reciprocal royal visits, military reviews and civic engagements. Hospital openings, prison visits, inspections of working-class housing and factories became the norm, setting a standard for future sovereigns and their families to emulate. All this was made possible by the revolution in transport and bolstered by the revolution in the newspaper industry, with the mechanization of production and the invention of photography and the telegraph ensuring them maximum, almost instant, coverage.

Reading about the Queen in the newspaper and looking at her picture became an everyday practice of collective identification with the sovereign a national figurehead and her family everyone's family. Visibility, the expectation that the sovereign must be visibly active, and public demand for value for money, equated with royal services rendered, all reached their apogee in the age of television, which itself received a boost with Elizabeth II's coronation.

'The more democratic we get the more we shall get to like state and show, what have ever pleased the vulgar,' Walter Bagehot predicted in the 1860s. Victoria's successor, Edward VII, was impatient with the drudgery of paperwork; his forte was royal ceremonial. An impotent but venerated monarch was a unifying symbol of permanence in an age of rapid industrial change and when Britain's position as an imperial power was already under threat. Under Edward's aegis, central London was transformed, with the widening of the Mall, the building of Admiralty Arch, the re-fronting of Buckingham Palace, and the construction of the Victoria Memorial, to accommodate a triumphant ceremonial way.

In the wake of the First World War, the British monarchy was one of the few to survive. Now it could be presented as something unique, which the British people could consider peculiarly theirs, their proud heritage.

The coronation of Elizabeth II in 1953 fulfilled several functions. It has been described as 'the last great ceremony successfully conflating monarchy and empire'; indeed, it was the last great imperial occasion. The ancient, Christian ceremony emphasized Britain's long, continuing tradition and political stability, in contrast to the new god of Communism and the Cold War which threatened the world. In postwar Britain, the emphasis on royal ceremonial was also a 'comfortable palliative' to a nation coming to terms with the loss of its world-power status.

Victoria's coronation had been a ramshackle affair. Significantly, at the time of her accession she held more political power than at her demise. As the power of the monarchy waned and its prestige grew, so too did the emphasis on royal ceremonial. No one did it better than the British, everyone agreed at subsequent coronations, royal weddings and funerals. The anachronistic grandeur of royal ceremonial, such as the coronation or the State Opening of Parliament, was emphasized in the age of the motor car by the use of horses, carriages, swords and plumed hats, not to mention the crown and regalia. So vital were these props to the whole mystique of monarchy that at the coronation in 1953 seven extra carriages had to be borrowed from a film company.

All monarchs are dependent on popular approval – no more so than in the present age of media exposure. Victoria, whose popularity dipped and rose in the course of her reign, feared she would be the last sovereign. 'How long will it last, we wonder?' asked the *Pall Mall Gazette* in the week of her 1887 Jubilee. 'As long as the Queen lasts, yes, but after the Queen, who knows.' Victoria would have been surprised and pleased to know that her great-great-granddaughter had taken the thousand-year monarchy into the twenty-first century. Will she be Elizabeth the Last, as one newspaper speculated on her eightieth birthday? Who knows.

Notes

INTRODUCTION

1 'Famous'. Cited in Pimlott, p.180.

1 'The English like'. Charlot, p.26.

1 happy anticipation. Pimlott, pp.33, 41.

2 a deep injury. See Marcus.

3 'I gyve no licence'. Wayne, p.19.

3 'It is a thing'. Knox, p.8.

4 authoritative as . . . male monarch. See Jordan.

4 'and though I am'. Elizabeth I, *Collected Works* (henceforth, *C.W.*), p.97.

5 'If by chance'. Maisse, p.11.

6 'Never any woman'. Bucholz, '"Nothing but Ceremony"', p.292.

6 'All the film'. Cited in Pimlott, p.181.

6 'The Queen is most anxious'. Hardie, *Queen Victoria*, p.140.

7 'I regret exceedingly'. Hibbert, *Queen Victoria in her Letters and Journals* (henceforth, *Journal*), p.126.

7 'We are not'. Hardie, *Queen Victoria*, p.159.

7 'the heart'. *C.W.*, pp.325–6.

7 'an old English'. Doebner, pp.107–9.

7 'As I know'. Gregg, p.152.

8 'I really cannot say'. *Journal*, p.34.

8 'There is a strong idea'. Levin, *Heart and Stomach of a King*, p.49.

8 'To conclude'. *C.W.* p.59.

8 tap into the emotional. See Bell.

8 bejewelled statue. McClure and Headlam Wells, p.64; Hackett, p.7.

8 England's impregnability . . . nation's welfare. Hackett, p.117.

8 'Whilst a female'. Munich, p.9.

9 'I am every day'. Munich, p.190.

9 'richly apparelled'. Carter, p.18.

9 'I think these ladies'. *Journal*, p.113.

9 'I will greatlie'. Knox, p.9.

9 fun in bed. Thompson, p.43.

9 Only Elizabeth II. Turner, pp.46–7.

10 'Queen and mother'. Malfatti, *The Accession*, p.66.

10 'though after my'. *C.W.*, p.72.

10 it 'shall be my endeavour'. Brown, p.232.

10 'There is no jewel'. *C.W.*, pp.335–40.

10 the legacy of childless. See Levin, 'Queens and Claimants'.

10 'sightings'. Ibid.

11 'I know also that'. *C.W.*, p.71.

11 'And for a woman'. *Journal*, p.228.

11 National Federation. Pimlott, p.188.

11 The *Lancet*, Ibid.

Part One: House of Tudor

Abbreviations

C.S. Camden Society

C.S.P. Dom. *Calendar of State Papers, Domestic Series, of the Reigns of Edward VI, Mary and Elizabeth, 1547–1580*

C.W. Elizabeth I, *Collected Works*

H.O. *A Collection of Ordinances and Regulations for the Government of the Royal Household*

L.P. *Letters and Papers, Foreign and Domestic, of the Reign of Henry VIII, 1509–47*

P.P.E. *Princess Mary. Privy Purse Expenses of Princess Mary, daughter of King Henry VIII, afterwards Queen Mary: With a Memoir of the Princess, and Notes*

Sp. Cal. *Calendar of Letters, Despatches and State Papers, relating to the Negotiations between England and Spain*

Ven. Cal. *Calendar of State Papers and Manuscripts, Relating to English Affairs, Existing in the Archives and Collections of Venice*

Mary I

CHAPTER 1: PRINCESS

15 glorious May. Hall, p.582.

16 'God give'. Erickson, p.18.

17 'Had it been a son'. Ibid.

17 deep injury. Marcus, p.403.

18 Katherine regaled. Richards, 'Mary Tudor: Renaissance Queen', pp.35–6.

18 Instructions for Mary's. P.P.E. *Princess Mary*, pp.xli–xlii.

19 gold spangles. Ibid., pp.xxv–xxix.

19 Feast of the Epiphany. Hutton, p.16.

20 'Priest, priest!' Giustinian, p.161.

20 Dressed in cloth of gold. Carter, p.9.

20 slipped the ring. Guistinian, p.225.

21 ladies at the hall. Hall, p.635.

21 'the young princess'. Strickland, Vol.V, p.145.

21 'to use moderate'. Madden, pp.xli–xlii.

22 Katherine herself . . . best educated. For Katherine's education see Richards, 'Mary Tudor: Renaissance Queen', pp.27–43.

22 Vives. See Watson.

22 'a woman is a fraile'. Scaglini, p.61.

22 'I gyve no licence'. Wayne, p.19.

23 'For it shall be'. Crawford, p.177.
24 'her cap and the net'. Erickson, pp.71–2.

CHAPTER 2: BASTARD

26 'Although we have had'. Strickland, p.157.
27 she might go to her daughter. *L.P.*, V, p.238.
28 clothes fit for a princess. Ibid., pp.210–11, 243.
28 christening robe. Eustace Chapuys to Emperor Charles. *Sp. Cal.*, IV, ii, p.756.
29 'give her too much dinner'. Ibid., p.1058.
29 'Am I not a man'. Ibid., p.629.
29 'Have you no message?' Ibid., p.894.
30 forced to dine. Ibid., pp.898–9.
30 leads of the roof. *Sp. Cal.*, V, i, p.4.
31 'even if Mary were only'. *L.P.*, VII, p.214.
31 'the cursed bastard'. *Sp. Cal.*, IV, ii, pp.898–9.
31 Mary haughtily. *L.P.*, VII, p.127.
31 cross the Channel. *L.P.*, X, p.116.
31 they hoped she would die. *L.P.*, VIII, pp.76–7.
31 'She is my death'. Prescott, p.83.
32 A little comfort. Queen Katherine to Cromwell. *L.P.*, VII, p.1126; Everett Wood, p.206.
32 'She is of such high courage'. Plowden, *Tudor Women*, p.67.
32 'for if I have a son'. Prescott, p.88.
32 a last loving. Crawford, pp.179–80.
34 'Nobody dared speak'. *L.P.*, X, p.402.
35 'humbly beseeching'. Ibid., p.424.
35 'most humbly prostrate'. Ibid., p.477.
35 'the utmost my conscience'. Ibid., p.466.
35 Furious, Cromwell. *L.P.*, X, p.467.
35 'without adding or minishing' Ibid., p.474.
35 'the said lady Mary . . . monster'. Ibid., p.422.
36 He would knock. *L.P.*, VI, p.69.
36 Chapuys advised . . . submit. *L.P.*, VII, p.254.
36 'There was nothing . . . conversing'. *Sp. Cal.*, II, p.199.
37 'such a child toward'. *L.P.*, XI, p.55.
37 bespoke wooden chair. Erickson, p.222.
37 Mary's Privy Purse expenses. Listed in *P.P.E. Princess Mary*.
38 'it is not comely for a mayde'. Cited in Wayne, p.23.

CHAPTER 3: REBEL

40 ejecting foul greenish-yellow. Scheyfve to Emperor Charles. *Sp. Cal.*, XI, p.35.
41 he had virtually eradicated. Hutton, p.85.
41 the parish churches. Wriothesley, ii, p.83.
42 'I will see my laws'. *Sp. Cal.*, X, p.212.
42 all ostentatiously sporting. *Diary of Henry Machyn*, pp.4–5.
43 'There are two things'. *Sp. Cal.*, X, pp.212–13.
43 'the Duke of Northumberland . . . went to receive her'. *Sp. Cal.*, XI, p.8.

43 Northumberland 'has found means'. Ibid., XI, p.35.

44 'What shall I do with it?' Plowden, *Lady Jane Grey*, p.80.

45 the baker. Ibid., p.82.

45 Roger Ascham. Williams, p.397.

46 It was obvious. *Sp. Cal.*, XI, p.46.

47 Ostensibly they were to enquire. Ibid., p.63.

49 'sightings' of the boy-King. Levin, 'Queens and Claimants.'

49 she was all for proclaiming. *Sp. Cal.*, XI, p.74.

50 'For whereas I might take upon me'. Statement of Lady Jane Grey to Queen Mary, 1553. Everett Wood, pp.274–9.

51 'Today I saw Lady Jane'. Cited in opening page of Plowden, *Lady Jane Grey*.

51 no one cried 'Long live'. *Sp. Cal.*, XI, p.80.

51 the senior men of her household. For a discussion of the assembling of Mary's Council see Hoak, 'Two Revolutions in Tudor Government'.

52 'to cause our right'. *Sp. Cal.*, XI, pp.82–3; Richards, 'Mary Tudor: Renaissance Queen', p.32.

53 He warned her to 'cease'. *Sp. Cal.*, XI, pp.82–3.

53 'the best manne'. *Chronicle*, p.5.

53 the only intention of the French. Harbison, p.49.

53 'the people press'. *Chronicle*, p.6; Wriothesley, ii, p.87.

53 'We believe that my Lady'. *Sp. Cal.*, XI, p.88.

54 that Mary's 'forces'. *Sp. Cal.*, XI, p.94.

54 'There was such a shout'. *Chronicle*, pp.11–13; Wriothesley, ii, pp.88–9.

54 'Men ran hither'. *Sp. Cal.*, XI, p.108.

55 'to recall that in all her own miseries'. Harbison, p.54.

55 'the English third estate'. Ibid., p.55.

56 '*Vox populi*'. Ibid., p.56.

CHAPTER 4: MARY THE QUEEN

57 Description of Mary. *Ven. Cal.*, V, p.532.

57 'she is a seemly'. Williams, p.398.

57 'a gowne of purple'. Wriothesley, ii, p.93; Carter; Richards, 'Mary Tudor as "Sole Quene"?', p.885.

58 'The queen's grace stayed'. *Chronicle*, p.14.

59 A royal entry. See Smuts, p.78.

59 'full of people shoutinge'. Wriothesley, ii, p.95.

59 'like great thunder'. Ibid.

61 to 'take great care at the outset'. *Sp. Cal.*, XI, pp.110–11.

61 'if she inaugurates'. Ibid., pp.116–17.

61 it forbade 'her subjects'. Williams, V, p.859.

62 The customary ritual. Richards, 'Mary Tudor as "Sole Quene"?', p.895.

62 'a litter decked'. Malfatti, *The Accession*, p.31.

63 Elizabeth followed close. Ibid., p.33.

64 'the Queen kept kneeling'. Ibid., p.34.

64 'Her Majesty ascended'. Strong, *Coronation*, pp.133–5.

65 'a stone chair'. *Sp. Cal.*, XI, p.262.

65 wild boar. Ibid., p.257.

65 Act declaring. An Act Declaring the Queen's Highness to Have Been Born in a Most Just and Lawful Matrimony. St.1 Mary, St. 2c.1, 1553 (Stat. Realm, IV, I, 201), Williams, pp.460–3.

65 allowed Arundel. *Sp. Cal.*, XI, p. 260.

CHAPTER 5: THE SPANISH MARRIAGE

67 Mary's natural advisers. See Hoak, 'Two Revolutions in Tudor Government', p.88.

68 'She is of very spare'. *Ven. Cal.*, V, p.532.

69 'Let her be in all things'. *Sp. Cal.*, XI, pp.110–11.

69 'Your Majesty could but be'. Ibid., p.131.

69 'As for the suggestion of marriage'. Ibid., XI, p.132.

70 she was 'thirty-seven'. Ibid.

70 'entering it by the gallery'. Ibid., p.288.

70 'If he were disposed'. Ibid., p.290.

70 'She would wholly love'. Ibid.

71 'She felt inspired'. Ibid., p.328.

71 Playing on Mary's pride. Ibid., p.364.

72 'it would burden'. Ibid., p.395.

73 'Parliament was not accustomed'. Ibid., p.364. Harbison, p.92.

73 anti-Spanish sentiment. Starkey, *Elizabeth*, p.129.

73 Small boys pelted. *Chronicle*, p.34.

74 'Queen and mother'. Mary's Guildhall speech is cited in Tytler, ii, p.281. Wriothesley, ii, pp.108–9; Malfatti, *The Accession*, p.66.

75 'considered herself his Highness's wife'. *Sp. Cal.*, XII, p.79.

76 The hundred-odd rebels. Harbison, p.136.

CHAPTER 6: EXIT JANE

78 Mary was forced to agree. Malfatti, *The Accession*, p.44.

78 Jane had dressed entirely. *Chronicle*, p.25.

79 'Woe worth him!' Ibid.

80 Jane told Feckenham. Malfatti, *The Accession*, p.44.

80 'Father, although'. Levin, 'Lady Jane Grey', p.101.

81 Guildford Dudley. *Chronicle*, p.55.

81 'sent her word', Malfatti, *The Accession*, p.48.

81 'Good people'. Ibid., p.56.

82 'What shall I do?' Ibid.

82 'Live still to die'. Ibid., p.57.

CHAPTER 7: THE PHANTOM PREGNANCY

83 Philip was bringing. *Sp. Cal.*, XII, p.85.

84 'often subject to'. Williams, p.400.

85 marriage treaty. *Sp. Cal.*, XII, p.287.

85 she metaphorically emasculated. Richards, 'Mary Tudor: Renaissance Queen'.

86 When he read the treaty. Harbison, p.106.

86 'You will send'. *Sp. Cal.*, XI, p.407.

86 'You have not privately'. Everett Wood, p.291.

86 'repayre to the Cittie'. Wriothesley, ii, p.118.

87 'He went straight'. *Chronicle*, p.140.

87 Philip's meeting with Mary is described in Malfatti, *The Accession*, pp.83–4.

87 'Good night'. *Chronicle*, p.140.

88 'The Queen is a very'. *Sp. Cal.*, XIII, p.2.

88 'To speak frankly'. *Chronicle*, p.140.

88 'The Queen, however'. *Sp. Cal.*, XIII, p.31.

88 'if she dressed'. Ibid., XIII, p.2

88 'The Queen is a good soul'. Ibid., p.35.

88 'her tailor'. Malfatti, *The Accession*, p.86.

88 'Interest is a powerful'. *Sp. Cal.*, XIII, p.2.

89 Like a queen consort. Richards, 'Mary Tudor as "Sole Quene"?' p.895.

89 'went forth with'. Malfatti, *The Accession*, p.86.

89 'she had her hair'. Ibid., pp.83–4.

89 Just as her mother. Starkey, *Six Wives*, p.59.

90 a simple gold band. *Chronicle*, p.141.

90 worldly goods. Richards, 'Mary Tudor as "Sole Quene"?' p.895.

90 the 'King went up . . . altar'. The wedding is described in *Sp. Cal.*, XIII, pp.10–11.

90 'Philip and Marie'. *Chronicle*, p.142.

91 'They are neither beautiful'. *Sp. Cal.*, XIII, p.31.

91 'What happened that night'. Malfatti, *The Accession*, p.88.

91 Philip's Spanish entourage. Ibid.

91 'This match'. *Sp. Cal.*, XIII, p.31.

91 'He treats the Queen'. Ibid., p.26.

92 unfitted for the task. Harbison, p.196.

92 Philip had no image. Loades, 'Philip II', p.192.

92 'The English hate'. *Sp. Cal.*, XIII, p.31.

93 'If it is true'. Ibid.

93 'The Queen is with child'. Ibid.

93 'A year has passed'. Ibid., p.53.

93 'Affairs are not settled'. *Sp. Cal.*, XII, p.125.

93 'There is no doubt'. *Sp. Cal.*, XIII, p.78.

94 'she is fatter'. Ibid., p.85.

94 phantom pregnancy. See Maclennan.

94 'And see how'. Richards, '"To Promote a Woman"', p.114.

95 'If it please the Queene'. *H.O.*, p.125.

95 A vast gathering of ladies. Maclennan, p.70; *Ven. Cal.*, VI, i, p.147.

95 'by private stairs'. Ibid., p.61.

96 Giovanni Michiel. Ibid., p.57.

96 'On the last day'. Ibid., p.60.

96 'Everything in this kingdom'. *Sp. Cal.*, XIII, p.51.

96 'one single hour's'. *Ven. Cal.*, VI, i, p.93.

96 'It is almost incredible'. *Sp. Cal.*, XIII, p.224.

96 Frideswide Strelly. *Ven. Cal.*, VI, i, pp.147–8.

97 drop down on a cushion. Erickson, p.415.

97 'is now unaccountably'. *Ven. Cal.*, VI, i, p.140.

97 'the pregnancy will end'. Ibid., p.148.

97 same dynastic marriage trap. See Marcus.
98 phantom pregnancy. For an explanation of pseudo (false), kyesis (pregnancy), see Brown and Barglow.
98 'As may be imagined'. *Ven. Cal.*, VI, i, p.174.
99 'she gave free vent'. Ibid., p.178.

CHAPTER 8: THE BURNINGS
101 Pole received the submission. *Sp. Cal.*, XIII, p.107.
102 'I cannot burn'. Ridley, *Bloody Mary's Martyrs*, p.118.
102 'Sire: the people'. *Sp. Cal.*, XIII, p.147.

CHAPTER 9: THE LEGACY
106 'In the name of God'. Mary's will is cited in Loades, *Mary Tudor*, Appendix 3, pp.370–87.
108 'many little children'. Henry Clifford, p.70.
108 the Catholic Queen. Ibid., p.71.
108 'The Calais question'. *Sp. Cal.*, XIII, p.437.
109 'nothing but mere'. Ibid., p.271.
109 'that she has been seen'. Erickson, p.447.
110 rarely went on progress. Henry Clifford, p.64.
110 ceremonial duties. Robinson, pp.25–6, 29–31.
110 'I am not moved'. *Sp. Cal.*, XIII, p.271.
111 'the Queen's desire'. Ibid., p.290.
111 summoning individual. Harbison, p.326.
111 'A woman is never'. *Sp. Cal.*, XIII, p.248.
111 'Not that only . . . Calais'. Erickson, p.479.
112 'in which you send me news'. *Sp. Cal.*, XIII, p.340.
112 'The one thing'. Ibid., p.367.
112 she 'now realized'. Ibid., p.379.
113 reign ended in sterility. Harbison, p.332.
113 Mary's reputation. See John King, 'Fiction and Fact', and Haller.
113 'Be of good comfort'. Cited in John King, 'Fiction and Fact', p.15.
114 the cruel practices'. Ibid., p.26.
115 'the horrible and bloudy'. Foxe, 1563 edn, p.889.
115 'by calling to his mercy'. Rowse, 'Accession of Queen Elizabeth I', p.297.
116 John Knox. Knox, p.12.

Elizabeth I

CHAPTER 10: THE LITTLE BASTARD
121 'to the great disappointment'. Mumby, p.3.
122 The Lord Mayor. The christening is described in Nichols, I, pp.1–2; Hall, pp.242–4.
122 'God of his infinite'. Cited in Starkey, *Six Wives*, p.510.
123 little caps of purple. Arnold, *Queen Elizabeth's Wardrobe*, p.3.
123 'his little bastard'. *L.P.*, X, p.51.
123 clad in yellow. Ibid.

124 her mother allegedly. Alexander Ales to Queen Elizabeth. *Calendar of State Papers, Foreign Series, of the Reign of Elizabeth*, 1303, p.527.

124 'neither potency'. *L.P.*, X, pp.374, 378.

125 'my lady Elizabeth is put'. Mumby, pp.16–18; *L.P.*, VIII, pp.172–3.

127 maleness. See Taylor-Smith, p.52.

127 'If she be no worse'. Starkey, *Elizabeth*, p.26.

127 'we are more bound'. *C.W.*, p.34.

129 It was almost certainly . . . eaten with him. Starkey, *Elizabeth*, p.30.

129 'She prides'. *Ven. Cal.*, VI, ii, p.1059.

129 'void'. Starkey, *Elizabeth*, p.49.

130 evidence of the handwriting. Ibid.

130 'which I know in many places'. Princess Elizabeth to Queen Katherine. *C.W.*, pp.6–7.

130 'To the most illustrious'. *C.W.*, pp.9–10.

131 'May I . . . be indebted'. Ibid.

CHAPTER 11: THE AFFAIR

133 'For the face'. *C.W.* p.35; Arnold, *Queen Elizabeth's Wardrobe*, p.18.

134 Elizabeth replied. Mumby, pp.32–3.

134 'Kat Aschlye tolde'. Sheila Cavanagh, 'The Bad Seed', p.10.

135 'He wold come'. Mumby, p.34.

137 'Although I could not'. *C.W.*, p.17.

138 'You may have him'. Ibid., p.25.

138 'When that comes'. Mumby, p.46.

138 'She hath a very good wit'. Strickland, IV, p.35.

138 When Sir Anthony Denny. Starkey, *Elizabeth*, pp.79–80.

139 'And as concerning Kat'. *C.W.*, pp.22–4.

139 'Master Tyrwhit and others'. Ibid.; Perry, pp.60–2.

139 'breeding of an evil'. Perry, p.63.

140 'because that she hath been'. Ibid., pp.64–5.

140 'it shall and doth'. Ibid.

141 'she read the orations'. Strickland, IV, pp.50–1.

141 'with respect to personal'. Ibid.

141 for the whole of Edward's. Arnold, *Queen Elizabeth's Wardrobe*, p.4; Strickland, IV, pp.54–5.

141 'with their hair'. Perry, p.72.

142 'with a great suite'. Ibid., p.69.

143 'but the best is'. Ibid., p.77.

144 an escort of 2,000. Ibid., p.83.

CHAPTER 12: THE SUSPECT

145 Kneeling before her. *Sp. Cal.*, XI, p.220.

145 'all the way to the church'. Strickland, IV, p.64; *Sp. Cal.*, XI, p.220.

146 'it would burden her conscience'. *Sp. Cal.*, XI, p.395.

147 'she very courteously'. Ibid., p.418.

147 'not to believe anyone'. Ibid.

147 'There is no persuading'. Ibid.

147 'ornaments for'. Ibid., p.440.

148 Mary had written. Mumby, p.99.

148 two of the royal. *Sp. Cal.*, XII, p.125.

148 'her countenance'. Ibid.

149 Elizabeth was not permitted. *Sp. Cal.*, XII, p.125.

149 'that she did thank'. *Chronicle*, pp.68–70.

149 Arms and provisions. Starkey, *Elizabeth*, p.126.

149 'that a king's word'. *C.W.*, pp.41–2; Perry, p.93.

150 Elizabeth Sandes. Freeman, p.109.

151 'Oh Lord! . . . yt needed not'. *Chronicle*, pp.70–1.

151 Elizabeth did not enter. Starkey, *Elizabeth*, p.143.

151 'she was a kinges'. Cited in Starkey, *Elizabeth*, p.144.

151 At first Elizabeth feigned. Starkey, p.145.

152 There is a pretty. Perry, p.97.

152 'This night I think'. Cited in Starkey, *Elizabeth*, p.150.

152 gifts of cakes. Perry, p.98.

154 'has contrived to ingratiate'. *Ven. Cal.*, VI, i, p.57.

154 Dudley–Ashton. Starkey, *Elizabeth*, pp.194–202.

155 Elizabeth contemplated leaving. Ibid., p.211.

156 When she moaned. Ibid., pp.224–5.

156 'we laughed . . . She is a very vain'. Perry, p.125.

157 The men he guessed. Ibid.

158 'My lords, the law of nature'. Harington, I, pp.66–7; *C.W.*, pp.51–2; Perry, pp.129–30.

CHAPTER 13: QUEEN

159 The first official act. Starkey, *Elizabeth*, pp.252–4, 257–8.

159 'Mary's accession speech' – and comparisons with Elizabeth's. See Richards, 'Love and the Female Monarch'.

160 'I give you this charge'. *C.W.*, p.51; Harington, I, p.68.

161 'to have more natural . . . multitude'. *C.W.*, p.3.

162 she 'seems to me incomparably'. Mumby, p.274.

162 'We princes are set'. *C.W.*, p.189.

163 'to succeed happily'. Cited in Starkey, *Elizabeth*, p.249.

163 the Queen stood up. Perry, p.132.

163 Elizabeth consulted the astrologer. Starkey, *Elizabeth*, p.265.

163–7 Richard Mulcaster's Account of Queen Elizabeth's Speech and Prayer During Her Passage Through London to Westminster the Day Before her Coronation, January 14, 1559, *C.W.*, pp.53–5.

164 'fyne payntynge'. Hoak, 'The Coronations', p.125.

164 props from the Great Wardrobe. Ibid.

165 the new monarch . . . east to west. See Warkentin.

165 'The whole court'. Hoak, 'The Coronations', p.131.

166 actors in a theatrical spectacle. Hackett, p.47.

166 to particular individuals. Hoak, 'The Coronations', p.135.

170 sensitive to strong. See Matthews.

170 'very cheerfully'. *Ven. Cal.*, VII, p.17; Rowse, 'The Coronation of Elizabeth I', p.303.

170 Lord Howard. *Ven. Cal.*, VII, p.18.

171 'Away with'. Mumby, p.311.

173 There was only one Jesus. Maisse, p.57.

174 personal book of prayers. See Haugaard.

CHAPTER 14: FOR A WOMAN TO BEAR RULE

175 use of rhetoric. See Green.

175 God's choice of a weak. Hoak, 'A Tudor Deborah?', p.77.

176 'God's Creature'. *C.W.*, p.52.

176 'Shall I ascribe'. Ibid., p.204.

176 the king's two bodies. Hackett, p.40.

176 'And as I am but'. *C.W.*, p.52.

177 'I care not for death'. Ibid., p.97.

177 'I thank God'. Ibid., p.97.

177 'defect' of her womanhood. Marcus, p.410.

177 'the body but of a weak'. *C.W.*, pp.325–6.

177 sets herself apart . . . careful to 'disable'. See Heisch.

177 'The weight'. *C.W.*, p.70.

178 the language of kingship. Marcus, p.411.

178 'To be a King'. *C.W.*, p.339.

178 she found power. Cole, p.5.

179 Groom of the Stool. Starkey, 'Representation Through Intimacy'.

180 'When the Queen'. Maisse, p.35.

182 receiving them into the Privy Chamber. Elizabeth's relationship with the nobility is discussed in Bell.

182 'she was both king'. Johnson, p.111.

CHAPTER 15: ONE MISTRESS AND NO MASTER

183 'For that she should'. Hackett, p.73.

183 'to remayne in that estate'. Ibid., p.52.

183 marriage 'is a thing'. Levin, *Heart and Stomach of a King*, p.49.

184 'happily chose'. *C.W.*, pp.56–8.

184 He who has 'preserved'. Ibid.

184 destitute of 'an heir'. Hackett, p.53.

184 'To conclude'. *C.W.*, p.59.

184 'Once I am married'. Ibid., p.65.

185 'to do nothing'. Ibid., p.57.

186 Elizabeth was intent. Marcus, pp.400–17.

186 Anne Twiste. Arnold, *Queen Elizabeth's Wardrobe*, p.105.

186 irregular menstrual. Levin, *Heart and Stomach of a King*, p.33; Jenkins, *Elizabeth and Leicester*, p.60.

186 nephritis. Maclennan, pp.70–1.

186 'She is vain'. Jenkins, *Elizabeth and Leicester*, p.142.

189 Kat Ashley begged. Perry, p.159.

189 advanced stages of. Aird, pp.75–6.

190 death was an accident. Ibid.

190 Cecil's part. Perry, p.159; Jenkins, *Elizabeth and Leicester*, pp.73–5.

190 'The Queen of England'. Jenkins, *Elizabeth and Leicester*, p.84.
191 she tickled his neck. Melville, p.92.
191 'God's death'. Jenkins, *Elizabeth and Leicester*, p.158.
192 'Nothing is increased'. Doran, 'Why Did Elizabeth Not Marry?', p.43.
193 'I stood in danger'. *C.W.*, p.96.
193 'I am your anointed'. Ibid., p.97.
197 'she danced'. Ross, p.176.
197 *I grieve. C.W.*, pp.302–3.

CHAPTER 16: TWO QUEENS IN ONE ISLE
199 'Howsoever it be'. *C.W.*, p.65.
199 'I know the inconstancy'. Ibid., p.66.
199 'No prince's revenues'. Ibid.
199 'And what danger'. Ibid.
200 'she was the fairest'. Melville, pp. 95–7.
201 'yonder long'. Ibid., p.92.
201 'no woman of spirit'. Ibid.
201 'I had secret'. Ibid.
201 'the lustiest'. Melville, p.107.
203 'I will that you do nothing'. Marshall, p.132.
203 'in great mirth'. Melville, p.131.
204 'Jesu, Paris'. Marshall, p.144.
204 'Pity me'. Ibid., p.147.
205 'My ears have been'. *C.W.*, pp.116–17.
206 'And then the Queen'. Melville, p.149.
206 'Madam, to be plain'. *C.W.*, p.118.
207 'Burn the whore!' Marshall, p.160.
207 'For which purpose'. *C.W.*, pp.117–19.
209 condemned without trial. Ibid., p.189.
211 'As a sinner'. Marshall, p.19.
211 'Princes, you know'. *C.W.*, p.189.
211 'since now it is resolved' Ibid., p.201.
211 'Yea, I protest'. Ibid., p.202.
211 'I shall pray you'. Ibid., pp.199–200.
212 'God forbid'. Marshall, p.200.
212 'the miserable accident'. *C.W.*, p.296.

CHAPTER 17: THE IMAGE OF THE QUEEN
214 power behind . . . wife-mother. See Heisch.
214 'though after my death'. *C.W.*, p.72.
214 progress to Norwich. Hackett, p.4.
216 Queen's birthday. Hackett, p.83; McClure and Headlam Wells, pp.63–4.
217 The jewel-encrusted. Frances Yates cited in Hackett, p.7.
217 'Hail Mary!' See Levin, 'Power, Politics and Sexuality'.
217 The royal wardrobe . . . state treasure. Arnold, *Queen Elizabeth's Wardrobe*, p.1.
217 Elizabeth . . . tailors. Ibid., pp.18, 115.
218 One of her ladies. Ibid., p.11.

220 virginity was powerful. Ibid., p.117.

220 the Queen's virginity . . . impregnability. Ibid.

220 The more precarious. Hackett, p.180; Belsey and Belsey, p.35.

221 Sieve portrait. Belsey and Belsey, p.35.

221 Kenilworth. Berry, p.66.

222 renewed 'sightings'. Levin, 'Queens and Claimants', p.41.

CHAPTER 18: ELIZA TRIUMPHANS

224 The defeat of the Spanish Armada. For a detailed description of the use of naval tactics and the winds and tides, see Hanson.

227 'My loving'. *C.W.*, pp.325–6.

227 Marvellous, rousing words. See Green.

228 *Cabala*. Frye, 'The Myth of Elizabeth', p.97.

229 It is salutary. Hanson, p.346.

229 The Queen was to be . . . unified political power. Frye, 'The Myth of Elizabeth', pp.107, 114.

230 The attack on England . . . rape. Ibid., p.107.

230 three extant Armada portraits. Ibid.; Belsey and Belsey, pp.11–35.

CHAPTER 19: THE SETTING SUN

232 she would constantly speak. Maisse, p.38.

233 'kept his arithmetic'. Cited in Somerset, p.555.

233 Lady Mary Howard. Harington, i, p.235; Arnold, *Queen Elizabeth's Wardrobe*, p.104.

233 'she preserves a great gravity'. Maisse, p.83.

233 'Her air was stately'. Arnold, *Queen Elizabeth's Wardrobe*, p.10; Rye, p.104.

234 'She was strangely attired'. Maisse, p.25.

234 'Men do adore'. *C.W.*, p.66.

234 the voices of reluctant. Cole, pp.89–93.

235 'my estate without'. Lee to Cecil cited in Cole, p.90.

235 'the Queen is troubled'. Somerset, p.490.

235 'if by chance she'. Maisse, p.11.

236 'When she is abroad'. Somerset, p.470.

238 'seek all England . . . solicitor'. Ibid., p.504.

238 'I have discovered'. Ibid.

239 'they laboured under'. Hackett, p.181.

240 even at the hands of Henry VIII. Somerset, p.518.

240 'sue, yield and submit'. Ibid.

240 'cannot princes err?' Hackett, p.181.

241 'You have prospered so ill'. Harington, pp.305–6.

241 Elizabeth 'newly up'. Somerset, p.534.

242 the Irish were laughing. Ibid., p.535.

242 'kiss her fair'. Somerset, p.537.

242 'The madcaps'. Harington, i, pp.317–19.

243 'I am Richard II'. Axton, p.2.

244 'I do see the Queen'. Harington, i, pp.314–16.

244 'The Queen smiled'. Ibid.

244 'There is no jewel'. Golden Speech, *C.W.*, pp.335–40.
245 'lively wit'. Somerset, p.566.
245 'When thou dost'. Perry, p.317.
245 'Little man'. Ibid.
245 'mildly like a lamb'. Manningham, p.146.
246 disgracefully neglected. Somerset, p.569.

Part Two: House of Stuart

Mary II

CHAPTER 20: PRINCESS OF ORANGE

250 Duke's whore. Edward Clarendon, Vol. 1, pp.377–81.
250 taken physick. Elizabeth, Queen of Bohemia, p.331.
251 the Duke's pimps. Pepys, Vol.III, p.419.
251 'just like an ordinary'. Ibid., Vol.II, p.471.
252 'a little child in hanging sleeves'. Ibid., Vol.IV, p.143.
252 venereal disease. Burnet, *History*, p.254.
253 'That she would'. Coke, Vol.III, p.116.
253 A courtier. Anthony Hamilton, p.329.
253 'Truth'. Burnet, *History*, p.207.
253 'it was much against'. Clarke, Vol.I, p.503.
254 'If I had any nuse'. Bathurst Papers, BL Loan 57/69 719B, 76.
254 patriarchal world. Zook, p.187.
254 'all covered'. Evelyn, Vol.II, p.99.
254 'Why dear cruel'. Bathurst, p.38.
255 'a new playfellow'. Russell, *Some Account of the Life*, p.7.
255 'Who can imagin'. Bathurst Papers, BL Loan 57/69, 168–9, p.51.
255 'be content'. Bathurst Papers, BL Loan 57/69 719B, 173; Bathurst, p.66.
257 'she wept'. Lake, p.1.
258 'Gather it up'. Lake, p.6.
260 light chatter. Anon, *Royal Diary*, p.50.
260 'the princess was'. Lake, p.22.
260 'a very tender parting'. Henry Clarendon, Vol.I, pp.11–12.
261 'I suppose you know'. Bathurst, pp.88–9.
261 'pray let her'. Dalrymple, Vol.II, Appendices p.155.
261 'so satisfied'. Ibid., p.202.
262 'had spent the nine'. Haile, p.82.

CHAPTER 21: UNNATURAL DAUGHTER

264 'The only thing'. Zee, p.209.
265 'I have found nothing'. Bowen, p.116.
265 'It gave me'. Burnet, *History*, pp.458–60.
266 'she did not know'. Ibid., p.140.
266 'I rendered thanks'. Bowen, p.117.
266 'This it has pleased'. Ibid.

266 'Besides the interest'. Ibid.

267 Mary decided to place. Ibid., p.118.

267 Anne gave or withheld her presence. Bucholz, 'Queen Anne', pp.110–11.

268 'We must presume'. Dalrymple, Vol.II, Appendices, Appendix Part I, p.231.

269 'never once'. Haile, p.192.

269 'This evening'. Strickland, Vol.VII, p.146.

269 'I am much put'. Haile, p.197.

269 'The consideration'. Baxter, p.227.

270 'for I cannot talk'. Bowen, p.126.

270 'And though I know'. Strickland, Vol.X, p.378.

270 'as if someone'. Zee, p.249.

270 'I assured him'. Ibid.

271 'What God intends'. Ibid.

271 cards and dancing. Doebner, p.5.

271 'Yet when I saw'. Ibid.

271 'the thought that'. Ibid.

CHAPTER 22: SOVEREIGN AND CONSORT

272 hand in hand. Schwoerer, pp.728–9.

272 'She came into Whitehall'. Evelyn, Vol.II, pp.289–90.

273 'She ran about it'. Marlborough, p.19.

273 'She rose early'. Evelyn, Vol.II, pp.289–90.

273 'put on a cheerfulness'. Burnet, *History*, p.523.

273 'only for a Regency'. Doebner, p.5.

274 François Poulain de la Barre, etc. See Schwoerer.

275 'gloriously'. Ibid., p.727.

275 'chuse a King'. Ibid.

275 Burnet even argued. Ibid.

276 'gentleman usher'. Speck, p.108; Strickland, Vol. X, p.414.

276 coronation ceremony . . . subtle details. Schwoerer, pp.729–30.

276 medals cast. Ibid., p.730.

277 'At night'. Strickland, Vol.X, p.414.

277 'She smiled'. Evelyn, Vol.II, p.289.

277 'a noisy world'. Doebner, p.11.

278 'Tell your princess'. Clarke, Vol.II (1816), p.270.

278 'I found myself'. Doebner, p.14.

278 'on no higher'. Chapman, p.183.

278 A 'Moll'. Zook, p.172.

279 'Female Parricide'. Ibid., p.172.

279 'In all this'. Doebner, p.45.

280 'I must tell you'. Marlborough, *Memoirs*, pp.31–4.

280 'women should not meddle'. Doebner, pp.22–3.

280 'a woman is but'. Ibid., pp.107–9.

281 'I ever fear'. Ibid., p.30.

282 'I must grin'. Bowen, p.222.

282 'I know I need not beg'. Ibid., p.200.

282 'he who I dare no'. Doebner, p.54.

283 'Will should have knotted'. Chapman, p.236.

284 'I thank you'. Schwoerer, p.740.

284 she did not 'reign'. Zook, p.176.

284 'never affected'. Ibid.

285 resembled Het Loo. Janssens-Knorsch, p.277.

285 Daniel Defoe. Chapman, p.345.

285 Daniel Marot. Janssens-Knorsch, p.285.

286 'to see so little'. Doebner, p.11.

287 Her account books. Queen Mary's Account Book, 1678–89, in the Royal Library, Windsor (RC IN 1142245) and The Household Book of Queen Mary II, the Royal Archives, Windsor (RA EB 13).

287 'during the whole course'. Burnet, *History*, p.606.

288 'The news will have'. Haile, p.310.

Anne

CHAPTER 23: LADY ANNE

293 'I am very glad'. Bryant, p.181.

295 'two braceletts'. Gregg, p.9.

296 'I abhor'. Brown, p.16.

296 'ignorant of everything'. Marlborough, *Correspondence*, Vol.II, p.146.

297 'I am not one'. Brown, p.6.

297 marrying . . . George of Hanover. Russell, *Some Account of the Life*, pp.44–5.

298 'had the Danish'. Evelyn, Vol.II, p.184.

298 'We talk here'. Bucholz, *The Augustan Court*, p.17.

299 'The Duke of York'. Brown, p.12.

299 'My frank'. Marlborough, *Memoirs*, pp.10–11.

299 'I believe you'. Bathurst, p.180.

299 the Jesuits. Gregg, p.37.

CHAPTER 24: THE CONSPIRATOR

300 'I am of your opinion'. Brown, p.17.

301 'I have always forgot'. Ibid., p.22.

301 'The good Princess'. Russell, *Letters*, p.103.

302 'to suffer'. Letter from John Churchill to Prince William of Orange, 17 May 1687, cited in Gregg, p.49.

302 'Pray don't'. Brown, p.27.

303 'I must tell you'. Ibid., p.34.

303 'the rumour'. Henry Clarendon, Vol.II, p.169.

303 'pressed her to go'. Burnet, *History*, p.477.

304 'Madam, I think'. Clarke, Vol.II, p.329.

304 'My dear sister'. Brown, pp.37–8.

305 'he would debar'. Clarke, Vol.II, pp.193, 202.

305 'depose her own'. Ibid., p.202.

305 Clarendon. Henry Clarendon, Vol.II, p.196.

305 'My lords'. Ibid., p.199; Clarke, Vol.II, p.202.

306 'Never was anyone'. Brown, p.44.

306 Sarah Churchill denied. Marlborough, *Memoirs*, p.14.
307 'I shall not trouble'. Brown, p.44.
307 'I have nothing'. Ibid., p.45.
307 'Nor did she think'. Marlborough, *Memoirs*, p.13.
308 'My own children'. Zee, p.258.
308 'King James was'. Strickland, Vol.VII, p.179.
308 'Can you think'. Brown, p.60.
309 'the same respect'. Marlborough, *Memoirs*, p.73.
309 'I have been'. Brown, p.52.
309 James rightly decided. Gregg, p.84.
310 acute infection. Dewhurst, p.40.
310 ten further pregnancies. Ibid., p.44.
312 'Some days before'. Haile, p.356.

CHAPTER 25: GOOD QUEEN ANNE
313 'As I know'. Gregg, p.152; Strickland, Vol.XII, p.40.
313 'Never any woman'. Bucholz, '"Nothing but Ceremony"', p.292.
314 'As for your'. Brown, p.125.
315 royal ritual. For the revival of royal ritual and ceremony see Bucholz, '"Nothing but Ceremony"', pp.288–323.
317 'There are now'. Ibid., p.298.
317 'I desire you would'. Brown, p.185.
317 'As long'. Anne to Godolphin, 1 May 1705, Ibid., p.232.
317 She 'rules a willing'. Bucholz, 'Queen Anne', p.100.
318 to 'be Queen of'. Ibid.
318 'ye Mercyless men'. Gregg, p.134.
318 'it has not been my fault'. Ibid., p.273.
319 'I beg my dear'. Ibid., p.173.
319 Anne 'wou'd not'. Bucholz, 'Queen Anne', p.112.
319 'I own I can'. Brown, pp.227–8.
320 'I must own'. Ibid., p.129.
320 'I can't forbear'. Ibid.
321 'he should do as'. Bucholz, 'Queen Anne', p.112.
321 'Whoever of the Whigs'. Ibid.
321 'All I desire'. Anne to Godolphin, 30 August 1706, Brown, pp.196–7.
322 'no more resentments'. Marlborough, *Memoirs*, p.155.
322 so lame that. Brown, p.127.
322 'Her Majesty'. Clerk, p.62.
323 'The poor lady'. Ibid., p.72.
323 'she laid down'. Lack of opportunities at court discussed in Bucholz, 'Queen Anne', p.100.
324 'hunting the stag'. Swift, *Swift's Journal*, p.219.
324 *When as Queen Anne*. Gregg, p.275.
325 'I remember you said'. Ibid.
325 'I believe no body'. Anne to Marlborough, 25 October 1709, Brown, pp.285–6.
326 'I can't help'. Gregg, p.302.

326 'when people are fond'. Sir David Hamilton, p.12.

327 'she would not build'. Gregg, p.329.

327 'is of the first quality'. Sir David Hamilton, p.38.

327 'the Pretender'. Ibid., p.44.

328 'I believe sleep'. Dr Arbuthnot to Jonathan Swift, 12 August 1714, Swif, *Correspondence*, Vol.II, p.122.

328 nostalgia for the days of 'Good Queen Anne'. Bucholz, 'Queen Anne', p.104.

Part Three: House of Hanover

Abbreviations

Journal. Christopher Hibbert, *Queen Victoria in her Letters and Journals*

Girlhood. Viscount Esher, *The Girlhood of Queen Victoria: A Selection from Her Majesty's Diaries 1832–40*

Letters. Queen Victoria, *The Letters of Queen Victoria,* First Series, 1837–61

Dearest Child. Roger Fulford, *Dearest Child: Letters Between Queen Victoria and the Princess Royal 1858–61*

Dearest Mama. Roger Fulford, *Dearest Mama: Letters Between Queen Victoria and the Crown Princess of Prussia 1861–64*

Your Dear Letter. Private Correspondence of Queen Victoria and the Crown Princess of Prussia 1865–71, edited by Roger Fulford (Evans Brothers, 1971)

Greville. The Greville Memoirs

Victoria

CHAPTER 26: KENSINGTON GIRL

332 'a pretty little'. Stockmar, Vol.1, p.50.

333 'As for the payment'. Cited in Charlot, p.20.

334 'Look at her'. Longford, *Victoria*, p.29.

336 'I never had a room'. Disraeli, Vol.1, p.309.

336 'I had led a very unhappy'. *Dearest Child*, p.111.

336 'I love him so'. Charlot, p.79.

337 'father, my protector'. *Dearest Child*, pp.111–12.

337 'No lady, and still less'. *Journal*, p.107.

337 crawling on a yellow. *Journal*, p.9.

337 'My dear little heart'. Charlot, p.58.

338 'You must not touch'. Longford, *Victoria*, p.33.

338 Lord Albemarle. Charlot, p.53.

338 'When we arrived'. *Journal*, p.10.

338 'Pop her in!' Ibid.

340 'extract about Queen Anne'. *Letters*, Vol.1, p.50.

340 'I see I am nearer'. Cited in Charlot, p.51.

340 'an accurate knowledge'. Ibid., p.50.

340 the plainness of the English. Ibid., p.51.

340 'Good heavens!' Thompson, p.93.

342 witnessing 'familiarities'. Charlot, p.55.
342 'I must tell you dearest'. Ibid., p.66.
343 'always on pins'. *Dearest Child*, p.72.
343 'I know the interest'. Charlot, p.67.
344 'I trust God'. *Greville*, p.113.
344 'Victoria has not'. Charlot, p.69.
344 a vow . . . to study. *Journal*, p.21.
345 'The courtyards'. Ibid.

CHAPTER 27: VICTORIA REGINA
346 'Since it has pleased'. *Journal*, p.23.
347 'The moment you get'. *Letters*, Vol.1, p.93.
347 'in my room'. *Journal*, p.23.
347 'He is a very honest'. Ibid., p.24.
347 'It is become his province'. Charlot, p.98.
347 her feelings for Melbourne. *Greville*, p.156.
348 'such jealous'. Ibid., p.116.
348 'There never was anything'. Ibid., p.118.
348 'I place my firm'. Charlot, p.83.
349 her 'perfect calmness'. *Greville*, p.119.
349 'your immediate successor'. Thompson, p.25.
349 'rather bewildered'. *Greville*, pp.118–19.
349 'an imbecile'. Cannadine, '"The Last Hanoverian Sovereign?"', p.130.
350 'Reginamania'. Plunkett, p.113.
350 'I am an experienced man'. Ibid., p.20.
350 'My object'. *Letters*, Vol.1, p.91.
351 'Monarchy to be'. Ibid., p.134.
352 'The best plan'. Ibid., pp.103–4.
352 'All I want'. Charlot, p.114.
353 'Take care Victoria'. Ibid., p.91.
353 'take no situation'. *Letters*, Vol.1, p.99.
354 'She has great'. *Greville*, p.133.
354 'I can assure'. Letters, Vol, 1, p.104
354 'no pretension to beauty'. *Greville*, p.120.
354 'A more homely'. Thompson, p.44.
354 One of her biographers. Lytton Strachey.
354 'The whole went off'. *Journal*, p.35.
355 less fulsome . . . industrial North. Plunkett, p.27.
355 'It was a fine'. *Journal*, p.34.
356 Lord Rolle. Ibid.
356 'You did it.' Ibid., p.35.
357 'Lady Flora'. Ibid., p.41.
357 'I found Lady'. Ibid., p.43.
358 'Nobody cares for the Queen'. Strachey, p.71.
358 'The state of agony'. *Journal*, p.45.
358 she sobbed and grasped. Ibid., p.46.
358 'The Queen ventures'. Ibid.

359 'Your Majesty better'. Ibid.
359 'I cannot give up'. Ibid., p.48.
359 'The Queen writes'. Ibid., p.49.
359 'Lord Melbourne must'. Ibid.
360 'Was Sir Robert so weak'. Strachey, p.76.
360 'It is a high trial'. *Greville*, p.155.
361 '*She* might be'. Ibid., p.157.
361 'it would be to impair'. Ibid., p.160.

CHAPTER 28: WIFE, MOTHER AND QUEEN

363 Benjamin Disraeli. Hardie, p.32.
363 'I must thank you'. *Journal*, p.18.
364 'I said, why need I'. *Journal*, p.52.
364 'Cousins are not'. Ibid.
364 'First of all'. *Letters*, Vol.1, pp.223–4.
365 'It was with some emotion'. *Journal*, p.55.
365 'tight cazimere'. Longford, p.167.
365 'much more comfortable'. *Journal*, p.57.
365 'Since the Queen'. Ibid., p.63.
365 fell into each other's arms. *Journal*, pp.57–8.
365 'be always near you'. Ibid.
366 'Oh! To feel'. Ibid.
366 'I signed some'. Ibid., p.58.
366 'Think of my position'. Charlot, p.180.
367 'It is, as you rightly', *Journal*, p.60.
367 'As to your wish'. Ibid.
367 'Now, though'. *Letters*, Vol.1, p.252.
367 'For God's sake'. Weintraub, p.133.
368 'England's fat queen'. Thompson, p.34.
368 'Party spirit'. Ibid., p.36.
369 'Monsters!' Weintraub, p.134.
369 'I wore a white'. *Journal*, p.63.
369 'I felt so happy'. Ibid.
370 'You forget, dearest'. *Journal*, p.62.
370 She had refused to play. Plunkett, pp.32–3.
370 'had such a sick'. *Journal*, p.64.
370 'When day dawned'. Ibid.
371 a fecund German stud. Plunkett, p.32.
372 'Her life has had'. Williams, p.145.
373 marriage was a lottery. *Dearest Child*, p.254.
374 'One becomes so worn'. Ibid., p.195.
374 'she will be very ugly'. Longford, 'Queen Victoria's Doctors', p.76.
374 fun in bed. Thompson, p.43.
374 'What you say'. *Dearest Child*, p.115.
374 'I positively think'. Ibid., p.195.
375 while Victoria had the title. *Greville*, p.223.
375 'I am every day'. Munich, p.190.

375 'If we are good'. *Journal*, p.89.

375 never put on a bonnet. *Dearest Mama*, p.23; Munich, p.68.

376 'an old woman'. Surtees, p.115.

377 a massive white silk. Munich, p.67.

377 'an ugly baby'. *Journal*, p.112.

379 'It is indeed'. David Cannadine, '"The Last Hanoverian Sovereign?"', p.147.

CHAPTER 29: THE DUAL MONARCHY

381 'Why, when one is'. Weintraub, p.190.

381 the 'dignified'. Kuhn, 'Ceremony and Politics', p.133.

382 'no authentic blue'. Smith, p.48.

384 'I regret exceedingly'. *Journal*, p.126.

384 'From the highest'. Ibid., p.132.

384 'swallowed in torrents'. Plunkett, pp.61–2.

384 Florence Nightingale. *Journal*, p.135.

385 'not to interfere'. Ibid., p.136.

386 'royal pleasure to land'. Tyrrell and Ward, p.113.

386 fact-finding visits. Ibid., p.119.

387 mechanization. Plunkett, pp.41–2.

388 'Our little humbug'. Thompson, p.xviii.

388 'a quiver full'. Plunkett, p.62.

389 'This day'. *Journal*, p.84.

390 Books of Beauty. Plunkett, pp.79–94.

390 *Windsor Castle in.* Schama, p.157.

391 'A *family*'. Smith, p.37; Thompson, p.139.

392 'It is a strange omission'. *Journal*, p.152.

392 'Whatever may be'. Ibid., p.100.

393 'The relief of tears'. *Dearest Child*, p.319.

394 'I do not cling'. *Dearest Mama*, pp.30–2.

394 'The Queen alone'. Hardie, *Queen Victoria*, p.73.

394 spider who eats. Munich, p.168.

394 'not fit to nurse'. Weintraub, p.297.

394 'never can I forget'. *Journal*, p.156.

394 'We have buried'. Thompson, p.50.

CHAPTER 30: THE WIDOW

396 'My reason!' *Journal*, p.157.

396 Sir James Clark. Longford, 'Queen Victoria's Doctors', p.85.

397 'I will do'. Ibid.

397 'The poor fatherless'. *Journal*, p.157.

397 'that no one person'. Ibid.

398 'as if he was'. Kennedy, pp.188–9.

399 The undemanding simplicity. Cumming, p.124.

399 'What a dreadful'. *Journal*, p.159.

399 'I am alas'. Ibid., p.167.

399 'Sweet little Beatrice'. Ibid., p.157.

399 a dangerous age. Munich, pp.104–9.

400 'I wish you would'. *Journal*, p.171.

400 'I have been so unwell'. Ibid., p.177.

400 'Wherever widowhood'. Munich, p.106.

401 Victoria's waist. Ibid., p.108.

401 'without a shudder'. *Journal*, p.158.

401 'He gives you his'. Ibid., p.172.

401 curiosity of Disraeli. Aronson, p.89.

401 'prayed by'. *Journal*, p.174.

402 Sitting very straight. Ibid., p.106.

402 'I who always hated'. Ibid., p.161.

402 'The Queen is a woman'. Hardie, *Queen Victoria*, p.135.

402 'The Queen is most'. Ibid., p.140.

402 'It is a subject which'. Ibid.

403 'The Queen has read'. *Journal*, p.180.

404 'I should deeply'. Ibid., p.184.

404 'The Queen asks'. Ibid., p.221.

404 'That was a woman'. Ibid., p.311.

404 'These commanding'. Aronson, p.94.

405 'The Queen would'. *Journal*, p.186.

405 'The Queen must'. Ibid., p.193.

406 'I fear you are already'. *Your Dear Letter*, p.187.

406 'Many were the'. Kuhn, 'Ceremony and Politics', p.148.

407 'The word distasteful'. *Journal*, p.198.

407 'Still, whatever'. Ibid.

407 'Eliza is'. Kennedy, p.248.

407 in future trust. *Journal*, p.194.

407 'the Queen must'. Ibid., p.197.

407 'Yesterday was a'. Ibid.

407 'The higher classes'. Ibid., p.201.

408 'To speak in rude'. Thompson, p.112.

408 'nourished by fantastic'. Harcourt, pp.22–5.

408 'the Queen has'. Ibid.

408 philanthropic and civic. See Prochaska, pp.100–5.

409 'I cannot find him'. *Journal*, p.209.

410 'Nothing could have'. Ibid.

410 'It is very gratifying'. Ibid., p.202.

410 'It is a real comfort'. Ibid., p.187.

410 'He comes to my room'. Ibid., p.188.

411 Queen's stallion. Munich, p.160.

411 'A woman can't'. Thompson, p.56.

412 sexually intimate. Sir Frederick Ponsonby, the Queen's equerry, believed that if the Queen had any sexual feelings for Brown, they were unconscious; their relationship was that of employer and devoted retainer. Sir Frederick Ponsonby, *Three Reigns*, p.38.

412 'Darling One'. Thompson, p.64.

412 Three hundred letters. Ibid., p.78.

412 'Leopold came'. *Journal*, p.280.

412 'The terrible blow'. Ibid.

412 'The Queen is trying'. Ibid.

413 'The Queen can't walk'. Ibid.

413 'Mr John Brown walked'. Williams, p.34.

413 The *Tomahawk*. Thompson, pp.79–80.

414 'I am not accustomed'. Cited in *Journal*, p.315.

414 Bagehot. Smith, p.34.

414 Bradlaugh. Thompson, p.106.

414 value for money. For a discussion of the arguments surrounding the 'value for money' issue and Gladstone's efforts to persuade the Queen to attend the public thanksgiving for the Prince of Wales's recovery see Kuhn, 'Ceremony and Politics'; on the civil list see Kuhn, 'Queen Victoria's Civil List'.

415 'select committee'. Kuhn, 'Queen Victoria's Civil List', p.645.

416 newspaper squares. Ibid., p.663.

416 'The conduct'. Kuhn, 'Ceremony and Politics', p.149.

416 'I shall take responsibility'. Ibid., p.150.

416 'the repellent'. Hardie, *Queen Victoria*, p.61.

416 'My foot much'. *Journal*, p.226.

416 'A most dreadful'. Ibid.

417 'My utter helplessness'. Ibid.

417 'Went to dress'. Ibid., p.216.

417 'The deafening cheers'. Ibid.

CHAPTER 31: THE GREAT WHITE EMPRESS

419 'India should'. Aronson, p.78.

420 'delight and duty'. Hardie, *Queen Victoria*, p.36.

420 'full of poetry'. *Journal*, p.203.

420 'Dizzy writes daily'. Aronson, p.106.

420 'cleverest man'. Ibid., pp.132–3.

421 'There is a freshness'. Ibid., p.107.

421 'lay it on'. Hardie, *Queen Victoria*, p.34.

421 'We authors'. Ibid.

421 'it entirely ruined'. *Journal*, p.299.

422 match tax. Hardie, *Queen Victoria*, p.134.

422 'The Queen therefore'. Aronson, p.125.

423 'I plight'. Ibid., p.126.

423 'Your Majesty's sceptre'. Ibid., p.135.

423 'flowers, crosses, vestments'. *Journal*, p.234.

423 'The Queen is deeply'. Ibid., p.237.

423 'I can only describe'. Disraeli, Vol.1, p.23.

424 'never to stand'. Ibid.

424 'Run away'. Ibid., Vol.2, p.57.

424 'fortunate . . . female sovereign'. Ibid., Vol.1, p.92.

424 'My head . . . shoulders'. Hardie, *Queen Victoria*, p.38.

424 'Nobody can'. Ibid.

425 'When?' Rothschild. Aronson, p.140.

426 'I *do not* think'. Ibid., p.146.

427 'You say you hope'. *Journal*, p.245.

428 'Then the Government'. Ibid.

428 'if the Queen were a man'. Aronson, p.162.

428 '*Der alte Jude*'. Ibid., p.106.

428 'If *we are to maintain*'. *Journal*, p.259.

428 'she would sooner abdicate'. *Journal*, p.260.

429 'no democratic leaning'. Ibid.

430 complained to Ponsonby. Sir Frederick Ponsonby, *Queen Victoria* (London, 1930), p.142.

430 'her experience of forty-three years'. Ibid., p.148.

430 'The Queen has never'. Ibid., p.145.

430 'Madam, and Most Beloved'. Ibid., p.155.

431 'Better not'. Thompson, p.122.

431 'The Queen does interfere'. Hardie, *Queen Victoria*, p.243.

432 'I cannot say'. Ibid., p.98.

432 'It would be a disgrace'. *Journal*, p.284.

432 'Gordon is in danger'. *Journal*, p.285.

432 'If only for humanity's'. Ibid.

433 'the worst I have ever'. Ibid., p.286.

433 'Khartoum fallen'. Ibid., p.289.

433 'The Queen would gladly'. *Journal*, p.327.

433 'I am sorry for'. Hibbert, *Queen Victoria*, p.377.

CHAPTER 32: MATRIARCH

434 'Fifty years'. *Journal*, p.304.

434 spared a while longer. Ibid., p.334.

434 'The crowds were'. Ibid., p.298.

434 'From the moment'. Ibid., p.303.

435 'The symbol that unites'. Munich, p.72.

435 'Then dressed'. *Journal*, p.305.

435 'It is impossible'. Ibid., p.307.

435 Marie Mallet. See Mallet.

435 James Reid. Longford, 'Queen Victoria's Doctors', p.85.

436 'The Queen is certainly'. Mallet, p.195.

436 breeding like the rabbits. *Journal*, p.211.

437 'My blood runs'. Ibid., p.329.

437 spontaneous mutation. See Potts and Potts, pp.63–84.

438 'He has been treated'. *Journal*, p.313.

438 'To describe this day'. Ibid., p.325.

439 'Georgie's first feeling'. Ibid., p.331.

439 She confessed to Marie. Mallet, p.77.

440 'The Queen is delighted'. *Journal*, p.257.

440 'The House of Lords'. Ibid., p.328.

440 'I have always felt'. Thompson, p.42.

441 'what a comfort'. *Journal*, p.308.

441 'Am making arrangements'. Ibid., p.313.

441 'I replied that Abdul'. Arthur Ponsonby, p.131.

442 'The Queen wrote'. *Journal*, p.328.
442 'God has guided'. Ibid., p.333.
442 'It is a very wonderful'. Ibid., p.334.
442 'Seventy-eight'. Ibid.
443 'A never-to-be forgotten'. Ibid., p.335.
443 'Before leaving'. Ibid.
443 'The more democratic'. Cannadine, 'The Context, Performance and Meaning of Ritual', p.121.
444 'We are not interested'. Hardie, *Queen Victoria*, p.159.
444 'I sincerely hope'. *Journal*, p.339.
445 'The news from Osborne'. Esher, *Journals*, Vol.1, p.275.
445 Arthur Balfour. Sir Frederick Ponsonby, *Three Reigns*, p.26.
445 three-decker ship. Ibid.
445 'Bertie'. Ibid.
445 stampeded. Ibid.

Part Four: House of Windsor

Elizabeth II

CHAPTER 33: LILIBET
449 'a little darling'. Pimlott, p.3.
450 'I like him'. Bradford, p.23.
451 'It almost frightens'. Ibid., p.31.
451 'an air'. Turner, p.1.
452 the Duchess told. Bradford, p.40.
452 'Do you usually'. Crawford, p.12.
452 obsession with orderliness. Ibid., p.87.
453 'If you want it'. Ibid., p.33.
453 nursery windows. Ibid., p.22.
453 'They all seemed'. Annigoni, p.82.
454 'What are we'. Crawford, p.70.
454 'Goodnight'. Ibid., p.37.
454 'Us four'. Bradford, p.132.
455 'I pray to God'. Ibid., p.49.
455 'Out of the mist'. Pimlott, p.32.
456 cipher-monarchy. Ibid., p.39.
456 praying for a baby. Ibid., p.41.
456 lady living. Ibid., p.28.
457 spoke to her as an equal. Crawford, pp.79, 87.
457 'the sweetest of'. Pimlott, p.110.
457 best biographer. Sir John W. Wheeler-Bennett. Cited in Bradford, p.85.
457 if 'you once gained'. Crawford, p.52.
458 bit of a show-off. Ibid., p.101.
459 'We went'. Pimlott, p.57.
460 broadening her social circle. Ibid., p.121.

460 'There is a motto'. Ibid., p.117.
463 not particularly maternal. Turner, p.39.

CHAPTER 34: ELIZABETH OUR QUEEN
464 an eagle hovered. Pimlott, p.175.
464 'My own name'. Ibid., p.179; Turner, p.41.
464 'hundreds of old'. Pimlott, p.180.
465 'All the film'. Ibid., p.181.
466 Jock Colville maintained. Ibid., p.183.
466 Lacking imagination . . . caution. Ibid., p.273; Turner, pp.15, 53.
467 'I am the only'. Pimlott, p.185.
467 initially opposed. Ibid., pp.204–7.
468 'She never thought'. Laird, p.35.
468 'She has a great'. Ibid., p.36.
468 degree of moral. Pimlott, p.195.
469 neither alienating. Ibid., p.239.
471 Queen's-speak. Turner, p.51.
471 'No further'. Ibid., p.183.
471 Rory Bremner's. Ibid., p.62.
471 an enigma. Martin Charteris quoted in Turner, p.10.
472 'impenetrably Delphic'. Ibid.
472 'Don't talk rubbish'. Turner, pp.11, 107.
472 King of Morocco. Confidential interview.
474 former Foreign Secretary. David Owen quoted in Turner, p.179.
475 Suez crisis. Pimlott, pp.253–6.
475 Butler . . . too complex. Ibid., p.332.
476 mind like a man. Turner, p.173.
476 'Her curtsey'. Ibid., p.181.
476 'tended to be'. Ibid.
477 editor of *Today*. Brian MacArthur.
477 *Sunday Times*. 20 July 1986.
477 *Guardian*. 21 July 1986.
477 ring up Thatcher. Turner, p.182.
477 'keeled over'. Ibid., p.183.
477 placed her duty . . . before her children. Pimlott, p.262; Turner, pp.113–17, 123.
478 no model. Turner, p.118.
478 The Queen's failure. Ibid., p.125.
479 'The idea of the film'. Pimlott, p.380.
479 'the Firm'. Turner, p.135.
479 If there were problems. Ibid., pp.118–19.
479 respected her authority. Ibid., p.118.
479 no guidance . . . partners. Ibid., p.138.
479 Charteris told the Queen. Ibid., p.125.
480 Charles was promiscuous. Ibid., p.126.
480 William and Harry. Ibid., p.153.
480 All four. Turner, p.139.

480 compensate for not giving them enough time. Ibid., p.90.
481 *The Times*. 2 November 1987.
481 A courtier who observed. Turner, p.9.
481 'Life imitating soap'. Pimlott, p.502.
482 'We did our best'. Brandreth, p.333.
482 'Where did'. Turner, p.113.
482 Robert Fellowes. Turner, p.155.

CHAPTER 35: AFTER DIANA
483 his main concern. Interview with Mark Bolland; Lacey, *Royal*, p.352.
484 whole family . . . drinking. Mark Bolland.
484 surprised by the strength. Lacey, *Royal*, p.367.
485 television crew's ideas. *Daily Telegraph*, 20 April 2006.
485 save her neck. Ibid.
486 Charles had denied. Interview with Mark Bolland.
486 justifiably angry . . . mess. Ibid.
486 Philip wrote. Ibid.
486 'Never mention'. Ibid.
486 encourage criticism. Ibid.
486 reinforced by her mother. The Queen's indulgence of her mother is discussed in Turner, pp.85–95, 97–9, 102.
487 homeopathic remedies. Interview with Harry Arnold, the *Sun*.
487 wilting press. Interview with Alan Hamilton, *The Times*.
488 touchy-feely. Turner, pp.57–8.
488 photograph of . . . George VI. Interview with Harry Arnold, the *Sun*.
488 The standing of the monarchy . . . partly responsible. Turner, p.194.
488 behaviour of her children . . . blame. Ibid.

EPILOGUE
489 'I will be'. *C.W.*, p.54.
489 'I declare'. Pimlott, p.117.
489 'My lords'. *C.W.*, p.52.
489 'that I with'. Ibid.
489 'At my Coronation'. Pimlott, p.190.
490 increase in secular. Starkey, 'Representation through Intimacy', p.188.
491 human body . . . aura . . . Groom of the Stool. Ibid., pp.187–224.
491 'such an awesomely' . . . sole use. Ibid., p.221.
493 'The more democratic'. Cannadine, 'The Context, Performance and Meaning of Ritual', p.121.
494 'the last great'. Ibid., p.153.
494 'comfortable palliative'. Cannadine, 'The Context, Performance and Meaning of Ritual', p.164.
494 use of horses . . . film company. Ibid., pp.123, 142.
494 'How long'. Thompson, p.119.
494 Elizabeth the Last. Jonathan Freedland in the *Guardian*, 21 April 2006.

Bibliography

All published in London unless otherwise stated.

Part One: House of Tudor

Primary Sources

Aylmer, John, *An harborowe for faithfull and trewe subjectes*, 1559

Barahona, Juan De, *Two Letters of Juan De Barahona Addressed to His Uncle Antonio De Barahona. I. The Journey to England and Marriage of Prince Philip of Spain. II. News from England October 1554*, in C.V. Malfatti, *The Accession Coronation and Marriage of Mary Tudor as Related in Four Manuscripts of the Escorial*, Barcelona, 1956

Calendar of Letters, Despatches, and State Papers, relating to the Negotiations between England and Spain, preserved in the Archives at Vienna, Simancas, Besançon and Brussels, ed. Pascual de Gayangos, G.A. Bergenroth, M.A.S. Hume, Royall Tyler and Garrett Mattingly, 13 vols., HMSO, 1867–1954

Calendar of State Papers, Domestic Series, of the Reigns of Edward VI, Mary, Elizabeth, 1547–1580, preserved in the State Paper Department of Her Majesty's Public Record Office, ed. Robert Lemon, 2 vols., 1856

Calendar of State Papers, Foreign Series, of the Reign of Edward VI, 1547–1553, preserved in the State Paper Department of Her Majesty's Public Record Office, ed. William B. Turnbull, 1861

Calendar of State Papers, Foreign Series, of the Reign of Mary, 1553–1558, preserved in the State Paper Department of Her Majesty's Public Record Office, ed. William B. Turnbull, 1861.

Calendar of State Papers, Foreign Series, of the Reign of Elizabeth, 1558–1603, preserved in the State Paper Department of Her Majesty's Public Record Office, ed. Joseph Stevenson et al., 1863–1950

Calendar of State Papers and Manuscripts, Relating to English Affairs, Existing in the Archives and Collections of Venice, and in Other Libraries of Northern Italy, ed. Rawdon Brown and Allen B. Hinds, 38 vols., 1864–1947

Camden, William, *A History of the Most Renowned and Victorious Princess Elizabeth*, ed. Wallace T. MacCaffrey, Chicago, 1970

The Chronicle of Queen Jane and of Two Years of Queen Mary, and Especially of the Rebellion of Sir Thomas Wyat. Written by a resident of the Tower of London, ed. John Gough Nichols, Camden Society, 48, 1850

Clifford, Henry, *The Life of Jane Dormer, Duchess of Feria*, ed. Joseph Stevenson, 1887

Elizabeth I, *Collected Works*, ed. L.S. Marcus, J. Mueller and M.B. Rose, Chicago and London, 2000

A Collection of Ordinances and Regulations for the Government of the Royal Household, made in Divers Reigns from King Edward III to King William and Queen Mary, ed. John Gough Nichols, Society of Antiquaries, 1790

Crawford, Anne, ed., *Letters of the Queens of England, 1100–1547*, Stroud, 1994

The Diary of Henry Machyn, Citizen and Merchant-Taylor of London, from AD 1550 to AD 1563, ed. John Gough Nichols, Camden Society, 42, 1842

Ellis, H., ed. *Original Letters, Illustrative of English History*, 2nd series, 4 vols., 1827

Everett Wood, Mary Anne, ed., *Letters of Royal and Illustrious Ladies of Great Britain*, 3 vols., 1846

Foxe, John, *The Acts and Monuments of John Foxe*, ed. Josiah Pratt, 8 vols., 1877

Guaras, Antonio de, *The Accession of Queen Mary: Being the Contemporary Narrative of Antoni de Guaras, a Spanish Merchant Resident in London*, ed. Richard Garnett, 1892

Guistinian, Sebastian, *Four Years at the Court of Henry VIII, Written by the Venetian Ambassador, Sebastian Guistinian and addressed to the Signory of Venice, January 12th 1515 to July 26th 1519*, 1854

Hall, Edward, *Hall's Chronicle; containing the History of England, during the Reign of Henry the fourth and the Succeeding Monarchs . . . in which are particularly described the Manners and Customs of those Periods*, 1809

Hamilton, W.D., *The Chronicle of England 1485–1559*, 2 vols., Camden Society, New Series, 11, 20, 1875, 1877

Harington, John, *Nugae Antiquae: Being a Miscellaneious Collection of Original Papers in Prose and Verse, written in the Reigns of Henry VIII, Queen Mary, Elizabeth, King James*, etc., ed. Henry Harington, 3 vols., 1804

Harrison, William, *The Description of England*, ed. F.J. Furnival, New Shakespeare Society, 1877

Intimate Letters of England's Queens, ed. Margaret Sanders, 1957

Jordan, W.K., *The Chronicle and Political Papers of King Edward VI*, Ithaca, New York, 1966

Knox, John, *The First Blast of the Trumpet against the Monstrous Regiment of Women*, Edinburgh, Akros Pocket Classics, 10, 1995

Letters and Papers, Foreign and Domestic, of the Reign of Henry VIII, 1509–47, ed. J.S. Brewer, R.H. Brodie and James Gairdner, 21 vols. and addenda, HMSO, 1862–1932

Madden, F., ed. *Privy Purse Expenses of Princess Mary, Daughter of King Henry VIII, afterwards Queen Mary: With a Memoir of the Princess, and Notes*, 1931

Maisse, André Hurault, Sieur de, *A Journal of all that was Accomplished by Monsieur de Maisse, Ambassador in England from Henry IV to Queen Elizabeth, Anno Domini 1597*, tr. and ed. G.B. Harrison and R.A. Jones, 1931

Malfatti, C.V., *Two Italian Accounts of Tudor England*, Barcelona, 1953

Malfatti, C.V., *The Accession Coronation and Marriage of Mary Tudor as Related in Four Manuscripts of the Escorial*, Barcelona, 1956

Manningham, John, *The Diary of John Manningham 1602–3*, ed. John Bruce, Camden Society, 1968

Melville, Sir James, *Memoirs of Sir James Melville of Halhill 1535–1617*, ed. A. Francis Steuart, 1929

Naunton, Sir Robert, *Elizabeth: Fragmentia Regalia*, ed. John S. Cerovski, Washington, 1985

Rye, William Brenchley, *England as Seen by Foreigners in the Days of Elizabeth and James the First*, 1865

Salter, Emma Gurney, *Tudor England through Venetian Eyes*, 1930

Williams, C.H., ed., *English Historical Documents, 1485–1558*, Vol. 5, 1967

Wriothesley, C.A., *Chronicle of England during the Reigns of the Tudors, from AD 1485 to 1559*, ed. William Douglas Hamilton, 2 vols., Camden Society, New Series, ii, 1875–7

Secondary Sources

Adams, Simon, '"Eliza Enthroned?" The Court and its Politics', in *The Reign of Elizabeth I*, ed. Christopher Haigh, 1985, pp. 55–77

Adams, Simon, 'The Patronage of the Crown in Elizabethan Politics: The 1590s in Perspective', in ed. John Guy, *The Reign of Elizabeth I, Court and Culture in the Last Decade*, Cambridge, 1995, pp. 20–45

Aird, Ian, 'The Death of Amy Robsart: Accident, Suicide, or Murder – or Disease?', *English Historical Review*, 71, 278 (1956), 69–79

Anglo, Sydney, *Spectacle, Pageantry and Early Tudor Policy*, Oxford, Clarendon Press, 1969

Anglo, Sydney, *Images of Tudor Kingship*, 1992

Arnold, Janet, 'The Coronation Portrait of Queen Elizabeth I', *Burlington Magazine*, 120 (1978), 727–41

Arnold, Janet, *Queen Elizabeth's Wardrobe Unlock'd*, Leeds, 1988

Axton, Marie, *The Queen's Two Bodies: Drama and the Elizabethan Succession*, Royal Historical Society, 1977

Barker, Felix, 'If Parma had Landed', *History Today*, 38 (May 1988), 34–41

Bassnett, Susan, *Elizabeth I: A Feminist Perspective*, Oxford and New York, 1988

Bayne, C.G., 'The Coronation of Queen Elizabeth', *English Historical Review*, 22 (1907), 650–73

Bell, Ilona, 'Elizabeth I – Always Her Own Free Woman', in *Political Rhetoric, Power, and Renaissance Women*, ed. Carole Levin and Patricia A. Sullivan, Albany, 1995, pp. 57–82

Belsey, Andrew and Belsey, Catherine, 'Icons of Divinity: Portraits of Elizabeth I', in *Renaissance Bodies: The Human Figure in English Culture c. 1540–1660*, ed. Lucy Gent and Nigel Llewellyn, 1990, pp.11–35

Berry, Philippa, *Of Chastity and Power: Elizabethan Literature and the Unmarried Queen*, 1989

Bloch, Marc, *The Royal Touch: Sacred Monarchy and Scrofula in England and France*, tr. J.E. Anderson, 1973

Brewer, J.S., *The Reign of Henry VIII: From his Accession to the Death of Wolsey*, ed. James Gairdner, 2 vols., 1884

Brown, Edward and Barglow, Peter, 'Pseudocyesis: A Paradigm for Psycho-Physiological Interactions', *Archives of General Psychiatry*, 24 (1971), 221–9

Carter, Alison, 'Mary Tudor's Wardrobe', *Costume, The Journal of the Costume Society*, 18 (1984), 9–28

Cavanagh, Sheila, 'The Bad Seed. Princess Elizabeth and the Seymour Incident', in

Dissing Elizabeth: Negative Representations of Gloriana, ed. Julia M. Walker, Durham and London, 1998, 9–29

Cerasano, S.P. and Wynne-Davies, Marion, eds., *Gloriana's Face: Women, Public and Private in the English Renaissance*, Detroit, 1992

Cole, Mary Hill, *The Portable Queen: Elizabeth I and the Politics of Ceremony*, Massachusetts, 2000

Collinson, Patrick, *Elizabethan Essays*, 1994

Cressy, David, *Bonfires and Bells: National Memory and the Protestant Calendar in Elizabethan and Stuart England*, Berkeley, 1989

Cross, C., Loades, D.M. and Scarisbrick, J.J., *Law and Government under the Tudors: Essays Presented to Sir Geoffrey Elton*, Cambridge, 1988

Dennis, Kay, 'She Was a Queen, and Therefore Beautiful: Sidney, His Mother and Queen Elizabeth', *Review of English Studies*, n.s. XLIII, 169 (1992), 18–39

Denny, Joanna, *Anne Boleyn*, 2004

Dewhurst, Sir John, *Royal Confinements*, 1980

Dewhurst, Sir John, 'Royal Pseudocyesis', *History of Medicine*, 8 (1980), 12–17

Dewhurst, Sir John, 'The Alleged Miscarriages of Katherine of Aragon and Anne Boleyn', *Medical History*, 28 (1984), 49–56

Dickens, A.G., *The English Reformation*, 1964

Dickinson, J.C., *The Shrine of Our Lady of Walsingham*, Cambridge, 1956

Dobson, Michael, *England's Elizabeth: An Afterlife in Fame and Fantasy*, Oxford, 2002

Doran, Susan, 'Religion and Politics at the Court of Elizabeth I: The Habsburg Marriage Negotiations, 1559–1567', *English Historical Review*, 104 (1989), 908–26

Doran, Susan, *Monarchy and Matrimony: The Courtships of Elizabeth I*, 1996

Doran, Susan, 'Why Did Elizabeth Not Marry?', in *Dissing Elizabeth: Negative Representations of Gloriana*, ed. Julia M. Walker, Durham and London, 1998, pp. 30–59

Doran, Susan, ed., *Elizabeth, the Exhibition at the National Maritime Museum*, 2003

Doran, Susan and Durston, Christopher, *Princes, Pastors and People: The Church and Religion in England, 1529–1689*, London and New York, 1991

Doran, Susan and Freeman, Thomas S., *The Myth of Elizabeth I*, 2003

Dovey, Zillah, *An Elizabethan Progress: The Queen's Journey into East Anglia, 1578*, Stroud, 1996

Duffy, Eamon, *The Stripping of the Altars: Traditional Religion in England c.1400-c.1580*, New Haven, 1992

Dunlop, Ian Geoffrey David, *Palaces and Progresses of Elizabeth I*, 1962

Dutton, Ralph, *English Court Life: From Henry VII to George II*, 1963

Eccles, Audrey, *Obstetrics and Gynaecology in Tudor and Stuart England*, London and Canberra, 1982

Elston, Timothy G., 'Transformation or Continuity? Sixteenth-Century Education and the Legacy of Catherine of Aragon, Mary I, and Juan Luis Vives', in *'High and Mighty Queens' of Early Modern England: Realities and Representations*, ed. Carole Levin, Jo Eldridge Carney and Debra Barrett-Gravel, New York, 2003, pp.11–23

Elton, Geoffrey, *England under the Tudors*, 1955

Erickson, Carolly, *Bloody Mary: The Life of Mary Tudor*, 2001

Freeman, Thomas S., '"As True a Subject Being Prysoner": John Foxe's Notes on the Imprisonment of Princess Elizabeth, 1554–5', *English Historical Review*, Vol.1, 17, No.470 (February 2002), 94–116

Froude, J.A., *The Reign of Mary Tudor*, 1924

Frye, Susan, 'The Myth of Elizabeth at Tilbury', *Sixteenth Century Journal*, 23 (1992), 95–114

Frye, Susan, *Elizabeth I: The Competition for Representation*, Oxford, 1993

Glasheen, Joan, *The Secret People of the Palaces: The Royal Household from the Plantagenets to Queen Victoria*, 1978

Green, Janet M., '"I Myself". Queen Elizabeth's Oration at Tilbury Camp', *Sixteenth Century Journal*, XXVIII, (1997), 421–45

Guy, John, 'The 1590s: The Second Reign of Elizabeth I?', in *The Reign of Elizabeth I: Court and Culture in the Last Decade*, ed. John Guy, Cambridge, 1995, pp.1–19

Guy, John, ed., *The Reign of Elizabeth I: Court and Culture in the Last Decade*, Cambridge, 1995

Hackett, Helen, *Virgin Mother, Maiden Queen: Elizabeth I and the Cult of the Virgin Mary*, Basingstoke, 1995

Haigh, Christopher, *Elizabeth I: Profile in Power*, 1988

Haller, W., *Foxe's Book of Martyrs and the Elect Nation*, 1963

Hammer, Paul E.J., 'Patronage at Court, Faction and the Earl of Essex', in *The Reign of Elizabeth I: Court and Culture in the Last Decade*, ed. John Guy, Cambridge, 1995, pp.65–86

Haugaard, W.P., 'Elizabeth Tudor's Book of Devotions: A Neglected Clue to the Queen's Life and Character', *Sixteenth Century Journal, 12.2* (Summer 1981), 79–106

Hanson, Neil, *The Confident Hope of a Miracle*, 2004

Harbison, E. Harris, *Rival Ambassadors at the Court of Queen Mary*, Princeton, 1940

Harris, Barbara J., 'Women and Politics in Early Tudor England', *Historical Journal*, 33, (1990), 259–81

Heisch, Alison, 'Elizabeth I and the Persistence of Patriarchy', *Feminist Review*, 4 (1980), 45–56

Hentzer, Paul, *Travels in England during the Reign of Elizabeth I*, ed. H. Walpole, tr. R. Bentley, with *Fragmentia Regalia* by Sir Robert Naunton, 1889

Hibbert, Christopher, *The Virgin Queen: Elizabeth I*, 1991

Hoak, Dale, 'Two Revolutions in Tudor Government: The Formation and Organisation of Mary I's Privy Council', in *Revolution Reassessed: Revisions in the History of Tudor Government and Administration*, ed. David Starkey and Christopher Coleman, Oxford, 1986, pp.87–115

Hoak, Dale, 'A Tudor Deborah? The Coronation of Elizabeth I, Parliament and the Problem of Female Rule', in *John Foxe and His World*, ed. Christopher Highley and John N. King, Aldershot, 2002, pp.73–88

Hoak, Dale, 'The Coronations of Edward VI, Mary I, and Elizabeth I, and the Transformation of the Tudor Monarchy', in *Westminster Abbey Reformed 1540–1640*, ed. C.S. Knighton and Richard Mortimer, Aldershot, 2003, pp.114–51

Hogrefe, Pearl, *Tudor Women, Commoners and Queens*, Iowa, 1975

Hole, Christina, *English Shrines and Sanctuaries*, 1954

Horton-Smith, L.G.H., *Dr William Baily, Physician to Queen Elizabeth*, 1952

Hume, Martin, 'The Visit of Philip II', *English Historical Review*, VII (1892), 253–80

Hutton, Ronald, *The Rise and Fall of Merry England: The Ritual Year 1400–1700*, Oxford, 1994

Ives, Eric, *Anne Boleyn*, Oxford, 1986

Jenkins, Elizabeth, *Elizabeth the Great*, 1958

Jenkins, Elizabeth, *Elizabeth and Leicester*, 1961

Johnson, Paul, *Elizabeth I: A Study in Power and Intellect*, 1976

Jordan, Constance, 'Woman's Rule in Sixteenth-Century Political Thought', *Renaissance Quarterly*, 40, No.3 (Autumn 1987), 421–51

King, John, 'Fiction and Fact in Foxe's *Book of Martyrs*', in *John Foxe and the English Reformation*, ed. David Loades, Aldershot, 1997, pp.12–35

King, John N., 'Queen Elizabeth I: Representations of the Virgin Queen', *Renaissance Quarterly*, 43.1 (Spring 1990), 30–74

Knighton, C.S. and Mortimer, Richard, *Westminster Abbey Reformed 1540–1640*, Aldershot, 2003

Lee, Patricia-Ann, 'A Bodye Politique to Governe: Aylmer, Knox and the Debate on Queenship', *The Historian*, 52 (1990), 242–61

Levin, Carole, 'Lady Jane Grey: Protestant Queen and Martyr', in *Silent But for the Word: Tudor Women as Patrons, Translators, and Writers of Religious Works*, ed. Margaret Patterson Hannay, Kent, Ohio, 1985, pp.92–106

Levin, Carole, 'Queens and Claimants: Political Insecurity in Sixteenth Century England', in *Gender, Ideology and Action: Historical Perspectives on Women's Public Lives*, ed. Janet Sharistanian, Westport, Connecticut, 1986, pp.41–66

Levin, Carole, 'Power, Politics and Sexuality: Images of Elizabeth I', in *The Politics of Gender in Early Modern Europe*, ed. Jean R. Brink, Allison P. Coudert and Maryanne E. Horowitz, Kirksville, MO, 1989, pp.95–110

Levin, Carole, *The Heart and Stomach of a King: Elizabeth I and the Politics of Sex and Power*, Philadelphia, 1994

Levin, Carole, 'Gender, Monarchy, and the Power of Seditious Words', in *Dissing Elizabeth: Negative Representations of Gloriana*, ed. Julia M. Walker, Durham and London, 1998, pp.77–95.

Levine, Mortimer, 'The Place of Women in Tudor Government', in *Tudor Rule and Revolution: Essays for G.R. Elton from His American Friends*, ed. Delloyd J. Guth and John W. McKenna, Cambridge, 1982, pp.109–23

Loades, David, *Two Tudor Conspiracies*, Cambridge, 1965

Loades, David, *The Tudor Court*, 1986

Loades, David, 'Philip II and the Government of England', in *Law and Government under the Tudors: Essays Presented to Sir Geoffrey Elton*, ed. Claire Cross, David Loades and J.J. Scarisbrick, Cambridge, 1988, pp.177–94

Loades, David, *Mary Tudor: A Life*, Oxford, 1989

McClure, Peter and Headlam Wells, Robin, 'Elizabeth I as a Second Virgin Mary', *Renaissance Studies*, 4.1 (March 1990), 38–70

McCoy, Richard C., '"This Wonderfull Spectacle": The Civic Progress of Elizabeth I and the Troublesome Coronation', in *Coronations: Medieval and Early Modern Monarchic Ritual*, ed. János M. Bak, Berkeley, 1990, pp.217–27

MacCulloch, Diarmaid, *Reformation: Europe's House Divided, 1490–1700*, 2004

McLaren, Angus, *Reproductive Rituals: The Perception of Fertility in England from the Sixteenth to the Nineteenth Century*, London and New York, 1984

Maclennan, Sir Hector, 'A Gynaecologist Looks at the Tudors', *Medical History*, XI (1967), 66–74

MacNalty, A.S., *Elizabeth Tudor: The Lonely Queen*, 1954

Maltby, William S., *The Black Legend in England: The Development of Anti-Spanish Sentiment, 1558–1660*, Durham, North Carolina, 1971

Marcus, Leah, 'Erasing the Stigma of Daughterhood: Mary I, Elizabeth I, and Henry VIII', in *Daughters and Fathers*, ed. Lynda E. Boose and Betty S. Flowers, Baltimore and London, 1989, pp.400–17

Marshall, Rosalind K., *Queen of Scots*, Edinburgh, 1986

Matthews, Leslie, G., 'Royal Apothecaries of the Tudor Period', *Medical History*, 8 (1964), 170–9

Mayer, Thomas F., *Reginald Pole, Prince and Prophet*, Cambridge, 2000

Mears, Natalie, '*Regnum Cecilianum*? A Cecilian perspective of the Court', in *The Reign of Elizabeth I: Court and Culture in the Last Decade*, ed. John Guy, Cambridge, 1995, pp. 46–64

Mellor, Walter Clifford, *The Boy Bishop and Other Essays*, 1923

Moorhouse, Geoffrey, *The Pilgrimage of Grace: The Rebellion that Shook Henry VIII's Throne*, 2003

Mumby, F.A., *The Girlhood of Queen Elizabeth*, 1909

Neale, J.E., *Queen Elizabeth I*, 1934

Neale, J.E., *Elizabeth I and Her Parliaments*, 1953

Neale, J.E., *Essays in Elizabethan History*, 1959

Nichols, John, ed., *The Progresses and Public Processions of Queen Elizabeth, Compiled and Illustrated with Historical Notes by John Nichols*, 3 vols., 1823

Perry, Maria, *Elizabeth I, the Word of a Prince: A Life from Contemporary Documents*, Folio Society, 1990

Planche, J.R., *Regal Records: Or, A Chronicle of the Coronations of the Queens Regnant of England*, 1838

Plowden, Alison, *Tudor Women, Queens and Commoners*, 1979

Plowden, Alison, *Lady Jane Grey and the House of Suffolk*, 1985

Pomeroy, Elizabeth W., *Reading the Portraits of Elizabeth I*, Hamden, Connecticut, 1989

Prescott, H.F.M., *Mary Tudor, The Spanish Tudor*, 2003

Rice, George P., *The Public Speaking of Elizabeth I*, Columbia, New York, 1951

Richards, Judith M., '"To Promote a Woman to Beare Rule": Talking of Queens in Mid-Tudor England', *Sixteenth Century Journal. The Journal of Early Modern Studies*, Vol. 28, No.1 (Spring 1997), 101–21

Richards, Judith M., 'Mary Tudor as "Sole Quene"?: Gendering Tudor Monarchy', *The Historical Journal*, 40, 4 (December 1997), 895–924

Richards, Judith M., 'Love and the Female Monarch: The Case of Elizabeth Tudor', *Journal of British Studies*, Vol.38, No.2 (April 1999), 133–60

Richards, Judith M., 'Mary Tudor: Renaissance Queen of England', in *'High and Mighty Queens' of Early Modern England: Realities and Representations*, ed. Carole Levin, Jo Eldridge Carney and Debra Barrett-Graves, New York, 2003, pp.27–43

Ridley, Jasper, *Bloody Mary's Martyrs: The Story of England's Terror*, New York, 2002

Ridley, Jasper, *Elizabeth I: The Shrewdness of Virtue*, Harmondsworth, 2002

Robinson, Brian, *The Royal Maundy*, 1977

Ross, Josephine, *The Man Who Would Be King: Suitors to Queen Elizabeth I*, 2005

Rowse, A.L., 'The Accession of Queen Elizabeth I', *History Today*, 3, (1953), 293–300

Rowse, A.L., 'The Coronation of Elizabeth I', *History Today*, 3 (1953), 301–10

Rye, W.B., *England as Seen by Some Foreigners in the Days of Elizabeth and James I*, 1865

Scaglini, Paula Louise, 'The Scepter or the Distaff: The Question of Female Sovereignty, 1516–1607', *The Historian*, 42, No.1 (November 1978), 59–75

Scarisbrick, J.J., *Henry VIII*, 1968

Scarisbrick, J.J., *The Reformation and the English People*, Oxford, 1984

Schenk, W., *Reginald Pole, Cardinal of England*, 1950

Schramm, Percy Ernst, *A History of the English Coronation*, Oxford, 1937

Shephard, Amanda, *Gender and Authority in Sixteenth Century England: The Knox Debate*, Keele, 1995

Simpson, Helen, *The Spanish Marriage*, Edinburgh, 1933

Smuts, R. Malcolm, 'Public Ceremony and Royal Charisma: The English Royal Entry into London, 1485–1642', in *The First Modern Society: Essays in English History in Honour of Lawrence Stone*, ed. A.L. Beier, David Cannadine and James Rosenheim, Cambridge, 1989, pp.65–79

Somerset, Anne, *Elizabeth I*, 1992

Starkey, David, 'Representation Through Intimacy', in *Symbols and Sentiments: Cross-Cultural Studies in Symbolism*, ed. Ioan Lewis, London and New York, 1977, pp.187–224

Starkey, David, *Elizabeth: Apprenticeship*, 2001

Starkey, David, *Six Wives: The Queens of Henry VIII*, 2004

Starkey, David and Coleman, Christopher, *Revolution Reassessed: Revisions in the History of Tudor Government and Administration*, Oxford, 1986

Starkey, David, et al., *The English Court: From the Wars of the Roses to the Civil War*, 1987

Stone, J.M., *The History of Mary I, Queen of England*, 1901

Strickland, Agnes, *Lives of the Queens of England*, Vols. IV and V, 1844

Strong, Roy, *The Cult of Elizabeth: Elizabethan Portraiture and Pageantry*, 1987

Strong, Roy, *Gloriana: The Portraits of Elizabeth I*, 1987

Strong, Roy, *Coronation: A History of Kingship and the British Monarchy*, 2005

Tapp, W.H., *Anne Boleyn and Elizabeth at the Royal Manor of Hanworth*, 1953

Taylor-Smith, Larissa J., 'Elizabeth I: A Psychological Profile', *The Sixteenth Century Journal*, Vol.XV, No.1 (Spring 1984), 47–72

Teague, Frances, 'Queen Elizabeth in Her Speeches', in *Gloriana's Face: Women, Public and Private, in the English Renaissance*, ed. S.P. Cerasano and Marion Wynne-Davies, Hemel Hempstead, 1992, pp.63–78

Tytler, Patrick Fraser, *England under the Reigns of Edward VI and Mary, with the Contemporary History of Europe, Illustrated in a Series of Original Letters Never Before Printed*, 2 vols., 1839

Veith, Ilza, *Hysteria: The History of a Disease*, Chicago and London, 1965

Waldman, Milton, *The Lady Mary: A Biography of Mary Tudor, 1516–1558*, New York, 1972

Walker, Julia M., ed., *Dissing Elizabeth: Negative Representations of Gloriana*, Durham and London, 1998

Warkentin, Germaine, ed., *The Queen Majesty's Passage and Related Documents*, Toronto, Ontario, 2004

Warnicke, Retha M., 'Queens Regnant and the Royal Supremacy 1525–1587', in Retha M. Warnicke, *Women of the English Renaissance and Reformation*, Westport, Connecticut and London, 1983, pp.47–66

Warnicke, Retha M., *The Rise and Fall of Anne Boleyn*, Cambridge, 1989

Watson, Foster, ed., *Vives and the Renascene Education of Women*, 1912

Waugh, Evelyn, *Edmund Campion*, Harmondsworth, 1935

Wayne, Valerie, 'Some Sad Sentence: Vives' *Instruction of a Christian Woman*', in *Silent But for the Word: Tudor Women as Patrons, Translators, and Writers of Religious Works*, ed. Margaret Patterson Hannay, Kent, Ohio, 1985, pp.15–29

Weir, Alison, *Henry VIII: King and Court*, 2001

White, Beatrice, *Mary Tudor*, 1935

Wilson, Derek, *A Tudor Tapestry: Men, Women and Society in Reformation England*, Pittsburgh, 1972

Wormald, Jenny, *Mary, Queen of Scots: A Study in Failure*, 1988

Wright, Pam, 'A Change in Direction: The Ramifications of a Female Household, 1558–1603', in *The English Court: From the Wars of the Roses to the Civil War*, David Starkey et al., 1987

Yates, Frances, 'Queen Elizabeth as Astraea', *Journal of the Warburg and Courtauld Institutes*, X (1947), 27–82

Yates, Frances, *Astraea: The Imperial Theme in the Sixteenth Century*, 1975

Youngs, F.A., *The Proclamations of the Tudor Queens*, Cambridge, 1976

Part Two: House of Stuart

Primary Sources

Abbadie, Jacques, *A Panegyric on our Late Sovereign Lady Mary Queen of England, Scotland, France and Ireland, of Glorious and Immortal Memory*, 1695

An Account of King William's and Queen Mary's Undeserv'd Ill Treatment of Her Sister, the Princess of Denmark, 1701

Anon, *The Life of that Incomparable Princess, Mary, Our Late Sovereign Lady, of ever Blessed Memory*, 1695

Anon, *The Royal Diary, Or King William's Interior Portraiture, To which is prefixt, The Character of his Royal Consort, Queen Mary II*, 1705

Bathurst, B., ed., *Letters of Two Queens*, 1924

Bathurst Papers on loan to the British Library, 57/69 & 57/71

Bentinck, Mechtild, Comtesse, ed., *Marie, Reine d'Angleterr, Lettres et Memoires*, The Hague, 1880

Brown, Beatrice Curtis, *The Letters and Diplomatic Instructions of Queen Anne*, New York, 1968

Burnet, Gilbert, *An Essay on the Memory of the Late Queen*, 1695

Burnet, Gilbert, *Bishop Burnet's History of His Own Time from the Restoration to Charles II to the Treaty of the Peace of Utrecht, in the Reign of Queen Anne*, 1838

Clarendon, Edward Hyde, 1st Earl of, *The Life of Edward, Earl of Clarendon, Lord High Chancellor of England, Written by Himself*, 3 vols., Oxford, 1827

Clarendon, Henry Hyde, 2nd Earl of, *The Correspondence of Henry Hyde, Earl of Clarendon and of his Brother, Laurence Hyde, Earl of Rochester; with the Diary of Lord Clarendon from 1687 to 1690*, ed. S.W. Singer, 2 vols., 1828

Clarke, James Stanier, ed., *The Life of James II, Collected out of Memoirs Writ in His Own Hand*, 2 vols., 1816

Clerk, Sir John, *Memoirs of the Life of Sir John Clerk of Penicuik, 1676–1755*, ed. John M. Gray, Edinburgh, 1892

Coke, Roger, *A Detection of the Court and State of England during the Reigns of the Stuarts*, Vols. II and III, 1719

Dalrymple, Sir John, *Memoirs of Great Britain and Ireland*, 3 vols., Edinburgh, 1771–88

Doebner, Dr, ed., *Memoirs of Mary, Queen of England, 1689–93, together with her letters and those of King James II and William III to the Electress Sophie of Hanover*, Leipzig, 1886

Elizabeth, Queen of Bohemia, *The Letters of Elizabeth, Queen of Bohemia*, compiled by L.M. Baker, 1953

Evelyn, John, *The Diary of John Evelyn*, ed. William Bray, 2 vols., 1901

The Form of the Proceeding to the Funeral of her late Majesty Queen Mary II of Blessed Memory, 1695

Hamilton, Anthony, *Memoirs of Count Grammont*, ed. Sir Walter Scott, 1846

Hamilton, Sir David, *The Diary of Sir David Hamilton, 1709–14*, ed. Philip Roberts, Oxford, 1975

Hanover, Sophie, Electress of, *Memoirs*, tr. H. Forester, 1888

Their Highness the Prince and Princess of Orange's Opinion about a general liberty of Conscience, etc, including Mijn Heer Hagel's First Letter to Mr Stewart, 1689

Jesse, John Heneage, *Memoirs of the Court of England from the Revolution in 1688 to the Death of George II*, 4 vols., 1901

Lake, Edward, *Diary of Dr Edward Lake in the Years 1677–78*, ed. George Percy Elliott, Camden Society, 1866

Marlborough, Sarah, Duchess of, *Private Correspondence of Sarah, Duchess of Marlborough Illustrative of the Court and Times of Queen Anne*, 2 vols., 1838

Marlborough, Sarah, Duchess of, *Memoirs of Sarah, Duchess of Marlborough together with her Characters of her Contemporaries and her Opinions*, ed. William King, 1930

The Other Side of the Question: Or, An Attempt to Rescue the Characters of Two Royal Sisters, Queen Mary and Queen Anne, out of the Hands of Dowager Duchess of M . . ., 1744

Pepys, Samuel, *Diary and Correspondence of*, deciphered by Rev. J. Smith, Life and Notes by Richard, Lord Braybrooke, 4 vols., New York, n.d.

Reresby, Sir John, *Memoirs*, ed. A. Browning, Glasgow, 1936

Russell, Lady Rachel, *Letters of Lady Rachel Russell in the Library at Woburn Abbey*, 1826

Russell, Lady Rachel Wriothesley, *Some Account of the Life of Rachel Wriothesley, Lady Russell*, 1819

Swift, Jonathan, *The History of the Last Four Years of Queen Anne*, 1758

Swift, Jonathan, *Swift's Journal to Stella 1710–13*, ed. Frederick Ryland, 1897

Swift, Jonathan, *The Correspondence of Jonathan Swift 1690–1713*, 2 vols., Oxford, 1963

Tennison, Thomas, Archbishop of Canterbury, *A Sermon Preached at the Funeral of Her Late Majesty Queen Mary of Ever Blessed Memory in the Abbey-Church in Westminster, 5 March 1694–5*

Secondary Sources

Baxter, Stephen, *William III and the Defence of European Liberty*, 1966

Bowen, Marjorie, *The Third Mary Stuart*, 1929

Boyer, Abel, *The History of the Reign of Queen Anne, Digested into Annals*, 1703

Bryant, Arthur, *King Charles II*, 1931

Bucholz, R.O., 'Queen Anne: Victim of her Virtues?', in *Queenship in Britain, 1660–1837*, ed. Clarissa Campbell Orr, Manchester, 2002, pp.94–129

Bucholz, R.O., '"Nothing but Ceremony": Queen Anne and the Limitations of Royal Ritual', *Journal of British Studies*, xxx (1991), 288–323

Bucholz, R.O., *The Augustan Court: Queen Anne and the Decline of Court Culture*, Stanford, 1993

Butler, Iris, *Rule of Three: Sarah Duchess of Marlborough and her Companions in Power*, 1967

Chapman, Hester, *Mary II, Queen of England*, 1953

Dewhurst, Jack, *Royal Confinements*, 1980

Fradenburg, Louise Olga, ed., *Women and Sovereignty*, Edinburgh, 1992

Green, David, *Queen Anne*, 1970

Gregg, Edward, *Queen Anne*, 1980

Haile, Martin, *Queen Mary of Modena: Her Life and Letters*, 1905

Hamilton, Elizabeth, *William's Mary*, 1972

Harris, Frances, *A Passion for Government: The Life of Sarah, Duchess of Marlborough*, Oxford, 1991

Janssens-Knorsch, Uta, 'From Het Loo to Hampton Court: William and Mary's Dutch Gardens and Their Influence on English Gardening', in *Fabrics and Fabrications: The Myth and Making of William and Mary*, ed. Paul Hoftijzer and C.C. Barfoot, Amsterdam, 1990, pp.227–96

Orr, Clarissa Campbell, ed., *Queenship in Britain 1660–1837: Royal Patronage, Court Culture and Dynastic Politics*, Manchester, 2002

Schwoerer, Lois G., 'Images of Queen Mary II, 1689–94', *Renaissance Quarterly*, Vol. XLII, No.4 (Winter 1989), 717–48

Speck, W.A., *Reluctant Revolutionaries*, 1988

Straka, Gerald M., *The Revolution of 1688: Whig Triumph or Palace Revolution?*, Lexington, Massachusetts, 1963

Strickland, Agnes, *Lives of the Queens of England*, Vol.VII, 1844; Vol.X, 1847; Vol.XII, 1848

Zee, Henri and Barbara, van der, *William and Mary*, 1973

Zook, Melinda, 'History's Mary: The Propagation of Queen Mary II, 1689–1694', in *Women and Sovereignty*, ed. Louise Olga Fradenburg, Edinburgh, 1992, pp.170–91

Part Three and Part Four: House of Hanover and House of Windsor

Primary Sources

Benson, A.C. and Esher, Viscount, eds., *The Letters of Queen Victoria: A Selection from Her Majesty's Correspondence between the Years 1837 and 1861*, First Series, 3 vols., 1907

Bolitho, Hector, ed., *Further Letters of Queen Victoria*, 1938

Bolitho, Hector (ed. with Albert Baillie, Dean of Windsor), *Letters of Lady Augusta Stanley*, 1927

Disraeli, Benjamin, Viscount Beaconsfield, *The Letters of Disraeli to Lady Bradford and Lady Chesterfield*, ed. Marquis of Zetland, 2 vols., 1929

Esher, Viscount, *Journals and Letters of Reginald, Viscount Esher*, ed. Maurice V. Brett, Vol.1, 1870–1903, 1934

Esher, Viscount, ed., *The Girlhood of Queen Victoria: A Selection from Her Majesty's Diaries, 1832–40*, 2 vols., 1912

Fulford, Roger, ed., *Dearest Child: Letters between Queen Victoria and the Princess Royal, 1858–61*, 1964

Fulford, Roger, ed., *Dearest Mama: Letters between Queen Victoria and the Crown Princess of Prussia, 1861–64*, 1968

Fulford, Roger, ed., *Beloved Mama: Private Correspondence of Queen Victoria and the German Crown Princess, 1878–85*, 1971

Fulford, Roger, ed., *Your Dear Letter: Private Correspondence of Queen Victoria and the Crown Princess of Prussia, 1865–71*, 1971

Fulford, Roger, ed., *Darling Child: Private Correspondence of Queen Victoria and the German Crown Princess of Prussia, 1871–78*, 1976

Greville, Charles, *The Greville Memoirs, 1817–60*, ed. Roger Fulford, 1963

Kennedy, A.L., ed., *My Dear Duchess: Social and Political Letters to the Duchess of Manchester 1858–1869*, 1956

Lutyens, Mary, ed., *Lady Lytton's Court Diary 1895–1899*, 1961

Mallet, Victor, ed., *Life with Queen Victoria: Marie Mallet's Letters from Court 1887–1901*, 1968

Ramm, Agatha, ed., *Beloved and Darling Child: Last Letters between Queen Victoria and her Eldest Daughter, 1886–1901*, Stroud, 1990

Stanley, Lady Augusta, *The Letters of Lady Augusta Stanley: A Young Lady at Court, 1849–1863*, ed. Hector Bolitho and the Dean of Windsor, 1927

Stanley, Lady Augusta, *Later Letters of Lady Augusta Stanley, 1864–76*, ed. Hector Bolitho and the Dean of Windsor, 1929

Stockmar, Ernst, Baron, ed., *Memoirs of Baron Stockmar*, 2 vols., 1872

Stoney, Benita and Weltzien, Heinrich C., eds., *My Mistress the Queen: The Letters of Frieda Arnold, Dresser to Queen Victoria*, 1994

Strachey, Lytton and Fulford, Roger, eds., *The Greville Memoirs, 1814–1860*, 8 vols., 1938

Victoria, Queen, *Leaves from the Journal of Our Life in the Highlands from 1848 to 1861*, ed. Arthur Helps, 1868

Victoria, Queen, *More Leaves from the Journal of a Life in the Highlands from 1862 to 1882*, 1884

Victoria, Queen, *The Letters of Queen Victoria, A Selection from Her Majesty's Correspondence*, First Series, 1837–61, ed. A.C. Benson and Viscount Esher, 3 vols., 1907. Second Series, 1862–85, ed. G.E. Buckle, 3 vols., 1926. Third Series, 1886–1901, ed. G.E. Buckle, 3 vols., 1930

Secondary Sources

Amies, Hardy, *Still Here: An Autobiography*, 1984

Annigoni, Pietro, *An Artist's Life*, 1977

Aronson, Theo, *Victoria and Disraeli: The Making of a Romantic Partnership*, 1977

Bagehot, Walter, *The English Constitution*, see Smith, Paul, ed.

Beier, A.L., Cannadine, David and Rosenheim, James M., *The First Modern Society, Essays in English History in Honour of Lawrence Stone*, Cambridge, 1989

Bogdanor, Vernon, *The Monarchy and the Constitution*, Oxford, 1995

Bradford, Sarah, *Elizabeth: A Biography of Her Majesty the Queen*, 1996

Brandreth, Gyles, *Philip and Elizabeth: Portrait of a Marriage*, 2004

Cannadine, David, 'The Context, Performance and Meaning of Ritual: The British Monarchy and the "Invention of Tradition" c. 1820–1977', in *The Invention of Tradition*, ed. Eric Hobsbawn and Terence Ranger, Cambridge, 1982, pp.101–64

Cannadine, David, '"The Last Hanoverian Sovereign?": the Victorian Monarchy in Historical Perspective, 1688–1988', in A.L. Beier, David Cannadine and James M. Rosenheim, *The First Modern Society. Essays in English History in Honour of Lawrence Stone*, Cambridge, 1989, pp.127–65

Cannadine, David, *The Pleasures of the Past*, 1990

Cannadine, David, *History in Our Time*, 2000

Charlot, Monica, *Victoria, the Young Queen*, Oxford, 1991

Colley, Linda, *Britons: Forging the Nation, 1707–1837*, New Haven, 1992

Crawford, Marion, *The Little Princesses*, 2002

Cumming, Valerie, *Royal Dress: The Image and the Reality, 1989*

Cunningham, Hugh, 'The Language of Patriotism, 1750–1914', *History Workshop*, Issue 12 (Autumn 1981), 8–33

Dimbleby, Jonathan, *The Prince of Wales*, 1994

Dimond, Frances and Taylor, Roger, *Crown and Camera: The Royal Family and Photography, 1840–1920*, Harmondsworth, 1987

Erickson, Carolly, *Her Little Majesty: The Life of Queen Victoria*, 2004

Guedalla, Philip, *The Queen and Mr Gladstone, 1845–1898*, 2 vols., 1933

Harcourt, Freda, 'Gladstone, Monarchism and the "New" Imperialism, 1868–74', *The Journal of Imperial and Commonwealth History*, Vol.XIV, No.1 (October 1985), 20–51

Hardie, Frank, *The Political Influence of Queen Victoria, 1861–1901*, 1935

Hardie, Frank, *The Political Influence of the British Monarchy 1868–1962*, 1970

Harris, Kenneth, *The Queen*, 1994

Hibbert, Christopher, *Queen Victoria: A Personal History*, 2000

Hibbert, Christopher, ed., *Queen Victoria in her Letters and Journals*, Stroud, 2000

Hooey, Brian, *All the Queen's Men: Inside the Royal Household*, 1992

Kuhn, William M., 'Ceremony and Politics: The British Monarchy, 1871–1872', *Journal of British Studies*, Vol.26, No.2 (April 1987), 133–62

Kuhn, William M., 'Queen Victoria's Civil List: What Did She Do With It?', *The Historical Journal*, Vol.36, 3 (September 1993), 645–65

Lacey, Robert, *Majesty: Elizabeth II and the House of Windsor*, 1977

Lacey, Robert, *Royal: Her Majesty Queen Elizabeth II*, 2002

Laird, Dorothy, *How the Queen Reigns*, 1959

Longford, Elizabeth, *Victoria R.I.*, 1964

Longford, Elizabeth, 'Queen Victoria's Doctors', in *A Century of Conflict 1850–1950, Essays for A.J.P. Taylor*, ed. Martin Gilbert, 1966, pp.73–87

Longford, Elizabeth, *Elizabeth R*, 1983

Marie Louise, Princess, *My Memories of Six Reigns*, 1956

Martin, Kingsley, *The Magic of Monarchy*, 1937

Martin, Kingsley, *The Crown and the Establishment*, Harmondsworth, 1963

Master, Brian, *Dreams about HM The Queen and Other Members of the Royal Family*, 1972

Moneypenny, William Flavelle and Buckle, George Earle, *The Life of Benjamin Disraeli, Earl of Beaconsfield*, 2 vols., 1929

Morton, Andrew, *Diana: Her True Story*, 1992

Munich, Adrienne, *Queen Victoria's Secrets*, New York, 1996

Nairn, Tom, *The Enchanted Glass: Britain and its Monarchy*, 1988

Pimlott, Ben, *The Queen*, 1996

Plunkett, John, *Queen Victoria, First Media Monarch*, Oxford, 2003

Ponsonby, Arthur, *Henry Ponsonby: Queen Victoria's Private Secretary: His Life and Letters*, 1942

Ponsonby, Sir Frederick, *Sidelights on Queen Victoria*, 1930

Ponsonby, Sir Frederick, *Recollections of Three Reigns*, 1988

Pope-Hennessy, James, *Queen Mary*, 1959

Potts, D.M. and Potts, W.T.W., *Queen Victoria's Gene: Haemophilia and the Royal Family*, Stroud, 1999

Prochaska, Frank, *Royal Bounty: The Making of a Welfare Monarchy*, New Haven and London, 1995

Rohl, John C.G., Warren, Martin and Hunt, David, *Purple Secret: Genes, 'Madness' and the Royal Houses of Europe*, 1999

Schama, Simon, 'The Domestication of Majesty: Royal Family Portraiture, 1500–1850', *Journal of Interdisciplinary History*, 17, 1 (Summer 1986), 155–83

Smith, Paul, ed., *Bagehot, The English Constitution*, Cambridge, 2001

Steinach, Susie, *Women in England, 1760–1914*, 2004

Strachey, Lytton, *Queen Victoria*, Harmondsworth, 1971

Surtees, Virginia, *Charlotte Canning: Lady-in-Waiting to Queen Victoria and Wife of the First Viceroy of India, 1817–1861*, 1975

Thompson, Dorothy, *Queen Victoria, Gender and Power*, 2001

Turner, Graham, *Elizabeth, the Woman and the Queen*, 2002

Tyrrell, Alex and Ward, Yvonne, '"God Bless Her Little Majesty", the Popularising of Monarchy in the 1840s', *National Identities*, Vol.2, No.2 (2000), 109–25

Vickers, Hugo, *Elizabeth the Queen Mother*, 2005

Watson, Vera, *A Queen at Home: An Intimate Account of the Social and Domestic Life of Queen Victoria's Court*, 1952

Weintraub, Stanley, *Victoria: An Intimate Biography*, New York, 1986

Williams, Richard, *The Contentious Crown: Public Discussion of the British Monarchy in the Reign of Queen Victoria*, Aldershot, 1997

Wilson, Christopher, *The Windsor Knot: Charles, Camilla and the Legacy of Diana*, New York, 2002

Index